Jennie

Jennie

The American beauty who became the toast—and the scandal—of two
continents, ruled an age and raised a son—Winston Churchill—
who shaped history

RALPH G. MARTIN

SOURCEBOOKS, INC.®
NAPERVILLE, ILLINOIS

Acknowledgment is made for permission to reprint excerpts from the following works:
My Early Life by W. S. Churchill, published by Charles Scribner's Sons and by Odhams Books Ltd. (The Hamlyn Group).
My Life and Loves, by Frank Harris, reprinted by permission of Grove Press, Inc. © 1925 Frank Harris, © 1953 Nellie Harris, © 1963 Arthur Leonard Ross, as executor of the Frank Harris estate.
Winston S. Churchill: Youth, 1874–1900, by Randolph S. Churchill, reprinted by permission of the publisher, Houghton Mifflin Company.
The author gratefully acknowledges permission granted by C & T Publications, Ltd., to quote from the letter written by Winston S. Churchill about his mother's death.

Published by Sourcebooks, Inc.
P.O. Box 4410, Naperville, Illinois 60567-4410
(630) 961-3900
Fax: (630) 961-2168
www.sourcebooks.com

Originally published by Prentice Hall in 1969 and 1971

Cataloging in Publication data is on file with the publisher.

Printed and bound in the United States of America.
BG 10 9 8 7 6 5 4 3 2 1

Acknowledgments

I AM DEEPLY AND PERSONALLY GRATEFUL to British historian Martin Gilbert, Fellow at Merton College, Oxford University, whose help was constant, advice invaluable and criticism important; to British historian Robert Rhodes James, whose assistance was vital to making the whole project possible by opening the first doors to important research sources and material; to Sir Shane Leslie and his charming wife, who gave me so much of their time and memory and made available to me letters, documents, and photographs; to the Duke of Marlborough for so graciously giving me permission to examine and copy the enormous file of family letters and papers held in the big black box in the Muniments Room of Blenheim Palace; and to the Duke's private secretary, Mrs. Eva Sharpe, for her constant cooperation; and to Miss K. M. Gell and her staff at the Muniments Room, Charles G. Dennis and Helen Wannerton, for their kindness and their patience; to Peregrine Churchill for making freely available his large collection of family letters and photographs, and for permitting me to make quotation from *The Reminiscences of Lady Randolph Churchill* on other material on which he holds the copyright; to Mrs. John Sloane and her husband, for allowing me access to the Jerome family bible and albums and for giving me copies of Jerome family pictures; to Mrs. Oswald Frewen, for freely permitting me use of her husband's diaries, as well as of the family letters; to Prince Clary of Venice and the Countess Kinsky in London, for their excellent background information on Count Kinsky; to Allen Andrews, who was so kind as to make available to me the then-unpublished manuscript of Moreton Frewen's collection of letters, entitled

The Splendid Pauper; to British publisher Mark Goulden, who helped me gain entrance to so many important research facilities in London; to Thomas Blackburn, managing director of the London *Express*, and Andrew Edwards of Beaverbrook Newspapers Ltd., who permitted my examination of their files and provided copies of material I requested; and to Michael Wybrow and his dear wife in Guildford, England, who provided me with lardycake and gave me unlimited use of their excellent Churchill library—one of the finest private libraries of its kind—and who helped me on some of the early research.

My gratitude also to Miss Marie Berry, Executive Secretary of the New York Genealogical and Biographical Society; Dr. Blake McKelvey, city historian of Rochester, New York; Mrs. Margaret H. Merhoff and Mrs. Dorothy S. Facer of the Wayne County Division of Archives and History in Lyons, New York; Rex Schaeffer, Library Director of the Rochester *Times-Union*; James Kelly, historian of Brooklyn, New York; Mrs. Kenn Stryker-Rodda, archivist of the Long Island Historical Society; Wayne C. Grover, archivist of the United States; Mason Tolman, Associate Librarian, and Ida M. Cohen, Senior Librarian, of the New York State Library; Alexander P. Clark, Curator of Manuscripts, Princeton University; Donald W. Marshall, town historian of Bedford, New York; Mrs. Miner C. Hill, Oyster Bay Historical Society; Miss Lenore Wysong, Empire State Society, Sons of the American Revolution; Dr. E. Taylor Parks, Historical Office of the State Department of the United States; Mrs. Elaine Mann, National Museum of Racing, Saratoga Springs, New York; Gertrude Annan, New York Academy of Medicine; Timothy Beard, Genealogical Room of the New York Public Library; Rutherford Rogers, chief of the Reference Department of the New York Public Library; G. Gelman, editor of the Wallingford (Connecticut) *Post*; Gerald Harrington Miller, town clerk of Wallingford; Mrs. Graham Wilcox, Curator of the Stockbridge Library Association, Stockbridge, Massachusetts; J. Guadagno of the Museum of the American Indian; Hope Emily Allen, historian of Pompey, New York; Virginia S. Hart, Chief of Information of the Bureau of Indian Affairs, United States Department of Interior.

My appreciation also to Robert Mockworth-Young, Librarian at Windsor Castle; R. J. Hill, Lord Chamberlain's Office at St. James Palace; Cleanth Brooks of the U.S. Embassy in London; Miss A. J. Fraser, Public Record Office in London; Miss M. Winder, Wellcome Historical Medical Society in London; the Staff of the Main Reading Room and the Manuscripts Room in the British Museum, who were most kind and patient; the Registrar of Somerset House in London; R. Rickinger of the Austrian Institute in London; Dr. Helmut Rumpler, Historiches Institut, Vienna; Mlle. Nelly Coadou and Mme. Claire Launois of the Institut Français du Royaume-Uni; the staff of the London Library and the Department of Archives in Paris.

For varied help and information, my thanks to Clara Booth Newell, Mrs. V. Colby, Mrs. Margot Levy, Hugo Dyson, Michael O'Connell, Adrian Bergson, Elsie Herron, Mrs. A. Verne Flint, Russell Bryant, Mrs. S. B. Morgan, Doris M. Nesbitt, Mrs. Sarah S. Dennen, Ray Rebhann, Emil Steinhauser, A. M. Keebler, Marion E. Snedeker, Kay Halle, Vera Curtis, Mrs. Arthur A. Corcoran, Dr. J. M. Spitzer, Dr. Robert Edelman, H. A. Cahn, Mrs. Alice L. Parker, D. W. Smythe, Jacqueline Bray, Erno Straus, Samuel Clarke, John Quinn, Charlotte Young, Len Slater, Mrs. Meryl Riecken, Mrs. Eleanor Claar, Philip Rosenberg, Carl Foreman and Alan Pizer.

My thanks, as always, to Director Ruth P. Greene and her staff at the Oyster Bay Public Library; particularly my deep gratitude to the very patient Mrs. Christine Lane, whose help has been constant and invaluable, and to the other staff members, Mrs. Annette S. Macedonio, Helen Baldwin, Ellen Coshignano, Gene McGrath, Patricia Stirrat, and Rosemary Burlew. As always, too, my thanks to Romana Javitz and her staff at the Picture Collection of the New York Public Library.

My personal thanks again for help beyond the call of friendship to Paul S. Green; Mrs. Pearl Bernier and the staff of Colony Offset Printing Company in Boston; Ruth Tropin; Peggy Leder; Sidney Shore; Abba P. Schwartz, former Undersecretary of State, U.S. State Department; Ed Plaut; David Lewin of the London *Daily Mail,* and his secretary Jean Cagienard; Irma Remsen; and to Mrs. Mari Walker who again, as always, had the difficult job of translating my handwriting, my notes, my tape recordings, and my manuscript into finished copy.

My warm appreciation to my good friend Harry Sions, who gave the manuscript the benefit of his sharp editorial wisdom; Mrs. Betty Copithorne, whose comments were similarly penetrating; and to my wife, Marjorie Jean, who was involved in some of the early research and criticism and who had the tedious job of deciphering the difficult handwriting in the letters of Lady Randolph Churchill.

A special note of thanks to my dear friend Howard Byrne, who believed in this book long before anybody else and who always placed the full facilities of his offices and the resources of his staff of Transatlantic News Features Ltd. at my disposal—my added thanks there to L. S. Symons and Mrs. Zena Fry.

A final personal note of thanks to Elizabeth Ruth Martin, Maury Martin, and Tina Suzanne Martin for their special help.

The judgments and opinions expressed in this book are entirely the author's own.

Prologue

VEN IN HER HOSPITAL BED, THIS WOMAN of sixty-seven looked almost a generation younger, her face nearly free of wrinkles, her smile dazzling, and her eyes, "great wild eyes," still luminous and eager.

In her time, she had been "the most influential Anglo-Saxon woman in the world."[1]

Out of her strength, she helped transform a social dilettante husband into one of the most important men in the British Empire; out of her love and ambition, she helped shape her son Winston into one of the great men of his century.

She sent her son the books that moulded his style of writing and speech; used her enormous influence to get him transferred from one war to another; got him his early assignments as a war correspondent; acted as agent to sell his first story and his first books; campaigned alongside him in his early elections; opened doors for him to all the important people of his time. But most of all, she gave him her courage and her stamina.[2]

It was a brassy kind of courage. In the last dramatic scene of her life, the doctor told her he would have to amputate her infected leg. This was a woman whose lovely legs and tiny feet were her special vanity—she had even displayed her collected evening shoes in a glass case. Yet, her answer came calmly and quickly: "Make sure you cut high enough."

Her stamina was also remarkable. In the course of a lifetime, Jennie was editor and publisher of an international literary magazine; organized a hospital ship for the Boer War and traveled with it for its first shipload of wounded; was a pianist of professional ability; took turns as playwright, author, reporter; directed national expositions and theatricals; single-handedly conducted political campaigns at a time when most women were not even permitted to attend the theater alone.

She married three times and characterized her second marriage as romantic but not successful, her third as successful but not romantic. At sixty-three, she had married a man younger than Winston, but her beauty was still so extraordinary that the marriage caused only a minimum of surprise.[3]

Jennie had few saintly qualities. She was, of course, what her world was. It was a world of hypocritical morals, as faked as the bustle, thinly gilded with pretentious propriety. She was also what her parents were: a snob like her mother, a sensualist like her father.

But what made her unique in her time was the drive, the special force that was her own. A Prime Minister's wife once said of Jennie, "she could have governed the world."[4]

In a sense, she almost did.

One

EONARD JEROME MAY WELL HAVE SERVED as the model for many of the men in his daughter's life. He was a man of considerable charm and extraordinary energy, a tall, handsome, bony-faced man with an impressive walrus mustache. He was also a fanatic lover of the horse and the race as well as of the woman and the chase. Nearly all the men Jennie loved, including the three she married, had most of those qualities, particularly the fierce zest for living.

At various times, Leonard Jerome was lawyer, newspaper editor, U.S. Consul at Trieste, art collector, part-owner of *The New York Times*.[1] Newspapers called him "The King of Wall Street," because he was a fabulous speculator who could make and lose millions of dollars, and then make them again. They also called him "The Father of the American Turf," because, almost single-handedly, he raised the social status of the horse race in the United States.

His private passion was music, and he financed the careers of many promising young singers–particularly if they were female and pretty. When the current love of his life was the famous singer, Jenny Lind, he had the audacity to persuade his unknowing wife to name their second daughter "Jennie."

Of his four daughters, Jennie was Leonard Jerome's favorite. When he was dying he said, "I have given you all I have. Pass it on." Much of what he gave her was a pattern of living, a conviction that life must be lived to the hilt, a sense that it was a waste to move through time without love.

That was part of his own heritage. The early Jeromes were among the thousands of Huguenot Protestants who fled France in search of religious freedom. But some failed to find it even in England and the Reverend William Jerome was burned at the stake in 1540. His descendents sailed to America. The first Jerome to become an American was an Englishman named Timothy, who came from the Isle of Wight in 1710.[2] In the strange completion of a circle, it was on the Isle of Wight, 164 years later, that Jennie Jerome took her first romantic step toward becoming an Englishwoman.

Timothy Jerome arrived at Meriden, Connecticut, with a royal grant for a monopoly on the salt-making in the area. He died rich and was buried on Buckwheat Hill overlooking the land he owned.[3] An inventory of his estate included a beaver hat, a punch bowl, a silk handkerchief, a large number of books, and four slaves named Pomp, Prince, Rose, and Jenny.[4]

During the American Revolution, Timothy's son Samuel fought alongside his own five sons. One of them, Aaron, married a cousin of George Washington. Since Washington had no lineal descendents, Leonard Jerome later claimed, "We are the closest of kin!"[5]

Aaron's son Isaac was also a soldier and a farmer, a quiet, conservative man, but his wife was a young Scotswoman, bright, witty, and ambitious. Her name was Aurora and she was the daughter of Reuben Murray, a soldier in the American Revolution,[6] a ready wit, a writer and balladeer, a tall, commanding figure full of drive and imagination who had made and lost several small fortunes. Isaac and Aurora Jerome had nine sons and three daughters.[7] Their fifth son, born in 1817, was Leonard Walter.

The Jeromes lived on a farm in the hill country of Pompey, New York. Isaac wanted to keep his sons on the farm, but the energetic Aurora insisted on packing the boys bundles and sending them out to seek their fortunes. Like his brothers, Leonard first worked at his farm chores. Later he got a job in the village store for a dollar a week and learned to dicker with the shrewd farmers who came to exchange their produce for store products.

Two of Leonard's older brothers had gone to the College of New Jersey, (which later became Princeton), and Leonard followed them there in 1836. A handsome boy who made friends easily, Leonard was involved in a number of college pranks. His most spectacular feat was to organize a group of a hundred students to return to the campus a huge cannon that had been captured during the War of 1812. The cannon is still there in the quadrangle, a prominent symbol of Princeton tradition.[8]

Princeton records also reveal that Leonard Jerome was suspended from school "for going to Trenton without permission."[9] He was caught tarring the seats in the prayer hall and sabotaging the chemistry teacher's test tubes so that they exploded in class. Perhaps in an attempt to compensate for all this ungentlemanly behavior, Jerome later offered Princeton an annual sum of $5,000 to be awarded to the best gentleman in the graduating class.[10] (*The New York Times* applauded the gesture and recommended that a similar award be offered in Congress, where, they felt, it was even more needed.) Princeton, however, rejected the award because "all Americans are equally born gentlemen."

Family financial pressure forced Leonard to transfer to the less expensive Union College in Schenectady, New York, where he sang a loud clear tenor in the college chorus and graduated near the top of his class. One of his cousins, who attended Union College several years later, was James Roosevelt, father of Franklin Delano Roosevelt.[11]

Leonard Jerome soon went to work for his uncle, Hiram Jerome. A former law partner of Abraham Lincoln, Hiram had become the first judge of the Wayne County Court in Palmyra, New York. Palmyra was then a thriving town of broad streets, gay shops, and elegant hotels facing the Erie Canal, where the painted packet boats passed in a continual flow. Leonard not only became a partner in his uncle's practice but was appointed notary public for the county and bought 170 acres of land north of Mud Creek. He and his younger brother Lawrence double-dated the Hall sisters, Clarissa and Catherine.

Clarissa, who later shortened her name to Clara, was a quiet young woman with a full figure and a substantial inheritance. She had a lovely oval face, brooding black eyes, beautiful black hair carefully parted in the middle. Some called her secretive and shy; her aunts claimed they could not tell what the girl was thinking and that she was a judicious flirt "who would fall into moods."

The Hall sisters had been orphaned early, and now lived with their aunts. Their father, Ambrose Hall, a tall, strikingly handsome man, had been a wealthy landowner and a prominent member of the New York State Assembly. Their mother, Clarissa Willcox, came from a Massachusetts family of early settlers. All the Hall women had black hair, dark features, and high cheekbones, which they referred to as "Hall-marks." The whispered family legend was that these features were a result of Indian blood, that their grandmother had been raped by an Iroquois.[12]

These Hall-marks seemed to become accentuated with age. In her later years, Jennie's mother Clara looked so much like an Indian that her kin referred to her as "Sitting Bull," just as they called Aunt Catherine "Hatchet Face." Even when Jennie's blonde sister died, a member of the family noted that "a strange change in her face gave her the look of an Indian. . . ." A nephew insists that Jennie herself took on the same look at her death.[13]

Uncle Hiram crimped the Jerome-Hall courtship by moving his law practice to Rochester and taking his nephews with him. A Rochester socialite[14] later remembered the Jerome brothers as "screamingly funny boys . . . very popular with the ladies owing to the dashing manner in which they rode high-spirited horses." Lawrence Jerome, however, soon married Catherine Hall, but Leonard Jerome took five years before proposing to Clara.

They were married on April 5, 1849. Leonard was thirty-two and Clara was twenty-four. The Jerome brothers bought houses alongside each other and built a connecting passage so they could visit without going outside. They lived in the fashionable Third Ward, the "ruffled-shirt ward," separated from the business district by the Erie Canal. Houses there were large, postcolonial homes, some with pretentious facades of Greek revival architecture, and most fitted with the newest convenience, the Bates Patent Chamber Shower Bath.

Rochester was a major shipping point for wheat and had a thriving upper-crust society with its own snob system. Clara Jerome fit in easily, decorating her home with red plush, expensive ormolu mirrors, white marble fireplaces, and carpets from Brussels. Clara's money also helped her husband buy the Rochester *Daily American*, which resulted in his deeper involvement in Whig politics. Political activity led to political patronage, and Leonard was soon offered an appointment as Consul to Ravenna. He turned down the appointment, however, because he had become involved in a telegraph line company in New York. To be close to his new business, he sold his interest in the Rochester newspaper in 1850 and moved with his wife to Brooklyn.

Brooklyn, then a legally independent city, had a population of some 120,000, and thirty-five miles of paved and lighted streets. Streetcars wouldn't arrive until 1853. The Jeromes lived in the section later known as Brooklyn Heights, where Jerome had rented a fifteen-room red brick house on Henry Street just a block from the East River. His older brother Addison, a New York stockbroker, moved in with them, and the two men commuted by ferry across the river to Wall Street.

Near the Jerome home was Plymouth Church, made famous because its preacher was one of the country's loudest and most dramatic voices against slavery, Henry Ward Beecher. Beecher's sister, Harriet Beecher Stowe, later wrote "the little book that started the Civil War."[15] In one of his most powerful sermons, Beecher yelled, "Sarah, come up here!" A small mulatto girl came to the pulpit and took his hand as Beecher said, "This little girl is a slave, and I have promised her owner 1200 dollars, his price for her, or she will be returned to slavery. Pass the baskets!" People threw in money, watches, and jewelry, and Beecher was able to announce, to their thunderous applause, that Sarah was free. Despite a notorious and scandalous affair with the wife of one of his parishioners, Beecher stayed on as pastor for some forty years, and kept his 2,800 church seats almost always full.

After a short time, Leonard sold his telegraph company and joined Addison in a full-scale plunge into stockmarket speculation. Leonard called Wall Street "a jungle where men tear and claw," but he thrived in it. When the New Haven Railroad was involved in a scandal over forged stock, Jerome helped lobby for and pass a railroad-reform bill to "clear up the chaos." He soon got a Wall Street reputation as a man who knew how to get things done.[16] A rival was even quoted as saying, "That damn fellow has cashed in on honesty."

Courage and a calculating coldness were the prime requisites of a Wall Street speculator. Jerome made much, because he was willing to risk much.

"How's business today, Leonard?" a friend remembered asking him.

"Oh, dull," said Jerome, "confoundedly dull. I have only made $25,000 today."[17]

He specialized in "selling short"—selling stock he did not yet own, to be delivered at a future date. The expectation was that in the interim the price would drop and he could then buy the stock more cheaply to fulfill his sale.

Leonard and Addison spent most of their evenings in Manhattan, either working hard or playing hard. Clara Jerome felt very much on the fringe. Her husband flourished financially and she had a houseful of servants and all the clothes she could buy, but she never really knew how to create excitement, as Leonard always did. Nor was she able to compete with her husband's diversions. Even her interest in music was so minimal that she seldom accompanied him to concerts.[18]

Clara was further restricted when her first child was born on April 15, 1851, a daughter they named Clarita. Less than a year later, Leonard blithely announced that they were all going to Trieste, where he had been appointed U.S. Consul, and that a Miss Lillie Greenough would accompany them.

Lillie was one of the several Rochester girls who had fallen in love with Leonard, and she was coming along, he said, to study Italian singing techniques. Clara was not overjoyed. Lillie even moved into their Trieste villa with them, but Clara branched out on her own, collecting her own covey of courtiers.[19] A visitor described her as "an elegant brunette with American vitality and Paris gowns." Soon Clara summoned enough courage to banish Miss Greenough and her piano to the attic.

Trieste was then the Austro-Hungarian Empire's only outlet to the Mediterranean, a city-state replete with Italian counts and castles. Leonard was not impressed. "They spoke more languages than I," he wrote, "but surely it is more important to think clearly in one idiom than to chatter in five." He continued his special interest in the opera (a visitor wrote that Jerome had gone to see Verdi's new opera, *Rigoletto*, some thirty times), in opera singers, his small white yacht, a pair of prize Lipizzaner stallions, and Lillie.

The Trieste interlude lasted only sixteen months. Back home there had been a national election, and Democratic President Franklin Pierce replaced Republican President Millard Fillmore. Jerome's resignation was promptly accepted. After a tour of Europe, the family was in Brooklyn by November 1853 in a rented house at 8 Amity Street, directly on the promenade facing the river view of New York.

Lillie was gone and Clara was pregnant again. But Leonard had renewed an earlier relationship with the Swedish Nightingale, Jenny Lind. Of her many admirers, Jenny Lind once remarked that Leonard Jerome was the best looking. Of Jenny, Leonard said, "Her voice is indescribable, like the dawn. Who wants more?"[20]

According to the family Bible belonging to Leonard's parents, the second daughter of Leonard and Clara was born on January 9, 1854.[21]

"Why not name her Jenny?" Leonard asked his wife.

Clara refused at first, but then reluctantly agreed. Only months later did she realize why he had insisted on the name.

They lived at Amity Street four more years. Jennie (shortened from Jeanette) had no memories of Brooklyn, but she must have walked along the promenade, gazed at the sailboats and paddleboats, fed the pigeons, occasionally watched volunteer firemen racing along with their ruffled shirts, high beaver hats, and long-tailed coats. It was in Brooklyn that still another Jerome daughter was born, Camille, in November 1855.

Leonard Jerome became a millionaire during the Panic of 1857, again by selling short. According to Oliver Guthrie, New York society now knew Jerome as "a great Don Juan, a great sportsman, and a beautiful whip." But he also increased the fund he had settled on his wife, bought her a magnificent diamond necklace, rented a summer home in Newport, and bought a yacht so he could sail there to visit his family.

Newport was the summer site of elegance, and the hub of its society was the Vanderbilt family, who later built a seventy-room stone Italian palazzo called "The Breakers." The Breakers had hot and cold running water (also hot and cold running saltwater) from silver taps. Bathtubs were carved out of solid marble, and the dining room was large enough for a dinner party of two hundred.[22]

Cornelius Vanderbilt was a big, bumptious man, a strong friend and a rough enemy, and he had taken a liking to Jerome. The two had been allies in the fight for control of the Harlem Railroad.[23] Many years later, Jennie was an honored guest at The Breakers staring at the huge chandeliers, each big enough to hold four men, and marveling at the sixteen footmen wearing silk breeches. The friendship between the Jeromes and Vanderbilts lasted several generations.[24]

The Jeromes moved to Paris in 1858, settling in a posh apartment on the Champs Elysées. Leonard Jerome noted briefly in a letter to his brother, "We have been to the Grand Ball at the Tuileries and were presented to the Emperor and the Empress. It was universally conceded that Clara was the handsomest woman there. I never saw her look so well."

Clara was blooming. "I have found the court I want," she wrote. But Archduke Maximilian, whom she had known in Trieste, was more critical. "The whole impression is of a make-believe court occupied by amateurs who are not very sure of their parts." One of these amateurs was Clara Jerome. She collected French aristocrats in small dinner parties and attended a series of salons that were "delightful" and "intimate." Another pregnancy slowed her pace only slightly. Leonard, however, was bored. "Paris is not as agreeable to me as New York," he wrote his brother. "I think I shall spend next summer at the Isle of Wight. It is a great place for yachting, horses. . . ."

Their fourth child was another daughter, and they named her Leonie (French feminine for Leonard). In 1859 Jerome brought them all back to New York.

New York was the nation's largest city, with a population of some 500,000, but Fifth Avenue was still unpaved north of Twenty-third Street, and most of Manhattan was rolling farmland spotted with summer estates. Jerome bought a piece of land on the southeast corner of Twenty-sixth Street in Madison Square, the new center for the sedate and the social. The Square's six acres had once been a pauper's burying ground, the site of the city circus, a playing field for the first organized baseball club, and was still the address of the fanciest bordello in town, "The Louvre," which advertised itself as "the most refined of its sort in the world."

Madison Square had begun its transformation when four-story private homes started to take over the fringes. Delmonico's Restaurant added splash to the area. Newly completed a few blocks away was the spectacular Fifth Avenue Hotel, with "a perpendicular railway intersecting each story" (later known as an elevator), a central heating system, and the startling innovation of indoor toilets—which some critics considered "not only unsanitary but immoral."[25]

Jerome had promised his wife, "I'll build you a palace yet." And he practically did.[26] His plot of land was close to the splendid new house of

Mrs. Schermerhorn, who had snubbed the Jeromes earlier. To outshine their neighbor, Clara insisted they design their house in the style of Napoleon III's Paris. The handsome six-story, red brick house trimmed with marble, with a steep mansard roof, tall windows, and delicate ironwork contrasted sharply with the more simple brownstone homes on the Square. It had a white and gold ballroom that could accommodate some three hundred people, a breakfast room that could seat seventy, a huge drawing room that Clara decorated in flaming red.

Leonard lavished most of his attention on the adjacent stable. Built at a cost of some $80,000, it was three stories high, thickly carpeted and paneled with black walnut. "Except for the Emperor's Mews in Paris, it is doubtful if any stable in the world . . . surpassed Jerome's," reported *The New York Tribune*.

Attached to it was an equally unique private theater that seated six hundred. "As you entered, you were received by liveried servants, and by them, conducted to your seat where you found yourself surrounded by the most brilliant assemblage, and, on the stage, as amateur actresses supporting the fair singer, the fashionable beauties of that day." That opening-day party for Jerome's Theater was in the tradition of the grand gesture—walls of roses and gardenias, fountains spouting champagne or eau de cologne.[27]

For Jerome, all this grandeur was a form of direct competition with his good friend August Belmont. Belmont was the renowned Rothschild representative in the United States. He was a short, heavy-set man with a limp (caused by a duel) and a foreign accent which many mistook for French, although his heritage was German and Jewish. Like Jerome, Belmont was a self-made millionaire with a razor mind and a biting wit, and both men were connoisseurs of women, horses, art, and good food. Belmont was married to the lovely daughter of Commodore Perry, and the costume balls at the Belmont home on Fifth Avenue were the social affairs of the season.[28]

One of the fashionable beauties for whom Belmont and Jerome competed was Mrs. Fanny Ronalds, a Boston divorcée who had been a celebrated concert singer. Frank Griswold discreetly noted the contest in his privately printed memoirs:

> There were two outstanding men at that time who were most prominent in all social and sporting events. They both drove coaches and four, and had large racing stables; both were married and in the prime of life. These two men fell desperately in love with Mrs. R–. L– and A– were rivals who kept the house of their lady filled with flowers and attempted to satisfy her every desire. She proved to be an accomplished general, for she managed these two great men with much skill.

Both men helped manage her money and multiply it. Both taught her how to handle plunging horses, and Leonard let her give a concert in his private theater. Both also helped her produce the most sensational ball of many seasons, at which Fanny wore a harp-shaped crown lit up by tiny gas jets from a holder hidden in her hair.

Twenty years later, Jerome and Belmont lunched together with their friend Frank Griswold, who recorded the conversation:

"August," said Jerome, "do you remember Fanny's celebrated ball?"

"Indeed, I ought to," replied Belmont. "I paid for it."

"Why, how very strange," said Jerome slowly. "So did I."

Jennie was not quite six years old when she first met Fanny, but the early memory lingered. "Mrs. Ronalds, who was as gifted as she was lovely, and shared the reputation of being the reigning beauty, gave me a species of small dog-cart and two donkeys which rejoiced in the names of 'Willie' and 'Wooshey.'" The donkeys, of course, were kept at Newport.

The Jerome residence in New York was more of a display place than a home, and little girls were trained to sit gingerly on fine furniture, and never, never venture outside unless surrounded by servants. Little girls were supposed to move and act like little dolls, a studied part of the museum atmosphere. The upbringing of children was largely left to maids and nurses and teachers.[29]

Clara Jerome's major concern seemed to be clothes. Her diamonds and gowns now needed an inventory to keep them in order. William Allen Butler wrote a poem entitled "Nothing To Wear" about women such as Clara:

> *Miss Flora McFlimsey, of Madison Square,*
> *Has made three separate journeys to Paris,*
> *And her father assures me, each time she was there,*
> *That she and her friend, Mrs. Harris . . .*
> *Spent six consecutive weeks without stopping*
> *In one continuous round of shopping.*
> *And yet, though scarce three months have passed since the day,*
> *This merchandise went in 12 carts up Broadway,*
> *This same Miss McFlimsey, of Madison Square,*
> *The last time we met, was in utter despair,*
> *Because she had nothing whatever to wear!*

Jennie cared more for horses than for clothes, and spent as much time as she could in her father's stable. Her father insisted that his daughters learn to play the piano, and Jennie's first teacher was Stephen Heller, a friend of Chopin. It was Heller who told her that if she practiced seriously enough, she might someday be a concert pianist. Her father's theater made its own impact on the imaginative Jennie. When there was a rehearsal in progress, young Jennie was often an avid audience, and the dramatic excitement of an opening night stirred the entire household.

In 1860 Jerome was an organizer of the Grand Ball for the Prince of Wales. The visiting Prince was nineteen, handsome, and bored. The Duke of Newcastle, his guide and guard, noted disapprovingly that the way American women pressed themselves upon the Prince was "not in strict accordance with good breeding." One of the would-be admirers was seven-year-old Jennie, who announced her determination to attend the ball and dance with the Prince. It was a tearful night for Jennie when she was not permitted to go. As for the Prince, it was reported in the gossip sheets that he escaped the watchful eye of the Duke of Newcastle one night "and disported himself riotously in the most luxurious brothels."

Clara Jerome kept her daughters within a strict social framework. "Unlike most American children, we were seldom permitted to go to boy-and-girl dances," Jennie later wrote.[30] But there was a costume ball given by August Belmont which Jennie did attend, and she even took a photograph to prove it. She was costumed as a *vivandière*. "For days I did not sleep with the excitement of anticipation, but on the eventful night I was found in a flood of tears, the explanation being that I did not look 'at all as I thought I was going to'—a situation which alas! has often repeated itself."

The fun for Jennie was not on Madison Square, but at the Jerome summer house at Newport, a charming seaside villa. "We were allowed to run wild and be as grubby and happy as children ought to be," Jennie wrote. Harnessed to a cart filled with a half-dozen children, Willie and Wooshey tore up and down Bellevue Avenue "at the risks of our necks and everyone else's." To urge the donkeys on, Jennie used a stick she called "The Persuader," which featured "the business end of a tack" at its tip. "The cart and its occupants soon became a terror to the smart folk in their silks and feathers. These were delightful days."

Clara Jerome unhappily told her husband that Jennie "should have been a boy." Yet to some extent, Clara encouraged Jennie's behavior. The regimen for her daughters included "plenty of milk, plenty of sleep and plenty of flannel"; to that, Clara added plenty of exercise, fresh air, and cold baths. "Strong women make beautiful women," she said.

One of their frequent summer visitors at Newport was Fanny Ronalds. Leonard Jerome often brought her along with him from New York on his new steam yacht named *Clara Clarita*, the interior of which was furnished in pale blue silk and hammered silver.[31] Clara seems to have become accustomed to her husband's extra-marital relationships: she was quoted as having said to Fanny when they first met, "I don't blame you. I know how irresistible he is."[32]

Fanny not only filled in as occasional substitute wife in the Jerome family, but also as substitute mother. Her own three children were apparently living with her former husband or away at school, so she gave some of her maternal love to Jennie and her sisters, who soon "allowed her to become a favorite." Long afterward, Jennie fondly remembered how Fanny Ronalds used to sing to the children in the evening before bedtime. Her relationship with Fanny would last their lifetimes, for Fanny had all the qualities Jennie admired most: beauty and talent and force and sensitivity.

Jennie's mother Clara had mainly beauty. It is small wonder that the many-faceted Leonard Jerome sought elsewhere for fulfillment. It is even less surprising that Jennie sought, and found, in other women the model of the mother she wanted.

Lillie Greenough, who had since married, summed up the lack in Leonard's life when she wrote him, "I love you more than ever because I feel you are never getting as strong love from anyone else." If Leonard didn't, it was hardly because he wasn't trying. His newest protégée was seventeen-year-old Adelina Patti, whose voice reminded him of Jenny Lind. Jerome launched her musical career in his theater and helped sponsor her first concert tour.

Jennie liked Adelina, too, but she liked young Minnie Hauk more. Minnie reportedly was Leonard Jerome's illegitimate daughter by an earlier romance. Jerome and Belmont both financed Minnie's musical education, promoted her sensational debut when she was only fifteen, and later put her under Adelina Patti's private tutelage. Minnie and Jennie looked very much like sisters, and Clara Jerome wrote on the back of Minnie's picture, "So like Jennie, but less good-looking."

Minnie reminisced in her memoirs[33] that "I was quite at home" in the Jerome house and remembered how warmly the Jerome girls accepted her. She also commented on the beautiful horses the girls had and their habit of riding many miles before breakfast. "They rode like Amazons."

Jerome had bought the old Bathgate estate at Fordham, in Westchester County. With 230 acres and a small racetrack of its own, the estate offered Jennie and her sisters even more freedom than Newport. Before Jennie was ten, the horse had replaced Willie and Wooshey, and at Bathgate Jennie had all the space needed to ride and race in the wild, free way she loved.

Jennie's younger sister Camille died of a sudden fever in 1863 at the age of six. The shock tightened Jennie's relationship with her older sister, Clarita, then twelve, and with Leonie, not quite five. Leonard's brother, Addison, also died about that time.

The country seemed full of death, for the Civil War had begun. "I remember nothing about it," Jennie reminisced, "except that every little Southerner I met at dancing school was 'a wicked rebel,' to be pinched, if possible." Her father, however, was deeply committed to the Union and must have brought his involvement home with him. Believing that one of the causes of the tragic war was the Negro's untenable position in American life, he helped with the government plan to start a colony of five thousand American Negroes on Haiti. When the government refused to support the Negroes financially while they organized themselves, and when he learned they were being maltreated on the island, Jerome withdrew.[34] (The scheme was finally a fiasco and most of the Negroes were returned.) Jerome also was Treasurer of the Union Defense Committee and paid for many of their activities. He personally contributed $35,000 toward the construction of the warship *Meteor*, served as an advisor to the government on its proposed Bank Bill, and was founder of the fund for families of the killed and wounded in New York's Draft Riots of 1863.[35]

The police had been unable to control the Draft Riots, and New York was overcome by looting mobs. Armed with torches, guns, and pikes, they roved in packs of several thousand, beating and hanging and burning Negroes, whom they blamed for the war. One gang broke into a Negro orphanage and threw children out of the windows. Jennie could not have been so sheltered that she did not hear of all this. And surely she must have known that her father, who owned a one-fifth interest in *The New York Times*, had manned one of the two new breech-loading machine guns given by the Army to the *Times* when a mob threatened to destroy the building. (Jerome never had to fire—when word of the guns at the windows reached the rioters, they moved on to the *Tribune,* singing "We'll hang old Horace Greeley to a sour apple tree." Two hundred police arrived to help the newsmen beat them back.[36])

Jennie was eleven years old when President Lincoln was assassinated. "I remember our house in Madison Square draped from top to bottom in white and black and the whole of New York looking like one gigantic mausoleum."

When the war ended, Jerome turned his full attentions again to music, art, money-making, women-chasing, and horse racing. "People like Belmont and Jerome do not enter Society," wrote Mrs. Frank Griswold, "they create it as they go along." As part of the creative process, the two formed The Coaching Club in an attempt to revive four-in-hand driving as a fashionable sport. "[Jerome's] horses were trained to caper and rear as they turned into the street," a reporter noted. "Gay and laughing ladies, in gorgeous costume, filled the carriage. Lackeys, carefully gotten up, occupied the coupe behind. Jerome sat on the box and handled the reins. With a huge bouquet of flowers attached to his buttonhole, with white gloves, cracking his whip, and with the shouts of the party, the four horses would rush up Fifth Avenue on towards the Park, while the populace said to one another, 'That is Jerome.' "[37]

With Belmont's help, Jerome also elevated the horse race from the rowdy to the social. On his Bathgate estate, he built the most elaborate racetrack in the country, sporting a grandstand seating 8,000 people, a luxurious clubhouse with a glittering ballroom, dining rooms, overnight guest rooms, and facilities for such diversions as trapshooting, polo, sleighing, and skating.

Opening day of the Jerome Racetrack on September 25, 1866, was described by the New York *Tribune* as "the social event of all time . . . a new era in the horse-racing world." Among the special guests was General Ulysses S. Grant. Adelina Patti and Fanny Ronalds were also there, and, it might be mentioned, so was Jerome's Madison Square neighbor, the madame of The Louvre. All three horses in the race were sired by the famous Lexington, and none had ever lost a race. One of them was Kentucky, for whom Jerome had paid forty thousand dollars. Clara Jerome left early, feeling faint, but Leonard insisted on keeping Jennie with him. Kentucky won, and Jerome lifted Jennie onto the horse's back while the crowd cheered. For twelve-year-old Jennie it was one of the unforgettable moments of her life.

Jerome built a small cottage near his racetrack, where his family could spend winter weekends. He even had an area flooded and frozen so that Clarita and Jennie could waltz on the ice while a band played in the cold air. Clarita, by then a young lady of fifteen, was a less venturesome skater than Jennie, who was called the "madcap." Fanny Ronalds, a superb skater, was often there, too, showing Jennie how to do figure eights in a shortened hoop skirt.

Jerome, Belmont, and Leonard's cousin and partner, William Travers, known as "The Stammering Wit of Wall Street,"[38] founded the American Jockey Club. *The New York Times* credited Jerome with "weeding out the blackguards who then controlled the Turf." It was then that reporters started referring to Jerome as "The Father of the American Turf."

When he wasn't racing horses, Jerome was racing yachts. He and his brother Lawrence proposed the first international yacht race across the Atlantic, with a ninety thousand dollar stake, winner take all. At the victory party with the Royal Yacht Squadron at Cowes on the Isle of Wight, observers noted that the Jerome brothers were the "life and soul of the party." During the dinner that night, Lawrence Jerome had a note delivered to him in a royal envelope, which he had picked up during a tour of the Queen's summer home earlier in the day. The Royal Yacht Squadron watched him open it, toss it carelessly aside, and then remark loudly to Leonard, "I am so sorry I cannot dine with the Queen, as we have a previous engagement which it would be ungentlemanly to break." The Royal Yacht Squadron's reaction was apoplectic. Lawrence finally pretended to let himself be persuaded to accept the Queen's invitation.[39]

After returning to New York, Leonard Jerome maintained his tradition of the grand gesture with a dinner at Delmonico's where each lady found a souvenir under her napkin—a gold bracelet.[40] "One rode better, sailed better, banqueted better when Mr. Jerome was of the company," noted a commentator of the time.[41]

Newspapers and magazines and gossip sheets were full of Jerome happenings. Clarita read them and passed on the nuggets to twelve-year-old Jennie. For Jennie, at least, all this notoriety and adventure made Jerome seem even more a romantic figure. Besides, her father somehow always found the time to take Jennie to the opera or a concert or a matinee, "to improve my mind." Father and daughter enjoyed each other deeply. Clarita's mind took a different turn; she shared her mother's concern for clothes instead of shows and spent more time having her hair fashionably frizzled by her French maid.

Clara Jerome had found herself unable to compete with Mrs. August Belmont, described in the press as the "Queen of High Life," whose high style, French manner, exquisite jewels, and flamboyant parties were constantly discussed. More than that, Clara could no longer countenance the publicity of her husband's flagrant affairs. She therefore told Leonard that she was moving with her daughters to Paris, permanently. He could visit them whenever he wished.

Two

$\mathcal{T}$HE YEAR WAS 1867, and jennie was thirteen years old. The impending break in her parents' marriage must have been traumatic, but Clara Jerome probably assured her daughters that their father's absence was only temporary. Indeed, she counted on her husband soon tiring of his many women and finally returning to his family.

They moved into an elegant apartment in the Boulevard Maesherbes, the most fashionable section of Paris. At forty-two, Clara was still a handsome woman, although she now needed flouncing gowns to hide her growing plumpness.

Paris had a population of some two million people, but it seemed like a city freshly finished. Napoleon III[1] had done for Paris what Queen Victoria had done for London—transformed a medieval town into a city of grandeur. He had built the best of the boulevards, created permanent structures for the famous Les Halles markets, designed the Etoile, given the Bois de Boulogne its final shape, and completed the monumental design of the Louvre—doing more in five years than his predecessors had done in seven hundred. A historian described his regime as "a government of cheap bread, great public works and holidays."[2]

By the time the Jerome women settled into their new home, the extravagant new Paris Exhibition was in full swing, the city full of national costumes and visiting royalty.[3] "Never had the Empire seemed more assured, the court more brilliant, the fêtes more gorgeous," Jennie later wrote. "The light-hearted Parisians revelled in the daily sights of royal processions and cavalcades. The Bois de Boulogne and the Champs Elysées were crowded with splendid equipages. . . ." Her mother's awed respect for any royalty had made its imprint on Jennie, and she used to watch and wait for the Empress driving in her daumont, "the green and gold liveries of the postilions and outriders making a brave show."[4]

The importance of all this was intensified for Jennie when in 1869 Clarita made her debut at the Imperial Court. For fifteen-year-old Jennie, it was as if Clarita were being given a key to freedom. No more governesses, no more rigid rules about bedtime and cold baths, no more "little girl" clothes. Everywhere outside was the world of romance and adventure, and the door was open. Jennie could hardly wait for her own years to race by.

Jennie described in loving detail how Clarita looked in her low-cut dress of billowing white tulle, and the way her blonde hair hung in ringlets on her neck. Then she continued,

> When the company was assembled, the doors were flung open and *Sa Mageste l'Empereur* was announced. Then, after a pause, *Sa Majeste l'Impératrice* appeared, a resplendent figure in green velvet, with a crown of emeralds and diamonds, spiked with pearls, on her small and beautifully shaped head. The Emperor and Empress walked around in the circle of curtsying and bowing guests, addressing a few words here and there, and proceeded to the ballroom.

Jennie not only actively identified herself with every step of her sister's debut, but thereafter served as a messenger, intermediary, and sister-confessor for the cluster of Clarita's beaus. One was the Duc de Lescera, a Spanish relative of the Empress, whom Clara Jerome had vetoed because he was a Catholic–she wanted only Protestant proposals for her daughters. Jennie one day acted as the Duke's guide through a side window into the drawing room. Mrs. Jerome unexpectedly marched into the room while the Duke and Clarita were together. Clarita and Lescera froze. Mrs. Jerome was so nearsighted, however, that she mistook Lescera for one of the servants and ordered him to deliver an immediate message to the cook about dinner that night. "Oui, Madame," said the Duke, and gratefully exited.

At the end of 1869, Jennie was almost sixteen, mature and ripe beyond her years. She was not simply budding, she was flowering. She had a figure that men's eyes lingered on, and her eyes had a dazzle and a magnetic impudence. Dreams of romance now held priority over horses, but her sister's complicated love life discouraged Jennie about marriage. "I am never going to marry," she told her father. "I'm going to be a musician."[5] She did practice at the piano four hours a day, but that was not a sufficient outlet for her energies. She was, after all, at the age of greatest susceptibility, open and warm, ready to accept any of the romance and wonder of life.

Her father was an ideal escort, particularly at this time. His need for her then was as great as her need for him. *Harper's Weekly*[6] had commented that if Leonard Jerome had been born in another age, "he would have led charges of dragoons." But Jerome had charged too deeply into the stock-market, badly misjudging its ability to absorb his huge amount of surplus railroad stock.[7] The price dropped suddenly, and Jerome found himself badly battered, most of his huge fortune gone.[8] He told his family nothing of the disaster but leased his Madison Square house to the Union League Club and came to Paris.

Jennie gave him the lift and love he needed. He took her horseback riding, to picnics, parties, the theater, opera, concerts. He was still an impressively handsome man, sophisticated in the ways of the world, and he gave her a grown-up look at the swirl of society that she had never had before.

Jennie soon found other men, older men, buzzing around her. Fanny Ronalds had come to Paris, so Leonard Jerome found it necessary to ask his good friend, the Prince de Sagan, a descendent of the Marquis de Tallyrand, to substitute as escort for Jennie. Sagan was charmed by the fresh, lovely Jennie on their frequent rides in the Bois de Boulogne. Mounted on a fiery chestnut horse, she remembered, "I fancied myself vastly." The Prince impressed Jennie enormously and she described him well:

> He was a remarkable looking man, about forty-five, with snow-white curly hair which stood out like a lion's mane, and through which he had a habit of passing his fingers. With a well set-up figure, irreproachable clothes, a white carnation in his buttonhole and an eyeglass to which he attached a black moiré ribbon which became the fashion, he was undoubtedly the ideal Parisian beau. His name, his fetes, his extravagances were on all lips. . . .

Jennie looked like a woman, rode like a woman, acted like a woman. The Prince, who was not the fatherly type, obviously made her feel like a woman.

After all, what was Jennie's frame of reference? Her father, with whom she felt closest? Certainly by then she was fully aware of the way of his life. Her sister Clarita? Jennie was completely informed of every detail of her many romantic maneuverings. Her mother? Clara Jerome had instituted a steady series of soirees, always fringed with a variety of suitors. The social circle of the Imperial Court? Emperor Napoleon set the pace, and everybody knew that he was a man of many women, had fathered a number of illegitimate children, and always seemed to be in the process of disengaging himself from one mistress in order to move on to another.

It was hardly surprising to Jennie, then, that the Duc de Persigny, a close friend and political ally of the Emperor, was also married, the father of five children, and yet one of Clara Jerome's most attentive suitors. Nor did Persigny's constant court of Clara deter him from playing the gallant to both Clarita and Jennie. During one dance, the Duke's interest in Jennie was so obvious—and Jennie's responsive smile so flirtatious—that the Duchess de Persigny walked over to Jennie and publicly boxed her ears. Such was the morality of the day that even while her ears were being boxed by the indignant Duchess, Jennie knew—as all the Court knew—that the Duchess had so many extramarital affairs that even the Emperor had felt obliged to warn Persigny about it.

Leonard Jerome did complain to his wife about the wildness of his daughters. "Well, dear," she responded, "they are *your* daughters."[9] Her point was well taken, of course, but they were also daughters of their time. The values, rules, and goals of women of their class were, with varying emphases, also theirs.

The standard was the Empress Eugénie, whom each of the Jerome women viewed from her own perspective. Clara saw the Empress Eugénie in terms of her incomparable social prestige; Clarita was overwhelmed by her elaborate wardrobe of some three hundred dresses and her magnificent jewels; ten-year-old Leonie saw her as the fairy queen come true; and Jennie marveled at her being not only the handsomest woman in Europe but a woman of power, who could move men, influence decisions of state, change history.

Marie-Eugénie Ignace Augustine de Montijo was tall, beautifully formed, and elegantly graceful. The Austrian Ambassador, Prince Metternich, himself a connoisseur of women, called her "all fire and flame." On the other hand, Maxime de Camp described the Empress Eugénie as "superficial . . . always pre-occupied with the impression she made, parading her shoulders and bosom, her hair dyed, her face painted, her lips rouged . . . with no passion but vanity . . . enveloped in a sovereignty which she didn't know how to wear. . . . To be in her proper sphere, she only lacked the music of the circus, the cantering decorated horse, the hoop through which to jump and the kiss to the spectators. . . ."[10]

There was a romantic story that the reason Eugénie did not marry until she was twenty-six was that she had had a frustrated love affair with a young man who preferred her sister. The story added that Eugénie even tried to poison herself and that the whole affair soured her on men. When she married Charles Louis Napoleon, he was some twenty years her senior, a short, squat man, with a disproportionately large head, a sharply-cut goatee, and a needle-point mustache. Napoleon had originally offered Eugénie his bed but not his throne. Only when she indignantly refused, did he propose marriage.[11] Their marriage, however, did not impede Napoleon's parade of mistresses. After two miscarriages, Eugénie gave birth to her only child, the Prince Imperial. After that, her relationship with Napoleon was purely platonic.[12]

"Destiny always has a sad side to it," the Empress wrote her sister. "For instance, I, who was always longing to be free, have chained my life; I shall never be alone, never free. I shall be surrounded with the etiquette of court, whose principal victim I shall be." Then she added, "Papa said to me one day, when we were talking politics: *'Las mujeres a hacer calceta!'* [Women are for knitting stockings]. I know very well I am not destined for that!"[13]

Eugénie showed an increasing favoritism for foreigners, particularly the Americans living in Paris. Her grandfather was an American, William Kirkpatrick, who had served as U.S. Consul at Malaga. Napoleon similarly enjoyed Americans. When he was still the young Pretender to the French throne, he had spent a happy, romantic exile in the United States and had even outlined a novel he hoped to write about a French grocer who emigrated to America.

Clara Jerome and her daughters were swept into the inner circle of the Empress. Eugénie found in Jennie the warmth and laughter that she herself had seldom had, and she and Jennie became close friends. For Jennie, this was another substitute mother-daughter relationship of considerable importance. She learned from the Empress not only the extravagances of power, but the loneliness of it. She learned, too, that majesty without love is hollow.

It was the Princess Mathilde who had introduced Eugénie to Napoleon. Mathilde was the daughter of the old roué King Jerome of Westphalia and a niece of Napoleon Bonaparte. She was a cousin of Louis Napoleon and had been engaged to marry him, but her father broke it off when Napoleon failed in his early coup to regain power. Instead, her father arranged a marriage for her with an immensely wealthy Russian, from whom she was soon separated. After Louis Napoleon became Emperor, he again proposed marriage, but Mathilde refused him. "I refused . . . without any hesitation and without the slightest regret," she said. "I should have been unable to give up my independence, and I should have felt that my heart was not in it." To a close friend, Mathilde later added, "If I had married him, I should have broken his head open to see what was inside."[14]

Jennie was fascinated with Princess Mathilde and called her "undoubtedly the most brilliant and intelligent woman of the Second Empire." When

Jennie knew her, Mathilde was in her late forties, a handsome, animated woman with a lively, piercing glance, a woman in the full flush of life, always surrounded by men.

"The Princess loved to surround herself with all those possessing wit and talent," Jennie later wrote, "and her salon had a world-wide reputation, comparing easily with the famous salons of the eighteenth century, with the added attraction and glamor of royalty and great wealth. . . . It was there that some of the young and pretty Americans in Paris . . . had the privilege of meeting such men as Dumas, Sardou, Théophile Gautier, Baudry and other habitués of the house." Some of the others included Proust, Guy de Maupassant, Anatole France, and Gustave Flaubert.

Sixteen-year-old Jennie was deeply impressed with the ease with which Mathilde could talk with men of intellect. Her soirees sparkled, unlike the dreary, formal "Little Mondays" of Empress Eugénie's set.[15] It was the difference, Jennie decided, between a bitter, lonely woman and a woman who loved life and loved love. Mathilde's men were always much younger than she was, but she once advised a friend who was tempted to marry a much younger man: "You are in love with him; he is good-looking and he pleases you; keep him at your side but do not marry him."[16] Those words meant little to Jennie then, but later they would mean more.

Jennie was also impressed with Mathilde's imagination and taste in decorating her two homes, a flair that Jennie soon found within herself. In fact, she saw in Prince Mathilde many facets of the woman she herself wanted to become.

If Empress Eugénie represented the majestic mother to Jennie, and Princess Mathilde the exciting aunt, Princess Pauline Metternich seemed like the older sister with whom Jennie most easily identified and whom she probably most admired. The Princess was about a dozen years older than Jennie, but the two had much in common: extraordinary beauty, strong will, warm heart, capricious moods, passionate speech, wit, and vivacity. "Her repartee and *bons mots* were on everybody's lips," said Jennie, "her dresses were the models all tried to copy and her company was eagerly sought by the greatest in the land."

The Princess and Jennie also shared a love of music and the theater. It was Pauline who was mainly responsible for presenting the first performance of *Tannhäuser* in Paris. And she organized theatricals and ballets and revues where she herself played some of the parts and sang some of the songs. One listener noted how surprised she was to hear Princess Pauline sing "broad—very broad—Parisian songs . . . with more dash and spirit than one has ever heard in any theater."[17]

Pauline was married to the handsome Austrian Ambassador, who was a chronic woman chaser. She herself became the discreet favorite of Napoleon III.

-◆◈-

Jennie's friend, the Duc de Persigny, was a caustic critic of the role that upper-class society played in French government—particularly the circle close to the Empress. He called them "brilliant and frivolous, chivalrous and war-loving, but lacking the virtues needed in a free state."[18]

The war-loving quality was quite in evidence by 1870. Prussian Chancellor Otto von Bismarck, the most calculating mind in Europe, had made Prussia the new center of the North German Confederation. "We could not have set up the German *Reich* in the middle of Europe without having defeated France . . ." he said.[19] Napoleon did not want war, but the Empress did, and so did most of the Court. Napoleon's misadventure in Mexico had cost the French dearly in men, money and material, and he knew that there were now horses without harnesses, cannon without ammunition, and machine guns without men who knew how to fire them. Besides, the French Army could only muster 300,000 men in the field with no reserves, while the Prussians had almost 500,000 ready men and large reserves. But when told that the Prussians represented the race of the future, Empress Eugénie answered icily, "We are not there yet."[20]

Meanwhile the Imperial social life never stopped. Jennie described the scale and style of one Royal weekend at Compiègne.

> It was much smaller than usual (less than a hundred people), on account of the Emperor's bad health and political worries.
>
> There was a *grande chasse* or stag hunt on the first day, at which all the guests appeared, riding or driving. Those who hunted wore the royal colors, the men in the green coats and the gold hunt buttons, the ladies in flowing green habits and three-cornered hats. The stag on this occasion was brought to bay in a lake, the Prince Imperial giving him the *coup de grâce*. At night there was a *curée aux flambeaux* in the courtyard of the chateau, the whole party assembling on the balconies in the glare of the innumerable torches. The carcass of the deer lay in the center, covered with its skin; the *hallai* was sounded; at the signal, the hounds were unleashed, and in a moment, every vestige of the stag had disappeared.

The men then escorted their ladies into the dining room where the table was set with Napoleon's magnificent initialed gold dinnerware. Since Napoleon disliked lingering over his meals, everyone ate quickly. Afterward, the Emperor staged one of his grand lotteries of prizes, which were usually rigged so that the most prominent guests won something. The American Ambassador, for example, seldom went home empty-handed. At this party, Clarita won an inkstand filled with gold Napoleon coins, while Clara won some valuable pieces of Sèvres china.

That spring of 1870, Leonard Jerome wrote from New York, "Everyone is getting tiresome here." His solution was to take Jennie and Clarita for a vacation in Nice. Clarita reported to their mother, still in Paris:

> Papa was very tired last night when he got here, but this morning he looked so fresh and handsome that we told him the ladies would all be after him. . . . We have arranged a little surprise for Pa. He has gone out and said he wouldn't be home till four. So Jennie and I have arranged a little salon so prettily, and brought home flowers to make it look "homey." . . . I suppose Jennie told you what a charming day we passed at Cannes . . . there was Lord-Someone-or-Another and his father, the Earl-of-Something-Else. . . . Madame Rothschild, from Vienna, asked me if I knew Mrs. Belmont. . . .

But even in the comparative calm of Cannes there was increased talk of the coming war with Prussia. Collision finally came on a point of pride—because Bismarck wanted it to come. He maneuvered a touchy political situation in Spain into a war crisis and then heightened the crisis by carefully editing a telegram from the French government to make it seem like a stinging insult to the German government. Unaware that the telegram had been altered, King William of Prussia sent a stiff reply to France. Bismarck called it "a red rag to the Gallic bull."[21]

Paris in the summer of 1870 was in high fever. "The war, the war, there is no other topic," noted a young American woman. "Utter strangers would stop to discuss the situation. The confidence in the generals and the army was immense. It was to be one long but straight march to Berlin; not a soul doubted it. . . . I shall never forget the excitement." Thousands packed the Place de la Concorde night after night with scenes of frenzied dancing. Boulevard windows were so thick with waving flags that one could hardly see the faces behind them. Anyone who dared openly question the wisdom of the war was called a "Prussian spy" and jeered and hooted at and chased. One mob overturned a beer cart and everybody filled glasses and toasted, *"Vive l'Empereur . . . Vive la France . . . Vive l'Armée!!!!"* Another stopped a bus and asked an opera singer inside to stand on top of it to sing the "Marseillaise." "There was a profound silence when she sang the first note," an American onlooker observed, "but all Paris seemed to take up the chorus after each stanza. . . . There were real tears in the singer's eyes, and her voice trembled with genuine emotion. . . ."[22]

Jennie had persuaded her mother to let her wander the streets and share in the excitement. Clara sent along Jennie's childhood nurse, Dobbie, a large American Negro woman who was visible in any crowd because of her green turban and red shawl. Jennie knew little of the real meaning of the war. The Duc de Persigny had filled in some of the background for the Jerome women, and the Empress had given them her highly emotional point of view. But Jennie was caught up in the drama of the moment, the deeply charged patriotism of the people. She was not a watcher; she was a participant, a sixteen-year-old girl who cried and clapped and cheered and waved.

Walking home from the Opera one evening, Jennie and her mother and sister saw crowds of men marching to the cry of, *"des chassepots . . . des chassepots . . ."* (*Chassepots* were the new French rifles supposedly superior to the Prussian guns.) "Poor devils," Jennie wrote many years later, "they soon had them, and all the fighting they wanted."

The Germans crossed the border into Alsace on August 4. Emperor Napoleon III went to see his cousin and former fiancée Princess Mathilde and fell weeping into her arms. Then he took his son, the Prince Imperial, and went to the front to take command. Jennie thrilled to the news that the Prince had received his baptism of fire by pulling the lanyard of the first French artillery shot of the war.[23]

The Prussian advance was so methodical that French towns were notified in advance that they would soon be occupied and that the Prussians expected them to furnish particular supplies. The list included everything from one-and-a-half pounds of bread per soldier for a specified number of soldiers, plus one pound meat and one-quarter pound coffee, to five cigars and either a pint of wine or a pint of beer per soldier. Towns unable to provide the supplies were burned to the ground.

After three successive major defeats, Napoleon wired home from the battlefront, "Hasten preparations for the defense of Paris." Paris became a city in panic. If there was one pervasive sound, it was the steady pounding of drums. Men and boys of all ages drilled in the streets, even at night under the gas jets. Some 40,000 oxen and 250,000 sheep were brought in from all directions to pasture in the Bois de Boulogne. Foods were packed into warehouses to prepare the city for siege. People clustered in crowds everywhere, noisily trading rumors. Everyone kept an eye out for Prussian spies, and all foreigners became suspect.

Most foreigners had left Paris by August. Among the few to remain were the Jerome women. Leonard Jerome wired his family from New York to flee to London. "Unfortunately my mother was laid up with a very severe sprain, and could not put her foot to the ground," Jennie wrote, "so we tarried. Besides we were incredulous of the Prussians ever reaching Paris, and every day we put off our departure. Our house became the rendezvous of the few of our French friends who had not gone to the front." Their most frequent visitor was still the Duc de Persigny, and the news he brought grew increasingly ominous. Prussia was advancing with three main armies, all reinforced with superior artillery. Then one day he rushed in, crying, *"Toul est perdu; les Prussiens sont à nos portes!"*

That was not exactly true. The Prussians were not yet at the Paris gates, but it was time to leave. Trains were moving irregularly, but he had managed to secure space for them to Deauville. They would have to pack within an hour, he said; they might tie some valuables in a sheet or a tablecloth. Since there were no cabs, Persigny rushed out to find a cart to carry the injured Clara.

Up to then, war for Jennie had meant flag-waving and songs, a game represented by a war map stuck with brightly colored pins. Now, suddenly the game had come alive, the drama had turned into fear edged with panic. Jennie tried to pull her mother away from her frenzied watering of the flowers and helped organize the packing. Clarita was more concerned with scribbling a short note to the Marquis de Tamisier, with whom she was currently in love. Jennie, more than anybody, kept the group in gear. Their maid Marie helped carry things to the train and then was sent back with instructions to pack the trunks and take them on the next day's train to Deauville. She never came. Their own train was the last out of Paris.

The end came for Napoleon III in the sleepy town of Sedan, where he surrendered his army of 80,000 troops.[24] Only seven months before, seven million Frenchmen had given their Emperor an overwhelming vote of confidence in a special plebiscite. Now they denounced him,[25] voted his Empire at an end, and proclaimed a new French Republic.

Friends of the Court finally persuaded the Empress to escape to England and join her son, who had been sent there earlier. Wearing a black veil and a dress of black cashmere, she went unannounced to the office of her dentist, a 46-year-old American, Dr. Thomas Evans. Together with another American friend, Dr. Crane, Evans managed to get a carriage and take the Empress to Deauville.

The Jerome women were still there waiting for passage on a ship across the Channel.

While at Deauville, a friend of ours, M. de Gardonne, called on us unexpectedly and asked if he might spend the day in our rooms—in fact, hide there [Jennie wrote]. He begged that on no account were we to mention his name or let anyone know we had seen him. Naturally we thought this very strange, and my mother grew suspicious; but he impressed upon us that it was for "state reasons," of which we would hear later. After dinner, when it was quite dark, he departed as mysteriously as he had come.

Later they learned that Gardonne had helped arrange for the Empress' escape from Deauville aboard a British yacht.[26] "I took her on board," Gardonne wrote, "and the only remark she made was, 'I know I am safe now, under the protection of an Englishman.' She also said, 'Poor France,' and became very hysterical for a time." After a rough crossing, the Empress landed on the Isle of Wight.

The Jerome women were able to leave soon afterward.

Three

$\mathcal{T}$HE JEROME WOMEN FELT like refugees when they arrived in Brighton. It was a resort out of season, the sky bleak, the winds brisk. They stayed at the Norfolk Hotel, still without clothes or servants, waiting for further word or direction from Leonard Jerome. Jennie remembered always the sorrow she felt as she walked along the stony beach. "Our friends scattered, fighting or killed at the front; debarred as we were from our bright little house and our household goods, it was indeed a sad time."

They all felt as the Prince Imperial did when he wrote to the Princess Mathilde: "I find England very dismal. The gray skies make me long for France more than ever. I hope 1871 will be happier; it cannot be worse."[1]

Leonard Jerome sailed immediately to England, swept his family into London, and settled them all into Brown's Hotel near Piccadilly[2]. As quickly as possible, they got clothes and governesses and established a routine of living that included the usual intensive piano practice. "A winter spent in the gloom and fogs of London did not tend to dispel the melancholy which we felt," Jennie wrote. They made few English friends that first year, and Clarita developed a fever which the doctors diagnosed as typhoid but which she described as frustration. Her Marquis sent messages by balloon[3] from the besieged Paris, but their romantic future seemed more dim than ever.

The Duc de Persigny came to call, and the Jeromes were saddened by the once-dashing diplomat now "broken-hearted, ill and penniless." When Leonard Jerome found the Duc selling his few possessions, he insisted on setting Persigny up in a room at Brown's and paying all the bills. "If it were not for you," Jerome told him, "my wife and daughters might yet be caught in a starving city."

The Jerome rooms became a haven for a vast variety of French refugees, each of whom brought his own rumors to trade. They all knew that the Empress had sold her jewelry, plus some royal real estate in Italy, and had settled in the country village at Chislehurst in Kent. She had leased a simple three-story house called Camden Place from a man who had been the trustee for the Emperor's former mistress, Harriet Howard. Unknown to the Empress, Camden Place held tender memories for the Emperor—he had paid heavy court to another young lady who had lived there, and was said to have been engaged to her for a short time.[4]

But now the Emperor had warmer feelings for his wife. From his prison in Prussia, on January 30, 1871, he wrote:

> Dearest friend, Today is the anniversary of our wedding. . . . I want to tell you that I am very fond of you. In good times, the links between us may have grown loose. I thought them broken, but stormy days have shown me how solid they are, and now, more than ever, I am reminded of the words of the Evangelist: "For richer, for poorer, in sickness and in health, to love, cherish, and obey. . . ."[5]

After seeing his family safely settled, Leonard Jerome had a United States government mission to perform. Paris was under siege. After Napoleon's surrender, the Government of National Defense had taken control with the public promise, "Not an inch of our soil will we cede, not a stone of our fortresses." The United States wanted Jerome to forward special proposals to Bismarck concerning an easing of the siege. They gave him a diplomatic passport and assigned the famous Civil War Generals Sheridan and Burnside to accompany him.

The three Americans found the city starving. The food hoarded in warehouses was long since gone, and so were the cattle and horses in the Bois de Boulogne. Some two months before, the Christmas menu at a Paris restaurant had listed: soup from horsemeat, mince of cat, shoulder of dog with tomato sauce, roast donkey and potatoes, mice on toast.[6] Sewer rats were considered "far more delicate than young chickens," according to young Charles Joseph Bonaparte, who stayed in the city throughout the siege.[7]

The Paris Journal described the purchase of the rats at the Rat Market in the Place de l'Hôtel de Ville:

. . . as the rats are shut up in a big cage, one has to choose the animal one wants out of the crowd. With a little stick the dealer makes it go into a smaller cage where it is alone, and then a bulldog is brought along. The little cage is shaken and the rat escapes; but it is promptly seized by the formidable teeth of the dog, which breaks its back and drops it delicately at the purchaser's feet.

One gourmet said that rat tasted like a "mixture of pork and partridge. . . ." Writing about his daily diet, a man named Labouchère noted in his diary:

. . . I have a guilty feeling when I eat dog, the friend of man. I had a slice of spaniel the other day; it was by no means bad, something like lamb, but I felt like a cannibal. Epicures in the dog-flesh tell me that poodle is by far the best, and recommend me to avoid bulldog, which is coarse and tasteless. . . .

Dog sold for four francs a pound, when it was available, compared to horse at forty centimes a kilogram. Cats were considered more of a delicacy, and the price was twenty francs a pound. A statistic supplied to the Chronique du Siège notes that the Parisians had eaten 25,523 cats during the siege, not counting alley cats. Mule was also considered superior to beef, but antelope wasn't regarded as good as stewed rabbit. When the zoo was closed, some elephant's trunk circulated at eight dollars a pound. Camel kidneys were much cheaper. Bread "seemed to have been made from old panama hats picked up in the gutter."[8] Jerome did not tell his daughters that a piece of bread was the price for a prostitute.

The prolonged siege so angered Bismarck that he ordered his troops to fire on the starving women and children of Paris, who often approached Prussian soldiers for food. When somebody suggested that his Prussian soldiers might refuse to do that, Bismarck answered, "Then you'll have to shoot the soldiers for disobedience," and added, "I attach no great importance to human life, because I believe in another world."[9]

The only plentiful food in Paris was mustard and champagne.[10] More Parisians—approximately 65,000—died of starvation and disease than of battle wounds. Of these, 3,000 were babies. After a four months' siege and a bombardment from heavy guns in the last few weeks, an armistice was arranged so that the dead could be buried.

Jerome visited the American Ambassador, Mr. E. B. Washburne, the only foreign representative who stayed in Paris throughout the siege. Washburne told him that the theaters had been turned into hospitals, then back again into theaters when human souls seemed sicker than bodies.[11] He described how Victor Hugo held recitals of readings from his books, and how hard the entertainers worked to stir the faint blood of the people.[12]

Jerome reported to his family that he had found their house intact, except for a cellar wall which had been blown open by a shell. The maid Marie was still there, guarding her mistresses' clothing.

He also described his visit with the two Civil War generals to Bismarck's headquarters in a large villa in Versailles. Bismarck worked and slept and smoked his endless cigars in a single overheated room, changing only from his doeskin-lined uniform to his dressing-gown, frequently working through the night and then sleeping to noon. He provided his guests with a simple dinner on tin plates, with candles stuck into wine bottles and one of his officers playing the piano.

The American group accomplished nothing, but it mattered little because soon it was all over. Paris surrendered. Bismarck dictated his terms to a French lawyer, and peace was signed at Versailles on February 26, 1871.

Upon his return to London, Jerome told his family of all he had seen in Paris, describing in dramatic detail the starvation, the despair, the courage. What affected seventeen-year-old Jennie most deeply and lastingly was the story of Paris' surrender. As the Prussians prepared to march down the Champs Elysées, the people emptied the streets, shuttered their windows, and waited in the dark silence of their defeat. Even the Bois de Boulogne was bare—the trees had long ago been cut down for fuel. Masses of Prussian troops wearing their spiked helmets marched past the Arc de Triomphe and down the deserted boulevards singing "Die Wacht am Rhein," the drum and fife corps playing in perfect unison. That day the Prussian soldiers were seen waltzing with one another in the Place de la Concorde.[13]

Had the Jerome women stayed in the United States, Jennie's life would have consisted almost entirely of the youthful gaieties of the rich. Those would still be the frame of her emerging womanhood, but the Paris interval had imposed a new understanding of the world.

Leonard Jerome decided to go again to Paris to safeguard his valuable collection of Italian paintings. Clara insisted on going along, even though Paris was in turmoil. When they arrived, they selected their favorite paintings and managed to pack and ship them just before the real riots started. The mob had moved on to the Palais de Justice and the Hôtel de Ville, set them afire, and after throwing furniture out the windows, held auctions on the lawn.

Auctions were still taking place the next morning when Clara ventured out to view the scene for herself. Outside the smouldering Tuileries, Napoleon's initialed gold dining plates were being offered for sale; Clara bid for them and bought them, then hired a wheelbarrow to carry the plates to her surprised husband. (Clara's grandson Winston later used those plates.[14])

It is easy to classify Clara Jerome as a social snob, a woman of limited imagination, firm prejudice, and pronounced ambition. She was. But she also had courage and high style—valuable attributes for the wife of Leonard Jerome and a resident of 1870 London.

※※

England in 1870 was still in the Victorian Age, with the Prince of Wales running gaily around the rim and Queen Victoria somber in the center. For the Queen, the guiding words were duty and self-denial. Her "dear Albert" had died nine years before, but she still wore the black silk dress of mourning, still had his clothes laid out every night on his bed at Windsor Castle, still ordered a fresh basin of water placed in his room every morning. And over her bed hung a framed photograph of Albert's head and shoulders, taken after he died.

Victoria had once complained to her daughter that, even in the happiest marriages, "the poor woman is bodily and morally the husband's slave. That always sticks in my throat." Still, Albert was much the stronger personality, and she a most willing follower. Soon after her first pregnancy, she gave him the keys to all her secret boxes and papers, allowed him the final word on all formal decisions—in effect made him her permanent prime minister.

After Albert's death, she suffered a nervous breakdown that lasted two years, then became a virtual recluse. For a long time, her preoccupation seemed to be setting up memorials to her dead husband.[15] She seldom made public appearances, held few receptions—at which no refreshments were served. All that her guests had to look forward to was their chance to kiss her "soft, small, red hand."[16] Court life was strict, stuffy, and dull. The public was royally bored.

The British people had loved her once, loved the young Queen who was fascinated by the glitter of court ceremonies. And when she married Albert, mothered nine children, and reigned with pomp and ceremony, the people respected her. But when she became a widow, sad and sour and solitary, they ignored her, mocked her, even demanded her abdication.

Disraeli, of the purple waistcoat and the flowery speech, had said that England was "a country of two nations," the classes and the masses; and that was true. It was also partly true, as The Spectator had printed, that "The country is once more getting rich. The money is filtering downwards to the actual workers."

Not enough, however. Charles Dickens died in 1870 but Oliver Twist did not. Too many children still went hungry. A favorite family potion was

Godfrey's Cordial, a drink compounded of opium, treacle, and sassafras, which brought quick, painless death to unwanted children for whom there was neither space nor food. Almost half the country's children were not in school. They worked in the factories at the age of ten, in the mines at twelve, six days a week. The legal age of consent for girls was thirteen, and many were soon drafted as part-time prostitutes, as were their mothers. The white-slave traffic traveled from England to Paris, and not vice versa.

Workers were not only fined for laughing on the job, but many factory workers were even charged for the use of hot water and the cost of cleaning the lavatories. As for women factory workers, when somebody tried to campaign for shorter working hours for mothers on Saturday, one newspaper editorialized: "To pretend that women wish to have their hours of work restricted by legislation is not honest." The favorite tune was, "Home, Sweet Home."[17]

At the Salvation Army, sleeping space was provided for the destitute in coffin-like boxes under a big sign that read, "Are you ready to die?" Most of them weren't. At least their world was now lit by gaslight, the slum of Porridge Island was torn down and replaced by the spacious Trafalgar Square, and if they could not ride the new taxicabs, they could watch them. They still had their pubs—and both beer and whiskey were cheap, but that hardly provided much comfort.

Jennie, of course, knew nothing of all this. England to her was Brown's Hotel, governesses, piano lessons, French aristocratic refugees, Hyde Park, the opera, and some carefully selected young people in British high society. It would be years before she really learned about the other England, where one-fourth of the people couldn't write their names and more than half couldn't read. She lived in the world of the "upper 10,000," highly social, quite stuffy, with a rigid schedule of "seasons." Besides the London Season, there was the Hunting Season, the Shooting Season, and the Season at Cowes.

Fortunately for the Jerome women, their entry into London society was considerably eased by the sponsorship of the Duc de Persigny, who had once been French Ambassador to England. The Emperor had been released from his comfortable Prussian prison and had joined his wife at Chislehurst in Kent. The collected gaggle of French aristocratic refugees quickly integrated into the London Season.

Although the London Season officially started in the spring, the prime period was summer. A Paris visitor was dazzled by how this "race of gods and goddesses descended from Olympus upon England in June and July . . . appeared to live on a golden cloud, spending their riches as indolently and naturally as the leaves grow green."

It was a steady round of opera, ballet, theater, and parties, with little variation in the schedule. Most of the entertaining, however, took place at home. For the many social Charitable Committees, there were breakfast invitations, usually from 8:30 to 10. Guests left promptly after the meal because most of them had to get ready for luncheon elsewhere. These luncheons ran into several courses with matched wines, often much more formal than today's dinners. More informal were the afternoon teas, always at five, usually featuring one of the accomplished guests at the piano. Jennie was often on call.[18]

A *Punch* joke on the subject of amateur pianists told of two matrons, one asking the other:

> "Do your daughters play, Mrs. Jones?"
> Mrs. Jones: "No."
> "Sing?"
> "No."
> "Paint in water-colors?"
> "No," said Mrs. Jones, smiling. "We go in for beauty."[19]

Beauty was essential, conversation desirable, piano-playing optional. The best female guests managed all three.

Dinner was usually the high point of the day, and the preparations were elaborate. Seating arrangements represented an art, equal to the selection of the proper vintage and bouquet of each of the various wines to suit the several courses of the lavish menu. The meal usually consisted of a thick soup or a sherry-fortified clear soup, one or two fish dishes, a choice of four entrées, followed by some poultry or game, then puddings, sweets, cheese, and dessert. Thanks to the influence of the Prince of Wales, champagne gradually replaced claret as the main dinner wine.

Hostesses invariably checked each other to avoid conflicts of dinner dates, and particularly of parties, since most of their guests came from the same two hundred governing families of England, whom Winston Churchill called "that brilliant and powerful body." Invitations were usually sent three weeks in advance, and the only excuses for nonattendance were death or contagious disease.

The rules were precise: all guests were to arrive no sooner or later than fifteen minutes after the time specified on the invitation, and all guests divided into male and female groups immediately after dinner. The women gathered in the drawing room, while men lingered behind at the table for their cigars and drink and manly conversation. Social "tail" of the evening was the arrival of other guests after ten, followed by some scheduled entertainment, such as a brief recital by an opera singer or a dance.[20]

"To make a ball successful," Lady Cowper once told Lady Dorothy Nevill, "three men should always be asked to every lady—one to dance, one to eat and one to stare—that makes everything go off well." Competition for guests and entertainers was incessant, with three or four balls—or "drums" as they were called—almost every night. The challenge to a guest was to transform night into day, crowd in as many parties as one could.

Even the afternoon social parade in Hyde Park had the fixed pattern of a pirouette. The time and place were between five and seven in the afternoon on a broad southern avenue that led past the Albert Gate and paralleled Rotten Row—a British contraction of the French, *Route en Roi*, the Avenue of Kings.

Rotten Row was actually nothing more than an unsurfaced road of loose sand and gravel, but nonetheless, the Row was regal. Heavy, old family coaches showed off their revarnished panels and relacquered brasswork. In a House of Commons debate, it was jokingly suggested that houses be built on both sides of the Row, so that ladies in the balconies could look at the riding gentlemen. The need to be seen was a matter of first importance.

All proper coaches had powdered lackeys and meticulously uniformed coachmen, usually dressed in blue coats with brass buttons. "It was not etiquette to handle the reins oneself in the afternoons," noted the Countess of Warwick in her memoirs,

> so we sat . . . chatting and behaving as if the world we knew, bounded by the Smart Set, was a fixed orbit, as if London— our London—was a place of select social enjoyment for the Circle, as if nothing could change in this best of delightful worlds. Then there would be a clatter of faster horses, and down this mile of drive came the well-known royal carriage, the beautiful Alexandra, Princess of Wales, bowing right and left as only she could bow, and hats were raised and knees curtseyed before seats were resumed and interrupted chatter continued.[21]

Jennie was among those who curtseyed to the Princess of Wales. Accompanied by a governess, she made the Hyde Park walk part of her ritual. There is little likelihood that it ever crossed her mind that one day she might compete with this Princess to whom she curtseyed for the affection and attention of the Prince of Wales.

In 1871, the Prince was thirty years old and had been married to the Princess Alexandra of Denmark for eight years. His taste in women was as varied as his taste in clothes, and he often set the style in both categories. The fashionable constantly copied the cut of his clothes, the shape of his goatee, his habit of cigarette-smoking after dinner. After an attack of rheumatism, Prince Edward was forced to shake hands stiffly, his elbow pressed against his side. Within a short time, the watchful fashionable men of London even copied that. Everyone knew that the Prince always traveled with two valets while two others stayed home to clean and care for his huge wardrobe. As for his women, the British penny-press gave special space to his Paris sprees with a beautiful French actress, Mademoiselle Hortense Schneider, and a prominent prostitute called "Skittles." He was also named as one of the adulterers in several celebrated British divorce cases (the Court accepted his denials). There were many other affairs that were hushed up. In fact, it was on a trip to settle one of his son's affairs that Albert, Queen Victoria's Consort, caught the fever from which he died. It was said the Queen never forgave Prince Edward.

The Queen once confided to a friend that sometimes she could hardly bear to be in the same room with her son. She also refused him access to any important papers or to make any important decisions. Prime Minister Disraeli agreed with her. He called the Prince "Chitter Chatter" and advised the Queen not to let him see any private papers because "he lets them out and talks to his friends about them."[22] During the Franco-Prussian War, Prince Edward had pleaded with his mother to let him act as her emissary to try to negotiate a peace. "I cannot bear sitting here doing nothing whilst all this bloodshed is going on," he wrote her. But she refused. One of the classic cartoons of the day showed him at the castle, standing in a corner like a bad little boy in a schoolroom, with his mother glaring at him.[23]

Denied any prerogatives of power, the Prince became more completely a "heavy swell" and an habitué of the racetracks. When his mother pointedly asked him not to attend the Ascot Races, he wrote her:

> I am always most anxious to meet your wishes, dear Mama, in every respect, and I always regret if we are not quite d'accord–but I am past 28, and have some considerable knowledge of the world and society; you will, I am sure, at least I trust, allow me to use my own discretion in matters of this kind. . . . [24]

But the most serious mother-son arguments concerned his parties–wild affairs that lasted until dawn, with guests tobogganing down the stairs on trays or engaging in slapstick battles with soda-siphons. Unwanted as guests were the literary people or intellectuals, because the swells "did not want to be made to think."

"We acknowledged that pictures should be painted, books written, the law administered," wrote the Countess of Warwick.

We even acknowledged that there was a certain class whose job might be to do these things. But we did not see why their achievement entitled them to recognition from us, whom they might disturb, overstimulate, or even bore. On rare occasions, if a book made a sufficient stir, we might read it, or better still, get somebody to tell us about it, and so save us the trouble.[25]

Most of the parties were at Marlborough House, the Prince's London home. His social group was called the Marlborough House Set, and it was quite fitting, therefore, that one of the Prince's newest recruits, a young man who became a particular favorite of his, was the second son of the Duke of Marlborough, Lord Randolph Churchill. Lord Randolph was a popeyed young man with an intense face and a handsome mustache. He was fresh out of Oxford by way of a Grand Tour of the Continent.

Marlborough House became the important meeting place for the fashionable beauties, particularly the Americans, in whom the Prince was especially interested. Of the many women who wandered into the Prince's orbit, few denied him their favors. In return, many of them tucked into their purses such expensive princely gifts as a gold sharkskin cigarette case with a diamond-and-sapphire clasp.[26] *Town Topics* said of the Prince, "He wastes nothing, and gives no favors without the assurance of favors in return." It added, "The attentions of H.R.H. to any woman means indignity and scandal." Such gossip was grist for the public mill, and the public loved it. To them, Prince Albert Edward of Wales was "good old Bertie." "The Prince of Wales is loved," said Lord Granville, "because he has all the faults of which the Englishman is accused."

The Cowes Season began with the end of the London Season in the first week of August. Cowes is a tiny village on the Isle of Wight. An intimate island with rocky coasts, cliffs of colored sands, chalk hills, and well-kept flower gardens whose fragrant scents tempered the sea air, Wight's physical setting resembled an impressionist painting. Here Queen Victoria had spent her young womanhood, and here she would come to die. Here also were the 300 members of the Royal Yacht Squadron, the most exclusive yacht club in the world, housed in a castle built by Henry VIII.

"In those days," Jennie wrote,

it was delightfully small and peaceful. No glorified villas, no esplanade or pier, no bands, no motors or crowded tourist-steamers. . . . The Royal Yacht Squadron lawn did not resemble a perpetual garden party, or the roadstead a perpetual regatta. People all seemed to know one another. The Prince and Princess of Wales and many foreign royalties could walk about and amuse themselves without being photographed or mobbed.

But in that first week of August, the Royal Yacht Squadron held regattas of such sweep and magnificence that they transformed the sleepy island into the social center of all Europe. It was *the* place in England to see and be seen.

Graphic Magazine described for Jennie the newly expanded social world in which she would soon move:

> For the fashionable beauty, life is an endless carnival, and dress a round of disguises. She does everything and the wings of Mercury might be attached to her tiny bottines, so rapid are her changes of scene and character. She is a sportswoman, an athlete, a ballroom divinity. She is alternately a horsewoman, a huntress, a bold and skillful swimmer; she drives a pair of horses like a charioteer, mounts the roof of a four-in-hand, plays lawn tennis, is at home on a race course or the deck of a fast yacht. She is aware of the refinements of dining and has a pretty taste in vintages. She is a power at the theater or the Opera; and none is more brilliant at a supper party. Of the modern young lady *à la mode*, who wields alike the fiddle-bow, the billiard-cue and the etching-needle, who climbs mountains and knows the gymnasium, none but herself can be the prototype.

Graphic, of course, was focusing on a highly favored few. More generally, the Victorian woman was not only considered the weaker sex in body and mind, but was presumed to have a purity and spirituality that needed to be protected from male coarseness. Women of polite society were expected not to travel either by cab or railway without a chaperon or to attend any public entertainment unescorted.[27] Except for the flouting, fashionable beauties, most of whom filtered into the Marlborough House Set, the Queen kept her women in a strict social straitjacket.

Sex was a dirty word, but an increasing number of society women smuggled Swinburne's poems into their bedrooms. One magazine referred to the poet as "Swineborn" and classified his sensual writings as the "Fleshly School of Poetry."

Jennie's occasional contact with young men was still carefully chaperoned and restricted entirely to parties and dances. Typical of her limited social correspondence was a note from the young French Prince Imperial, who was two years younger than she and lived with his parents in Chisle-hurst: "Will you please forgive my negligence in the last few days? . . . I got measles from a young lady with whom I danced a mazurka, and I really should not dance with any other girl."

Leonard Jerome rented Rosetta Cottage at Cowes, a small house with pretty gardens facing the sea. It was often a rough sea, as the Jeromes discovered one day when they were invited for a cruise around the island in the Emperor's yacht. Most of the small group became sick and remained in their cabins. The young, gangly Prince Imperial unsuccessfully tried to lift everyone's spirits with his store of mild jokes. Only the Empress seemed to flourish in the fierce sea, but it was the Emperor whom Jennie best remembered: "I can see now the Emperor leaning against the mast looking old, ill and sad. His thought could not have been other than sorrowful and, even in my young eyes, he seemed to have nothing to live for."

The Emperor's long mustache had begun to droop badly now, his hair was ragged around his ears, his speech softer and more hesitant than ever. He spent his time developing long-range schemes for old-age pensions for the French people and outlining drawings for an economical stove for poor families. He also conceived a plan to abolish war by which a council of nations would meet regularly to decide critical issues on the basis of international law. While he kept his social life carefully cloistered, limited to a few old friends and an occasional visit to Queen Victoria, his great pleasure was in the time spent with his son. He had already enrolled the Prince Imperial in the Royal Military Academy.

Napoleon's staff organized a stratagem for a Royalist return to France through Switzerland to spark a Bonapartist uprising. But Napoleon was too sick to mount a horse. He told his old associates he would not return to France even if the Army revolted in his favor; he would return only if recalled by a plebiscite. Organizing a *coup d'état* was something "one does in one's youth," he said.[28]

Later in the fall of 1871, Jerome took his family back to France. "But what changes in Paris itself!" Jennie wrote.

> Ruins everywhere: the sight of the Tuileries and the Hô-tel de Ville made me cry. St.-Cloud, the scene of many pleas-ant expeditions, was a thing of the past, the lovely chateau razed to the ground. And if material Paris was damaged, the social fabric was even more so. In vain we tried to pick up the threads. Some of our friends were killed, others ruined or in mourning, and all broken-hearted and miserable, hiding in their houses and refusing to be comforted.

The statues at the Place de la Concorde, representing the most important towns of France—Strasbourg, Lille, Nancy, Orleans—swathed in crepe, . . . reminded one daily, if one needed it, of the trials and tribulations France had just gone through. Only the embassies and a few foreigners, principally Americans, received or entertained. . . . A few opened their houses, but the French on the whole were shy of going out at all, and if Paris had any gaiety left in those days, it was owing to her cosmopolitan character.[29]

What does an energetic seventeen-year-old girl do in a sad city? Her younger sister Leonie had been sent off to school in Wiesbaden, and Clarita was still mooning over the Duc de Lescara, toward whom her mother would not relent. Persigny returned to Paris, but Jennie no longer saw him as anyone to flirt with—he was just an old man of fifty, bitter and boring. He would die that year. Dismayed by Clarita's stolen romance with Lescara, Mrs. Jerome was more watchful than ever of Jennie and established stricter limits on her social life. So Jennie went riding in the Bois with her father or his friends, and with little else to do, studied music and languages more intensively.

Paris seemed so quiet for Clara Jerome, too, that she welcomed her husband's suggestion that they all return to Cowes in the summer of 1872. Jerome continued on to New York alone.

The time had come for Jennie's debut. During Regatta Week at the start of the August season she would be presented to the Prince and Princess of Wales at the annual Royal Yacht Squadron Ball.

Her dress, of course, had to be white. Dressing was an ordeal. A maid pulled the corset laces as tightly as pain would permit. A seventeen-inch waist was a thing of pride, but anything over twenty-one inches was considered an enormity. The tight lacing also caused an artificial enlargement of the bust—augmented when necessary by padding of horsehair or inflated rubber. For Jennie that was not needed. To offset the artificially enlarged curve of the bust (well-exposed by an extreme decolletage), there was an even more artificially enlarged posterior, produced by the bustle hidden under a full flounce, and further complicated by the yard-long trailing skirt. All this extra fabric and artificial enlargement was in sharp contrast to the dress material stretched over the woman's flanks and loins with an almost violent tightness. Whatever the attractions of the bigger bust and the exaggerated posterior, it is true that statistics indicated a considerable increase of marriages in the 1870's.[30] The only make-up permitted Jennie, however, was a little powder on her nose—she could keep the puff wrapped in her handkerchief.

Throughout the presentation, her manner was easy, her enjoyment obvious. It was a gay evening and Jennie danced through the hours, never lacking for partners. A British guest described her vitality as "American."

Throughout the Cowes Season, Clarita and Jennie applied the same vigor to piano duets at dinner parties. "Such a lovely sight it made, those two young heads, one blonde and one dark, bent raptly over the keys," an admirer recorded years later.[31]

The two sisters were kept so busy socially that they seemed to have little time for writing letters—either to Leonie at school in Wiesbaden or to their father in New York. Jerome complained:

> Mrs. Clit, Miss Clarita, and Miss Jennie,
> Dearly beloved, it is nearly two weeks since I had a letter. You must be sure to write me particulars of all that is going on. I have no doubt you will see many nice people and will have Cowes all to yourselves as far as Americans are concerned. Did you get the tent from London? And do you make it lively and have you secured the Villa Rosetta for another year? etc. I rather like the idea of Cowes next summer and a yacht. Don't forget while sitting under your own vine and eating up your own fig tree that I am awfully disappointed if I don't get my weekly letters.[32]

Four

$\mathcal{B}$Y THE TIME OF THE 1873 Cowes season, the Jerome women were firmly entrenched on the scene. Clara Jerome felt her position strong enough on the Cowes social list to pick and choose most selectively among the many invitations. But one of them was obviously a must: a deckle-edged invitation from the officers of the guardship _Ariadne_ to a ball on board in honor of the Czarevich and the Czarevna of Russia.

The invitation read:

To Meet
Their Royal Highnesses, the Prince and Princess of Wales
and
Their Imperial Russian Highnesses
the
Grand Duke, Cesarewitch and Grand Duchess Cesarevna,
Captain Carpenter and the officers of H.M.S. "Ariadne"
request the honour of the Company of
MRS. AND MISSES JEROME
On board, on Thursday, August 12th, from 3:30 to 7:30 P.M.
DANCING
Boats will be in attendance at the RYC Landing Place.
R.S.V.P.

Jennie long afterward wrote between the lines of the invitation:

To Meet—Randolph.

Until then, the social life at Cowes had been a steady hum, but this was high spectacle and Clara was all aflutter about it. Barges took the guests from shore to ship. the women having to negotiate the ship's ladder with their full skirts. Canopied with bobbing lanterns, the ship's deck was draped with the national colors of England and Imperial Russia, and the Royal Marine Band played in the background.

The two sisters were quickly crowded around by admirers. Both bare-shouldered and beautiful, they effectively complemented each other: Clarita, blonde and dreamy; Jennie, dark and sparkling. Jennie was swiftly swept away into her first dance, a waltz with a lieutenant, then again surrounded by a host of admirers wanting a place on her dance-card.

Her friend Frank Bertie pushed through the crowd, bringing with him a pale young man. Jennie had noticed him before, standing aside and staring at her. She had smiled slightly at him, and when he simply kept staring, she had blushed. "Miss Jerome," said Frank Bertie very formally, "may I present an old friend of mine who has just arrived in Cowes, Lord Randolph Churchill."[1]

He was slim, not tall, with a large head and a walrus mustache, attractive but not handsome. He had been a Lord since he was eight years old (when his father became the Duke of Marlborough), and he looked the part. Impeccably dressed, almost dandified, he had the elegant polish of his class but also much of its pomposity. His manner with strangers was brusque and his sense of humor occasionally cutting. At twenty-three his was the life of the pleasure-seeker of turf and town. He had neither deep convictions nor high ambitions. In fact, he had hardly any deep passions except for the horse and the hunt.

His mere membership in the Marlborough House Set served as intriguing credentials as far as Jennie was concerned. It provided him with an aura of attractive danger. If he belonged to the Set, he could hardly be *too* proper! The floor was full of pompous dandies, but beneath the surface of this one there might be something special.

After proper small talk, Randolph rather reluctantly asked Jennie to dance. Like most Churchills, he was not a man of music, and he detested dancing. But it seemed the only way he could keep with him this strikingly lovely young woman in the white dress with the fresh flowers and the dark hair.

Lord Randolph had such noticeable problems in matching his feet to the intricate figures of the quadrille, that he finally admitted to Jennie that dancing made him dizzy, and wouldn't she prefer sitting somewhere? In this case, she definitely would. So he found some seats on the open deck in the soft breeze and they sat and sipped champagne and talked.

Randolph had a way of speaking with great rapidity and vehemence and a compelling intensity. It was as if his words were trying to catch up with his thoughts. It intrigued Jennie. A beautiful woman who knows she's beautiful, who always has been openly admired for her beauty, is often more captivated by the man who regards her as someone with a mind as well as a body. They had much to talk about, much to interest each other. They had traveled to the same countries; they both loved horses; they had both mingled with the great of the world. Jennie had a lively mind and was easily bored. He obviously did not bore her. When he wished, Randolph could be charming, witty and jaunty. This was one of those nights.

The two talked so long, so oblivious to the dance and the dancers, that Jennie's mother searched them out. Without many words, she clearly indicated that there was such a thing as spending too much time with one man at such a ball. But before the evening was over, Jennie had persuaded her mother to invite Lord Randolph, along with their mutual friend, Colonel Edgecumbe, to dinner the next night.

Jennie seemed particularly nervous the following day. She insisted that she and Clarita spend extra time rehearsing their piano duet and even asked Clarita to decide what dress she should wear.

The evening air was gentle, with an occasional breeze and bright stars, and the lights of the many boats flickered in the harbor. The small dinner was very pleasant, and afterward Jennie and her sister "played duets at the piano and chattered merrily." When Colonel Edgecumbe commented to Randolph on both the performance and the players, Randolph answered quietly and seriously, "I admire them both tremendously. And, if I can, I mean to make the dark one my wife."[2]

After their guests had gone, Jennie asked her sister in private what she had thought of Lord Randolph. Clarita had not been very impressed. She thought he had been trying too hard to be clever, and she didn't particularly like his fancy mustache. "I'm sure you'd like him if you knew him better," Jennie answered while she brushed her hair. Then she suddenly stopped brushing, looked at her sister very seriously and added, "Please try to, Clarita, because I have the strangest feeling that he's going to ask me to marry him. . . . I'm going to say yes." Clarita was incredulous and laughed out loud.

The next day, Jennie was so unusually quiet that her mother commented on it to Clarita. It was then that Clarita mentioned Jennie's confession of interest in the young Lord. Clara was not happy about it. She was aiming higher for Jennie than a mere Lord who, as a second son, was not even in direct line of succession to the dukedom.

But Jennie already had arranged her next rendezvous with Randolph. It was ostensibly a meeting "by accident." During their conversation the night before, she had told him of her daily habit of walking along a certain path at a certain time. Naturally, he was there. For the first time, they were quite alone.

He was supposed to leave the next day for Blenheim Palace. Could he see her again that night? She would ask her mother. Perhaps he might come to dinner again.

Forewarned of Jennie's interest in young Churchill, Clara regarded this new request most critically. "Are we not inviting that young gentleman rather often?" she asked. But Jennie persisted, and her mother scribbed on a small, printed card:

Mrs. Leonard Jerome
The Misses Jerome

I shall be most happy to see you
at dinner this evening truly yours

C.H. Jerome.

(Lord Randolph later preserved that card in a black metal box in Blenheim Palace among his most intimate possessions.)

After dinner that night, Mrs. Jerome unwillingly excused herself with a headache, and Clarita more willingly excused herself with a smile. In a short memorandum to herself, Jennie remembered the night as being beautiful and described how she and Randolph strolled into the garden, "when, finding ourselves alone for a moment, he asked me if I would marry him and I said yes. We agreed not to say anything to my mother, as she would not understand the suddenness of it."

It was probably not so matter-of-fact—not with these two passionate people. There must have been many promises made and sealed, love freely given, dreams shared.

Randolph postponed his departure another four days. Just before he left, they broke the news to Mrs. Jerome. "She thought we were both quite mad," Jennie later commented, "and naturally would not hear of anything so precipitous."

At Blenheim, when Randolph told the news to his mother, the consternation was even more intense. Those were the days when the great houses of England had closed their doors to "dollars and impudence."[3] As Jennie herself later put it, "In England then, the American woman was looked upon as a strange and abnormal creature with habits and manners something between a Red Indian and a Gaiety Girl."

The Duchess of Marlborough was a commanding woman. She was, after all, the former Lady Frances Anne Emily Vane, eldest daughter of the Third Marquis of Londonderry. *The Complete Peerage* described her as "a woman of remarkable character and capacity, judicious and tactful." Few denied the quality of her character, but many questioned her judiciousness and tact. Her face had more strength than beauty and her eyes were hard or warm, depending on whom she looked at, but they were never lackluster. "She ruled Blenheim and nearly all those in it with a firm hand," Jennie wrote later. "At the rustle of her silk dress, the household trembled."[4]

Joined with a frequent temper and an occasional rage, the spirited Duchess had breathed new life into the moribund Blenheim. Her entertainments were lavish and exciting. She also produced two sons and six daughters (three other sons died in infancy). As a mother, she was both domineering and devoted. Her grandson Winston later wrote of her: "She was a woman of exceptional capacity, energy and decision."

But her eldest son, Blandford, was a sharp disappointment both to her and to the Duke. He had married a beautiful, pious, stupid woman who now bored him, and he openly showed his boredom by hedge-hopping with any other beautiful woman he could find. He was a restless, unhappy man, a rebel against the propriety of his parents. The Duke and Duchess, therefore, had turned their hopes and love to Randolph. At the very least, Randolph always had been a warm, affectionate son.

Most of Randolph's early life had followed the fixed upper-class pattern. When he was only ten, he rode his first pony on a fox hunt and came back "blooded" with the fox's tail. As soon as he was old enough, he bought and bred his own hounds, raced his own horses. Everything else was subsidiary, including school.

For the English aristocracy, the horse was a symbol of social, political, and economic dominance. Those who rode and those who owned horses viewed society as composed of "a small, select aristocracy, booted and spurred to ride, and a large, dim mass, born, saddled and bridled to be ridden."[5]

At Eton, Randolph had been called "a scug." A scug was an untidy, ill-mannered, and morally undeveloped boy, a shirker at games, bumptious and arrogant. If not naturally vicious, a scug was considered degenerate. One teacher called Randolph "idle to the extreme"; another called him a "little blackguard." He liked to recline langorously with his feet on the desk, where he had carved his name, and he seemed to dress for effect, getting particular pleasure from the startled looks when he wore a gaudy violet waistcoat. One of his few close friends, later Lord Redesdale, insisted that he had no real evil in him, that he was "the most delightful of boys, bubbling over with fun and the sweetest deviltry." However, Randolph did manage to organize one of the largest of the groups of personal "fags"[6] to do his bidding. He had fifteen lower-form boys to fulfill his every wish.

Even his father wrote of his "pain and displeasure . . . to find you ignore every promise you have made to me as to your conduct." And, in another letter: ". . . To tell you the truth, I fear that you yourself are very impatient and resentful of any control . . . and allow both your language and manner a most improper scope. . . ."

As to Randolph's manners, a family friend noted that Randolph called attention to his needs at the Eton dinner table by banging his spoon. The battered spoon later became a family memento. Randolph himself wrote about his manners in a letter home, describing the local parade by the Prince of Wales and his new bride, Princess Alexandra. When determined to crash through the parade line and reach the royal coach, "Several old genteel ladies tried to stop me but I snapped my fingers in their face . . . crying 'Hurrah' and 'What larks!' I frightened some of them horribly."

He then added that he charged through the barricade and broke it (". . . it was a second Balaclava,") knocked down the police in front of him, lost his hat, and pushed on to the door of the carriage. He was perfectly certain, he said, that the Prince of Wales bowed to him, all of which made him shriek louder.

In a biography of his father, Winston Churchill was most generous when he wrote, "He dreamed no dreams at Eton."[7] It took Randolph a long time to dream any dreams at Oxford, either. In fact, it took him a long time to be admitted. Despite the cram help of a tutor, he failed on the first try. "The truth is, he does not care for scholarship and is horribly inaccurate," the tutor reported to the Duke.

Oxford was located so close to Blenheim, that after Randolph was admitted he practically lived at home, making full use of his hunting hounds. At Merton College in Oxford[8] he organized a select social group of students called "The Blenheim Harriers."[9] They hunted regularly and kept a careful account of their kill. Of his own accomplishments one season, Randolph recorded, "Killed altogether last season twenty-nine brace of hares and one fox."

His sister Cornelia later wrote of the fun he had at Oxford: "luncheons in his rooms . . . gatherings full of fun and amusement . . . and many a party, which I, as a girl, accompanied. . . ."

Classmates called him "Gooseberry" Churchill because of his protruding eyes. Among other things, "Gooseberry" was fined for smoking while in academic dress, and again for breaking the windows of the Randolph Hotel.[10] He was also once arrested for drunkenness.

Years later, Frank Harris, then editor of the *Fortnightly Magazine*, reported that Louis Jennings, one of Churchill's closest friends, had told him of a far more serious incident: A small group had had a lively discussion of the master-servant relationship, and Randolph had expressed his views so well that the group had cheered him. As the party broke up, one of the members filled a huge stirrup-cup of champagne for Randolph and he drained the drink. Randolph insisted to Jennings later that he remembered nothing more of what happened that night.

"Next morning," Jennings reported Randolph having told him,

> I woke up with a dreadful taste in my mouth, and between waking and sleeping was thunder-struck. The paper on the walls was hideous—dirty—and, as I turned in bed, I started up gasping: there was an old woman lying beside me; one thin strand of dirty gray hair was on the pillow. How had I got there? What had happened to bring me to such a den? I slid out of bed and put on shirt and trousers as quietly as I could, but suddenly the old woman in the bed awoke and said, smiling at me, "Oh, Lovie, you're not going to leave me like that?"
>
> She had one long yellow tooth in her top jaw that waggled as she spoke. Speechless with horror, I put my hand in my pocket and threw all the money I had loose on the bed. I could not say a word. She was still smiling at me; I put on my waistcoat and coat and fled from the room. "Lovie, you're not kind!" I heard her say as I closed the door after me. Downstairs I fled in livid terror.[11]

Randolph described to Jennings how he rushed frantically to the doctor, who examined him and then treated him with a strong disinfectant. But, after a 21-day incubation period, a syphilitic sore became apparent. The doctor treated him with mercury, pronounced him cured, and warned him to abstain completely from alcoholic drink. But the cure proved only temporary.

Syphilitic treatment was still highly primitive, not far removed from the so-called "Greek water," an arsenic treatment which had been granted a patent by King George II more than one hundred years before. Those unable to afford the half-guinea for a bottle used the cheaper substitute called "Hot Hell Water" and often died of arsenic poisoning.

About that time, when he was twenty years old, Churchill's whole tone of life seemed to change. He suddenly gave up the Blenheim Harriers, turned seriously to a study of history and law, wrote Latin verses, and helped organize a chess club. He also discovered Gibbon's *Decline and Fall of the Roman Empire*, and was so fascinated by it that he read it again and again, memorizing whole pages.[12]

A frequent visitor at Blenheim in the 1860's was the family friend, Benjamin Disraeli, leader of the Conservative Party and soon to be Prime Minister. It was Disraeli who told the Duchess that "it rested with Randolph to become a distinguished man."

But that seemed increasingly unlikely. After his graduation, Randolph returned to Europe, this time on a Grand Tour through France, Italy, and Austria that lasted eighteen months. If he had indeed received any doctor's order to avoid alcohol completely, he no longer followed it, and he smoked cigarettes "until his tongue hurt." On his return to England, he seemed oppressed by dark moods. Even the hilarity of the Marlborough House Set failed to pull him out of his depression. The future seemed vague and unshaped. The army, maybe, or the diplomatic service, perhaps, but not for a while. He was a young man with neither purpose nor direction.

Then he met Jennie.

Randolph's mother soon conceded that she would be unable to sway her son's decision to marry this American girl but hoped her husband might have more influence in the matter. Not only did Randolph have extraordinary affection and respect for his father, but his father represented Randolph's sole source of income. The Duke was on a fishing and hunting trip in Scotland when Randolph wrote him from Blenheim. Part of his long and carefully worded letter said:

> I must not keep you in ignorance of a very important step I have taken—one which will undoubtedly influence very strongly all my future life. I met, soon after my arrival at Cowes, a Miss Jeanette Jerome, the daughter of an American lady who has lived for some years in Paris and whose husband lives in New York. I passed most of my time at Cowes in her (Jeanette's) society, and before leaving asked her if she loved me well enough to marry me; and she told me she did. I do not think that if I were to write pages I could give you any idea of the strength of my feelings and affection and love for her; all I can say is that I love her better than life itself, and that my one hope and dream now is that matters may be arranged that soon I may be united to her by ties that nothing but death itself could have the power to sever.
>
> I know, of course, that you will be very much surprised, and find it difficult to understand how an attachment so strong could have arisen in so short a space of time, and really, I feel it quite impossible for me to give any explanation of it that could appear reasonable to anyone practical and dispassionate. I must, however, ask you to believe it as you

could the truest and most real statement that could possibly be made to you, and to believe also that upon a subject so important, and I must say so solemn, I could not write one word that was in the smallest degree exaggerated, or that might not be taken at its fullest meaning.

He then apologized for not having written to his father before proposing to Jennie, but explained that he could not restrain his emotion. He added that they had broken the news to her mother before he left Cowes. ". . . And she [Jennie] said in her letter that her mother could not hear of it. That I am at a loss to understand."

Randolph then got down to the hard fact:

> I now write to tell you of it all, and to ask whether you will be able to increase my allowance to some extent to put me in the position to ask Mrs. Jerome to let me become her daughter's future husband. I enclose you her photograph, and will only say about her that she is as nice, as lovable, and amiable and charming in every way as she is beautiful, and that by her education and bringing-up she is in every way qualified to fill any position.

To reinforce his argument,

> Mr. Jerome is a gentleman who is obliged to live in New York and look after his business. I do not know what it is. He is reputed to be very well off, and his daughters, I believe, have very good fortunes, but I do not know anything for certain. He generally comes over for three or four months every year. Mrs. Jerome has lived in Paris for several years and has educated her her daughters there. They go out in Society there and are very well-known.
>
> I have told you all I know about them at present. You have always been very good to me, and done as much and more for me than I had any right to expect; and with any arrangement that you may at any time make for me, I shall be perfectly contented and happy. I see before me now a very happy future, almost in one's grasp. In the last year or so I feel I have lost a great deal of what energy and ambition I possessed, and an idle and comparatively useless life has at times appeared to me to be the pleasantest; but if I were married to her whom I have told you about, if I had a compan-

ion, such as she would be, I feel sure, to take an interest in one's prospects and career, and to encourage me to exertions and to doing something towards making a name for myself, I think that I might become, with the help of Providence, all and perhaps more than you had ever wished and hoped for me. On the other hand, if anything should occur to prevent my fondest hopes and wishes being realized (a possibility which I dare not and cannot bring myself to think of), how dreary and uninteresting would life become to me! No one goes through what I have lately gone through without its leaving a strong impress on their character and future. Time might, of course, partially efface the impression and recollection of feelings so strong as those I have tried to describe to you, but in the interval, the best years of one's life would be going, and one's energies and hopes would become blunted and deadened.

Finally, he concluded with:

I will not allude to her. I believe and am convinced that she loves me as fully, and as strongly as possible, as I do her; and when two people feel towards each other what we do, it becomes, I know, a great responsibility to assist in either bringing about or thwarting a union so closely desired by each.

Randolph's letter demonstrated insight into his own potential, but more than that, it stated clearly why he had chosen Jennie—not simply for her beauty but for the strength he knew she had and he needed. He counted on her to "encourage me to exertions and to doing something towards making a name for myself."

The Duke replied quickly. "My dearest R.," he wrote, "You have indeed taken me by surprise, and to use a Cowes speech, you have brought up all standing." After some short, noncommittal generalities, he continued, "Your letter is in a very affectionate tone and I appreciate all your feelings but I cannot say more. I only hope you will be willing to be guided by your mother and me."[13] As always, in the family tradition, he signed the letter "Marlborough."

This was not the answer Randolph had hoped to get. But his father could not then be more encouraging, for he was after all the seventh Duke of Marlborough, and his was a heritage among the richest in England. The first Duke of Marlborough had been John Churchill, who commanded the

English armies for Queen Anne and fought France in ten campaigns. He won every battle he engaged in, took every fortress he besieged. His greatest victory was the Battle of Blenheim in 1704, when he broke the French line on the left bank of the Danube with a cavalry attack. The grateful Queen Anne presented him with the royal manor of Woodstock, rich in history for more than a thousand years. Here the Saxon and Norman and Plantagenet kings, from Ethelred the Unready to Alfred the Great, held their Courts. From the time of Henry I, there was scarcely an English king or queen who did not stay in the manor house. It was here that Princess Elizabeth was imprisoned for nearly a year by her sister Mary. And it was here that the Roundheads besieged the Royalist Forces during the Civil Wars, and then ravaged the place.

When Queen Anne gifted the area to Marlborough, the manor house was an old ruin and Parliament voted the British equivalent of more than a million dollars for a new home, not only as a personal reward to the victor of Blenheim, but as a massive national memorial. "It was his achievements, not himself, that were to be recognized by a grateful country," Winston Churchill wrote in a biography of his ancestor.[14]

Set on 2,700 acres, the building finally had 320 rooms, soon filled with treasures of the world. King George II said of it, "We have nothing to equal this."

One approaches Blenheim through the arched stone gateway at the edge of town and down the winding path until one reaches a scene out of time, a setting as of a King Arthur legend. The peaceful lake, the enormous old trees, and the palace itself, spread over a huge area, severe and symmetrical with an almost ominous power. Winston Churchill called Blenheim "an Italian palace in an English park." He was referring to the balanced wings, the geometrical flower beds, the matched monuments. But the heritage of Blenheim is constructed of the bones and hot blood of England.

If there was ever a woman to match a man, it was the wife of the first Duke of Marlborough. Some say the Duchess Sarah not only ruled her roost but occasionally helped run the British Empire. As Queen Anne's closest confidante (until she angered the Queen), Sarah was even credited by some with masterminding the final decision to make war with France. The poet Alexander Pope wrote scathingly of her:

> Offend her, and she knows not to forgive;
>   Oblige her and she'll hate you while you live.

She was also highminded. When she read a biography of her famous husband, she remarked in a letter: "This History takes a great deal of pains to make the Duke of Marlborough's extraction very ancient. This may be true for aught I know. But it is no matter whether it be true or not in my opinion. For I value nobody for another's merit."

Despite her sometimes disagreeable character and her commanding presence, Sarah's numberless possessions attracted many suitors after the Duke's death. To one of them, the eminent Duke of Somerset, she wrote: "If I were young and handsome as I was, instead of old and faded as I am, and you could lay the empire of the world at my feet, you should never share the heart and head that belonged to John, Duke of Marlborough."[15]

Since there were no surviving sons, the dukedom passed to a nephew, Charles Spencer—Spencer thereby becoming part of the family name. The Spencer family crest was a griffin, the fabulous half-eagle, half-lion; the Churchill crest was a lion.

After Spencer and then the third Duke, the fourth Duke succeeded to the dukedom at the age of twenty and held it for fifty-eight years. He hired "Capability" Brown to create at Blenheim an artificial lake of a hundred acres, the largest such lake on any British private property. He also collected antique gems, staged elaborate amateur theatricals, and had Sir Joshua Reynolds paint the family portraits. The fourth Duke, however, became a confirmed hypochondriac. For three full years he maintained complete silence, not saying a single word. He broke his silence when he was informed of the scheduled arrival of a noted woman author. "Take me away," he roared, "Take me away. . . ."[16]

The most noteworthy comments on the fifth and sixth Dukes concern their fantastic extravagance, which necessitated their selling the most important Blenheim art treasures. The sixth Duke ended up so broke that he was forced to live in a remote corner of the palace.

The seventh Duke, George Charles, the father of Randolph, was described as "a man of formidable facade who was gentle and understanding but with an obstinacy and singlemindedness that characterized the Churchills."[17] Unlike his immediate predecessors, the seventh Duke led a useful life of public service. He was Conservative Member of Parliament for Woodstock and later served as Lord President of the Council.

With his eldest son and successor seemingly so irresponsible, Marlborough had pinned high hopes on Randolph. And now, here was a letter from Randolph asking his permission to marry an American. Who were these Jeromes, anyway? Marlborough sent off a stream of inquiries to key contacts in various countries.

While Randolph was trying to obtain his parents' approval for the marriage, Jennie was using all her powers of persuasion on her mother. At first, her mother was firmly opposed to the idea. She already had written her husband a hurried resumé of what had happened, using such phrases as, "hasty . . . rash . . . headstrong . . . unconsidered . . . impulsive," and adding,

"You must return to England by the next boat." Clara Jerome felt that Lord Randolph simply wasn't good enough for Jennie, Lord or no Lord, Marlborough or no. Still filled with romantic memories of the Imperial Court of Napoleon III, she envisioned a long parade of Princes and other royalty just waiting to pay court to her daughter.

Jennie drafted the strong support of Clarita. With incessant arguments and tears, the girls pursued their mother relentlessly. The combined force of two daughters was too much for Clara Jerome. Finally, but reluctantly, she consented to the marriage. She wrote her husband of her view and also answered Randolph, who had written her a pleading letter: "I must acknowledge that you have quite won my heart by your frank and honorable manner." But toward the end of her letter, she also added, "I hope you will listen to your father's advice, whatever it is. He can only have your happiness at heart. As a good son, your first duty is to him."

Marlborough, in the meanwhile, had begun to receive reports about Leonard Jerome. A London lawyer wrote:

> I am advised . . . that the gentleman named is at the present time doing one of the most extensive stockbroker's businesses in New York but that he lives very extravagantly and it is not unlikely that his income, large as it is, may be absorbed in his expenditure.

Another contact reported:

> I know Leonard Jerome of New York slightly. He has been a successful speculator and is what would be called by boon companions a "jolly good fellow"; but I have never heard that he holds a prominent position in either public or social life. Still, I believe he is a thoroughly respectable person.

An American friend contributed:

> Jerome is a well-known man with a fast reputation, has been a large stock speculator and was a few years ago supposed to be well cleaned out and managed to hold onto some purchases of real estate heavily mortgaged. As to his social position, I don't know what to say "*comme ça*" not good except among a fastish set. The daughters, who have been abroad several years with their mother . . . are, I hear, much admired.

One correspondent noted that Jerome's credit on the stock exchange was good, that nobody would "hesitate to execute any order of his." But another discussed his lavish expenditures, "the worst inference being that he spends as much as he makes."

Such reports were enough for the Duke. On August 31st, he finally wrote Randolph:

> It is not likely that at present, you can look at anything but from your own point of view but persons from the outside cannot but be struck with the unwisdom of your proceedings, and the uncontrolled state of your feelings, which completely paralyzes your judgment. Never was there such an illustration of the adage, "*love is blind*" for you seem blind to all consequences in order that you may pursue your passion; blind to the relative consequences as regards your family and blind to trouble you are heaping on Mamma and me by the anxieties this act of yours has produced. . . .
>
> Now as regards your letter I can't say that what you have told me is reassuring. I shall know more before long but from what you tell me and what I have heard, this Mr. J. seems to be a sporting, and I should think vulgar kind of man. I hear he drives about six and eight horses in New York (one may take this as a kind of indication of what the man is).
>
> Everything that you say about the mother and daughters is perfectly compatible with all that I am apprehensive of about the father and his belongings. And however great the attractions of the former, they can be no set off against a connection, should it so appear, which no man in his senses could think respectable. . . . I am deeply sorry that your feelings are so much engaged; and only for your own sake wish most heartily that you had checked the current before it became so overpowering.
>
> May God bless and keep you straight is my earnest prayer. Ever your affectionate father,
>
> Marlborough.

That was crushing for Randolph. A double-barreled blow came from his sister Cornelia and his brother Blandford. Cornelia wrote a long letter, part of which said:

> . . . when one feels how serious a step marriage is, one can't help feeling anxious that you should have chosen

hastily . . . and whether affection so quickly found would be likely to last and get stronger, as one sees how miserable marriage is when the reverse is the case. All I can say is one can't be too careful in taking a step which is so irrevocable. . . . I am afraid that there are many difficulties in the way, and that money will be a great obstacle. . . . Do, dearest Randolph, think calmly and sensibly over the whole matter, and do not let yourself be carried away by what might only be a passing fancy. . . . I think that when one hears people say that marriage is a mistake, and indeed madness, it is a hasty, ill-considered marriage that has made them say so.

Since Cornelia was staying with the Duke in Scotland, her words were particularly meaningful.

Blandford was much more blunt. He sent his younger brother a poem he had written, entitled, "An Elegy on Marriage."

> *Twas yours and not another's hand that built*
> *The funeral pyre near which you tarry.*
> *The dagger's plunged into its bleeding hilt*
> *Thy fate is sealed if thou dost marry . . .*
>
> *Remorse shall seize upon thy stricken soul*
> *When tinselled charms begin to pall,*
> *Thy part is strife, a fractious grief thy whole*
> *If thou dost thus in weakness fall . . .*
>
> *Perambulators and the babies' rusks*
> *Shall be among thy chiefest cares.*
> *See thou to the bottle that it sucks,*
> *Revolt Thy spirit will not dare.*
>
> *And when thy better half shall whine or fret*
> *Because thou dinest not at home,*
> *Perchance the scene will turn into a pet,*
> *Then! Wilt thou at thy fortunes moan! . . .*

It went on like that for fifteen stanzas, all of which pointed up the perils of a marriage in haste repented at leisure.

Randolph was infuriated. He sent copies of Blandford's poem to Cornelia and to the Prince of Wales. Cornelia answered soothingly:

> You must not think he means to be unkind. It is only his love of writing pieces that makes him give expression to such

ridiculous sentiments, and I think he fancies himself enormously. You know him as well as I do and can make allowances for him. . . .

The Prince of Wales, with even more extensive experience with marriage and mistresses, replied that Blandford's poem "is certainly one of the
most extraordinary productions I have ever read." But he advised Randolph not to take it too seriously, that he himself would write to Blandford.

Another letter came from his parents. His father had gone from Scotland to Cowes, where his mother had joined him. The Duchess wrote the
letter, which the Duke, who was a little tired, dictated.

> Your mother and I are only anxious for your happiness.
> I am quite willing, my dear boy, to give you credit for all you
> say . . . to make allowances for the state of mind in which
> you say you are. I only hope it will not lead you . . . to treat
> your mother and me ungratefully. . . .
> This Mr. J. seems to be a sporting, and I should think you must
> imagine to yourself what must be our feelings at the prospect of
> this marriage of yours. You cannot regard yourself alone in the
> matter and disassociate yourself from the rest of your fam-
> ily. . . . Under any circumstances, an American connection is
> not one that we would like. . . . you must allow it is a slightly
> coming down in pride for us to contemplate the connection. . . .

In New York Leonard Jerome similarly had qualms. After receiving his
wife's letter about the rushed romance, he was highly skeptical. He had a
strongly biased opinion against the inbreeding and overbreeding within the
British aristocracy, and he felt this was not a fit match for his fiery and
beautiful daughter.

"You quite startle me," he wrote Jennie.

> I shall feel very anxious about you till I hear more. If it has
> come to that—that *he* only "waits to consult his family" you
> are pretty far gone. You must like him well enough to accept
> for yourself which for you is a great deal. I fear if anything
> goes wrong you will make a dreadful shipwreck of your af-
> fections. I always thought if you ever did fall in love it would
> be a very dangerous affair. You were never born to love
> lightly. It must be *way* down or nothing. . . . Such natures if
> they happen to secure the right one are very happy but if dis-
> appointed they suffer untold misery. . . .

Jennie was at her best in a situation such as this. It was a romantic drama and she was the heroine. The accumulating obstacles only sweetened the prize. The opposition only fortified her determination. Life had generally been smooth for her. Now for the first time she was forced to fight for what she wanted, fight for the man she loved. And she discovered that she was most effective when she was doing battle for a cause.

Leonard Jerome read his favorite daughter's protestations of her love, and ultimately he wrote her:

> You know my views. Great confidence in you, and still greater in your mother; and anyone you accept and your mother approves, I could not object to, provided he is not a Frenchman or any other of those Continental Cusses.

He would have preferred to take the next boat to England and survey the situation himself, but the Duke's financial reports on Jerome were quite accurate. A financial scandal early in 1873 had rocked the stockmarket and panicked the country. Stephen Fiske described an evening at a restaurant with Leonard Jerome host to a large group of friends. A waiter delivered a telegram to Jerome, who excused himself to read it silently. Only after dinner was over did Jerome apologize for his rudeness in reading the telegram, and added, "But, gentlemen, it is a message in which you are all interested. The bottom has fallen out of stocks and I am a ruined man. But your dinner is paid for and I did not want to disturb you while you were eating it."[18]

Jerome was not quite ruined. He long ago had settled a sufficient sum of money on his wife to assure her financial independence. He also had salvaged some real estate. And out of the wreck of his major speculations, he recovered enough to keep him going on Wall Street, but on a much slower and smaller scale. His greatest ruin was in his loss of status. He was no longer one of those who ruled Wall Street, no longer in the top group of Vanderbilt, Gould, and Fisk.

Jerome, however, wrote little of the financial problems that were preventing an immediate trip to Europe. He had seldom discussed his financial affairs with his wife, "who hates money, or thinks she does." But the likelihood of Jennie's formal engagement, too, hinged on the money question. "I telegraphed your mother immediately that I was 'delighted' and that I would arrange £2,000 per year for you which she says in her letter will do," Jerome wrote.

> I cannot imagine any engagement that would please me more. I am as confident that all you say of him is true as though I knew him. Young, ambitious, uncorrupted. And

best of all you think and I believe he loves you. He must. You are no heiress and it must have taken heaps of love to over-come an Englishman's prejudice against "those horrid Amer-icans." I like it in every way. . . . I must say I have been very happy all day. I have thought of nothing else.

To his wife, Leonard outlined suggested terms of the dowry. By this time, Clara and her daughters were again at their house in Paris.

Learning of the Duke's disapproval of the match, Clara Jerome promptly wrote Randolph:

Of course, dear Randolph, he [Leonard] knows nothing of you except what I have written, which I need not say was most favorable. Taking for granted that what I said must be true, and listening to his daughter's earnest appeal, who thinks all her happiness in life depends on her marrying you, he gives his formal consent. I must say that my husband has not the slightest idea of any opposition from your father. And I wrote him very particularly what you told me at Cowes, that there would be none. I can only repeat that both Mr. Jerome and myself have too high an opinion of our daughter and too much love ever to permit her to marry any man without the cordial consent of his family. . . .

If your father gives his consent, I shall wish you to see more of each other before taking such an important step, and if there is any engagement at all, it must be a long one.

She appended a financial comment from her husband: "If the settlement of £2,000 a year and the allowance of one-third of all my fortune later is satisfactory, this can all be easily arranged."

However, nothing was to be easily arranged, and money was one of the critical keys. Randolph's financial dependence on his father made any mar-riage without Marlborough's consent impossible, for he had neither the in-clination nor the training to hunt for a job. And Jennie, though possessed of some "original, if arrogant, opinions," would not dream of disobeying her parents.

Blandford at this time followed up his poetic advice with some perish-able prose. In a greater attempt at brotherliness, he addressed it, "My dear old chap . . ."

I feel that what I am about to say is like words scattered at a raging gale. . . . You are my only brother and what you do affects me far more than anything that can befall anyone else. . . .

I don't care if your demoiselle was the incarnation of all physical beauties on God's earth, my opinion is the same. . . .

Do you marry for a fortune? No!

Do you marry to get children? No!

Do you marry because you have loved a woman for years? No!

You really only want to marry because you are in love with an *idea*.

. . . Damnation! . . . here you are a sensible man, no longer a child . . . you are a d- -d fool. Excuse my plain speaking, old chap. . . .

The Prince of Wales in the meanwhile had written Blandford and sent a copy to Randolph. The letter so impressed Randolph that he asked the Prince's permission to forward it to the Duke and Duchess. The Prince hesitated, then agreed only to let Randolph apprise his parents of the contents, without showing them the letter itself. He must have worried that the Duchess might pass the letter back to his own mother the Queen. But the Prince did write Randolph, "I quite understand how low you must feel under all this suspense."

Leonard Jerome had now heard of the Duke's disapproval of the proposed marriage and cabled his wife, "CONSENT WITHDRAWN."

At this low point in their ebbing fortunes, it was Jennie who served as their common source of strength while Randolph vacillated between exhilaration and despair. Jennie gently chided him for it, and Randolph answered, "You certainly have great powers of perception. I cannot but own that there is a great deal of truth in what you say about my being one moment very despairing and another moment very sanguine. I cannot help it; I was made so."

In another letter, he explained some of the antidotes for his moods:

> When I feel very cross or angry, I read Gibbon, whose profound philosophy and easy though majestic writing quiet me down, and in an hour, I feel at peace with all the world. When I feel very low and desponding, I read Horace, whose thorough epicureanism, quiet maxims and beautiful verse are most tranquilizing. Of late, I have had to have frequent recourse to my two friends, and they have never failed me. I strongly recommend you to read some great works of histories. . . . Novels, or even travels, are rather unsatisfactory,

and do no good, because they create an unhealthy excitement, which is bad for anyone. I wonder whether you will understand all this, or only think me rather odd.

But she did not think him odd; she prided in his mind and boasted of his intellect.

Fortunately for Randolph, reports were still flowing to the Duke about the quality and character and cash of Leonard Jerome, and the details now seemed more favorable. These reports added strength to the unceasing pressure of his favorite son—who was desperate enough to propose that he might even seek a job, "in England or out of it."

The Duke demurred but eventually felt compelled to acquiesce—provisionally—"for the sake of his son's peace of mind and his own authority."

> The great question is still unsolved, whether you and the young lady who has gained your affections are, or can be, after a few days' acquaintance, sufficiently aware of your own minds to venture on the step which is to bind you together for life. What I have now to say is that if I am to believe that your future is really bound up in your marriage with Miss Jerome, you must show me proof of it by bringing it to the test of time. I will say no more to you on the subject for the present, but if this time next year you come and tell me that you are both of the same mind, we will receive Miss Jerome as a daughter, and, I need not say, with the affection you could desire for your wife.

Reporting to Jennie, Randolph referred to his father's "unnecessary rigamarole and verbosity," and added:

> . . . I do not mind telling you that it is all humbug about waiting a year. I could and would wait a good deal more than a year, but I do not mean to, as it is not the least necessary; for though we have only known each other a short time, I know we both know our minds well enough, and I wrote a very long and diplomatic letter to my father yesterday, doing what I have done before, contradicting him and arguing with him, and I hope, persuading him that he has got very wrong and foolish ideas in his head. You see, both he and my mother have set their hearts upon my being a Member for Woodstock. It is a family borough, and for years and years a member of the family has sat for it. The present Member is a stranger, though a

Conservative, and is so unpopular that he is almost sure to be beaten if he were to stand; and the fact of a Radical sitting for Woodstock is perfectly insupportable to my family. It is for this they have kept me idle ever since I left Oxford, waiting for a dissolution [of Parliament]. Well . . . a dissolution is almost sure to come almost before the end of the year. I have two courses open to me: either to refuse to stand altogether unless they consent to my being married immediately afterwards; or else, and this is still more Machiavellian and deep, to stand, but at the last moment to threaten to withdraw and leave the Radical to walk over. All tricks are fair in love and war. . . .

Finally, came good news:

The clouds have all cleared away, and the sky is bluer than I have ever seen it since I first met you at Cowes. It is exactly six weeks tomorrow since we met on board the *Ariadne*, and I am sure I seem to have lived six years. How I do bless that day, in spite of all the worry and bother that has come since, and I am sure you will not regret it. I have not had a further conversation with my father since I wrote you, for I think it is best to leave things for the present as they are. Our early golden dreams of being married in December won't quite become realized, but still it won't be very long to wait; and I shall be able to see you from time to time, and write as often as I like; in fact, we can be regularly engaged, and all the world may know it. . . .

Jennie dutifully wrote to her prospective mother-in-law, and Randolph was quick to compliment her on it.

My dearest, what a nice letter you wrote to my mother, she was so pleased with it. You have the happiest and nicest way of expressing yourself of anyone I know. You will be happy to hear that my father is very much struck with your handwriting, which he assures me has a deal of character.

Now he was also able to reassure her that his father had

promised to give his consent to our marriage when he is sure we are fond of each other. As to the year, I have every right to say that I do not think he will insist on it. . . .

There are three new elections to come off, owing to death vacancies; and if they go against the government, as they very probably will, we are sure to have a dissolution, and then I shall become a Member for Woodstock.

But, after all, public life has no great charms for me, as I am naturally very quiet, and hate bother and publicity, which, after all, is full of vanity and vexation of spirit. Still, it will all have greater attractions for me if I think it will please you and that you take an interest in it and will encourage me to keep up to the mark.

To stir her interest in politics, he wrote in another letter, "I advise you to get a copy of today's *Times* if you can, and read Disraeli's great speech. He has made a magnificent one to the Conservatives of Glasgow . . . it is a fine specimen of perfect English oratory."

Jennie not only read Disraeli's speech but everything about British politics she could. On Randolph's recommendation, she also read Gibbon and Horace. She was determined to make her mind a match for his.

For Jennie, life was more exciting and fruitful than it was for Randolph. Paris was seething with rumor and whisperings by Royalists and Bonapartists wanting to be back in power. To dampen any smouldering fire, the new French Assembly accused Marshal Bazaine of treason for having surrendered his army to the Prussians. Jennie attended the Bazaine trial at Versailles, and wrote her partisan impressions:

A long, low room filled to suffocation with a curious crowd, many of whom were women, a raised platform, a table covered with green baize and holding a bottle of water, a few chairs arranged in semi-circles, completed the *mise-en-scène*, which seemed a rather poor one for the trial for life or death of a Marshal of France.

She related that some women had jumped onto their chairs and peered through their opera-glass to get a better look at Bazaine, so that the gendarmes "pulled the offenders down unceremoniously by their skirts," reproving them by saying, "*C'est pas gentil.*" And Jennie added, "Nor was it."

What had impressed her was how impassively Bazaine sat while his defense lawyer dramatically gestured toward him, exclaiming that Bazaine was no traitor but merely an imbecile. "How the mighty have fallen!" Jennie wrote.

I thought of him and his wife in the glittering throng of Compiègne only three years before, and of him again as the Commander-in-Chief of a huge army, which now he was supposed to have betrayed and sold. I say supposed, for although he was found guilty and condemned to death [later commuted to twenty years' imprisonment], there were many who believed in him and thought him a hero. . . . I doubt if posterity will place a halo around his head.

Somewhere in her long letter about the trial, Jennie incorrectly used the word *prorogue*. Randolph chided her for it. Instead of accepting his correction, Jennie consulted a young French nobleman, Count de Fénelon, whose name she had seemed to mention often in her letters. Fénelon agreed with her definition of the word. Randolph's reply was sharp:

> . . . Hang *le petit* Fénelon, little idiot! What do I care for him. He may be a very good authority about his own beastly language, but I cannot for a moment submit to him about English . . . To prorogue means to suspend something for a definite time, to be resumed again in exactly the same state, condition and circumstances. Therefore to talk about proroguing the Marshal's powers would mean that they were to be suspended for a certain time and then resumed again exactly as before. Parliament is prorogued; L'Assemblée is prorogued; that does not in the least mean that the powers of either are lengthened or increased in any way, but that they are temporarily suspended.

Jennie, however, refused to let the matter drop. She showed Randolph's letter to her mother, who merely commented, "What a very English letter." Then she again consulted Fénelon, and continued her semantic cause. Randolph finally answered,

> I am looking forward particularly to utterly suppressing and crushing *le petit* Fénelon. We must really, tho', drop this argument when I am with you, as it is likely to become a heated one, I fear. We will therefore "prorogue" it.

Jennie complained about the tone of his letters, and he responded,

My darling Jennie,

You heap coals of fire upon my head by YOUR DEAR LOVING LETTER received this morning. I remember now I did write a rather cross letter last Tuesday, but you must make allowances for me as I have been awfully hustled and worried. . . . I hope your sister is quite well, comforts you and sticks up for me when you abuse me to her or doubt me. . . .

Jennie then informed Randolph that her father had arrived in Paris and planned to visit his future son-in-law in England. Randolph promptly wired "Miss Jeanette Jerome" on January 1, 1874:

HAS YOUR FATHER STARTED? WHERE DOES HE STOP WHEN IN LONDON? HAVE LEFT SANDRINGHAM. MY AUNT DANGEROUSLY ILL IN IRELAND.

His aunt's illness came at the worst time for the young lovers, because Randolph had finally received permission from his parents to visit Jennie in Paris. But Lady Ely Partington was a favorite aunt, and his parents depended on him to be in Ireland with them. First, however, he had to meet his future father-in-law. In his daily letter to Jennie, Randolph wrote:

I am just going to dinner with your father, and then I am off to Ireland. There is no change in Lady Partington's state, and I doubt whether she will be alive when I arrive. It is very, very sad; and I do so dread a house of mourning . . . I have been going about with your father all day. . . . I had a very pleasant afternoon . . . and helped him to make his different purchases. . . . I really like him so much, the more I see of him. I am sure we will always be the best of friends. I had it all out with him about the abuse of me that had been sent from America. I am glad to find that such nonsense does not seem to have made any impression on him. Fancy people saying that I drank!!!! What next?

P.S. You will not get a letter from me till Sunday night or Monday morning, as the post takes longer going from Ireland. But, really, *you* might write a little more. It makes me think your head is full of everything and everybody else but me. . . .

Before he left for Ireland, Randolph sent another telegram to Jennie, saying that he had dined that night with her father, and, "AFRAID THERE IS NO CHANCE OF MY BEING IN PARIS MONDAY."

Throughout that month, Randolph's depression deepened considerably—his Aunt Alice would seem to get better, he would prepare to leave, then she would slip into another crisis, and he would unpack again. He set specific dates for his arrival in Paris several times and each time had to postpone the trip.

His letters to Jennie poured forth in a daily stream:

> . . . These ups and downs are more trying and depressing than anything you can imagine. I am so unhappy and low. . . . There are only my father and mother and Lady Londonderry here. . . . I don't think I ever witnessed anything so trying. Everyone is in a state of continual apprehension, never knowing what to expect from one moment to another. I would give anything to be with you, darling, quiet and happy. I was thinking last night, what would I do, if, supposing we were married, and you were to fall ill like this? I am sure I should go quite mad. . . .

> . . . I should be more distressed than I am at your loneliness if I did not know that you did not have Kevenhuller to pass your time with. He must be very charming, as you write so much about him. . . .

> . . . My darling Jennie, I am sure you don't care for me as much as you did. I don't wonder; I am not wonderfully brilliant when I am with you that you should remember me very much when I have been away. I don't think, if we had been prevented from seeing each other for a year, we should have had a chance of being married . . . you seem to let anything come between you and your letter to me. It is never the least trouble to me to write to you, because I love you and am always thinking of you. I wish it was the same to you. . . . I am certainly a fool. I began this letter intending to say nothing reproachful, and I find I have written ten pages. I can't help it. . . .

> . . . Try to write one letter in which that . . . Austrian should not appear. It would be curious to see if you could do it. I don't think you could. . . .

> . . . My dearest, I hope and trust you are really not looking ill or worried, as you say. I wish you could get out of that

horrid habit of sitting up so late. You can't imagine how bad it is for you. If you could go to bed early, you will soon get into the habit of going to sleep after a few nights; but you never do anything I ask you—at least, not often. *Good-bye, darling, dearest, loving, good, affectionate Jennie. . . .*

Here I am detained again, at the very last moment. I'd actually started; but I'd left my aunt in the most critical state. A sudden relapse had come on and everyone was much alarmed. I could not bear the idea of disappointing you, but, still, I did not like to leave the house at such a moment. If she had died . . . it would have looked so unfeeling, my having to go off. . . . My mother was quite sorry at my being obliged to stay, on your account, and insisted on telegraphing herself to you, that you might know it. . . .

(The telegram read: GRIEVED TO SAY RANDOLPH CANNOT LEAVE HIS AUNT TILL THIS CRISIS IS OVER. DUCHESS OF MARLBOROUGH.)

Really, my dearest, you must not get afraid of my getting tired of you. . . . So far, dearest, from my learning to do without you, this prolonged separation of ours is showing more forcibly than ever before that I *cannot* get on or do without you. . . .

Do try to amuse yourself, and do something to make the time pass. Go to Fontainebleau and play, and anything to occupy your thoughts; even try Kevenhuller, if he can amuse you. . . .

. . . I cannot bear you to think that my letters have been "cold." I am sure it is only your fancy. They may, and most probably have been, stupid, as I have nothing to write about except this sad illness, which could not interest you much; but I am sure they were never cold. I could not write you so if I wished to. . . . I don't know what I would not give to get away, but here I am tied by the leg. She is still alive and conscious, but that is all one can say. There is no hope of the slightest recovery; but how long this state may last, it is impossible to say. . . . Yet, every evening and morning follow each other and she is still alive. . . .

A month after Randolph had arrived in Ireland, Lady Partington died. The funeral at her castle in Emo was one of much pomp and ceremony. The night after the funeral, Randolph hurried across the Irish Channel and on to Dover, intending to take the first boat the following morning to France.

Just then the news came that Parliament was dissolved. Gladstone's Liberal Party had been enervated by factionalism among its leaders. A Conservative Party leader referred to the Prime Minister's administration as "a range of exhausted volcanoes . . . not a flame flickers on a single pallid crest. . . ." The tide that had swept the Liberals into power in 1868 now turned against them, and the Government lost a series of important by-elections. Finally, Gladstone, old, exhausted, and ill, used poor political judgment in attempting to override a Parliamentary action and then found that on the pinprick of a legal technicality, he had consented to the dissolution of Parliament.

So Lord Randolph was suddenly called back to Blenheim to begin his campaign for Member from Woodstock. The situation allowed no postponement—that very afternoon there was to be an open-air meeting of all the farmers in his area, and his attendance was mandatory.

"It was perfectly impossible to get any letter off by last night's post, as I have not had a moment to spare," he wrote Jennie from Blenheim.

> Since ten this morning, I went and saw several people at Woodstock, and had, on the whole, satisfactory answers and assurances of support. It was a most fortunate circumstance that the Annual Coursing Meeting, which my father allows every year in the Park, had been fixed for today; all the farmers were there, and as they had a good day's sport, were all in great spirits. I took the chair at their dinner at the Bear Hotel, and you cannot imagine how enthusiastic they were for me. They all go as one man. I hear nothing certain as to any opposition; there are no end of rumors, but no one as yet has appeared publicly; I suppose we shall know for certain tomorrow.
>
> I am off now to a part of the borough four miles distant, to see more people, and I have a large meeting of my committee at four in Woodstock. I think that I may say that for the present everything is satisfactory. There are 1,071 voters, and I do not think that more than 800 will poll; out of these I calculate at least on 460, which will be enough. But this is, of course, mere guesswork; it is all still very uncertain, and I am glad I lost no time in arriving.

His Liberal opponent was George Brodrick, who had been a don at Merton College in Oxford when Randolph was a student there. In 1868, when running for Parliament from Woodstock, Brodrick had charged the

Duke of Marlborough with bribery, intimidation, and dishonest interference with the vote. After that, Randolph had refused to attend any more of Brodrick's lectures. Called to the office of the School Warden to explain his absence from Brodrick's lectures, Randolph had said, "How, sir, could I attend the lectures of one who has called my father a scoundrel?"[19] Whatever his memories, Randolph again met Brodrick, and wrote Jennie, "We shook hands and were very friendly. The contest will be a hard one and the result doubtful; it is impossible to say how the laborers will go. However, I have made a very good start and have nothing to complain of as yet."

The politically inexperienced Randolph needed help, and Edward Clarke, a well-known Tory barrister from London, came to his aid. Meeting Clarke at the station was the retiring Member of Parliament, Henry Barnett, who fully outlined all of Randolph's handicaps. Clarke soon catalogued them himself:

> He had little knowledge of literature, none of science, no familiarity with political history and very slight acquaintance with foreign affairs.... Lord Randolph Churchill was a rather nervous, awkward young man who certainly seemed to have the most elementary ideas about current politics. We had some talk about the subjects he was going to deal with in his speech. I wrote out four or five questions which were to be put in friendly hands and asked from the back of the room, and gave Lord Randolph the answers.... When we came to the meeting, Lord Randolph was very nervous. He had written out his speech on small sheets of paper, and thought if he put his hat on the table and the papers in the bottom of the hat, he would be able to read them. This of course he could not do. There was a rather noisy audience who gibed at him and shouted to him to take the things out of his hat, etc., and the speech was far from a success. But the questions and answers went very well; then I made a speech, and, taken together, the meeting went off very well.[20]

Clarke also edited Churchill's campaign speech for the press, and Randolph later wrote him, "I really am confident that many of the votes, if not the majority, may be attributed to your excellent speech."

Randolph's letter to Jennie failed to mention the disturbance at the meeting but said:

> We had a great meeting last night which was very successful; we had a speaker down from London and I made a speech.

How I have been longing for you to be with me! If we had only been married before this! I think the reception you would have got would have astonished you. The number of houses I have been into—many of them dirty cottages—the number of unwashed hands I have cordially shaken, you would not believe. My head is in a whirl of voters, committee meetings and goodness knows what. I am glad it is drawing to an end, as I could not stand it very long; I cannot eat or sleep. . . .

Brodrick must have been sleeping even more poorly. Randolph had all the Marlborough money and influence on his side. The Duke had rented the town's three leading hotels for his son's cause, and that left Brodrick with what Randolph described to Jennie as "a wretched, low, miserable pothouse." Coming to help Brodrick was a bright young man named Asquith.[21] But Woodstock was a family borough, and in one way or another many of the local people were dependent on the Marlboroughs. Not all were, however, and Randolph was realistic, if not pessimistic.

"How this election is going," he wrote Jennie,

I really can form no opinion and the uncertainty of it makes me quite ill. Yesterday I was canvassing all day in Woodstock itself. People that I think know better than anybody tell me it will be very close. You see, with the [secret] ballot, one can tell nothing—one can only trust to promises, and I have no doubt a good many will be broken. Our organization and preparations for Tuesday are very perfect, and the old borough has never been worked in such a way before. . . . I have a presentiment that it will go wrong. I am such a fool to care so much about it. I hate all this excitement. . . . I saw my opponent today in church. He looks awfully harassed. I feel quite sorry for him, as all his friends here are such a disreputable lot. . . .

Interspersed among his letters to Jennie, Randolph kept up a barrage of telegrams, several of them in French, one of which worried aloud, "I BELIEVED ALL GOES WELL, BUT IT IS GRAVE ENOUGH." But on February 4th, he sent her a telegram which read: "I HAVE WON A GREAT VICTORY BY 569 VOTES AGAINST 404. GREAT ENTHUSIASM. EXPECT ME SATURDAY."

Jennie's excitement was almost explosive. She exultantly showed everyone the victory telegram and constantly quoted Randolph's remarks about everything.

He now wrote her:

... Ever since I met you, everything goes well with me–too well. I am afraid of a Nemesis. I always hoped I should win the election, but that under the ballot and against a man like Brodrick I should have that crushing, overwhelming victory never entered into my wildest dreams. It was a great victory–we shall never have a contest again. The last two contests–in '65 and '68–were won only by 17 and 21 majorities; so just conceive the blow it is to the other side. You never heard such cheering in all your life. The poll was not declared till eleven, and hours of suspense were most trying; but when it was known, there was such a burst of cheers that must have made the old Dukes in the vault jump. I addressed a few words to the Committee–and so did Blandford–and was immensely cheered; and then they accompanied us, the whole crowd of them, through the town and up to Blenheim, shouting and cheering all the way. Oh, it was a great triumph– and that you were not there to witness it will always be a source of great regret to me. . . .

. . . There is nothing more to be done except to pay the bill, and that I have left to my father. . . .

Leonard Jerome wrote his future son-in-law a letter on Jockey Club stationery from New York:

You are very good indeed to write to me the particulars of your canvass. They are interesting indeed. You do not tell me how much you were pelted with eggs and stones etc. That I suppose you leave to my imagination. But the great fact of your election, I assure you I appreciate, and I congratulate you most heartily. It is really a great thing, great to anyone; and just at this period of your life, it is immense. It opens to you a magnificent field–a field wherein, with only half an effort, you are bound to play no ignoble part.

. . . I think of the many talks we shall have in the course of time. You will find me quite ready to impart to you, if not words of wisdom, at least my notions of the problems of life gathered from experience. . . . Could we have "a few words in private" you might get a liberal dose tonight, but situated as we are, that may not be. What a fortunate fellow you are.

Jerome hoped Jennie and Randolph would visit him in America after their wedding that summer. "I will take you on the rounds of this 'great republic' and do my best to implant in your bigoted Conservative brains some liberal Yankee notions (including a buffalo hunt)."

The victory had created for everyone, including the Marlboroughs, a warmer, more amenable mood. The situation seemed even more agreeable when the Duke went along with his son to Paris to meet Jennie. Jennie charmed him. She played the piano for him—Beethoven's "Sonata Appassionata"—and even talked about British politics, backed up by a surprisingly large fund of information. The Duke was openly impressed and pleased. Jennie was similarly pleased with her future father-in-law. As for Mrs. Jerome, she found the Duke "a perfect dear."[22]

The Duke of Marlborough's income from his Oxfordshire estates then totaled about £40,000 a year. Considering the size and upkeep of his estate and allowances to his daughters and two sons, this was not a great fortune. In fact, he had felt forced to sell the ancestral Marlborough gems for some 35,000 guineas, as well as a major part of Blenheim's famous Sunderland Library.[23]

Nonetheless, he offered a preliminary wedding present to his son: ". . . I observe your bills," he wrote.

> Therefore, if you wish me to clear you, it must be done at the expense of the fund I have proposed to put into settlement, and I will go so far as to raise now £2,000 [$10,000] to clear your present and previous debts, without charging you the interest so that I shall be giving you actually £1100 . . . and in addition to this, I will pay your annual expenses for the representation of Woodstock. . . . I shall have done as much as my means and income will admit of. . . . As you must be well enough aware, my income is not large enough to bear the continual and heavy charges which are continually accruing. . . .

Randolph himself could offer Jennie only his titled name, the pitifully small salary as a Member of Parliament, a town house in London, and two fine horses (but not his own carriage).

The Duke advised him that he was forwarding to his lawyer Jerome's proposed marriage settlement and then commented, "I do not wish to say anything harsh or unkind, but the inference is not hopeful unless Miss Jerome takes the finance department under her own control. . . ."

Randolph sent his gratitude for "your offers *most* kind and *most* liberal and more than I at any time expected . . . in clearing off my debts before starting on what one may call a new life. . . . I did not like Mr. J. should think I had married Jennie to get my debts paid. . . ." Then he added:

> I am quite decided that Jennie will have to manage the
> money, and I am quite sure she will keep everything straight,
> for she is clever, and like all Americans, has a sacred, and I
> should almost say, insane horror of buying anything she can-
> not pay for immediately.

Actually, though Jennie had learned about many things, money management was not among them.

There was only one item left to settle—the details of the dowry. Lord
Randolph never concerned himself with money matters, but the Duke did.
His ancestors had left him financially strapped. Unfortunately, Leonard
Jerome was in similar financial straits, and while he was far from flattened,
he now had to consider more carefully which money went where. Consequently, the dowry negotiations were long and legal and messy. Jerome
wrote to the Duke and the Duke wrote to Randolph and all of them wrote
their lawyers, who all then wrote to each other.

Marriage, then, was arranged not simply by informal family agreement
but by contract, often incredibly detailed, full of all kinds of clauses and
whereases intended to anticipate every eventuality. Particularly in the great
families of England, such a contract was an accepted formality, making
marriage an economic union as well as a physical one. No one really questioned its need, even those who resented it.

Randolph stayed in Paris, and wrote long, daily letters to his "dearest
Papa" and constantly asked his father's advice on all the qualifying clauses
in the contract. Things became not only increasingly complicated but increasingly bitter. ". . . Affairs are come to a most unpleasant pass." he wrote
his father. "Mr. and Mrs. Jerome and myself are barely on speaking terms
and I don't quite see what is to be the end of it. . . . I think that his conduct
and Mrs. J's is perfectly disgraceful . . . and I am bound to say that Jennie
agrees with me entirely. . . ."

Leonard Jerome returned to Paris for the final negotiations. With his
two daughters pressuring him in one direction, his wife in another, and
Randolph set in the center glaring, it was not a friendly family picture. Finally it was agreed that if Jennie died before Randolph and there were children, the money would be apportioned among them. If Jennie died before
Randolph and there were no children, half the money would go to Randolph and the other half to the Jerome family. Jubilantly, Randolph wrote
his father the good news:

> . . . I must thank you for your letter to him, which was
> so nice in every part. I really don't think there is anyone
> who can write such nice letters as you can. Mr. Jerome was

immensely pleased with it, and I have no doubt it had the effect of making him behave properly. . . . Please don't be very angry with Mr. Jerome, though I cannot be surprised if you think he behaved rather curiously. . . . The fact of the matter is that Mrs. Jerome twists him round her finger. She was furious at the whole of the after-dinner agreement, and declared that Mr. Jerome did not know what he was doing, and tried to make him back out of it. When, however, for two days, I would not speak to her or him, except to tell them both my mind, when Mr. Jerome became so worried, he actually never came down for dinner or breakfast, and when he finally declared he was going to London the next morning, and America the next day, she became frightened and alleged all the difficulties could easily be overcome. You will not tell anybody except Mama about this, will you? It is not very pleasant. Poor Jennie has been most awfully worried about it all, and I believe she had several hours up with her mother. . . .

That, however, was not the end of it. The lawyers took over, and negotiations reached an incredible nadir of haggling over who should pay for the telegrams and postage ($61), the title search on the Madison Square property (then under lease to the Union League Club of New York), and even the charges for preparing the abstract (102 pounds, 15 shillings, and sixpence—in American money, at five dollars a pound, $545.85). There was also a major wrangle over an allowance for Jennie. To the Marlborough's lawyer, Jerome wrote: "I have conceded considerably more than Lord Randolph declared to me by letter . . . was entirely satisfactory (and nearly all required by his father . . .)."[24]

The pile of legal letters grew. One dated February 23, 1874 and written to Lord Randolph by one of Marlborough's lawyers on Savile Row noted,

> The Duke says that such a settlement cannot as far as you are personally concerned be considered as any settlement at all, for as I explained in my former letter, Miss Jerome would be made quite independent of you in a pecuniary point of view, which in my experience is most unusual. . . . Although in America, a married woman's property may be absolutely and entirely her own, I would remark that upon marrying an Englishman, she loses her American nationality and becomes an Englishwoman so that I think that the settlement should be according to the law and custom here. . . .

That, too, was resolved, and the fathers-in-law-to-be exchanged more friendly letters. Jerome wrote:

> In regard to the settlement, . . . I beg to assure you that I have been governed purely by what I conceived to be the best interests of both parties. It is quite wrong to suppose I entertain any distrust of Randolph. On the contrary, I hope there is no young man in the world safer. Still, I can but think your English custom of making the wife so entirely depend- ent upon the husband, is most unwise. In the settlement, as it is finally arranged, I have ignored American customs and waived all my American prejudices, and have conceded to your views and English customs on every point, save one. That is a somewhat unusual allowance of money to the wife. Probably the principle may be wrong, but you may be very certain my action upon it in this instance by no means arises from any distrust of Randolph. . . .

Randolph was then able to report to his mother, "Things are all going now as merrily as a marriage bell."

The wedding would take place in Paris on April 15, 1874. That was also the Duchess' birthday, but the Duke and Duchess excused themselves from attending. The Duchess was presumably not well. The absence of both of Randolph's parents was not only unusual—it was incredible. Randolph was their favorite son. Despite their early disapproval of the marriage, they had given their final consent and their blessing. Even if one of them were ill, the other would have been expected to participate in the wedding.

Leonard Jerome tried to put the best possible face on the awkward situation. In a letter addressed "Dear Duke," he noted,

> I am very sorry you are not able to come over for the wed- ding. We had all hoped to have the pleasure of seeing both yourself and the Duchess. . . . I have every confidence in Ran- dolph, and while I would entrust my daughter to his sole care alone in the world, still I can but feel reassured of her happi- ness when I am told that in entering your family, she will be met at once with "new affectionate friends and relatives. . . ."

Blandford, however, did come, as did three of Randolph's sisters and his aunt, Lady Camden. Leonard Jerome arranged a resplendent family dinner for all of them the night before the wedding.

The trousseau had long ago been ready: twenty-three French-made dresses, seven Paris bonnets, piles of delicately embroidered white underlinen. "These will have to last me a long time," Jennie told Clarita and Leonie, thinking of her limited budget.

The night before her wedding, Jennie wrote: ". . . This is the last time I shall wind this clock . . . this is the last time I shall look in this old mirror. Soon nothing will be the same for me anymore: Miss Jennie Jerome will be gone forever."

On the wedding morning, Randolph received a letter from his father:

> I must send you a few lines to reach you tomorrow, one of the most important days of your life, and which I sincerely pray will be blessed to you, and be the commencement of a united existence of happiness for you and your wife. She is one whom you have chosen with rather less than usual deliberation, but you have adhered to your love with unwavering constancy, and I cannot doubt the truth of your affection, and how I hope that, as time goes on, your two natures will prove to have been brought not accidentally together. May you both be "lovely and pleasant in your lives" is my earnest prayer. I am very glad that harmony is again restored, and that no cloud obscures the day of sunshine; but what has happened will show that the severest faith is not without its throes, and I must say ought not to be without its lesson to you . . .
>
> . . . We shall look forward shortly to seeing you and Jeanette here, whom I need not say, we shall welcome into her *new family*. . . .

It was a morning wedding, and the maid hurried in early with a breakfast tray for Jennie. The corset had to be pulled more tightly than usual, but not so tight as to cause the bride to faint at the ceremony. A hairdresser arrived to arrange her thick black curls.

Jennie's dress was of white satin with a long train, all lavishly trimmed with Alençon lace. She wore white silk stockings, white satin slippers, and long white kid gloves. There was a knot of white flowers at her breast and a fine tulle veil covering her from head to foot. Her only jewelry was a string of pearls, a wedding gift from her father.

As his best man, Randolph had chosen Francis Knollys, secretary to the Prince of Wales. Jennie's bridesmaid was her sister Clarita. The ceremony was swift and simple. The marriage certificate read:

> I hereby certify that Lord Randolph Henry Spencer Churchill, bachelor of the parish of Woodstock and the county of Oxford, now residing at Paris, Hotel d'Albe, and Jennie Jerome, spinster, of the city of Brooklyn, in the state of New York, U.S.A., were duly married according to the rites of the Church of England in the House of Her Most Historic Majesty's Ambassador at Paris this 15th day of April in the year of our Lord one thousand eight hundred and seventy four. . . .

The brief wedding was startlingly unadorned. This, after all, was one of the first great international marriages of the time. Considering the prestige of the families, the historic nobility of Marlborough and the national eminence of Jerome, one would have expected the social splash of the season. Despite his diminished fortune, Leonard Jerome certainly had the friends and funds to stage an elaborate wedding. Instead, there was just a simple ceremony in the British Embassy before a handful of people, with the Duke and Duchess of Marlborough conspicuously absent.

Certainly it was not the way Mrs. Jerome would have wanted it. In addition to her hopes of steadily rising social splendor, this was the first marriage among her daughters, and no wedding preparations could have been too lavish for her. Nor could it have been the ordinary wish of Jennie, whose recent memories were still captivated by Napoleon III's Imperial Court and who had her own sense of large-scale romantic drama.

Furthermore, why had Clara Jerome, hardly blissful about Jennie's less-than-royal choice, suddenly become instrumental in eliminating all settlement obstacles?

Was there a connection with the birth of Winston Churchill seven months later? It is a fact, of course, that Jennie's second son was also a seven-month baby. But is it not also possible to imagine that the two lovers, with passions intensified by their long separation and the fear their chances of marriage were dribbling down the legal drain, might determine to force the marriage, or simply let their emotions overwhelm them?

Anyway, there they were, after a hearty wedding breakfast, climbing into a beautiful coach with handsome gray horses. Jennie wore a dark blue-and-white striped traveling dress with a stylish bonnet. She held a lovely, fragile parasol of white lace frills mounted on a tortoise-shell stick rimmed with gold, a gift from her father. "Thought it looked like the sort of bit of nonsense you liked," he told her.

The last comment Jennie made to her mother before leaving was "Why, Mama, don't cry, life is going to be perfect . . . always . . ."[26] It would not be, for her future held heartbreak as well as splendor, terror as well as triumph.

$\mathcal{T}$HIS WAS A LOVE MATCH if ever there was one, with very little money on either side," wrote Winston Churchill of his parents' marriage. "In fact, they could only live in the smallest way possible to people in London society."[1]

That was only partly true. Randolph and Jennie did feel a financial pinch, but such was their ignorance of money and budgets that it scarcely interfered with the extent of their social life. Everything to them seemed gay and glittering.

The Duke of Marlborough had given them a 37-year-lease on a four-story house at 48 Charles Street in London, a graceful building complete with balconies and window boxes.[2] It would not be available, however, until the late summer of 1874, so for the intervening months, the young Churchills had rented a house at 1 Curzon Street. Randolph suddenly cut short their French honeymoon in order to attend the opening of Parliament. Since the Curzon Street house was not quite ready, the young couple decided to visit Blenheim Palace.

They were met at the railroad station by the assembled townfolk, who unhitched the horses from the Churchill carriage so that the people themselves might pull the young couple to the palace. Woodstock was a quiet place of small, old houses and a single main street. The people waved and cheered as the Churchills went by. Through the town, under the tremendous stone archway, past a porter holding a long wand topped by a red-tasseled, silver knob—and then the park and palace of Blenheim. Jennie gazed at it with awe and expectancy; the view of the monumental bridge across the valley, miles and miles of magnificent park, green glades edging an ornamental lake, the palace partly hidden by the trees in the distance, and the trees themselves, thousand-year-old oaks once part of a royal forest where so many kings had come for their private pleasures.

For Jennie it was overwhelming, the hugeness of it, the splendor and formality, the dramatic suddenness of it.

They moved up the broad and shallow steps, past the oversize doors, and into the immense hall, with its domed ceiling so high that Jennie had to crane her neck to see the painting of the first Duke of Marlborough, dressed in a Roman toga and driving a chariot.

The initial impression of grandeur, however, was quickly overridden by the less pleasant reality. Alexander Pope had written of Blenheim:

> See, sir, here's the grand approach;
> This way for his Grace's coach:
> There lies the bridge and here's the clock;
> Observe the lion and the cock,
> The spacious court, the colonnade,
> And mark how wide the hall is made!
> The chimneys are so well designed
> They never smoke in any wind.
> This gallery's contrived for walking,
> The windows to retire and talk in;
> The council chamber for debate,
> And all the rest are rooms of state.
> "Thanks, sir," cried I, "'tis very fine,
> But where d'ye sleep and where d'ye dine
> I find by all you have been telling,
> That 'tis a house, but not a dwelling."

The first Duchess, Sarah, had referred to Blenheim as "a wild and unmerciful house."[3]

"We slept in small rooms with high ceilings," complained the American guest who later became mistress of the palace. "We dined in dark rooms with high ceilings; we dressed in closets without ventilation; we sat in long galleries or painted saloons."[4] Novelist Horace Walpole had likened it to "the palace of an auctioneer who has been chosen King of Portugal," and Voltaire had called it simply "a great mass of stone."[5]

Jennie's nephew, Hugh Frewen, who played there as a child, called

Blenheim "a bastard of a building."[6] One of his strongest memories was the clatter of eating from gold plates. "I always worried for fear some of the gold would chip off and get mixed with the vegetables." He also remembered that there was about it a "palace smell . . . rather like the weighty smell of locked-in history . . . with hints of decaying velvet." All visiting children were kept outdoors as much as possible, an understandable system in a palace filled with irreplaceable Brussels tapestries, Meissen china and countless mementoes each worth a fortune.

Formality and order ruled at Blenheim, guided by tradition. The Duchess dictated everything to her guests, including the arrival train they must take and the time of their departure. "When the family were alone at Blenheim," Jennie remarked later,

> everything went on with the regularity of clockwork. So assiduously did I practice my piano, read or paint, that I began to imagine myself back in the schoolroom. In the morning an hour or more was devoted to the reading of newspapers, which was a necessity, if one wanted to show an intelligent interest in the questions of the day, for at dinner, conversation invariably turned on politics. In the afternoon a drive to pay a visit to some neighbor, or a walk in the gardens, would help to wile away some part of the day. After dinner, which was a rather solemn full-dress affair, we all repaired to what was called the Vandyke room. There one might read one's book, or play for love a mild game of whist. . . . Many a glance would be cast at the clock, which sometimes would be surreptitiously advanced a quarter of an hour by some sleepy member of the family. No one dared suggest bed until the sacred hour of eleven had struck. Then we would all troop out into a small anteroom, and lighting our candles, each in turn would kiss the Duke and Duchess and depart to our rooms.[7]

Even breakfast was ceremonial, women dressing in velvet or silk and no one beginning to eat until everyone was assembled. Luncheon was dignified, formal, with rows of entrée dishes filling the table and the Duke and Duchess carving joints of meat for the whole company, including governesses, tutors, and children. The children filled food baskets for poor or sick cottagers in the surrounding area, a traditional family gesture of *noblesse oblige*.

Afternoon tea was solemn. The gold tea service was used mainly in honor of visiting royalty. Yet no matter who the guests were, the exchange of tea-time small talk always concluded when the hostess said, "I am sure you must need a little rest." It took a visiting Princess to answer icily one day, "Thank you, it is now half-past five. I will go to my room at seven."

"Furs and hot-water bottles kept us warm," wrote one guest.[8]

> The Duchess sat, evidently racking her brains for some subject of conversation, but was unsuccessful in finding any sufficiently interesting. . . . The Duchess seems a kindhearted, motherly sort of person—neither clever nor at all handsome. The Duke also is a "plain" man in all its meanings, but it is in itself an immense merit to be a religious Duke of Marlborough, and this, His Grace has.[9]

For Jennie, however, the Duke was not "plain" and the Duchess was not "motherly." Jennie got along far more easily with her father-in-law, seeing in him a man of grace, courtesy, and kindness, the *grand seigneur*, with an acute sensitivity toward his heritage. Marlborough told her the story of the French Ambassador touring Blenheim during the time of the fifth Duke. The Ambassador expressed curiosity in the sources of the various art treasures, impressed by the fact that so many had been gifts. "The house, the tapestries, the pictures—were they all given? Was there anything that had not been given?"

Highly irritated, the Duke quickly led the French Ambassador out to the south side of the palace, showed him the stone trophies and the effigy of Louis XIV, and said simply, "These were *taken*, not given, by John, Duke of Marlborough, from the gates of Tournai."

Despite the Duke's pride in the past, Jennie observed that the family rarely looked at the magnificent art surrounding them. "If familiarity breeds contempt," she remarked, "it also engenders indifference."

Blenheim was occasionally opened to tourists who came to stare more appreciatively at the art treasures. On those days, the Marlboroughs remained in their private rooms. But not Jennie. "Occasionally, for fun, some of us would put on old cloaks and hats, and, armed with reticules and Baedekers, walk around with the tourists to hear their remarks, which were not always flattering to the family," she wrote. "One day, we nearly betrayed ourselves with laughter at one of my compatriots exclaiming before a family picture: 'My, what poppy eyes these Churchills have got!'"

Jennie recorded only one other excitement during her initial stay at Blenheim. It occurred one day while the family was out shooting with the Lord Chief Justice of England, Sir Alexander Cockburn. His gun went off by accident, the bullet just missing her head. "I must be careful," he calmly apologized.

It was still May when the young Churchills moved into their home on Curzon Street. The early swing of the London social season had just begun and would continue ceaselessly until the end of July. Curzon Street was in the middle of Mayfair, the heart of London's most fashionable district, not far from Piccadilly and quite close to Marlborough House on Pall Mall where the Prince of Wales lived. Perhaps representing the tone of Mayfair was a handsome fountain with figures representing Tragedy, Comedy, Poetry, surmounted by a statue of Fame. The life of Jennie and Randolph Churchill would have each in full measure, particularly the first and last, but who might have guessed it then? They were a young couple gifted with all the graces: beauty, charm, social position, wit, intelligence, spirit, and energy; and the Prince himself had provided them social entrée everywhere.

Soon after Jennie and Randolph had settled in Curzon Street, the Duchess of Marlborough arrived to help her daughter-in-law pay her preliminary visits to the city's social leaders. "The Duchess came for me at two, and we went off in grand style in the family coach," Jennie wrote her mother. "The Duchess was very kind, and lent me some rubies and diamonds, which I wore in my hair, and my pearls on my neck. I also had a bouquet of gardenias which she sent me."

The Set had a prim rule about newlyweds. Before presenting themselves socially, young married couples were required to hibernate for a few months. The young Churchills violated that rule—as they would so many others—by appearing at a ball in honor of Czar Alexander II. Notified that they had been married barely a month, the Czar looked at Jennie, and indicated rather shocked surprise at the social breach.

Jennie soon discovered other rules: "Having been brought up in France, I was accustomed to the restrictions and chaperonage to which young girls had to submit; but I confess to thinking that as a married woman I should be able to emancipate myself entirely." She learned, however, that a lady never traveled alone without taking her maid with her in the railway carriage. "To go by oneself in a hansom was thought very 'fast,' " she noted. "Not to speak of walking, which could be permitted only in quiet squares or streets. As for young girls driving anywhere by themselves, such a thing was unheard of."

But Jennie had a way of disintegrating strictures. Freed first from her mother's watchful eye, and now from the formality of her mother-in-law's palace, Jennie went the blithe way of her own sweeping wings. With a high spirit let loose and a loving, indulgent husband who also relished the swiftness of free flight, the horizon was unlimited.

Jennie envisaged her life as a never-ending schedule of fun: garden parties, the fashionable races at Ascot and Goodwood, the regatta at Henley, the pigeon-shoots at Hurlingham,[10] the Princess Cricket and Skating Club. (". . . There's a slight loss of lady-like complacency among female beginners, but none are so ill-bred as to remark their tumbles.") And of course the balls, the opera, concerts at Albert Hall, theater at the Old Empire and the Alhambra, the ballet, the new Four-in-Hand Coaching Club, and the sequence of royal and nonroyal parties that lasted until five in the morning.

Jennie's sister Clarita (who now called herself Clara) came to visit for part of the summer in 1874 and reported to their mother, "I don't know why, but people always seem to ask us [to parties] whenever H.R.H. [His Royal Highness] goes to them. I suppose it is because Jennie is so pretty. . . ." At one of the Prince's exclusive affairs, to which women came decorated as cards, he asked Jennie to come as the Queen of Clubs. Almost as much as Jennie's beauty, the Prince enjoyed her fresh wit and frankness. Discussing the bridegroom of an Anglo-American marriage, the Prince told Jennie, "The family is very poor, but it is in its favor that it came over with the Conquerer."

"That's all very well," said Jennie, "but if I were the girl, I'd prefer to marry into a family that had done a little conquering on its own account."[11]

The Prince had a particular fondness for American women. "I like them because they are original and bring a little fresh air into Society," he said. "They are livelier, better educated and less hampered by etiquette . . . they are not as squeamish as their English sisters and they are better able to take care of themselves."[12]

With the Prince around, they had to. He had a notorious reputation with women and was accused of being "a prominent actor in almost every scene of aristocratic dissipation and debauchery which has been encountered in the British metropolis."[13] He seemed to make a specialty of the wives of friends, and he was seldom to be denied. His early attention to Jennie was noticeable, and he made it more obvious by inviting the Churchills to most of his frequent parties. Most British society, however, regarded the Anglo-American marriage "as experimental as mating with Martians."[14] Jennie aptly described the reactions of British women toward the American female invader:

> Anything of an outlandish nature might be expected of her. If she talked, dressed and conducted herself as any well-bred woman would, much astonishment was invariably evinced, and she was usually saluted with the tactful remark: "I should never have thought you were an American." Which was regarded as a compliment.
>
> As a rule, people looked upon her as a disagreeable and even dangerous person, to be viewed with suspicion, if not avoided altogether. Her dollars were her only recommendation,

and each was credited with the possession of them—
otherwise what was her *raison d'tre* ? No distinction was ever
made among Americans. They were all supposed to be of
one uniform type. The wife and daughters of the newly-
enriched California miner, swathed in silks and satins, and
blazing with diamonds on the smallest provocation; the cultured, refined and retiring Bostonian; the aristocratic Virgin-
ian, . . . all were grouped in the same category, all tarred with
the same brush. . . .

Shortly after the Churchills' marriage, there was a sudden increase in
Anglo-American unions. The American press was generally scornful of this
marital quest for English titles. "They should have sought noble hearts instead of noble names," was a typical comment. *Town Topics* once noted in its
columns that there was a Polish Prince looking for an American beauty with
ten million dollars. "He is Prince Poniatowske, and a Polish Prince is about
as marketable as last year's hat. I strongly advise Ward to bring on additional Dukes." However, observing the significance of the American woman
in England, former Prime Minister Lord Henry Palmerston prophetically
remarked, "Before the century is out, these clever and pretty women from
New York will pull the strings in half the chancelleries in Europe." Minnie
Stevens became Lady Paget, Consuelo Iznaga (of Cuban and American
parentage) became Lady Carrington,[15] Mrs. Arthur Post became Lady Barrymore, all of them with pretty faces to match their attractive fortunes.

These were only a small influential sprinkling of the flood that followed,
and Jennie knew them all. There was, in fact, an obvious kinship among
them. Outstanding among the American beauties circulating the same parties with Jennie were a Mrs. Standish and a Mrs. Sandys. So often were the
three together that the press dubbed them "The Pink, the White and the
Black Pearls." Raven-haired Jennie, of course, was the Black Pearl and generally acknowledged as the most gifted and the prettiest.[16]

She was also the most individual. At the Gold Cup races of 1875, she
daringly wore her wedding dress, newly embellished with crepe de chine
trimmings. The low decolletage of some of her other dresses caused even
more comment. And to the theater, where traditionally women wore only
black, Jennie insisted on wearing a pale blue dress, even though Randolph
begged her to change because it was "so conspicuous."[17]

At one fancy-dress ball, Clara introduced a young Lord to Jennie. "Introducing him to me, she [Clara] pretended I was her mother," wrote Jennie.

> Later in the evening I attacked him, saying that my
> daughter had just confided to me that he had proposed to

her, and that she had accepted him. To this day I can see his face of horror and bewilderment. Vehemently he assured me that it was not so. But I kept up the farce, declaring that my husband would call on him next day and reveal our identity, and that meanwhile I should consider him engaged to my charming daughter. Deficient in humour and not overburdened with brains, he could not take the joke, and left the house a miserable man.

"Generally speaking," Jennie added, "there is no doubt that English people are dull-witted at a masked ball, and do not understand or enter into the spirit of intrigue which is all-important on such occasions. . . ."

A woman's social success greatly depended on her gift for badinage, and it was a gift Jennie had in abundance. To counter the constant flow of aggressive flattery from most men, she displayed a special talent for arch banter, a lilt and a quip and a laugh that made her everywhere popular, with women as well as men.

Jennie's mother was in Paris, with her own social circle, and Clara continued to write: "Jennie and R. have quite decided to come to Deauville . . . and R. after depositing Jennie and I with you, will go off for a cruise with the Duke on his new yacht." As an afterthought she added, "You must not think that we are at all fast . . ." But "fast" is what they were, and "fast" is what they wanted. "We seemed to live in a whirl of gaieties and excitement," Jennie commented.

Typical of their style was a small dinner party featuring a parlor game called "thought reading." Blindfolded in the middle of the room, Randolph heard Lady de Clifford tell him, "Don't resist any thought that comes into your head; do exactly as you feel." Without hesitating, Randolph grabbed the Lady and embraced her. Lady Jeune described him then as "a great schoolboy, full of fun and mischief. . . . I have seen him lie back in his chair and roar with laughter at things he had done and said."[18]

Lady Jeune was originally Mary MacKenzie who married a Colonel Stanley in 1871 and lived for a year in Utah and Nevada where her husband helped operate a mining company. After her husband's death, she married Sir Francis Jeune, a member of the Privy Council, and quickly became one of the prominent hostesses of London. George Smalley quoted a noted socialite who told him, "I go to Lady Jeune's because I never know whom I shall meet, but I always know there will always be somebody I shall like to meet." Lady Jeune's thesis was that the interesting people are the exceptional people, and among her good friends was Theodore Roosevelt.

To Jennie and Randolph Churchill, the social life counted for almost everything. Even Randolph's membership in Parliament seemed mainly a social gesture. His maiden speech about a railway works at Oxford was very "maiden" indeed. Professor Benjamin Jowett said at the time, "It is only the speech of a foolish young man who will never come to any good."[19]

Punch Parliamentary critic Henry Lucy was more perceptive than Jowett in his analysis of Randolph's speech. ". . . The young member was so nervous, his voice so badly pitched, his delivery so faulty, that there was difficulty in following his argument. But here and there, flashed forth a scathing sentence that made it worthwhile to attempt to catch the rest."[20]

Disraeli described Randolph's speech more kindly to both the Duchess and Queen Victoria:

> Lord Randolph said many imprudent things, which is not very important in the maiden speech of a young member and a young man; but the House was surprised, and then captivated by his energy, and the natural flow, and his impressive manner. With self-control and study, he might mount. It was a speech of great promise.[21]

Perhaps Disraeli was kind because he well remembered the reaction to his own first effort. He had stood wearing his black velvet coat, purple trousers with gold braid running down the outside seam, a scarlet waistcoat, and white gloves outside of which he wore diamond rings. Disraeli's friends insisted this dandified dress was part of a deliberate pattern to attract attention. "At heart, I think he always despised that sort of thing," said his friend Lady Dorothy Nevill. He did attract attention, but he was so laughed at by the members of the House, that he finally sat down, his speech unfinished. "I will sit down now," he said then, "but the time will come when you will hear me."[22]

A similar "dandy" and wit, Randolph Churchill wore a smartly cut dark blue frock coat with colored shirts, and sometimes startled his friends by wearing tan shoes and an excess of jewelry. His favorite was a large diamond ring in the shape of a Maltese Cross that Jennie had given him.

Like Disraeli, too, Lord Randolph could be impertinent and blunt. While women often found this fascinating, men found it a little frightening. Randolph often seemed to be dancing on the edge of hysteria, his nerves taut, his speech brittle. And since he had learned so well from Gibbon "to finger the phrase and marshal the paragraph,"[23] guests could never be completely sure what devastating remark might come from him, almost at whim. Buttonholed at his club once by some boring friend who seemed unable to finish his story, Randolph rang the bell for a footman whom he told to "listen until his Lordship finishes," while he himself left.

Lady Jeune told of another example of his annihilating arrogance. Churchill had quarreled with an old friend who had been his classmate at Eton. "Every time they met," she wrote, "I had to go through the same little farce of introducing them to each other, Lord Randolph saying to him in a very innocent, irritating manner: 'Ah! Yes, I believe I do recollect you at Eton.'"[24]

Jennie's warmth complemented her husband's cutting coldness. It was Jennie who gave Randolph whatever resilience and calm sureness he thereafter occasionally showed. He, in turn, gave her the polish of his class and access to the most brilliant and important people of their time, while broadening her political education so she could ask pertinent and intelligent questions.

Disraeli had become Prime Minister the year the young Churchills were married. He was seventy years old and his wife had died the previous year, but he enjoyed Lord and Lady Randolph and visited them often. Jennie appreciated Disraeli's wit, which could be cutting to rude people he disliked. When one young woman tapped him with her fan, Disraeli turned to Jennie and asked, "Who is that little ape?" But he was always charming and kind to Jennie. Comparing the effect of sitting next to Disraeli or Gladstone, one woman wrote: "When I left the dining room after sitting next to Gladstone, I thought he was the cleverest man in England. But when I sat next to Disraeli, I left feeling that *I* was the cleverest woman!"[25]

Jennie always enjoyed Gladstone as a dinner companion. However,

> having once started him on his subject, an intelligent "yes" or "no" was all that was required. But if you ventured a remark (to which he listened in grave silence) he had a disconcerting way of turning sharply round, his piercing eye fixed inquiringly upon you, and his hand to his ear, with the gesture so well known in the House of Commons. His old-world manner was very attractive, and his urbanity outside the House remarkable.

At one of the Churchills' parties, the Prince of Wales noted that Jennie and the Prime Minister had been in deep conversation for an extended period of time, and afterward asked her, "Tell me, my dear, what office did you get for Randolph?"[26]

But the truth was that at that time Lord Randolph wanted no office. He just did not find politics fun. He considered himself as merely one of the fifty members of the House who supplied Disraeli's majority, with slight need for either his vote or his voice. Compared to his frenetic social life, parliamentary politics seemed too calm, too formal, and too sluggish.

The social world was also most important for Jennie. Along with other prominent society newcomers, she was presented to Queen Victoria at Court. The Queen was reported to have taken a dim view of Anglo-American marriages.

"I was dreadfully frightened," Jennie wrote. "Making my curtsies for the Queen quite put me out. As I went to kiss her hand, she pulled me towards her and kissed me, which proceeding so bewildered me that I kissed her in return, and made comical little bows to the other Royalties instead of curtsies."

Of course Jennie was awed by the experience, but years later she fondly remembered a comment made by a maid of Mrs. J. Comyn-Carr upon first seeing the Queen: "So that's the Queen? Who'd have thought she'd look so much like an old apple woman?"

Years after the Prince Consort had died, one of the Queen's daughters wrote her husband Crown Prince Frederick of Prussia:

> Mama is dreadfully sad . . . and she cries a lot; then there is always the empty room, the empty bed, and she always sleeps with Papa's coat over her and his dear, red dressing gown beside her and some of his clothes in the bed! . . . Poor Mama has to go to bed, has to get up alone—for ever. She was as much in love with Papa as though she had married him yesterday . . . and is always consumed with longing for her husband. . . .

It was her daughter Alice who brought John Brown from Scotland to be the Queen's manservant. He was a rugged, mountain of a man, a rough-talking Highlander who liked his pipe and his whiskey. In Jennie's social circle, rumors soon whirred like arrows: Did you know that John Brown slept at Windsor in a bedroom right next to the Queen's? Did you know that John Brown was quoted everywhere saying, "The Queen and I"?

Their intimacy increased after John Brown saved the Queen from a would-be assassin. One cartoonist depicted Brown putting his boots on the mantelpiece in the Queen's room. Another showed him leaning against the vacant throne, pipe in hand, while below him the British lion roared. *Punch* parodied the court circular by reporting the daily routine of John Brown instead of the Queen's. One of the many critics commented on the coarseness of the former stableboy, observing that the Queen "clings to him with more warmth and tenacity than becomes a lady who carried her sorrow for a deceased husband previously to such an extravagant pitch." And every woman in Jennie's set knew about the scraps of a letter from the Queen found in John Brown's room which were pieced together to read, ". . . you are so indescribably dear to me, so precious and so adored that I can't bear you misunderstand things. . . ." And she signed it, "Your own ever-loving and devoted one." Much of all this was hashed together into a best-selling pamphlet called *Mrs. John Brown.*

Years later, when Prince Edward became King, one of the first things he did was smash the china figurines of Brown that Victoria had kept in a cabinet. Brown not only had boxed the Prince's ears when he was a boy but once kept him waiting two hours before letting him see his mother.

With the beginning of August, the London Season was over and Jennie Churchill's life changed completely. She was pregnant, and her world was suddenly quiet. "We are very humdrum and stay a great deal at home," Clara wrote their mother. Home was now their own house on Charles Street, in a "très chic" location, as Jennie said, just three houses from Berkeley Square, and complete with butler, footman, and housemaid. It was a famous street. Lady Dorothy Nevill had lived there for thirty-eight years, and that was enough to make it a social center. In 1792, "Beau" Brummel had lived just a few doors away from the Churchills' new home. Bulwer–Lytton had a house on Charles Street, with a room fitted as an exact replica of a Pompeian apartment.[27]

"You see, dear Mama," Jennie wrote,

> now that we have this house, we must look after it, and tho I should be delighted to pass September in Paris with you, I think I had better be in London till after my confinement. . . . We only mean to furnish at the present, two bedrooms and the sitting room downstairs, which we shall use also as a dining room. . . . There is one good thing, we have our *batterie de cuisine* and china, glass and plate and linen, all things which are very expensive. . . . I am so delighted to have a fixed abode at last, and it is such a nice house. . . . Randolph had no settlement made on him when he married, and this of course, makes a settlement. If anything was to happen to him, this house comes to me. . . .

She had another mercenary note: "I do so hope Papa will be able to give me the £2,000 he promised. . . . And, of course, he need not send it all at once, but gradually, as it is convenient."

Jennie must have chafed at having to live quietly. After all, she was only twenty-one and the past few months had been filled with high excitement and her rising importance as a welcomed young woman of beauty and wit. September and October of 1874 were among the most inactive, contemplative months of her life.

There were a few parties and dances, but Jennie became tired of sitting with the chaperons, so the young Churchills went to Blenheim for a change of scene. There is a Visitor's Book at Blenheim Palace, an enormous volume bound in heavy red leather, worn at the edges. It has the signature of the first Duke of Marlborough, dated 1708, and then the signatures of most of Europe's royalty, the kings, the queens, the emperors, and their collective royal kin, as well as those of the prime ministers of England and the leading social, literary, and political luminaries of European history. The name of Jennie Spencer-Churchill makes its first official entry on October 22, 1874.

November was a peaceful month at Blenheim but it was climaxed by the annual St. Andrews Ball. Her grandniece, Anita Leslie, claims that Lady Randolph was dancing when suddenly she had to hurry away while the party was still at its height, ". . . past the endless suite of drawing-rooms, through the library, 'the longest room in England,' down the longest corridor in the world, the quarter-mile of dark-red carpet that led to her bedroom. . . ." In his book on Blenheim, historian David Green states that Jennie was out on a shooting party when she suddenly felt ill and hurried back to the palace. The facts are that while out on a shooting party with her husband on a Tuesday, she fell. "A rather imprudent and rough drive in a pony carriage brought on the pains on Saturday night," Randolph wrote to his mother-in-law. "We tried to stop them, but it was no use. They went on all Sunday."

They had put her up quickly in a room on the ground floor, just outside the Great Hall. It had once been the room of Dean Jones, a fat cleric with a florid face who had served as chaplain to the first Duke of Marlborough. Since that time, several guests swore they had been wakened in the night by a blaze of light to see the ghost of the cleric bending over them. That Saturday night, the small room had been converted into a ladies' cloakroom, the bed covered with the feather boas and velvet capes of guests who had come for the ball.

Since there were few trains on Sunday, the London obstetrician failed to arrive when needed, and a local Woodstock doctor, Frederic Taylor, performed the historic delivery on November 30. "The baby was safely born at 1:30 this morning after about eight hours labor," Randolph continued. "She [Jennie] suffered a good deal poor darling, but was very plucky and had no chloroform. The boy is wonderfully pretty so everybody says dark eyes and hair and very healthy considering its prematureness."

He had an upturned nose and protruding Churchill eyes, and they named him Winston Leonard Spencer-Churchill, after his American and English grandfathers.

Attending Jennie were her mother-in-law, Randolph's Aunt Albertha, Lady Clementine Camden, and Randolph's sister-in-law, Lady Blandford.

Lady Camden was named godmother, and Randolph asked Leonard Jerome to be godfather. As the birth was unexpected at that time, there was no layette ready at Blenheim. So young Winston Churchill started out life in clothes borrowed from a local attorney's wife, whose own expected baby had not yet arrived.

Early the next morning, the bells of Woodstock Church rang to announce the arrival of a new Churchill, a new heir presumptive to the Marlborough dukedom. "A merry peal was rung," according to the signed document handed to Jennie as the first written record of her son's birth. To make it even more official, the *Times* of London reported at the head of its birth notices:

> On the 30th Nov., at Blenheim Palace, the Lady Randolph Churchill, prematurely, of a son.

The *Times* announcement caused some snickers, because no one had ever stated that the baby looked premature. He was obviously healthy and robust.

The young family spent Christmas at Blenheim with the Marlboroughs, and the baby was baptized in Blenheim Chapel by the Duke's chaplain. Shortly afterward they moved back into their home on Charles Street.

One of the clichés compounded by biographers of Winston Churchill presses the point that his mother ignored him as a child until he grew old enough to be interesting. Like many such clichés, this is a half-truth. The real intimacy between mother and son did develop during Winston's early manhood, when indeed he was interesting, but it is also true that Jennie's concern for her child was constant, as her many letters and memoranda fully testify. But as Lady Randolph Churchill, she had become basically adapted to the British way of life and one of the most permanent fixtures in this way of life, particularly among the upper classes, was the institution of "Nannies."

Nannies were substitute mothers, who usually came into the family when the infant was hardly a month old. They took care of the dirty diapers and kissed away the infant tears; they provided love and authority, watchfulness and devotion throughout the child's youth and often longer. One recent sociologist has termed the system a "prostitution of maternity," but that is unfair. It is true, nonetheless, that nannies were paid more in love than in money.

In his novel *Savrola*, Winston Churchill described a nanny:

> She had nursed him from the birth up with a devotion
> and care which knew no break. It is a strange thing, the love
> of these women. Perhaps it is the only disinterested affection

in the world. The mother loves her child; that is maternal nature. The youth loves his sweetheart—that, too, may be explained. The dog loves his master, he feeds him; a man loves his friend, he has stood by him perhaps at doubtful moments. In all there are reasons; but the love of a foster-mother for her charge appears absolutely irrational. It is one of the few proofs, not to be explained even by the association of ideas, that the nature of mankind is superior to mere utilitarianism, and that his destinies are high.[28]

Winston's "Nanny" was Mrs. Elizabeth Ann Everest, a plump, friendly 41-year-old widow who liked to wear dark silks and a bonnet. "My nurse was my confidante," Winston later wrote. "Mrs. Everest it was who looked after me and tended all my wants. It was to her I poured out my many troubles." As for his mother, "She shone for me like the evening star. I loved her dearly—but at a distance." She would come up to kiss Winston goodnight, usually dressed for dinner, shimmering like "a fairy princess from afar."

Victorian children were seldom seen and almost never heard. Nannies provided a physical barrier between children and parents. Jennie bridged that barrier more than most mothers in her social set, although she did exempt herself from the chores of early motherhood. She also happily maintained a total ignorance of the art of housekeeping, "the ignorance I often had cause to bemoan."

Jennie was desperately trying to become as British as she could. She was aware of the focus on her every action. She was, after all, one of the very first American women to make such a prominent international match.[29]

But something happened to Jennie at this time that was not revealed in her letters. She was more than just a social butterfly. From the letters of her sister Clara, who stayed with her then, it appeared almost as if there was an element of frenzy in her social life. In most of her accounts of their intense socializing, Clara makes no mention of Randolph's presence. Indeed, at most of the reported parties, Clara and Jennie were on their own, always the instant focus of a variety of men. Clara's letters to her mother in Paris revealed much:

> . . . Lord Hartington took me to lunch in a private room with the royalties, the Prince himself giving his arm to Jennie. . . . Jennie took her Sir William Cumming all to herself, he being the swell of the party and does not let anyone else talk to him. . . . Sir Cumming . . . began *très sérieusement à faire la cour* to Jennie last night . . . There was a party for the

Prince [afterward Emperor Frederick] and Princess of Prussia . . . we came away about three o'clock . . . escorted by a whole troop of men!

At a dance after the races, ". . . Jennie wore her dark blue and the men were all *very* nice to us. . . ."

Where was Randolph Churchill all this time? He was certainly not being kept busy at Parliament, where he had only made two speeches the first year. Had there been a rift because of the Prince's obvious amorous advances to Jennie? Or had Jennie discovered the dark secret of Randolph's syphilis?

The second stage of syphilis manifests itself in headaches, fevers, recurrent illness coming suddenly and diminishing slowly, annoying rashes, and pimples on the genitals, the palms of the hands, and the soles of the feet. Sores appear and disappear repeatedly on the mouth, and the lymph glands of the groin become swollen and tender. Even if Randolph did not confess the nature of his illness to her, she had the right to expect the truth from Dr. Robson Roose, who was not only Randolph's doctor but hers.[30]

There might have been an added factor in the rift. Medical opinion agrees that sexual guilt can cause frigidity, which may evolve into a strong aversion to the opposite sex. That may well have been the case with Randolph Churchill, and may explain the frenetic behavior of his beautiful 21-year-old bride.

The Jeromes made separate trips to Charles Street to inspect their new grandson, Leonard traveling from New York and his wife coming from Paris. "The Baby is *too* lovely," Clarita had written her mother. "He is so knowing. I wish you could see him on the piano stool, playing the piano!" Still a handsome woman, Mrs. Jerome had her own salon on the Rue de Roi de Rome, catering mostly to minor royalty, faded diplomats, unappreciated artists, and unpublished poets. She soon returned to them, but Leonard Jerome lingered awhile in London. Fanny Ronalds had deserted the court of the Bey of Algiers to set up her salon on Cadogan Place. It was occasionally highlighted by the Duke of Edinburgh playing the violin and His Royal Highness, the Prince of Wales, playing the piano while Fanny sang the songs of "dear, dear Sir Arthur Sullivan."

Jennie and Fanny Ronalds became close friends in the course of time. Fanny was a sophisticated advisor and offered needed warmth. Her long relationship with Jennie's father was an added fillip. For a troubled Jennie trying to handle some extramarital affairs, Fanny served as a familiar model of the easy morality of the time.

Despite the obvious tension in their marriage, Jennie and Randolph maintained a proper social face. They took Leonard to the races, which they all equally loved. "R. is in very good humor as he made £200 at the Derby and Jennie £20 on her own book," Clara gleefully wrote her mother. Leonard probably supplied his daughters with some extra money while he was there: "Boxes of hats and gowns seemed to arrive every hour," he wrote. Leonard also met for the first time the Duke and Duchess of Marlborough. His reactions are unreported.

There is, however, no lack of report on the growing strain between the Duchess and Jennie. Clara wrote to her mother about some of the signs. "...I can't tell you how jealous Randolph says the Duchess is of Jennie and I. She is always very kind and amicable but *une certaine aigreur* in the way she talks...."

The Duchess exacerbated the tension to a critical point the first year after the marriage. Blandford, who had campaigned in both prose and poetry against Randolph's marriage, now became increasingly captivated with his American sister-in-law. His own marriage had long ago grown sour. His wife, Lady Albertha Hamilton, related by blood to half the great peerages of England, was a confirmed practical joker. At various times she served slivers of soap among the cheese for her guests, and put inkstands over her bedroom door to drop onto her husband's head as he entered. But if her sense of fun was acute, her wit was not.

Blandford, a middle-sized man with a smooth face, a strong jaw, and a formal manner, was also a French scholar, a connoisseur of art, a student of science, a constant correspondent with the great minds of his time, and a devoted lover of beautiful women. So taken was Blandford with Jennie that he gave her a ring, and Jennie made the mistake of showing it to her mother-in-law. The Duchess exploded. Blandford had no right to give Jennie that ring, said the Duchess, because it belonged to his wife. Jennie promptly repeated that to Randolph, who promptly told Blandford, who promptly wrote his mother an unprecedented letter, blisteringly angry, which said in part:

> Well acquainted as I am with the intense jealousy that you often display in your actions and the mischief which you so often make . . . I should not have thought you would have allowed yourself to be so carried away as to descend to mistruth to substantiate an accusation [so] as to give color to a fact.

To try to calm the situation, Jennie offered to return the ring, but the issue had become a matter of family principle. The Duke stepped in, writing to Randolph:

Your mother has received today the enclosed correspondence.

I have only three words to say upon it.

1st. You have grossly misrepresented facts to Blandford.

2nd. You have while being received with kindness, yourself, wife and child dishonorably and treacherously abused
the confidence which you yourself pretended you shared
with [your] mother about Blandford.

While you were much aware that she never entertained
any motives but those of the truest affection for you both.

3rd. You have thus induced your brother to pen to his
mother an unparalleled letter, which I do not trust myself to
characterize in words.

Randolph's answer was hardly meek:

My dearest Papa,

I most respectfully remark with regard to your letter of
this afternoon that I think you have formed a hasty judgment
of the enclosed correspondence. I venture to think that expressions such as "*dishonorable*," "*treacherous*" and "*liar*" are hardly
applicable to me. As long as these expressions remain in
force further communications between us are not only in
your remark useless but impossible.

In contrast with the warm and loving relationship that had existed between Randolph and his parents, this exchange came as a terrible blow,
particularly to the Duchess. She might have understood Blandford's explosion, as she and the Duke had always made obvious their displeasure at
Blandford's actions, and this could be seen as Blandford's resentment finally peaking. But Randolph's response was an injury for the Duchess that
would never heal. It was smoothed over in the course of time, but it was always there and always sensitive. In perhaps typical motherly fashion, the
Duchess transferred all the blame and hostility to her daughter-in-law. This
hostility, like the injury, was often carefully camouflaged and sometimes
even seemed to disappear, but it was a live coal, buried deep, always ready
to flare again.

ORD AND LADY RANDOLPH had been swept into the social vortex of
the Prince of Wales. Where he went, they went. In the course of nine
months, a newspaper critic commented that the Prince attended thirty
plays, twenty-eight races, and more than forty social functions.[1] Just as
Prime Minister Gladstone had continually urged the Queen to let the
Prince help her in the "visible duties of the monarchy,"[2] Gladstone's successor, Prime Minister Disraeli, continued to encourage the Queen in her
refusal, commenting that the Prince was "a thoroughly spoilt child who
can't bear being bored."[3]

Disraeli had suggested that the Prince might be sent to live in Ireland
where he could hunt, socialize (out of sight and sound), and perhaps even
learn something about government administration. But the Prince decided
he would prefer a long trip to India. He assembled a group, more social
than political, to accompany him. The Queen and Disraeli both objected to
the make-up of the group, as well as to the itinerary, and Disraeli proposed
a parliamentary allotment for expenses which the Prince felt was too meager. In support of the Prince, Randolph wrote a letter to *The Times* defending the trip. Disraeli called this letter "a mass of absurdities." The issue
became rather heated, and Disraeli commented in a letter, "I dined this evening at the Somers'. . . . There were the Randolph Churchills; he glaring
like one possessed of the Devil, and quite uncivil when I addressed him

rather cordially. Why?"[4] The situation straightened enough, however, for the Prince and his party to make their trip. Jennie and Randolph did not join them. The reasons may have been partly financial, but Randolph might well have had more personal grounds for not going. The Prince's attention to Jennie had become increasingly obvious.

Randolph would not have wanted to become another "Sporting Joe." "Sporting Joe," who was going with the Prince to India, was the Earl of Aylesford, a champion polo player, whose lovely Welsh wife had been having a prolonged but intermittent affair with the Prince. "Sporting Joe," however, did not let the affair interfere with his friendship for the Prince. Randolph was not then as compliant. This attitude could well have explained Randolph Churchill's strange behavior in the sensational scandal that followed.

While the Prince of Wales and "Sporting Joe" and their group were in India, Randolph's brother Blandford moved his horses and himself to the inn closest to Lady Aylesford's house. Word of this soon traveled to India, and it was even intimated that Lady Aylesford was pregnant with Blandford's child. (Blandford's wife at this time played one of her more pointed practical jokes by serving him his usual breakfast tray—but instead of his poached egg underneath the silver cover there was a small pink baby doll.[5]) The Prince and "Sporting Joe" were equally outraged at Blandford's intrusion on their mutual preserve. The Prince insisted that Blandford had openly compromised the good Lady and should therefore divorce his wife and marry her.

Randolph entered into the argument, but in a surprising way. Ordinarily one might have expected him to intervene as a soft-spoken mediator, a friend of both parties. Instead, he openly threatened to publish some love letters that the Prince had written to Lady Aylesford unless the Prince withdrew his adamant support of "Sporting Joe" on the matter. Randolph even went so far as to visit the Princess of Wales to warn her of the undesirable publicity of any proposed divorce suit, suggesting she pressure the Prince to pull out of the affair. "I have the Crown of England in my pocket," Churchill later told Sir Charles Dilke.[6]

But his father and mother both counseled Randolph to be cautious in any row with the Prince of Wales. At the Queen's request, the Prince had forwarded to her Randolph's threatening letter, and now Randolph faced the royal wrath. Randolph was in Holland when he received a demand from the Prince for either an apology or a duel to be held in Rotterdam. Ironically, it was Lord Knollys, en route home from India, who delivered the message from the Prince. Just two years before, Knollys had served as best man at Randolph's wedding. Randolph refused to fight against his future Sovereign and offered to duel anyone else of the Prince's choice. In the interim, Jennie wrote him: "Do you think the Queen will have an interview with Disraeli? If so perhaps you will have one with him. . . . and you may get him on your side (in a way) before HRH returns. Am I talking nonsense? . . ."[7]

"Even Jennie's iron nerves began to fray," reported a member of the family.[8] Then Queen Victoria intervened. "What a dreadful, disgraceful business," she wrote the Prince of Wales. ". . . Poor Lord Aylesford should not have left her. I *knew* last summer that this was going on."[9]

Randolph received a royal emissary, the distinguished Lord Hartington, later to become the Duke of Devonshire. George W. Smalley, who was present when Hartington arrived, afterward described the events that followed and said of Hartington, "There are Dukes and Dukes. This was the greatest of all. None was more sagacious, none had a sounder judgment of affairs and of men." A tall man with a long face and a high nose, who was seldom angry but often bored, Hartington belonged to one of the great governing families of England and was immensely wealthy. His life was given to public service and he held more Cabinet offices under more governments than any other man in his time. Three times Hartington would be offered the position of Prime Minister, always to refuse it. He was above ambition, above corruption, and was therefore perfect for this delicate assignment. What made him even more suitable was his experience in these matters: he himself had for thirty years been maintaining a quiet extramarital affair with a beautiful Duchess.

Smalley reported that Hartington said he would do nothing for either side until he first saw the Prince's letters to Lady Aylesford. Randolph gave them to him.

> "Are there any more?" Hartington asked.
> "No."
> "I have your authority to make such use of these letters as I think best?"
> "Yes."

Lord Hartington then walked to the fire, put the letters through the grate, saw them become ashes, and said, "I do not think it will be necessary to carry this much further." Then he notified Randolph, "You are at liberty to say what you like and do what you like. I have acted in what I consider to be the interests of both sides."

"Hartington," Smalley commented, "is the only man I know who could have done it without question. But that is because he is Hartington."[10]

Whispers and rumors about the episode spread everywhere. The major mystery was Churchill's role. Why had he reacted so intensely when his friendly mediation might have solved it all quietly? The most plausible explanation seems to reside in Randolph's resentment of the Prince's feeling for Jennie, and the fact that everyone knew of it. Jennie's other escorts could easily be dismissed as "flirtations," but the Prince's attention toward any woman attracted an enormous social spotlight, and Randolph became angered by the glare.

The Prince was similarly angered. He let it be known that he would not visit any home in which the Churchills were guests. It was a strict boycott, seldom broken. In one instance, Randolph and Jennie were guests at a ball given by Lord Fitzwilliam when the band stopped playing at the height of the festivities and there followed the hush that always preceded the royal entry. The harassed host begged Jennie and Randolph to leave quickly, and the two were rushed through the servants' quarters, down through the basement to the back stairs. When the Prince arrived, he couldn't understand why the gaiety had gone out of the party.

British society, which had so warmly welcomed the Churchills, now just as coldly ostracized them. There were a few exceptions. When the Prince reprimanded John Delacour, saying, "I hear you are continuing to see the Randolph Churchills," Delacour answered, "I allow no man to choose my friends."[11] And the American-born Duchess of Manchester coolly informed the Prince, "I hold friendship higher than snobbery." Then she added smilingly, "I couldn't possibly, Sire, even for you, neglect poor Jennie. We were at school together."

Without describing the details, Winston Churchill's biography of his father said, ". . . Lord Randolph incurred the deep displeasure of a great personage. The fashionable world no longer smiled. Powerful enemies were anxious to humiliate him. His own sensitiveness and pride magnified every coldness into an affront. London became odious to him." It became odious to Jennie, too. She had been so near the summit of Society, and suddenly she was a social pariah. "Most people in the course of a lifetime get to know the real value of the Mammon of Unrighteousness," she wrote, "but few learn their lesson so early. We both profited by it."[12]

Winston regarded the incident in retrospect as "a spur" to his father. "Without it, he might have wasted a dozen years in the frivolous and expensive pursuits of the silly world of fashion; without it he would probably never have developed popular sympathies or the courage to champion democratic causes."[13] There is little question that the incident "altered, darkened, and strengthened his whole life and character," and that it converted "a nature originally congenial and gay" into a man of "stern and bitter quality" with "a harsh contempt for what is called 'Society' and an abiding antagonism to rank and authority."

As for Jennie, she realized that her own future impact on Society could no longer depend on her beauty or personality or her husband's heritage or friends, but strictly on the weight of accomplishment. That realization, more than anything else, tightened their marriage. No more parties, no more balls, no more suitors, and only a few friends. All they truly had left was each other, and their need was great. Toward the end of the crisis with the Prince, she had written Randolph, "... if we are to have all these worries—do for Heaven's sake let's go through them together. As long as I have you I don't care what happens. . . ."[14]

"Randolph felt in need of solace and distraction," Jennie wrote. So did she, and nobody knew this better than her father. He sent them a sympathetic invitation to come to the United States "to sail and drive and see what I have left in the way of horses."

Leonard Jerome was then fifty-eight years old and still an attractive man. That was the year he had imported polo from England, introducing it at Jerome Park in New York. He himself was unable to play after having strained his back by impulsively challenging (and beating) a weightlifter at a circus.

Jennie and Randolph arrived first in Canada, and went from there to Niagara Falls and Newport before going to New York. With them was an intimate friend of Randolph's named Harry Tyrwhitt.[15] "Although the life there was a great contrast to that of Cowes, savoring more of the town than of the country," Jennie said of Newport, "we found it one of the most fascinating of places, and the hospitality and kindness shown us by the friends of my family were most gratifying."

In the United States 1876 was a presidential election year and Rutherford Hayes barely won. Jennie understood the Hayes character when she heard his nickname: "Queen Victoria in Breeches." Much wilder news that year came from the West, news of everything from Custer's Last Stand at Little Big Horn to frequent and daring stagecoach robberies. Mark Twain had written: "This country is fabulously rich in gold, silver, copper, lead, coal, iron, quicksilver . . . thieves, murderers, desperadoes, ladies, children, lawyers, Christians, Indians, Chinamen, Spaniards, gamblers, sharpers, coyotes. . . ."

Newspapers in New York were lively and unrestrained. They played up horrifying crimes, such as those which left bodies dismembered by "THE HUMAN FIEND . . . A THIRST FOR BLOOD." Some criminals were even caught trying to steal the bones of Abraham Lincoln to hold for ransom. Central Park was described as "a ruffian's refuge where ladies, children and the unprotected generally are at the mercy of villains." On the same page with ads promising "ugly girls made pretty" with French corsets, or "beautiful artificial teeth for only eight dollars," there was the item, "150 FINE PLATES AND ENGRAVINGS OF THE ANATOMY OF THE SEXUAL ORGANS." And, in the Page One personal column:

> 7th Avenue Car. Saturday evening, seven o'clock . . . Was
> the fall in my lap when getting out accidental. If not, address,
> in honor, BACHELOR Box 139, appointing interview.

Broadway between Madison Square and Forty-second Street was lined with theaters, so the area was referred to as The Rialto. Seven years later, in 1883, the Metropolitan Opera House would open on Broadway at Thirty-ninth Street. Cars were still horse-drawn, but an elevated was being built on Third Avenue where Jennie's father used to race horses, and the Brooklyn Bridge was under construction to span the river which once had only ferries to connect Brooklyn with Manhattan.[16]

"We went also to Saratoga," wrote Jennie, "where the beauty of the ladies, and the gorgeousness astonished the men." An article in *Harper's Magazine* that year noted that "The fountains of Saratoga will ever be the resort of wealth, intelligence and fashion." Jennie, however, thought the obvious wealth too rich for their pocket. "Having found the hotel at that place absurdly expensive, I asked my father to remonstrate with the proprietor, who replied: 'The Lord and his wife *would* have two rooms, hence the expense.'"

Philadelphia was more fun. The hundredth anniversary of American Independence was being celebrated with a Centennial Exposition featuring everything from the greatest steam engine ever built to the first public demonstration of Alexander Graham Bell's telephone, from the hand of the unfinished Statue of Liberty to George Washington's false teeth. Other demonstrations included an automatic baby feeder, an eagle eating live chickens, and the new typewriting machine.

One of the places that particularly interested Jennie was the Women's Pavilion featuring a woman operating a six-horse-power steam engine, which powered a press producing a weekly eight-page magazine that boasted, "No masculine hand had any part in its production."

"For heaven's sake, keep them diverted," Leonard Jerome asked his brother Lawrence, who served as their guide. And so he did. Acting as a volunteer salesman for products at various outdoor booths, Lawrence not only kept the young couple laughing but collected huge crowds, sold many items, and even accepted the commission from appreciative booth owners.[17] Had Lawrence done anything like that in England, he would have been thought drunk or insane. Public fun in England was strictly for the "lower classes."

Jennie might have sighed at the contrast. America was her childhood, Europe her adolescence; and she had flowered as a mixture of both. Years later, she remembered of this visit that she had been "invigorated and refreshed by contact with the alert intellects of my compatriots." But that has the settled sound of time. How different it must have been when she was actually there, free from the vise of British formality. How exhilarating to come from an old city to a growing one, from austere in-laws to a warm, laughing, vibrant father who could never say no to her.

There had been, of course, the fairyland quality of the past few years, emperors and princes and the high minds of Europe knowing her, dancing with her, calling on her. That now seemed lost, the social future bleak. She felt free and alive in America; going back to England held a chilly uncertainty. Yet there was no choice—she could not ask Randolph to stay in her country. Some Englishmen had become Americans, but Randolph was a Member of Parliament. He had no other trade or talent.

Upon their return to England, the young Churchills' bleak future seemed brightened. The Duke of Marlborough had accepted an appointment as Viceroy to Ireland, a position he had previously refused. Disraeli had pressed it on him again, urging that the social air of Dublin Castle might prove more friendly to his family than that of England. The particular point was that Randolph would accompany his father as an unpaid private secretary. It was a happy solution to all the problems brought on by the Aylesford affair.

"Not being in favor with the Court, from which London society took the lead," wrote Jennie, "we were nothing loath to go." Jennie looked forward to Ireland. She had heard the Irish were a people of warmth and passion, that theirs was a country of rich speech, green fields, mist, and mystery.

They arrived in December 1876. It was a dramatic entry, full of the panoply and pomp that royal England attached to a Viceroy—full dress parade, carriages with outriders and postilions, the booming of cannons. Jennie didn't know where this new twist in her road would wind, but she was eager for the adventure.

Seven

$\mathcal{J}$ ENNIE, RANDOLPH, AND WINSTON MOVED into "the little White Lodge," a low, white building with green shutters and veranda. Set in Phoenix Park, it was only a few minutes' walk from Viceregal Lodge, the home of the Viceroy. This enormous park of 1,700 acres, an ancient place of dramatic duels and tame deer, was originally set up as a hawking ground for the viceroys, then became the great public pleasure grounds of Dublin.

Preceding the Duke of Marlborough as Viceroy had been the Duke of Abercorn, better known as "Old Magnificent," a delightful and handsome man who scented his beard and had the debutantes pass by in a kissing review, asking the pretty ones to return for an encore. What made Marlborough's replacement of Abercorn embarrassing was that Abercorn's daughter was Blandford's wife, deserted in the Aylesford scandal. Nevertheless, the Marlboroughs and the Churchills moved in for a three-year stay.

Jennie liked Ireland. She viewed the green island with the romantic eyes of a 23-year-old woman of privilege. Instead of a poor, rocky land, it was for her a lovely, lonely place with stone fences lining the green meadows "like veins on a time-worn hand." Instead of the wretched mud hovels, she saw the slender, circular stone towers that had given shelter from foreign raiders during the Middle Ages, the profusion of flowers and sea-swept rocks, the bright oats stacked next to black peat. Instead of the hopelessness of hungry people, she saw barelegged colleens in red petticoats riding sideways on the backs of donkeys. For Jennie, it was a singing land of poetically lilting names—Inishmore, Tipperary, Limerick, Blarney, MacGillicuddy's Reeks.

She would soon learn the harsher truth of Ireland, but now she knew only the pleasure. Hers was primarily the outdoor life: sailing on the lakes of Killarney and the wide stretches of rivers called loughs, trout fishing in Galway and Connemara, snipe hunting at Lord Sligo's place in Westport, shooting near Muckross Abbey, catching lobsters along the natural harbors of the irregular coastline, weekending at Lord Portarlington's home near Emo (where Randolph had spent so many weeks waiting for his aunt to die), hard riding in the wild woods and open fields. Riding, in fact, became such a passion for Jennie that she "begged, borrowed or stole any horse she could find," to go whenever she could. With a brown mare she had bought in Oxford, she could manage most of the "trappy" fences of the Kildare country, as well as the banks and narrow doubles of Meath "as though to the manner born."[1]

Riding often and everywhere gave her the outlet she needed for her enormous physical energy, as well as a sense of freedom—freedom from the watchful eye of her mother-in-law, freedom from the polite but dull duties at the Viceregal Lodge, and the freedom of feeling that she belonged to herself.

Randolph occasionally rode with her. Once she was going through an opening in a fence when the heavy gate swung and caught the horse broadside.

> Luckily I fell clear, but it looked as if I might be crushed underneath him, and Randolph, coming up at that moment, thought I was killed. A few seconds later, however, seeing me all right, in the excitement of the moment he seized my flask and emptied it. For many days it was a standing joke against him that *I* had the fall, and *he* had the whiskey.

One photograph of Jennie shows her wearing a closely fitting, black riding habit and a rakishly set, black silk hat. Winston, two years old when the family went to Ireland and six when they left, retained that image through his adulthood. "My picture of her in Ireland is in a riding habit, fitting like skin and often beautifully spotted with mud."[2]

Lord D'Abernon remembered her differently. The former Sir Edgar Vincent, D'Abernon was a statesman and philosopher, former Ambassador to Berlin, an international banker in Turkey, and regarded by many as one of the most handsome men in England. He wrote:

I have the clearest recollection of seeing her for the first time. It was at the Viceregal Lodge at Dublin. She stood on one side, to the left of the entrance. The Viceroy was on a dais at the further end of the room surrounded by a brilliant staff, but eyes were not turned on him or his consort, but on a dark, lithe figure, standing somewhat apart and appearing to be of another texture to those around her, radiant, translucent, intense. A diamond star in her hair, her favorite ornament—its luster dimmed by the flashing glory of her eyes. More of the panther than of the woman in her look, but with a cultivated intelligence unknown to the jungle. Her courage not less great than her husband—fit mother for descendents of the great Duke. With all these attributes of brilliancy such kindliness and high spirits . . . she was universally popular. Her desire to please, her delight in life and the genuine wish that all should share her joyous faith in it, made her the center of a devoted circle.[3]

He and Jennie were to be intimates for a long time.

Jennie was impressed with all the men of Ireland: their warmth and wit, their conviction that life and living were more important than form. "During those three years we lived there," she wrote, "I cannot remember meeting one really dull man. From the Lord Chief Justice to the familiar car-man, all were entertaining."

Randolph Churchill was away at Parliament much of the time. Jennie wrote him dutiful letters: ". . . Winston is flourishing, though rather cross the last two days—more teeth, I think. Everest has been bothering me about some clothes for him, saying that it was quite a disgrace how few things he has, and how shabby, at that. . . ."[4]

In his first three years as a Member of Parliament, Randolph spoke a total of one-and-a-half hours on the House floor, his speeches unimportant and unimpressive. On January 28, 1878, he wrote Jennie from London:

> . . . I am sure the debate will be very stormy. I am in great doubt what to do. I think I could make a telling speech against the Government, but old Bentinck got hold of me today and gave me a tremendous lecture. Of course I have my future to think of. . . . It is very difficult. . . .

It did not seem much of a future then, but that made it easier to surrender on various points of principle. The Duke of Marlborough was finally able to persuade Randolph to sign a full and formal apology to the Prince of Wales. The Queen and Lord Chancellor, however, had prepared for Randolph an even more contrite letter of apology, and he signed that, too.

That still did not heal the rift. Jennie, therefore, seldom went with Randolph to London. She had no wish to suffer any snubs, or defend herself against sneers. During that summer of 1878, however, she did accept an invitation to the "Peace with Honor" banquet given for Disraeli, (who three years before had been created Earl of Beaconsfield) and for Lord Salisbury, who had returned from a Berlin Conference where peace had been made with Russia over the Dardanelles. Jennie accompanied the Duchess of Wellington. "It was a wonderful sight," she said of the banquet, "and the enthusiasm was boundless when Lord Beaconsfield, looking like a black sphinx, rose to speak. It was on that occasion that, pointing with a scornful finger at Mr. Gladstone, he declared that he [Gladstone] was 'inebriated with the exuberance of his own verbosity.' "

Another newcomer to Parliament, elected the year after Randolph, was Ireland's fiery Charles Stewart Parnell. Like Randolph, his initial speeches were characterized by bad delivery and obvious nervousness. But unlike Randolph, his convictions were strong and his passions intense, particularly when he insisted on Ireland's right of self-government: "Ireland is not a geographical fragment," he said, "She is a nation."[5] Parnell gradually organized a small band of Fenian followers in Parliament to obstruct all proposed legislation until their own demands were met. Randolph once remarked, "How very troublesome the Fenians are," and called them "a great, secret, silent army." He overestimated their strength, however.

Born in the United States as a movement to export revolution to Ireland, Fenianism had become more of a symbol than a breed. Its uprisings were few and frustrated. The most formidable of them, in 1867, just seven miles out of Dublin, resulted in 960 arrests and practically destroyed the movement. Another Irishman, the brilliant Isaac Butt, accepted leader of Parliament's sixty representatives favoring Home Rule for Ireland, was a more moderate man. He believed in the power of words and reason; Parnell believed in force. Parnell saw the House of Commons as an English institution and hated it; Butt loved the House.

Randolph and Jennie knew both men. Butt, however, was their good friend and had begun to influence their opinions on the Irish issue. Other Irish friends, Lord Justice Fitzgibbon and Father James Healy, also worked to convert the Churchills to the cause of Home Rule.

Jennie must have been impressed by the fact that these Irish leaders thought of her not only as a woman, but as a thinking person, as someone worthy of conversion. Men of experience, older and wiser than she, they easily might have considered her simply a charming lady to be hand-kissed and ignored. That they did not, and that she felt capable of debate with them, gave her a growing sense of individuality, even apart from her husband.

While the Churchills remained unconverted on Irish Home Rule, his familiarity with that crucial issue not only made Lord Randolph strongly sympathetic to Irish problems but served as a springboard for his future. In one of his early speeches, which had been in answer to an Irish member of the House who had sneered at the first Duke of Marlborough, Randolph had retaliated by calling Dublin "a seditious capital." He now publicly apologized, saying, "I have since learned to know Ireland better." Then in an inflammatory speech at his home borough of Woodstock, Randolph blamed a generation of British misgovernment and neglect of Ireland as the real cause of the crisis between the two peoples. "There are great and crying questions which the government has not attended to," he warned, "and as long as these matters are neglected, so will the government have to deal with obstruction from Ireland."[6]

This unprecedented criticism from a Tory aristocrat caused considerable furor in the press. Newspaper editorials blistered Randolph as a traitor to his country and his class. In obvious disapproval of Randolph's Woodstock speech, Disraeli wrote to the Duke of Marlborough that the seeds of the Irish Home Rule movement seemed to him a menace "scarcely less disastrous than pestilence and famine." A family friend asked Marlborough for an explanation of Randolph's remarkable speech. "The only excuse I can find for Randolph," the Duke replied, "is that he must either be mad or have been singularly affected with local champagne or claret. I can only say that the sentiments he has indulged in are purely his own."[7]

Jennie, however, believed as her husband did. It was true that she and Randolph had lost most of the fire of their early love and that their marriage had been pulled together by the social disaster of their encounter with the Prince. But more important in maintaining a sense of unity was their abiding mutual respect. Churchill knew the strength of his wife's will, the extent of her energy, and the value of her astuteness; Jennie was keenly aware of the potential of Randolph's intelligence and passions, however fitful. Certainly Randolph himself, at this unsure time in his political career, could not have stood against the austere force of his father and the pleading of his mother had he not had Jennie's full support.

Famine had come to Ireland with the failure of the potato crop in 1877, resulting in two years of hunger, terror, and ruin. Official aid being insufficient, the Duchess started a Famine Fund. It was largely aimed at supplying the basic essentials to the aged and the ill, with a sum of money to help keep at least a few families out of the workhouse and provide food and clothing for children in school. Jennie and Randolph both joined in the effort and traveled throughout the country, from the moors to the mountains. They were profoundly moved by the desperateness, especially in southern Ireland. "In our walks, we had many opportunities of seeing the heart-rending poverty of the peasantry who lived . . . more like animals than human beings," Jennie wrote.

They found people living in one-room huts furnished only with some straw and blankets, eating nothing but potatoes and salt, and having meat but twice a year, at Easter and Christmas. Pigs could not be raised because there was no garbage to feed them—garbage was a luxury. "There are many houses in this parish at present," wrote one priest at the time,

> in which the last pound of meal has been consumed. the last bed-covering worth a shilling has been deposited in the pawn office, and the last fire of turf collected from the saturated heap upon the bog has died upon the hearth, the dying embers being a vivid emblem of that death from starvation which is already creeping upon the threshold.

Together the Churchills toured almost every county in Ireland. What they saw and learned had a permanent effect upon them both.

The experience was particularly significant for Jennie. This was the first time she had been drawn outside of herself. While it was true that she and Randolph lived on limited funds compared to others of their social level, it was still a financial pinch of the gentlest kind, a pinch with a wink in it. She had never seen the horror of hunger, of children without shoes, of homes warmed by huddled bodies for lack of coal. It was a new view of an old world that shocked and hurt her. She never forgot. Nor would she ever let Randolph forget.

Her son, however, also demanded attention. ". . . Winston has just been with me," she wrote Randolph, "such a darling he is. 'I can't have my Mama go—and if she does, I will run after the train and jump in,' he said to me. I have told Everest to take him out for a drive tomorrow, if it is fine."[8]

Mrs. Everest, whom Winston called "Woom" or "Woomany," was the one who took him to the pantomime shows, helped teach him to read, and introduced him to the "tangle of arithmetic." In *My Early Life,* Winston wrote of the latter:

> These complications cast a steadily gathering shadow over my daily life. They took one away from the interesting things one wanted to do in the nursery or the garden. They made increasing inroads upon one's leisure. . . . My mother took no part in these impositions, but she gave me to understand that

she approved of them and she sided with the Governess almost always.[9]

British tradition relegated Jennie's job with Winston to that of overseer,
at a prescribed distance. Children appeared briefly at breakfast, at lunch,
and shortly before bedtime. Nannies, at that time especially, cultivated in
children a sense of strain because they repeatedly emphasized that all children must be on their best behavior during any appearance before parents.
Parents were to be regarded as special personages of unpredictable moods.
Any undesirable behavior on the part of a child, whether a sob or a sudden
laugh, could cause immediate banishment to the nursery and even the dep-
rivation of dessert. Thus children of this time and this class found they
could really relax only with their nannies.

Commenting on a British children's book at the time, a London critic
wrote: "Little boys and girls ought not to regard themselves, as these stories teach them to do, as possible personages. . . . They should be left to the
happy humility of unspoiled children who do not discover that they are
worth thinking about. . . ."

While Jennie deviated somewhat from the pattern of the upper-class
British parent, Randolph followed it in the extreme. She demonstrated love
and concern, but Randolph seemed to determinedly maintain a distance
from his son. Part of that, too, was the standard of British upper-class fathers. But Randolph Churchill's attitude toward Winston, from his earliest
years to the time of his death, was more—or rather, less—than austere
reserve—it was calculated coldness. Children of a disappointing marriage,
of course, are often the objects of resentment, and if Winston had been conceived before the marriage, guilt may have further embittered Randolph.[10]
Moreover, had there been no marriage and no son, the nature of Randolph's illness might have remained secret and his shame unexposed. In
the family, however, it was also said that Randolph generally disliked children. Whatever the origin, the fact is clear: Randolph Churchill did not
like his son.

Although the marriage was still intact, it was severely rent. Jennie was
happy to go riding with nearly any attractive and interesting man. One of
her most frequent escorts was Colonel Forster, then Master of the Horse to
the Viceroy. Jennie wrote of him only that he was "a beautiful rider, and
many were the pleasant hunting days we had together."

Hunting trips seemed to consume an increasing amount of time. Jennie
went on many, but primarily for the ride. She had a particularly strong
aversion to the killing of any living creature. Years later, she described the
way a young, charming-looking woman killed a stag:

With the aid of a powerful pair of field-glasses, I watched her stalk. . . . First she crawled on all fours up a long burn; emerging hot and panting, not to say wet and dirty, she then continued her scramble up a steep hill, taking advantage of any cover afforded by the ground, or remaining in a petrified attitude if by chance a hind happened to look up. The stag, meanwhile, quite oblivious of the danger lurking at hand, was apparently enjoying himself. Surrounded by his hinds, he trusted in their vigilance, and lay in the bracken in the brilliant sunshine. I could just see his fine antlered head, when suddenly, realizing that all was not well, he bounded up, making a magnificent picture as he stood gazing round, his head thrown back in defiance. Crash! Bang! and this glorious animal became a maimed and tortured thing. Shot through both forelegs, he attempted to gallop down the hill, his poor broken limbs tumbling about him, while the affrighted hinds stood riveted to the spot, looking at their lord and master with horror, not unmixed with curiosity. I shall never forget the sight, or that of the dogs set on him. . . . If these things must be done, how can a woman bring herself to do them?

During this hectic time in Ireland Jennie still managed to maintain a smooth relationship with her in-laws. From the first time they met, she and Marlborough shared a mutual admiration. As for the Duchess, Jennie was an obvious asset during the considerable entertaining that was required of the Duke's position. Jennie also had worked hard for the Duchess' Famine Fund, for which the Duchess had received flattering appreciation from Queen Victoria. But most of all, the cooling relationship between Jennie and Randolph had strengthened Randolph's ties to his mother. The Duchess was most happy to have it that way.

On April 15, 1879, Randolph wrote to his mother from London: "I write to wish you very many happy returns of your birthday tomorrow, which is also, as perhaps you may remember, our wedding day; and having been married five years, I begin to feel highly respectable."

The importance of respectability was certainly one of the pressures that kept his marriage intact and one reason he blinded himself to the constant rumors about Jennie and her men.

While Randolph was away at Parliament, Jennie had met the visiting 42-year-old Empress Elizabeth of Austria. Elizabeth had once been considered the most beautiful princess in Europe. She was an eccentric, who always carried a large fan to hide her face from the crowd, and who for a time had lived on a diet of blood and milk. On one occasion during her youth, she had received her Greek teacher by wearing black, flowing clothes and hanging upside down from a trapeze. Her father had once told her, "If you and I had not been born princes, we would have been performers in a circus." On her arrival in Ireland, Elizabeth converted her boudoir into a gymnasium. She wore a riding habit so tightly fitted that whenever she fell from a horse, she had to be unbuttoned before she could stand up.

Elizabeth had married the Emperor Francis Joseph when she was only sixteen. Not only had she been infected by him with syphilis, but she had passed on the disease to their only son, Rudolph. Once this was discovered, the Emperor refused her nothing. He catered to her every whim, even let her choose his chief mistress.[11] Perhaps Randolph catered to Jennie's whims out of his own guilt, for her influence over him continued, despite her affairs.

Randolph's trips to London increased considerably, both in quantity and duration. During his stays in London, Randolph wrote often to his mother but less often to his wife. The tone of affection was marked in the letters to his mother; those to Jennie were mainly of politics.

Even when Randolph was back in Ireland, he and Jennie rode separately as often as they rode together. In his memoirs, Winston Churchill noted, "She and my father hunted continually on their large horses; and sometimes there were great scares because one or the other did not come back for many hours after they were expected."[12]

One of the favorite friends of the young Randolph Churchills for many years was Lieutenant-Colonel John Strange Jocelyn. Jennie had met him at Blenheim Palace on that first day she signed the Guest Book. Strange Jocelyn was the third son of the third Earl of Roden, born in Dublin, educated at Harrow. He and his wife had an 8,900-acre estate close to the shores of the Irish Sea.[13]

Jennie was again pregnant in the summer of 1879, and her second son was born in Dublin on February 4, 1880. John Strange Jocelyn was asked by the Randolph Churchills to be a godfather,[14] and they named the boy John Strange Spencer-Churchill.

WOMEN HAD FEW LEGAL RIGHTS in England in 1880. so long as a wife remained under her husband's roof, she was legally subject to him. As late as 1899, a man suffering from syphilis could legally insist upon sexual intercourse with his wife and could not be accused of rape if he forced her. For any upper-class woman of the time, the stigma of divorce was overwhelming. To the outside world the strange thing was that here was a country ruled by a woman, and yet the Victorian Age represented the last stand of British male supremacy.[1] For example, the first British Marriage and Divorce Act was passed in 1857, but society women generally steered clear of it, because the stigma was too strong. While the Queen had no qualms about inviting men to Court ceremonies who were known to be unfaithful to their wives, she would never—until 1887—invite any woman who had the temerity to petition for divorce, no matter how justified the woman's reasons.[2] The Married Women's Property Act would not pass Parliament for another two years. Until then, a husband could demand and collect the whole of his wife's income and spend it any way he wanted—even if she had left his bed and board, and even if their children were starving.

Private lives were considered private, with only a single social rule—no scandal. Divorce meant scandal, and scandal damaged society's image with the mass of people. "We saw to it," said Lady Warwick, "that five out of every six scandals never reached the outside world."[3] As soon as it seemed there might be an appeal to the Divorce Court, social pressure converged on the couple to avoid the final step. If the name were famous enough, such pressure often came from the highest quarters.

But there were other factors. Jennie, of course, was not unfamiliar with compromised marriage. Her own mother, after all, had nearly always been cognizant of her husband's flagrant infidelity and had made no attempt at divorce. The London society of which the Churchills were a part abounded in such situations, where marriage merely served as a social convenience long after love had gone. Moreover, if Jennie did not respect Randolph as a husband, she did respect his other qualities—his courage, his charm, his wit, and his potential. Jennie was then only twenty-six years old, and she felt a lingering tenderness for Randolph. Leaving her husband then would have meant abandoning him at a time of his greatest need.

Divorce for Randolph was similarly out of the question. He still loved Jennie in his own way, and there were never any other women connected with him in whispered scandal. He needed Jennie as an anchor, a source of strength, a sympathetic advisor. He always had been physically frail, but now the recurrent specter of syphilis also kept him mentally insecure.[4] In addition, divorce would have seriously crippled any political future Randolph hoped to have.

In March, 1880, Jennie and Randolph and their ménage of two children, nanny, cook, and servants set up house at 29 St. James Place, a very desirable address.[5] It was a small, prestigious street, set in an area of quiet dignity on a high piece of ground that on a clear morning afforded a view of the distant Surrey hills. The cream of the social elite were gathered there. St. James Palace and Marlborough House were just on the other side of Pall Mall; around the corner were two of the city's most exclusive clubs: White's, with its famous big bay window, and Boodle's.

The English club was even more a castle for the English gentleman than his home. More whims were catered to more completely—and more quietly. An occasional snorer was awakened either by a heavy weight dropped near his feet or by an attendant asking him loudly, "The gentleman in the armchair has rung for something?"

Each club had its distinctive style. Boodle's had a rule that silver given in change must first be plunged into boiling water and then twirled in a leather bag to ensure proper cleanliness. In the St. James Club, which catered to the Diplomatic Corps, Lord Knightley refused to accept silver at all, telling the waiter, "Please bring me gold for that." The Caledonian Club featured a snuffbox; the Orleans Club specialized in bread-and-butter puddings; the Turf Club catered to the sportsmen and furnished a meeting place for the new rich and the old landowners; the Aetheneum saw itself as the club for men of national distinction. All the clubs offered rich libraries, fine wines, careful cuisine, unlimited stationery, guarded privacy, and some of the most scintillating conversation in London.[6]

At the bottom of St. James Place, in the cul-de-sac bounded on one side by Green Park, was the lovely home that had belonged to Lord Spencer, the noted Home Secretary in the time of Pitt and Burke. Next door to the Churchills lived Sir Stafford Northcote, who replaced Disraeli as leader in the House of Commons, after Disraeli's elevation to the House of Lords in 1876. A man of dignity and patience, with a puckish sense of humor, Northcote was too tolerant of the turbulent spirit of his times to maintain a position of party leadership. Lord Randolph later made Northcote his personal target for political destruction, and succeeded. They must have been interesting neighbors for one another.

England had a General Election in April 1880. The country had changed significantly during the previous generation. The population had jumped from 27 to 35 million and liberalized election laws had extended the franchise. After its success with Russia over the Dardanelles, Disraeli's government had suffered some severe setbacks, particularly in the unpopular Afghan Zulu wars (in the latter of which the Prince Imperial, son of Napoleon III, was killed). There had also been serious problems in farm areas following the arrival of cheap wheat from America. Conservatives seemed to be in serious trouble everywhere. Even the family borough of Woodstock no longer seemed safe, and Randolph hurried there to work for votes.

"The outlook here at the outset was very alarming," he wrote his mother. "I think I must attend more regularly this session. Hall hit me rather hard on account of my slack attendance."

In *My Early Life*, Winston Churchill reported his boyhood estimate of the election:

> In 1880 we were all thrown out of office by Mr. Gladstone. Mr. Gladstone was a very dangerous man who went about rousing people up, lashing them into fury so that they voted against the Conservatives and turned my grandfather out of his place as Lord-Lieutenant of Ireland. . . . Lord Beaconsfield [Disraeli] was the great enemy of Mr. Gladstone, and everybody called him "Dizzy." However, this time Dizzy had been thoroughly beaten by Mr. Gladstone, so we were all flung out into Opposition and the country began to be ruined very rapidly. Everyone said it was "going to the dogs."[7]

Randolph, however, had won, but by a mere sixty votes. "Starting with many advantages," his son later wrote, "he was still, at thirty-one, obscure. . . . His party was now humbled in the dust. . . . Grave and violent dangers beset the State, and no one troubled to think about an undistinguished sprig of the nobility. Nevertheless his hour had come. . . ."[8]

That summer of 1880 Winston was six years old and a troublesome boy. Jennie wrote her mother that he was a "most difficult child to manage." It was probably partly a little boy's frustration with the seeming lack of parental affection. Randolph Churchill was involving himself more deeply in politics and Jennie faced the delicate job of again ingratiating herself with London society after a three-year absence. Winston and his baby brother Jack were still primarily looked after by their nanny Mrs. Everest. Many years after, Winston Churchill would write, "If there be any, as I trust there are some, who rejoice that I live, to that dear and excellent woman, their gratitude is due."

Jennie occasionally took over, particularly when Mrs. Everest was ill or on holiday. On one such night, Winston was unable to fall asleep and Jennie exhausted herself playing "Pirates and Indians" with him.[9]

Vacation plans soon had to be made, but since Parliament was not expected to recess till September, Jennie sent Winston and Jack to Ventnor, on the Isle of Wight, for the month of August. Mrs. Everest had a sister who lived there. Her sister's husband was a prison warder who filled Winston with all sorts of exciting stories of prison mutinies, and took him for long walks out on the cliffs overlooking the sea. One day, Winston wrote, "We saw a great splendid ship with all her sails set, passing the shore only a mile or two away." "That is a troopship," the prison warder told him, "bringing the men back from the war." Then there was a sudden storm and Winston afterward learned the ship had capsized and three hundred soldiers had drowned. He was told divers had gone down searching for the bodies, "and it made a scar on my mind—that some of the divers had fainted with terror at seeing the fish, eating the bodies of the poor soldiers . . ."

Winston then wrote what was probably his first letter: "My dear Mama I am so glad you are coming to see us. I had such a nice bathe in the sea today. love to papa your loving Winston."[10]

Shortly after his return from Ventnor, he was readied to go off to school for the first time.

> It appeared that I was to go away from home for many weeks at a stretch in order to do lessons under masters. The term had already begun, but still I should have to stay seven weeks before I could come home for Christmas. . . . I was no more consulted about leaving home than I had been about coming into the world. . . .

The fateful day arrived. My mother took me to the station in a hansom cab. She gave me three half-crowns, which I dropped onto the floor of the cab, and we had to scramble around in the straw to find them again. We only just caught the train. If we had missed it, it would have been the end of the world. However, we didn't, and the world went on.

St. George's was a fashionable, exclusive school that prepared students for fashionable, exclusive Eton.

It was a dark November afternoon when we arrived at this establishment. We had tea with the Headmaster, with whom my mother conversed in the most easy manner. I was preoccupied with the fear of spilling my cup and so making "a bad start." I was also miserable at the idea of being left alone among all these strangers in this great, fierce, formidable place. After all, I was only seven, and I had been so happy in my nursery with all my toys. I had such wonderful toys: a real steam engine, a magic lantern, and a collection of soldiers already nearly a thousand strong. Now it had to be all lessons.[11]

Winston soon learned that St. George's was a school where flogging was a regular practice. "Two or three times a month the whole school was marshalled in the Library," he remembered,

and one or more delinquents were haled off to an adjoining apartment by the two head boys, and there flogged until they bled freely, while the rest sat quaking listening to their screams. How I hated this school, and what a life of anxiety I lived there for more than two years.

Winston was once flogged for taking sugar from the pantry. Afterward he was reported to have found the Master's straw hat and kicked it to pieces. In her *Life of Roger Fry,* which purportedly describes St. George's, Virginia Woolf described floggings by a sadistic headmaster with a hatred of red-haired boys.[12] Red-haired Winston, however, kept the fact of the headmaster's sadism to himself and wrote his parents, "I am very happy at school."

In those next years, Jennie lived with a different anxiety. London was always a part of it. Their house was expensive, Winston's school was expensive, everything was expensive, and their income never seemed to cover everything. "London is very gay now," she wrote her mother.

> I haven't been to many balls; as I simply cannot afford to
> get dresses and one can't wear always the same thing. Be-
> sides I was not bidden to the one I wanted to go to [because
> of the Prince] and I did not care about the others. . . . Money
> is such a hateful subject to me just now . . . don't let us talk
> about it. . . .

Fortunately, Jennie was able to furnish her house "on the cheap." She
had a collector's instinct as well as a decorator's flair, and she had made the
rounds of the Dublin antique shops during her Ireland years, buying
mostly choice pieces from ancestral homes. Blandford referred to her collection as "Jennie's stage props." Her most expensive acquisitions were silk
panels for her drawing room—but they were soon ruined by the damp London fog.[13]

Mrs. Jerome had left Paris to live again with her husband in New York,
and Jennie wrote them there:

> . . . Our money affairs are pretty much like everyone
> else's, it seems to me, hard up, notwithstanding Papa's most
> generous "tips."
>
> Randolph is obliged to spend so much in a political way,
> going to these meetings etc., and this big public dinner in
> Woodstock will cost a lot . . . the building alone costs
> £120 . . . But this demonstration is of great importance to R.
> and the thing must be well done with Lord Salisbury and a
> lot of big swells coming. You don't know how economical we
> try to be. I've not bought but one winter dress, and that we
> bought in Woodstock for twenty-five shillings and made over
> by my maid—dark red thin flannel. . . .
>
> P.S. R. sends his best love—Bye and bye couldn't you
> send me a barrel of American eating apples to St. James
> Place? I'm so fond of them.

Up to then, Jennie Churchill was many things: beautiful, fascinating,
witty, but her positive impact upon others had been primarily social and
mainly among men. She had broken out of the small, rigid frame that limited the mind and activity of the average Victorian society woman. Her
conversations were not confined to the female trivia of her time, and few
topics were beyond her ken. Yet the hard fact was that at twenty-seven she
was neither a successful wife nor a successful mother. But the year of 1881
was a turning point in her metamorphosis, just as it was for Randolph. It was
as if both had suddenly realized that success in politics could influence so

much else—their self-respect, their position in society, and particularly their marriage. Their common enthusiasm for the nature of politics and the rewards it offered could generate a way of life to be discussed and planned together. Jennie had a gift for the written word, and could help her husband with his speeches—read them, listen to them, suggest changes, and perhaps even write some of them. Randolph also relied on Jennie for her manipulative mind and her intuitive judgment of people.

Randolph Churchill, the quiet back-bencher, meekly accepting most party orders, suddenly became aggressive, sarcastic, gay, heedless of consequences. The social dilletante who seemed to care little about anything suddenly became a political figure with the principles and courage of a Scarlet Pimpernel.

He was still ill-equipped, however, to cope with a new-found future, having had only the slightest background in foreign affairs and almost none in political history, except for the Irish question. As a speaker, too, he appeared to be ill-suited to success. His voice was guttural, with "a curious rolling effect, as if his tongue was too big for his mouth."[14] (Winston Churchill later copied his father's voice and style.) It was also rather disconcerting that Randolph used head movements instead of arm movements to emphasize a point. And his physical figure, too, was hardly impressive: slim, slightly smaller than medium height, his main distinction a fashionable walrus mustache, but one that seemed disproportionate to his face.

Yet what gave his speech particular force and made one forget the face and the figure and the guttural sounds was a smoldering fury that often exploded. It was the same fury of the small boy who, as Shane Leslie described it, once "took a silver spoon, twisted it, stamped on it, bit it and crushed it out of all recognition." The direction of this fury was unpredictable. Neither his enemies nor his friends knew what he might say or do next, nor whether his reason might be lofty or confused, based on conviction or self-sacrifice.

Attacking a government pamphlet on one occasion, Randolph threw the pamphlet down on the floor of the House and stamped on it, to the long, loud cheers of his fellow Conservatives. After that speech, Jennie wrote in a letter to her sister, "Everyone . . . rushed up and congratulated me to such an extent that I felt as tho' I had made it."

His humor was barbed, his phrasing incisive, his mode of thought cynical and sparkling, his charm persuasive. At a political meeting in Paddington, a woman in the audience asked a question that caused an uproar. Churchill asked for quiet, then said, "Gentlemen, there is only one reply to a lady when she argues with you—Silence." The audience laughed in approval. It was little wonder that he soon gathered around him a small circle of kindred spirits. He and three others became a pressure group in the House and were soon nicknamed the "Fourth Party." A long-time family friend, fifteen years older than Randolph, Sir Henry Drummond Wolff was the most flippant and unflappable of the four. Jennie, who had met Wolff at Cowes before her marriage, later described him as "the best of the company . . . with a pink-and-white complexion that a girl might have envied, and a merry twinkle which hid behind a pair of spectacles . . . a godsend if anything went wrong, and a joke from him saved many a situation." It was Wolff whose warmth always gave the group's meetings the tone of a family gathering.

Then there was John Eldon Gorst, a serious, calculating man in his late forties, a member of the House for fourteen years, and a close friend of Disraeli. In her *Reminiscences*, Jennie said of Gorst that he always seemed stern but that "he could make himself very pleasant."

> I remember [Gorst] defending me in some trivial case in the County Court, and winning it; the appearance of a Queen's Counsel in silk gown and wig creating a sensation. Randolph accompanied us, and we drove away in a four-wheeler, feeling very triumphant until the wheel came off and we were ignominiously precipitated into the street.[15]

A see-saw member of the Fourth Party, 32-year-old Arthur James Balfour moved in and out, depending upon the political climate. Balfour served as secretary to his uncle, Lord Salisbury, whom he kept fully posted on Lord Randolph's plans. Balfour seemed to need nobody. Among contemporary public figures, his blood was the bluest—he was a Cecil and son of a prominent member of Parliament, his wealth was extensive, and behind his bland face and indolent, charming demeanor worked "the finest brain that has been applied to politics in our time."[16] He had moved into Parliament from a family-controlled borough, as Randoph had, at the age of twenty-six.

Balfour was later quoted as saying that one of the reasons he joined the Fourth Party in the front seats of the House was that it gave him more room for his legs. Six feet tall with a willowy figure, Balfour always seemed to be sitting on his spine. *Punch's* Henry Lucy described the position by saying that Balfour appeared to be trying to discover "how nearly he could sit on his shoulder blades." Winston Churchill in later years called Balfour "the most courageous man alive. I believe if you held a pistol to his face, it would not frighten him." Still, some Irish members of the House called him "Miss Balfour" and even "Clara," because of his unmistakable effeminacy.

Jennie particularly admired Balfour's knowledge of music, and the two of them frequently played Beethoven and Schumann piano duets. She saved this note from him, written at the House of Commons:

> I'm groaning and swearing on this beastly bench: while you are listening to Wagnerian discords, I am listening to Irish grumblings—there is a great deal of brass in both of them; otherwise there is not much resemblance! I *am* sitting next——, I *might* be sitting next you! I am an unhappy victim. . . .

She and Balfour shared their mutual interest in music with Gorst, and the three of them often went together to concerts, particularly the "Monday Pops." "My fashionable and frivolous friends, spying the three of us walking together, often teased me about my 'weird' companions," Jennie wrote, "one solemn with beard and eye-glass, the other aesthetic with long hair and huge spats."

Jennie was practically a fifth member of the Fourth Party. "Many were the plots and plans which were hatched in my presence by the Fourth Party," she said. "How we used to chaff about the 'goats' as we called the ultra-Tories and followers of Sir Stafford Northcote! Great was to be their fall and destruction."

Lady Jeune described one of the group's meetings at her house when "Randolph looked like a great schoolboy, full of fun and mischief, his busy brain devising means by which he could upset his political opponents, and then bubbling over with fiendish glee at the traps he was setting for the unaware politicians of his own side. . . ."

Five months after the national election, in August 1880, the Liberals solemnly rebuked the Fourth Party for "obstruction," noting that since the election the Fourth Party, collectively, had made 247 speeches and asked seventy-three questions.

A junior member of the Liberal Government found himself being kidded at one of Jennie's soirees because he was absenting himself from the House that night. The guest finally admitted that he had asked his Leaders for permission to come to this party and they told him that he could stay as long as he liked—provided he managed to keep the four members of the Fourth Party away from the House.

The first cartoon about the Fourth Party featured a faithful likeness of Randolph which emphasized his popeyes and showed him gazing upward while his three bewildered companions murmured, "We wonder where he is taking us to?" Parliamentary critic Lucy described the group's mood as "one of youth, as of boys playing at politics, and in their undisciplined revels plucking the beards of grave and reverend seigneurs. . . ."

House members always expected the unexpected from Lord Randolph. Who else but he would ride a bicycle on the terrace of the awesome House of Commons, just to get some exercise? Or accept a bet that he could run back and forth across nearby Westminster Bridge while Big Ben was striking midnight, and do it? Who but Randolph would tell another Conservative Party member in the House lobby, "You had much better join us. Sitting up there behind the old Goat [Northcote] you will never have any fun at all."

Always the dandy, his frock coat open, looking correct yet frivolous, Randoph could pose his questions in the most charming but insinuating way and invariably evoke an emotional reaction from Prime Minister Gladstone. Gladstone's was the classic manner of speech and debate, and it was his eloquence that was largely responsible for his great victory in overthrowing the Disraeli Government. But he was easily provoked, although he quickly regained his calm to answer the question at length. Then, as soon as Gladstone had concluded, another Fourth Party member would pop up with still another question. And so it went.

Gladstone had serious problems with Turkey and Greece and Cyprus and South Africa, problems that would still plague Winston Churchill's Government in the next century, but the Fourth Party's point of most concentrated attack was the Irish question. Unrest in Ireland had intensified, and the Gladstone Government seemed unable to cope with it.[17] The Fourth Party was convinced that coercion was unnecessary to quell the Irish troubles, that proper education and social welfare were more effective. It was a concept central to the Fourth Party's doctrine of "Tory Democracy."

Charles Stewart Parnell was soon attracted into Randolph's orbit. Parnell felt strongly that Lord Randolph was more likely to be genuinely touched by the Irish cause than any of his Conservative Party compatriots. By aligning himself with Churchill now, Parnell shrewdly calculated that he could stir the Liberals into moving in his direction.[18] Parnell's support would give the Fourth Party a strength out of proportion to its size, particularly since Gladstone's Liberal parliamentary majority was unruly and unpredictable.[19] And the Fourth Party would provide a critical weight to the House's Irish group, as a motion for adjournment "on a matter of urgent public importance," required forty supporters. Parnell had a personal following in the House of thirty-seven; with the addition of the Fourth Party, the Irish group would have its necessary forty.

Churchill soon moved into the corner of the coveted front bench of the House, the focal point of House attention. In one of his more celebrated speeches, he said:

People sometimes talk too lightly of coercion. It means that hundreds of Irishmen, who if the law had been maintained unaltered and had been firmly enforced, would now have been leading peaceful, industrious and honest lives, will soon be borne off to prison without trial; the others will have to fly the country into hopeless exile; that others, driven to desperation through such cruel alternatives, will perhaps shed their blood and sacrifice their lives in vain resistance to the forces of the Crown. . . .

Of this performance, Henry Lucy wrote: "Few spectacles have been more sublime than that of this young man of fashion devoting himself assiduously to the affairs of the state, sitting up long hours in the House of Commons, and doing violence to a naturally retiring disposition by bearding the Premier. . . ."[20]

Randolph began to put more sting into his speeches against the elderly Gladstone. He called Gladstone's Government, "these children of revolution, these robbers of churches, these friends of the lawless, these foes of the loyal. . . ."

"On one occasion," Jennie noted,

I had been at the House hearing Randolph make a fiery attack on him [Gladstone], this he answered with equal heat and indignation. The hour was late, and Randolph and I had just time to rush home and dress to dine at Spencer House with Lord and Lady Spencer. The first person I met as I went in was Mr. Gladstone, who at once came up and said: "I hope Lord Randolph is not *too* tired after his magnificent effort."

Dinner at the Gladstones often featured readings from Shakespeare and Macaulay. The typical gentleman of the day was still the Gladstone type: devoted to duty, an excellent landlord, anonymous contributor to charities, regular attendant at Sunday church.

Jennie sometimes sat next to "picturesque and dignified" Mrs. Gladstone in the Ladies Gallery at the House of Commons. For special debates, the small gallery might be filled with fifty women crowded "into the small dark cage to which the ungallant British legislators have relegated them." The Ladies Gallery in the House—or "parliamentary cage," as it was called—had three rows. Jennie described how the ladies in the front row had to sit in a cramped attitude, their knees against the grills, their necks craned forward, and their ears painfully on the alert if they wish to hear anything. . . . Those in the second row, by the courtesy of the first, may get a peep of the gods below. The rest have to fall back on their imagination or retire to a small room in the rear, where they can whisper and have tea. . . .

Next to speaking in public oneself, there is nothing which produces such feelings of nervousness and apprehensions as to hear one's husband or son make a speech. There is no doubt, however, that the frequent recurrence of it minimizes the ordeal, particularly if the speakers are sure of themselves. In this respect I can claim to be specially favored, though Randolph, even after years of practice and experience, was always nervous before a speech until he actually stood up.

. . . [That] reminds me of a painful sight, . . . a young member of Parliament with more acres than brains, who sat for a family pocket borough. Shutting his eyes tight and clenching his hands, he began in a high falsetto voice . . . and for thirty minutes he recited, or rather gabbled, the speech he had learned by heart, while his wife, with her eyes riveted on him, and with tears pouring down her cheeks from nervousness, unconsciously, with trembling lips, repeated the words he was uttering.[21]

Jennie did not suffer from such fears. She had a tough, hard mind, which she used to full advantage. By the spring of 1881, she had helped Randolph acquire a supreme self-confidence he had never known before. He relied on her more for that than for anything else. It was this self-confidence that imparted to Randolph Churchill an aura of excitement and a political magnetism that propelled him suddenly into national prominence.

In a letter to her mother, Jennie wrote,

You will be glad to hear that R. has been covering himself with glory and I'm told he has made himself a wonderfully good position in the House. . . . When this Government goes out (which they say will be soon) I fancy R. and his boon companion Sir Henry Drummond Wolff must be given something. . . .

Disraeli was less reserved in his predictions. He told Sir Henry James, a Liberal Party friend of Randolph's, that the Conservatives would soon be swept into power again. "When they come in," Disraeli said, "they will have to give him [Randolph] anything he chooses to ask for, and in a very short time they will have to take anything he chooses to give them."[22]

Disraeli served as the early advisor for Randolph's group, and remarked to them, "I wholly sympathize with you, because I never was respectable myself." The former Prime Minister, though now Lord Beaconsfield and a member of the House of Lords, was still titular head of his Party and the man to whom the Fourth Party went for final advice on key questions, the man who served as intermediary to forge compromise with their own Conservative Party leadership in the House of Commons. He still sat in Parliament as he always had, impassive, his crossed legs covered by his long frock-coat, his body slumped, his arms folded across his chest, his chin drooping as if he were about to fall asleep. But he was acutely aware of everything.

Disraeli died at the end of April, 1881. Young Winston later recalled:

> I followed his illness from day to day with great anxiety, because everyone said what a loss he would be to his country and how no one else could stop Mr. Gladstone from working his wicked will upon us all. I was sure Lord Beaconsfield was going to die, and at last the day came when all the people I saw went about with very sad faces because, as they said, a great and splendid Statesman, who loved our country and defied the Russians, had died of a broken heart because of the ingratitude with which he had been treated by the Radicals. . . . [23]

With Disraeli's death, Lord Randolph became even less temperate. His attacks on Gladstone became more bitter, more personal, often vitriolic. One friend said to him: "You will kill Gladstone one of these days."

"Oh no!" answered Randolph, "he will long survive me. I often tell my wife what a beautiful letter he will write to her, proposing my burial in Westminster Abbey."[24]

In the meantime, there was happy news from Jennie's sister Clara, who had become engaged to be married. Moreton Frewen came from an old Sussex family and was known as one of the best gentleman riders in England. A tall, assured sportsman, he had also spent a year driving cattle in Colorado, had explored the buffalo trails of Texas, and had known every one there from Buffalo Bill to Sitting Bull. "A bad man with brown eyes need not be feared," Frewen once wrote, "but the fellow with gray eyes or gray-blue whose eyes grew darker as they looked down a gun—that was the sort of man to reckon with." Moreton described himself as "lean and hard and tough as pin-wire." He had a natural gift of gab, all of it highly opinionated, and moved easily into the Leonard Jerome circle in New York. "My pre-destined father-in-law, Leonard Jerome, one of the kindliest of men, was the centre for a brilliant coterie to which I had entrée." Of his future mother-in-law, Moreton had less kindly comment. He called her "Sitting Bull," be-cause "she looked like a hatchet-faced squaw, and she never got up during my courting visits."[25]

To his future sister-in-law Jennie, whom he carefully called, "Lady Ran-dolph," Moreton wrote,

> For fear you may think me ungracious enough to bear malice, let me write you a few lines to say how right and rea-sonable you were to oppose Clara's selection. I should have thought you a careless sister indeed had you done otherwise. Still, I am not inclined to admit that she is doing a foolish thing. . . . [26]

Jennie did not consider Frewen good enough for her sister, and she made her opinion known. Clara was four years older than she, but Jennie never had any compunction about expressing her views on anything to anyone. She felt that Frewen offered neither the security nor the stability that her sister needed. Earlier that year, Moreton had been one of the more active suitors of Lily Langtry, who had caught the public imagination throughout England after her 1881 debut in *She Stoops To Conquer*. Langtry had a classic profile, golden hair, and a startling figure, and crowds followed her wherever she went. (Lord Houghton had introduced Jennie to Lily Langtry, saying, "I am proud to introduce the two most beautiful women in Europe to one another.") Women at all levels of society were soon wearing their hair in Langtry knots, buying Langtry shoes and Langtry hats. "The Jersey Lily" was seen riding in the park long after dark with the Prince of Wales. The King of Belgium came to call for her at the unusual hour of nine in the morning, and Crown Prince Rudolph of Austria deluged her with flowers. Frewen gave Lily a beautiful horse named Redskin, but bowed out of the competition with all that royalty. He later wrote, "But I had the joy of seeing her ride my horse when out exercising with H.R.H. Anyway, lilies can be dreadfully boring when not planted in bed!"[27]

His association with Langtry was only one factor in Jennie's opposition to Frewen; but Jennie was in London and Clara and he were together in New York. The marriage plans were set.

Frewen and Clara were married in New York's Grace Church in 1881. The young couple spent their honeymoon in Moreton's pine-log house on a beautiful knoll overlooking the Powder River in Wyoming. They lived entirely on fresh meat and fish, a far cry from the elegant sustenance on which Clara had been bred. But she still kept her French maid. Moreton invited Jennie to come and visit their Big Horn home:

> I can promise your husband A-1 shooting and a glimpse of the nicest life in the world. What an incongruous century this is: we've got a telephone connecting this house with our store and post office twenty-five miles below on the river, and last week there were a lot of Redskins—more naked than ashamed—talking to one another through it. I never saw such ludicrous astonishment. . . .

Visiting the Churchills later in London, Moreton wrote to his wife that he admired the "quiet force" of Randolph, ". . . but Jennie is an angel as she has whooping cough and the children too and R. is ill and rather snappish but she takes it all so well." In another note, contrasting Jennie and Leonie, Frewen commented, "Jennie has not got Leo's depth of character."

Jennie's character was strengthened with the imminent tests of time and tragedy. Randolph's syphilis had been in remission, but now suddenly worsened. It had reached the stage of recurrent headaches and fevers, lowering his threshold of irritability. His friends saw it as a kind of subterranean hysteria, and Jennie had the added job of soothing her husband and calming the ruffled feelings of puzzled friends.

"It was a most bewildering enterprise to follow the course of his friendships," wrote Lady Jeune.

> Sometimes he was inseparable from his friends; at other times he would hardly speak to them, and although this added greatly to the excitement of a visit he might happen to pay, it had its drawbacks in the fact that you were never certain for twenty-four hours when the change from one extreme to the other might take place.[28]

One by one, Randolph cut himself off from some of his closest associates, even breaking bitterly with Gorst on the Irish issue. It reached a point where Lord Hartington felt impelled to denounce Randolph publicly as "vile, contumacious and lying." Instead of responding with his customary scorn, Randolph dispatched an emissary to Hartington to demand a retraction or satisfaction in a duel. His emissary was even stranger than his demand—Captain O'Shea, an Irish Member of the House of Commons, and the husband of Parnell's mistress. Hartington apologized for his language, and the incident was closed. Friends, however, regarded Randolph's behavior as still another sign that he was poised at the edge of a breakdown.

As his illness worsened, Randolph insisted on spending more time at Blenheim—back with his horses and his dogs, back with the scenes of his boyhood. Now that the Duchess felt renewed control over her son, she made life increasingly bitter for Jennie. In a letter from the Palace that winter, Jennie confided to her mother:

> I quite forget what it is like to be with people who love me. I do so long sometimes to have someone to whom I could go and talk. Of course, Randolph is awfully good to me and always takes my part in everything, but how can I always be abusing his mother to him, when she is devoted to him and would do anything for him—The fact is I *loathe* living here. Its not on account of its dullness, *that* I don't mind, but it is gall and wormwood to me to accept anything or to be living on anyone I hate. It is no use disguising it, the Duchess hates me simply for what I am—perhaps a little prettier and more attractive than her daughters. Everything I do or say or wear is found fault with. We are always studiously polite to each other, but it is rather like a volcano, ready to burst out at any moment. . . . [29]

Jennie rented a small cottage near Wimbledon in the spring of 1882, and she and Randolph stayed there for several months, out of public sight. It was a lovely house with a long, green lawn and a rose garden. This peaceful period drew them closer together again, and Randolph's disease again went into remission.

Early that summer, when he had recovered enough, Jennie took Randolph to New York to stay with her family. Her letters had revealed her need to be close to them, a need to return to her roots. In a letter to a friend, Leonard Jerome wrote of his son-in-law: ". . . frail but fiery . . . I think Jennie is wonderful for him, he draws on her strength. I love having them here. I believe in R."[30]

These were the Elegant Eighties in the United States, a time of national tranquility between wars. One era had ended five years before with the death of Sioux Chief Crazy Horse, the last of the warring Indians, and another with the withdrawal of the final contingent of Federal occupation troops from the South. James A. Garfield had been shot and killed in 1881, and the new President was Chester A. Arthur. If the Presidents then were nondescript, perhaps it was because the times demanded no great leaders.

The Churchills stayed in the United States for two months, long enough to see Edison's electric lights transform the streets of Manhattan. New York was then a city of small brownstone or red brick houses, of pot-bellied stoves and horse-cars, of organ-grinders and strolling bands and the ubiquitous wooden Indian. Men wore scratchy paper collars and preachers denounced baseball as a game for oafs and "ill-mannered persons." Harlem was a quiet suburb and the Bronx was considered countryside; a skyscraper was a building twelve stories high. But most people worked a twelve-hour day, six days a week, for an average of ten dollars, and many worked longer for less. Even a short illness spelled family disaster, and a father's death often meant orphanages for the children. Immigrants jammed the slums, each national group in its own ghetto, with some 500,000 of New York's two million population unable to speak English. Some sections of the city had so much violence and crime, so many gang wars that police seldom ventured into them unless they went in strength. A few teen-age street gangs had a thousand members, armed with guns, knives, and blackjacks. Murder on the Bowery was common and expected, but any thug found in the so-called respectable part of town could expect a thorough beating in the backroom of the nearby police station.[31]

None of these things penetrated the social conversation within the charmed circles of Astor or Vanderbilt. Novelist Edith Wharton said that talk among their members "was never intellectual and seldom brilliant, but it was always easy and sometimes witty." Conversation concentrated on "food, wines, horses, yachts, cotillions, marriages, villas at Newport. . . ."[32]

The search for sensation became outlandish: a dinner eaten on horseback, with the favored horse fed flowers and champagne; a banquet given in honor of a small black and tan dog who wore a diamond collar worth $15,000; fine black pearls placed inside oysters and served at a dinner party; monkeys alternating with seated guests at a dining-room table; a complete orchestra hired to serenade a newborn child.

But the most widely-discussed town topic was a social war between Mrs. William Backhouse Astor and Mrs. William Kissam Vanderbilt. Mrs. Astor, "a tall, formidable woman of commanding dignity," had long been the single arbiter of New York society. It was she who had given the famous ball to which only four hundred guests were invited because there was room for no more in her ballroom. This limitation had prompted Ward McAllister's remark that there were only about four hundred people in fashionable New York Society. "If you go outside that number," McAllister had informed reporters, "you strike people who are either not at ease in a ballroom or else make other people not at ease." As far as Mrs. Astor was concerned, the number did not include Mrs. William Kissam Vanderbilt.

As pugnacious as she was plump, Mrs. Vanderbilt made her supreme challenge. She had built, at a cost of three million dollars, a replica of a French chateau, and then announced she would inaugurate her new palace with a ball. In reporting on guests' preparations for the ball, *The New York*

Times wrote that they had "disturbed the sleep and occupied the waking hours of social butterflies, both male and female, for over six weeks." Dress designer Lanouette estimated that the 150 gowns he had designed had cost more than thirty thousand dollars and had kept 140 dressmakers working day and night for five weeks. Naturally expecting to be invited, Mrs. Astor's daughter Caroline organized a special dance for the ball. However, Mrs. Vanderbilt gently let it be known that she could hardly invite the young Miss Astor since Mrs. Astor had never called on her. Faced with her daughter's disappointment, Mrs. Astor made the humiliating drive in her carriage up Fifth Avenue to call on Mrs. William Kissam Vanderbilt, and the war was won.

The Churchills did not attend the Vanderbilt ball because Randolph was ready to return to England, as was Jennie. The social life would always be a part of her life, but its allure now seemed to pall before the exhilaration of politics. The Astor-Vanderbilt feud did not compare with the fury of the Fourth Party. It was good rediscovering the openness and love of her family, and she enjoyed the free vitality of the United States; perhaps her heart was still in America, but her spirit and ambitions were in England.

Just before Jennie and Randolph departed, the Irish troubles were again in the headlines. "I remember a reporter calling at my father's house in Madison Square and telling me the news. We were greatly shocked and could hardly believe it until it was confirmed the next day. . . . Mr. Burke . . . and his sister ·. . . we knew quite well." Thomas Burke, the Permanent Under Secretary and an old friend of the Churchills, and Lord Frederick Cavendish, a close friend of Gladstone, had both been assassinated in Phoenix Park by a group called the Irish Invincibles.

When Jennie was in Dublin the following season for the Horse Show, she was invited by an official of the Kilmainham Gaol to meet the convicted assassins.

> I confess that I did not feel any great desire for this entertainment, but being told that it was nearly impossible to get permission to see them, and that without exception no one was allowed in the prison, I began to feel more interested.

She was taken to a small room in the jail and stood behind the man who interviewed each murderer. As he was being led back, the youngest of them turned suddenly to Jennie and asked her to help his wife if he "had to go." "This depressed me dreadfully," Jennie noted afterward,

> nor were my spirits raised by being taken round the prison by the Governor. . . . The tier upon tier of tiny cells, each

containing a miserable-looking man, the food brought in baskets which I saw prodded through and through with swords for fear that something might be smuggled in them, were a more than unpleasant sight.[33]

The Inspector General, however, arrived unexpectedly at the jail and Jennie was hidden in a bleak cell to avoid explanations. It was a cell without windows, and in the utter blackness Jennie was certain she saw "the little beady eyes" of rats. "The door opened just in time to save me from screaming." But later she could not help laughing when she thought of the expression that would have appeared on the face of the Inspector General if he had happened to visit her dungeon, especially as he had previously met her on a more social occasion. It would have made a fine dinner party anecdote, but Jennie revealed the story to no one for more than three years after the assassins were executed, for fear of compromising the Governor of the jail.

*J*ENNIE MUST HAVE BROUGHT BACK to England a gift of money from her father, for she and Randolph moved to a larger house at 2 Connaught Place early in 1883. Friends soon called the Connaught home "House Tyburnia," because it sat in the square terrace of the new Tyburn area, the residential quarter of the new society. The more fashionable, more proper society was beyond them, over the invisible line that enclosed some 350 homes in Mayfair and Belgravia. The novelist Thackeray described Mayfair-Belgravia as "that pale and polite district where all the inhabitants look prim and correct, and the mansions are painted a faint white-brown."

The Connaught house faced onto Hyde Park with an unobstructed view of the area from Marble Arch to Knightsbridge Corner. Within sight of the front window, back in 1724, an estimated 200,000 people had watched the hanging of Jack Sheppard, one of the most notorious criminals of his time. At the same place, Catherine Hayes, convicted of murdering her husband, was burned at the stake by a mob who refused to wait for a hangman. Here, too, the corpse of Oliver Cromwell, having been torn from its tomb at Westminster Abbey, was hung by a mob on the anniversary of the death of King Charles I, whom Cromwell had helped execute in 1649. Shortly after the Churchills moved into their new house, a mass grave was uncovered in the cellar. Because of all this notoriety, the house was generally thought to be haunted.

The Connaught Place house was even more of a curiosity for being one of the first homes in England to be lit by electric lights. Since Randolph was a traditionalist in the home, the idea of having the electricity undoubtedly came from Jennie. "The light was such an innovation that much curiosity and interest were evinced to see it, and people used to ask for permission to come to the house," Jennie said. "I remember the fiasco of a dinner party we gave to show it off, when the light went out in the middle of the feast, just as we were expatiating on its beauties, our guests having to remain in utter darkness until the lamps and candles, which had been relegated to the lower regions, were unearthed."[1]

That was characteristic of Jennie, always restlessly seeking out the different and the new. Her home was striking evidence of her spirit. The traditional Victorian home, like the Victorian female body, was, as one critic observed, well covered. Window curtains three deep; thick drapes, elaborately fringed; and dark, dull, expensive wallpaper matching the dark, dull brown paint on most walls. Furniture was usually mahogany, massive and solid. Living rooms were cluttered with enormous clocks, huge vases, stuffed birds and wax flowers under glass domes.[2] Jennie, however, startled her friends—and set a style—by using white paint and simple paneling, delicate pieces of French and Italian furniture, art from China and Japan, as well as electric light.[3]

Randolph was politically on the rise again, but the rise and fall of his emotions more and more resembled a runaway ferris wheel. At times he seemed drained and dispirited. "One evening I came home from the House of Commons very anxious and rather discouraged," he wrote,

> because . . . among people whom I ought to look upon as my political friends, I had met nothing but gloomy looks; and I felt very much inclined to retire from the game, thinking I was doing more harm than good, and rather—to use a slang expression—disposed to cut the whole concern.

Upon recovering his self-confidence, he frequently acted recklessly, as when he referred to a parliamentary opponent as "a damned fool"—unheard of language in the House of Commons. The press called him "Cheeky Randy" and "Little Lord Random,"[4] and mocked the way he perpetually twisted his walrus mustache. His popularity, however, was enormous. At outdoor rallies, he tailored his style of speech to his audience, often combining wit and abuse, epigram and harangue, while flailing his arms for emphasis. "Give it to 'em hot, Randy," the crowd would sometimes yell.

His effectiveness in Parliament, too, was vastly broadened. "Lord

Randolph dominated the House of Commons in all its moods," reported historian Robert Rhodes James.

> When it was gay, he stirred it into laughter; when it was flippant, no one could exceed him in droll irreverence; when it was united and determined, he spoke with seriousness and moderation; when it was angry, he fanned the flames until they spread into an ugly glow; when it craved a leader who would "show them game," Lord Randolph Churchill stood in the van.[5]

When his popularity led to overconfidence, Jennie acted as a balance wheel. She wrote her mother, "I am only so afraid of R. getting spoilt . . . he would lose half his talent if he did. I keep reminding him of it."

Jennie went with him on speaking tours around the country in the early 1880's, but was always exasperated when required to sit for hours with other politicians' wives who wanted to talk trivia when she wanted to talk politics. It was a bit more lively at Aston Park outside Birmingham, where a rioting group of Liberals threw potatoes, chairs, and stones at them.

Jennie was saved from the crush of another crowd by a Colonel Frederick Gustavus Burnaby, six-foot-four with a 47-inch chest. She described him as also having laughing eyes and a heavy dark mustache. "He was a gentle-voiced amiable man, notwithstanding an enormous frame and gigantic strength." Then she added cryptically, "I had occasion to see a good deal of Colonel Burnaby."[6]

Randolph's renewed success in politics animated their social life. "We were bombarded with invitations of every kind," Jennie wrote. "The fashionable world, which had held aloof, now began to smile upon us once more."

This fashionable world that the young Churchills reentered had long been an inbred circle of several hundred people. One could neither push in nor buy in nor break in—one could only be born into it. By the 1880's certain specially favored individuals—favored by royalty or marriage or celebrity or wealth—were gradually admitted, on a conditional basis. If the drastic change could be attributed to one motive, it was the desire for novelty. "In the old days we rather dreaded the social influence of a people we did not know," Lady Dorothy Nevill, London's most celebrated hostess, commented, "but many old families, both in mind and pocket, have been completely revivified by prudent marriages with American brides." She described most of the American female influx as bright and vivacious, and added, "it is by the American girl that we have been conquered." Lady Dorothy was an elderly but vital Victorian lady, well known for her quaint caps and quick wit. She loudly proclaimed her disapproval of "the lip salve and muck" that some women then put on their faces, and she believed all women should wear veils and gloves so that their skin would not look "like a bit of mahogany veneer. . . . I should think," she added, "that the young men would as soon think of kissing a kipper."[7]

Lady Dorothy was very fond of the young Churchills, who had been her neighbors on Charles Street. At her frequent parties she gathered together some of the most vibrant people in London, and Jennie and Randolph were often among them. She was also among the guests at a dinner party given by the Churchills on March 18, 1883 in honor of the Prince and Princess of Wales. The occasion marked the final reconciliation between Prince Edward and Randolph. Others attending included Prime Minister Gladstone and his wife and a small group of similar distinction. "The conversation proved so animated that there was no possibility for awkward thoughts, or looks, or even silences to occur."

There was small question in Lady Dorothy's salon that the gentle persuasion of Jennie had much to do with Prince Edward's decision to be reconciled with Lord Randolph. Shortly before his death, Disraeli had predicted the reconciliation would come about when Randolph was a rising star. "The Prince is always taken by success," he said. It was also the wish of Queen Victoria, who was concerned about any hostility between the royal family and a man who might soon be a Minister of the Crown. Four days before the dinner party for the Prince and Princess, Jennie was invited to the Queen's drawing room.

The Prince of Wales was pleased with his renewed friendship and let it be known: "R. Churchill's manner was *just* what it ought to have been." But he was even more pleased that his relationship with Jennie could be revitalized, and more openly. Prince Edward was soon giving Jennie presents of expensive jewelry; and it was well known that he seldom gave such gifts to a woman with whom he was not having an affair.

Jennie was a frequent guest at the Prince's great, rambling, country home at Sandringham, even though Randolph did not always accompany her. "One felt at home at once," she wrote.

> Indeed, the life was the same as at any pleasant country house. Breakfast, which began at nine o'clock, was served at small, round tables in a dining-room decorated with Spanish tapestries given by the late King of Spain. The men were in shooting get-up, and the ladies in any dress they chose to affect–short skirts and thick boots or elaborate day-gowns. No one cared or noticed. None of the Royalties appeared before midday, although the Prince of Wales joined the shooters, who made an early start after breakfast.

While the men were shooting, the women moved into the large hall to the writing tables, books, magazines, piano. Most often, too, they separated into cliques, usually formed on the first day and kept firm until the final day.

Country-house parties customarily lasted four nights, the guests arriving Tuesday and leaving Saturday. The discreet hostess usually took into account unacknowledged liaisons in assigning bedrooms, each of which had a name in a brass frame outside the door so that after-hours visitors would make no embarrassing mistakes.

The extravagances involved in country-house entertaining were so considerable that some friends of royalty could not afford it. In certain houses of unlimited wealth, it had become customary to have a royal suite especially refurnished for each visit and to replace the regular chef with a specialist. "I could tell stories of men and women who had to economize for a whole year, or alternatively get in debt so that they might entertain royalty for one weekend," wrote Lady Warwick in her memoirs. "Added to the cost of entertaining guests was the cost of caring for accompanying servants, which might mean as many as four hundred more mouths to feed."

A typical lunch for six might include cold pheasant, a couple of partridges, two hot roast fowls, and hot beefsteaks. Dinner always featured a choice of at least two soups, whole salmons and turbots, vast saddles of mutton and sirloins of beef, roast turkeys, several kinds of game such as woodcocks, plovers, and snipe, a large array of vegetables, perhaps some deviled herring and cream cheese, an assortment of pastries, the ever-present, enormous Stilton and Cheshire cheeses, a profusion of wines followed by nuts and preserved fruits, and then some port, madeira, or sherry. Luncheon at Sandringham was usually served in a big tent and was always animated.

> Five o'clock was a feature at Sandringham. The simplicity of the day attire was discarded in favor of elaborate tea gowns . . . Sometimes I played duets with the Princess, who was particularly fond of Brahms' Hungarian Dances, which were just then in vogue. Or it might be that we would go to Princess Victoria's sitting-room, where there were two pianos, and struggle with a Concerto of Schumann. The pace set was terrific, and I was rather glad there was no audience. . . .
>
> Although no uniforms were worn at dinner, this was a ceremonious affair, with everyone in full dress and decorations.

The Queen's Magazine, on the rules of etiquette at such dinners, noted, "The guests are sent into dinner on their first evening according to their rank (except for their Royal Highnesses)." On the second night, however, it became the fashion for gentlemen to draw lots to determine which of the ladies they would escort in to dinner. "Rather unpunctual in those days, I was always on the verge of being late," Jennie remarked.

> . . . When everyone was assembled, Their Royal Highnesses would be announced. . . . The dinner, which never lasted more than an hour, was excellent and admirably ordered, which is not always the case in royal households where indiscriminate profusion is often paramount. Conversation was fairly animated; there was none of that stuffiness which pervaded Windsor and made one fear the sound of one's own voice.
>
> . . . The evenings were not prolonged. . . . The Prince would have his rubber of whist, while the rest of the company sat about and talked until the Princess made a move to go to bed, when the ladies would troop off together, stopping to laugh and chatter in the passages. . . .

The men, meanwhile, moved into the smoking room for a couple of hours before retirement. Prince Edward preferred company who played a good game of bridge or baccarat, knew how to tell good jokes, liked light music rather than classical. Lady Warwick, who knew the Prince intimately, summed up his taste when she said, "As a class, we did not like brains." Of the exceptions, Lady Warwick herself was one and Lady Randolph Churchill another.

Despite her slight deafness, the Princess of Wales was an astute woman who knew how to hide her intelligence, just as she knew how to hide the scar of a burn on her throat with a broad dog-collar of diamonds that soon created a fashion called "La Belle Alexandrine."

(Jennie also had a distinguishing mark, the tattoo of a snake on her wrist, which she usually covered with bracelets. Tattooes were somewhat of a fad at the time—the Prince of Wales had one, as did Czar Nicholas II.[8])

Princess Alexandra's resentment against the many women involved with her husband somehow never extended to Jennie, who always remained her good friend. Sometimes Jennie would be invited into the Princess' room.

> On the perch in the center of the room was an old and somewhat ferocious white parrot, which I remember made disconcerting pecks if you happened to be within his radius.
>
> At other times the Princess might surprise you by coming

to your room, ostensibly "to see if you had everything you
wanted," but in reality to give a few words of advice, or to offer her sympathy if she thought you needed any.

In the midst of this calm sea came a rough shock for Randolph. His father died suddenly in early July 1883. Randolph had dined with him just
the night before. Marlborough had been the steadying influence that Randolph had relied upon, a source of solid, conservative opinion that leav-
ened his own. This contrasted with Jennie's influence, which served as both
a spur and a brake, depending upon his need and his temper.

Randolph and Jennie went to Blenheim for a time, where Randolph
brooded over his father's death, and spent hours rereading the early letters
his father had written him. The *Dictionary of National Biography* termed the
Duke of Marlborough "a sensible, honorable and industrious public man."
Jennie included this description of him in her own memoirs:

> He had always been most kind and charming to me. If
> he seemed rather cold and reserved, he really had an affec-
> tionate nature. Although his children were somewhat in awe
> of him, having been brought up in that old-fashioned way
> which precludes any real intimacy, they were devoted to
> him.

The formality of Randolph's relationship with his father was exceeded
only by Randolph's relationship with his own sons. Years later, Winston
wrote,

> I would far rather have been apprenticed as a bricklayer's
> mate, or run errands as a messenger boy, or helped my fa-
> ther to dress the front windows of a grocer's shop. It would
> have been real; it would have been natural; it would have
> taught me more; and I should have got to know my father,
> which would have been a joy to me.[9]

Aside from generalized animosity toward his son, Randolph had little
faith in Winston's potential. He felt that his son was a boy of small matter
and less mind. Winston's school reports were mixed. He was good in English and history but little else. His teachers complained that he did not
work hard enough, was often late to class, had little ambition. As for his
conduct, it ranged from "troublesome" to "*very* naughty." In a letter to her
husband, Jennie had written, "As to Winston's improvement, I am sorry to
say I see none." She had made a similarly critical comment about Winston

to Leonard Jerome, who promptly answered, "Let him be. Boys get good at what they find they shine at."

"My teachers saw me at once backward and precocious, reading books beyond my years and yet at the bottom of the Form," Winston Churchill reflected. "They were offended. They had large resources of compulsion at their disposal, but I was stubborn. Where my reason, imagination or interest were not engaged, I would not or I could not learn."

School was loathsome. It seethed with brutality, yet somehow he could not or would not transmit to his parents the details of this brutality. How his father would have snorted at him had he complained! The practices of fagging and flogging were typical of the entire British public-school system. "I counted the days and the hours to the end of every term when I should return from this hateful servitude, and range my soldiers in line of battle on the nursery floor."

He was nine years old then, and his private army of 1,500 toy soldiers represented a kind of final retreat, a make-believe world where he could convert his loneliness into dramatic action which he alone controlled. His soldiers were all of the same size, and he had arranged them as a British infantry division with a cavalry brigade.

He organized wars, maneuvered the soldiers into battle, committed great casualties with peas and pebbles, stormed forts, charged his cavalry, destroyed bridges, surrounded the enemy with real water tanks.

His visiting cousins would watch with wonder, but Winston never allowed them to touch anything. However, when a plaything broke, he would let one of the younger children keep it. Among the things the other children thus collected was a mastless ship, a model theater whose figures could be manipulated from the wings, and some tattered copies of boys' adventure magazines.

Toddling along with the children was three-year-old brother Jack Churchill. The two brothers would always be separated more by their difference of personality than by their difference in age. Nonetheless, Jack's admiration for his older, more adventurous, more successful brother remained so unbounded and uncritical that their family feeling was strong and affectionate.

Winston vented some of his frustration in make-believe battles, but more was manifested in his public behavior. Some of his cousins remembered him as "full of fun and quite unself-conscious." Others, though, saw him as "a little upstart" who had even taught Jack how to use a pea-shooter. His dancing teacher, Miss Vera Moore, called him "the naughtiest small boy in the world." The future Lady Barlow, then a little girl, remembered a party that year during which the footman came in to tell Winston, "Your nurse has called for you, sir." Winston told the footman, "Tell her to wait."

The little girl asked with awe, "Can you make your nurse wait?" And Winston answered, "Everything and everybody waits for me."

That year was one of rebellion, of antagonism toward a world that had given him little. At another children's party, Winston arrived dressed in a sailor-suit, protesting aloud. One of the young women wanted to know, soothingly, what was wrong. "My clothes," he said. "I told them they were wrong, and of course they are!"

If Winston was in danger of being a prig, he was in greater danger of being a suppressed, embittered little boy, full of frustrations, and hungry for affection. He idolized his mother. She was still his own fairy princess, even more perfect in his imagination because he saw her so seldom. He considered every visit a privilege, every excursion a special pleasure. Jennie gave him little of herself then. In 1883, she was twenty-nine years old, but she wrote, "I shall not acknowledge it to the world, twenty-six is quite enough!" Women considered thirty the deadly age, especially those who concerned themselves more with men than with children, more with love than with schools, more with the enticements of life than with its chores.

Jennie crowded her life that year with politics, the Prince of Wales, her husband's illness, her house, the pulsing whirl of an intense social life, and a new lover. During the summer of 1883, Count Charles Kinsky rode his own chestnut mare, "Zoedone," in the Grand National and became the first amateur ever to win that race—despite 14–1 odds. They toasted him in all the racing clubs, named drinks after him, made him the social hero of the hour.

The handsome, dashing Charles Rudolf Ferdinand Andreas Kinsky was twenty-five—four years younger than Jennie—had served as honorary attaché at the Austro-Hungarian Embassy in London since 1881, and had been made Imperial Chamberlain early in 1883. His father was Ferdinand, seventh Prince Kinsky, whom Jennie probably met when he toured Ireland with the Empress of Austria in 1879. Count Kinsky's mother was a Lichtenstein Princess, and the whole family was branched deep into the heritage of European history.[10]

The most fashionable party place in London then was the New Club at Covent Garden, and Count Kinsky was host at a small dance attended by the Prince of Wales, the Duke of Braganza (who later became King of Portugal), the King of Greece, and Archduke Rudolph of Austria. Kinsky invited Jennie;[11] there is no record of her husband being there. Jennie described the evening as "most animated . . . we danced till the early hours of the morning, to the music of Tziganes, then a new importation."

She wrote nothing more about that evening, but Count Kinsky had come into her life to stay. He was a fiery young man, highly romantic and impulsive. Emotionally, he and Jennie were a matched pair.

Nonetheless, Jennie was deeply conscious of her position and her children. She often had guilt feelings about Winston. His health was still "very delicate," and his complaints about St. George's School were now frequent, so she found him a smaller, more informal school in Brighton, close to where the family doctor, Robson Roose, lived. The Brighton school was run by two kind ladies who promoted an atmosphere of permissiveness. Jennie also insisted to Randolph that they take Winston with them on their vacation that summer to the Austrian Alps.

They all went to Gastein, a well-known "watering place" where the accent was on the simple life. There was little to do besides climbing mountains and taking mineral baths, but there were some interesting people. "In our walks we frequently met Bismarck with his big boar-hound, two detectives following him closely," wrote Jennie. "One day as he was walking rather slowly, we tried to pass him, whereupon, much to my annoyance, the detectives rushed forward in a most threatening manner. I had no idea we looked like anarchists."

One afternoon the Churchills were invited to tea with Emperor William I.

> The Emperor was a fine-looking man, notwithstanding his age, and he had that old-world manner which is as attractive as it is rare. He was full of gaiety, and chaffed some of the young people present. It was a mystery to me how he survived what he ate and drank, although he was doing a cure. He began with poached eggs, and went on to potted meats and various strange German dishes, added many cups of strong tea, and ended with strawberries, ices, and sweet, tepid champagne. We talked *banalities*; it was not very exciting.

In a letter to his friend Wolff, Randolph also described the meeting:

> The Emperor I must admit was very guarded in his conversation, which was confined to asking me how long I had been here, and whether I had come for my health. I imitated his reserve. My wife, however, sat by him at tea, and had much conversation which, I have ascertained, was confined to the most frivolous topics. I have reason to believe, though it is humiliating to confess it, that the fame of the Fourth Party has not yet reached the ears of this despot. I must say he is a very fine old fellow and the Germans seem to love him. There are several other Prussians and Austrians present; but I was rather bored on the whole and so was my wife.

> They wanted us to go the next night, when they had arranged some tableaux for the old boy, but I sent an excuse on the ground that I was in deep mourning. We did not come here to kowtow to monarchs.

Toward the end of their stay, Blandford, now the eighth Duke of Marlborough, joined them for some mountain climbing. Their father's death had brought the brothers close together again.

Blandford had been divorced by his wife that year. Even though Lady Aylesford had given birth to his child in Paris, he had decided not to marry her.[12] Now Blandford insisted that Randolph and Jennie join him at Blenheim for the rest of the year with Jennie to act as Blenheim's hostess. Jennie hesitated. "My American efficiency will out," she said, "and they will call me bossy." But they decided to go. Because of Randolph's recurring depressions, the attraction of Blenheim was strong. And Jennie was probably intrigued with the idea of being mistress of a palace.

As Blenheim's hostess, Jennie had trouble remembering the names of the 200 great governing families of England, as well as their lineages and titles. It was equally difficult to keep straight the detailed protocol of servant duties. For example, if a fire needed to be lit, you *never* rang for the butler. If you did, he would inform you, coolly but politely, "I shall send for the footman."

One of their frequent guests was George Nathaniel Curzon, a Fellow at Oxford who later became Viceroy of India. Over six feet tall and proportionately broad, Curzon had a head too small for his large body, and a face incongruous to it—chubby and exceptionally young-looking. He could be cordial; but more often he affected the grand manner, his demeanor cold, hard, completely lacking the "common touch." His conversation, often bordering on the brilliant, flashed with wit and laughter and fine phrases. Margot Asquith considered him "a remarkably intelligent person in an exceptional generation," but others regarded him as an intellectual fop, often obnoxious in his icy arrogance and limitless vanity. He was the subject of a widely circulated doggerel:

> *I am a most superior person,*
> *My name is George Nathaniel Curzon.*
> *My face is pink, my hair is sleek,*
> *I dine at Blenheim once a week.*

Curzon added his name to the long list of men who fell in love with Jennie. She appreciated his intelligence and natural eloquence, but she had too many prior claims on her affections to consider Curzon.[13]

HE FOURTH PARTY was in a kind of limbo in 1883, and sir Henry Wolff proposed an idea. The primrose had been Disraeli's favorite flower, and Wolff was given one to wear on the anniversary of Disraeli's death. In Parliament that day, he was struck by the number of other House members also wearing the primrose.

Why not start a Primrose League? "Let's go off and do it at once," Randolph answered.

The League became fully operational that winter and was a complicated affair with distinctive titles and badges and decorations. Men were Knights, women officers were Dames, and clubs were called Habitations. Randolph had his mother made president of the Ladies Grand Council and Jennie made a Dame.[1] "As a Dame I was determined to do all I could to further its aims," Jennie said. "The wearing of the badge exposed me to much chaff, not to say ridicule, but we persisted."

The Primrose League was a brash innovation, a kind of political-social organization through which Conservatives could gather, no matter what their class, to discuss issues, listen to their leaders, and participate in election work. Churchill's critics at first regarded the League as "another of Randy's pranks," but it soon had almost two million members, a large portion of the Tory Party.

The most startling result of the Primrose League was that it put women into politics. British women in the 1880's were already reading "Modern Love," going to the new colleges, some even practicing as doctors.[2] They were not, however, emancipated enough for the House of Commons to pass an amendment to the Reform Bill of 1884 to the effect that "words importing to the masculine gender" should be interpreted as embracing the fair sex. Englishwomen were still generally considered the "fags and fans" of their pretentious men, waiting only for their husbands' command. Englishmen were supposed to show a similar reaction to their women as to their horses, using the same word to describe both. The word was "fine."[3]

It is not difficult to imagine that the force that created the Ladies Grand Council of the Primrose League was the highly persuasive force of Lady Randolph herself. She knew from her own experience the stimulation and fascination of politics for women eager to escape the routine of running a household and to move away from personal problems into the realm of the unexpected, of association with people of all classes and kinds, of commitment to a cause. As a fifth member of the Fourth Party hierarchy, she would not have found it hard to convince them.

> I became Dame President of many Habitations and used to go all over the country inaugurating them. The opening speeches were often quaint in their conceptions, a mixture of grave and gay, serious and frivolous—speeches from members of Parliament, interspersed with songs and even recitations, sometimes of a comical nature. The meeting would end with the enrollment of converts.
>
> A strange medley, the laborer and the local magnate, the county lady and the grocer's wife, would troop up to sign the roll. Politics, like charity, are great levelers.

She told how Lady Salisbury rebuked a member who complained that some proposed entertainment might be attractive to the masses but was really slightly vulgar. "Vulgar? Of course it is vulgar," said Lady Salisbury, then president of the Ladies Executive Council, "but that is why we have got on so well."[4]

Jennie not only traveled the Primrose League trail for her own purposes, making her own speeches, but she also continued to accompany her husband on his major political trips. By the beginning of 1884, Randolph again had energized his passion for politics. Speaking in Blackpool, he made a blistering speech, one of his best:

> Gentlemen, we live in an age of advertisement, the age of Holloway's pills, of Coleman's mustard, and of Horniman's

pure tea; and the policy of lavish advertisement has been so successful in commerce that the Liberal Party, with its usual enterprise, has adopted it to politics. The Prime Minister is the greatest living master of the art of personal political advertisement. . . . Every act of his, whether it be for the purposes of health, or of recreation, or of religious devotion, is spread before the eyes of every man, woman and child in the United Kingdom on large and glaring placards. . . . For the purposes of recreation, he has selected the felling of trees; and we may usefully remark that his amusements, like his politics, are essentially destructive. Every afternoon the whole world is invited to assist at the crashing fall of some beech or elm or oak. The forest laments, in order that Mr. Gladstone may perspire. . . . [5]

So similar in style and tone were the speeches Jennie and Randolph made that some of their closer friends openly wondered about it. One friend of particular courage, Cecil Spring–Rice, made mention to the Dowager Duchess of Marlborough of this apparent wifely influence. The Duchess bristled and answered icily that the only real influence on Lord Randolph's career was his mother.

It was true that the Duchess was a growing influence. With the death of the Duke, she concentrated completely on furthering the fame and fortune of her second son. "She idolized him," observed George Smalley. "She talked of him often to those whom she knew to be his friends, and she thought of him continually. She made sacrifices for him; to her they were none because they were for him. In him, her life centered . . ."[6]

Randolph, in turn, visited his mother more often, especially after she moved to her London house in Grosvenor Square. And when he traveled, his letters to his mother still were longer and more affectionate than those to his wife. Yet he continued to deeply respect Jennie's judgment and advice. The fight between Jennie and the Duchess for control over Randolph ended only with his death.

Whatever Jennie did, she did with high style. One of her widely copied social inventions was the "dinner of deadly enemies." A guest at her first such dinner, Smalley later described it:

It was thought a hazardous experiment. It proved a complete success. They were all well-bred people. They all recognized their obligations to their hostess as paramount for the time being. They were Lady Randolph's guests; that was enough. As guests, they were neither friends nor enemies.

There were no hostilities. The talk flowed on smoothly. When a man found himself sent in to dinner with a woman he did not speak to, his tongue was somehow unloosed; it was a truce. In some cases, ancient animosities were softened. In all, they were suspended. The guests all knew each other; and as they looked about the table, they all saw that Lady Randolph had attempted the impossible, and had conquered. A social miracle had been performed.[7]

Part of the challenge was to eliminate all consciousness that these dinners had a political purpose. Yet there could hardly be any such dinner without political discussion, even argument. At one affair, attended by Joseph Chamberlain, Liberal Party leader and President of the Board of Trade under Gladstone, Randolph was expounding on the connection between class and character in the ruling of India: "He [a typical member of the upper class] knew how to govern because he came of a governing class," Randolph said. "And he was a gentleman. Whereas now," he added, looking directly at Chamberlain, "instead of gentlemen, you get men from–Birmingham and God knows where."

Chamberlain was a man of elegant features who wore a monocle and faultless attire. A self-made millionaire, he had retired from business at thirty-eight, and gone into politics. After achieving a brilliant record as a reform mayor of Birmingham, he had moved into Parliament at the age of forty. The public called him "Pushful Joe," and Randolph's verbal knife had plunged deep. But cool and smiling, Chamberlain simply noted that it was time to join the ladies. "Instantly the clouds cleared," said Smalley. "India was forgotten. The two combatants walked up the stairs arm in arm, and the storm was as if it had never been."

Jennie's own remarks often had a more caustic edge now. During one hectic political crisis, a visiting political leader told her he had not yet made up his mind whether to vote for or against Randolph the next day. "I shall be a man or a mouse," he told her.

"Or a rat," she responded, with only the smallest smile.[8]

One reported comment that reached her was that a Mrs. Stephens had told a Mrs. Farquhar that she "hoped little Lady Randolph had better manners than she had last year." But that acerbic quality had become one of Jennie's weapons and she kept it sharp for ready use. She had started to paint seriously that year and was once cornered at one of her house parties by Joseph Chamberlain, Sir William Harcourt, and Sir Charles Dilke–all political rivals of Randolph. The three men begged her to paint their portraits. "Where can you find more attractive models?" they asked.

"Impossible," said Jennie smiling. "I should fail."

They wanted to know why.

"I could never paint you black enough," said Jennie, still smiling.[9]

Sir Charles Dilke was an impressive-looking man with a brilliant political future and an obvious charm for women. When Mrs. J. Comyns-Carr mentioned to Lady Lindsay that she would like to meet Dilke, she was told, "There's always a waiting list, you know." But Dilke was so smitten with Jennie that he got down on his knees and begged her to be his mistress. Jennie afterward related the incident to Lord Rosebery, pointing out how ridiculous Dilke looked on his knees, and Rosebery wrote the story in his private papers. Randolph heard of the incident and physically attacked Dilke. Reference to all this was obliquely made by Dilke, who, without supplying details, told of his friendship with Randolph which was ended when Randolph attacked him.

Dilke later was caught in a messy scandal involving prostitutes, bizarre sex practices, and adultery, and it killed his career.[10] Years after, Jennie wrote in a published essay that there were many British society leaders who could "live down scandals, whereas the less-favored go under emphasizing the old saying, 'One may steal a horse while another may not look over the wall.' "[11]

She may have been referring to herself or the Prince of Wales or a dozen other people. As for Randolph, however, there were almost never any women remotely connected with his name. One of the few was Lady Gladys de Grey, a good friend of Jennie's, "a luxurious woman with perfect manners, a kind disposition and a moderate sense of duty." She was also beautiful, perceptive, and charming. Emotionally, however, she was so high-strung and easily agitated that even the cry of the cuckoo made her feel ill. She hardly seemed a candidate for the affections of the even more volatile Randolph.[12]

It further seemed that the growing danger and doom of his syphilis had alienated him from all women, except his mother. Much whispered comment was made of the fact that Randolph took a great many short trips on the Continent without Jennie—always with individual men friends, always the same ones reappearing. They were not political friends, nor were they generally invited to the Churchills' dinners or parties—they were Randolph's personal friends.

"Randolph is a woman and I never seem to manage women,"[13] Lord Salisbury told a friend of Lady Constance Leslie. Her friend added, "Indeed, it is quite true that Lord Randolph has a feminine side, and a large side, to his nature."

That would clarify many things—failure of his marriage with Jennie, her search for other men, her newly acquired harshness. It would also explain his utter lack of relationship with his sons and his very strong ties to his mother. If this were the case, it was certainly not so when he married Jennie, for theirs was initially a physical love. The catalyst for the growing change was the resurgent syphilis.

At this time, Jennie was taking lessons in painting from Mrs. E. M. Ward,[14] the wife of a noted artist. Among Mrs. Ward's pupils were the Princess of Wales, the Duchess of Albany, and assorted other royalty. Jennie was occupied "very violently" with her painting and was soon "martyrizing many models, paid and unpaid, covering miles of canvas with impossible daubs, and spending a small fortune in paints and pigments." Whenever he was home on holiday, Winston liked to watch his mother paint, and he soon tried it himself. It became one of the few subjects at school that he really liked and excelled in. From school he soon wrote how he had begun "shading. I have been drawing little landscapes and bridges, and those sorts of things."

Jennie was soon herself made a model of sorts, one of the so-called PBs, the Professional Beauties, an elite group of England's most beautiful women, whose photographs were sold in shops all over the country.[15] "The first time mine found its way into a shop," she said, "I was severely censured by my friends, and told I ought to prosecute the photographer." Of course, she didn't—the flattery apparently counterbalanced the notoriety. In addition to the photographs, there were persistent publicity, interviews, and magazine articles about the PBs. A poem about these women named a dozen of them. About Jennie, it said,

> *Then Lady Randolph Churchill, whose sweet tones*
> *Make her the Saint Cecilia of the day . . .*

The PBs became a highly prized asset at all social affairs. Hostesses would tack onto invitations, "Do come; the PBs will be here." Lily Langtry was one of the most celebrated PBs, and was once so crushed by her admiring crowd that she needed an ambulance to rescue her. "Whatever happens, I do not intend to grow old," Langtry told Lady Warwick.[16] The man who most approved of that sentiment was Leonard Jerome. He courted Langtry heavily when she came to New York, introduced her and Oscar Wilde to the city society at a round of his famous dinners. Langtry called him "Uncle Leonard."

Leonard's daughter Clara would have qualified as another PB, but she and her French maid and Moreton Frewen were far distant in their log house at Big Horn, Wyoming, with few visitors except bears, buffalo and such friends as Lord Queensberry and Buffalo Bill.

A number of Englishmen had invested heavily in American cattle and real estate. The Duke of Sutherland alone owned some 500,000 acres, and two English syndicates had bought seven million acres in Texas. But the big attraction for the British visitors was the hunting of American bear. Moreton's interest, however, was in his 45,000 head of cattle. But the story is that, wise as he supposedly was to the ways of the West, Frewen once stood on a hilltop and bought the same herd of 7,000 cattle three times while the herd was driven in a circle around the hill.

Something more serious at the time was Clara's pregnancy. The nearest doctor was in Cheyenne, two hundred miles away, a four-day trip by the Deadwood Coach. The child was stillborn, and was sent back to the family burial plot in Greenwood Cemetery in Brooklyn. Clara went to recuperate in New York. Moreton stayed behind, until his father-in-law ordered him to return to Clara.

Leonie now announced her own marriage plans. Her fiancé was Lieutenant John Leslie of the British Grenadier Guards, whom she had met four years earlier while visiting Jennie in Ireland. The romance had been discouraged because Mrs. Jerome wanted at least one French son-in-law and Lady Leslie preferred an English bride for her only son. It hardly helped matters that the former Elizabeth Livingston of Staatsburgh, New York, who had married British socialite George Bentinck, had told the Leslies that Leonard Jerome was a dustman whose coach was used to remove offal. Lady Leslie's friends also informed her that Mrs. Jerome was three-quarters Indian. Sir John Leslie promptly warned Leonard Jerome that his estates were his own, and not necessarily willed to his children. Jerome's answer was curt: "Letter received."

The wedding was posh. Wedding gown by Worth; the famous Bishop Potter of New York performing the service in Grace Church; guests including the Astors, the Belmonts, the Livingstons, the Van Burens. A society reporter noted, somewhat inaccurately, "Mr. Leslie [is] an intimate friend of Lord Churchill's, and his income amounts to 30,000 pounds a year. Miss Jerome is worth a quarter of a million in her own right."[17] The press did not note the Leslie family's disapproval—the bridegroom's sisters were not even allowed to cable their congratulations.

Ritzman's in London meanwhile added the photographs of Leonie and Clara to their window display of Professional Beauties, but *Town Topics* commented, "Pretty as these two heads are, neither can compare in beauty with the second sister, Jennie."

The reunion of the Jerome sisters at Leonie's wedding was a short one, but that must have been the time when Jennie persuaded her sisters to move to England so that they could all live close together. Mrs. Jerome would follow her daughters shortly.

Only Leonard Jerome stayed behind. He rented his house on Madison Square as a gaming club for $25,000 a year. The club specialized in baccarat and poker, and featured a big blackboard posted with racing results from Paris and London. Jerome moved to the Brunswick Hotel on Fifth Avenue, considered the headquarters of the aristocratic "horsey set." It was also the meeting place for Jerome's Coaching Club, which he still conducted wearing a whole bouquet in the buttonhole of his bright green coat.

Upon her return to England, Jennie found Randolph's health and disposition worsening. About that time, Randolph's friend Frank Harris came to visit. Born in Ireland, educated in Kansas, where he had become an American citizen. Harris was editor of the *Evening News*. "While we were talking the door opened and Lady Randolph appeared," Harris remembered.

> Naturally, I got up as she called out, "Randolph," but he sat still. In spite of his ominous silence, she came across to him, "Randolph, I want to talk to you!"
>
> "Don't you see," he retorted, "that I've come here to be undisturbed?"
>
> "But I want you," she repeated.
>
> He sprang to his feet. "Can't I have a moment's peace from you anywhere?" he barked. "Get out and leave me alone!" At once she turned and walked out of the room.[18]

It was a single, small incident. By itself, it might have little meaning, but it was part of a pattern.

Randolph's mind was now tormented and his health tortured. His syphilis apparently was entering the third stage.

During this stage, the disease can take many forms. Decay may penetrate to the bone or erode the membranes of the mouth and rectum or form dead areas in the liver, kidney, brain, or heart. No organ is immune to the danger. Erosion of the brain's fragile blood vessels or a gradual disintegration of the cerebrum can stretch out interminably. As the infection increases, the syphilitic brain gradually becomes detached from reality, disconnected from the evidence of its senses. It functions with intervals of fantasy that can be either pleasant or violent. These fantasies are often patterned on a distorted imitation of reality, but gradually they become progressively abstract and meaningless.

It was then Randolph decided to travel to India and Egypt—without Jennie. He was trying to escape something from which there was no escape.

ANDOLPH'S STAY IN THE EAST LASTED four months. with him was
Thomas Trafford, his favorite traveling companion. Trafford had
been in the Churchill party on Randolph's visit to the United States in 1876
and had accompanied him on a number of shorter trips. Friends had
thought it strange that Randolph did not delay his departure a few weeks
so that he could spend the Christmas holidays with his family at home. Jennie had wanted to go to India and was bitter about being left behind. Soon
afterward, she met G. E. Buckle, editor of *The Times*, who had written a critical editorial about Randolph that morning. Buckle smilingly approached
Jennie and asked if she would still speak to him, or whether she was too angry.

"Angry? Not a bit," she said. "I have ten volumes of press cuttings about
Randolph, all abusive. This will only be added to them."[1]

"I cannot remember one friend of mine who was really happy," said
Frances, Countess of Warwick, a close friend of Jennie's who shared with
her the unofficial title of the prettiest young matron in London. Both were
women of sharp minds and rounded figures, often diaphanously draped.
They were both unhappy in their marriages and had competed for the intimacy of the Prince of Wales. "Each of us knew that disillusion must follow . . . ," she wrote. "In the feverish search for pleasure, any woman might
lose her lover."[2]

Jennie was not lonely during those winter months. Lucille, the heroine of Winston Churchill's novel *Savrola*, was modeled after his mother.

> . . . her life had been a busy one. Receptions, balls and parties had filled the winter season with unremitting labor of entertaining. Foreign princes had paid her homage, not only as the loveliest woman in Europe, but also as a great political figure. Her salon was crowded with the most famous men from every country. Statesmen, soldiers, poets and men of science had worshiped at the shrine. She had mixed in matters of State. Suave and courtly ambassadors had thrown out delicate hints, and she had replied with unofficial answers. Plenipotentiaries had explained the details of treaties and protocols, with remarkable elaboration, for her benefit. Philanthropists had argued, urged and expounded their views and whims. Everyone talked to her of public business. Even her maid had approached her with an application for the advancement of her brother, a clerk in the Post Office; and everyone had admired her until admiration itself, the most delicious drink that a woman tastes, became insipid.

Lucille's husband "saw her less and less frequently," and she then took a lover.

Jennie saw much of the Prince of Wales during that time, and she saw even more of Count Kinsky. Kinsky was still the hero of the hour in England because of his victory in the Grand National. Every man wanted him at his table and a long waiting list of women wanted him in their boudoirs. He had not only brawn but brain. He was handsome, charming, a rising diplomat with a talent for words, a sparkling pianist, a man with an easy laugh and a firm grip. Jennie's brother-in-law Moreton Frewen called Kinsky "the best Austrian that ever was," and printed his photograph in his memoirs;[3] Leonie named Kinsky godfather to her second son. Randolph Churchill himself was proud to call Kinsky his friend through the years, despite the fact that Jennie's romance with the Count was an open secret all over London.

But it was still a furtive romance. Kinsky could only visit her when Randolph was away. Not only was she a married woman, but her husband had become one of the most important politicians in England.

Though Kinsky concentrated on Jennie, therefore, his attentions were not exclusive. He was a womanizer, and the women were always available. Jennie frankly exploited some of her own anxious admirers to stir up Kinsky's jealousy. One of them was an extremely handsome horseman and boxer named Peter Flower. Leonie hinted to Kinsky that Jennie liked

Flower "dangling about" and noted that Kinsky promptly went to Jennie and demanded an explanation.[4]

To help fill the big house at Connaught Place, Jennie invited her sister Leonie to stay while John Leslie was serving with the Guards in England. Clara had settled in nearby Sussex, in a bleak and beautiful stone house of Brede Place at the edge of the Frewen estates. Built in 1350, it had been occupied only by gamekeepers for more than two hundred years and still had wells from which the water was hauled and old-style privies. Moreton Frewen's anticipated fortune in cattle had disappeared in a severe drought. In the course of coming years, Moreton would spend most of his time away from home in every part of the world, searching for a fortune he would never find.

Leonie, also, was having her troubles, mainly with her mother-in-law, Lady Leslie. For many months, her mother-in-law refused even to recognize Leonie's social existence. A formidable woman of firm opinions, Lady Leslie also had a terrible temper. Relatives still remembered her as the headstrong Constance who jumped onto the windowsill of her Berkeley Square home and threatened to "dash herself down if not yielded to in a dispute." Her language could be similarly strong. Leonie noted in her diary that she had received "a vile letter" from Lady Leslie and "it makes me . . . feel so wretched. . . ."[5]

So there they were, the three Jerome sisters, an exceptional trio of beauty, talent, energy, and character—each woman undergoing a variety of misery in her marriage, each skimming along on a financial shoestring, each unable or unwilling to alter her way of life. They went everywhere together. A critic called them "The Beautiful, the Witty, and the Good"[6] (Jennie, Leonie, and Clara in that order). Others called Clara "beautiful, blonde, and brainless"; Jennie, "flashing, brainy, and social"; and Leonie, "the one with the most character."

The three sisters shared a love of music and the theater. Fanny Ronalds still held her Sunday afternoon salons for music lovers, and the Jerome sisters were often in attendance. They were also constantly at the opera. As they couldn't afford boxes of their own, their good friend, Covent Garden manager Harry Higgins, often let them sit in various boxes to "paper" the house, where they "could see without being seen."[7]

Leonard Jerome's fortune had almost disintegrated. He had settled $10,000 a year on Jennie, part of the income from rental of the Madison Square house. In addition, he sent $2,000 a year now to the improvident Leonie and John. Moreton still pretended to provide for Clara, and occasionally did, but Leonard told his wife that he himself hoped to send $2,000 a year to Clara. He did rent a house for her on Aldford Street, close to Jennie. And Leonie soon moved to nearby Seymour Street.

But the three Jerome sisters lived as if money would always be available. It was true that Jennie spent little on jewelry. One of her few pieces, and her favorite, was a large diamond star which she wore low on the brow. It was remarkably similar to the diamond star worn by the heroine of one of Disraeli's novels, *The Divine Theodora*. What Jennie and the others did not spend on jewelry, they spent on clothes. Leonie, however, whose husband was still a poorly paid officer in the Guards, was happy to accept Jennie's cast-off Worth gowns.[8]

Following in his famous father's tradition, Jean Worth in Paris was Europe's most distinguished dress designer. With his pointed beard and his steady smile, Worth was an impressive figure. He seldom met his clients, except a few favored ones from the French Empire days, such as the Jerome women. He would study them as a painter might, until inspiration came. Quickly, then, he would outline the dress in the air, order special fabrics in particular colors from his anxious assistants, and make his expectant customers pose for him while his dress creation evolved. The cost was proportionate to the creation—up to five hundred dollars for a dress. He frankly confided to one of his clients that the reason he was so interested in every gown he made was that "every Worth creation must be the advertisement for other Worth creations. Every costume has its advertising value."[9] So strong was the female urge to insure the absolute uniqueness of each Worth dress, that Jennie's future sister-in-law Daisy, Princess of Pless, even had a fringe of real violets sewn into the train of a gown. (It was a gown of transparent lace, lined with blue chiffon and a sprinkling of gold sequins—which would seem to have been unique enough.)

The style in women's clothing had changed considerably in the ten years since Jennie's marriage. The huge bustle moderated gradually, then temporarily disappeared by 1878. Replacing it was a narrowed but highly elaborate skirt fitted tightly over the hips and thighs. Gone was the gown so full that a wind could almost carry a woman away, as Gladstone's daughter Mary once described in her diary. Gone too was the dress so heavily petticoated that it made tennis playing almost impossible—especially when the woman had to use one hand to hold down her hat. The bustle, however, reappeared in 1883, looking more like a camel's hump. The earlier bustle had shot out from the spine like a shelf, on which one could actually place a glass of water or a plate of soup. Back, too, was the wasp waist, which demanded that women corset their ribs so tightly into their liver that it often caused an anemia called "green sickness." Dr. Wardrop's heavily advertised corset featured a light, strong plate, for which he claimed medical approval, "which gives the stomach flatness and grace. . . . The figure is entirely remodeled without undue pressure." The crinoline, or hoop-petticoat, also had been improved to eliminate its "creaking or rattling" and its tendency to sway from side to side as a lady walked. Jennie was one of the first to wear looser dresses of richly colored material, falling in straight lines from a more natural girdle.

At an exhibition in 1882 of "hygienic wearing apparel," the bloomers, introduced unsuccessfully by Mrs. Amelia Jenks Bloomer in the 1840's, were reintroduced, but it took another ten years before they came fully into vogue. Women outdid themselves with their cotton stockings, decorating them with horizontal stripes of green, yellow, or red.[10]

Single women were still not allowed to go anywhere without chaperones. Even married women were never expected to lunch alone in London, and no proper ladies, single or married, were ever expected to walk past the big-windowed private clubs from which men could watch them. In 1882, women were the subject of a national symposium entitled "Our Freedom and its Results." Mary Agnes Hamilton said that there were "very large numbers of otherwise intelligent persons who did sincerely endorse the view that members of the female sex were not human, as members of the male sex were."[11]

Little of this, of course, impeded Jennie. She was thirty years old and long before had broken barriers, stretched rules, ignored conventions. Just as she set her own style in clothing and house decoration, so she set her own pace. She was no fluttering female, and she seldom minced words or suppressed her feelings. "Whenever I want to think of an outstandingly brilliant woman, my mind leaps immediately to Lady Randolph Churchill," later wrote Lady Warwick. ". . . One never thought of giving a party without her. She was as delightful to women as to men. . . . Lady Randolph was like a marvelous diamond—a host of facets seemed to sparkle at once."[12] And Victorian era chronicler Thomas Escott, editor of the *Fortnightly Review*, had commented, "London possesses no more accomplished or charming hostess. . . ."

Wherever Jennie went now, she was questioned about Randolph. His letters to her from India and Egypt were educational rather than emotional. Though he dismissed the Suez Canal as a "dirty ditch," he praised the elephant highly:

> I think the elephant is the best mode of conveyance I know. He cannot come to grief; he never tumbles down nor runs away (at least not on the march); nothing stops him; and when you get accustomed to his pace, he is not tiring. You would not believe what steep places they get up and down or what thick, almost impenetrable jungle, they go through. If a tree is in the way, and not too large a one, they pull it down; if a branch hangs too low for the howdah to go

under, they break it off. They are certainly most wonderful animals, and life in many parts of India would be impossible without them.

Letters to his mother were more exciting: "I have had the great good fortune to kill a tiger. . . ." He told her of riding his elephant and coming across

> the recently killed carcass of a pig, half devoured. Hersey, when he saw it, declared it was quite fresh, and that the tiger must be close by. You may imagine the excitement . . . All of a sudden out bundled this huge creature, right under the nose of Hersey's elephant, and made off across some ground which was slightly open. Hersey fired and missed. I fired and hit him just above the tail. (A very good shot, for he only showed me his stern, and he was at least forty yards off.) Hersey then fired his second barrel, and broke his shoulder, which brought him up (literally with a round turn). He took refuge in a patch of grass about fifty yards from us where we could just see bits of him. Heavens, how he growled, and what a rage he was in! He would have charged us but that he was disabled by Hersey's last shot. We remained still, and gave him four or five more shots which on subsequent examination, we found all told; and then, after about five minutes more awful growling, he expired. Great joy to all! The good luck of getting him was unheard of this time of the year; the odds were a hundred to one against such a thing. He was a magnificent specimen, nine feet seven inches in length, and a splendid skin—which will, I think, look very well in Grosvenor Square. . . . [13]

Randolph did not mention the possibility that the skin would look equally well at his own home in Connaught Place.

To Randolph, Jennie noted petulantly, "You never mentioned me in your letter to your mother . . . ," but throughout his four-month trip, Jennie kept Randolph posted on the family: "The children are flourishing. I hear a much better account of Winston. . . . He is working so much harder this term." Winston's handwriting also had improved slightly, she noted, and "the spelling is not too bad. . . ."

Randolph also got reports from ten-year-old Winston, about the Christmas party, his stamp book getting filled up (but would his father please send him more stamps), how he was learning to dance "and I like it very much," and that the dog Chloe "is very fat indeed. I give her a run every day to take her fat down." He also remarked how nice it was for his father to be "sailing all over the sea," and had a variety of other questions: "Are the Indians very funny?" "Are there many ants in India if so, you will have a nice time, what with ants and mosquitoes . . ."

His father answered few of Winston's letters.

Jennie kept her husband advised, too, on the course of British politics. Gladstone's Liberal Government was in serious trouble on a number of issues: a fiasco in Sudan, a series of dynamitings in Ireland, trouble with Russia over the Afghanistan border, and the failure to reinforce General Gordon at Khartoum. Even the Queen sent her Prime Minister a bitter telegram about Gordon's defeat and death, and Randolph wrote: "Any Hindu who dies at Benares and whose ashes are thrown into the Ganges, goes right bang up to Heaven without stopping, no matter how great a rascal he may have been. I think the G.O.M. [Gladstone] ought to come here; it is his best chance."[14]

In the strange way of politics, Randolph's four months' absence only increased his public popularity. In a *Punch Magazine* cartoon, Fourth Party members Wolff and Gorst stare sadly out to sea, crying, "When *will* he come?" Commenting on this to Jennie, her father wrote:

> I have watched with wonder Randolph's rise in the political world. Over and over he was smashed, pulverized, so ruthlessly squelched that he was considered done forever. And yet, little after, up he comes smiling, as though he had never been hit at all. I confess, I am amazed. So young! So reckless in experience, so impulsive! That he should have fought his way up through the fiery elements without, as the trotters say, a "skip or a break," is indeed wonderful. I hope he will come home soon, and that he will find himself in accord with Lord Salisbury. . . .

It seemed likely that the Gladstone Government would soon fall. In that event, Salisbury would become Prime Minister and Randolph would inevitably be offered an important position.

One of England's men of distinction, Robert Arthur Talbot Gascoyne-Cecil, Lord Salisbury, had twice held the India Office and the Foreign Office and would serve three times as Prime Minister. He had firm opinions, a penetrating mind, a tactless manner. Leadership, he felt, belonged to the men of birth, wealth, and intellectual power. What he said, he usually said with virulence, and sometimes with imprudence and even insolence. He was not a man who measured his phrases.

A massive man—six feet four—with stooped shoulders, almost bald but with a curly gray beard, Salisbury preferred solitude to society, liked to ride a tricycle in St. James Park for exercise, hated hunting or shooting, and was always reluctant to visit the Queen because he thought she kept her castle too cold. An intellectual with a sharp interest in science, Salisbury had fitted up his own chemical laboratory; a melancholy and deeply religious man, he attended his private chapel every morning before breakfast.[15]

Curzon called Salisbury "that strange, powerful, inscrutable, brilliant, obstructive deadweight at the top." In the best of times, it would have been difficult to be "in accord" with Salisbury. But these were the worst of times. Salisbury recognized Randolph for what he then was: brilliant but sick, irresponsible and unpredictable.

At his first appearance in the House after returning from his trip, Randolph was cheerfully greeted by the Tory Party, and even Gladstone walked over to shake his hand. So did Sir Stafford Northcote, whose resignation as the Tory Party leader Randolph had been demanding. Questioned as to what place he would give Lord Randolph if he were asked to form a government, Northcote replied, "Say, rather, what place he will give me."[16] Northcote's point was well made. Not only had Randolph demanded Northcote's dismissal, but he had insisted that if Salisbury became Prime Minister, he should give prominent posts to Fourth Party members. "He had won no battle, negotiated no peace," wrote Winston Churchill of that time. "He had passed no great measure of reform; he had never held public office; he was not even a Privy Councillor; yet he was welcomed on all sides with interest or acclamation."[17]

Winston wrote from school that he had been out riding with a gentleman who "thinks that Gladstone is a brute and thinks that 'the one with the curly mustache' [Randolph Churchill] ought to be Premier." Jerome also wrote a complimentary letter:

> . . . I want to congratulate you on your safe return from the East, and especially on the great good the trip seems to have done you. They all say you are in splendid condition. I should be glad to believe you would keep so, but I fear, from what I read of your doings lately, you will soon put yourself down again. A little less work and not quite so many cigarettes, I fancy, would be better for you. . . .
>
> I might indulge in some complimentary remarks on the "wonderful rise of the young statesman" and how very gratifying . . . but I know it would only bore you.

But Randolph was far less optimistic about his "wonderful rise." When a friend told him that Salisbury could not form a government without him,

Randolph answered, "He can form a Ministry, if necessary, with waiters from the Carleton Club."

After a defeat for Gladstone on a critical vote, Randolph jumped onto the bench in the House of Commons and like a small boy waved a blue handkerchief over his head, yelling taunts at the Liberals. But with Gladstone's overthrow imminent, Churchill's depression grew quickly deeper. "I am very near the end of my tether," he told a friend.

> In the last five years I have lived twenty. I have fought Society. I have fought Mr. Gladstone at the head of a great majority. I have fought the Front Opposition Bench. Now I am fighting Lord Salisbury. I have said I will not join the Government unless Northcote leaves the House of Commons. Lord Salisbury will never give way. I'm done.[18]

Much of this sudden shift from boyish joy to deep depression was a typical symptom of his degenerative disease. The smell of Tory success was in the air, and Jennie was enthusiastic about her husband's new possibilities. She tried to buoy him up as best she could. The rumor was that Randolph would be offered the post of Secretary of State for India when the Conservatives came in.

Randolph had discussed India's problem at a banquet of the Primrose League, shortly after his return.

> Our rule in India is, as it were, a sheet of oil spread out over the surface of, and keeping calm and quiet and unruffled by storms, an immense and profound ocean of humanity. Underneath that rule lie hidden all the memories of fallen dynasties, all the traditions of vanquished races, all the pride of insulted creeds. . . .

Home barely a month, however, Randolph decided he needed still another holiday abroad, this time to France. Going with him was his friend Sir Henry James.

Caught up in the political turmoil which might heighten their need of each other, Jennie and Randolph now wrote more affectionate letters. "Darling dearest petit R . . ." "Petit R." was her most endearing nickname for him. And he answered, "My dearest Jennie."

Shortly upon Randolph's return from France in June, Prime Minister Gladstone resigned after a parliamentary defeat on an unimportant budget amendment. The Queen asked Lord Salisbury to form a government.

Many felt that Randolph might now compromise his demands for North-cote's removal and Fourth Party rewards. But he remained adamant. Salisbury seemed stymied. This angered the Queen, who wired Salisbury that she did not think Lord Randolph Churchill should be allowed to dictate his own terms, especially since he had never before held a Cabinet office. Even the Dowager Duchess intervened, appealing to Randolph by letter to reconsider his demands and to reconcile himself with the new Salisbury Government. Randolph refused, and his reinforced resolution won out. Northcote was eased upstairs into the House of Lords, and Fourth Party members Wolff, Gorst, and Balfour were all brought into the Government. As for Randolph, Salisbury appointed him Secretary of State for India after Queen Victoria said she had "no insuperable objection."

Randolph's term as M.P. (they called him "The Wasp from Woodstock") was up at the same time. He had neither the time nor the energy to work for votes there, so Jennie took charge and single-handedly supervised his reelection campaign, to insure his seat in the House. It was a key election. Randolph Churchill's defeat at that particular time would have meant an enormous victory for the Liberals, who mounted an energetic campaign to overthrow him. True, it was a family borough, and Marlborough support had considerable meaning. But at first Jennie did not even have that vital help. Shortly after Blandford had succeeded to the Dukedom, he had sold many of the family treasures at Blenheim. He and Randolph had quarreled bitterly about it, and the Duke was not anxious now to help Randolph's reelection. Though Blandford permitted Jennie to stay at Blenheim, she had to maintain her committee rooms at the nearby Bear Hotel. Pressed by Jennie's pleas, he finally relented enough to loan her his carriages to help bring voters to the polls.

"We held daily confabulations with the friends and Members of Parliament who had come to help," she wrote.

> We were most important, and felt that the eyes of the world were upon us. Revelling in the hustle and bustle of the Committee rooms, marshaling our forces, and hearing the hourly reports of how the campaign was progressing, I felt like a general holding a council-of-war with his staff in the heat of battle. A. was doubtful, B. obdurate, while C's wife, a wicked abominable Radical, was trying to influence her husband whom we thought secure, to vote the wrong way. At once they must be visited and our arsenal of arguments brought to bear on them.

Jennie traveled in her sister-in-law's tandem, the horses decorated gaily with the ribbons of Randolph's racing colors, pink and brown. There were a thousand voters to be reached.

> The distances to cover were great. . . . Sometimes we would drive into the fields, and getting down, climb into the hayricks, falling upon our unwary prey at his work. There was no escaping us. . . . Sometimes with these simple country folk a pleading look, and an imploring "Oh please vote for my husband; I shall be so unhappy if he does not get in," or, "If you want to be on the winning side, vote for us; as of course we are going to win.[19]

The Primrose League was still in the embryonic stage in Woodstock, with no Habitation to supply Jennie with Primrose Dames. She therefore had to scour up her own workers. This was the first time that Primrose badges were worn in an actual political campaign. "Party feeling ran high," said Jennie, "and in outlying districts we would frequently be pursued by our opponents, jeering and shouting at us; but this we rather enjoyed."

Reception committees greeted her with jingling rhymes about her campaigning. One of them went this way:

> *But just as I was talking*
> *With Neighbor Brown and walking*
> *To take a mug of beer at the Unicorn and Lion,*
> *(Because there's somehow a connection*
> *Between free beer and election)*
> *Who should come but Lady Churchill, with a turnout that was fine.*
>
> *And before me stopped her horses,*
> *As she marshaled all her forces,*
> *And before I knew what happened I had promised her my vote;*
> *And before I quite recovered*
> *From the vision that had hovered,*
> *'Twas much too late to rally, and I had changed my coat.*
>
> *And over Woodstock darted*
> *On their mission brave, wholehearted,*
> *The tandem and their driver and the ribbons pink and brown.*
> *And a smile that twinkled over,*
> *And that made a man most love her*
> *Took the hearts and votes of all Liberals in the town.*

Bless my soul! That Yankee lady,
Whether day was bright or shady,
Dashed about the district like an oriflamme of war.
When the voters saw her bonnet,
With the bright pink roses on it,
They followed as the soldiers did the Helmet of Navarre.[20]

Randolph could not have been more pleased. "I should be very glad if you could arrange to stay in Woodstock till Friday," he wrote Jennie. "If I win, you will have all the glory."

Widely covered by the press, the election was considered important enough for newspapermen to send some six hundred "result" messages on the final victory. Randolph had received a majority of 127 votes, more than twice the majority he had received five years before.

The lady from Brooklyn had traveled a long, strange road to where she now stood in front of the historic Bear Hotel in this old English village, thanking the large, enthusiastic crowd for her husband's victory. One day her son Winston would stand at that same place thanking the people for his own victory.

"I surpassed the fondest hopes of the suffragettes," Jennie reflected,

and thought I was duly elected, and I certainly experienced all the pleasure and gratification of being a successful candidate. I returned to London feeling that I had done a very big thing, and was surprised and astonished that the crowds in the streets looked at me with indifference. . . . I often think that these must be the sensations of a newly made Member of Parliament when he first goes to the House of Commons, fresh from the hustings of his own meetings, where his dullest and silliest inanity is listened to and applauded. In the House he finds his level, alas! only too soon, and in a cold and inattentive audience realizes that perhaps he may not be the born orator he was led to believe.

There was a note awaiting her from Sir Henry James:

You must let me very sincerely and heartily congratulate you on the result of the election, especially as that result proceeded so very much from your personal exertions. Everybody is praising you very much.

But my gratification is slightly impaired by feeling I must introduce a new Corrupt Practices Act. Tandems must be put down,[21] and certainly some alteration—a correspondent informs me—must be made in the means of ascent and descent therefrom; then arch looks have to be scheduled, and nothing must be said "from my heart." The graceful wave of a pocket handkerchief will have to be dealt with in committee.

Still, I am very glad.

The Prince of Wales also sent his congratulations, adding that reading some of Lady Randolph's speeches had converted him, in some respects, to her views. In answer, Jennie wrote, "It is a further source of infinite satisfaction to Lady Randolph to know that possibly by action on her part she may have been fortunate enough to influence in any degree your Royal Highness's view on a subject of large political importance."

In those days, when women were generally thought of in terms of kitchens and bedrooms, Lady Randolph Churchill's political campaigning received international attention. As Leonard Jerome proudly wrote to his wife, "You have no idea how universally Jennie is talked about and how proud the Americans are of her."

Paradoxically, Randolph's weakness had become Jennie's strength. If her husband had possessed the strength of a Salisbury or a Gladstone, Jennie would have been forced into the role of the assured social hostess, the tea-pourer, the smiling, decorative ornament in the background. She would have been a wallpaper wife, as were the wives of most leading politicians. But Randolph's lack was the irritating sand that created the pearl. It forced Jennie into areas where she otherwise would not have tread. Even the Marlborough House Set, for all their irreverence of rules, could not have imagined that path for a woman.

Jennie was now not only the mistress of her house but often the master. Randolph's trips were so frequent and often so extended that she found herself in a role of increasing independence. Unlike other wives who went into a solitary confinement when their husbands were absent, Jennie kept her house alive with friends and parties. More and more, too, she was faced with daily decisions normally resolved by the man in the house. Decisions about money, decisions about the children's education, decisions and evaluations concerning her own purpose in life.

Jennie's successful electioneering prompted her good friend, the Baroness Angela Georgina Burdett-Coutts, to ask her to help conduct her new husband's first campaign for office. Jennie agreed.[22] The Baroness had lived through the entire Victorian era and the Duke of Cambridge had called her "an English institution." Inheriting a fabulous fortune, great common sense, and lofty ideals, she had sought the advice of the Duke of Wellington and Charles Dickens on how to put her money to the best use.

She founded schools, replaced English slums with model housing, even helped feed, clothe, and revive whole districts in southwest Ireland during the famine.

As the wife of the new Secretary of State for India, Jennie went to work for the National Association for Supplying Medical Aid to the Women of India. The Association built dispensaries, provided medical treatment for the poor, and spurred the medical careers of many Indian women. In those days, even in England, the woman doctor was a rarity.[23]

Taking his third vacation that year, Randolph went to Scotland and Ireland with his secretary Cecil Wolff. He wrote Jennie concerning the Medical Association for India, advising her that the best means of promoting more publicity for the fund-raising was to "get hold of Mr. Buckle [editor of *The Times*], and fascinate him and make him write you up." She fascinated Buckle, and many others, so well that the Association's finances became brighter than they had ever been.

Jennie was also involved with determining policy for the Primrose League. The League proved so successful that Jennie got letters from her friend, the elegant Comtesse de Paris, asking advice on forming a similar group in France, aimed at restoring the monarchy. The Comtesse, who was the sister of the Queen of Spain and the mother of the Queen of Portugal, did start the "White Rose League" with gilt badges shaped as roses—but it never grew out of the seedling stage.

Jennie's most crucial problem, however, was not the Primrose League but Randolph. Despite his repeated and prolonged vacations, his disease was sapping his strength. "I have no longer any energy or ideas," he told a friend in August of 1885, "and I am no more good except to make disturbance." One such disturbance was his threat to resign because the Queen appointed her younger son to an office in India without consulting him. "However, he has returned to reason 'having taken calomel,'" Salisbury wrote Queen Victoria, "and is not going to resign." The Queen then expressed the hope that Lord Salisbury "would restrain Lord Randolph as much as he can," and Salisbury warned Randolph, "If you once go a step too far—if you once break the spring—you may take years to get over it."

Caring for a sick, temperamental husband left Jennie little time for her sons. Five-year-old Jack was still under a nanny's care, but eleven-year-old Winston needed more special attention. Jennie's theory about children was that they should be given as much responsibility as they could handle. George Smalley remembered Winston inviting him and Jennie and Jack to go boating. "He took command of the party," wrote Smalley, "first on land and then on water. But nobody thought of disputing his claim. I'd lived enough in boats to see that Winston, though no great skill in watermanship, knew what he was about; and though he ran some needless risks, it was never necessary to interfere."[24] Jennie realized how important it was to let Winston take command without her interference or suggestions. For part of the summer, though, she sent him to Chesterfield Lodge on the east coast of England. He wrote her unhappy letters, wanting to come home, asking "Do you miss me much?" and despairing, "The governess is very unkind, so strict and stiff, I cannot enjoy myself at all. I am counting the days until Saturday. Then I shall be able to tell you all my troubles. . . ."

While Winston had to fight for attention in his mother's crowded schedule, he knew he could always reach her and that she would always listen. When St. George's School was too hateful to him, she was the one who transferred him to another school. When he begged to go to Europe on vacation with them, it was she who insisted on taking him. When he had a special request or needed more money, it was she who attended to it. She wrote to him regularly, visited him when she could, brought him home when there was time. Winston always felt sure of her love. His father, however, was merely a famous person to Winston, someone he could boast of to his classmates, whose autograph was a valuable commodity to trade or sell, but not someone he could talk to or touch.

Grandfather Jerome always proved to be a refreshing change for Winston. His was a love and pride shown openly and freely. Jerome had come to England for a visit late in the summer of 1885, in time to observe some of Jennie's political campaigning.

Everyone had realized that the Salisbury Government was simply filling a caretaker role until the General Election. The Voting Reform Bill had expanded the electorate by some two million voters and no one could predict whom they would want. Randolph's Woodstock constituency had been abolished, so he now challenged the highly popular John Bright in the Radical stronghold of Birmingham. In a not-very-anonymous article in the popular *Fortnightly Review*, Randolph had disclosed his own radical attitude toward the leadership of the Tory Party:

> Unfortunately for Conservatism, its leaders belong solely to one class; they are a clique composed of members of the aristocracy, land owners and adherents whose chief merit is subserviency. The party chiefs live in an atmosphere in which a sense of their own importance and the importance of their class interests and privileges is exaggerated and which the opinions of the common people can scarcely penetrate. They are surrounded by sycophants who continually offer up the incense of personal flattery under the pretext of conveying political information. They half fear and half despise the common people. . . .

Churchill offered the British people an alternative. His banner was "Tory Democracy," a phrase he coined. ("Tory Democracy," he later confided to a friend, "is a democracy which supports the Tories.") His slogan was "Trust the people and they will trust you."

Randolph trusted them so much that he did not campaign and again let Jennie take charge. This time, however, Jennie's mother-in-law, the Dowager Duchess, joined her. During the campaign, the two women grew as close as they would ever be, and each somewhat revised her opinions of the other. Afterward, the Duchess for a while even defended Jennie to some of her society friends, emphasizing how much Jennie had "matured" since she had entered politics.

"It was the first time that women had ever indulged in any personal canvassing in Birmingham," wrote Jennie,

> and we did it thoroughly. Every house in the constituency was visited. The Duchess would go in one direction, and I in another; the constituency was a large one and the work arduous. The voters were much more enlightened than the agricultural laborers of Oxfordshire; the men particularly were very argumentative and were well up on the questions of the day. . . . The wives of the Radicals were also admirably informed, and on more than one occasion routed me completely.

She told of an incident which occurred when she visited a factory to talk to the men during their lunch hour.

"I was received in sullen silence. When I inquired why, one, speaking for the rest, said they did not like being asked for their vote."

"But you have something I want," she told them, and added, "How am I to get it if I do not ask for it?"

"This struck them as quite reasonable, and when I left they cheered me."

Not all her receptions became as friendly. Visiting a pub, Jennie talked to the wife of the owner, who called to her husband in the cellar, "Lady Churchill wants to see you."

"Well, tell Mrs. Churchill to go to—"

"At which time," said Jennie, "I beat a hasty retreat."

She had greater success with a butcher to whom she gave a flower. He not only gave her his vote, but afterward sent her half a sheep.[25]

The excitement of politics had infected Winston—his father fighting a vital election, his mother hot on the campaign trail. And even his grandmother, the highly proper Dowager Duchess, ringing doorbells and soliciting votes. Winston found a classmate whose father was also a parliamentary candidate. If both fathers won, Winston wrote, he and his friend were going to have a victory supper.

But there was no victory supper. Bright beat Randolph Churchill by 773 votes. Randolph took his defeat gracefully. "Gentlemen," he said, "the man who can't stand a knockdown blow isn't worth a damn." The blow was quickly countered. A Churchill admirer in South Paddington, a safe Conservative district, withdrew in Churchill's favor, and Randolph was promptly elected there the next day.

The over-all election result, however, was that the Salisbury Conservatives were out and the Gladstone Liberals were in again, with 335 seats to 249. Randolph's opposition friend, John Morley, met Randolph in St. James Park after the election.

"You look a little pensive," said Morley.

"Yes, I was thinking—I have plenty to think of. Well, we're out—you're in."

"Yes, we're in for three months; then we dissolve and you're in for six years."

Shortly after that, another friend asked Randolph:

"What will happen now?"

"I shall lead the Opposition for five years," answered Randolph. "Then I shall be Prime Minister for five years. Then I shall die."[26] Randolph's prediction was to be less accurate than Morley's.

Twelve

Windsor Castle, November 30, 1885

Dear Lord Randolph:

The Queen wishes to personally confer the Insignia of the Order of the Crown of India on Lady Randolph Churchill on Friday next the fourth of December at three o'clock.

Will she come back here to luncheon?

The 1:10 train from Paddington is the most convenient one, and if Lady Randolph will let me hear whether she comes by that or another train, I will send the carriage to meet her here.

Yours very truly,
Henry Ponsonby.

Jennie then received a note from the Queen's lady-in-waiting, advising her of correct attire and procedure:

LADY RANDOLPH CHURCHILL:

Bonnet and morning dress, gray gloves.

To kiss the Queen's hand after receiving the decoration, like the gentlemen to-day. A room will be prepared for her.

For any woman of the time an audience with the Queen was a highlight in her life. The curtsy and a kiss of the Queen's hand were considered by some as second in importance only to their marriage. The main test was of grace, and any awkwardness became a badge of shame.

The Queen, with one of her daughters and a lady-in-waiting, received Jennie in a small room:

> She stood with her back to the window, wearing a long white veil which made an aureole around her against the light. Addressing a few kind words to me, to which in my embarrassment I made some inaudible answer, she proceeded to pin the order on my left shoulder. I remember that my black velvet dress was thickly embroidered with jet, so much so that the pin could find no hold, and unwittingly the Queen stuck it straight into me. Although like the Spartan boy, I tried to hide what I felt, I suppose I gave a start, and the Queen realizing what she had done was much concerned. Eventually the pin was put right and I curtsied myself out of the Royal Presence. As I reached the door, her majesty suddenly stepped forward saying with a smile, "Oh! You have forgotten the case," holding it out to me at the same time. This little touch of nature relieved an otherwise somewhat formal ceremony. Remarking afterward to the lady-in-waiting that I was afraid that I had been awkward, and nervous, she answered, "You need not be troubled. I know the Queen felt more shy than you did."[1]

The pin was a pearl and turquoise cipher attached to a pale blue ribbon bordered with white. The next day Jennie received a note from the Queen's lady-in-waiting:

> "My dear Lady Randolph,
>
>   I hope you got home quite comfortably yesterday, and took no cold. The Queen told me she thought you so handsome, and that it had all gone off so well.
>
> Believe me ever,
Yours truly,
Jane Ely,

Victoria remarked in her Journal, "Lady Randolph (an American) is very handsome and very dark."[2]

Within a few months, the Randolph Churchills were invited to dine with the Queen at Windsor and spend the night. Jennie remembered the dinner as being in a small room surrounded by family portraits on the wall, the conversation carried out in hushed whispers almost oppressively quiet. "I tried to keep my tongue under control," she said later.

> You know how I tend to rattle on, and I was terrified of saying a word too much, and arousing that dread "We are not amused." . . .
>
> When the Queen spoke, even the whispers ceased. If she addressed a remark to you, the answer was given while the whole company listened.

Victoria's first impression of Randolph was "his extraordinary likeness to darling Leopold, which quite startled me." Both had an arrogant mustache and protruding eyes. Prince Leopold's sculpted figure in Oxford Cathedral indeed bears a considerable resemblance to Storey's marble of Randolph at Blenheim. Another time, she noted in her diary after a conversation with Randolph, "We remained talking in the corridor until half past ten. . . . He said some strange things to me which I will refer to later." The strange things concerned the Government's conduct in India and his strong feelings against Lord Hartington. "The Queen thought it looked as if he [Randolph] was likely to be disagreeable, and wanted the Queen to agree with him." She also commented, "Lord Randolph was looking very ill."[3]

Of that evening, Jennie wrote her mother on Windsor Castle stationery that "dinner was a very solemn, ghastly affair. . . . I was the only 'strange lady.' " But if Victoria was concerned about Randolph, she was obviously pleased with Jennie. "The Queen was most amiable last night and talked to me for some time."

During the following spring, eleven-year-old Winston suddenly became critically ill of pneumonia—a disease whose recurrence would plague him all his life. Jennie rushed to her son's bedside, and Dr. Roose sent reports to Randolph. "We are still fighting the battle for your boy. His temperature is 103 now, but he is taking his nourishment better. . . ." The doctor advised that the right lung was infected and the left lung strained from the overwork.

> This report may appear grave, yet it merely indicates the approach of the crisis which, please God, will result in an improved condition, should the left lung remain free. . . . I am in the next room and shall watch the patient during the night, for I am most anxious.

Three days later the delirium ceased and the fever subsided. "Winston has had six hours of quiet sleep." The crisis had passed, but Roose warned Jennie, "I am so fearful of relapse, knowing we are not quite out of the woods yet." Winston, he said, must have absolute quiet, and even Mrs. Everest should not be allowed in the sickroom the first days because "the excitement and pleasure of seeing her might do harm!"

Jennie's mother-in-law sent a note of sympathy: "Such hours make one years older, and one feels how one's happiness in this world hangs on a thread. . . . I am so thankful for God's goodness for preserving your dear child. . . ."[4] Moreton Frewen wrote, "Poor, dear Winnie, and I hope it will leave no troublesome after-effects, but even if it leaves him delicate for a long time to come, you will make the more of him after being given back to you on the very threshold of the unknown. . . ."[5]

But during that year of 1886 Jennie was not able to concentrate love and attention on her son. That was the critical year that shattered all hopes for her husband and herself. Randolph's syphilis seemed in a recessive stage, but Jennie was always aware of its specter. Dr. Roose did not hold out excessive hope for Randolph. Perhaps to insure that Roose would maintain professional silence, Randolph kept their relationship close and friendly. Roose was deeply appreciative:

> When I realize, as I do daily, that through *you*, I have op-
> portunities, introductions and a kindly sympathy . . . I feel I
> cannot do too much for you and yours. And with this feeling
> of deep gratitude, I accept your cheque, almost with pain! . . .
> Please do not be offended with me for saying again and
> again that I have no desire nor anticipation of fees from you,
> and that no amount of work I can do for you will redeem the
> immense service you have and do render to me by your men-
> tion of my name to so many.[6]

A member of the Royal College of Surgeons in England, Robson Roose had studied at Quebec and Edinburgh Universities, had served as physician to the Ottoman Embassy as well as the St. Andrews Home for Boys in Brighton.[7] A prolific writer on medical subjects, he authored one book entitled *Nerve Prostration* and another on *The Waste and Repair in Modern Life*. In the latter work, Roose noted the different capacities of individual men for hard mental work.

> Previous training, constitution and temperament are po-
> tent factors in determining the amount which each is capable
> of doing. Some men can stand an enormous amount of

mental strain without any apparent injury; others, from what may be called, for want of a better term, "weakness of the brain," are incapable of anything requiring mental tension.

The fact, however, remains that not a little of the brain-work of the world is done by men whose standard of health is extremely low; and the weak and ailing condition of body has been proved to be quite compatible with great ability for severe mental exertion. Such cases are, however, the exception.[8]

Lord Randolph at this time had his own concept of the ideal life: "to lie in bed all day, dozing over a book, to dine in one's dressing gown, and then with all convenient speed to find one's way back to bed again."[9] But Jennie's persistence kept him from idling.

Returning as Prime Minister with a narrow majority, Gladstone promptly announced that his Liberal Government would propose a Home Rule Bill to give Ireland its own Parliament. The House of Commons immediately became a setting of high drama, the chamber so packed that Members of Parliament sat on the steps leading up from the floor, even on the arms of benches and on each other's knees. Side by side in the jammed galleries were the famous of the world, from English bishops to Indian princes. Frank Harris sat between two of Jennie's intimates, the Marquis de Breteuil and Herbert von Bismarck. Harris described Gladstone:

> His head was like that of an old eagle—luminous eyes, rapa-
> cious beak and bony jaws; his high white collar seemed to
> cut off his head of a bird of prey from the thin, small figure in
> conventional, black evening dress. His voice was a high,
> clear tenor; his gestures rare, but well chosen; his utterance
> as fluid as water; but now and then he became strangely im-
> pressive through some dramatic pause and slower enuncia-
> tion, which emphasized, so to say, the choice and music of
> the rhythmic words.[10]

The predominant mood of Parliament was hostile when he started, and Gladstone was tired. He began speaking slowly:

> I do not deny that many are against us whom we should
> have expected to be for us. . . . You have power, you have
> wealth, you have rank, you have station, you have organiza-
> tion, you have the place of power. What have we? We think
> that we have the people's heart; we believe and we know we

have the promise of the harvest of the future . . . I believe
that there is in the breast of many a man who means to vote
against us tonight a profound misgiving, approaching even
to a deep conviction, that the end will be as we foresee, and
not as you–that the ebbing tide is with you, and the flowing
tide is with us. Ireland stands at your bar, expectant, hopeful,
almost suppliant. . . . She asks a blessed oblivion of the past,
and in that oblivion our interest is even deeper than hers. . . .
She asks also a boon for the future; and that boon for the future, unless we are much mistaken, will be a boon to us in respect of honour no less than a boon to her in respect of
happiness, prosperity and peace. . . ."

The theme was one he would return to again and again: "It is liberty alone
which fits men for liberty."[11]

The House cheered for five minutes. Bismarck told Harris it was the
greatest speech he had ever heard.

The Home Rule Bill split Gladstone's Liberal Party. Churchill saw it as
the political opportunity of his lifetime. "Let him defeat us [the Conserva-
tives] with the aid of the Parnellites, and then let us dissolve and go to the
country with the cry of, 'The Empire is in danger!' " Randolph even queried
Frank Harris for more details on Parnell's affair with Mrs. O'Shea–for possible use as political ammunition. His friendly association with Parnell was
automatically dissolved in the expediencies of politics. Ambition was the
key and the Prime Ministership was the prize.

Randolph admired Gladstone personally and afterward called him
"the wisest, cleverest and most experienced parliamentarian that ever
lived." But now his invective against the Prime Minister was almost savage. He referred to the Home Rule Bill for Ireland as "a conspiracy against
the honor of Britain . . . startlingly base and nefarious . . . to gratify the
ambition of an old man in a hurry. . . ." In his biography of his father,
Winston Churchill said of that speech, "If the address was vulgar, it was
also popular."[12]

"The moment the very name of Ireland is mentioned," said critic Sidney
Smith, "the English seem to bid adieu to common feeling, common prudence, and common sense, and to act with the barbarity of tyrants and fa-
tuity of idiots."

Gladstone had gone out on a precarious political limb for the benefit of
a people he had hardly seen–he had been to Ireland only once on a short
visit. The issue to him, however, was one of practicality as well as principle.

Randolph called the speech "a piece of premature gush," and to an ally
predicted, "we shall roll the old man over."

Manchester proved to be the barometer of the country's mood. "Among the many political meetings I attended with Randolph during those two years," Jennie recounted,

> I think the biggest and most imposing was that held in the Manchester Drill Hall. Eighteen thousand people filled the place to suffocation—no singer that ever lived can command the audience of a popular politician. If the building had held 40,000 or 50,000, it would still have been crowded. Most of the people had been standing two hours before we arrived. Manchester gave Randolph a magnificent reception; thousands lined the streets and covered the roofs of the houses as we slowly drove through the town in a carriage drawn by four horses. Over 200,000 people were said to have turned out that day. I felt very proud. Randolph's speech lasted for over two hours. The heat was great and on leaving the building the crowd pressed round the carriage to such an extent that two men were killed.

Because Manchester was a traditional Liberal stronghold, Jennie opened a new Primrose Habitation there, and spoke before the large crowd that had met:

> When Mr. Gladstone appears in his new role of undertaker, let us hope, with the exception of a few hypocritical mourners, he may be left to bury his doomed Bill alone. When that melancholy rite is accomplished, and he appeals to the country, I trust with all my heart that it will answer with one voice in favor of that party which is pledged to support all that is dear to England—religion, law, order, and the unity of the Empire.

Posters advertising the meeting had billed Arthur Balfour as the star speaker. Newspaper reports, however, treated the meeting differently. One gave a glowing account of Jennie's speech, adding the postscript, "Lady Randolph was ably supported by Lord Salisbury's nephew, Mr. Balfour, M.P." That was a considerable compliment for her, since critic John Buchan later called future Prime Minister Balfour "the best talker I have ever known."[13]

Commenting on the speech, a reporter noted the strong resemblance in style and tone between Jennie's public addresses and Randolph's.[14] London society wondered again whether Jennie wrote Randolph's speeches, just as she ran his campaigns. They also wondered about Randolph's remarkable reversal on the Irish issue, and whether Jennie had played any part in that.

It was true, as later events proved, that Jennie had the greater talent as a writer and editor, and it is quite possible that she helped him with his speeches more than other people knew. But if she did pressure him on the issue of Ireland, ambition would have been her motive. If her husband could ever become Prime Minister, as she felt he could, she knew that it must be soon. Immersed in politics as deeply as she now was, it was obvious to her that the Home Rule issue stirred so much public sentiment in England that it could quickly kill the Gladstone Government.

Of course Randolph was subject to many other pressures concerning this issue, and he had his own ambition, his own timetable. But it does not seem unreasonable to assume that if he trusted his wife enough to let her run his campaigns, he would also seek out her judgment on political questions. If that was so, who and what most influenced Jennie?

First was Balfour. A tall, elegant figure of a man, Arthur Balfour had all the silken, deprecatory manners of the Court. He was not a man to carry bold standards. Detached and philosophical, he was highly impersonal in his dealings with most people. Ramsay MacDonald later said of him, "He saw a great deal of life from afar," and Winston Churchill remarked, "Arthur Balfour did not mingle in the hurley-burley. He glided upon its surface." Jennie admired Balfour's intellect, his political philosophy, his considerable charm for people he liked. Margot Tennant had called him "irresistible" and Lady Battersea had said, "What a gulf between him and most men!" Balfour's admiration for Jennie was probably more platonic than romantic. (He reputedly had concentrated his emotional fire on Gladstone's niece, May Lyttleton, some years before, and was said to have "exhausted his powers in that direction." Closer friends claimed it was not so much that Balfour was cold to women as that he was warm to his freedom.) In any event, Jennie highly respected Balfour's judgment, and Balfour was the policy pipeline from his uncle Lord Salisbury. Salisbury realized, better than most, that the Irish issue was the pivot that could return him as Prime Minister.

In addition to Balfour, Jennie was friendly with many respected politicians who were in revolt against Gladstone on the issue. Among them was Joseph Chamberlain, who some said was tired of waiting for Gladstone's retirement and felt he could rise faster with the newly formed Liberal-Unionists, a faction split off from the Liberal Party. Salisbury, always suspecting Chamberlain's convictions, once told a friend, "Mr. Gladstone was hated but he was very much loved. Does anyone love Mr. Chamberlain?" Chamberlain thought cool and hit hard, and he and Jennie each admired the other's strength. Jennie's energy made such an impression on Chamberlain that he ultimately went to America to seek a wife.

Then there was the venerable Lord Hartington, dedicated to government service rather than ambition. "How can we have a more honest guide?" Balfour had said of him. Hartington's split with Gladstone on Home Rule caused an explosive political reaction. Moreover, Jennie not only respected Lord Hartington but was a good friend of his wife, who provided the drive for her own husband.

Jennie's affection for Ireland and the Irish people was fervent, but her commitment to England and Empire and to her husband's political future was more so. Conducting Randolph's campaign for reelection in South Paddington, Jennie now operated with the panache of a professional. As one critic noted, the "American wife flashed hither and thither—not a butterfly, but a comet, influencing the orbits of even the greater planets."[15] It went so well that Randolph contented himself with sending a written statement to his electorate, and they swept him into office by a majority of better than three to one.

Winston wrote his mother a congratulatory note, "I'm very glad Papa got in for South Paddington by so great a majority. I think that was a victory." He also wanted her professional opinion on whether the Conservatives would win the General Election scheduled to take place within a couple of weeks. And he added, "I should like you to come and see me very much."

But Jennie still had no time. As a leading official of the Primrose League, she had a major role to play in the national election, and she plunged into it. Not Randolph.[16] He was on a fishing trip in Norway with Tom Trafford, and money seemed much more on his mind than election results. "It seems to me," he wrote Jennie, "we want the £5,000 a year badly. But really we must retrench. I cannot understand how we got through so much money." (A letter from his bank some months earlier confirmed a six months loan for a thousand pounds, based on a note he and Jennie had signed. His secretary that month also noted the payment of some racing bets, including £25 to Count Kinsky.)

Parliament was dissolved on June 27, 1886, after only four months of Gladstone's stewardship. The General Election in July brought back the Conservatives, now united with the Unionist faction.

Randolph had predicted both the cause and shape of the victory, and the public question was what would be his prize? Gladstone's comment was a bitter one: "If I were in a dying condition, I confess I should have one great apprehension in my mind—what I conceive to be the great danger to my country . . . It is the men of the future—personalities of the stamp of Randolph Churchill." Queen Victoria expressed similar concern. "Lord

Salisbury came to me again at four," the Queen's Journal reads for July 25th, "and we talked about everything. He feared Lord Randolph Churchill must be Chancellor of the Exchequer and Leader, which I did not like. He is so mad and odd,[17] and also in bad health. . . ."

Randolph was given both appointments. Lady Jeune described the Dowager Duchess' reaction:

> I shall never forget the bright ecstasy and joy with which she welcomed his being made Leader of the House of Commons. I . . . shall always remember the passionate delight with which she spoke it. He had reached the height of his ambition, and she was content.[18]

Randolph felt otherwise. Asked by a friend, "How long will your leadership last?" Randolph smiled and said, "Six months."

"And after that?" asked the friend.

"Westminster Abbey," answered Randolph.[19] He was then thirty-seven years old.

"So Lord Randolph has secured the object of his ambition," a friend wrote to George Curzon, who had been elected to Parliament in the Conservative sweep. "I hope he will use his great position wisely. I must confess to being a wee bit anxious as to how he will lead. A leader requires angelic temper—this, I fear, Lord Randolph has not."[20] More than ever, Randolph was sensitive, impulsive, moody, impatient, petulant. Much later, Jennie wrote:

> Personality exercises a vast influence, and it is not the prerogative of great people. Without it, it is true, the front rank can never be reached, but, on the other hand, its complete fulfillment is only possible where it combines with the power to achieve.[21]

Randolph's health flagged. If he still had the skills for leadership, he often no longer had the will. Of the duties of Members of Parliament, Dr. Roose wrote:

> Work begins in the committee-rooms at noon; the House assembles at four, and the sittings are often prolonged till midnight. Before the adoption of the 12-o'Clock Rule, readers of the debates became quite familiar with the announcement, "The House was still sitting when we went to the press!"

... Besides his duties at Westminster, he must attend to his constituents, show himself among them from time to time, and must be ever-ready to listen to complaints, suggestions or even dictates. . . . a Cabinet Minister . . . begins the day by making himself acquainted with the contents of the daily papers, and perhaps by giving a few minutes to his private correspondence. The study of official papers . . . will occupy him till eleven o'clock, the ordinary time of attendance at his office, where he remains until the meetings of the House to which he belongs. . . . In addition to official work, not a few hours are required for preparing parliamentary speeches and extra parliamentary discussions of various kinds. . . . If in charge of any important measure in Parliament, he must be present during any debates on it, and often make speeches in its support. Replies to questions have to be carefully prepared. . . . Attendance is at Cabinet councils and meetings of the Privy Council, at state balls and concerts, at dinners and meetings of every conceivable kind . . . , and if to these items be added the multifarious duties of a private character, which almost necessarily devolve upon him, it will be readily admitted that the work of a Cabinet Minister at the present day is such as to tax to the utmost even the highest degrees of mental and physical vigor. The diversified character of his work would appear to be its redeeming feature.

Many a man enters upon parliamentary life under the idea that he has an important mission to fulfill; but session after session passes, and he finds himself no nearer to the goal. Meanwhile, he has had to listen, night after night, to an incessant flow of talk, the larger portion of which is unattended by any practical result. . . . There are, at times, other reasons for disappointment and disgust. Speeches made and votes given for party purposes, in support of measures believed to be mischievous, must, in some cases at least, be productive of no ordinary amount of self-contempt. A certain amount of anxiety—the sensation which Dr. Hughlings Jackson has happily described as "fright spread out thin," is of course unavoidable. . . . Many a man might ask himself whether the game he is playing is really worth the candle, and whether less bustle and hurry, or even one of the quieter walks of life would not, after all, be much more conducive to happiness than the constant whirl of excitement and anxiety. Mr. Greg remarked, "A life without leisure and without pause—a life of haste and excitement—a life so full that we have no time to re-flect where we have been and where we intend to go, what we have done and what we plan to do, can scarcely be deemed an adequate or worthy life."[22]

When his mood was good, Randolph still demonstrated a contagious gaiety and exercised a facile, audacious control of conversation. Except from his close friends, however, he resented any attempts at familiarity. While he usually maintained an Old World courtesy and manner, his rude-ness increased—more against his seniors than his juniors. He could be so abusive that Jennie once made him apologize to a hostess whose food and drink he had criticized excessively. If he disliked a person at a dinner, he was apt to take his knife and fork and move to another place at the table. A few timorous hostesses even sent him their guest lists for his approval be-cause they wanted to suffer no scene.[23] High society, however, loved social "lions," and Randolph Churchill was a prize lion. His rudeness was part of the price a hostess paid, for the quintessence of a successful dinner was the quality of conversation. Conversation did not mean chatter or flippancy, and there was seldom anything casual about it. Conversation meant perti-nent politics interlaced with wit and the subjects that moved the world.

Of course, cuisine of the highest quality was requisite. The Churchills knew many people who had worked their way into society through the ac-complishments of a gifted chef.

Rosa Ovenden, the Churchills' cook, had been a pretty kitchen maid for the cigar-smoking Comtesse de Paris before being hired by Jennie as an occasional cook, to fill in for the busy chef. Rosa soon ruled the kitchen with a choice set of Cockney expletives which quickly circulated among the Churchills' friends. Still, Rosa was a perfectionist in her own way, as was Jennie. "Lady Randolph Churchill only wanted a few things, but those things she wanted the most perfect, and perfect things to eat," Rosa ex-plained. "She was one of the most perfect women herself that I have ever met. She always put all her money in a few things."

Jennie regularly checked the menus with Rosa before a party. Mrs. Hofa-Williams, for example, could not eat lobster patties because "it always brings her out in spots." As for Randolph, Rosa wrote that he "would rather eat a perfect dish of his favorite *oeufs brouillés aux truffes* than have a seat in the Cabinet." A favorite dish of the Prince of Wales, who had be-come portly enough to be known as "Prince Tum-Tum," was plain broiled truffles "served like little ebony apples on a silver dish wrapped around with a white linen napkin."[24]

The Prince also liked Rosa. In the course of time, he gave her many little gifts of brooches and bracelets in appreciation of her affections. Years later, Rosa even maintained a suite of rooms for the Prince in the Cavendish Hotel, which she then owned. In the course of time, too, Rosa became the model for characters in several novels, including one by Evelyn Waugh, who always remembered her commanding him, "Take your arse out of my chair."

Rosa remembered the Churchills' Connaught House as "a social merry-go-round" but their marriage as "not a very happy one." It pained her to see her mistress "treated badly by Lord Randolph," and she was shocked to see Randolph "running up such huge gambling debts." Rosebery once quoted Randolph as saying, "I have a great horror of gambling in any form." But the gossip columns often reported Randolph as participating in baccarat games, either with the Prince of Wales or "a group of gilded youths." And no one better enjoyed betting on horses. Rosa summed up the Churchills by saying that "although he was a very clever man, he would never have been half the man he was if it had not been for her."

Rosa's earliest memory of Winston was the time he came home for a short vacation and wandered into her busy kitchen, surprised to find so many people at work. He asked her whether the Prince was coming for lunch, and she chased out the little red-haired boy, saying, "What the devil are you messing about here for? Hop it, copper-nob."[25]

Winston was a lonely boy then, with few friends. His brother Jack was six years old, too young for Winston to play with more than occasionally (though Jack once told a guest that his brother was teaching him to be naughty). Leonie noticed that Winston roamed about the house with a kind of aimlessness and wrote her father that the boy "flitted in the background."

His health better now, Winston reassuringly wrote his mother from the Brighton school, "We had gymnastic examination on Monday, and I find, in addition to gaining back my strength, I have gained more than I possessed before. . . . It is superfluous to add that I am happy. . . ." Other news included his learning *Paradise Lost* for elocution, his having had a lecture on astronomy, the fact that he could now swim the length of the pool—some sixty feet, that he wanted to learn to play the violoncello instead of the piano, that he planned to have "some fine barricades" with Jack the next time home, and that "I am very sorry to say that I am bankrupt, and a little cash would be welcome."

His mother had criticized the slangy language in some of his letters, and he answered, "I intend to correspond in the best language which my small vocabulary can muster."[26]

Winston later wrote of more formidable problems he had begun encountering that year of 1886.

> I had scarcely passed my 12th birthday when I entered the inhospitable regions of examinations, through which, for the next seven years, I was destined to journey. These examinations were a great trial to me. The subjects which were dearest to the examiners, were almost invariably those I fancied least. I would have liked to have been examined in History, Poetry, and writing essays. The examiners, on the other hand, were partial to Latin and Mathematics. And their will prevailed. Moreover, the questions which they asked on both these subjects were almost invariably those to which I was unable to suggest the satisfactory answer. I should have liked to be asked to say what I knew. They always tried to ask what I did not know. When I would willingly have displayed my knowledge, they sought to expose my ignorance. This sort of treatment had only one result: I did not do well in examinations.[27]

Winston continued his pleading for affection and attention. In one letter, he begged his mother to give up a dinner party at her home and come to Brighton School to see an "English play, French play, Latin and Greek, Recitations, Supper, Dancing. Commencing 4:30 P.M., ending 12:00 P.M." He particularly wanted her to see him act in one of the plays at which he was "working hard," and also asked if she would possibly play the piano, in which case the teacher promised to double the admission prices. Or, at least, he said, she could distribute the prizes. "It would give me tremendous pleasure, do come, please." Then he made a final appeal: "Now you know I was always your darling, and you can't find it in your heart to give me a denial. . . ." The dinner, however, was important and she could not cancel it.[28]

Winston wrote a note to his father, too, tinged with sadness and bitterness: "You never came to see me on Sunday when you were in Brighton."

But the son's problems seemed of less consequence than his father's. At first flush, Randolph appeared firmly entrenched politically. *The Times*, in fact, editorialized that it could "not think there is much chance of turning out Randolph for a long time to come." And Queen Victoria, who had been so reluctant to accept him as a Cabinet member, wrote him a note of thanks:

> Now that the session is just over, the Queen wishes to write and thank Lord Randolph Churchill for his regular and full and interesting reports of the debates in the House of Commons, which must have been most trying.

> Lord Randolph has shown much skill and judgment in
> his leadership during this exceptional session of Parlia-
> ment.[29]

But the Exchequer was a post of intricate difficulty for Randolph. He
was unable to cope with all the statistics. Commenting on the columns of
decimals he had to struggle with, he once said, "I could never make out
what those damned dots meant." Holding that same Cabinet position, Winston Churchill would one day have similar trouble.[30]

Randolph often quarreled with his fellow Cabinet members on budget
economies, and found himself increasingly alone in his opinions. He outlined some of his new financial proposals to George Smalley, the New York
Tribune correspondent in England. "You break with all tradition," said Smalley, himself a great Bohemian and individualist. "What do you suppose I
am here for?" Randolph answered. "Have you ever known me to adopt an
opinion because somebody else had adopted it?"[31]

He further isolated himself from his colleagues with ever more critical
speeches, even against some of his friends. To one of his closest friends,
Lord Rosebery, who had given him an icy stare after an irritating remark,
Randolph roared out in the House of Commons, "Don't think you are going to terrify me with that poached-egg eye of yours." (The simile, however,
was apt. Rosebery, who later became Prime Minister, had the classic poker
face, a remarkable control that enabled him to maintain a bored, blank look
to great effect.) Lord Rosebery thought Randolph was broaching disaster,
and privately predicted that "Randolph will be out of the Cabinet or
smashed up before Christmas."

Even his most loyal adherent, Louis Jennings, a Conservative member
of the House from Stockport, often found it impossible to follow the sudden zigzags of Randolph's tactics. Jennings, who had been an editor of both
The New York Times and *The Times* in India, was the man Randolph later
named in his will as the co-executor of his private papers. It was Jennings
who had edited a book of Randolph's speeches and to whom Randolph
had confided the full story of how he had contracted syphilis. But not even
Jennings could persuade him to guard his political power and wait for a
more propitious time to move.

With his continued arrogance and belligerence, Churchill soon painted
himself into a political corner. "No man is so entirely alone and solitary as
I am," he told T. H. S. Escott.[32] George Curzon, himself a snob, said of
Lord Randolph then, "I used to know him well, and to be on familiar terms
with him. But since he became a swell, he will scarcely look at his subordi-
nates, and the barest civility is all that one can expect."[33]

Not only did Randolph constantly quarrel with his political cohorts, but he openly and strongly disagreed with his party boss, Prime Minister Salisbury, on most foreign policy issues. Salisbury wanted to ally England with France against Russia, and Churchill loudly urged an alliance with Germany. In a revealing letter, Salisbury described his difficulty in "leading an orchestra in which the first fiddle plays one tune, and everybody else, including myself, wishes to play another."

Arthur Balfour, who still played the part of Randolph's friend, wrote his uncle:

> My idea is that at present we ought to do *nothing* but let Randolph hammer away. . . . I am inclined that we should avoid, as far as possible, all "rows" until R. puts himself entirely and flagrantly in the wrong by some act of Party disloyalty which everybody can understand and nobody can deny. . . .

The conflict with Salisbury was heightened that fall of 1886. Randolph went abroad with Tom Trafford and received enormous publicity on the continent. "I am hopelessly discovered," he wrote Jennie. "At the station yesterday I found a whole army of reporters at whom I scowled in my most effective manner. Really it is almost intolerable that one cannot travel about without this publicity."

He soon was forced to realize the division within the Party was heavily weighted against him—he, almost alone, poised on one side, the full strength of the Salisbury Government on the other. "I can't go on at this rate," he wrote W. H. Smith, head of the War Ministry. "Whether on foreign policy or home policy or expenditure, I have no influence at all. The Government are proceeding headlong to a smash and I could be connected with it. . . ." Insisting on certain economies in the War Ministry Randolph added, ". . . nothing will induce me to give way on this matter and if I cannot get my way, I shall go." Analyzing his father's position, Winston Churchill would write, "It is no doubt that he rated his own power and subsequent responsibility too high."

Salisbury made it plain that he sided with Smith and told the Queen, "We are not a happy family." Victoria answered that Churchill "must not be given way to."

During the growing tempest, Jennie was outside her husband's confidence. He had drawn everything more and more into himself, everything into his weakened brain with its fitful fevers and delusions, into his enervated body, into his depressed and irresolute personality. As love is akin to hate, Jennie had said, so perhaps is success akin to failure. She and Randolph were never more far apart.

"How often in matrimonial difficulties," Jennie later wrote, "the more culpable of the two is given all the sympathy. . . ." In this case, the rumor-mongers noted Lady Randolph and her assorted escorts and gave Lord Randolph the sympathy.

With the increased political pressures, the chaos in Randolph's mind finally had shaped a decision. One afternoon he stopped off at Connaught Place for his bag, as the Queen had invited him to spend the night at Windsor Castle. En route to the station, he saw his fellow Cabinet member Lord George Hamilton, who was also going to Windsor. Randolph invited Hamilton to share a train compartment. Hamilton later remembered that Randolph had an almost spectral air about him, his mood artificially gay, almost cheerful.

"I am going to resign," Churchill said.

"What are you going to resign about?" asked the thunderstruck Hamilton.

"Smith's and your estimates."

"But we have practically settled everything."

"No," said Churchill. "I cannot go on any longer."

He wrote his letter of resignation to Salisbury at Windsor Castle and even read it aloud to Hamilton. In it he detailed some controversial budget items for the Admiralty and War Office and added,

> I know that on this subject I cannot look for any sympathy or effective support from you. I am certain I shall find non-supporters in the Cabinet. I do not want to be wrangling and quarreling in the Cabinet; and therefore must request to be allowed to give up my office and retire from the Government. . . .

Lord Randolph had his audience with Queen Victoria after dinner, telling her nothing of his intentions. She noted that he was "gloomy" and "tired."

At a luncheon in town the next day, Randolph was in fine form. Afterward, he confided to Wolff what he had done, but to nobody else. Randolph already had received word from Smith that Salisbury would accept his resignation were it offered. He soon received a letter from Salisbury himself, saying, "In presence of your very strong and decisive language I can only again express my profound regret." There was no hint of a further meeting to discuss the situation.[34]

Jennie was later to write:

> . . . So little did I realize the grave step Randolph was contemplating, that I was at that moment occupied with the

details of a reception we were going to give at the Foreign Office which was to be lent to us for the occasion. Already the cards had been printed. The night before his resignation, we went to a play with Sir Henry Wolff. Questioning Randolph as to the list of guests for the party, I remember being puzzled at his saying: "Oh! I shouldn't worry about it if I were you; it probably will never take place." I could get none of his meaning and shortly after the first act he left us, ostensibly to go to the club, but in reality to go to *The Times* office and give them the letter he had written at Windsor Castle three nights before. In it he resigned all he had worked for for years, and, if he had but known it, signed his political death warrant.[35]

Appropriately enough, the play at the Strand was *The School for Scandal*.

There are two versions of Randolph's interview with G. E. Buckle, the editor of *The Times*: one insists that Buckle tried to persuade him not to send the letter and that Randolph replied, "It is gone." The other version claims that Randolph tried to persuade Buckle to support him in a leading editorial and that Buckle refused. "There is not another paper in England that would not show some gratitude for such a piece of news," Randolph is alleged to have said, with Buckle answering, "You cannot bribe *The Times*."[36]

Randolph's letter of resignation was delivered by messenger to Salisbury at Hatfield, where the Prime Minister was host at a ball. Among his guests were Randolph's mother and sister. The letter arrived at 1:30 A.M. in a red dispatch box. Salisbury read it without altering his composure, then resumed his conversation with the Duchess of Teck. Later he simply went to bed without telling anyone of the letter. The Dowager Duchess of Marlborough spent the night with the Salisburys.

Early the following morning, Salisbury was awakened early by his wife and reminded that he had to see the Duchess off. "Send for *The Times* first," was his sleepy response. "Randolph resigned in the middle of the night, and if I know my man, it will be in *The Times* this morning."[37] Lady Charles Beresford described the morning scene at Hatfield to Lady Leslie:

Can you picture to yourself the bomb that exploded. . . . Fanny [the Dowager Duchess of Marlborough] . . . wept large tears of fury and mortification . . . and was conveyed to London speechless. . . . I traveled up by later train with the Premier, who seems as much astonished as anyone, and declares he cannot account for it. Liver or madness? Charles said it must be a woman!! (Of course.)

"Liver or madness?" answered Lady Leslie. "Let us hope the latter, and that he will be shut up before he can do further mischief. It is a cruel blow just before Christmastime."

"When I came down to breakfast," wrote Jennie,

> the fatal paper in my hand, I found him calm and smiling. "Quite a surprise for you," he said. He went into no explanation, and I felt too utterly crushed and miserable to ask for any, or even to remonstrate. Mr. Moore [the Permanent Under Secretary at the Treasury], who was devoted to Randolph, rushed in, pale and anxious, and with a faltering voice said to me, "He has thrown himself from the top of the ladder, and will never reach it again!" Alas! he proved too true a prophet.

Jennie's reaction was one of horrified shock, almost as if a loved one had suddenly died. What had died was her dream of someday being the wife of the Prime Minister of England and providing the support he needed to rule an Empire. She would then have been one of the most important women in the world. And how hard she had worked for it, how much she had endured. Now, in a single stroke, it was made futile. Not only had he never discussed his decision with her, but his twisted mind had planned it as a brutal surprise.

The general response to Churchill's resignation was steeped in bitterness and outrage. Said *The Times'* lead editorial:

> Lord Randolph Churchill declared not long ago that the whole basis of the government to which he belonged was to maintain the union of the party. . . . We may well ask what has become of that conviction concerning the paramount duty of unity, when he himself drives a wedge into the very center of the party at the most critical moment of its existence. . . . [38]

The Vienna *Tagblatt* was more scornful:

> Lord Salisbury's patronage did a great deal for Lord Randolph Churchill, who, if he stood alone, would have small weight. Lord Randolph has played the frog, blowing himself out to look like the bull. It may surprise him, however, when he joins the Radical Party, to find that he is received simply as a frog, and not as a bull. . . . He has not the stuff of a leader in him. . . .

Queen Victoria was incensed. Writing to a friend on Christmas Eve, she said:

> The resignation of Lord Randolph Churchill has placed Lord Salisbury in considerable difficulty; and its abruptness and, I am bound to add, the want of respect shown to me and to his colleagues have added to the bad effect which it has produced. Lord Randolph dined at my table on Monday evening and talked to me about the Session about to commence, and about the *procedure*, offering to *send me* the proposed rules for me to see! And that *very night at the castle*, he wrote to Lord Salisbury, resigning his office! It is unprecedented![39]

Assessing his father's action years later, Winston Churchill wrote that Randolph undoubtedly "had chosen bad ground at the worst time," that he had acted with "the highest imprudence."

> If he had put away for a season his pledges and his pride, both might have been recovered with interest later on. As it was, he delivered himself unarmed, unattended, fettered even, to his enemies; and therefrom ensued not only his own political ruin, but grave injuries to the causes he sustained.[40]

Reginald Brett visited Randolph at Connaught Place the day after the public announcement in *The Times*. He found Randolph sprawled on the sofa in his library looking "completely prostrated." Randolph told Brett he had been "shunned like a pest" and visited by almost nobody, "not even those who owe everything to me." Brett noted that Randolph not only looked drawn and ill, but also seemed doubtful that he had done the right thing.

More courteous than candid, Salisbury wrote to the Dowager Duchess of Marlborough, who had made a personal and passionate appeal to him.

> Do not think I gave up the hope of converting Randolph to views in which his colleagues could go with him at once. I had a very long correspondence with him as you recommended, before he wrote those final letters, and I did all in my power to persuade him. I am afraid that he was, as you say, suspicious that my sentiments toward him were changed, that made him assume so inflexible an attitude. He is very amiable, very fascinating, very agreeable to work with, as

long as his mind is not poisoned by any suspicion, but men inferior to himself are able to invest suspicions which seem to madden him. Nothing has happened seriously to injure or damage a career of which you are so justly proud, or to deprive the country of the value of his services in the future.

But to a friend inquiring of Randolph's possible return to the Cabinet, Salisbury said, "Did you ever know of a man, having got rid of a boil on back of his neck, wants another?"

In a desperate attempt to search for a way to alter the situation, Jennie soon afterward attended a dinner and dance, just to see Prime Minister Salisbury and talk with him about it. "But he was very nervous," Jennie wrote Leonie in Ireland, "and I had the greatest difficulty to get him to speak of Randolph. I rather had the impression that they could never come together again." And then she sadly added, "Snippy, I feel very sick at heart."

At the age of thirty-seven, Randolph Spencer–Churchill had killed himself politically with one brief letter. The Salisbury Government shook for eleven days, but did not crack. Lord Goschen, a frequent house guest of the Churchills', an old admirer of Jennie's, and a strong critic of Randolph's, was asked to take the position at Exchequer. "I forgot Goschen," Randolph told Lady Jeune.[41]

On January 14, 1887, several weeks after Randolph's resignation, Jennie received a letter from Arthur Brisbane, London correspondent of the New York *Sun*, who later became a prominent editor. Writing from the Hotel Metropole in London's Charing Cross, he said:

My Lady,

An article furnished me this week for enclosure in my Saturday cable to the New York *Sun* deals with the details of a separation which the writer alleges to be pending between yourself and Lord Randolph.

Unwilling to publish so grave a statement without having first made every effort to verify its exactness, I called twice, hoping to see either Lord Randolph or yourself, in order to be guided in correcting or entirely withholding the article in question, by what you might wish to say. If you will make an appointment for me before noon tomorrow, when my dispatch is sent, I shall be pleased to wait upon yourself or Lord Randolph. I endeavored to see your father, Mr. Jerome whom I have met, but could not learn whether he had gone from the Langham. I may add that a cable received today

informs me that rumors are current there of the story, of
which the article sent to me purports to be a confirmation.

Believe me, my lady, very truly yours.

Jennie passed the letter on to Randolph, who promptly wrote a blistering reply to Brisbane. Whatever his matrimonial problems, he had no intention of resolving them publicly, particularly at that time. Brisbane answered that he had simply tried "to save a lady and a compatriot from the uncontradicted publication of scandalous gossip."

"Scandalous gossip" increased when Randolph decided to go off on holiday to the Mediterranean, again without his wife—this time with Harry Tyrwhitt, "a most amiable companion." More rumors of separation or divorce reached public print. The American magazine *Town Topics* ran a leading article, flatly declaring that the real reason Randolph had resigned was his alleged involvement with Lady Brooke, who was suing her husband for divorce and predicting the affair would cause a more explosive scandal than the Dilke case. All kinds of other ill-founded rumors kept cropping up.[42]

In *Savrola*, Lucile's husband plans to abdicate leadership in his government and she asks herself: "Can I do nothing, nothing? Have I played my part? Is the best of life over?" And then, with a hot wave of resolve, "I will do it—but what?"

When a representative from Parliament came to collect the official robes Randolph had worn as Chancellor of the Exchequer,[43] Jennie refused to surrender them, saying, "I am saving them for my son."

Thirteen

HOW DARK THOSE DAYS seemed! Jennie wrote:

> In vain I tried to console myself with the thought that happiness does not depend so much on circumstances as on one's inner self. But I have always found in practice that theories are of little comfort. The vicissitudes of life resemble one of those gilded balls seen in a fountain. Thrown up by the force of the water, it flies up and down; now at the top catching the rays of the sun, now cast into the depths, then again shooting up, sometimes so high that it escapes altogether, and falls to the ground.[1]

Randolph saw it quite differently. "It is certainly very pleasant to get away from the cold and worry of London," he wrote his wife from Algiers. And from Palermo, "In any case, I am in no hurry to come home—and, am, too, thankful I went away." His tour of the Mediterranean lasted two months. It apparently mattered little to him that he had left Jennie behind to face the gaggle of gleeful enemies, the smirks of society, to conduct herself with grace under pressure.

Let us not paint the picture of the sad, mournful wife. Jennie was not that. She had as many friends as her husband had enemies; London society was full of people who would say: hate him, love her. Her friends swarmed around her, her admirers assumed an almost belligerent stand in her defense, her family closed ranks. Soon there were more invitations than ever. She almost became a cause.

"We are sorry Randy is in the muck, less for his own account than for that of the gallant American girl he had the luck to marry," wrote *Town Topics.* "She had worked so hard to popularize him and forward his ends. . . ."[2]

Not that she was dependent on any of that—she had her own strength and courage, her own ability to be flauntingly defiant. She reserved her sadness for letters, revealed her sorrow to her sisters. Everyone else knew only the gay, witty, lovely woman. And she never gave up searching for the slimmest rays of political hope.

In his private diaries, Sir Algernon West recounted his meeting Jennie coming away from Devonshire House and the two of them discussing the Gladstone Government. He told her he doubted the rumors of Gladstone's immediate retirement, but said it was inevitable "that a man whose eyes were gradually getting worse . . . could not last . . . very long."[3] Jennie asked what he thought of the possibility of a dissolution of Parliament. "I said there would be none, unless unforeseen circumstances, such as a defeat, were to happen."

Politics was still on Randoph's mind, much as he tried to blot it out in the hot Mediterranean sun. "When a politician dwells upon the fact that he is thankful to be rid of public cares, and finds serene contentment in private life, it may usually be concluded that he is extremely unhappy," remarked Winston Churchill years later. Tyrwhitt wrote Jennie that Randolph sat brooding and silent for hours, smoking cigarettes incessantly. "What a fool Lord S. was to let me go so easily," Randolph wrote.[4] To Lord Rosebery, who met him in Rome, Randolph confessed, "There is only one place, that is Prime Minister. I like to be boss. I like to hold the reins." Churchill's political tragedy was that when he had the strength to be Prime Minister, he did not have the opportunity; when he had the opportunity, he did not have the strength.

After a short time, the Randolph Churchill affair was overshadowed by the accelerating excitement of the Jubilee Year, Victoria's fiftieth anniversary as Queen of England. "Everything that year was dubbed 'Jubilee,'" wrote Jennie,

> from knights and babies to hats and coats. "God Save the Queen" was heard *ad nauseam* until the tune became an obsession. This led to a practical joke at the Castle which caused much amusement. One morning, speaking of the Jubilee craze, I pretended that I had received as an advertise-

ment a "Jubilee bustle" which would play "God Save the Queen" when the wearer sat down. This, of course, created much curiosity and laughter. Having promised to put it on, I took my hosts into my confidence. An aide-de-camp was pressed into the service, and armed with a small musical box was made to hide under a particular arm-chair. While the company was at luncheon I retired to don the so-called "Jubilee wonder," and when they were all assembled I marched in solemnly and slowly sat down on the arm-chair where the poor aide-de-camp was hiding his cramped limbs. To the delight and astonishment of everyone the National Anthem was heard gently tinkling forth. Every time I rose it stopped; every time I sat down, it began again. I still laugh when I think of it and of the astonished faces about me.

This musical bustle quickly became a London craze, almost "a perfect nuisance."

Winston wanted to come home and share the fun. His Brighton teacher did not want to let him go, because, she said, his parents would be too busy to be with him. But Buffalo Bill had brought his Indian show to London, and Winston was desperate to meet this celebrated friend of his Uncle Moreton. "I shall be very disappointed," he wrote his mother. "Disappointed is not the word, I shall be miserable, after you have promised me, and all, I shall never trust your promises again." He was "in torment" and had many things "pleasant and unpleasant" to tell her. "I must come home, I feel I must. . . . I love you so much dear Mummy and I know you love me too much to disappoint me." He even enclosed the draft of a letter she should write to his teacher. Then in a final postscript, "For Heavens' sake Remember!!!"

She let him come. June 21, 1887, was a memorable day. Jennie described it:

London was crowded to its utmost, and people came from all parts of the world to see the pageant and the crowded ceremony in Westminster Abbey. The day was blessed with the proverbial "Queen's weather." Rarely had I seen London look so festive–blue sky and bright sunshine, flags everywhere and an excited yet patient crowd filling the thoroughfares and the route of the procession. As the wife of an ex-Cabinet Minister, I was given a good place in the Abbey. The magnificent sight impressed me greatly. Gorgeous uniforms and beautiful dresses were enhanced by the "dim religious light," pierced here and there by the rays of the summer sun as it streamed through the ancient stained-glass windows. The Queen, representing the glory and continuity of England's history, sat alone in the middle of the great nave, a small, pathetic figure surrounded by that vast assembly, whose gaze was riveted upon her.

Instead of a black bonnet, which she had worn for twenty-six years of mourning, the Queen wore a coronet-shaped bonnet of white lace covered with diamonds, making her look many years younger. Royalty and the leaders of the world were there, from Queen Emma of Hawaii to the Imperial Prince of Japan.

Gentlemen wore cocked hats and black velvet Court attire, admirals wore uniforms of blue, white, and gold, generals came dressed in brilliant scarlet, judges wore their wigs and robes. Sheriffs were there from the fifty-two counties of England, mayors from all the main cities, representatives from the twelve million square miles of the British Empire. "I think that for once the English were not taking their pleasure sadly," said a writer in the *Monthly Packet.*

Except the Queen. "A wave of emotion passed over the crowd," Jennie wrote, "as silent tears were seen to be dropping one by one upon the Queen's folded hands." Victoria later explained her tears to her Journal:

> The day is come, and I am alone, though surrounded by many dear children. . . . Fifty years today since I came to the throne! God has mercifully sustained me through many trials and sorrow . . . I sat *alone* (Oh, Without my beloved husband, for whom this would have been such a proud day!)[5]

Winston saw his Queen and Buffalo Bill and was taken sailing with Jennie and the Prince of Wales on the royal yacht, where he met a young man whom he would later know better as King George V. His Uncle John also took him to the circus to see the strong man and "the boneless wonder." But Winston was obviously not on his best behavior that holiday because he later felt impelled to write a note of apology to his mother: "I hope you will soon forget my bad behavior while at home, and not make it alter any pleasure in my summer holidays."

He asked his mother to send him a book by Rider Haggard,[6] his favorite author, and notified her that he liked literature "tremendously," was getting along in Euclid "capitally," and enjoyed collecting butterflies "immensely." Proudly he informed her, too, that he had learned to dive off the top springboard and was getting along very well in his role as Robin Hood, but ruefully admitted he was still weak in Greek and added how much he would like five shillings "as I am absolutely bankrupt." He also asked his mother if he and his friends could join her chapter of the Primrose League. "I want to belong to yours most tremendously." A further request was for six autographs from his father and six from his mother. (He apparently did a brisk business in these autographs, as he constantly asked his parents for more of them.)

Jennie and Randolph decided that Winston must have a tutor for the summer to prepare for the entrance examinations to Harrow. When Winston was told of this, he quickly replied that he would be happy to go to Harrow and would tolerate a tutor, but only under one condition, "Not to do any work." It was "against my principles. . . . I have never done work in my holidays and I will not begin now. . . . Even if it is only one hour a day . . . it would hang like a dark shadow over my pleasure. . . ." Then he asked his mother to please visit him, as he had not seen her for three weeks "and I want to see you very very much."

Increasingly bored with politics and himself, Randolph again turned his attention to horses. Jennie gladly joined him. Randolph bought horses in partnership with Lord Dunraven, the only member of the Salisbury Government who had resigned when he did. (Some rumors intimated that their partnership extended beyond horses and included Jennie, whom Dunraven openly admired and frequently escorted.)

The shining light of their shared stable was a beautiful black mare for which they had paid three hundred guineas. Jennie described her as "a gallant little thing with a heart bigger than her body." She had been one of five yearlings up for sale at Doncaster, and one of the reasons Randolph had chosen her was that she was the cheapest of the five. Jennie had been reading a French book by Renan entitled *L'Abbesse de Jouarre* and named the horse after the book. The public, however, nicknamed it "Abcess of the Jaw." But the Abbess soon proved a startling moneymaker,[7] winning the Prince of Wales Handicap, the Portland Plate, and the coveted Manchester Cup (which paid more than $11,000 to the winner). The Churchills, though, both failed to see The Abbess win her biggest victory, the Oaks at Epsom ($13,000), because Randolph was on another fishing trip and Jennie was away visiting with friends. What made it worse was that they had not had any money bet on The Abbess, and the odds against her were twenty to one.

Usually Randolph sat for hours prior to a race, checking his calculations in Ruff's Guide before making his bet. But once he had a dream about a race in which he saw a number hoisted on the board. Checking his race card the next morning, he saw only one horse with that high a number, bet on it heavily, and won. When word of this dream leaked to the press, Lord Hartington was quoted as saying that Lord Randolph "had better give up politics and stick to dreaming."

Of all the racing parks, Newmarket was the best. Ascot was more social and stilted, with its elaborate garden parties and its pageantry of fashion. Goodwood, equally picturesque, with a short racing season during July, was even more famous for its deer, pheasant, kennels, and tennis courts. Epsom Downs, of course, had the Derby and the Oaks in May and June, and the Prince of Wales always made them social events, taking a crowd down on his "Royal Special" train. But Newmarket was the home of horses. Here on the Heath more than a thousand racehorses always seemed to be in some stage of training. Here was the home of the Jockey Club, whose members were the best jockeys of the best horses. The racing tradition at Newmarket was more than two hundred years old, and there was always more talk of animals than of people. It was not the place for Duchesses to come and do their needlework. In fact, of the racing habitués like Jennie, there were hardly a dozen women, and all of them wore country clothes instead of velvets and feathers.

"We would ride out in the early morning from six to seven to see the horses do their gallops," wrote Jennie. "It was a most healthy and invigorating life." It was a good time for both of them. Away from parties and people, away from the friction of politics and the responsibilities of their position, they shared the peace of a country home, the daily conversation that centered on the horses they loved. Riding was so exhilarating that it buoyed them, perhaps brought them closer together than they had been for a long time. "Very pleasant and very fresh it was," Randolph wrote his mother from Newmarket. He also told her that he and Jennie were going to Cowes.

Perhaps they reminisced at Cowes about their first meeting aboard a yacht in the harbor and wondered about the guests of honor at the party—now the Czar and Czarina—for they decided to travel together to Russia the coming winter. But the plan probably did not illustrate the cliché of romance born afresh at the site of a first meeting, as they decided to take along with them two more people. It was an odd ménage—almost as if they had chosen someone for him and someone for her: Tom Trafford and the Marquis de Breteuil.

Like most of Jennie's admirers, Henri Charles Joseph le Tonnelie, the Marquis de Breteuil, was a man of great distinction. Six years older than Jennie, dashing, handsome, brilliant, he had been a much-decorated Captain in the Cavalry during the Franco-Prussian War, a prominent member of the Chamber of Deputies,[8] a strong spokesman for the restoration of the monarchy. Son of a family of distinguished French diplomats, one of Breteuil's ancestors had been the French Ambassador to the Imperial Court of the Empress Catherine of Russia. Had the monarchy returned to power in

France, Breteuil would have become Foreign Minister. He was a dynamic speaker, extremely popular, and a spectacular horseman.

Marcel Proust later knew Breteuil, as well as Jennie, and modeled the "Marquis de Bréauté" in *Remembrance of Things Past* after him. Portraying Bréauté wearing "pearl gray gloves, his crush hat and white tie," Proust further remarked that the Marquis looked through his monocle with "an infinitesimal gaze that swarmed with friendly feeling and never ceased to twinkle at the loftiness of ceilings, the delightfulness of parties, the interestingness of programs and the excellence of refreshments." But the charming Bréauté was also a "would-be connoisseur of art who loved to give advice with an air of expert knowledge on things he knew nothing whatever about, recommended marriages which always failed, suggested interior decorations which looked hideous and urged investments which usually slumped."

Queen Victoria was uneasy about the proposed trip to Russia. She wrote Lord Salisbury, on December 7, 1887, "Think it of great importance that the Foreign Governments and the country should know that Lord Randolph is going simply on a private journey, in no way charged with any message or mission from the Government, nor is likely to return it. . . ."

Reports of the Queen's concern reached Randolph, who wrote to the Prince of Wales repeating that the trip had no political connotations. The Prince forwarded Churchill's letter to the Queen and also expressed his own opinions:

> I know that Lord Randolph's visit has no political object of any kind, as I saw him, the day before he started, at Ashridge. . . . I know he wanted to be out of England till Parliament met, so as to avoid making speeches at meetings, though he entirely supports Lord Salisbury's Government, and I own, I regret that he is not asked to rejoin it, because in spite of his many faults and constant errors of judgment, he is very clever and undoubtedly a power in the country. . . . My impression is that he will be careful, and I expect shortly to hear from him.

The Queen answered:

> I cannot, I own, quite understand *your* high opinion of a man who is clever, undoubtedly, but who is devoid of all principle, who holds the most insular and dangerous doctrines on foreign affairs, who is very impulsive, and utterly unreliable. . . .

Pray don't correspond with him, for he really is *not* to be trusted and is very indiscreet, and his power and talents are greatly overrated. Sir R. Morier agreed with me as to the danger of his visit to Russia and his total unreliableness. I don't state all this from any personal enmity toward Lord Randolph; but I *must* say what I *know from experience* to be the case. Let the subject drop now.

The Prince, however, asked his wife Alexandra to give Randolph and Jennie a letter of introduction to her sister, the Czarina. Upon their arrival in Russia, that letter opened wide every Imperial door and so swept up the Churchills in the orbit of Russian society that they saw only the glitter of the country and none of its sordidness. Jennie was fascinated with Russia:

> Everything was new and attractive to us. The people were charming and hospitable, and seemed full of *bonhomie*, and we saw no signs of that grinding despotism and tyranny which is supposed to be synonomous with Russian life. My first impression of the scenery was one of disappointment, the country between Berlin and St. Petersburg, or rather, the part beyond the Russian frontier, being flat and uninteresting. The waste and dreary expanse, when covered with snow, inspires a feeling of deep melancholy. To live for months every year, buried in that cold, monotonous silence, is quite enough, I should imagine, to account for the vein of sadness which seems to be the basis of the Russian character, and which betrays itself in all Russian music and painting. As our snow-laden train crawled into the station in St. Petersburg, we stepped out joyfully, and stretched our cramped and tired limbs. The broad streets, full of life and animation, and as bright as day with electricity, seemed a delightful contrast. I do not know what I expected to see, but the city disappointed me with its modern appearance. Looking at the houses of rather mean exterior, with their small double windows and tiny doors, little did I dream of the splendor within. Space, however, seemed to be immaterial, and this struck me the more forcibly, accustomed as I was to London, with its narrow streets and considered inches. . . .
>
> I thoroughly enjoyed the outdoor life of sleighing and skating. Comfortably seated in the sleigh, behind the good fat coachman to keep the wind off, I never wearied of driving about. The rapidity with which one dashes noiselessly along

is most exhilarating, notwithstanding a biting wind or blind-
ing snow.

She also admired the coachman, with his furlined coat gathered in at the
waist, his bright red or blue octagonal cap with gold braid, and the way
he did the driving with his arms extended forward in order to preserve
his circulation.

> I was much impressed with the fact that the coachmen
> hardly ever seemed to use their short, thick whips, which
> they kept carefully hidden. A footman stands on a small step
> behind, his tall hat and ordinary greatcoat looking a little in-
> congruous, I confess, and marring an otherwise picturesque
> sight. The horses are so beautifully broken that a word will
> stop them. The whole time I was in Russia, I never saw a
> horse ill-used.

Jennie wrote long descriptive letters about all this to her sisters and her
sons. Those letters became the basis of a magazine article which she later
wrote about Russia and which afterward she developed as part of a book.

The Randolph Churchills had an audience with the Czar and the Czarina in the Winter Palace at Gatchina, about an hour's trainride from St.
Petersburg and approached from the station through a series of small
parks. The Czarina took Jennie on a tour of the palace:

> Among many rooms, I remember a large hall, worthy of
> an old English country-house, full of comfortable armchairs
> and writing tables, games and toys. In that room, their
> Majesties often dined, I was told, even when they had guests;
> and after dinner, the table would be removed, and they would
> spend the remainder of the evening there. This seemed
> strange to me, when I thought of the many hundred rooms in
> the enormous building. But their tastes were the simplest,
> and the Czar particularly affected tiny rooms, though they
> were much at variance with his towering frame and majestic
> bearing. His manner impressed me with a conviction of sin-
> cerity and earnestness.

In his interview with the Czar, Randolph advised the Czar not to take
any notice of the English national press, since "no public man in England
ever cared a rap for anything they said." Randolph later reported that "the
conversation began in French, which was a great disappointment to me, for

he can speak English perfectly; and sometimes he talked rather low and in his beard, so that I, who do not hear very well, missed some of his remarks." Balfour once had described the Czar as "an immense, big fellow, with a good-humored countenance, but not much mind in it." Randolph, however, found much more mind than he expected.

The Czar told him:

> With regard to the Black Sea and the Dardanelles, if you desire peace and friendship with Russia, you must not mix yourselves up there against us. We will never suffer any other power to hold the Dardanelles, except the Turks or ourselves; and if the Turks ultimately go out, it is by Russians that they will be succeeded.
>
> ... You have a great task before you on your return to England—to improve the relations between Russia and England.

Randolph reported that to the Prince of Wales, adding, "I feel certain that they not only do not desire war, but will do much to avoid it." The Queen heard of the correspondence and complained to her son, saying it was dangerous for him to write to Lord Randolph, much less support him. In that, too, the Prince ignored his mother.

Jennie and Randolph, meanwhile, received disturbing news from the Dowager Duchess. Mrs. Everest had contracted diphtheria, and the Duchess had whisked the boys away to Blenheim. "I hope neither of you worry about the children," she wrote.

> Do not mind if you hear I am strict and discourage going out and keep Winston in order. . . . I only do as if they were my own. I do not like Winston going out. . . . I really think he goes out too much and I do object to late parties for him. He is so excitable. . . . He is a dear boy but wants a firm hand.[9]

Winston's letters were unhappy. "I feel very dull—worse than school. It is very dull without you. I do so long to kiss you, my darling Mummy. How I do wish I was with you in the land of 'pink, green and blue Russe.' "

When Winston returned to school, the Duchess wrote Randolph:

> I do not feel sorry for he is certainly a handful. Not that he does anything seriously naughty except to use bad language which is bad for Jack. I am sure Harrow will do

wonders for him for I fancy he was too clever and too
much the boss at that Brighton school. He seems quite well
and strong and very happy–Jack is a good little boy and not
a bit of trouble. . . .

Before leaving St. Petersburg, the Churchills were again invited to
Gatchina. They traveled on a special train with about 150 other guests. Entertainment at the palace featured three short plays, each in a different language, after which supper was served. "I had been given a seat in the third
row," Jennie wrote, "but when the Royalties came in, I was bidden to sit behind the Empress, who every now and then would turn round and make
some pleasant remark."

A woman with a graceful figure and a small head, the Czarina resembled her sister, Princess Alexandra, "though not so beautiful." She asked
Jennie "endless questions about England," and Jennie remembered the Czarina from Cowes as a wholesome normal girl with a love of laughter. Jennie
noted the mass of attendants, some with black, white and orange feathers
in their caps, "giving a slightly barbaric appearance to the scene." Outside
the Czarina's audience chamber were two Nubians dressed in white, with
turbans and scimitars, making the scene even more bizarre.

A New Year's reception was held at eleven in the morning at the Winter
Palace and attended by the whole Court. The procession began as the
Czar, dressed in the uniform of the Gardes du Corps, gave his arm to the
Czarina, who wore a magnificent tiara and a blue velvet and ermine train.
The couple were followed by the Imperial Family. Four young officers car-
ried the train of each Grand Duchess. "I remember that of the young
Grand Duchess Vladimir's was of silver brocade, with a sable border, half-
a-yard in depth," Jennie wrote.

> These were followed by long files of ladies-in-waiting,
> dressed in green and gold, and maids-of-honor in red and
> gold. The procession ended when all the court officials, re-
> splendent in gorgeous uniforms and covered with decora-
> tions, walked with measured steps through the long suite of
> rooms, and lined up on each side with officers in the red,
> white, or blue of their regiments. To these, the Czar spoke as
> he passed, saying, "Good morning, my children," to which
> they replied in unison, "We are happy to salute you."

Jennie observed that most Russian ladies smoked cigarettes, and one of
the reception rooms at a party was always set apart for this purpose,
"which caused a continual movement to and fro–taking off the stiffness of

a formal party and enabling people to circulate more freely . . ." She also noted that Russians had enormous appetites, and were very fond of good living, good eating, and hard drinking.

> Drinking in Russian society is not considered a heinous offense. The night we went to Gatchina, the officer in charge, the Colonel of the Probejensky Guards, the smartest regiment in Russia, who was responsible that night for the safety of the Czar, was so drunk that he fell heavily on my shoulder when presented to me. Those nearer laughingly propped him up, evidently thinking nothing of it.

She found Moscow more striking than St. Petersburg.

> Everything was a source of interest, from the narrow streets filled with a motley crowd of fur-clad people, the markets with their frozen fish or blocks of milk, from which slabs would be chopped off, and carcasses of beasts propped up in rows against the stalls, to the Kremlin, with its palaces and churches. . . . We visited the Trichiakoff Picture Gallery, belonging to a retired merchant, where I was amazed to see depicted all the grimmest and most gruesome incidents of Russian tyranny and cruelty: Ivan the Terrible murdering his son, or receiving on a red staircase of the Kremlin, a hapless envoy, whose foot he transfixed to the floor with a spike ferrule of his walking-stick, while he read some unwelcome passage; Siberian prisoners; horrible deeds perpetrated in the Fortress of Peter and Paul; and many other atrocities.[11]

She also visited a museum, where she found an Italian cabinet which had been at Blenheim before being sold.

All their visits were fully covered in the *Moscow Gazette*, which paid high compliment to Lord and Lady Randolph. It reported that they visited Prince Dolgoroukoff, Governor-General of Moscow and attended the opera with him, after which the Prince gave a grand dinner in honor of his guests. Dolgoroukoff was a charming old man of 80; a "*Grand Seigneur* of the old school, he looked very smart and upright in the uniform of the Chevalier Gardes. He told me that he had been 22 years Governor of Moscow, and had served 56 in the Army under three Czars."

The Prince had issued an order requiring all beggars to be off the streets so that the Churchills would not be annoyed by them. And the couple was also followed throughout Moscow by two detectives, not, as we at first imagined, to spy upon us, but to see that, as distinguished strangers, we were not molested in any way.

Before leaving, we attended the "Bal de la Noblesse," in the Assembly Room. It was a fine sight, the floor excellent, and the music most enspiriting. . . . Officers would be brought up to me, clicking their spurs together and saluting; then they would seize my waist without a word, and whisk me around the enormous room at a furious pace, my feet scarcely touching the ground. Before I had recovered, breathless and bewildered, I would be handed over to the next, until I had to stop from sheer exhaustion.

Just before the Churchill's departure, there was a last round of gala parties in their honor, including one at the British Embassy for six hundred people.[12] "It would bore me dreadfully to go to all these dinners and parties and things," Lord Randolph wrote to his mother, "but here it amuses me. I wonder why it is." The day they left Moscow, the Governor came to see them off, and presented Jennie with a lovely bouquet of orchids. The temperature, however, was twenty-two degrees below zero and the flowers shriveled before she had time to sit down.

While the men of Russia had impressed her, so had the women:

Not indulging in any sport and taking little or no exercise, they stay a great deal indoors, and in consequence, have much time to educate themselves, to read, and to cultivate the fine arts. Speaking many languages, and reading widely, they form a most attractive society. . . . It was, however, a matter of surprise to me that women so eminently fitted by nature and education to influence and help those struggling in the higher vocations of life, should have seemingly but one ambition, to efface themselves, to attract no attention, to rouse no jealousies. Yet I doubt not that their influence is felt, though it may not be open and fearless, as in England or America.

One woman of influence was the Dowager Duchess of Saxe-Coburg-Gotha, the only daughter of the previous Czar, Alexander II. She had married the Duke of Edinburgh and had lived in England until his death. As the Czar's daughter, it had been her duty for two hours daily to read her father's correspondence and the secret news of the world. She and Jennie were dear friends, and Jennie maintained an extensive correspondence with her throughout the years.

On their way home, the Churchills spent five days in Berlin. It was perhaps not a coincidence that Count Kinsky was there. He had been transferred to the Berlin Embassy in September 1887, after having been recalled to the Foreign Office in Vienna some months earlier. He would become the Secretary of the Berlin Embassy by March 1888 and would again be transferred to London. For Jennie and Kinsky their time in Berlin allowed a brief reunion.

Randolph wrote his mother that upon seeing Otto von Bismarck he had noticed that the "old Emperor was looking very brisk." In 1886 Prince Otto von Bismarck had made his son Count Herbert von Bismarck-Schonhausen Secretary of State, putting him in full charge of foreign affairs. Discussing Herbert von Bismarck, Randolph wrote, "We talked very freely for a long time and drank a great deal of beer, champagne, claret, sherry and brandy! H. B. is delightful, so frank and honest. . . ."

Jennie wrote of a private dinner the Count gave in Berlin for the Churchills: "I remember that at this dinner he had an argument on the subject of Mr. Gladstone, whom he cordially hated." Count Herbert quoted his father as saying, "Gladstone would drag England to the lowest ground of Hell." In later years, Herbert would change his mind about Gladstone and yet become increasingly anti-British, favoring an alliance instead with Russia. But at that time the Bismarcks were friends of Great Britain.

Herbert von Bismarck was a giant of a man with a long, blond mustache and blue eyes. He and Jennie were quickly attracted to each other, and the attraction grew over the years into a long-lasting affair. It was typical of Jennie that she found herself in Berlin ardently surrounded by three suitors—Bismarck, Breteuil, and Count Kinsky. Bismarck's reputation for women-chasing was as celebrated as Kinsky's and Breteuil's—he had just been involved in a divorce scandal with a popular singer. The jealousy and competition of the three men for Jennie was natural, but what was not natural was Randolph's obvious friendships with all three men, friendships he maintained throughout his lifetime.[13] It was almost as if there were an unspoken arrangement: Jennie could have her lovers and Randolph had Tom Trafford and Henry Tyrwhitt, among others.[14]

Jennie and Randolph visited the palaces, galleries, and museums of Berlin. In one of the galleries, they saw three paintings which had been at Blenheim, one of them the famous "Bacchanalia" by Rubens, which had covered one wall of the dining room.

On the gala performance night at the opera, the Churchills were taken into a small room where the Emperor William stood surrounded by the Royal Family, Court officials, and the Diplomatic Corps.

> The Emperor, looking most upright in a smart uniform,
> welcomed me in a few well-chosen words, also referring to

our tea party at Gastein and the jokes we had had with the children. Little did I or anyone else present think that this was to be his last entertainment, and that in a few weeks, the kind and noble old monarch would be no more. Suddenly, a side door opened; the Empress Augusta, sitting in a small bath-chair, was wheeled in. Dressed in pale blue satin, with jewels to her waist, her venerable head crowned with a magnificent tiara, she made a brave, if somewhat pathetic, figure. She asked me many questions in excellent English, addressing me as "Lady Churchill," and inquiring after the Czarina, whom she understood I had just seen. She also asked so much after her "dear Queen Victoria," that I came to the conclusion that she was mistaking me for Queen Victoria's lady-in-waiting, Jane, Lady Churchill. Her remarks were almost inaudible; and I had to answer in a very loud voice, as she did not hear well. I do not recollect ever having felt more embarrassed or uncomfortable than during this conversation at cross-purposes, carried on before the whole Court, which was listening in respectful silence.

In a letter to Leonie, Jennie described the Emperor and Empress as

both half alive only and their ancient bodies covered with Orders. The Empress a thin mummy with her whole breast removed from cancer, yet it was covered with jewels, her head tied on! And she jerked out her orders like an automaton, and was then carried off and put to bed! And the Emperor was not allowed to dine.

After leaving Berlin, Randolph and Jennie stopped off in Paris to meet General Boulanger, the French "man on horseback," who intended to return royalty to power in France. Boulanger impressed Randolph but not Jennie. He was a handsome man with a fierce mustache, immensely popular, particularly with rich French widows, but Jennie sensed that he was "a man not quite sure of himself." He later came to dine several times at their home in London, but only confirmed Jennie's original impression. She proved to be right. Boulanger had a single moment in the French plebiscite of 1889 when he could have swept himself into power, but prolonged his hesitation until it was too late. A French critic described him as "a comet crossing the skies—an empty-headed thing with a fiery tail."

Fourteen

𝒰PON THE CHURCHILLS' RETURN to London, Randolph dutifully reported his observations of Russia to Prime Minister Salisbury. A few short years earlier, Salisbury would have been respectful of Lord Randolph's opinion, but now he passed them on to the Queen with the curt comment, "It seems odd that so clever a man should attach the slightest value to such a promise on the part of Russia."[1]

Salisbury had moved up his nephew, Arthur Balfour, to fill the vacuum left by Randolph. The appointment was not mere nepotism; Balfour had served as Chief Secretary in Ireland, made a record of clear accomplishment, and revealed a tough core beneath his genteel features. "The Conservative Party are evidently tired of Lord Randolph," wrote *Punch* critic Henry Lucy, "and turn with favor to welcome a rising young man, who, they say, at least, has never betrayed them."

Balfour was also the central sun of an intellectual group called "The Souls." The Earl of Ronaldshay, George Curzon's official biographer, credits Jennie with inventing the name. British Society had split off into three main streams, and only a handful, like Jennie, swam in all of them. First, there was the Queen's Set, also called the Court Set or The Incorruptibles—old families of conservative lords and lineage, the quiet, class-conscious crowd of form and tradition. Then there was the Smart Set, the group that clustered around the Prince of Wales, also known as the Marlborough

House Set, the Party Set, or the Horsey Set. And finally there were The Souls. Instead of playing bridge or baccarat, this small, select group preferred to meet regularly to "talk about each other's souls."[2]

Lady Warwick, who was more body than soul, described them this way:

> This little coterie of Souls loved literature and art and were perhaps more pagan than soulful. They were decidedly ambitious, clever and well-read, and exercised great influence on London society for five or six years. I think they sent us all back to reading more than we otherwise should have done, and this was an excellent thing for us.[3]

The world of the intellectual had increasingly become Jennie's world. Most of the men in her life had intellectual qualities of the first rank. She could talk to them on their own terms, just as she could the jockeys at Newmarket on theirs, and just as she could discuss Society with Lady Dorothy Nevill or music with Paderewski or clothes with the Countess of Warwick or the theater with Sir Henry Irving.

She already had created something of a small literary stir with her magazine article about her Russian trip. A British publisher later thought enough of her French and her literary style to contract her to translate a French book into English. But her real literary prominence would come after the turn of the century, when she would be best known as an author, playwright, editor, and publisher of *The Anglo-Saxon Review*.

Describing a Souls dinner party at the Bachelor's Club, the *World* wrote: "This highest and most aristocratic cult comprises only the youngest, most beautiful and most exclusive of married women in London. . . ." Asked to sum up these Souls, Sir William Harcourt said, "All I know about The Souls is that some of them have very beautiful bodies." The fact was that women Souls were supposed to be different from "all those people who have lovers," but the main difference was their discretion, not their abstinence.

One of the pastimes of the Souls was for each participant to write a parody on half an hour's notice. George Curzon wrote one of Edgar Allan Poe's "The Bells":

> *I sing the attraction of the Belles,*
> *   London Belles,*
> *   Society Belles.*
> *Of the manifold allurement of the Belles.*
> *Oh what rhapsodies their charm deserves;*
> *How delicious and delirious are the curves*

With which their figure swells—
Voluptuously and voluminously swells—
To what deed the thought impels.

Curzon had an opinion on everything, and it was always an absolute opinion. Debating with Curzon in Parliament, a Thomas Bowles dissolved the House into laughter when he pointed to Curzon and said, "That is my difficulty which I am sure you all share. He has been everywhere; he has seen everything; he has read all the books—he has written most of 'em."[4] Years later, Winston Churchill said of Curzon:

> Commons found something lacking in him. It was certainly not information nor application, nor power of speech nor attractiveness of manner and appearance. Everything was in his equipment . . . yet somehow or other the total was incomplete . . . The House considered him from the earliest day of his membership a lightweight. He aroused both admiration and envy but neither much love nor much hatred.

Oscar Wilde would be even more devastating, calling Curzon a "plodding mediocrity." Though he may often have been more hardworking than brilliant, more fluent than witty, Curzon's later record as Viceroy of India was largely a distinguished one. There is small question that he was one of the most popular Souls.

Jennie Churchill could attend a meeting of The Souls—at The Clouds, the home of Sir Percy Wyndham, for example—settle back in a sofa, and count a whole cluster of men there who had courted her, including their leaders, Balfour and Curzon. Among the more interesting men for her, was the handsome, six-foot-four future Ambassador to Berlin, Lord D'Abernon.[5] Freshly returned from a visit to the United States, D'Abernon had received the red-carpet treatment from a horde of social matrons eager to capture him. His abilities as linguist, horseman, and fencer were celebrated. He had recently served as financial advisor to the Khedive. He refused to touch liquor, abhorred ice, and liked to talk about his brother, who was the Chief of Detectives of London police.

Soul-member Margot Tennant (later the wife of Prime Minister Asquith) wrote of D'Abernon, "His face was even more conspicuous than his height and the beauty of his countenance can never be forgotten."

Another of Jennie's conquests, one who lingered longer than most, was Henry John Cockayne Cust, whom his Soul-mates called Harry. Sir Ronald Storrs, his nephew, years later referred to an Eton professor who had taught in succession Rosebery, Curzon, and Cust and who, of the three, had chosen Cust as the future Prime Minister. Cust was not only "irresistibly fascinating" to women,[6] but in many ways the most brilliant and enthusiastic of all the Souls. A sensitive poet, an athlete, a scholar, a fastidious critic, a handsome man with a flowing mustache, he was also reckless and self-indulgent and the heir to the Brownlow barony.

Cust wrote considerable love poetry, most of it privately published, and each of his women friends felt each poem was privately for her. It was thought that "To a Portrait," was for Jennie:

> *Beautiful Face!*
> *Is your heart broken that you look so sad*
> *Is there no heart of earth that once made glad*
> *Your heart, to hearten yet your flower of grace*
> *Is God untender toward you*
> *Or can Man,*
> *Loving such dear eyes. Or, save despairing*
> *For too much caring,*
> *Grudge his uncrownedness in the race he ran,*
> *And squandered life and loved, and lost the prize*
> *They pay the worthiest cost,*
> *Whose lives for you were lost."*

And "Amictus Amoris":

> *About the perfect body of my love*
> *A Vesture clings, wherefrom no force may free her.* . . .

And "Immortal End":

> *It matters not what life we spend,*
> *What anguish we inspire,*
> *So there be one immortal end*
> *To one immense desire.*

Cust once gave a dinner for some twenty guests, including Balfour and probably Jennie. The talk was so absorbing that when a fire broke out upstairs, both the dinner and the conversation continued. While the firemen were fighting the blaze, the footmen passed out bath towels to the dinner guests to protect them from the water of the hoses.

Little towels could not protect the Souls, however, from the steady stream of criticism. A satire by W. H. Mallock was representative of the kind of attack generally made on them:

You keep talking of faith, of devotion and purity,
Things deep and things high are your favorite themes;
We have dreamed of them, too; but our song, in maturity,
Has sunk to one burden, "Goodbye to our dreams."
Oh sons and Oh daughters of art and of culture!
Forget for a moment your play and your parts;
And take pity upon us, for whom time is a vulture,
Which leaves us our livers and feeds on our hearts.

The criticism was well taken. The world of Jennie's Souls was the world of the abstract and the intellectual and had little to do with the livers and hearts of London.[7] Although Jennie moved easily among the varied levels of society, and although she had penetrated to the level of the working people during her political campaigning, her understanding of their living conditions was superficial. Times were changing. Among the English masses there was restlessness as well as fear. The poet and essayist Matthew Arnold feared that England was "on the verge of anarchy."[8] When London dockworkers asked for an additional sixpence an hour, most employers considered this a "monstrous wage increase." Many of Jennie's friends thought that laborers must be kept in their place, for "the more you give them, the more they will ask." But the dockworkers won public sympathy when they paraded the London streets carrying pikes upon which they stuck samples of the horrible food their pitiful pay forced them to eat.[9]

This was a time when the poverty line for a family of five was put at fifty-five pounds ($275) a year, and almost 16 million English workers (including postmen and policemen) earned less than fifty pounds a year. Most of the white-collar class (about 3 million people) earned an average of seventy-five pounds a year. Farm workers still used the scythe and the sickle, working from 5 A.M. until dark. Indoor servants still slept in basements without windows or in attics without fresh air. And those too old to work almost inevitably faced the end in a poorhouse.

If Jennie knew little of this, Randolph knew less. What they did know was there were 115 persons in England who each owned more than fifty thousand acres, half of these landowners with an annual income of fifty thousand pounds. Of the forty-five who owned 100,000 acres, half of them had an annual income of 100,000 pounds. Of the 45 million people then in Great Britain, there were 2,500 landowners, each of whom owned more than 3,000 acres.

Randolph had talked of "Tory democracy," criticizing the inbred rule of the aristocracy, and Jennie had sympathized with and encouraged his view, but both nonetheless had gravitated toward the powerful rather than the weak. The Reverend Benjamin Jowett, Master of Balliol College at Oxford, had said, "We must study the arts of uniting Society as a whole, not cling-ing to any one class of it." Jennie was still a snob and would remain so the rest of her life, but more and more now she and Randolph chose their friends on the basis of intelligence, talent, accomplishment, charm, but not social class.

Lord Randolph was still a member of the House of Commons for the safe seat of Paddington, but he was a quiet member, most often absent. De-spite the depth of his political dive, however, there were still many who ex-pected him to bounce back to the surface. Randolph himself, however, seemed disgusted with the interplay of politics and found himself in oppo-sition to the Salisbury Government on a growing number of issues. When a friend told him he hoped to live to see Randolph back again in the Cabi-net, Randolph answered swiftly, "I sincerely hope you will not."

He now limited his horizons. The Prime Ministership was a dead dream, but what about the position of Viceroy of India? He knew India and had many friends there. It would restore glitter to his name, fame to his family, and provide an end to his increasing financial worries. Salisbury heard about Randolph's great expectations and wrote to the Queen:

> I understand he [Randolph] has told two of his friends
> that the post above all others he desires is that of Viceroy of
> India. Of course it is impossible; his reputation for rashness
> is too pronounced, but it is odd that he should desire it. It is
> said that his pecuniary position is very bad.[10]

Salisbury was right about the Churchills' "pecuniary position." Their Russian trip had been expensive and they had borrowed from banks to make it possible. Randolph even felt impelled to borrow money from his sister Cornelia's husband.

Whatever the deterioration of his mind and personality and the bleak-ness of his future, Randolph maintained a sense of the fitness of things. At any time he could have lent his renowned name to the Board of Directors of a number of corporations and lived well from the fat payments. Many of his friends had done so, but he would have none of it. His dignity and his code and his heritage were immutable.

They thankfully had Jennie's annual income from the rental of the Madison Square house, as well as frequent "tips" from her father. Of all the Jerome women, Jennie received the most money and love from their father. From the content of his letters, however, it is clear that Jerome did not know of Randolph's fatal disease. He realistically evaluated the futures of two of his sons-in-law—seeing John Leslie's clear road to respectability, Moreton Frewen's cloudy road to despair—but Randolph's road supposedly full of great promise of political achievement. So if he financially coddled Jennie and Randolph whenever he could, if he catered to their needs more than the others', it was not only because of his special relationship with Jennie but also because he regarded the Churchills' future as greater than the others'.

Jerome came to visit them that year, as he often did, and more carefully inspected his grandson Winston, whom Mrs. Jerome had described as "a naughty, sandy-haired little bulldog." Mrs. Jerome preferred Jack, who was much quieter, more polite, more predictable.

Winston was thirteen years old, working hard to prepare himself for the entrance examination to Harrow, scheduled for March 1888. "You will be pleased to hear," he wrote his mother, "that we are learning the geography of the U.S. When I come home, you must question me."

Miss Charlotte Thomson of the Brighton School, who escorted him to the examinations for Harrow, wrote Jennie afterward that Winston had a "severe attack of sickness" after the exam, due "to the nervous excitement."

In his reminiscences, Winston Churchill remembered that he had not answered a single question on the Latin paper. "I wrote my name at the top of the page," he noted.

> I wrote down the number of the question, "I." After much reflection I put a bracket round it thus, "(I)." But thereafter I could not think of anything connected with it that was either relevant or true. Incidentally, there arrived from nowhere in particular a blot and several smudges. I gazed for two whole hours at this sad spectacle: and then merciful ushers carried it up to the Headmaster's table. It was from these slender indications of scholarship that Mr. Welldon drew the conclusion that I was worthy to pass into Harrow.[11]

As headmaster, Welldon had considerable latitude in evaluating the tests. While Winston had blanked out in the Latin exam, his marks in arithmetic had been "the best." The thirty-four-year-old Reverend J. E. C. Welldon was new at the job, but he was not so new that he was unaware Winston Churchill was the son of one of the most important men in England who still, conceivably, might one day be Prime Minister. Before the examinations, in fact, Welldon had received a letter from one of the Marlboroughs, informing him about Winston's application. Welldon had answered that it would be a pleasure for him to find room at Harrow for the son of Lord Randolph Churchill.

"I have passed," Winston wrote his mother, "but it was far harder than I expected."

Winston Churchill later liked to exaggerate his schoolboy stupidity, perhaps to make his eventual metamorphosis seem all the more astonishing. But his dullness was a fiction. Like most boys, Winston did well in some subjects, poorly in others. Latin and Greek he had never liked, but at Brighton School he had won prizes in English and in Scripture, and he had always come out high in History. Welldon wrote Jennie that Winston was not "in any way wilfully troublesome," and "I do not think he is idle, only his energy is fitful, and when he gets to his work, it is generally too late for him to do it well." The headmaster described Winston as "a remarkable boy in many ways . . . as far as ability goes, he ought to be at the top of his form, whereas he is at the bottom."

Later the headmaster also reported to Jennie that Winston's slovenliness was "phenomenal," and added, "if he is unable to conquer this slovenliness . . . he will never make a success of public school." Furthermore, Winston's

> forgetfulness, carelessness, unpunctuality and irregularity in every way have really become so serious, that I write to ask you, when he is at home, to speak very gravely to him on the subject. . . . He is so regular in his irregularity that I really don't know what to do.

Jennie's letters to Winston at Harrow usually accentuated the positive but not always. She knew when to prod and when to approve, just as she understood the need for absolute sternness. She was, after all, not only the mother of her two sons but had to take the role of father as well. Randolph at best was indifferent to them. Winston's letters to his father were usually either pleading or apologetic. "I have written a very long letter and have taken up a lot of your time," he once respectfully wrote, adding, "When do you think you'll be able to come and see me?"

Discussing his father with Frank Harris years later, Winston Churchill said, "He wouldn't listen to me or consider anything I said. There was no companionship with him possible to me and I tried so hard and so often. He was so self-centered no one else existed for him." And then he added quietly, "My mother was everything to me."[12]

While Jennie did try to help organize Winston's mind and discipline his behavior, she never tried to stifle his spirit. Lady Warwick noted this during one of Winston's weekends home: "True to her American training, she did not check Winston when he asked questions or argued with her."[13] When he felt that he was being treated unfairly at school, he begged his mother to come to Harrow and argue with Welldon about it. "You must stick up for me, because if you don't, nobody else will. . . . Now you know Mama you told me to rely on you and tell you everything so I am taking your advice."

He had no one else. He loved Mrs. Everest deeply, but she was a simple, uneducated woman. As a child, he had been able to confide in her fully, but he could not as a growing young man full of new ideas. Both grandmothers were stiff martinets. He loved his American grandfather, but saw him only seldom. He saw his own father hardly more. His aunts were lovely and interested, but busy with their own broods. His mother was the only one he could always reach. She often kept her own distance and she did not always fall in with his wishes, but he knew how to focus on her guilt feelings, knew how much he could persist. But most of all, he was sure of her love. More than just a mother's love, her devotion was part of another love she was gradually transferring from her husband to her sons.

Jennie did go to Harrow to defend her son against the headmaster's severity, but she still maintained a severity of her own with him. When she considered his letters too slangy, she tried to stir in him a greater readiness of expression, a greater concern for language. When his reports were poor, it was she who wrote the letter that his father should have written: "You know darling how I hate to find fault with you, but I can't help myself this time." His report was "a *very* bad one." His work was fitful and "inharmonious." If only he were a little more methodical, she said, she would *try* to find an excuse for him.

> You make me very unhappy. I had built up such hopes about you and felt so proud of you—and now all is gone. My only consolation is that your conduct is good, and that you are an affectionate son—but your work is an insult to your intelligence. If you would only trace out a plan of action for yourself and be determined to do so—I am sure you could accomplish anything you wished.

His thoughtlessness was his biggest enemy, she wrote. He was old enough to understand the seriousness of this and realize that what he did in the next year or two could affect his whole life. "Stop and think it out for yourself and take a good pull before it is too late. You know dearest boy that I will always help you all I can."

Winston's reply was contrite: "My own Mummy I can tell you your letter cut me up very much." He admitted he had been "rather lazy" and promised to "do my *very best* in what remains."[14]

Randolph was more concerned about his horses. His references to Jennie in his letters at this time concerned her coming from somewhere or going to somewhere else, but he mentioned very little about their going anywhere together. He was soon off to Tarbes, France, where he was a guest of the Marquis de Breteuil. "Here we are, peaceable and comfortable," he wrote Jennie. "Beautiful weather, splendid mountains, nothing to worry about." He told of the arrival of a Parisian actress traveling with two men—one who was "her first and original lover, who is now only her friend, and with another young man, who is the present lover. These three travel about together. So French!"

It would be difficult to imagine Randolph's remarks were simply innocent gossip, rather than at least an oblique reference to the parallel in his own life. Jennie was never blatant about her relationship with Breteuil or anyone else, but neither was she furtive. Whenever Randolph was away, which was often, there were men who escorted her everywhere. The names of all of them were linked with hers in the press, in society living rooms, in family letters. News of all this certainly reached Randolph from a dozen directions.

Why, then, would he pay a prolonged visit to Breteuil? For the same reasons, perhaps, that he had invited the Marquis to join them on their trip through Russia. The simple, strange fact was that, despite their obvious relationship with Jennie, he liked Breteuil, Kinsky, the Prince of Wales, Herbert von Bismarck—and they all liked him and honestly admired the qualities in him that could have made him greater than they. It is true that Randolph had occasional rows with some of them, open clashes that reached public print. The Prince of Wales acted as mediator in one heated argument between Randolph and Count Kinsky, and again intervened when Randolph threatened to thrash the Prince's 23-year-old son for too open and too ardent courting of Jennie. The Prince packed his son off to Malta. And Jennie's nephew, Shane Leslie, remembered the evening that Randolph ordered the 48-year-old Prince of Wales out of his house for paying similar attention to Jennie.[15]

But all these were quarrels soon repaired. Randolph had long ago resigned himself to the status of cuckold, and he surfaced in anger only when the gossip became too blatant and unbearable or when his strained nerves tore him apart. Most important, he wanted to preserve a proper social face on his marriage for the few remaining years of his life. He was too tired for scandal, too drained to face divorce, and ever-aware of the demands of his heritage.

He did have one platonic, female friend, who also became one of Jennie's closest friends—Pearl Mary Teresa Richards, daughter of a New York merchant who had settled in England. She was a dozen years younger than Jennie, but they shared a passion for music and had known unhappiness in marriage. She had married Reginald Craigie in 1887, borne him a son in 1890, and divorced him the same year. Later she became a prominent novelist under the pseudonym John Oliver Hobbes.

Randolph's brother Blandford, on the other hand, wanted more than platonic female friends. During that summer of 1888, he went to New York, where Leonard Jerome had lined up a prospective new bride, a good-natured, very wealthy widow named Lily Hammersley. She had gained some notoriety by covering the walls and ceiling behind her opera-box with orchids. "I hope the marriage will come off," Jerome wrote his wife, "as there is no doubt she has lots of tin."

The New York press gave Blandford a mixed greeting. One of the more gossipy journals wrote, "Where the great Marlborough conquered campaigns, the little Marlborough conquers courtesans; the man of the past won battles, the man of the present wins bawds." Another magazine, noting Blandford's thirty-five pieces of luggage, remarked, "Everything His Grace of Marlborough brought with him was clean, except his reputation."[16]

Blandford's visit was not confined to bride-hunting and "boozy" parties. He met Thomas Alva Edison and talked of his plans for a scientific laboratory at Blenheim. Edison wrote of him to Moreton, "I thought the English Duke was a fool with a crown on his head. But this man knows a great deal which I do not intend inventing till next fall."[17]

Before the month was out, Jerome reported, "Well, Blandford is married! I went with him to the Mayor's office in the City Hall at one o'clock today and witnessed the ceremony. I took charge of his cable to the Duchess. Also sent one of my own to Jennie."

The new Duchess of Marlborough came in for much critical comment. Snidely observing that the Duke had obviously been smitten "by her manifold charms and her multifarious millions," one magazine noted that the Duchess Lily weighed some 160 pounds, was "a common looking and badly dressed woman with a mustache, but yet a pleasant face." It then pointed out that she also had an annual income of 150,000 dollars a year and a personal fortune of some five million dollars. "And ready cash buys Norman blood." Another report proclaimed that her spaniels dined on chicken fricassee, cream, and macaroons, and slept on silk sheets under satin blankets.

The press also observed that the Duke's first wife had been a god-daughter of Queen Victoria, and as the Queen was still incensed about the scandalous divorce, it seemed quite unlikely that Duchess Lily would be presented at Court. "The Lord Chamberlain must rue the day when the Queen consented to receive American women at Court," added *Society Magazine*. "The poor man has been so besieged with applications." Discussing "the successful raids made by our American sisters-in-law on the English marriage market," *Society* further commented: "The American republic was founded, it has been said, by housemaids out of place, and mechanics out of employment. It is being solidified by English aristocrats out of elbows."

"I like the Americans very well," said Lady Dorothy Nevill, "but there are two things I wish they would keep to themselves—their girls and their tinned lobster."[18]

Blandford, however, had no complaints. His wife's money enabled him to make many badly-needed repairs at Blenheim and to convert the palace's top floor into a giant laboratory for his experiments in chemistry and metallurgy. Randolph described the improvements to his mother:

> Well! Have seen everything here, and am not very much impressed. All the electric-lighting and heating in stables have been well-done, and are no doubt great improvements. Although there may have been heaps of money spent on the drawing-rooms, I cannot see much, if any, improvement; they might just as well have been left alone. I have been rather bored here. The Duchess Lily talks about Blandford and to Blandford all day long, flatters him and exalts him to his heart's content. He believes himself to be a beneficent genius. . . . I never knew anything like the unpunctuality here; yesterday, we did not get breakfast till eleven, lunch until three, and dinner till nine; most tiresome. I don't think the Duchess Lily looking at all well in health, and the mustache and beard are becoming serious. . . . [19]

But Jennie moved quickly to ease Duchess Lily's entry into English social life. In the course of years, Jennie had become a kind of bridge between the new American brides and the old British. She recognized that a new arrival must maneuver to make an entry. In the case of the visiting Mrs. Cornelius Vanderbilt, Jennie simply arranged for a small dinner party with the Prince and Princess of Wales. In the case of Duchess Lily, it was not so simple. It took all of Jennie's assets to help launch the Duchess. Jennie realized better than most that it mattered little to most Englishmen whether an American woman's father was a landowner or a streetcleaner—as long as the American woman was bright, beautiful, witty, and rich. In Duchess Lily's case, her money had to make up for her other obvious deficiencies, although Jennie did manage to persuade her to diet twenty pounds from her heavy figure and remove some of the excessive hair from her face. In all this, Jennie had the determined help of her five sisters-in-law—Lady Wimborne, Lady De Ramsey, Lady Marjoribanks, Lady Curzon, and the Duchess of Roxburghe—as well as the Dowager Duchess, all of whom pressured their friends to accept the new Duchess of Marlborough.

Jennie was soon concerned with other family problems—news of her father was discouraging. He had been forced to give up Jerome Park, had witnessed the deterioration of the American Jockey Club, and was searching fruitlessly for funds to build a new race course. Past seventy, Jerome was often rakishly called "The Squire," but his letters had begun to show him as a beaten and bitter man. He complained to his wife that he had just paid the year's "ugly bill" for taxes of $4,551.90 and that he had mailed Leonie a hundred pounds. To Leonie he had felt impelled to write:

> I think you must give up your Newport excursion. It would be very charming, but unavoidably expensive. It's the first time I refused any of you girls anything on the ground of expense. I must really know how some things are going to turn out before spending any more than we can reasonably help.

Leonie and John Leslie made a dramatic decision. John resigned from the Guards and he and Leonie moved to Paris so that he could study art at Julien's Academy. But John Leslie's painting would never be as successful as his marriage. Even years later, Leonie's letters to her husband were always full of her love, as when she wrote him, "The more I think of you, the more adorable do you appear. I mentally kiss you from head to foot."[20]

And enduring passion also kept Clara married to her everwandering Moreton. He would write her:

> Lovers we are always . . . so often, half awakening, I feel for the soft fair beauties that were my own, and I find them not. But sometimes a dear dream of love comes to me and once again I hold you in my arms and press long lingering kisses on your lips, your neck, your glowing bosom . . . when I return—I pray late very late—may I wanton with the lovely masses of that bright hair, may I kiss you anywhere everywhere at my own dearest will. May I sink all my life and strength in fervent passion. . . . [21]

Leonard Jerome was particularly fond of Frewen. "I don't wonder you are in love with him," he told Clara. "I am in love with him myself." As for Moreton's failure to make a fortune, Jerome wrote, "It is nothing here. It is a common saying that one must fail once or twice here before he learns how to make or keep a fortune."

Moreton had a new hope now. Randolph had recommended him as financial advisor to Sir Salar Jung to help clear up the mess in his Indian state of Hyderabad. The elder Jung had allied his Mohammedan subjects to the British, and his son had shot tigers with Randolph. Sir Salar was a huge man, six feet four and weighing 330 pounds at the age of twenty-four. He was also charming, intelligent, ambitious. But he drank too much, and the Nizam of Hyderabad had displaced him as Prime Minister and sent him into exile. Frewen had to try to arrange a rapprochement between Sir Salar and the Nizam, and then worry about improving the state's finances, as well as his own.[22]

Upon joining Sir Salar in Cairo, one of Frewen's first assignments was to bargain in a Turkish harem for a bride for Sir Salar. And when Sir Salar wanted to go to England to see a big horse race. Moreton had Leonie rent Cardinal Manning's large house near Goodwood and collect a cheerful party. Among the guests were the Duke of Marlborough, who spoke Urdu, Jennie, and Count Kinsky. Kinsky brought along an Hungarian band, whose discordant notes caused two Indians to hurry away from the party.[23]

After returning to India with Sir Salar, several of Morton's letters to Leonie contained urgent messages:

> Ask Jennie to write Sir Salar how sorry she was not to see him to say goodbye and a little civil regret that she and Randolph were out of town. If R. would write a form of letter of this sort, it would do heaps of good. . . .
>
> . . . I hope Jennie has written to thank Sir Salar for that silver work, if not please remind her and ask her to write an exceptionally friendly letter. . . . I am feeling grateful even to Randolph, and if I make a million here in railroads, I will send Jane a "bit." [Moreton often called Jennie "Jane."]

Sir Salar never was reinstated as Prime Minister, even though he kissed the Nizam's boot. So Moreton, without a fortune, headed for America to work on his project to create a new town out of a natural port in Canada, a project in which he had persuaded Count Kinsky to invest.

Moreton's first letter home carried sad news about Lawrence Jerome. "Dear, kind Uncle Larry . . . is sinking fast. Everyone feels that a great friend is going from the world." When Lawrence died, the New York *Tribune* obituary said, "The merriest spirit in all the world goes when Lawrence Jerome crosses the dark river."[24] Leonard Jerome was heartbroken over the death of his favorite brother. The two had married sisters, lived in adjoining houses, made, lost, and risked fortunes together; they were not only men of the same blood but of kindred natures.

Lawrence Jerome was buried in the family mausoleum in Greenwood Cemetery, Brooklyn, in a massive vault overlooking the water. Nearby rested Jennie's seven-year-old sister Camille.

Lawrence left his wife, the vinegary Catherine Hall, and two sons. (It was Catherine whom some in the family called "Hatchet Face.") When Alderman Murphy of the Bronx renamed Jerome Avenue after himself, Catherine ordered new signs made and hired a crew of workmen to change all the "Murphy" signposts back to "Jerome"—and so they stayed. Lovell Jerome, the elder son, had been in the Army unit that arrived too late at Little Big Horn and became a burial party for the massacred victims of Custer's Last Stand. For his charge against Chief Lame Deer in the Battle of the Big Muddy, Lovell had received the Congressional Medal of Honor. William Travers Jerome later so distinguished himself as New York District Attorney[25] in his fight against Boss Tweed's Tammany Hall that he was prominently mentioned as a presidential possibility. Jennie would tell Travers it was her ambition to see her son as Prime Minister of England and William Travers Jerome as President of the United States.

Moreton Frewen's trip to the United States was prolonged and typical of his dozens of trips all over the world, on which he almost always went alone. Clara had been particularly jealous of the fact that Moreton had gone to America on the same ship with his former flame, Lily Langtry, and was reportedly seeing her in New York.

> Oh Lord what a creature you are—I don't see any nice women out here—and I fear I am getting . . . a little beyond that game! But if it were otherwise, and some nice creature took care of me while I am 5,000 miles away—you ought to be rather pleased than otherwise. On the other hand, if someone looks after you while I am that distance off, well . . . that is quite another pair of shoes.

But the beautiful Clara had acquired one of Jennie's suitors, King Milan of Serbia. A striking looking man, King Milan was thick-set with bulging black eyes, inky black hair and heavy mustache. A newspaper of the time described him as "a man of many faults and some virtues." Among his virtues were intelligence and an agreeable personality. Jennie had encouraged his courtship, partly perhaps to make Kinsky jealous, for he and Milan were close friends.

Although she liked him, Jennie described Milan as "certainly one of the most uncivilized beings I have ever encountered." At one of Jennie's many small dinner parties, King Milan told of his early years as a goatherd, barefoot, clad in rags, often starving, fighting wild beasts. "He became so excited that, suddenly forgetting he was not in his native wilds, he began to eat with his fingers, tearing the meat on his plate." But Jennie also remembered dining with him at the Amphitryon in a private room he had ordered covered with orchids. Milan was separated from his Queen, and for that reason was not welcomed by Queen Victoria. "His life on the whole was a sad one," wrote Jennie.[26]

For Jennie, King Milan was in the same category as such men as Ernest Cassel and William Waldorf Astor, dynamic men whom she admired, who could challenge and help her, but whom she could not love. The men she wanted were the few who combined strength and sensitivity, body and brain. But these others—Milan, Cassel, Astor, and a host like them—fit into only a small part of her life.

"Personally, I feel my acquaintance can never be too large," Jennie wrote, "when I reflect that there are thousands of delightful and interesting people one may be missing, no opportunity ought to be lost in cultivating as many as possible. Friends are in another category. Time alone can prove friendships."

King Milan, perhaps wanting more than friendship, turned his attentions to Clara. One advantage in this was that Kinsky was not competing for Clara. Another was that Clara's husband was on another continent, while Jennie's husband did make occasional appearances. Besides, the blonde Clara may have been even more attractive to him than Jennie.

Milan arrived daily at Clara's doorstep with a box of gardenias for her and presents always for her children. Among the surviving gifts is an exquisite tortoise shell music box with a tiny golden bird that pops out and sings. In Serbian, Milan's surname meant "bird." But he was hardly birdlike; Clara referred to his "overpowering ways."[27]

Jennie, meanwhile, had had a distant, exotic admirer in the Shah of Persia. He had heard of Jennie's beauty and specifically asked that she be presented to him during the Court Ball in his honor. Later she was informed, however, that she did not meet the Shah's expectations—she was not fat enough.

Clara often felt alone, increasingly dependent on Jennie for affection and money. With her creditors growing more insistent, Clara also was sent some money by her mother, who took the opportunity to warn, ". . . Be sure that Moreton knows nothing about it, as he would leave it all for us to do and his money would go to someone else. *Write urgently* to him for money to *live on.*"

The financial scene began to change again for Leonard Jerome. Years ago, he could have had millions for the asking, but it had become a local joke to ask Jerome if he had found $400 to build a new track. Finally, he was able to answer, "No, I have not found the $400; but I have found 40 millions." He had met John A. Morris and persuaded him to build the new race course they would call Morris Park Course. The *Tribune* later described it as "an immensity. . . . The enclosure seems to have no bounds, the stables may be measured in miles. The betting ring would hold all the bookmakers in the United States." That winter of 1888 Jerome was flush enough to make a proposal to his wife:

> How would it do for you and Clara to go over to Paris
> and establish yourselves alongside Leonie and Jack? I would
> come over by the French Line and spend Christmas and a
> week or two or more with you. Besides, I will pay all extra ex-
> penses, whatever more it may cost you to live three months in
> Paris. . . . For Christmas week, Jennie and Randolph might
> come over and visit us. The scheme strikes me as very sensi-
> ble, very possible and very jolly. What do you say?

Hearing the news, Moreton promptly wrote his wife urging her to accept her father's offer and leave London. He also asked her to send his
stuffed buffalo head and his stuffed eagle, among other trophies, to Jennie's
house for safekeeping. "I'd like her to have them," he said; besides, "it will
more likely be six [years] before we can 'show our head' in London."

When they agreed to go, Leonard wrote Leonie in Paris to tell her
about it and advise her, "Don't try to live together. You have done it several times heretofore, and successfully, but it is not good policy." He then
mentioned that Jennie and Randolph were also expected to come, and
added, "Tell me how you propose to live, how to amuse yourselves in
Paris. It is the place of all others for young people capable of enjoying the
world's pleasures without running to excess. A hundred pound bill
enclosed."

The three Jerome sisters did live together, however, on Avenue Kleber,
and it made quite a ménage–Grandmother Clara, Leonie with her four
boys, Clara with her two boys and a girl, Jennie occasionally bringing over
her two boys. With their fluent French, their elegant pianism, and their
charisma, the three Jerome sisters were at their social peak in Paris. Theirs
was the lively life–theaters, parties, restaurants, seldom eating meals in
their apartment. The Marquis de Breteuil was in constant attendance;
Count Kinsky,[28] too, of course; and the Prince of Wales dropped in.

By that time, Prince Edward was very stout, and his tight clothes emphasized his girth. He had cut down on his drinking, but not on his eating.
One critic had started calling him "Spuds," insisting that his head looked an
enormous potato ready for the pot. His tremendous hands, his outsize nose
and ears, and his large gray codfish eyes hardly helped dispel the Spuds impression. But he was nonetheless an impressive man, whose full beard and
mustache and German-accented English lent him a continental distinction.
He still lived the sensuous life of a *bon vivant* and still set the style. The called
him "Collars and Cuffs" because he always showed more linen than any
other Englishman. If H.R.H. arrived at a party one evening wearing three

shirt studs instead of two, as he once did, men automatically scurried to search for another stud. A serious kidney disease was said to have slowed down his dalliances with the ladies, but the decrease was barely discernible.

Two new admirers for the sisters, particularly for Clara and Jennie, were Widor, the famous French organist, and Alexandre Eiffel. Eiffel escorted Clara to the uppermost part of the tower he was building for the Paris Exhibition (his "construction of amazement"), telling her she was the first woman in the world to have been so high. Widor often gave a private recital for each of the Jerome sisters in his organ loft at St. Sulpice.

Always available for escort duties was Count Kinsky's friend, the 60-year-old Baron Maurice de Hirsch, a financier and philanthropist who had made his fortune in Balkan railways.[29] The rumor of the time was that Baron Hirsch was an illegitimate son of the Emperor of Austria. In addition to his charming house on the rue d'Elysée, Hirsch also had a vast estate in Hungary, where the Prince of Wales often went to shoot partridges and the Jerome sisters were frequent guests. Just the year before, the Marquis de Breteuil, then treasurer of the Orleanist Party, had gone to Hirsch for a campaign contribution. Hirsch pulled at his Napoleonic mustache and then wrote out a check. "My knees shook under me," said Breteuil. "It was for six million francs." Hirsch came often to the Jerome parties, and Jennie said that he "was one of the few millionaires I have met who knew thoroughly how to enjoy life."

Fifteen

BY EARLY NOVEMBER, 1888, the Churchills were back in London and Randolph introduced to Jennie a Colonel John North, also known as "The Nitrate King," intimating that North was a man with the Midas touch who would help them accumulate their own fortune. Though his nitrate mines were in Chile, Colonel North kept a large London house where he entertained lavishly. He was a vulgar man, however, boisterous and ostentatious. When he told Jennie he had paid £8,000 for a painting, she asked him the name of the artist. North could not remember; nor could he remember the subject of the painting, but he did know that "it is twelve feet by eight."

For a time, Randolph planned a series of trips to South America, and the Churchills arranged a number of parties at which North was their guest of honor. A gossip sheet[1] reported that the grateful Colonel North "put Lord Randolph into some snug little schemes to enable him to realize quite a handsome fortune." If so, it was not the oversize fortune that Randolph had so rosily expected.

Another friend of Randolph's, among the richest men in the world, was former American Minister to Italy William Waldorf Astor, impolitely known as "Wealthy Willie."[2] Gossip writers coupled his name with Jennie's almost regularly throughout the years. After the death of Astor's wife and Jennie's husband, it was even reported that Astor and Jennie were engaged to marry. He was a big, blue-eyed, handsome man with a blond mustache, a rugged build, and an overpowering personality, aided and abetted by eighty million dollars. They called him "Walled-Off Astor," because he had built high walls topped with glass around his 300-acre Cliveden Estate on the Thames, had barred his windows, and had actually used the draw-bridge at his Hever Castle to keep everyone out.[3] The real wall, though, was around his soul.

Addicted to timetables, minutes mattered more to him than people. For weekend guests, Astor would arrange a schedule that suffered no possible deviation. When it was letter-writing time and one guest chose to roam the garden, she was approached by a nervous servant who timidly suggested that perhaps the lady had forgotten that it was letter-writing time and Mr. Astor would be unhappy to know that she was not following the schedule. When the angry guest told the servant she would not stay in such a house and asked him to call her carriage, the stammering servant said he would not dare to do so before Mr. Astor's scheduled time for guests to leave.

Such a formalized man hardly fit well into Jennie's free-moving ways. Nor did she like his views on the America he had left. After his unsuccess-ful campaign for Congress Astor had been quoted as saying, "America is good enough for any man who has to make a livelihood, though why trav-eled people of independent means should remain there more than a week is not readily to be comprehended. . . . America is not a fit place for a gentle-man to live."[4]

Astor's main attraction for Jennie was his power and money, and she in-troduced him into the orbit of the Prince of Wales, who was attracted by the same things. Jennie and Astor were, however, friends, and they re-mained so. It may have been coincidence, but when Astor bought the *Pall Mall Gazette* in 1892, he offered the editorship to Harry Cust; and when he bought *The Observer*, he said it was mainly to retain the services of its editor, James Garvin. In addition to Cust, Garvin was another of Jennie's con-quests. How much Jennie influenced Astor's choices is not known.

❖❖❖

Suddenly an unexpected opportunity for the Churchills loomed large and ripe. John Bright, the grand old man of Birmingham, died in March 1889, and a Birmingham delegation invited Randolph to run for Bright's seat. Randolph was safely settled in his Paddington seat, but a victory in Birmingham, the heart of the Liberal stronghold, would be spectacular. It would mean for him a political revival of the first order, catapulting him into the forefront of the Conservative Party where the Prime Minister's job would again be within reach. To make it more tasty, Randolph's friends guaranteed him a safe seat elsewhere in the event he lost Birmingham.

Jennie was exultant. Everything was possible again. Certainly Randolph was often ill, but she would always be there to help him. She could not speak for him, but she could write and maneuver for him even more than she had before. She knew the most important men of her time; she had traveled throughout Europe and met the royal rulers, and she understood the intricacies of continental diplomacy. She had conducted political campaigns throughout England and was familiar with the vital issues that confronted the country. She could be her husband's right hand, his common sense, his strongest supporter and advisor. After all, he was only forty years old. His disease had been quiescent for some time, and perhaps it would stay that way long enough for him to become Prime Minister. Jennie recruited all their closest friends to pressure Randolph into accepting the candidacy. Even Colonel North cabled from Santiago, "BE SURE CONTEST BIRMINGHAM."

Randolph was stirred by the possibilities. He asked Louis Jennings[5] to write him a farewell speech for the voters of Paddington South and a campaign speech for Birmingham.

"When do you want them?" asked Jennings.

"This afternoon," answered Randolph.

While Jennings was busy with the speeches and arrangements, Churchill was caving in under the pressure of Joseph Chamberlain. A sometime friend and occasional rival of Randolph, Chamberlain was still boss of Birmingham. During his three terms as Mayor, he had cleared city slums and vastly improved water and gas service. As an M.P., he had broken with Gladstone on the Home Rule issue, quitting his Cabinet post as President of the Board of Trade, yet Balfour said of him that he "does not completely mix, does not form a chemical combination with us." Twelve years younger than Chamberlain, Balfour also commented, "The difference between Joe and me is the difference between youth and age; I am age."[6]

Chamberlain was a man of firm intellectual control who seldom deceived himself. He knew the complications that would ensue if Randolph Churchill moved into his arena of Birmingham. He liked Randolph personally, but he did not want to share political prominence in Birmingham with anyone.

Once firm and fierce, Randolph's mind was now weak and malleable, and after their second meeting he succumbed to Chamberlain's arguments. "It's all over," Randolph told his supporters. "I cannot stand for the seat."[7] In another time, in another England, Joseph Chamberlain's son Neville would count on the loyalty of Winston Churchill.

"It was a great blow to his friends and supporters in Birmingham who felt that they had been offered up on the altar of Mr. Chamberlain's ambitions," Jennie confided in her memoirs.

Bearing in mind the political campaign of 1885, and the hard work in which I had taken part and which now seemed a waste of time and energy, I felt very incensed. On the day when Randolph returned from the House of Commons and informed me of the pressure brought to bear on him, and how he had given in, I accused him of showing the white feather for the first time in his life. He had, he said, "made up his mind to abide by the opinion of the leaders of the party." "But not when those leaders are your political enemies," I cried. Arguments, however, were useless. If he was right, he got no thanks for it, and a great opportunity was lost for him to show his strength and power.[8]

Writing to Salisbury about the situation, Balfour said:

He [Chamberlain] now goes the length of saying that the Conservative Party are not so strong in the central ward of Birmingham as they were when Randolph Churchill fought the seat in 1885. At that time, the Conservatives were far better organized than they are now, and there was a very active Primrose League, under the direction of the Duchess of Marlborough and of Lady Randolph, which did great service in the most radical ward of the constituency. All this, according to him, is now at an end, and the Conservative organization is, for all practical purposes, worthless.[9]

The Birmingham incident marked a milestone in Randolph's decline, much more than the speeches and articles that attacked and insulted him. Here was the great opportunity for which his supporters had worked so hard, and he had missed it—his followers felt he had been betrayed by Chamberlain. "After Randolph left the Government, our relations with Lord and Lady Salisbury became gradually more and more strained," Jennie said.

Outward appearances were kept up, such as our still being invited to the political parties given in Arlington Street, but all real cordiality ceased. Mutual friends indeed tried to bring about a rapprochement, and eventually we were asked to dine. Much against his inclination, Randolph was persuaded to accept. The dinner, which was a large one, was a fiasco, so far as the object of our being there was concerned. For beyond a bare greeting, neither Lord nor Lady Salisbury exchanged a word with Randolph. This he resented very much, and regretted having gone. I do not think this was intended as a slight.

Shortly after, Jennie received a very friendly letter of invitation from Lady Salisbury to a garden party which was to feature speeches by Chamberlain and Lord Randolph.

> Great was to be the gathering of Unionists, and a solid front was much desired. At the last moment, however, Randolph flatly refused to go. No arguments moved him; he insisted that I should keep the engagement alone. As I drove up to the historical Elizabethan house, an ideal residence for the Prime Minister of England, my feelings were anything but enviable. I shall never forget the look of blank dismay and the ominous silence with which my feeble excuses for Randolph's absence were greeted. That night at dinner, in the splendid banqueting-hall, I sat next to Lord Salisbury. Courteous as ever, he talked pleasantly to me, but made no allusion to the subject uppermost in my mind. The next day was fine, and masses of people, brought by special trains from London, filled the beautiful gardens, crowding round the various speakers. Cries for Randolph were heard on every side, many had come expressly to hear him, and bitter was the disappointment when they realized that he was not there. No adequate reason could be given for his absence, and the "rift within the loot" was made more apparent than ever. I confess I was very glad when I could slip away, for rarely had I felt so uncomfortable or experienced anything more disagreeable.[10]

So much had Randolph alienated himself from his party's policy, that when he asked for a glass of water during one of his speeches in the House of Commons, no one stirred. Thinking that he had not been heard, he repeated the request. No one moved. After a prolonged silence, a young Tory M.P. went out for the water. Taking the glass from him, Randolph said solemnly, "I hope this will not compromise you with your party."

"Many of those who witnessed this incident," wrote Robert Rhodes James, "could not help but remember the gay evening in the palmy days of the Fourth Party, when Randolph demanded a drink in the middle of a speech, and called out cheerfully after the departing Gorst, 'Remember, Gorst, brandy and seltzer.' "[11]

Randolph lost his last loyal friend, Jennings, when he unexpectedly switched his position on an upcoming bill—without telling Jennings, who had made a preliminary speech in favor of it. Jennings considered it a "stab in the back."

Jennie spent a great deal of time in Paris in 1889, visiting her mother and sisters and Count Kinsky. She was also a regular guest at the popular literary salons of Mrs. Ferdinand Bischoffsheim, an American. "It was there that I first met Monsieur Bourget, then unmarried," she wrote later. Paul Bourget, who wrote mainly about intellectuals and aristocrats, was then an important and popular literary figure. He and Jennie developed a close friendship that grew more intimate in the coming years. They exchanged an extensive correspondence, and in one letter Bourget wrote her, "Arrived at a certain point in life, one knows too much about it, wishes to do too much, and is not able to express what one has to say. Do you know that Turgenev has summed it all up when he said, 'Life is a brutal affair.' "[12]

Jennie was 36 years old, reaching for younger men and more excitement. There seemed nothing now to hold her back except hypocrisy, and she had little of that. *Town Topics* reported that a footman saw Jennie dancing the Can-Can at a party given in Dublin by the Viceroy. "She suddenly touched the mantelpiece with her foot, making a dreadful exposé," the magazine wrote, and added, "This is only one of her many freaks which have caused much scandal."

Randolph, in the meanwhile, had his own routine, his own private friends. In the fall of 1890, he and Harry Tyrwhitt leased a houseboat on the Nile for several months. "The days slip by as if they were hours, . . . life on the Nile is ideal," he wrote Jennie. It was a life of "good food, hock, champagne, Pilsener beer, Marquis chocolate, ripe bananas, fresh dates and literally hundreds of French novels."

"These few months were decisive to his fortune," wrote Robert Rhodes James. In the strange way of politics, Randolph's political fortune was tied to the strength of Charles Stewart Parnell and his pivotal group of M.P.s in the House of Commons. Together they held a balance of power. Faced with that fact, Salisbury needed unity within his own party, and this meant a cagy treatment of the popular Randolph Churchill.

Ten-year-old Jack wrote his father about a story in the *Graphic*: "It said you had a hot temper, and yet everyone was willing to hear what you had to say. It said you were going to be in office again, and that the office suited you very well. What it all means, I do not know." It meant that Randolph's disease was still largely a family secret and that in the public's view his political power was inevitable and growing. But the power crashed finally and utterly with the fall of Parnell.

Parnell had survived the smear of a highly publicized facsimile reprinted

JENNIE   •   235

in the *Times* in 1887, supposed to have been a letter he had written approving the Phoenix Park murders. He denied he had written the letter, but it took him two years to win public vindication.[13] Then in 1890 Captain O'Shea, the husband of Parnell's mistress, sued for divorce based on adultery, naming Parnell as co–respondent. Parnell and Kitty O'Shea had lived together for ten years, with the Captain's blackmailing knowledge. The Captain finally had offered a divorce for 20,000 pounds. When Parnell was unable to raise the money to buy him off, the Captain filed suit.[14]

Parnell refused to defend himself,[15] refused to resign the leadership of his group of Home Rulers, and consequently split both his party and his country into bitter factions. "Don't throw me to the wolves," pleaded Parnell, the "Uncrowned King of Ireland," to his Irish Parliamentary Party. "The Irish did not throw him to the English wolves," James Joyce later wrote, "they tore him to pieces themselves." Even Gladstone felt forced to turn against Parnell, though he once remarked that he had known eleven former Prime Ministers, every one an adulterer. Parnell's sin, later wrote Mrs. O'Shea, was that he had violated the Eleventh Commandment, "Thou shalt not be found out."

Parnell married Kitty O'Shea the next year. He died that same year, at the age of forty-five.

The scandal set back any possibility of passing the Home Rule Bill for many years. Gladstone said of it sadly, "For five years, I have rolled this stone patiently uphill. And now it has rolled to the bottom again and I am 81 years old."[16]

With Parnell's fall and the collapse of Irish unity in the House, Salisbury no longer thought it necessary to consider any future impact of Randolph Churchill on the Conservative Party. Realizing what had happened, Randolph wrote Jennie from Egypt of

> my decision to have done with politics and try to make a little money for the boys and for ourselves. I hope you do not all intend to worry me on this matter and dispute with me and contradict me. More than two-thirds, in all probability, of my life is over, and I will not spend the remainder of my years in beating my head against a stone wall. I expect I have made great mistakes; but there has been no consideration, no indulgence, no memory or gratitude—nothing but spite, malice and abuse. I am quite tired and dead sick of it all, and will not continue political life any longer. . . . It is so pleasant getting near home again. I have had a good time, but now reproach myself for having left you all for so long. . . .

Of this, Lord Rosebery wrote,

> Surely a tragic letter. The revelation of a sore and stricken soul. He was sick of heart and body when he uttered this burst of melancholy candor . . . and all that may be written about the tragedy of Randolph's life, there will be nothing so sad as this letter of his.[17]

It was some time in 1891 that Lord Randolph had copied out some famous lines by Dryden:[18]

> *Happy the man, and happy he alone,*
> *He, who can call today his own;*
> *He who, secure within, can say:*
> *"Tomorrow do thy worst, for I have lived today.*
> *Be fair, or foul, or rain, or shine,*
> *The joys I have possessed, in spite of fate, are mine.*
> *Not Heaven itself upon the past has power;*
> *But what has been, has been, and I have had my hour."*

For all his many and varied faults, for all the injury and disappointment he had heaped on her life, Randolph had given Jennie her "hour," too. He had opened the door of a new world for her. His name and his title had given her access to the finest minds and most fascinating personalities of her time. His prominence in politics had given her a position of clear visibility at the hub that moved the wheels of the British Empire. But if he had provided the entrée, she had made the friends—and she had kept those friends when he could not. If his political position had revealed the hub to her, she had supplied to him the drive to help turn the wheel.

Now his letter from Egypt struck a responsive chord. He had found himself in an enormous, lonely void, and he was reaching out to her for a point of purpose. Jennie brightened her letters with cheer and encouragement. She wrote good news about Jack, then at Elstree School. Ten years old, he was a model student, always near the top of his class, despite poor vision in one eye. Jack himself wrote his father, "I wish I'd come to Egypt with you, and roam and see all the world. I wish a good many things which do not occur."

There was good news about Winston, too. He had written his mother that he was "working very well," and "very hard." "Arithmetic and Algebra are the dangerous subjects." He also reported to her that there was a good chance of his winning a chess tournament, and "I have been drawing little landscapes and bridges, and those sort of things." In addition, he had passed the test for Corporals in the Rifle Corps.[19]

Winston's focus on an Army career had begun one day in his room when he and Jack had their opposing armies of 1,500 toy soldiers arrayed against each other, ready for war. Randolph came into the room and surveyed the impressive scene.

> At the end he asked me if I would like to go into the Army. I thought it would be splendid to command an Army, so I said "Yes" at once: and immediately I was taken at my word. For years I thought my father with his experience and flair had discerned in me the qualities of military genius. But I was told later that he had only come to the conclusion that I was not clever enough to go to the Bar.[20]

After that incident Winston's education was geared toward entrance into Sandhurst. Jennie went to Harrow and then reported to Randolph that Welldon thought Winston was working as hard as possible and perhaps now might pass the preliminary examination for Sandhurst in the fall. Winston, she wrote, was "looking pale, but he was very nice and full of good resolutions which I trust will last."

That fall Winston did take the preliminary examination. In commenting on the tests, Winston thought his mother might be pleased that with a choice of subjects for the essay test, he had chosen the one on The American Civil War.[21] Then he added his customary footnote, "A remittance would not be altogether misplaced."

Shortly afterward, Jennie was able to write her husband:

> I am sure you will be delighted to hear that Winston has passed his P.E. [Preliminary Examinations for entrance into Sandhurst] in *everything*—one of the only four boys of Harrow who got in. . . . I think you ought to make him a present of a gun as a reward. He is pining for one and ought to have a little encouragement.

Randolph returned from Egypt in February 1891 wearing a beard but with little else changed. His loneliness and his yearning for home and family seemed to have disappeared with the sea voyage. His life with Jennie did not improve.

Winston wrote his father, pleading with him to visit at Harrow. "You have never been to see me and so everything will be new to you." He even told him of a fast train that only took half an hour from Baker Street. "P.S. I shall be awfully disappointed if you don't come." He was awfully disappointed.

If Randolph had changed his mind about his need for family closeness, he had not changed his mind about his need for money. The magic word was "gold," and the magic place was South Africa. Within a short time, he announced his intention to leave for South Africa at the end of April, the trip to last some nine months.[22] The *Daily Graphic* had agreed to pay him two thousand guineas (more than $10,000) for twenty articles of four thousand words each. His good friend Lord Rothschild loaned him five thousand pounds ($25,000) and sent along his best mining engineer, a Mr. Perkins, to help in the gold hunt.

Randolph originally intended to take his brother-in-law Moreton with him. Frewen's latest prospective fortune-maker was a gold-crushing machine he had patented and in which the Churchills had bought some stock. The *Western Daily Mercury* scathingly deemed the invention most appropriate to Frewen, "seeing that he is a prominent bi-metallist and therefore anxious to crush gold as far as possible out of existence." But Randolph had good advice and second thoughts on the crusher, and wrote Moreton that he could not continue investing in the machine:

> All my available resources are taken up with my journey to Mashonaland. . . . On reflection I am of opinion that you and I had better not go to South Africa together. . . . We shall not agree on business matters and . . . we might quarrel and separate out there which is a result to be avoided.

Realizing the Frewens' financial straits, Jennie refused to accept back any money she and Randolph had given Moreton for their gold-crusher stocks. Moreton wrote Randolph, "Jane threatened to return this second check to Clara, which was very kind of her, very; but it would hurt my feelings if she did."

Randolph, however, had no such qualms about accepting the money. "I have had so many accounts to settle and payments to make before leaving that I am rather short and racing has been distinctly adverse. . . . If you will pay the £200, I will be much obliged. . . .[23]

As Randolph was making his final preparations for departure, Leonard Jerome came to England for his final visit. Here was a man who had packed his life full: the loveliest women had loved him, the finest minds had listened to him, and a whole generation of Americans were richer in spirit because of him. His was the kind of remarkable energy and imagination that was so much a part of the growth of the American republic. When his health had begun to fail, his wife had urged him to hire a servant. "I have no use whatever for a servant," Jerome answered. "He would only be a nuisance. When one has been in the habit of putting on one's own shoes and stockings for 60 or 70 years, it would become rather awkward to have another do it."

Now he was seventy-three, tired and dispirited, and he had come to die among his family. As his nephew Eugene Jerome had written to Moreton from New York, "It must have been something of a shock to you to see how much he has failed and how helpless he has become. From all I have learned of his doctor here, he will never recover the use of his leg."

Leonard moved into Clara's house on Aldford Street. The street opened onto Park Lane, and from Clara's windows one could see the trees and the nearby Grosvenor Chapel. Jerome sat in a big, black velvet chair behind a screen, tended by his wife, nursed by his daughters, observed by his many grandchildren. The children were told that their American grandfather had "galloping consumption."

"It is thawing today, and we hope Papa has a good day," Leonie wrote her mother-in-law in January. "If Papa is well enough, Jennie wants to go and meet Randolph at Marseille, but I doubt her getting away."

Leonard grew worse and the family decided to move him to Brighton for the sea air. He and his wife stayed at the Lyon Mansions and the daughters were there almost daily. Shane Leslie wrote that in his last days Jerome lived on champagne and oysters. He died in a big brass bed, surrounded by his wife and daughters. His final words were, "I have given you all I have. Pass it on."

Of all his daughters, Jennie had been closest to him. He had given her most—not only of money, but of himself. She had the most of his drive, imagination, and courage—and she would pass it on.

But at that moment, she felt drained and lonely. For one of the few times in their marriage, Jennie needed Randolph more than he needed her. Her needs, however, were no longer his.

In addition to the family at the funeral in Grosvenor Chapel, were the United States Minister, the Hon. Robert T. Lincoln (son of President Lincoln), the German Ambassador, and some thirty friends. The New York *Daily Tribune* carried a large headline, "LEONARD JEROME DEAD," and the New York *Herald* noted, "At Leonard Jerome's death, a warm feeling of sorrow awakened in English social circles."

Moreton Frewen agreed to take the body back to the family mausoleum in Greenwood Cemetery, Brooklyn.

Instead of a fortune, Leonard Jerome left behind only debts. Among his effects was a diamond necklace he had bought for his wife during the days of the Imperial Court of Napoleon. Moreton, however, persuaded his mother-in-law to part with it, along with other heirlooms, as a sure investment in his gold-crusher, which would make millions for everyone. "When I return, I will build a big yacht for you," he wrote Clara, "and you shall take a year's holiday!"

Jerome's death did not deter Randolph from sailing the next month, but Jennie would not be alone. She would have her sons and her sisters and her friends. As her husband had become more and more a shadow in her life, she would have to find the substance elsewhere.

Sixteen

HE MONTHS THAT FOLLOWED her father's death in 1891 were
months of anguish for Jennie. "I feel as though I were living in an
atmosphere of disease, funerals, graves!" she wrote Randolph. "It is too
much for me—the black fog on top of it makes me feel too depressed for
words. . . . I am making myself too melancholy. . . ."

"It is wet and cold here," she said in another letter, "and I fight against
depressions the whole time . . . I am always saying to myself that life is too
short for the blues."

She was troubled, too, about Winston, who at sixteen was seriously in
need of a man with whom he could walk and ride and talk, someone he
could use as a model. Later that year, Jennie wrote Randolph of Winston,
". . . Honestly he is getting a bit too old for a woman to manage. . . . He really requires to be with a man. . . ." While his father was distant and dim,
Count Kinsky was visible and available.[1] Kinsky's nephew, Prince Clary[2]
remembers him as a man of charm and kindness, handsome and bright, the
kind of man a boy quickly accepts as a hero. His outstanding characteristic
was an absolute fearlessness, a quality he demonstrated many times in his
life—on the hunt, in a race, and during the war. For a boy whose only adventures were lived through the imaginary actions of 1,500 toy soldiers,
Kinsky was a model larger than life. Winston vividly described the day
that Kinsky took him to the Crystal Palace and someone tried to stop them

as they moved out of a waiting line: "The Count whom you know is immensely strong grew furious and caught hold of the blackguard's hand
crushing the fingers in his grasp," Winston wrote his brother. Kinsky also
took him to the zoo, the fire brigade drill, and to dinner. Winston delight-
edly reported that at the restaurant the head waiter said there were no tables "but Count K. spoke German to him and it had a wonderful effect."
Kinsky even decided that Winston was old enough to share some champagne.[3]

Winston and Count Kinsky developed a close friendship. "What a
wonderful stepfather Kinsky could have made for Winston," remarked
Winston's cousin Shane Leslie, who knew Kinsky. "Kinsky could have
given Winston so much that he badly needed." Kinsky would have been
able to provide Winston an earlier sense of self-confidence, a greater emphasis on manliness. Jennie could advise and influence her son, but she
could not transform his softness into steel. Without a father's love, Winston wanted more of his mother, and even into early maturity his letters to
her were gushy, as if he were still a child pleading for her kisses. He was a
mama's boy, and Jennie knew it and worried about it. She could give him a
great deal but she could not give him his manhood.

Jennie, her mother, her sisters, and all the children spent the summer of
1891 at the Churchills' home at Banstead. For part of the summer, Kinsky
was at his country estate adjacent to the Churchills'. All the sisters' husbands were elsewhere: John Leslie with his family in Ireland, Moreton
Frewen in America en route to Australia ("I don't ask their plans as they
change every week," wrote Jennie), Randolph in South Africa.

Winston and Jack, their visiting cousins, Shane Leslie and Hugh
Frewen, and the gardener's son worked together to construct a large two-
room hut of mud and wood which they called The Den. They also built a
moat and filled it with water, a drawbridge that actually pulled up and
down, and a catapult that used unripe apples as ammunition (one of which
hit a cow). Not quite seventeen, Winston was the general who drilled his
soldiers and organized the battles.[4]

The boys also looked after their chickens. "My hens have had one
brood of four chickens and laid eighty eggs," Winston wrote his father. He
also had two hens sitting on some turkey eggs, but the guinea pig died, as
did two of the captured rabbits. Jennie supplemented the Banstead news
somewhat in her own letters to Randolph. "The boys are very happy. Kinsky has gone out with them to put up a target. I am going to try to buy a
gun for Winston."

Kinsky occasionally roamed elsewhere. Lady Warwick happily mentioned in her memoirs that Count Kinsky had shared many "of my horsey
adventures." Even Jennie's cook Rosa later reminisced, "Kinsky had a great

time of it in London."[5] But at this time, he seemed to concentrate completely on Jennie.

Randolph's letters home were longer now and more frequent. He was a wasting and disappointed man. In a letter to Winston, he tried to make his South African adventure sound gay, describing it as "a regular gypsy life" which included sleeping on a mattress in a tent, dressing and washing in the open air, eating round a campfire, shooting a variety of wild game, examining gold mines, traveling in "a spider"—a wagonette with eight mules, capable of doing about fifty miles a day. He then added a rare fatherly footnote: "Take care of yourself, don't give Mama any trouble."

But in fact, Winston was causing her some trouble. Jennie described him in a letter as being "just at the 'ugly' age—touchy and tiresome." He often seemed to be working himself up to a bilious attack. "I fear his blood is out of order."

Welldon at Harrow wrote Jennie that he thought Winston should spend some of his holidays abroad and live with a French family to improve his skill at the language. Winston reacted violently to the idea, and Jennie wrote to Randolph, "I am going to try to find a little governess (ugly) who wants a holiday. . . . Just to talk and read with him. . . . If I can't I will have to send him away." Finally she did find a young man from cambridge ("rather nice") who came at the end of August to tutor Winston for several weeks.

But Jennie was quite concerned about their dwindling finances. The horses which had often brought in much-needed cash were not doing well, either. "The stable seems to have been very unlucky at the Derby. Three horses beaten. . . . Old Sherwood is rather disgusted." Furthermore, she had to pay two hundred pounds for forage, stables, trainers, and so forth. "I thought it best to settle all I could as it is better to owe money to the bank than to a man like Slater." She also wanted to buy a pony for Jack from a certain Billy for fifteen pounds. "He says he won't send it until I send him the money." Jack ultimately got his pony, however. Lack of money occasionally slowed down Jennie, but seldom stopped her. She wrote her husband that she thought she could manage until November. "I have been obliged to pay a few bills, one big one, and of course, the boys' school bill and the tutors will have to be paid. . . ." And later, "I'm afraid you must feel that our future is in a bad way, as regards money. . . . But we must not despair. . . ." At a recent party where everyone had to make a wish, she also told him, "I wished that you might make a lot of money."[6]

While Jennie had her annual income, however inadequate, Clara never seemed able to keep clear of creditors. "Cannot your mother help you?" Moreton wrote. ". . . Your mother seems to think R and Jenny's future is alone of any consequence, that whether we sink or swim is nothing!"[7]

Mrs. Jerome, in fact, was rapidly becoming a niggardly recluse. Her grandchildren later remembered her as a sad, silent, and lonely woman who looked increasingly like an Indian squaw they had seen in picture books. Hugh Frewen described her as an old lady

> severe and exacting to my young mind. She laid down the law, and did not seem kindly disposed to us children. She was a great disciplinarian. One day I said to her, "Grandmama, when are you going to your *own* home?" My mother thought this was a great joke.

Though Clara Jerome still had her own fund of money, she kept it mostly to herself, except for paying her daughter Clara's critical expenses. Finally she settled into a cheap boardinghouse at Tunbridge Wells and economized to the point where she refused to have fires in the fireplace, even during some of the coldest days of the winter. She had long ago left the Society to which she had so snobbishly clung. The real sadness was that this woman—who had never been able to talk the same language or live in the same world as her husband—now was incapable of reaching into the lives of her children and grandchildren. Jennie's shared confidences were with her sisters, not with her mother, but she always remained loyal and affectionate toward her.

With the summer's end, Jennie wrote her husband that she was seeing the boys off to school. "They have been as happy as kings, riding and shooting." Winston was "in tearing spirits. . . . I know Jack was quite worn out rushing after Winston . . . the difference in their ages is beginning to tell. . . . I shall be very dull without the boys. . . ." Her loneliness wasn't helped by the fact that Kinsky had gone to Austria on a shooting trip.

While in Africa Randolph also did considerable shooting, but his most telling shots were in the *Graphic*. His columns hit at all kinds of people, traditions, institutions, and soon stirred up considerable public reaction.[8] Jennie quoted Salisbury as saying, "Since when has Randolph become the correspondent of a penny-paper!" Arthur Balfour complained to Jennie that Randolph's critical column on the Land Bill had caused him to have "a tiresome time with mutual friends in Parliament."

Jennie herself offered some personal comments on his columns: "It was very interesting to me," she wrote of one of them, "but perhaps not very to the general public. I marveled at your writing so much with so little to go upon." Another time she observed, "I am afraid people think your letters a bit prosy—but I don't see how you can write differently."[9]

Caricaturists lampooned Randolph daily, a mustache-twirler among the lions. At their annual conference, delegates of the National Union

Convention booed his name. Editorialists poked fun with barbed jabs. The Gaiety Theater so burlesqued him that the Lord Chamberlain forbade one of their more satirical songs. "Everyone is much amused," wrote Jennie.

The Dowager Duchess was not amused. A comic paper called *Funny Folks*, she informed her son, "has a stupid thing every week about 'Randy on the Rampage.'" And she was sending him "some poisonous remarks of the *Pall Mall* which I feel to be utter lies and therefore you should see. . . ." She also mentioned that some had praised his first letters in the *Graphic* but "people laughed at your botany." The Duchess herself disapproved of the *Graphic* columns because "they seem to bring them out so as to help the sale of the papers."

The Duchess felt that "there is a great desire to get you back. I must own, however, that your name is not always well received." The Salisburys were guests at a party she had attended, but "I never went near them." Even months later, she would write, "I cannot make up my mind to go to any of Lord S's parties." Her grudge was deep. "I fear a trap was laid for you into which you fell, and I know you must get out and confound your enemies. God help you . . . I long to get you back again, dearest, and think of nothing else."

Winston was also disturbed by the criticism of his father. "The papers are exceedingly spiteful and vicious . . . You cannot imagine what biles of wrath you have uncorked. All the papers simply rave. But oh! I will not bore you with the yappings of these curs . . ." He did tell him, though, that "*Punch* has got a very stupid article in which they announce that Capt. Gwynydd writes the letters and reads them to you for approval."[10] But Winston was more worried about something else. He knew a Harrow boy, he said, who had been to Kimberley for the summer holidays "and he told me the people out there said you were looking ill."

In one letter, Winston drew a picture of a man with a rifle, facing a mean-looking lion, with the heading, "I imagine you." Under another heading, "Don't forget my—" he drew an antelope head. He then explained to his father that he didn't expect him to bring home a live antelope, just a stuffed head for his room. At the end of that letter, he wrote, "Wishing luck, sport, amusement and health." And in another, "Mama has got a big map of S.A. on which she follows your route. I wish you had taken me. What fun I should have had." Then, in printed capital letters: "HAVE YOU FOUND A GOLD MINE? HAVE YOU SHOT A LION YET?"

Jennie had other questions for Randolph: Was there really going to be a war in Mashonaland? Was it true that a friend of theirs had had his body mutilated by tribesmen before having a bullet put into his head? Could he tell her more about the Dutch Parliament? "What creatures those Boers must be!" His column on the Boers, she commented, was the best he had written. "I hope they won't make it too hard for you."

She passed on whatever political news she could corral. Gladstone had told a mutual friend that he felt certain to be returned to office in the next General Election. (Jennie added she could not see what he would do when he got there.) The press was starting to pick on Balfour for some of the bills he proposed. The Irish seemed to have no "go" left after the Parnell-O'Shea scandal. Everybody she talked to seemed "so bored with the government." Lord Hartington had been quite pleased with himself for telling the Queen that all the government had done was "Thanks to Mrs. O'Shea."

Interviewed by a reporter somewhere in South Africa, Randolph was asked, "What quality do you consider most necessary for success in an English politician?"

"Nimbleness," he replied.[11]

His most interesting letters home still were written to his mother. Jennie complained, "I have not seen your letter about the lions, so am rather in the vague as to your encounter." And then she added that it seemed "such ages since I had heard from you." Again Jennie remarked that Randolph failed to mention her, even in some of his longest letters to his mother.

Despite the occasional adventures with wild animals and the potential excitement of finding gold, time often dragged for Randolph in the monotony of so many months of camp life. "It is rather tiresome here," he wrote his mother once. The coffee was very bad, the water dirty, the food "piggy," the meat rationed, the flies ubiquitous.

Jennie seemed little happier. "London does not seem to be very gay. Hardly anything going on—even the Opera is a failure."

She had moved into her mother-in-law's house on Grosvenor Square, to save expenses, and rented out their Connaught house. It was a galling situation for Jennie. She and her mother-in-law had settled into a quiet rapprochement, but within each of them was an uneasiness toward the other, a lingering resentment. "I know beggars can't be choosers but I feel very old for this sort of thing," Jennie wrote Randolph. "I shall be so glad to get you back," she offered in another letter. "I feel rather low and lonely at times." Randolph had used most of their funds and had borrowed money to finance his trip to South Africa. Yet, whether from guilt or sympathy, he did respond to Jennie's unhappiness by sending her a diamond, which she had made into a pin and later into a ring. "It is quite lovely," she wrote him. "Everyone admires it immensely. . . . I never dreamed of it. . . ."

One of the activities that kept Jennie busy was music. She and Leonie organized "a pilgrimage" to Bayreuth for the Wagner Festival. To help familiarize everyone with the Wagner scores, Jennie drafted a noted German musician and a Wagnerian singer to perform for their small group. She also arranged for a series of lectures on Wagner, but the professor's English was so limited and his accent so thick that an unexpected note of hilarity was added to the meetings.

Only a half-dozen finally made the trip to Bayreuth, including her sisters and Lady de Grey.

> Our little party was settled to meet between the acts and exchange opinions, but so great were our emotions that we all fled in different directions, avoiding one another, until the performance was over, when we should be more calm.

Parsifal's wig fell off in the third act, but the audience was such a serious one that there was not a titter.[12]

Jennie afterward helped lay the groundwork for the premiere performance of *The Ring* in London and later met Siegfried Wagner, the composer's son, at a small dinner in his honor. Guests were asked to select their two favorite composers. "I was the only one who did not name Wagner," said Jennie. "Partly out of contradiction and partly because I think so, I mentioned Bach and Beethoven." Amid the room's embarrassed confusion, Siegfried Wagner smiled and proclaimed, "My father would also have chosen them."

Ignace Paderewski was Jennie's personal pride.[13] Shane Leslie remembered being in a car with his mother Leonie, Aunt Jane, and "Paddy," as they all called Paderewski. They were all excited about the prospect of launching him in London.

> I was lying on the seat, but everytime I woke I could see Jennie and my mother trying to guess the tunes that Paderewski played in the air with his fingers. It was a curious game but they were all in high, tearing spirits and Paddy's fingers never seemed to stop. . . . [14]

Jennie arranged Paderewski's first London performance.

> I invited to meet him a select few whom I knew to be capable of appreciating and judging him. Needless to say, their admiration and enthusiasm was unbounded. A few days later, he gave his first concert in St. James Hall. The place was only half-full, and behind me were two musical critics, taking notes for their papers. "There's not much in this fellow," said one. "He would be all right," said the other, "if he would leave Chopin alone, which he plays against all traditions."

Jennie would like to have informed them that Chopin's friend Stephen Heller had told her the great composer never played his works twice in the same way. "The following year, Paderewski, having had a gigantic success in Paris and elsewhere, returned to London, where he received an ovation from an excited and enthusiastic audience, who stormed the platform to kiss his hands!"

Paderewski particularly enjoyed playing duets with Jennie, said Shane Leslie, but was musically in love with all the Jerome sisters and told them that whenever any of their children got married, he would be happy to come and play at the wedding.

Jennie also met Abbé Liszt at the Russian Embassy in London:

> I sat next to the great man, whose strong, characteristic face, so often delineated both by brush and chisel, seemed strangely familiar. He was so blind that he ate his asparagus by the wrong end, until I pointed out his error. . . . After luncheon, notwithstanding his gouty fingers, he was prevailed upon to play . . . I never heard him at his best.
>
> Anton Rubinstein I well recollect, with his long hair tossed about, the perspiration pouring down his face, as his big hands tore up and down the piano. Full of tricks—to which so many artists become addicted—when he reached the culminating *fortissimo*, wild with excitement, he would hit with his palms or his forearm as many notes as he possibly could, until he seemed positively to get to the end of the instrument, making the strings snap and the wood sound.[15]

Several months earlier, Jennie's mother-in-law had asked her to undertake a concert for one of her favorite charities, the Paddington Recreation Center. "It will be a great trouble and care," Jennie wrote Randolph, "but I suppose I must."

Soon she was swept up in its excitement. The Princess of Wales sent her a note offering help. The famous actor-manager Sir Henry Irving offered her the use of his Lyceum Theater. Artist Julian Story set to work designing three tableaux—one Venetian, one French, and one in which the figures moved.[16] Following a small notice in the paper, Jennie began receiving "an avalanche of mail from tiresome people all wanting to act or recite." After the Prince of Wales agreed to sponsor the performance, many of the lovely ladies of London started to compete for the right to appear in the tableaux. "H.R.H. was very kind and has fussed greatly about it all," Jennie wrote. "It *must* be a success. It is no use doing anything unless one is sure of success."

It was a great success, some nine hundred people packing the theater, the platform covered with palms and flowers. Even Nellie Melba was one of the performers. "The Paddingtonians seemed very pleased," Jennie wrote of the evening.

> I had an awful moment when two of the performers who had to begin the concert did not appear. I had to take the place of one of them. . . . Thank goodness it is over. . . . [17]
>
> Personally, I have never been able to surmount the nervousness one feels in playing before the public, whether in concerted pieces or alone. What musical performers, good, bad or indifferent, have not at some time felt their nerve giving way as they approach the difficult passage? Only to think of it is fatal! Once, at some concert for charity, I was playing a classical piece, the first movement of which had a few bars of some difficulty. The first time for the *da capo*, I got over it all right, but to lead for the next movement, it had to be repeated with variations in another key. To my consternation, I found myself embarking on the same one, which, of course, led me to repeating the first movement. Again, as I came to the fatal passage, I trembled and did the same thing. Three times did I repeat that movement, until the audience were becoming quite familiar with the tune. As for me, I felt in a hideous nightmare, and was on the verge of jumping up from the piano and rushing off the stage, when oh! joy! the fourth time, I mechanically played the right bars and was able, eventually, to bring the piece to its conclusion. Hans von Bülow is supposed to have done the same thing once, with a sonata of Beethoven, until, in desperation, he had to send for the music.

Something equally embarrassing happened to her at a concert before a large audience at the Mansion House. She and another woman were to play a Chopin Polonaise on two pianos.

> As our turn came, the mademoiselle, who was the professional of some experience in execution, said hurriedly to me, "At the 11th bar on the 6th page, when I make you a sign, stop, as I mean to put in a little cadenza of my own." Before I could remonstrate, or point out that it would be unnecessary addition to one of Chopin's masterpieces, the lady had seated herself at the piano, and perforce I had to follow suit. When she arrived at the 11th bar of the 6th page, she nod-

ded violently to me, and then proceeded to dazzle the company with arpeggios, runs and trills, until I began to wonder if I should ever find a propitious moment to re-enter. I finally did, and had the pleasure of hearing from the occupants of the front row as I went out, "Poor Lady Randolph, what a pity she lost her place for so long."[18]

Randolph's prolonged stay in South Africa stirred up snickering rumors. "With such a charming wife and so many political and social inducements to remain in England," a magazine reporter remarked, ". . . and as he has been out of England a great deal of late, . . . I sincerely hope that nothing has gone wrong in the Churchill household." At the same time Jennie was linked in the press with more and more men of reputation, although many of them were of no real meaning to her.

She and the Prince of Wales had often been guests of the Baron Hirsch at his home in Paris, and he invited them now to attend an international shooting party at St. Johann, his Hungarian estate. It was a chance for Jennie to get away from the gossip and from the dismal Grosvenor Square home of her mother-in-law.

"Life at St. Johann was simple and healthy," she wrote.

> Shortly after breakfast, a parade of victorias appeared, the horses in gay harness and the postilions in hussar-like blue jackets, Hessian boots and shiny, high-crowned hats. The guests then drove to the rendezvous. There an army of 600 beaters were waiting. The guests started off at the sound of a bugle, advanced in line, walked for miles over the sanded, stubbled plains, saw enormous blue hares and the plentiful partridges, roe-deer, blackcock and pheasants. Luncheon was always out-of-doors, regardless of weather.

Jennie particularly remembered one shooter: "As the huge coveys flew over him, seemingly from every point of the compass, he kept calling out to them in his excitement, 'For heaven's sake, stop! Oh, do wait one moment!'" The total bag of partridges for one day reached three thousand.

Passing through Paris on her return home Jennie had an unpleasant but exciting experience. She was standing by the midday train, in one of the busy archways in the Gare du Nord,

> when I suddenly heard a shot fired, followed by two or three more in rapid succession, and a man with a hand to his hip and an agonized expression on his face, ran, or rather hob-

bled, past me from behind one of the pillars of the archway. He was closely followed by another man who held a revolver, which he again fired off, this time so close to me that I fled in terror, seeing, as I ran, the victim fall to the ground, the murderer still firing at him. A large crowd, which had scattered in every direction at the first shots, now rushed to the spot. Meanwhile, fearing that the man was running amok, and that I might be the next recipient of his wild firing, I ran down the platform as fast as the heavy fur coat and various encumbrances permitted me. Unfortunately, I dropped my muff, which happened to be a sable one, adorned with tails, containing my purse and ticket. Before I could pick it up, a man pounced on it and made off at top speed toward the swinging glass doors leading out of the station. As I followed, calling out, I saw him vanish through one of the doors and reappear by another like a clown in a pantomime. Calm and unconcerned, he was swinging a cane, and no muff was visible. While I stared at him in utter amazement, I spied one of the tails of the muff sticking out from his coat, which he was endeavoring to keep closed. At that moment, the bell, which announced the departure of the train, began to ring. There was no time for words; it was a case of "do or die." I rushed at the thief, seized the tail of the muff, and jumped into the train, which I just managed to catch, leaving the man with his mouth wide open, still staring as we crawled out of the station. As to the wretched victim of the shooting, I heard afterward that the assassin had shot him seven times before he was overpowered, and then tried to beat out his brains with the butt-end of the revolver, so great was his determination to kill him. A passenger received a stray shot in his leg, and altogether it was a scene of wild excitement and confusion. From the paper which gave an account of the fray, it appeared that both men were Americans, the murderer having stalked his prey for more than a year, and caught him as he was leaving France for America. It was proved at the trial that love and money were the motives of the crime.[19]

After returning to London, Jennie was apparently quite upset to learn that the Marquis de Breteuil had found an American heiress named Miss Garner and was going to be married. The wedding ceremony was at Pau, and Jennie did not attend. Writing to Randolph of the Marquis' marriage, she commented snidely, "I hope Breteuil's wife will keep sane." Back from a visit to the United States with his bride, Breteuil wrote Jennie an enigmatic letter. "I am happier every day and I will never forget that you had pushed me. . . . What I miss is not seeing you anymore . . . believe me again of my attachment. . . ." This letter somehow fell into Randolph's possession and was found among his final papers.

Jennie now moved back to her home on Connaught Place and was hardly bereft of male companions. John Strange Jocelyn, "the delightful Strange," had come from Ireland and visited. The newly arrived King of Greece took her to a concert. The Prince of Wales came to tea, "but not the Princess." She and the Prince went to the Fitzwilliams' for a weekend. After she and Kinsky had been out for an evening, Winston arrived unexpectedly to find them breakfasting together. George Curzon took her to dinner. She spent an evening with Arthur Balfour "A.B. sends you his love," she wrote Randolph.

Town Topics, which gobbled up all the gossip, reported: "Society has invented a new name for Lady R. Her fondness for the exciting sport of husband-hunting and fiancé-fishing, when the husbands and fiancés belong to other women, has earned her the title of 'Lady Jane Snatcher.' "

The rounds of pleasure were soon replaced by pain. "Those pains I used to think were in my 'mind' were really the thing beginning. I've got lots of pain," she wrote Randolph. The doctors found that she had a growth in the rectal area, "a lump about the size of a pullet's egg." They were unable to tell if it would grow or not, she reported, but if it did, it would have to be cut out and that would be a serious operation.

> I can't remember anything else he said—but I am not to give way to nerves and depression. Thank goodness I have done with doctors for the present. I was going down to see the boys today, but Clara has gone. . . . Recommend me some good books, will you? I feel better than I did, though somewhat bruised by those doctors.

Jennie's illness did not cause Randolph to hurry his return. Nor did he attend the wedding of sister Sarah (for whom Jennie had acted as matchmaker). He would return only after he found gold.

Randolph traveled from Kimberley and Johannesburg to Bechuanaland and Mashonaland. Depressed that the gold remained at the end of the rainbow, he wrote to Prime Minister Salisbury and to Balfour asking for appointment to the vacant Ambassadorship at Paris. Balfour, certainly pressed by Jennie, urged his uncle to give Randolph the post: "It would take him out of a sphere where, in these days of reckless electioneering promises, he is really dangerous and put him in one where he would be relatively powerless from mischief." Salisbury refused.

"I have been horribly low ever since," Jennie wrote when she heard of the refusal. "I have not breathed it to anyone, not even your mother. You can tell her when you get home. . . . The idea is too galling that the only thing you ever asked for should be refused!"

Randolph was also bitter at the parade of events. In November, Balfour had been made Leader of the Party in the House, and Randolph wrote to Jennie:

> So Arthur Balfour is really the Leader—and Tory Democracy, the genuine article, at an end. Well, I've had quite enough of it all. I've waited with great patience for the tide to turn, but it has not turned, and will not now turn in time.

Jennie's problems with Winston also had multiplied by the winter of 1891. He was approaching his seventeenth birthday, and he seemed to have reached the age of indecision. "Really I feel less keen about the Army every day," he wrote his mother. "I think the church would suit me much better." He then decided to be confirmed in the Church of England. "Perhaps it will steady him," Jennie wrote her husband. However, she added that she suspected the main reason he wanted to be confirmed was "only because it will get him off other work!" She knew her son well. His interest in the Church gradually became remote. (As an adult he liked to quote Disraeli: "All sensible men are of the same religion.")

Winston had a persistent way of converting an invisible crisis into an imagined catastrophe. "I can't tell you what trouble I have had with Winston this last fortnight. He has bombarded me with letters, cursing his fate and everyone," Jennie wrote Randolph. The crisis concerned Welldon's renewed suggestion that he spend the coming Christmas holidays with a family in France, in order to better prepare himself for the French examination for Sandhurst admissions. Winston objected vehemently: "I beg and pray that you will not send me to a vile, nasty, fusty, beastly French 'Family.'" Jennie partly surrendered and persuaded Welldon instead to make arrangements at the Paris home of one of Harrow's French teachers. Winston now attacked from another angle.

> Darling Mummy, I shall think it will be very unkind and unnatural if you allow him to do me out of my Christmas. . . . Please don't *you* put any pressure on me. . . . Mummy,

don't be unkind and make me unhappy . . . I have firmly
made up my mind not to go abroad until after the 27th.

Jennie answered firmly, "You can be quite certain my darling that I will
decide for what is best, but I tell you frankly that *I* am going to decide and
not *you*."[20]

Winston enjoyed Paris much more than he had imagined he would.
The Marquis de Breteuil invited him to lunch and Baron Hirsch took him
on a visit to the morgue, then a favorite Parisian pastime. "I was much interested," Winston wrote, except that he was disappointed at finding only
three bodies there that day—"not a good bag."

As was her custom, Mrs. Everest wrote long, solicitous, loving letters.
In one she told him she was sending his big tweed coat, "some fine flannel
shirts to sleep in," and his new suit. "Winny dear do try and keep the new
suit expressly for visiting, the brown one will do for everyday wear, please
do this to please me. I hope you will not take cold my darling take care not
to get wet or damp."

In another she described her Christmas supper at Connaught Place
with the house help.

> After supper they all sang songs and then we went into
> the kitchen and they put aside the table and danced for dear
> life. Edney whistled and I played the comb like we used to do
> in our good old nursery days . . . and we drank to the health
> and happiness of Mama and Papa, Mr. Winston and Mr.
> Jack which of course I heartily joined in you may be sure.

She continued, "Cheer up old Boy enjoy yourself try and feel contented
you have very much to be thankful for if you only consider and fancy how
nice it will be to *parlez vous francais* . . ."[21]

Jennie had kept Jack with her in London. "Jack's holidays are so much
shorter, I must have him with me," she had written Randolph. A studious
boy, Jack continued to do well at school, and his admission to Harrow appeared certain.[22]

Randolph was finally returning with gold. "Pa" Perkins, the American
engineer representing Rothschild, had found the goldbearing reefs and
determined the direction and depth necessary for Rand Gold-Mining
Company shafts to reach the area. Before the news caused a price rise,
Rothschild had loaned Randolph five thousand pounds to buy Rand
shares. Even after selling two fifths of his shares to pay debts, within three
years Randolph's remaining stock was still worth more than 70,000
pounds.

Just before the discovery, Esme Howard reported how drastically changed Randolph was when she saw him there. "He seemed to be a man who knew he was finished." Afterward, Lord Winchester saw Randolph crossing a river in Mashonaland in a litter laden with champagne.

"Papa arrived yesterday morning looking very well but with a horrid beard," Jack wrote his brother in Paris on January 9, 1892. He and his mother had missed the train to the ship by six minutes and had to wait two hours for the next one. The *Globe* had noted, "Lady R. Churchill nimbly ran across the dock."

Randolph's beard was a "terror," Jennie wrote Winston; "I think I shall have to bribe him to shave it off." But Randolph kept his ragged beard. Shane Leslie later wrote:

> To a child, Randolph was then a grizzled and bearded hunter returned from South Africa. . . . I ventured once to offer him the fruits of my own hunting in the local bush: an empty bird's nest. He stared at me long and sadly, perhaps madly, without uttering a word. It looked a harassed and haunted face; and when he came into the room, everyone started whispering, as in a church.[23]

Randolph did write Winston a reasoned letter, however, although the handwriting revealed a severe tremble. Winston had asked that his father visit him in Paris or get him an extra week's vacation so that he could come home and hear the stories of lions and tigers and gold. Randolph answered that it was much more important for Winston to get back to school and start studying again for the Sandhurst examinations. "After you have got into the Army you will have many weeks for amusement and idleness should your inclinations go in that direction."

Answering another money request from Winston, Randolph was more caustic: "If you were a millionaire, you could not be more extravagant. . . . If you are not more careful . . . it will see you in the Bankruptcy Court."[24]

Randolph extended his bitterness to Jennie, and Clara must have witnessed some angry scenes between them, for she described them in a flow of detailed letters to her husband. Moreton answered:

> . . . What a fright you must have had. That of itself was enough to make you ill. . . . I am so sorry for dear Jane; very sorry; but good times are at hand and when they come in full measure we shall be able to make things much more comfortable for her also. She is a great dear, and with all her faults, I am devoted to her. . . . Poor dear kind Jennie, I shall

so long to know things are tolerable with her again. She, of all people, must be fretting under such circumstances. He is a very hateful creature in many ways.

. . . Dear sweet Jenny, I am so sorry for her worries; worries too, not like ours to be got over; he is an impossible man that; a bad-natured man essentially; but the sense of the mistakes he has made would embitter a much better disposition than he has.[25]

Even Jennie's mother was now aware of the situation. "I have just seen Randolph in the park," she wrote Leonie hurriedly. "He is in a frantic state of mind about the state of affairs. . . . I must see you, I am so worried. Randolph is going out of town. . . ." But Jennie left town first, together with Clara, for an extended trip to southern France.

Anything disagreeable or disruptive within an upper-class British family of the time was always submerged and kept from the children. Winston knew nothing of his family's continual financial and personal crises and continued writing requests for money and for visits. He had become an expert fencer, with a "quick and dashing attack which took his opponents by surprise," and which made him the school's fencing champion. It was one of the few times he had ever won anything, but his father's congratulation was curt, "I only hope fencing will not too much divert you from the army class." Nor would his father come to see him compete for the Public School Fencing Championship, because he said he had to attend the Sandowne Races that day. Winston won that championship, too, against "much taller and more formidable" opponents.

It was at this time, too, that his first words reached print—in an anonymous letter to the *Harrovian*, signed "Junius Junior," urging more student participation in gym activities.

Winston was less successful with the final entrance examination for Sandhurst. His tutor thought it was a creditable first try, and noted that Winston would have another chance at it within six months. But Randolph, highly skeptical, wrote his mother, "If he fails again, I shall think about putting him in business."

Jack seemed to be everything Winston was not, conscientious, responsible and placid. He was also far more popular with his older relatives. But he, too, was lonely. He wrote his father, "I waited all afternoon for you. . . . You might come down and see me. You have been here only once, the whole time I have been down here [three years]." Jennie tried to make up for Randolph's obvious lack of affection for his sons. Still in France, she remembered to send Jack a box of tangerines and a dispatch case for his twelfth birthday. She also wrote him how delighted she was when he was admitted to Harrow. Jack and Winston were reunited at Harrow in 1892 and shared a room.

The many who did not know of his disease still considered Randolph Churchill a potential political force. Salisbury asked him to dinner: "We shall be very glad to see you." Arthur Balfour invited him to sit with him on the honored front bench in the House: "*Everyone* desires that you should do so, and *most of all* yours ever, A.J.B." Party leaders invited him to attend their meeting on parliamentary tactics. Joseph Chamberlain could not have been kinder. And even the press adopted a friendlier tone. Requests for him to speak publicly came from everywhere again. Randolph, however, confided to an associate, "Politics interests me less and less."

Despite his apparent disinterest in politics, Randolph was plainly delighted when the Gladstone Liberals defeated Salisbury's Conservative government in the General Election of July 1892, by a bare parliamentary margin of forty. Randolph never forgave Salisbury for gleefully accepting his resignation and refusing to appoint him as either Viceroy of India or Ambassador to France. As for the Conservative Party, Randolph wrote that it had "boycotted and slandered me . . . for five years."

His health was failing again. "I have been very seedy . . . with giddiness," he told Rosebery. Jennie had returned from France, and she also was ill. "Her condition is so full of serious possibilities," Dr. Roose wrote Randolph, "that I felt it my duty to advise her Ladyship seeing at once Dr. Keith."

Jennie made light of it. She journeyed to Scotland for a short visit with friends, while Randolph stayed close to his horses at Newcastle. But her pain suddenly increased, and she went to Dr. Keith for a more detailed examination.

A tall, gentle man with a full beard, long hair, intense eyes, and a musical voice, Dr. Thomas Keith not only became Jennie's physician but later advised on Randolph's case in its final stages. He was a prominent surgeon, educated in Boston and Edinburgh, a specialist in the genital and ovarian areas, and widely known for his use of electricity in treating uterine tumors.[26] His examination of Jennie revealed a swelling in the right groin near the uterus, a pelvic peritonitis and cellulitis. Operations for such a condition were rare and dangerous. There was, however, hope that the whole thing might quiet down, Keith pointed out. "Rest is essential in order to avoid the risk of an acute attack. . . . In moving about, she must keep within the limits of pain."

"We have to face many months of terrible anxiety . . . and there is no margin for mistake," Roose wrote Randolph at Newcastle. "Her Ladyship is holding her own, but has a great deal of suffering."

"He said if I wished to avoid an operation, I must be very quiet," Jennie wrote her husband. "By that he meant no mental worry or physical exertion. It is rather gloomy here and I miss you much."

Randolph, who knew all about suffering and gloom, suddenly realized that Jennie might die. Despite the wide drift of their marriage, he had always been certain that she was there and that she would always be there when he truly needed her. That knowledge had buoyed him through his steady series of crises. But with her gone, there would be no one but his mother; there would be emptiness. No matter how self-centered he was, this was a time to turn away from self-pity in concern and care for his wife. He must have been moved, torn by the fact that despite all her lovers, she still wanted her husband near her.

Jennie's crisis also converted Randolph into a father again. He promptly returned to London and wrote his sons,

> Your dear mother was extremely ill yesterday and we were rather alarmed. But thank God today there is an improvement and the doctors are very hopeful. I only got up to town this evening. I will keep you informed as to how your dear mother progresses.

Since Winston was busy preparing for his repeat examination for Sandhurst, Randolph added, "Your mother would be in such good spirits if she thought you were going to do well in your examination." Then in an affectionate, paternal note, "Kiss Jack for me."

Winston replied immediately, "I am awful sorry to hear that Mama is so bad. I hope that she will soon be better, and that you will let us know every day how she is. Is it very good writing to her?"

It was a time of trouble and death. Blandford, the eighth Duke of Marlborough, died unexpectedly in 1892 at the age of forty-eight. It was a shattering shock and hurried Randolph's own physical disintegration. Troubles piled upon troubles. Shortly after his brother's death, Randolph received a desperate note from Blandford's widow. Some time before, she said, Blandford had written an article on "The Art of Living" for the *Fortnightly*. "I am anxious to get it back," she wrote. "I could not have it appear in print. See Mr. Frank Harris, and get this article from him at any price."

Blandford had done the piece for the *Fortnightly* in order to get Frank Harris to publish a dull article by his mistress, Lady Colin Campbell, the unorthodox lady with the tweed knickerbockers who had decided to become an actress. In his will, Blandford had left Lady Campbell the sum of 20,000 pounds "as a proof of my friendship and esteem." Blandford's article was full of personal revelation in which he wrote, among other things, that he thought women were the only things in life worth winning.

Randolph sent for Harris. "When he came across the room to shake hands with me," said Harris,

> I was appalled by his appearance. In a couple of years he had changed out of character, had become an old man instead of a young one. [Randolph was then forty-three years old.] His face was haggard; his hair grayish and very thin on top; his thick beard, also half-gray, changed him completely. He held himself well, which added dignity, but the old boyish smile was gone.

Randolph asked Harris not to publish his brother's article. Harris protested, but Randolph answered, "You won't refuse an old friend's last request," and held out his hand.

"As I took his hand," said Harris, "and looked at him I felt sick: the deep lines on his face, the heavy gummy bags under his miserable eyes, the shaking hand—it might well be his *last* request!"

"It shall be as you wish," promised Harris.

Before Harris left, he told Randolph to get well and strong. "I fear the dice are loaded against me," Randolph replied.[27]

Randolph had vertigo, numbness of the hands, palpitations, increasing deafness, and a growing difficulty in articulating. His letters, once clear and concise, now rambled on in all directions and were written in a tremulous script. His behavior was increasingly erratic and moody. On one occasion he had a most congenial dinner with his old friend and political enemy, Joseph Chamberlain; then at another dinner in the same week, for no apparent reason, he snarled at Chamberlain and ordered the waiter to put a bowl of flowers between them.

He was equally unpredictable with his family. When his sons put on an amateur theatrical at Banstead for a small family audience, Randolph said frostily, "I shall preserve a strong and acid silence." Then again, he might show a much softer side of himself. Late in 1892 when his boys were on winter vacation, the family was at Banstead for a weekend. Winston fired a double-barreled shotgun at a rabbit that appeared on the lawn, and the sound startled Randolph.

"He had been very angry and disturbed," Winston wrote later.

> Understanding at once that I was distressed, he took occasion to reassure me. I then had one of the three or four intimate conversations with him which are all I can boast. He explained how old people were not always very considerate towards young people, that they were absorbed in

their own affairs and might well speak roughly in sudden annoyance.

In a quiet, fatherly, almost affectionate tone, Randolph told Winston how glad he was that he liked to shoot, and that he would arrange for him to shoot partridges on their small property.

> Then he proceeded to talk to me in the most wonderful and captivating manner about school and going into the army and the grown-up life which lay beyond. I listened spellbound to this sudden departure from his usual reserve, amazed at his intimate comprehension of my affairs. Then at the end, he said, "Do remember things do not always go right with me. My every action is misjudged, and every word distorted . . . so make some allowances."[28]

Perhaps Jennie was making more allowances, too. She had been very dangerously ill, and her recovery was slow. Deeper than ever now, she understood the mood and the mind of her husband, whose suffering and closeness to death was so intense and shameful and predictable. And in her time of real danger, he was the one she had wanted to be with her. She was thirty-eight. Her beauty was still rich but no longer fresh. The young men she had known were now no longer young and most of them married. Though her husband was only a remnant of the man she had married, he was still her husband.

"My dear sweet old Jane," her brother-in-law Moreton wrote from America:

> Troublous times at least do this—they turn us back upon those really near and dear with a feeling of gentle reliance and that is why I am writing to you. . . . I am anxious that you have these worries, not only these abominable money troubles, vile and vulgar as they are. Please God, good times are near and I will take a house in Leicestershire, and a lot of horses for you, and we will renew youth and health also at the dear old game.[29]

A dream, to be sure, but this was a time when she needed such dreams. Count Kinsky was not available to console her, as he had been summoned by the Archduke Franz Ferdinand, the heir to the Austro-Hungarian throne, to accompany him for three months travel in India and Ceylon as part of a world tour. The two men formed a fast friendship, and the Archduke would again ask for Kinsky to come with him on future tours.[30]

Jennie, however, did receive sympathy from an unexpected source—her mother-in-law, the Dowager Duchess. Their conflict had lost its sharp edge, and although there was still a large reservoir of resentment left, it did not prevent the Dowager Duchess from offering Jennie the Marlborough home at 50 Grosvenor Square whenever Randolph was away nor Jennie from accepting the offer. Now, with Jennie's illness and Randolph's worsening health, the Duchess suggested that they both move in with her because "it might be much more comfortable and economical." And so they did.

No sooner did Jennie begin slowly improving than things started happening again to Winston. Late in January 1893, she was informed that he had failed his final examination for Sandhurst for the second time. He wrote that he was "awfully depressed." Randolph asked Welldon for further advice about his son and Welldon recommended a "crammer," a Captain Walter James. Winston later wrote that with the crammer's help "no one who was not a congenital idiot could avoid passing thence into the Army."

But before Winston could begin the cram course, he had a serious accident in which he was almost killed. The Churchills had given up Banstead, but Randolph's adoring sister Cornelia, Lady Wimborne, had lent Jennie and the boys her comfortable estate in Bournemouth for January. The estate had some fifty acres of pine forest ending in sandy cliffs and smooth beach. Playing a game of chase with his twelve-year-old brother and fourteen-year-old cousin, Winston found himself trapped in the middle of a bridge, so he climbed the balustrade and tried to jump onto the top of a nearby fir tree. He missed and fell almost thirty feet to the ground. It was three days before he regained consciousness and two months before he was back at school.

Randolph had gone to Dublin for a reunion with friends, when Jennie summoned him home with the news. Among other injuries, Winston had a ruptured kidney. As he put it, "I looked at life round the corner." The Harley Street specialist whom Dr. Roose had brought told Jennie that her son "should not return to hard study any more than he should take vigorous exercise."

This suited Winston perfectly. He was brought to the home of the Dowager Duchess on Grosvenor Square, and it turned out to be a truly happy time for him. Jennie gave her son solicitous attention and kept his mind stirred with the excitement of parliamentary politics.

> My mother gave me full accounts of what she heard, and
> Mr. Edward Marjoribanks, afterwards Lord Tweedmouth,

Mr. Gladstone's Chief Whip, was married to my father's sister, Fanny. We thus shared, in a detached way, the satisfaction of the Liberals at coming back to power after their long banishment. We heard some, at least, of their hopes and fears. Politics seemed very important and vivid to my eyes, in those days. They were directed by statesmen of commanding intellect and personality.

It seemed a very great world in which these men lived; a world where high rules reigned and every trifle in public conduct counted; a duelling ground where although the business might be ruthless, and the weapons loaded with ball, there was ceremonious personal courtesy and mutual respect.[31]

Jennie invited most of these "statesmen of commanding intellect" for dinner, and Winston listened in awe as they discussed "the burning topics of the hour." Among the guests were three future Prime Ministers—Rosebery, Balfour, and Asquith—all of whom, in one way or another, would help shape Winston's future. Jennie encouraged Winston not simply to listen, but to ask questions, and even politely argue.

"In those days, people could not see any definite principle behind Jennie Churchill's upbringing of her sons," wrote Lady Warwick.

They did not realize that she was developing in them qualities, which, in the ordinary course, take years to show themselves. She always found time to encourage her boys to express themselves. . . . I still chuckle when I remember how, as a schoolboy, he [Winston] would comment to his face upon the views of such a politician as Lord Hartington.[32]

In addition to filling her house with the most important political figures of her time and encouraging Winston to involve himself in the discussions, Jennie explained at length all the intricacies of political maneuver which so fascinated him. She supplemented that with her own estimates of the political leaders of both parties. So vividly and excitingly was the way of politics described that it enveloped him enough to help pattern the direction of his life.

As soon as Winston was allowed to go out, Jennie encouraged him to visit the House of Commons to listen to the debates and watch the great men he had observed in private conversation now acting their parts in public. One thing immediately struck him as remarkable: political opponents did not allow even their most violent parliamentary clashes to hurt their friendly social relations. Winston particularly remembered one interchange between his father and Sir William Harcourt in Parliament.

> Sir William seemed to be quite furious and most unfair in his reply, and I was astonished when only a few minutes later, he made his way up to where I sat, and with a beaming smile, introduced himself to me and asked me what I thought of it all.[33]

Frank Harris once asked Winston Churchill about his father. "Did you never talk politics with him?"

"I tried," Winston told him, "but he only looked with contempt on me and would not answer."

"But didn't he see you had something in you?"

"He thought of no one but himself. No one else seemed to him worth thinking about."

"You didn't like him?" Harris continued.

"How could I? I was ready enough to as a boy, but he wouldn't let me. He treated me as if I had been a fool; barked at me whenever I questioned him. I owe everything to my mother; to my father, nothing."[34]

During those early months of 1893, Winston could see the effects of his father's condition. "As time wore on, I could not help feeling that my father's speeches were not as good as they used to be. There were some brilliant successes; yet, on the whole, he seemed to be hardly holding his own." Henry Lucy reported one painful episode:

> He had, at the proper moment, taken some drug to "buck up" his frail body through the hour he intended to speak. But someone raised the question of privilege, discussed for a full hour, through which Lord Randolph sat, fuming. When the hour had sped, the tonic effects of medicine were exhausted. It was a decrepit man who, with bowed figure, and occasionally inarticulate voice, at length stood at the table—a painful spectacle, from contemplation of which Members gradually withdrew. The chamber which once filled at the signal, "Churchill is up," was almost empty when he sat down.[35]

At Jennie's urging, Liberal M.P. Edward Carson had a private dinner with Winston at Harrow and explained to him at length how the Liberals planned to overcome the opposition of the House of Lords to the Home Rule Bill (which they did not do). Carson also invited Winston to dine with him at the House of Commons. "If you would rather I would not go, please send me a wire," Winston wrote his father.[36]

Jack wrote Jennie from school that Welldon had told him "if I worked like Winny did his first three years here, it would turn his hairs white." When she visited at Harrow, she learned that Jack was "the youngest boy in the school," but was happily settled. Welldon's report was excellent.

Winston, however, still was not a serious student, and Captain James complained that he was "casual," "inattentive," and "rather too much inclined up to the present to teach his instructors instead of endeavoring to learn from them. . . ." Furthermore, Winston had developed other distractions. At eighteen, he was a good-looking young man with a ruddy face, an aggressive manner, and an eye-catching crop of red hair. He had caught the eye of Mabel Love, a young actress at the Lyric Theater, who sent him some pictures and notes—much to the envy of his Harrow friends.

Finally, on his third try, Winston passed the entrance examination into Sandhurst, but barely. He later said of that:

> If this aged, weary-souled Civil Service Commissioner had not asked this particular question about these cosines or tangents in their squared or even cubed condition, which I happened to have learned scarcely a week before, I might have gone into the church and preached orthodox sermons in a spirit of anxious contradiction to the age.
>
> I might have gone into the City and made a fortune. I might have gravitated to the Bar, and persons might have been hanged to my defense. Anyhow, the whole of my life would have been altered and I suppose would have altered a great many other lives.

His marks, however, were not high enough to qualify him for an infantry cadetship, so he was assigned to the cavalry.

> I had already formed a definite opinion at the relative advantages of riding and walking. What fun it would be, having a horse!
>
> I say to parents, and especially wealthy parents, "Don't give your son money. As far as you can afford it, give him horses." No one ever came to grief—except honorable grief— through riding horses. No hour of life is lost that is spent in the saddle. Young men have often been ruined through owning horses, or through backing horses, but never through riding

them; unless, of course, they break their necks, which, taken at a gallop, is a very good death to die.[37]

Winston wrote his father a letter of youthful exuberance about his success in entering Sandhurst, and he got this caustic response:

> The first extremely discreditable feature of your performance was missing the infantry, for in that failure is demonstrated beyond refutation your slovenly happy-go-lucky harum scarum style of work for which you have always been distinguished at your different schools. Never have I received a really good report of your conduct in your work. . . .
>
> With all the advantages you had, with all the abilities which you foolishly think yourself to possess . . . with all the efforts that have been made to make your life easy and agreeable . . . this is the grand result. . . .

Randolph went on to say that if Winston kept up his past performance, "you will become a mere social wastrel, one of the hundreds of the public school failures, and you will degenerate into a shabby, unhappy and futile existence."

How much of that bitterness was a reflection of his own frustrations and failures? How much resulted from his having asked the Duke of Cambridge to reserve a place for Winston in his regiment of the 60th Rifles, and now having to face the embarrassment of rescinding the request? But part of his resentment was based on the fact that the Cavalry meant an expense of two hundred pounds a year, plus the cost of several horses and a string of polo ponies.

Randolph ended his diatribe to Winston with, "Your mother sends her love." It was a venomous letter, and Winston never forgot the pain it caused him.

Randolph also wrote to the Duchess his views of Winston:

> I have told you often and you never would believe me that he has little [claim] to cleverness, to knowledge or any capacity for settled work. He had great talent for show-off exaggeration and make believe. The whole result of this either at Harrow or at Eton [was] to prove his total worthlessness as a scholar or a conscientious worker. He need not expect much from me.

Just as Winston had not known at thirteen whether his father had gone to Harrow or Eton, neither did Randolph seem to know now that his son had never been to Eton.

Jennie had small illusions about any hope of a cure for her husband, but she did think the mineral baths at Kissingen might quiet his nerves and give him some needed rest. Most of all, though, she wanted to get him away from London, where he was making more and more a pitiful spectacle of himself at public and social affairs.

For her sons that summer of 1893, Jennie arranged a walking tour of Switzerland with a young Eton tutor. Of the Matterhorn Winston wrote, "I don't wonder that people want to go up, in spite of the numerous graves in the churchyard."

At Kissingen, Jennie and Randolph were visited by Prince Otto von Bismarck, who by then was out of power. "He came up to our rooms—which luckily are on the first floor—and sat down and we began to converse," Randolph wrote to his mother.

> I had sent off a message to Jennie, who had gone to the Kurhaus to see a friend, so I had about a quarter of an hour in which to talk to the Prince. . . . He is 78—so he told me afterwards—but he looks so much younger than Mr. Gladstone . . . He struck me as being very nervous. Perhaps it was meeting with a total stranger, because he had never seen me before. However, he was most gracious and seemed very anxious to please. You may imagine that I did my very best to please him, for I thought it a great honor for this old Prince to come and see us. . . . He further in conversation said that he should be very alarmed and anxious if such a man as Mr. Gladstone governed "my country." Then Jennie arrived, and he talked mainly to her for a few minutes, when he announced that his son Herbert and his recently-married wife arrived that afternoon to stay a few days with them, and that he hoped we should see something of them.[38]

They later had dinner together, Prince Otto and the Princess, Jennie and Randolph, Count Herbert and his new wife. The Countess was the former Marguerite Hoyos. Herbert had earlier intended to marry Princess Elisabeth of Carolath-Beuthen, but the scandal of their affair and the Princess' divorce of her husband had forced the Count to give her up. The social stigma remained so acute, however, that Count Herbert and Countess Marguerite would be snubbed by Berlin Court Society for some time.[39] Jennie described the dinner in detail:

We dined with him at the old *Schloss*, where he was living, its picturesque red roof making a landmark in the flat Bavarian scenery. . . . At dinner, I sat on one side of the Prince, and Randolph on the other, the huge boar-hound, our host's constant companion, lying on the ground between us. Conversation was animated. Bismarck spoke excellent English, but very slowly; and if he could not find a word he wanted, he would pause and think until he did.

His family looked up to him with awe and admiration, and listened with the greatest attention to every word he uttered. The old Princess, who seemed very feeble, did not take much part in the conversation. After dinner, we adjourned to another part of the room, where we sat round a long table covered with books and newspapers. There were a great many illustrated papers, full of caricatures of Bismarck, which in answer to a question, he assured me he did not mind in the least. Later, however, Count Herbert contradicted this, saying that his father was really very sensitive, and disliked being caricatured.

Speaking of the country and the long walks he took daily, Bismarck said he loved nature, but the amount of life he saw awed him, and that it took a great deal of faith to believe that an "all-seeing Eye" could notice every living atom, when one realized what that meant. "Have you ever sat on the grass and examined it closely? There is enough life in one square yard to appal you," he said. When we were about to leave, his great dog fixed his fierce eyes on mine in so persistent a manner that I became alarmed and thought that he was going to spring upon me; but the Prince reassured me, saying, "He is looking at your eyes, because he has not seen any like them."

During the two months the Churchills were at Kissingen, Winston started Sandhurst and Jennie kept in close touch with him. Things went very well for Winston from the start. Gone were the "discomfort, restriction and purposeless monotony. . . . One could feel oneself growing up almost every week." He was given an infantry cadetship, after all, which pleased his father. His grades were consistently good. "It shows that I could learn quickly enough the things that mattered," he said.

Randolph still seemed skeptical of Winston, however, and pointedly criticized both the content and style of his son's letters. Almost in retaliation, Winston let his mother know how happy he was to be able to write to

her "unreservedly instead of having to pick and choose my words and information." He closed with, "Do come back as soon as you can as I am
longing to see you. . . . Goodbye dear darling Mummy. Ever so much love
and more kisses from your ever loving son." The sentiment seems overripe
for a young man nearing nineteen. The emotion more properly belongs to
a boy lonesome for his mother, or to a young man pining for his sweetheart. Seen in the context of his father's constant rejection of him, however,
Winston's longing for love reflected a continuing need.

Jack shared his brother's need. Jennie did not return to London with
Randolph but went to Paris to visit Leonie, and Jack asked his father repeatedly, "When is Mama coming home?" And with repressed anger he
said, "I suppose that you are too busy to come and see me one day this
term. Even a Sunday would do." Randolph promised he would go, but then
Jack wrote his mother, "Papa changed his mind or something and did not
come to see me although he sent me one pound but I would rather he
would come down."

Randolph finally did visit Jack at Harrow and brought along his much
bemedaled friend Lord Roberts. The three had dinner with Welldon.
("Such an honor," Winston wrote his mother. "I can never remember a
lower boy going before.")

When Jennie wired Randolph for money so she could stay in Paris
longer, he simply answered that their bank balance was overdrawn. She returned home. Jack's letter was waiting for her, telling her about his father's
visit and declaring that he needed "a little money," a new silk hat, and was
tired of wearing Winny's "shabby" coat which was "awful."

But Jennie's more serious worries concerned Winston. During the past
year she had continually made mention to Randolph of Winston's need to
be made a man, to have the advantage of fatherly advice and male companionship. Finally her campaign had effect. Winston's new status as a gentleman cadet improved his position with his father. Examining his son in
this new light, Randolph informed the Dowager Duchess, "He has much
smartened up." In the coming months, Winston's relationship with his father reached its peak. Conversations were minimal and there was still no
sign of emotional feeling, but there was more contact.

Randolph began taking his son to the theater, a few racing parties, and
some political affairs. He even sent Winston two boxes of his favorite cigars, advising him though, "Keep down the smoking, keep down the drink
and go to bed as early as you can," Winston answered, "I shall take your
advice about the cigars, and I don't think I shall often smoke more than
one or two a day–and very rarely that."[41]

Winston's letters now had a more worldly air. He thought his father's
remarks on the coal strike "were splendid." Had his father read a new novel

called *Euthanasia* "It seems well written." Would his father please put his name down for a good club? And also, "Am now in tails according to your instructions."

There was going to be a ball at Sandhurst, he wrote. "If Mama is home, I shall ask her to come." Both boys were proud of their mother's beauty, talents, social position, and striking personality. "She didn't seem to be like other women at all," said Shane Leslie. "I think her sons and I looked on her as something far more beautiful than any of the actresses we were called on to admire."

But Winston was not so awed by his mother that he could not raise his voice in indignation toward her. The reason now was that the Dowager Duchess had fired Mrs. Everest, who was, he wrote, "In my mind associated—more than anything else—with *home.* . . . She is an old woman who has been your devoted servant for nearly twenty years—she is more fond of Jack and I than of any other people in the world." She had fed them, clothed them, nursed them, kissed them, played with them, cried with them, fought for them, loved them. ("I am going to make Winnie's box cover tomorrow. . . . I am longing to see my darling Jackie to have some kisses. . . .") They were, in a sense, her cubs more than Jennie's.

The Dowager Duchess had sent Mrs. Everest on holiday, and while she was away had stopped her wages and sacked her. The Duchess never had liked Mrs. Everest, considering her a barrier between herself and her grandsons. With Jennie and Randolph living with her, she used the excuse of inadequate space to fire Mrs. Everest. Winston called it "cruel and mean."

"I know you have no choice in the matter and that the Duchess has every right to discharge a servant for whom she has 'no further use,'" he wrote his mother. But "it is in your power to explain to the Duchess that she *cannot* be sent away until she has got a good place." He was not asking his mother, he was insisting. If she did not see that Mrs. Everest was provided for, he said, he would go directly to his father.

Jennie, of course, was in no position to ask for anything. She and Randolph were in the Duchess' home on pure sufferance. She tried to find Mrs. Everest a place, and finally did, at the home of a Bishop in Essex, "an outlandish part of the world," and also continued to send her a small, separate check.

Mrs. Everest was most unhappy away from her boys and away from the lively life of the Churchills. For the short remainder of her life, Elizabeth Ann Everest maintained a constant and motherly correspondence with Winston and Jack and saw them whenever she could. (She had visited both her boys at Harrow when their parents could not come. Jack's son Peregrine insists that it was his father, not Winston, who met her at the station, kissed her, and openly escorted her throughout the campus.[42] One of his class-mates commented, "I wish I had the courage to do that with my nanny.")

With Mrs. Everest at Essex and their parents so often either traveling or socializing, Winston and Jack still had a host of homes where they could visit for weekends or short vacations. Their family was large and quite closely-knit. The aunts were the anchors, the grandmothers the bedrock, and the horde of cousins provided a ready intermingling of companionship and love. They were always welcome at Blenheim, Ireland, Paris, and the town and country homes of a dozen close relatives.

After his flurry of concerned fatherhood, Randolph retired again to his racing horses, which were having an excellent year. For the previous four years, in fact, Randolph and his partner, Lord Dunraven, had been among the biggest winners of the British turf. Jennie again substituted for him in visits to Sandhurst and her letters to Winston were longer now.[43] But it was soon time to be more wife than mother.

"In the spring of 1894, it became clear to all of us that my father was gravely ill," Winston Churchill wrote.

> He still persisted in his political work. Almost every week, he delivered a speech at some important center. No one could fail to see that these efforts were increasingly un-successful. The verbatim reports dropped from 3 to 2 columns, and then to 1 ½. On one occasion, the *Times* mentioned that the hall was not filled.[44]

Just before he was scheduled to address Parliament in March 1894, his friends John Morley and Arthur Balfour talked about it. "He told me that Randolph was going to make a speech two hours long," Morley said afterward.

"What about?" Morley asked.

"Heaven only knows," answered Balfour.[45]

When Randolph got up on that occasion to speak, his face prematurely aged, his hands shaking, his speech so garbled that it became unintelligible after the first sentence, members of the House fled into the lobby. To check their onrush, the parliamentarian yelled, "Order, order!" A friend described the speech as a waking nightmare. Randolph's face had a terrible, mad look, and he even screamed, "You damned fools! You're playing the devil with the Tory Party and making hell of the House of Commons." But it was he who was making the hell, and Arthur Balfour sat next to him, his head bowed, his hands over his face in pity and shame.

"There was no curtain, no retirement," wrote his dear friend, Lord Rosebery. "He died by inches in public."[46]

Rosebery replaced Gladstone as Prime Minister in March of 1894. The Queen had coolly accepted the resignation of the proud old eagle—she had never liked Gladstone. Silver-tongued Rosebery was more to her taste. Even Gladstone had once called him the cleverest man in politics. Rosebery possessed a remarkable voice with natural authority, and he could be as terrible to his enemies as he was irresistible to his friends. His smile could be playful, his silence freezing. He could also discuss Greek poets or race-horses with equal skill (his horses would win the Derby three times). He seemed to have everything, except ambition. But Rosebery had come into power when Liberal fortunes were at their lowest. It was the end of an age, and he was not the man to begin a new one.

Randolph was Rosebery's personal sadness. "Why recall those last days except to recall the pity of them," Rosebery wrote. He begged Jennie to keep Randolph away from the House of Commons, stop his public appearances, prevent any further speeches. Jennie tried. Winston Churchill later wrote:

> I heard my mother and the old Duchess, who so often disagreed—both urging him to take a rest, while he persisted that he was all right and that everything was going well. I knew that these two, who were so near and devoted to him, would never have pressed him thus without the gravest need.

"I don't think any wife could have played a greater part than Jennie did," Shane Leslie said. "She had tremendous powers; she had a touch of Cleopatra in her and she never lost heart."[47] There were numberless times when she almost did. To maintain her own equilibrium, Jennie took frequent trips to Paris to be with Leonie. Clara was often there, too.

Randolph's public conduct was completely unpredictable. After sitting alongside him at a dinner, Lord Carnarvon had written that Randolph's conversation was "as mad a one as I ever listened to from mortal lips." Attending another dinner at Sir Henry Thompson's, Frank Harris sat opposite Randolph. Harris had seen him only a couple of months before, but now Randolph was far worse. His face was drawn and his skin leaden gray; there were gleams of hate, anger, and fear in his eyes, "the dreadful fear of those who have learned how close madness is."

> All through the next course Lord Randolph didn't speak a word. As the game was being taken round, the footman noticed that it was not properly cut, so he passed Lord Randolph quickly to get it dispieced at the sideboard. At once Randolph pointing with outstretched hand, squealed out as if in pain, "E-e-e-e-e-e!"

"What is it, Lord Randolph?" asked the host in utter solicitude.

"E-e-e-e!" He repeated the high squeal, while pointing with his finger after the footman. "I want that—e-e-e! Some of that—!"

"It shall be brought back," said Sir Henry. "I'm very glad you like it." The grouse was brought back: Randolph helped himself and began to eat greedily. Suddenly he stopped, put down his knife and fork and glared at each face round the table, apparently suspecting that his strange behavior had been remarked. He was insane, that was clear. From that moment on I could drink but not eat. Randolph Churchill mad! Like Maupassant![48]

On May 27, Wilfrid Scawen Blunt visited Churchill at Grosvenor Square and then described his condition:

He is terribly altered, poor fellow, having some disease, paralysis, I suppose, which affects his speech, so that it is painful to listen to him. He makes prodigious efforts to express himself clearly, but these are only too visible. He talked of his election prospects at Bradford, and the desire of the Conservatives to delay the turning out of the Rosebery government.

About Egypt, Randolph said, "You know my opinion is unchanged, but my tongue is tied." He walked his friend Blunt to the door, trying to say something about Egypt, but finally broke down, almost in tears. "I know what to say, but damn it, I can't say it."[49]

Randolph was still saddened by the death of his closest friend Louis Jennings, who had succumbed to cancer at the age of fifty-six. Jennings had been his constant support in Parliament, and had made his own reputation as an editor of the London edition of the New York *Herald*, as a crusading editor of *The New York Times* during the Tweed Ring exposé, and as the author of a three-volume novel, *The Philadelphian*. In his will, Randolph had named Jennings as one of his literary executors, and never changed the designation, even after Jennings' death.

Seventeen

HE DOCTORS DECIDED that Randolph should go with Jennie on a world tour, then changed their minds,[1] worried that he would need a doctor's attention, and finally agreed that Dr. Keith[2] would accompany him. Randolph had sold his Connaught Place house plus some of his gold stocks to pay his bills and provide funds for the trip. He had also sold his share of the Abbess to Lord Dunraven for some $40,000.[3]

Down to the dregs of his life, Randolph still had the stamp of the patrician, a sense of fitness and dignity. His had been a life of pleasure, sport, and fashion, but he had left his mark as a stormy statesman with a record of sporadic brilliance. His temper was imperious, his disdain overbearing, his rudeness vicious. No man had made more enemies. Yet he demonstrated—when he chose—gifts of grace and charm. He showed vestiges of those graces at a dinner for some of his oldest friends just before leaving on the tour. He talked little and worried excessively about the comfort of his guests. But "one noticed how nervously his hand beat on the table, as he gazed round."

"I cannot even now make up my mind whether I wish that I had dined or stayed away," Lord Rosebery later wrote. "It was all pain, and yet one would not have liked to have missed his good-bye. I still cannot think of it without distress."

Before leaving, Randolph contracted to write a series of columns for a

Paris journal describing his world tour, but they were columns he would never write.

It was not a trip Jennie wanted to make—a whole year away from the world she loved, a year with a husband nearly insane. In addition, she had had a showdown with Count Kinsky. He could not and would not lose her for a whole year. He had waited too long, and a year out their lives now was more than he could tolerate. The whole world would understand if she were to leave Randolph, a virtual madman. Kinsky had already requested and received permission to transfer to the legation in Brussels. From there they could transfer together to any embassy in the world, a new world, their own. They were entitled to the rest of their lives together. But Jennie turned away. Randolph was the man she had once loved. He was her husband and he was dying, and he needed her because he had no one else. She could not leave him now.

They started their world tour on the S.S. *Majestic* on June 27, 1894. A few old friends came to see them off, among them Prime Minister Rosebery and Mr. Goschen and Lady Jeune, as well as their sons.

"I was making a road-map . . . when a cyclist messenger brought me the College Adjutant's order to proceed at once to London," Winston Churchill later wrote.

> My father was setting out the next day on a journey round the world. An ordinary application to the college authorities for my being granted special leave of absence had been refused, as a matter of routine. He had telegraphed to the Secretary of State for War . . . and no time had been lost in setting me on my way to London.
>
> We drove to the station the next morning—my mother, my younger brother and I. In spite of the great beard, which he had grown during his South African journey four years before, his face looked terribly haggard and worn with mental pain. He patted me on the knee in a gesture which, however simple, was perfectly informing.[4]

Leonie later talked about Randolph with Frank Harris:

> Randolph was quite mad when my sister took him on that last trip round the world. We all knew it. No one but Jennie would have trusted herself to go with him, but she's afraid of nothing and very strong. Yet from things she has let drop, she must have had a trying time with him. Why once, she told me, he drew out a loaded revolver in the cabin and

threatened her, but she snatched it from him at once, pushed him back in his berth, and left the cabin, locking the door behind her. Jennie is the bravest woman I ever knew.

Harris reported that Jennie herself told him, "At first, when he was practically a maniac and very strong it was bad enough, but as soon as he became weak and idiotic, I didn't mind."[5]

Perhaps her words were actually less harsh, but even if not, they can be understood with sympathy. He was mad and she knew it, yet she went with him—and she did not have to. The decision was hers and the strength was hers. And so was the final horror.

Jennie's cousin William Travers Jerome, then an assistant district attorney in New York City, met her for the first time when the Churchills arrived in New York. "Shall I call you Aunt Jennie or Cousin Jennie?" Jerome asked her. She answered, "Why don't you just call me Jennie. It will make you feel older and make me feel younger."[6]

What might have made Jennie feel older in New York was to note that there was a new Madison Square Garden, designed by Stanford White, directly across the street from the old Jerome house on Madison and 26th Street. Even newer was the Metropolitan Life Insurance headquarters only three blocks away, foreshadowing the change of the Madison Square area from a residential to a commercial center.[7]

The weather was hot in the city, and the Churchills stayed only two days. Perhaps they were speeded on their way by the pressure of the social invitations they could not face. A local magazine reported:

> His Lordship is much changed from the gay, clever and vivacious young man who gained wide popularity here and at Newport, 10 or 11 years ago, when he came to visit the family of Mr. Leonard Jerome. He is restless, nervous and irritable, and walks feebly, with jerky steps, like a man uncertain of where he is putting his feet. His whole manner indicates a painful nervousness and mental irritation, from the querulous tones of his voice to his compressed lips, which he keeps drawn over his teeth in an apparent effort to control their trembling.[8]

Chauncey Depew, one of the few people they saw, put his private railroad car at their disposal for their journey to Bar Harbor. After the dust and heat of New York, Bar Harbor was a haven of fresh sea breezes, lovely drives and mountain walks. But Jennie commented, "As far as I could gather, life there was very much a second edition of Newport, and consisted in perpetual dressing, dinner, and dances, and that horror of horrors, the leaving of cards."

The Churchills and their party then traveled across Canada by train.[9]

> On an average, our train stopped every half-hour, with much whistling, ringing of bells, and exchange of greetings between the engine-driver and the inhabitants. Every log-cabin was the station, and every platform the club of these poor people whose only excitement was the daily arrival of the train. . . . Life on one of these prairies, although probably monotonous, must have the compensations which come with peace and the close study of nature. . . . At Banff, we had our car put into a siding, and passed two days there, which well repaid us. For the first time, we saw the Rockies and all their grandeur. We could not resist the "call of the wild," and drove about all day in uncomfortable buckboards and "cut-unders."[10]

During one of those drives, Jennie insisted on getting down and touching some "hoodoos" for luck. These were curious natural monuments, half earth, half stone, some seventy feet high, looking like the half-formed figure of a man seated on a pedestal. Indians treated them with great superstition and awe.

During the trip through Canada, they also saw great forest fires,

> and at times we would wend our way through burning trees on every side. It was a melancholy sight to see the miles of black stumps and leafless skeletons, their twisted and tortured branches standing out against the background of snow, while the bright-green ferns and variegated flowers made a carpet at our feet. . . . In some places we saw trees burning down close to the stations on the railway track, but no one attempted to put the fires out.

At Victoria she found an excellent Steinway piano in the hotel and played it frequently, to the evident delight of some old ladies who congregated to hear her.

> On one occasion, however, I scattered them like frightened wood-pigeons when, to the inquiry, what was the "sweetly-pretty" tune I was playing, I answered, "Gotter-dammerung!" with an emphasis on the third syllable. With

one look of pained surprise, they gathered up their skirts and fled.

They arrived at San Francisco on a windy and sunless day, amazed at the innumerable electric tramways, "which seem to come upon one from every direction." They visited Chinatown with a detective, finding the joss-houses, opium dens, and gambling places very stuffy and astonishingly small. "The opium smokers lie on bare boards, and in such uncomfortable attitudes that it is a mystery to me how they can find enjoyment in the pernicious practice."

Jennie was awed by the gardens of Monterey.

> I was never tired of walking about and admiring the splendid trees, shrubs, and plants of all kinds, while the flowers were in a profusion I have never seen equaled anywhere. . . . After several miles of forest, the ocean suddenly came into view, and a quantity of seals were seen disporting themselves on the rocks. while an exciting fight was going on between two. We watched them for a long while—sometimes they would tumble off into the water, but quickly scrambled up again, to have a few more rounds. I proposed to wait and see the end, but our driver informed us they might go on for a couple of hours. On our way back, we passed through the celebrated Cypress Grove, a very entrancing spot, full of mystery and charm. These ancient trees, so old that generations have lost count of them, twist their gnarled trunks away from the sea, their dark green heads embellished by long, pale strands of the feathery moss which eventually strangles them.

She smiled when the driver pointed out several buildings and seriously said that they were very ancient, dating from 1850.

The Churchills and their party went on to Japan. They were fascinated by the country, particularly the theaters in Yokohama, with their plays of fourteen or fifteen acts that lasted all day, and sometimes two.

Occasionally Randolph would go berserk, buying up whole shopsful of goods. Jennie would patiently and quietly make explanations and then cancel all the orders. She described an incident of another kind that occurred in a shop evidently not frequented by Europeans:

> As the little maids who waited on us hovered about me with the greatest curiosity, and before I could stop them, one

had put on my gloves, another had seized my hat, which I'd taken off . . . and a third was strutting about with my parasol.

Jennie also told about peasant women in some of the small villages.

The married ones were easily recognized by their shaved eyebrows and blackened teeth, in which hideous custom they indulge, in order to remain faithful to their husbands, but which conceivably might produce the reverse effect on the husbands themselves. Among them were a number of girls, their shiny hair stiff with camelia-oil, and adorned with combs, tiny chrysanthemums and coral beads, their painted faces breaking into a smile, if you looked at them.

They traveled quite extensively through Japan.

I never tired of the mountains, with their changing shadows, deep gorges, and rushing streams and cascades, with here and there a peep of the sea in the distance. The vegetation was a great source of interest and pleasure, it was all so new and so attractive: On our journey up, I counted 55 different kinds of agricultural products and shrubs.

Randolph suddenly worsened at Yokohama. Dr. Keith reported "a transient paralysis of the left arm." The doctor and Jennie wanted to take him home, but Randolph insisted on continuing the trip.

Jennie did not write her sons about their father, but Winston was now a young man of twenty with a mind of his own. "I persuaded Dr. Roose to tell exactly how Papa was. . . . He told me everything and showed me the medical reports. I have told no one. . . . I need not tell you how anxious I am."[11] The ugly reality was a shock for Winston. The psychological impact of the word "syphilis" might explain much of Winston's future way of life, his own relations with women, and his sympathy for his mother's troubled life.[12]

Winston wrote constantly after that, and Jennie found in his letters a renewed tenderness and concern:

Darling Mummy, I do hope that you are feeling well and that the fatigues of traveling as well as the anxiety you must feel about Papa—are not telling on you. I can't tell you how I long to see you again and how I look forward to your return.

He wanted to go there himself to help her handle his father, and he wanted her to confide everything in him.

> Do, my darling Mama, when you write let me know *exactly* what you think. . . . You know you told *me* to write to *you* on *every subject* freely.
>
> I fear that much worry will tell on you–and that the continual anxiety and added to the fatigues of traveling will deprive you of any interest and pleasure in the strange things you see. If I were you I would always try to look on the bright side of things. . . . Above all, don't get ill yourself. . . .

She tried hard to follow his advice and filled her letters with colorful description of all she saw. "Your letters are a treat," he wrote encouragingly.

> We made a flying visit to Canton, going up the Pearl River in a large steamer which had an English captain. As I entered the ship, I caught sight of stacks of rifles in the saloon, with printed instructions to the passengers to use them, if necessary. This did not make me feel at all safe, these river-steamers having been known to be attacked by pirates. At Hong Kong, we were advised not to go to Canton, since owing to the war and their defeat, the Chinese were in rather a turbulent state. We thought, however, as we meant to spend only the day there, we should be safe enough. The steamer was obliged to anchor at the mouth of the river, as there were torpedoes laid across it, and the Chinese pilots were rather vague as to their locality. It was a lovely, moonlight night, and I remember the ghostly effect of a searchlight from a fort nearby, which was constantly being turned on us, lighting up strange crafts and great, lumbering Chinese junks with square sails, which hovered near.
>
> . . . The streets were full of open shops, banners, Chinese lanterns and gaudy signs. A continuous stream of people hurrying along made it a most animated scene. They scowled and glared at us as we passed, calling us "Frankwei" ("foreign devils"); and they spat at one of our party and hit another, who luckily did not retaliate. Otherwise, we might have been made into mincemeat. The shops were very attractive; and Randolph bought me one of the green jade bangles, which have since become fashionable. It is supposed to keep the devil away.

A visit to the execution ground was not so attractive. Eight men had been decapitated a few days before, and the blood was still on the ground. We were asked if we would like to see the heads, which had been placed in jars, an offer we declined with thanks.

They next went to Singapore, where the heat "was like a vapor bath and so enervating that one felt absolutely incapable of doing anything."

The Sultan of Johare gave them a sumptuous luncheon, and showed them through his palace. In one room, the tables and chairs were made of cut glass, upholstered in bright blue velvet with glass buttons.

After luncheon, the Sultan, who's a charming and courteous old man, sent for his Sultana to come and see us. She was a very pretty Circassian of about 25, a present from the Sultan of Turkey. Enormously fat, we were told that she was fed every two hours, the Sultan admiring large proportions. Her costume was most peculiar, to say the least–a Malay sarong of silk; a blouse with huge diamond buttons; round her neck a rivière of diamonds and one of sapphires; and on her short black curls, cocked over one ear, a velvet glengarry cap with an eagle's feather and a diamond aigret. The Sultan, thinking, I suppose, that she had been seen enough, suddenly pointed with a stern gesture to the door. Casting a frightened glance at him, she fled as fast as her fat little feet could take her.[13]

Jennie and Dr. Keith again tried to persuade Randolph to end the trip and return home. The heat had intensified and they were afraid he would not last much longer. But he had been the man in the British Cabinet most responsible for annexing Burma to the British Crown and "he would have gone alone," said Jennie. The sea was rough and very hot, the ship full of beetles, ants, and rats.

"I have met very few people one could talk to since we left England," Jennie wrote Clara.

I can't tell you how I pine for a little society. It is so hard to get away from one's thoughts when one is always alone. And yet the worst of it is I dread the chance even of seeing people for his sake. He is quite unfit for society . . . one never knows what he may do. At Government House Singapore he was very bad for two days and it was dreadful being with strangers. Since then he has become much quieter and some-times it is quite pathetic but Keith thinks it is a bad sign. . . . [14]

It was so bad a sign that they added to their luggage a lead-lined coffin.[15]

It was at Rangoon that one of the major lights went out of Jennie's life. She received a telegram from Count Charles Kinsky. He had given up the long wait for her and was now engaged to be married.[16] Jennie wrote of it to Clara: "I *hate* it! I shall return without a friend in the world and too old to make any more now." She would not then have appreciated an epigram by her friend Oscar Wilde, who said, "Women spoil every romance by try-ing to make it last forever."

Randolph had deteriorated. His disease had reached the final stage in which walking becomes stumbling and the feet move sideways, hitting the ground with a stamp. Sores break out all over the body and refuse to heal. The victim loses control of his bladder; the joints in his legs and feet swell into painful masses of deformed bone. The brain is mostly imbecilic. With Ran-dolph, the syphilitic germs seemed highly unselective—they attacked every-where. "You cannot imagine anything *more* distracting and desperate, than to watch it and see him as he is and think of him as he was," Jennie wrote.

Winston sent her a gay letter about his first public-speaking experience at the Empire Theater. A crowd of several hundred people had started tear-ing down the barricades put up to separate the bars of the Empire from the nearby promenade where women liked to walk. Winston then jumped on top of the broken barricade and shouted to the crowd, "You have seen us tear down these barricades tonight; see that you pull down those who are responsible for them at the coming election."[17] The Countess of Abercon-way was there and quoted Winston as saying, "Ladies of the Empire! I stand for Liberty!"

The Westminster Gazette printed Winston's letter on the subject. "It was I who led the rioters—and made a speech to the crowd," Winston wrote, en-closing a newspaper clipping to prove it.

Winston celebrated his twentieth birthday at Hindlip Hall in Worcester as Lord Hindlip's guest at the local Hunt Ball. In the post office the follow-ing morning, he was handed a letter with the news that his father was dying.

"The collapse of an airplane in mid-air is always more terrible than the overturning of a hackney cab in the street," said Shane Leslie. "Randolph fell from meteoric heights."

Yet Churchill's mind and body had been tearing apart for too long to al-low for any surprise. His family and friends had seen the final collapse coming for many years—only the vast public were unaware of what was happening to him. To them his was a magic name. The *Dictionary of National Biography* would say of Lord Randolph Churchill:

His personality had fascinated the masses, who admired his courage, his ready wit, and the brilliant audacity with which he dealt his blows at the loftiest crests, whether those of friends or adversaries. Moreover, it was perceived by this time that there was a fund of intellectual power and a genuine depth of conviction behind his erratic insolence and reckless rhetoric.

The small, sad group arrived back in London just in time for Christmas. Winston saw that his father was "as weak and helpless in mind and body as a little child." For a month Randolph lingered. Clara Frewen wrote Leonie of the misery of the final days, of how Randolph "groaned and screamed with pain and instead of the dose of morphia they gave him acting in five minutes it took 20 before he got relief and went into a sleep which lasted 4 hours. Jennie never left him . . . she hasn't eaten or slept since she arrived. . . ."

The hope had died long before. The hope of living. The hope of a good marriage. The hope of being Prime Minister and of shaking the world. His had been an agony protracted, a genius long misguided, a promise unfulfilled.

In *Savrola*, Winston Churchill has his leading male character say to his wife just before dying,

> And you—will you forget? . . . do not allow yourself to mourn. I do not care to be remembered for what I was. If I have done anything that may make the world more happy and more cheerful and more comfortable, let them recall the action. If I have spoken a thought which, rising above the vicissitudes of our existence, may make life brighter or death less gloomy, then let them say: "He did this, or he did that." Forget the man; remember, perhaps, his work.

Sir Richard Temple remembered an elderly Tory saying of Randolph, "He made the people believe in us."[18] The whole of his spectacular political life had lasted less than six years, the brilliance of an exploding rocket leaving nothing. Dante Gabriel Rossetti, who had died a dozen years before, had summed up one such as Randolph Churchill in the couplet:

> My name is Might-have-been;
> I am also called No-more, Too-late, Farewell.

The press gave prominent coverage to Randolph's daily health bulletins. There were many callers. On January 23, 1895, he sank into a coma.

In the early hours of the next morning, Winston was summoned from a nearby house where he was sleeping. "I ran in the darkness across Grosvenor Square, then lapped in snow." At 6:15 the next morning, January 24, Randolph died in his sleep at the age of forty-five. On that very day, seventy years later, Winston Churchill would die.

Moreton Frewen wrote Leonie:

> So poor R. has flickered out; dear sweet little Jane my mind runs on her very much. I wish I could hear that she is left comfortably off, and that life might look smilingly on her after many days. . . . Love and luck sweet Kali. . . . Oh! To have got rid of that hair shirt–poor fellow–for ever. . . . There was much nice about him, but he was mad always. . . .

When Lord Salisbury sent a letter of condolence to the Duchess of Marlborough, she answered bitterly. Within a period of eighteen months, she had lost both her sons:

> Dear Lord Salisbury: I thank you for your sympathy with this terrible sorrow. But oh, it is too late, too late. There was a day, years ago, when in my dire distress, I went to you and asked you, as a father, to help me–for my Darling had no father. He had but *me*, and I could do nothing, though I would have given my life for him. I went to you–I would have fallen at your feet if you could have helped me, and sympathized with me. He knew not what I did, but I was desperate, and I knew he had been misled and made a fatal mistake; and yet I knew all his real cleverness and real goodness and what he had been and could be to his Party. . . . Your heart was hardened against him. I suppose he had tried you, and worry and anxiety beset you for it was Fate.
>
> But from that Hour, the Iron entered into his soul. . . . He never gave a sign, even to me, of disappointment, but for Days and Days, and Months, and Years, even it told on him and he sat in Connaught Place, brooding and eating his Heart out and the Tory Press reviled him, and the Tory Party, whom he had saved, abused and misrepresented him, and he was never the same. The illness which has killed him is due, they tell me, to overwork and acute mental strain, and now he is gone and I am left alone to mourn him and the Grace. . . .

It's all over now. My Darling has come Home to die, and oh, it seems such bitter mockery that *now* it is too late, he seems to be understood and appreciated.

They did not bury Randolph in the Marlborough family vaults in Blenheim but in the small cemetery behind a tiny church in nearby Bladon. There, too, his wife and sons would be buried.

Shane Leslie described his uncle's funeral:

I was due to go to school for the first time, but I was kept for the funeral in Westminster Abbey. It was immensely solemn; and the great roof stretched over us in icy space. It was like a cathedral of the arctic. I heard the lugubrious choir and the voice of Dean Farrar, and then the Dead March from "Saul" crept into our shivering souls. When it was over, I caught sight of Parliamentary heroes only known through their caricatures in *Punch*. Down the aisle passed Arthur Balfour, and a grizzly "Black Michael" Hicks-Beach. Both had been Irish Secretaries; and there was a certain queer look which distinguished English statesmen who had ever held that office. Sir William Harcourt, looking like Jumbo, and Lord Rosebery followed. There was a flag half-mast at St. Margaret's; and in Parliament Square, we were told to rise and bow from the carriage to a gray-bearded gentleman of prophetic appearance who returned our bows solemnly. It was Lord Salisbury, who no doubt mistook us for Randolph's brood. It was well known that he was one of those who could not tell a heron from a handsaw. The haggard Sir Henry Irving also passed down the aisle. In youth, Randolph was said to have asked Irving in Dublin how the play of "Hamlet" finished! Randolph was finishing like Hamlet, himself. There were four captains to bear him to his grave. "For he was likely, had he lived, to have proved most royal." The funeral procession passed through Paddington, followed by Walden, the faithful valet, and thence under the shadow of Blenheim, into the endless Nirvana which swallows the short and agitated lives of statesmen, if they could only realize it.

It was the first death I had ever heard announced. I was swung off my hinges. I did not believe grown-ups could die. This was a fate I believed reserved for the heathen, for pirates, and enemies of the Queen. . . . It was my first funeral; and as godson to the deceased, I thought myself bound to observe the strictest mourning. I became susceptible to the grief of my elders. In hushed whispers, they mentioned Randolph's last miseries and madnesses; and I recorded the event in my first diary, January 24, 1895: "Uncle Randolph became a saint in Heaven.[21]

As Jennie lay in her widow's bed, her face pale, her eyes burning, the inevitable death of her mad husband perhaps seemed in part a vast relief.[22]

Only two weeks before, however, on January 7, Count Charles Andreas Kinsky had married Countess Elisabeth Wolff Metternich zur Gracht, a lovely woman twenty years younger than Jennie. After Kinsky's marriage, Jennie had written Leonie:

> The bitterness, if there was any, has absolutely left me. He and I have parted the best of friends and in a truly *fin de siècle* manner. So darling don't worry about me on that score. . . . Pity or mere sympathy even from *you* is wasted on me. No one can do me *any* good. He has not behaved particularly well and I can't find much to admire in him but I care for him as some people like opium or drink although they would like not to. . . .

Thus did the hope seem dead for her, too. She had given of herself to her world without reservation. She had offered her best to a husband who could not accept it, so she had scattered among others her wit, her charm, her drive, her imagination, her love. But Charles Kinsky had been the romantic drama of her life; the many other men had merely filled the intermissions. He would not forget the love she had given him, and she would not forgive his relinquishing it. It was a concentrated, fiery love, a love accumulated from many neglected sources. If not for Kinsky she might have had more for her sons.

Now she was forty, and what was there left? Ardent admirers all married, sons at school, house empty.

"Why do you always wear black?" asks Medvedenko in Chekhov's *The Sea Gull.*

"I am in mourning for my life."

The clouds surrounding her were dark. She could not know that the world was just beginning to open for her.

Eighteen

OR JENNIE, THE YEAR 1895 began bitter and bleak. after a lingering illness, her husband had died of syphilis, raving mad. Only weeks before, her lover, unwilling to wait any longer, had married.[1] Her sons Winston and Jack both had problems that required her full attention.

Physically and emotionally, she felt drained.

Was it any wonder? She had taken a maniacal husband on a year-long world tour to keep him out of trouble at home, and his final illness had been prolonged and excruciatingly painful. "You would have thought it was some wild animal," Jennie's older sister Clara wrote her husband, describing Lord Randolph Churchill's terrible groans.[2]

The deathbed scene took place at the London home of Randolph's mother, the Dowager Duchess of Marlborough. She and her daughters never left Jennie alone with Randolph for a moment, ". . . all of them criticizing every word she says, everything she does . . . it is positive torture. . . . I sometimes think that if it isn't soon over she will soon go mad herself."

When Jennie's younger sister Leonie reported to her that the doctors did not think Randolph would live through the day, Jennie herself had reached the point of near hysteria and "burst out *laughing*."

". . . Poor, poor little Jane," Clara wrote to her husband, "when I think of the future, I shudder for her . . ."[3]

❧❧

"Man is justified by the greatness of his acts," it is written in the Koran, "but woman, through the magnitude of her illusions." What were Jennie's illusions?

She had none about her husband's death. It was a relief and a blessing. She had done all her mourning and paid her penance many years before.

Nor did she have illusions about her financial security. Lord Randolph Henry Spencer Churchill left an estate whose gross value was £75,971 ($379,855), but much of it was needed to pay off his debts. Of the remaining portion, most of it was in trust funds for their two sons. Lord Randolph's last will and testament allowed Jennie a slim legacy of £500 ($2,500) plus all their "horses, carriages, plate, linen, china, glass, books, pictures, prints, furniture and other household effects."[4]

To make matters worse, as Clara explained to her husband, the fact that Randolph had died before his mother meant that the Duchess was free to leave the family money to whomever she pleased, "and she isn't likely to befriend Jennie, whom she doesn't like, or the boys, whom she never liked either."[5]

But nothing had shattered Jennie's illusions and darkened her future more than the sudden marriage of the man she had loved most, Count Charles Rudolf Andreas Kinsky. Jennie had once written that Kinsky was "like opium" for her. A young Austrian diplomat of noble lineage, he was extraordinarily handsome, with the kind of good looks that won a woman without his making any effort. A brilliant young man, he wrote books about international diplomacy; musically talented, he played the piano excellently. He was charming, with old-world manners but a modern wit. Above all, he was a spectacular horseman and a national hero in Great Britain, the first foreigner to have won the Grand National on his own horse. And he was in love with Jennie, desperately so.

Theirs was a fiery, intense love, lasting as long as they lived. Kinsky had begged Jennie to leave her husband and marry him, but she felt she could not abandon Randolph when he needed her most. Long afterward, Jennie's nephew noted what a marvelous stepfather Kinsky would have been for Winston and how close and warm the relationship between young Winston and his mother's lover had been.[6] Winston so admired Kinsky that only two weeks after his own father's death he wrote his brother Jack at Harrow:

> I should very much like that picture of Count Kinsky on Zoedone [his Grand National winner]–very much. . . . If you send it down here, I will pay you a sovereign for it. . . .[7]

Kinsky might have waited for Jennie, but he was subject to enormous pressure from his father, Prince Kinsky. The Prince was one of Austria's great landowners with a family heritage that traced back through hundreds of years of aristocracy. He objected strenuously to Jennie because she was not of noble lineage, because she was not Catholic, but, most of all, because she was then forty years old and therefore unlikely to produce an heir. The Prince's candidate for his son was the young Countess Elizabeth Wolff-Metternich, who had all of the required qualifications. The Prince also had powerful leverage: he was the source of his son's lavish allowance, which was always quickly spent. And so, out of combined despair and pressure, Kinsky agreed to marry the Countess Elizabeth.

"I hate it!" Jennie wrote her sister Clara upon hearing of the announcement. As for Count Kinsky, although his marriage put a great gulf between himself and Jennie, it never dampened his love for her. At Kinsky's death many years later, the one picture found hanging over his desk was a portrait of Jennie.[8]

So here was Jennie, with the man who had loved her most now married to someone else, little money and not even a home of her own. She had once said in a note to Clara, "Your life is not *couleur de rose*. Whose is?"

And yet, such was the inner resource and resilience of this woman that her life soon took on an excitement and vitality such as she had never dreamed of. As her friend Lady Curzon said in a letter to her, "You are the only person who lives on the crest of a wave."[9]

That she lived on the crest of a wave was certainly true, and to do so she had to rely upon two of her most fundamental traits: her courage and her drive. The result was a vital force that was seldom smothered. It could be blunted or stalled, but never obliterated.

She seemed to have, deep within her, a feeling of exhilaration for all the unknown things to come, a sense of adventure. Jennie had a touch of Cleopatra about her. Her determination was strengthened whenever she faced crises in her life—and they often came in a parade. These were qualities she passed on to her son Winston. "Never give in," Winston later told the boys at Harrow, "never, never, never, never, in nothing great or small, large or petty—never give in except to the convictions of honor and good sense."[10] That could have been Jennie speaking.

Certainly it would take more than a lack of funds to stop her. She still had the annual $10,000 from the rental of her family's home on Madison Square in New York City.[11] For a woman in upper-class British society with two young sons, however, that was very little income. But she had somehow managed before, and she would manage again.

She was a woman of superb taste who appreciated the best and recognized it when she saw it—whether it was in clothes or books or furniture or men. She was a woman of such high style that one felt that she was meant to have money. And yet she never really did. The amazing thing was that essentially it did not matter.

What else could Jennie's future lack besides money? Friends? Never. Tolstoi had written in his diary in 1853: "The means to gain happiness is to throw out from oneself like a spider in all directions an adhesive web of love, and to catch in it all that comes." An adhesive web of love was Jennie's great gift. It was instinctive in everything she did, and it drew women as well as men to her. This was part of the reason for her effectiveness in political campaigns, in fund-raising, in organizing. She had more than charisma; there was a kind of radiation from within her so full of warmth and sincerity that it reached almost everyone she met. Two generations after her death, a woman whose life she had touched only tangentially would say with a glisten in her eyes, "I *loved* her."[12]

Shortly after her death a British magazine tried to detail all of Jennie's qualities:

> Beauty and brains, wealth and social position are admirable things, but they would not of themselves have won for Lady Randolph Churchill her preeminence among the women of her time. . . . To be greater than one's peers is not possible without personality of the outstanding type. . . . It may be magnetism, it may be charm, it may be strength of will, it may be vitality, it may be arrogance of temper, it may be supreme sweetness of disposition, it may be the ability to smile or to frown at the right time or in the right place. Tact may have something to do with it, foresight may be a help, belief in oneself counts for something, a certain ruthlessness comes in useful, perhaps. . . . [13]

In 1895 a new era was beginning which called for all these qualities. Queen Victoria was in her last years, and much of the old magnificence that had been associated with her reign was now in decline. Aristocrats no longer commanded sweeping social power. Dynamic wealth was creating its own aristocracy, capturing Park Lane. Many British peerages had come up for sale and the new aristocracy was described by some as "a religion of gold.[14] Even back in the days of King James, in the early seventeenth century, £10,000 could buy a barony.[15] Benjamin Disraeli described how the younger Pitt, in the eighteenth century, "created a plebeian aristocracy and blended it with the patrician oligarchy. He made peers of second-rate squires and fat graziers. He caught them in the alleys of Lombard Street, and clutched them from the counting-houses of Cornhill."[16]

"There is no country where so much absolute homage is paid to wealth," wrote Ralph Waldo Emerson about England.[17]

"It is not fair to say that they were wholly wrapped up in materialism, and the pursuit of wealth," countered Herbert Asquith. "But it took a great deal to make them realize that they might be paying too high a price for capturing the markets of the world in a system of production which crippled and stunted and decimated the women and children of the country."[18]

Great Britain owned twelve million square miles around the world and was by far the strongest power.[19] Yet a scullery maid in London still started at only sixty dollars a year,[20] and the law allowed women factory workers to add three nights to their six-day week. What is more, with the average working woman expected to experience ten pregnancies, child labor was considered necessary to help support large families. For children under five, the death rate in industrial Birmingham was 95.6 per thousand.[21] Even years later, over twelve million people in the country were living on the verge of constant hunger and "in the grip of perpetual poverty."[22] Human beings were still cheap in England.

It was the Golden Age, though, for the rapidly-growing moneyed middle class, and it was no longer easy to answer the question: Who rules Britain? It was certainly not the 150 great families. Tory gentility could no longer hand down an undiminished tradition, and along with their power went much of the British pomp and plush. Gone, too, were the carriage flunkeys whose overcoats swept to their feet, and the boyish grooms with cockaded hats and white breeches. And going rapidly were more and more of the magnificent mansions.

The Victorian Age had made its mark. It had created or nurtured many British institutions—public schools, the professional civil service, military regiments, political parties, universities—and it had given the British a sense of stability and supremacy. British constitutional government was a model for the world. But the world was changing.

The new era also brought a new Prime Minister. At the age of eighty-five, the distinguished William Gladstone had resigned after sixty-one historic years in politics and government. His successor could scarcely have been more of a contrast. Lord Archibald Philip Primrose Rosebery was the Prince Charming of politics. Everything came easily to him, perhaps too easily. "I think Lord Rosebery would have had a better nervous system and been a happier man if he had not been so rich," wrote his friend Margot Asquith. "Riches are overestimated in the Old Testament: the good and successful man received too many animals, wives, apes, she-goats and peacocks."[23]

It was a pertinent point. Rosebery reportedly had told a friend at Eton that he had three great ambitions: to marry an heiress, to win the Derby, and to become Prime Minister. He married not only an heiress, but a Rothschild; his horse won the Derby not once but three times; and the Prime Minister-ship was achieved without his having to fight for it—the Queen personally chose him for the post. "Only Heaven left," wired his American friend, the railroad magnate Chauncey Depew.[24]

But the nineties were a pleasure-loving time, and Rosebery was a pleasure-loving man. The Prime Minister's job required too much work to suit his taste—he likened it to "riding a horse without reins."

"There are two supreme pleasures in life," Rosebery said, "the one ideal, the other real. The ideal is when a man receives the seals of office from his Sovereign. The real pleasure comes when he hands them back.[25] Jennie understood all this about Rosebery because they had known each other well for many years. They shared a love of politics, horses, literature, and new ideas.

"Ideas were in the air," wrote Richard Le Gallienne in his study of this exciting decade. "People . . . were convinced that they were passing not only from one social system to another, from one morality to another, and from one religion to a dozen or none. . . . Our new-found freedom seemed to find just the expression it needed in the abandoned nonsense-chorus of 'Ta-ra-ra-boom-de-ay. . . . ' "[26]

The Elegant Eighties had become the Naughty Nineties. It was a time of growing contempt for old ideas, of willingness to challenge tradition and taboos, of a rather upstart arrogance. People were more fun-seeking, more emotional, more gregarious. It was a trying time for power in every area of society, from business and politics to social relations. It was a time when people thought anything could happen, that convention was a cage that you broke out of in order to live your own life in your own way.

"Not to be new in these days is to be nothing," wrote H. D. Traill in an essay on "The New Fiction." Magazines were filled with articles on everything new: The New Realism, The New Voluptuousness, The New Spirit, The New Woman.[27]

Jennie had been the new woman long before it became fashionable. She had little interest in such fads as microbe farming, which involved the bizarre practice of displaying such exotic germs as "a lovely purple cholera" in test tubes at afternoon teas.[28] But she had been one of the first to free herself from the steel-armored corset, and her house had been the first in London to use electric lighting.[29]

But, even more significantly, Jennie believed in the kind of new woman recommended by George Bernard Shaw:

> . . . unless you do something in the world, you can have
> no real business to transact with men; and unless you love

and are loved, you can have no intimate relations with them. And you must transact business, wire-pull politics, discuss religion, give and receive hate, love and friendship with all sorts of people before you can acquire the sense of humanity. . . . [30]

As a "new woman," Jennie would have been "as unsuitable as possible for a bishop's wife or the president of the YWCA," her nephew noted. "She saw no need for Victorian humility or modesty."[31]

Or hypocrisy, either. English society had been well aware of the romance between Jennie and the Prince of Wales. Its peak had passed, but some of the emotion was still alive, ready to be stirred. Of course, for the Prince there had always been others, many others. He was deservedly well publicized as "a professional lovemaker."[32] The Prince usually disassociated himself from his mistresses when his affairs with them ended, but with Jennie it was different. Unlike the women who told him only what he wanted to hear, Jennie always spoke her own mind, whatever the subject. The Prince was not a man of profound intellect, but he respected those who had it, particularly women. They intrigued and stimulated him.

In 1895, Albert Edward, the Prince of Wales, was fifty-four years old and portly, the picture of opulence. He was a heavy-lidded man, with protruding eyes, a sensual mouth, and an elegant goatee, and he was usually seen smoking an enormous cigar. Rudyard Kipling called him "a corpulent voluptuary." But his overfed body was always superbly attired, and he was still a vigorous man with an air of geniality and a certain charm and flair.

He liked the lavish show, the morning hunt, the good joke, the pretty ankle, and the uses of power. Jennie had a significant and lasting influence on him because he respected her judgment. He also knew he could rely on her. If he wanted a small private party arranged, he often asked her to oversee the compiling of the guest list and to decide on the menu. Jennie knew his particular friends as well as his favorite foods. She knew what kind of music he liked. She knew the level of his impatience and boredom, the danger point of his anger, and what to do about them. In return, he was lavish in his gifts and in his open affection for her.

Certainly nobody could have been more solicitous than the Prince during her husband's last days and after his death. He sent her a steady flow of notes: "Should you wish to see me, I could call at five tomorrow." And he dropped in often to spend a consoling hour with her.

Through the previous years the tone of their correspondence had been circumspect. He was, after all, the future King of England, and in the early days she had been the wife of a man who was in a position to become his Prime Minister. The Prince had to be particularly careful after his involvement in a widely publicized adultery suit, a matter over which he and Jennie's husband had almost fought a duel and which had forced the social exile of the Randolph Churchills to Ireland. But after Randolph's death, the Prince's letters began to address Jennie as "*Ma chère Amie*," and they were signed "*Tout à vous*, Albert Edward," or simply "A.E."

Alexandra, the Princess of Wales, was hard-of-hearing, but she was not blind. She knew all about her husband's many extramarital affairs. She probably even knew of his favorite London restaurants that thoughtfully equipped a private dining room with a settee as well as a panel button for a disappearing bed. Kettner's, in the Soho district, proudly named a room on the second floor "The Edward Room." Frances, Countess of Warwick, a close friend of Jennie's and the Prince's mistress for an extended period, wrote of the Princess: "Beneath her placid exterior there was shrewd judgment that expressed itself now and again in no uncertain terms."[33]

Whether out of shrewdness or resignation or for some other reason, the Princess maintained cordial relations with some of her husband's women. With Jennie especially Alexandra had a remarkably close friendship. After parties the Princess frequently invited Jennie to her room for a *tte-à-tte*, and Jennie was often a guest at the Princess's private soirées. The two women enjoyed and trusted each other. "She was always such a tried dear friend of mine," Alexandra would write of Jennie.[34] They shared a fine sense of humor, and both had generous and impulsive instincts, as well as a dislike of pretence and arrogance. Princess Alexandra, after all, had been brought up in the simplicity of the Danish Court where she had even been taught to darn her own stockings.

Alexandra and Jennie were both affectionate mothers, so they must have talked with each other about their children. There was a similarity in their sons; with the two older boys tempestuous, and the younger ones quiet and placid.[35]

Winston was then twenty years old but still a "mama's boy." For many years to come, nearly until his marriage, his letters to his mother would be gushingly affectionate, almost romantic outpourings. The boy's closeness to his mother is understandable, as his father had been a remote figure to him. "If ever I began to show the slightest idea of comradeship, he was immediately offended," Winston wrote in *My Early Life*, "and when once I suggested that I might help his private secretary to write some of his letters, he froze me into stone."[36]

Winston had known his father best as one of the important men of his time. But he was also a man who had died in political disfavor. What brave young man would not have dreamed of vindicating his father's memory, and therefore himself as well? What ambitious young man would not have hoped to emulate and perhaps even surpass the reputation his father had had at the height of his career?

Winston's feeling for his father revealed admiration, envy, and strong filial respect. He memorized some of his father's speeches, imitated his gesture of resting his hand on his hip while giving a speech, and ultimately wrote a two-volume biography of him.

Winston was now at Sandhurst military college, and more than anything else, he wanted to be able to join a cavalry regiment after his graduation.

"Horses were the greatest of my pleasures at Sandhurst," he later wrote. "No hour of life is lost that is spent in the saddle. Young men have often been ruined through owning horses, or through backing horses, but never through riding them; unless, of course, they break their necks which, taken at a gallop, is a very good death to die."[37]

One of his mother's ardent admirers, Colonel John Palmer Brabazon, commanded the Fourth Hussars, which was billeted at Aldershot near Sandhurst. Winston had dined with him several times at the regimental mess, where he was overwhelmed by the "glitter, affluence, ceremony and veiled discipline."[38]

"After some months, my mother told me that Colonel Brabazon was anxious that I should go into his regiment but that my father had said 'No.' . . ."[39] Lord Randolph decided long before that Winston should enter an infantry regiment. After his father's death, however, Winston lost little time asking his mother to contact Brabazon.

Brabazon was everything a man or a woman might admire. Jennie liked him not only because he was a magnificent figure of a man—six feet tall, with a strong jaw, symmetrical features, an elaborate mustache, and bright gray eyes—but also because he was genial, thoroughly good-natured, and adept at repartee. The Prince of Wales liked him because he was knowledgeable at the race course, good on the hunting field, and brave on the battlefield. Moreover, the Prince was a faultless dandy about his clothes, and *Vanity Fair* had called Brabazon, "The Beau Brummel of the day . . . equally exquisite in dress and manner."[40]

Women called him "Beautiful *Bwab*" because of his good looks and his inability to pronounce *r*'s. One of the best-known stories about "Bwab" concerned the time he was drawing heavy fire during a battle and refused to take cover, saying that he believed that certain people had cast aspersions "on my personal couwage and so I wish to show you all that my personal couwage is as good as ever it was."[41]

The love affair between Jennie and Brabazon had been brief, but they maintained a solid and reliable friendship, and Brabazon was devoted to her. Within a week after her husband's death Jennie sent him a telegram and Brabazon replied:

> Now this is what I want you to do *at once*. I have seen Sir Reginald Gipps, & have written to Fitzgeorge the Duke's private secretary—You must write to the Duke [of Cambridge] & at once. His address is
>
> Hotel Prince de Galles
> Cannes.
>
> . . . What I should say was that the boy had always been anxious to go into the Cavalry, but for certain reasons Randolph put his name down for Infantry. That latterly he completely came round to Winston & your wishes & was anxious he should join my regiment. . . . You can say there is *now* a vacancy in the 4th Hussars, that you are very anxious he should not be idling about London & that I personally knew the boy, liked him, & was very anxious to have him. I should add—which is the case—that Winston passed very much higher than any of the candidates for Cavalry & hope that the Duke will allow him to be appointed to the 4th Hussars, and thus fulfill one of Randolph's last wishes.
>
> The fact is, there are more men passed for Cavalry than there are vacancies, and that's the hitch, but I feel certain that if you write to the Duke, he will make a personal matter of it and that all will be arranged. . . . [42]

Jennie did as Brabazon suggested, and several days later there was a letter from the Duke of Cambridge:

> I will write home at once to the Military Secretary, and if it can be arranged, it shall be carried out. . . .
>
> I remain, dear Lady Randolph,
> Yours very truly,
> George.[43]

In less than two weeks, Winston was ordered to report to the Fourth Hussars at Aldershot, and on February 20th he received his commission. Several years after, he wrote, "Solitary trees, if they grow at all, grow strong; and a boy deprived of a father's care often develops, if he escapes the perils of youth, an independence and vigor of thought which may restore in after life the heavy loss of early days."[44]

But Winston was not a solitary tree. Just as he had relied on his mother to know a Brabazon or a Duke of Cambridge at this turning point in his life, so would he turn to her again and again, confident that she would know whom to call upon and which move to make. As Winston himself acknowledged, her range and her resources seemed limitless:

> My mother was always on hand to help and advise. . . . She soon became my ardent ally, furthering my plans and guarding my interests with all her influence and boundless energy. . . . We worked together on even terms, more like brother and sister than mother and son. At least so it seemed to me. And so it continued to the end.[45]

As Winston noted, she was more than his mother and ally. For a long time, she was his only confidante, the only one to whom he could pour out his loneliness, the only one he loved, the only one who really believed in him. And when sternness was necessary, she also had to be his taskmaster.

In Victorian England the conventions of mourning were strictly observed. The mourning period was supposed to last two years, during the first of which, the dress was to be completely covered with black woven crepe. During the second year, the crepe could be used just for trimming. Only after two years could the widow accept social invitations.[46] Queen Victoria set an extreme example by still wearing black in mourning for her Prince Consort, even though he had died nearly thirty-five years before. But widow's weeds were not for Jennie—not for long, at any rate. In February 1895 she would go to Paris, where it was perfectly permissible for a beautiful young widow wearing long black bloomers to bicycle in the Bois de Boulogne.

The weather in London that month was so cold that the Thames froze solid enough for an ox roast to be held on it. It had been a month of howling gales, heavy blizzards, and violent thunderstorms.[47] But Jennie was counting on the weather to be better in Paris.

PARIS WAS ALMOST AS FAMILIAR AS HOME TO JENNIE. Her birthplace was American, her manners British, but part of her was French. It was more than the family coat-of-arms that her French Huguenot ancestors had registered in Paris in 1699; it was her own memories of excitement in this city that had been so large a part of her life.

Here she had grown up in the fairyland court of Louis Napoleon and Empress Eugénie. The tall graceful Empress, whose grandfather had been American, had often been more of a mother to her than Jennie's own mother. Only sixteen then, Jennie had already bloomed and was being ogled and chased by men. Then in 1870 came the Franco-Prussian War, and Jennie and her mother and sisters barely caught the last train out of Paris before the enemy surrounded the city.[1]

Paris was also where she and Lord Randolph had played the final scene of their courtship. Here, too, they were married in a hurried, brief ceremony at the British Embassy. And several times during their long, unhappy marriage Jennie had come here alone. Paris was always the place where she could find the fullest freedom.

Much of this surely must have been in her mind as she rode in a carriage down the Champs Elysées. The scene along the Champs had long had both a reminiscent and an invigorating effect on her.

"If you look from the Arc de Triomphe to the Tuileries, you see a broken mass of glittering carriage tops and lace parasols, and what looks like the flashing of thousands of mirrors as the setting sun strikes on the glass of the lamps and windows and on the lacquered harness and polished mountings."[2]

The Champs was a boulevard of vivid vignettes: the young men on the upper deck of the horse-drawn omnibuses stooping to have a better look at the young women in the open carriages below; a young Marquis on a dog-cart proudly flaunting his coquettish passenger; a fashionably dressed, middle-aged woman, driving a Victoria, flourishing her whip while her pug-dog sat placidly alongside her on a cushion; and not too far away, a heavy and red-faced woman driving a wagon piled high with bright carrots—she, too, with a dog, this one big and threatening and chained beside her; and on the spacious tree-lined sidewalks fashionable women showing off their tightly corseted figures, their long dresses almost sweeping the ground as they sauntered among Indian maharajahs, New York millionaires, Egyptian pashas, Haitian nabobs, and English tourists dressed in flannel shirts, hunting caps, and knickerbockers "exactly as though they were penetrating the mountains of Afghanistan or the deserts of Syria." The Champs Elysées was still the best show in town.

As she rode by, Jennie knew that this still wasn't Paris at its peak. A few more weeks would make the difference for the city. For Paris, which looked like a vast ice-skating rink in winter, February was still the season of artificial flowers. Almost timed with Jennie's arrival, was the famous annual lace sale at *Bon Marché*, and the great store was accented with exquisite but artificial Parma violets. Within a few weeks, *Printemps* would give away thousands of bouquets of real violets to shoppers, and the old chestnut tree in the Tuileries would fulfill its tradition of being the first to put forth a spring bloom. For both Paris and herself, Jennie was looking forward to the first sign of a fresh spring.

"Americans go to London for social triumph, or to float railroad shares; to Rome, for art's sake; and to Berlin to study music and to economize; but they go to Paris to enjoy themselves."[3] Richard Harding Davis, the man who made that comment, was a handsome, adventurous war correspondent. He was then thirty-one years old, living in Paris, and writing a book about the city. Davis later wrote of Jennie and her son: "I do not remember Winston ever seeming young enough to be his mother's son, just as I do not remember Lady Randolph ever seeming old enough to be his mother."

Davis and Jennie were part of a large American colony in Paris. Americans had a firm social tradition in the city. An American had been one of the founders of the Jockey Club, which was, after the *Cercle de L' Union,* the most exclusive club in Paris; two of Empress Eugénie's ladies-in-waiting had been American and some of the most exclusive salons in Paris had been and still were run by Americans.[4]

Shortly after Jennie's arrival, a story appeared in the Paris edition of the *New York Herald* about a dinner given by Sir Clare Ford in honor of the Duchess of Manchester. The *Herald* quoted a conversation between a German Baron and the Duchess:

> "At last I am able to leave those Americans," the Baron asserted, "really, they haunt one, they are ubiquitous, it is impossible to get away from them. You cannot imagine what a relief it is to speak to you, there is such a contrast between the English and the American manner."
>
> The Duchess of Manchester smiled and answered, "You may be right, Baron, but, being an American, I naturally cannot see it."[5]

The Duchess was the former Consuelo Iznaga of New York, one of Jennie's closest friends, and the two women delighted in that story.

American expatriates were a special breed. Jennie knew a sampling of many of them. There were those who quickly became part of the French scene, such as Loie Fuller, a short, plump woman from Illinois who became a Paris celebrity after discovering that a certain combination of color and light lent an air of mystery to the serpentine wriggle of her dancing. Miss Fuller lived above the Folies Bergères in an apartment so small that she saved space by painting the chairs on the walls. During that early spring of 1895, she became a theatrical manager, producing a French-American version of *Salomé* in pantomime. The show flopped and Miss Fuller went back to her serpentine wriggle. Later that year, her French and American friends threw a gala party for her, the kind which Jennie might be expected to have attended.

Jennie's family friends, the William Kissam Vanderbilts, were also in town, but, having just been divorced, they stayed well away from each other. Commodore Vanderbilt, who had founded the family fortune, had been a friend and business partner of Jennie's father, the fabulous Leonard Jerome, and the two families had been close ever since. William Vanderbilt settled on the Champs in a plush apartment, complete with billiard room. Mrs. Vanderbilt arrived with her tall, charming, nineteen-year-old daughter Consuelo, whose future husband Mrs. Vanderbilt had already selected. He was Jennie's nephew, "Sunny," the twenty-one-year-old Duke of Marlborough.

"I forced my daughter to marry the Duke," Mrs. Vanderbilt testified many years later. "I have always had absolute power over my daughter. When I issued an order, nobody discussed it. I therefore did not beg, but ordered her to marry the Duke."[6] Mother and daughter did not linger long in Paris, as they were being hard-pressed by an American suitor, Winthrop

Rutherford. "Winty was outclassed," one magazine remarked. "Six-foot-two in his golf stockings, he was no match for five-foot-six and a coronet."[7] The Duke's hand in marriage cost the Vanderbilts $2.5 million in Battle Creek Railway Company stock, plus $100,000 a year for life: a dowry totalling $15 million.[8]

It was said by some that Jennie had played an important part in the matchmaking, but a letter to her son Jack indicates that at the time she was surprised by the engagement. Besides, it turned out to be a miserable, loveless marriage, and if Jennie had engineered it, Consuelo would not have remained her close friend.

The current society news when Jennie arrived in Paris concerned the Count Castellane and his young, newly arrived American bride. Jennie knew the whole clan of Count Boni de Castellane, particularly his uncle, the handsome Prince de Sagan, who had been a trusted friend of Jennie's father and the first mature man who had stirred any romantic feelings in her.[9] The Count's bride was Anna Gould, the daughter of the late celebrated international financier, Jay Gould, and the wedding had been appropriately lavish. Fifty florists had worked all through the night before the ceremony arranging wagonloads of orchids, roses, and lilies. Each guest received a solid silver, heart-shaped box lined with gold and containing a piece of wedding cake. However, the wedding was not as ostentatious as a birthday party that Count Castellane afterward gave for his wife in Paris, featuring eighty thousand Venetian lamps, an illuminated ballet by a cast of eighty on the banks of a lake, fifteen kilometers of carpet laid on the grass so the 250 guests representing "the bluest of blood in France" would not get their feet wet from the dew. There were also an orchestra of 200 musicians, 80 footmen in scarlet costume, and spectacular fireworks.[10]

That same spring, two of Jennie's other men friends, George Curzon and Sir Bache Cunard, were en route to the United States to meet their American brides. An American newspaper complained editorially that $161,653,000 had traveled to Europe in the form of American brides.[11] A magazine further suggested that it might not be a bad idea to establish a protective export duty on American heiresses.[12]

The Paris *Herald* noted a growing resistance to the American invasion[13] and reported that a set of prominent European matrons were forming a social boycott of unmarried American ladies, no matter how laudatory their letters of introduction. The newspaper, however, was always filled with ads offering a variety of liaisons:

> Young Literary Gentleman is Starving in Paris. Money gone,
> his wife has deserted him; lives luxuriously at leading hotel.
> Deep gratitude for temporary help.

> Young English Gentleman, through disappointments, tem-
> porarily dependent on wife's income, would act as confiden-
> tial secretary or traveling companion; would arrange business
> or financial matters for lady who finds them irksome.

> Platonic friendship–A lady holding the doctrine of Plato on
> the above subject, wishes to form a friendship, on purely pla-
> tonic principles, with a gentleman. He must be of good posi-
> tion and appearance, tall, dashing, of the type one calls chic.
> Lady is handsome (sparkling, brunette), an accomplished lin-
> guist and musician.

Jennie did not have to advertise for companionship, even though she was
alone at a hotel. She was still a great beauty and now in her prime. Her son
Winston later wrote of his mother that "She was still, at forty, young, beautiful, fascinating," and her nephew Shane Leslie was still more descriptive:

> I remember visiting her the week after Randolph died.
> She was haggard, but her beauty was never more apparent. I
> remember her so well, lying in bed, her face absolutely
> white, her black hair hanging, a marvel. It was the first time I
> realized how beautiful women could be.[14]

Hers was the kind of dark, full-figured beauty for which Parisians particularly had a passionate appreciation. That appreciation sometimes showed
itself in direct, but unorthodox ways. For example, Jennie awoke early one
morning in her hotel room to see a very corpulent French gentleman
slowly approaching her bed. The man had managed to get the room adjoining hers, which had a connecting door. Then he had very quietly removed the hardware from the door and entered Jennie's room. Now he
was slowly approaching his intended pleasure. Jennie watched him, waiting
until he was almost upon her. Then she hit him as hard as she could in his
overstuffed midsection. The man gasped and doubled over. Then he disappeared through the connecting door much more quickly than he had entered. When Jennie later told the story, she explained that she did not
believe in screaming, either in a hotel or in a foreign country.[15]

Jennie was planning a lengthy stay in Paris and soon found a more permanent place to live than this hotel, with its limited privacy. Her new home
was the kind of place one would expect her to find, on a quiet, fashionable,
tree-lined boulevard in a lively part of the city. Avenue Kléber radiated
from the Arc de Triomphe at the end of the busy Champs Elysées. The Arc
could be seen from her street, as could the six-year-old Eiffel Tower. (There

was talk in Paris at this time about tearing down the Eiffel Tower, as it seemed to have a magnetic attraction for would-be suicides.) The winding Seine was only several blocks away from Jennie's house and, fittingly enough, the Place des Etats-Unis was just around the corner. The sculptor Bartholdi, who had recently finished the Statue of Liberty, was completing a bronze of George Washington and Lafayette for the area.

Kléber was an avenue of large gray mansions. They were all homes with distinctive heavy doors and inner courts, in careful keeping with the *cachet*. The exiled Queen of Spain had lived on this street for more than thirty years. Number 34 was a handsome seven-story house, with gargoyles decorating the windows. Most of the windows had small balconies. But it was the interior that Jennie soon made her own. She had a passion and a gift for decorating, following no style but her own taste. She liked bright colors for curtains, hated heavy furniture, and loved to fill walls with paintings. She could move into a cold, formal house and very quickly convert it into a warm comfortable home.

Jennie's younger sister Leonie Leslie and her three sons were the first houseguests to arrive. Their older sister Clara was in Tunbridge Wells, taking care of their mother, who was ill. Clara, or Clarinette, as the sisters often called her, striking in her blonde beauty, was married to Moreton Frewen (who came to be called "Mortal Ruin" by his unfortunate financial partners). Never was there a more brilliant, eloquent man who failed so magnificently in so many schemes in so many places, from Kenya to Canada. Moreton was so often away that his marriage seemed more one of correspondence than contact. Clara's letters to him were full of loneliness and longing.

Leonie, the youngest sister, whom Jennie called "Sniffy," was dark, not as pretty as Clara, but twice as clever and talented. Her husband was John Leslie, who like Frewen also found it necessary to spend considerable time away from his family, but was more often found at the race course than in remote corners of the world. His three sons seldom saw him, and he was especially a stranger to the youngest boy, Seymour. Jennie often told of the first time John Leslie visited her Avenue Kléber home, and spent the night. The seven-year-old Seymour opened the door of his mother's bedroom in the morning and was so surprised to see John Leslie in bed beside her that he asked, *"Qui est ce Monsieur, Maman"* Seymour Leslie would later write of his father, "He had never domineered or been unkind, which would be forgivable; only completely indifferent, which is not."[16]

The three sisters were so close that they were a kind of spiritual unity. Each not only knew what the others thought and felt, but what they *would* think, what they *would* feel. They told one another their innermost secrets, shared their limited funds, and acted more like mothers than aunts over their various nieces and nephews. It was a mutual love and tenderness. And when outside trouble threatened any one of them, their compact formed a fortress against the world.

If Jennie unburdened herself somewhat more to Leonie, it was not only because Leonie was the wiser one, but also because the two were somehow more closely attuned, had more of the same interests, even preferred the same kind of men. "I do hope, my dearest mama," her son Winston had written, "that you will keep well and not give way to depression. I am sure Aunt Leonie will look after you and make the time pass pleasantly."[17]

Jennie, of course, had her periods of depression. What soon made Paris much brighter for her was that the city was filled with so many of her friends, as well as some of her lovers. Among them was Albert Edward, the Prince of Wales, who had come somewhat earlier aboard his own yacht, *Brittania,* which he was preparing to race in the Mediterranean Regatta.

"Our nurse was shaking in a paroxysm of loyalty when she woke my brother and myself, soaked us in eau de cologne, and led us into the drawing room," wrote Shane Leslie.[18] "We were told to shake hands with an enormous gentleman with a beard and a gutteral voice. We did not know whether he came out of pantomime or Grimm's Fairy Tales.

"The Prince was kind enough to enquire what we intended to be when we grew up. I was tongue-tied, but my brother had the presence of mind to answer: 'Please, one of your soldiers,' I suspect under the prompting from my mother. The Prince immediately felt in his pockets and gave him a Queen's shilling in the form of a gold piece. The sovereign was confiscated, and we were both returned to bed. In future years, my brother made good his word, for he was one of the first officers killed in October, 1914."

While he was in Paris, the Prince of Wales dropped in unexpectedly at the British Embassy. The Ambassador was having his tea, and when the groom burst in announcing, "His Royal Highness, the Prince of Wales," the startled Ambassador let his teacup fall as he jumped up exclaiming, "Good God!" The Prince, who was a marvelous mimic, later reenacted the whole scene, coming in and announcing himself, then jumping up, dropping his cup and saying, "Good God!"[19]

The Princess Alexandra had been left in London. This was not unusual. In Paris the Prince preferred his freedom, and he had become very adept at eluding his equerry.

Two other men in Paris who assuredly left their wives home when they visited Jennie were Paul Bourget and the Marquis de Breteuil. Jennie had known both men before they were married, and had she been free, each would willingly have married her. It must have seemed to Jennie as if life went round in concentric circles. It would always be that way for her. Those who had loved her never wanted to let her go.

Henri Charles Joseph le Tonnelie Breteuil, a member of the French Chamber of Deputies and a distinguished diplomat, would have been Foreign Minister of France if the monarchy had been restored. An ancestor of his had been French Ambassador to the Imperial Court of the Empress Catherine of Russia, which was one of the excuses Breteuil had used to accompany Jennie and her husband on their trip to Russia in 1887.[20] But their romance had predated that trip. When he married Marcelite Garner, an American girl, Jennie was caustic about it[21] and temporarily terminated their relationship. The Marquis then wrote to Jennie, "What I miss most is not seeing you anymore."

Jennie and Breteuil shared many things. They were both extraordinary equestrians, both were dynamic speakers, and he was as handsome as she was beautiful. Both also most enjoyed creative people. The great French novelist Marcel Proust later used Breteuil as a model for "Bréuté" in *Remembrance of Things Past:*

> ". . . A snob! But, my dear, you must be mad, it's just the opposite. He loathes smart people, he won't let himself be introduced to anyone. Even in my house! If I ask him to meet someone he doesn't know, he swears at me all the time."[22]

Proust added that "Bréuté" visited only those who had a certain reputation for intellect, "with the result that from his presence, were it at all regular, in a woman's house, one could tell that she had a 'salon.' "

It was obvious why Breteuil clung to Jennie. In addition to everything else, she was a fresh breeze in his formal world. The Prince of Wales, a good friend of Breteuil's, delighted in calling him, "Braces." Jennie had the same unstuffy spirit.

Paul Bourget was of a different cut, but equally distinguished and equally in love with Jennie. She had met him years before at the Paris literary salon of a fellow American, Mrs. Ferdinand Bischoffsheim. As Jennie discreetly put it in her memoirs, he was "then unmarried."

Bourget, just slightly older than Jennie, was one of France's most celebrated novelists. In June of that year he would be elected to the French Academy, taking the seat once held by Voltaire. Critics called Bourget a poet of delicate fancy, a writer of subtle psychological observation, a critic capable of "the finest shades of appreciation and discrimination." His novels, of which there would be fifty before he died, hinted rather than thundered, and always in elegant style. Women, particularly, admired his genteel analyses of their emotions and the delicate way he sought the secrets of their inner selves.

Bourget had just returned from a long visit to the United States, and he and Mark Twain—whom Jennie also knew—had tilted literary swords in the

North American Review. Bourget referred to American women as "the real Romans of decadence" and mocked the ladies of Baltimore and Philadelphia who wanted to cover up their cities' naked public statues. His American stories must have amused Jennie.

Bourget was a handsome, shaggy-haired man with an impressive mustache and an elegant manner. The celebrated American novelist Henry James noted in his diary at the time that Bourget's marriage was not going well and was unlikely to survive in the Paris scene.[23] His elaborate apartment was only ten minutes' walk from Avenue Kléber.

Bourget's correspondence with Jennie through the years was long and prolific. He had once written her, "Arrived at a certain point in life, one knows too much about it, wishes to do too much, and is not able to express what one has to say. Do you know that Turgenev has summed it all up when he said, 'Life is a brutal affair'?"[24]

The brutality of life reached Jennie that spring in Paris when she picked up the Paris *Herald* and noted two new arrivals at the Hotel Bristol: Count Charles Kinsky and his bride, fresh from their honeymoon.[25]

If Jennie was anguished, Kinsky was certainly as much so when he heard of her presence in Paris. There was no love in his marriage, but his heritage, his religion, and his father made divorce inconceivable. The disintegration of his marriage soon became publicly obvious.

As for Kinsky and Jennie, what would these two frustrated lovers do? Would he try to see her? Probably. And would Jennie see him? She was a unique woman. Her pride had not been merely damaged; it had been battered. As much as she loved this man—and she would love him until she died—she was stubborn enough to refuse for years to see him. But that, too, would change.

IT WAS JENNIE WHO WAS THE MOST influential factor in the development of her son Winston. Besides the courage, spirit, and drive she instilled in him, besides shaping his mind through their constant discussions and correspondence, besides introducing him to the people who helped determine his future, besides her own maneuvering for him in every area in which she could protect his interests and further his ambition—besides all of those things, at a crucial stage in his life Jennie provided Winston with the only real father figure he ever had, the one man who was most vital in helping him develop the greatest of all his gifts.

Several generations later, Democratic Presidential candidate Adlai E. Stevenson, himself a speaker of sparkling wit and elegance, asked Winston Churchill whose example had helped fashion the famous Churchill oratorical style. "It was an American statesman who inspired me . . . and taught me how to use every note of the human voice like an organ," Churchill answered. And then, to Stevenson's amazement, Churchill quoted long excerpts from speeches made by Bourke Cockran some sixty years before. "He was my model," Churchill said.[1]

In March 1895, Bourke Cockran was just a man who came to dinner one night at 34 Avenue Kléber. Leonie had invited him to Jennie's home because he was a good friend of their brother-in-law Moreton Frewen. Romanticists might say that Jennie and Bourke Cockran were fated for each other. Wasn't it more than strange, they might ask, that these two remarkable people, who had never met before, just happened to be in Paris at the same time for the same reason? Jennie had become a widow only a month before Cockran became a widower. His wife, like Jennie's husband, had died after a long illness. Cockran and Jennie both had come to Paris for a change of scene and mood. Both believed that their lives had reached an ebb. Both had lived so long with the dying and the dead that they were ripe for the freshness of loving and living. Seldom were two people more open and ready for each other.

"Live intensely and die suddenly," was Bourke Cockran's motto,[2] and no motto could have suited Jennie better.

The passport issued earlier that month to William Bourke Cockran noted simply:

Age, 41 years. Stature, 5 ft. 11 inches. Forehead, high. Eyes, gray. Nose, straight. Mouth, mustache. Chin, round. Hair, dark brown. Complexion, dark. Face, round.[3]

"Leonine" was the best word to describe him. Particularly when he was speaking, he truly looked like a lion ready to spring. The single most striking physical characteristic about him was his magnificent head, with its long dark hair that tossed like a flowing mane. A big, broad-shouldered man, he was a commanding figure with deep-set, widely spaced eyes, a strong jaw, and thoughtful brows that slanted upward and inward. He was not handsome, and Alice Roosevelt Longworth, Theodore Roosevelt's daughter, affectionately described him as "an enormous ogre."[4] But he moved with grace and energy, and his presence radiated charm and power. "When he entered a room, it was like somebody turning on the electric light," observed the great Irish statesman, Sir Horace Plunkett.[5]

Cockran and Jennie were so much of the same cut. They had the same sparkling wit, never barbed for injuring, and they were both generous givers of themselves—their time, their money, their strength, and most of all, their spirit. They both had penetrating intelligence, inner fire, and titanic vigor.

Cockran's voice was almost magical, "a low rumble of thunder that has the sweetness of the lute in it." It had the lilt of Irish laughter and vibrated with vitality. Despite his talents as a talker, he never tried to dominate conversation, although he was always ready to reply with a witty riposte. And when he wanted, he could be a swift, dangerous thruster in repartee.

"When I was a young man, we used to regard Carlyle as the greatest conversationalist of his time," wrote Lord George Ripon, a former Viceroy of India. "Then, later on, we spoke of Gladstone as the greatest conversationalist since Carlyle. Well, I heard Carlyle and Gladstone many times, and I am quite convinced that, in wit, wisdom, and elegance of expression, neither of them approached the American statesman Bourke Cockran."[6]

Jennie, too, knew the great conversationalists of her time. They had come to her parties and crowded her dinner table, Prime Minister Gladstone among them. Having been trained in that art herself, she was never simply the polite hostess who quietly poured the tea; she injected her opinions forcefully, and yet in a way which nobody really could find objectionable.

Jennie and Bourke had much to talk about.

There was the current news: Japan at war with China over Korea; Cubans rebelling against Spanish rule; 3,000 troops called in to quell violence caused by a trolley-car strike in Brooklyn; an abortive attempt by partisans of ex-Queen Liliuokalani to restore the monarchy in Hawaii; the anticipated United States Supreme Court decision declaring the income tax unconstitutional; and the strange, controversial case of Captain Alfred Dreyfus. As a lawyer, Cockran was particularly interested in the Dreyfus case. Having been convicted of treason in a secret court martial, Captain Dreyfus had been publicly degraded, stripped of his rank in front of 5,000 soldiers, and imprisoned in solitary confinement on Devil's Island. Proving Dreyfus' innocence had already became a cause, and the case would topple several French governments before Dreyfus would be exonerated.[7]

There were lighter items for table talk: a scheduled race of horseless carriages (at a predicted speed of sixteen miles an hour); an old-fashioned duel between a composer and a noted clubman caused by comments made during the dress rehearsal of a Paris play; Lady Wolseley's ball at which guests wore costumes copied from 18th-century paintings; and the opening match of the Ladies' Football Club, organized by a Miss Honey-ball at the Nightingale Lane Football Grounds.

Jennie and Cockran might also have talked about Ireland. She had lived there more than three years, when Randolph had served as secretary to his father, who was then Viceroy of Ireland. Jennie had loved Ireland. Her second son Jack was born there.

Bourke Cockran had been born in Ireland, in County Sligo which he called "the most Irish part of Ireland . . . the weird and solitary grandeur of Knocknarea, the music of the waterfall at Ballysodare, the moonlight on Lough Hill, and the perfumed breath of the Tyreragh meadows where we saw the swaying of the cowslips and daisies, not the movements of the senseless winds, but the capers of the dancing fairies. . . ."[8] He had emigrated from Ireland alone at seventeen, clerked in a New York department store, taught French and Latin, become principal of a public school, worked briefly as a foreign correspondent,[9] and got his law degree by studying at night. His first wife had died in childbirth and his second wife had been the daughter of a millionaire merchant. He himself was now a very successful lawyer.[10]

Jennie and Cockran shared a common love of horses, too. Both of them were born to it. As a boy, Bourke had lived on a farm and had moved almost from his cradle into the saddle. His father had had a similar love, and had died of a broken neck in a steeplechase run when young Bourke was only five years old.[11] Jennie, too, came to her love of horses through her father, for Leonard Jerome was "the father of the American turf" and the man largely responsible for making horse racing respectable in the United States.[12] In fact, Cockran often had attended the races at Jerome Park.

They also shared memories of New York City. Jennie had vivid memories of her father's luxurious home on Madison Avenue with its own private theater where Jerome personally auditioned young singers, and where she had strutted on the stage, pretending to be an actress. New York to Jennie also meant elegant balls where she had daydreamed of dancing with the Prince of Wales when she wasn't even a teenager yet.

Bourke Cockran, too, had had a home on Madison Avenue, near where Jennie had lived, and he could tell her about the changes in the neighborhood—the end of the trolley-car barn, new hotels replacing old mansions, the move of elegance northward.

And they could spend a whole series of evenings talking about Jennie's brother-in-law, Moreton Frewen, "the splendid pauper."[13] A friend of Presidents and Princes, Frewen had an unbroken record of fiscal failure, but he remained an indomitable optimist, a man of a thousand ideas, a visionary who forecast the Panama Canal and the St. Lawrence Seaway. Jennie and Bourke had both lost money in some of his schemes. Shane Leslie remembered sitting with Frewen and Cockran, who "could endlessly debate the Silver Question, the Irish Question and Tariff Question together, and when each was fought to exasperation, they would laugh and turn to one another. Often I was deafened between their rival torrentades. And, afterwards, Moreton would confide to me, 'Poor Bourke, such a windbag, but such a good fellow!' And Bourke would mutter, 'Was ever so much intelligence so sublimely misdirected!' "[14]

Politics was another field on which Jennie and Bourke could meet as equals. Not only did Jennie understand the intricacy of back-room dealings, but she had single-handedly conducted several of her husband's political campaigns at a time when other upper-class women didn't even go out on the streets unescorted. An American newspaper had referred to Jennie as one of three women in England "who were intelligent politicians."[15]

She had considerable knowledge of American politics, particularly New York's. In his capacity as assistant district attorney, her favorite cousin, William Travers Jerome, had served on the Lexnow Commission investigating New York City's political corruption.[16] His detailed revelations had helped destroy some of the power held by Tammany Hall, New York's Democratic organization, and in 1895 Jerome helped elect a reform Mayor. He himself would later become the state's Attorney General, a prominently mentioned candidate for Governor, and even a much-discussed possibility as a presidential nominee.

Cockran's connection with Tammany had been double-edged. He had fought them, joined them, and was now again against them. He had fought them during the corrupt Boss Tweed days, when everything was for sale and the price high. In the early 1870s a big, broad ex-soapstone cutter and amateur actor named "Honest John" Kelly succeeded Tweed and reorganized Tammany Hall. Kelly decided to recruit unimpeachable candidates and to work more subtly behind the scenes. "Honest John" even lectured on Jesuit Missionaries in North America, and it was he who persuaded Cockran to join the new Tammany team.[17]

West Side Tammany leader George Washington Plunkitt had remained skeptical of Cockran's convictions:

> I'll admit he's a grand gentleman and the greatest orator in the land, but take it from me, he's not a dependable politician. He calls himself a Democrat but his heart was never in Tammany Hall. . . . While he was in Congress, he never darkened the door of a Tammany clubhouse.[18]

Cockran's connection with Tammany grew weaker when Richard Croker succeeded "Honest John" as Tammany leader. Boss Croker was a mild-mannered, soft-spoken, sad-faced, small chunk of a man who believed that "To the victors belong the spoils." Within a short time, Boss Croker owned a Fifth Avenue mansion, a vast estate in England, a stock farm for race horses worth $250,000, and a well-bred bulldog which cost $10,000.[19]

Croker helped elect Cockran to Congress for several terms but then decided he was too independent and refused to endorse him for United States Senator in 1895. Charles Emory Smith, editor of the *Philadelphia Press,* editorially guessed at the reason: "Bourke Cockran has never been able to make his principles elastic. That is something that Boss Croker does not appreciate or even understand."[20]

Cockran had been an effective Congressman during his three terms in office, but he made the politically unforgivable mistake of voting on the basis of principles and issues, rather than political party. He later explained his independence by telling of the wandering Indian who refused to admit he was lost: "Me here; tepee lost!"

Boss Croker was vehement in his denunciation of Cockran, calling him the most objectionable man he had ever met in his political career. Pressed for a reply, Cockran said, "Croker never said anything that was worth replying to." Then he paused and added, "Except on a few occasions. That was up to a few years ago when I wrote what he was to say in advance."[21]

Nothing Bourke said as he sat alongside her at dinner that night at 34 Avenue Kléber could have stirred Jennie as much as she might have been had she been able to hear him speak from a public platform. Perhaps the best speech of his career was at the Democratic National Convention in Chicago in 1892.

"Not until the last delegate to the convention sleeps in his grave will the famous oration cease to be discussed with wonderment and ecstasy," one reporter wrote.[22]

The convention had been in continuous session for more than ten hours and it was then long past midnight. The more than fifteen thousand delegates in the enormous tent were hot and tired and hungry. The great majority of them clearly wanted Grover Cleveland as their presidential nominee. The song they had sung was:

> Grover, Grover,
> Four more years of Grover;
> Out they go
> In we go;
> Then we'll be in clover.[23]

In fact, everybody there wanted Grover Cleveland except Tammany Hall.

His audience seemed to him then like a wall of darkness, punctured with white spots. "The only person I recognized was Governor Flower[24] of New York. The rain was constantly coming through the roof, and he sat on the back of the chair to keep his feet from the wet floor, with an umbrella over his head. I remember that I thought he looked like a huge turtle."[25]

At first Cockran felt like a swimmer in a stormy sea. He started out with tender, mellow tones, with sorrow and pathos rather than anger. A reporter described it as "the tongue of gentleness, whose words ripple as flowing water . . ."[26] Then, with his eyes half closed, his eloquence came with a rush. The delegates sat on their hard, cramped seats "as silent as death." From outside could be heard the thunder of a storm and the whistle of a passing train.

The notes of his two-octave voice now picked up added purpose and passion, "the blood suffusing his great neck and his fiery Irish soul leaping from his wonderful eyes . . ."[27]

"I have said that I believe that Mr. Cleveland is a popular man," he intoned. The crowd broke into enthusiastic applause. Cockran stood still, a small smile on his mobile face. When the cheers subsided, he continued, "Let me say, a man of extraordinary popularity." Again, the audience cheered. A moment later, after taking a sip of water, Cockran completed his point, "A very popular man on every day of the year except one, and that . . ." (he paused dramatically) ". . . and that is Election Day."[28]

He had caught the delegates' complete attention. From then on, the vast audience alternated between agitation and stillness "as a field of summer barley is swept by gusts of summer wind." They were carried along "upon the melodious current of his speech, unconscious, and when he was done, they turned to one another like men who have awakened from a vivid dream."[29]

"The severest test of oratory is to compel applause from a hostile audience," said Senator Champ Clark. "I have nearly blistered my hands applauding William Bourke Cockran when I dissented from everything he said."[30]

Only after their thunderous applause did the delegates remember that they were tired, hungry, thirsty, and still pledged to Grover Cleveland, whom they afterward nominated.

⬦⬦

There is no knowing how much of his background Bourke revealed to Jennie that evening at dinner at 34 Avenue Kléber in March 1895. But that evening was just the first of many more evenings. The attraction was quick and mutual. The timing was perfect and the formula was right. They were free enough to do as they pleased, adult enough to know what they wanted in this summer of their lives.

Years before, when Jennie had rented an apartment in Paris on the Rue Marbeuf, she found an enormous snake drawn over the head of the bed, with the words:

J'enlace et jamais l'en lasse.
(*Entwine yourself with me, and never lazy shall I be.*)[31]

Filed away among Cockran's papers is a bit of doggerel he had copied. The original title was "The Rhyme on the Hungry Husband," but he had changed it to "Any Husband to Any Wife":

Feed me on victuals
For I'm sick of bran.
Feed me on bacon, eggs and coffee, too.
Feed me on beefsteak, if you can't get ham.

Feed me on beans and peas and Irish stew.
Feed me on custard,
And when at length the festive board is spread,
Just shut the door and hurry off to bed.[32]

In the language of the gypsies, a "jennie" is a merry-go-round, which is what life must have seemed like to her then. Part of the pleasure of being together in Paris that spring, for Jennie and Bourke, was that it was a natural habitat for both of them. They had spent their youth there, both spoke French as fluently as English, and they knew all the best places to go together. They knew where to walk for quiet conversation: the tree-lined quays on the Ile Saint-Louis, down the still streets near the Jesuit Church at the Place Saint-Sulpice. They knew what it was to walk the gaslit streets all night and greet the dawn, the Seine almost motionless in the sunrise, and the drifting mist lending a softness even to the skeletal steel of the Eiffel Tower.

They went riding and cycling in the Bois de Boulogne. Jennie loved cycling and everybody was learning it, even the portly Prince of Wales. Women wore *bicyclettes*–divided skirts[33] of which each leg was composed of alternating strips of lace and fabric. Even Queen Victoria was entertained by a group of women who performed a bicycle ballet set to music.

Jennie wrote her sons that she was "very busy," that Paris was "charming," and that, in her ice skating at the Palais de Glace, "I find I have not forgotten my various figures–Sea Breeze, etc. . . ."[34]

There was the theater, which she and Bourke both loved. Jennie was a frustrated playwright, and Bourke a frustrated actor. As a young man he had played bit roles, and his first speech, at sixteen, concerned the moral influence of drama.

Every new Paris play was a social event, and intermissions were noisy with comments. Everybody seemed to have some point to make and there hardly seemed time to savor the *glacé* sweetmeats from Boissier's, which the women ate from a pair of tongs so as not to soil their suede gloves.

One of the popular plays in Paris at the time was called *L'Age Difficile,* about the extramarital affairs of a woman named Jeanne. A critic said, "It is suggestive, but with dainty skill, cutting almost to blood flow, but yielding immediately a bit of pretty batiste to bind the wound." Another less successful play called *Mademoiselle Eve* was by "Gyp" (pseudonym of the Comtesse de Partel) and dealt with the several love affairs of a society lady and her unsuspecting husband.[35]

The most popular play in Paris at the moment was *La Princesse lointaine,* a sad, sumptuous, dreamy fantasy by a young playwright named Edmond Rostand. The play was considered slight, but Sarah Bernhardt was its star. The gossip was that "the divine Sarah," then fifty-one years old, had invested her own money in the play because the twenty-seven-year-old play-wright, whom she called, "*mon poète*," "hung from one of her rays."[36] Bern-hardt was still the actress with the golden voice that could move any audience to tears, and yet such was her perfect control of emotion that she could always wink at a stagehand.[37]

Paris was full of concerts, and Jennie and Bourke both loved music. Paderewski had just returned from a highly successful American tour and reported all the details to Jennie. Paderewski was indebted to Jennie. It was she who had arranged his premiere performance in London when he was yet little known. She called him "Paddy" and they played duets together.[38] Even then, he wore his hair long and flowing and reported, "How I hate my damned hair! But I have to wear it like this because the public have grown to expect it from my portraits."[39]

At the end of his Paris concert there was such cheering that the Paris *Herald* reported, "Not even Liszt received the ovations which were ac-corded to M. Paderewski."[40]

There was a different kind of music at the Ambassadeurs where Yvette sang her ballads. Yvette Guilbert was the rage of Paris, and Toulouse-Lautrec later immortalized her on canvas. Her songs were highly sugges-tive and more scoffing than subtle. Some people listened to them with a sense of outraged propriety, but they listened and loved her, because she had grace and audacity and style.[41] In one of her ballads she sang of a son who had killed his mother at the request of his sweetheart. As he held his mother's heart in his hand, he slipped suddenly and the heart said, "Don't fall, dear son, and hurt yourself. . . ."[42]

The Ambassadeurs was decorated like a roof garden, complete with gravel, lined benches, and gas jets. At the back were boxes where people dined and listened. The Dead Rat and the Black Cat were places with a dif-ferent mood. The Black Cat had massive rafters, heavy broad tables, an im-mense fireplace, and black cats everywhere—stuffed in their natural skin, carved in wood, cut out of wrought iron with gas jets flaming from their mouths, and depicted in illustrations as waltzing in the woods, running over red tiled roofs, racing over the ocean. In an informal theater upstairs local poets recited their verses in the dark. It was very romantic.

Artistide Bruant, another Paris personality, recited a different kind of poetry at his tiny café on the Boulevard Rochechouart. Bruant liked to re-fer to himself as a modern François Villon, a poet of the people. He always dressed in brown velvet, a red shirt, a broad sombrero, and high boots. There were only three long tables in his tiny place and guests needed to know the special knock to gain entry. Bruant sang in a swaggering style, his hands deep in his pockets, his long hair shaking. He also insisted on kissing the women—the pretty ones—goodbye when they left.[43]

Spring in Paris was carnival time, and that meant clowns, confetti, colored balloons, and a parade with mounted trumpeteers and the Queen of Queens, robed in white, her hair powdered, wearing a diadem and holding a scepter. It was a time when the students, singing and marching arm in arm, made the boulevards impassable. But one newspaper reporter described an argument between an angry *agent de police* and an equally angry student that was "hysterically funny" because they were both "so animated and at the same time so exquisitely polite."[44]

Jennie and Bourke were lovers of good food, and they never stinted. Then, as now, the specialty at the Tour d'Argent was pressed duck—the meat carefully carved off the skeleton, and the skeleton then put into a great silver press and crushed before the diners' eyes. The juice of the bones gave the sauce a particularly delicious flavor.

Jennie and Bourke probably also went to the receptions given by Madame Emile Straus. She was better known as Geneviève, the widow of composer Georges Bizet. Geneviève's salons featured sparkling conversation by the most eminent and fascinating people in Paris. Geneviève herself once said of a beautiful woman who had spread with age, "She is no longer a statue; she is a group." And when somebody said to her, "Madame, you may say what you like about *my* friends," Genevieve answered, "I didn't know you had any." But her most repeated remark, made to a woman whose name appeared on the Honours list, was, "The feminine chest was not made for hanging orders on."[45]

It is also possible that Jennie pulled Bourke along to the Fourteenth Annual Exhibition of Lady Painters. She herself had started to paint more often and more seriously. She was also often asked to pose for other artists. She must have told Bourke about the time she had posed for the French artist Hébert. They were at Hébert's studio and suddenly were almost overcome by a compelling odor. Hébert broke into the studio below to find the corpse of a fellow artist, "who had been lying dead for two weeks!"[46]

The weather in Paris had been lovely during the onset of spring, but in London the cold had helped spread an influenza epidemic. Jennie wrote her son Jack, "Go to bed early and take care of yourself . . . I don't like hearing of a cough. . . . I hope you won't get influenza. . . ."[47] Newspapers reported thirty-four dead, and 1200 London policemen and many members of Parliament, including Prime Minister Rosebery, had been incapacitated. A newspaper even blamed the influenza for causing a fit of temporary insanity in a respectable workman; he had murdered his wife and six children by cutting their throats with a razor and then committed suicide.

Jennie's mother was ill, but Clara was still there to take care of her. Winston had visited her and wrote to his mother that grandmama "looked very pale and worn. . . . She carped a little at your apartment in 'the gayest parts of Champs Elysées' but was otherwise very amiable—or rather was not particularly malevolent." He also wrote that he hoped to get a few days' holiday and come to Paris at Easter, "so you must keep a fatted calf for the occasion. . . ."[48] He told her that he was sending her three boxes of her favorite cigarettes, Royal Beauties. Jack was also planning to visit his mother for Easter, and she wrote him, ". . . Mind you bring a knickerbocker . . . for you will want to bicycle . . . and a pair of low shoes. . . . I will send an order for your coat. . . ."[49]

At the end of March 1895, Jennie's mother's health suddenly worsened, and the two sisters made preparations to hurry to her side. Jennie was to go first, and Leonie wrote Clara to tell their mother that Jennie was coming on business. "It will be everything for you having Jennie," Leonie wrote, observing that Jennie was "practical and helpful."

Winston wrote immediately to his mother. "What sad times you are having, my darling Mummy. I trust you may have strength to go through them. . . . I can come at an hour's notice if you feel you want to see me—so don't hesitate to wire. . . ."[50]

The weather also had changed, and a vicious gale was blowing over the English Channel. But their mother's condition was critical, and the two sisters rushed to leave. Several days later, the Paris *Herald* social column noted that Bourke Cockran, too, had left for England.

Twenty-One

ENNIE'S FATHER HAD PASSED on to her his drive, his imagination, his love of life, and she had adored him. But her mother was a cold, straight-laced woman. "Poor darling, she has had so little pleasure these last years," wrote Clara, the eldest daughter, the one who had been named after her and the one who had loved her most.

"She had grown very old and we had to be very quiet, for fear of disturbing her," recalled Clara's daughter Clare Sheridan, who became a noted sculptress. "At the end of her days, she became superbly squaw-like, and would sit impassively for hours, staring into the fire, her head shrouded in a shawl. A figure of great moral fortitude and self-oblation was gradually fading out. She had lived a selfless life."[1]

But it had not really been selfless. Leonard Jerome had been a man of many women because his wife could not give him the love and the life he wanted. Since divorce at that time was unthinkable, Clara moved with her daughters to Europe, while Leonard remained in New York.

Clara Jerome's goal in life was social prominence. She would have bought it if she had more money, or married it if she had been widowed. Her last hope, therefore, was to push her daughters into outstanding marriages and bask in their social success. But that, too, failed. She was bitterly unhappy with all three of her sons-in-law: Randolph terrified her; Moreton Frewen had wasted her family jewels for his ill-conceived ventures; and John

Leslie and his family always treated her with disdain. Was it any wonder then that she sat grimly over her teacups in a cheap boarding house in Tunbridge Wells, surrounded by the dregs of her life, pinching pennies until the end came?

"Poor Grandmama is to be buried tomorrow, Friday," Jennie wrote her son Jack on April 4th, 1895.

> You must meet us at Charing Cross at *eleven o'clock*. Please ask Mr. Welldon [Headmaster of Harrow] to allow you to come. Aunt Leonie returns to Paris Saturday and I will come, if possible, and take you over Tuesday. If you have no black gloves, get some at Harrow. I have ordered a wreath for you. Don't be late—*eleven o'clock*. The train is very punctual. Winston is here.

Jennie could not pretend an emotion she did not feel. She and her mother had long lived in separate worlds, and there had been no bridge between them. They had had different values, different insights, different dreams.

Clara Jerome's will designated that two-thirds of her estate was to go to Clara and one-third to Leonie. This meant an income of £1600 a year ($8,000) for Clara and £800 ($4,000) for Leonie.[2] "What breaks my heart, Moreton," Clara wrote her husband, "is that she sacrificed so much these last years of her life in economizing and saving just to leave me in comfort."[3]

Moreton was just then involved in another disastrous venture called Electrozone, and welcomed the chance to get at some more funds.[4] He urged his wife to go to America to try to raise some money on her share of the American estate, and he promised to come from Australia and meet her there in June.

The three sisters already had decided to take their mother's body back to America for burial in the elaborate family vault in Greenwood Cemetery in Brooklyn, where their father lay. They now agreed to postpone the trip until June, when Clara could meet Moreton.

London newspapers gave scant attention to the death of Clara Jerome. The front-page news was the sensational Oscar Wilde affair. The scandal sprang from Oscar Wilde's libel action against the Marquis of Queensberry for intimating that Wilde had persuaded Lord Queensberry's son into a homosexual act.

Jennie found herself in the awkward position of being good friends with both Oscar Wilde and the Marquis' attorney, Edward Carson. Carson was a brilliant, fiery M.P. from Dublin. At Jennie's suggestion, he had once journeyed to Harrow to lunch with Winston and talk to him about his future. He also invited Winston to watch Parliament in action "and dine with me then to view the scramble of a House of Commons dinner." Carson was probably one of the first men to talk with Winston about politics.

Edward Carson had a reputation for extraordinary courage and determination. In a discussion about him and another great lawyer, an admirer of Carson remarked, "I should be ready to hunt tigers with Carson; I wouldn't hunt cats with the other."[5] Another comment often repeated was "I would rather be defended by Carson when I was wrong than by any other man when I was right."[6]

Oscar Wilde, the plaintiff in this celebrated case, had been a frequent guest at Jennie's parties and dinners. In fact, there were few great London houses where he had not dominated the dinner table. He was, after all, famous, rich, flooded by commissions from theatrical managers, courted by the intelligentsia, constantly interviewed by the press, and aggressively imitated by a whole generation. Even captains of football teams were seen with the Wilde long hair style.[7] "I was a man who stood in symbolic relation to the Art and Literature of my age," Wilde wrote. "Few ever hold such a position in their own lifetimes and have it so acknowledged."[8]

He enjoyed Jennie's dinners because he had spent a year in the United States and genuinely liked American women. He thought they were "pretty and charming–little cases of unreasonableness in a vast desert of practical sense."[9]

Jennie did not fit easily into that generalization about American women, and Wilde had great respect for her. When she wrote and asked him to settle a bet she had made on the accuracy of a quotation from one of his plays, he promptly answered:

> The only difference between the saint and a sinner is that every saint has a past and that every sinner has a future!" That, of course, is the quotation. How dull men are! They should listen to brilliant women, and look at beautiful ones– and, when, as in the present case, a woman is both beautiful and brilliant, they might have the ordinary common sense to admit that she is verbally inspired.[10]

Wilde once said, "The first duty in life is to be as artificial as possible. What the second duty is, no one has yet discovered."[11] And he lived by this rule. At his trial, he was "as artificial as possible." Describing the first day in court, a *New York Herald* correspondent wrote that it was the first time in the history of Old Bailey that the dock of that court was occupied by a peer of the realm. "Yet, though it was the Marquis who was technically in the dock, it was quite evident that before the day's proceedings finished, it was his accuser, the heavily-jowled, broad-shouldered person, lounging ungracefully over the front of the witness box, who really stood on his defense before the world."[12]

"He made one think of an enormous doll, a preposterously exaggerated puppet, a rather heavy dandy of the Regency period," wrote Richard Le Gallienne.[13] Wilde had a large, loose face, thick sensuous lips, and his curly hair was modeled to his face, almost like a wig. "All his bad qualities began to show in his face," another reporter wrote.[14] His eyes, however, were haughty and humorous, and he modulated his strong voice with elaborate self-consciousness.

When asked whether iced champagne was a favorite drink of his, Wilde said that it was, though strictly against the doctor's orders. And when Carson rapped out, "Never mind the doctor, Mr. Wilde," he answered, "I don't mind the doctor."[15] "It was all very amusing, and there were roars of laughter," wrote E. F. Benson, "but the entertainment was madly out of place, and most prejudicial to him, for these answers were given to questions which clearly had a very ugly significance, and a more unsuitable occasion for jests could not be imagined."[16]

Carson cut into Wilde's witty quibbles "with his bitter, shameless questionings, like an apple corer plunging down into the heart."[17] The questioning revealed that Wilde's father had been an alcoholic oculist in Dublin, his mother a poetess who wanted a daughter and consoled herself by dressing and treating Oscar as if he were a girl.[18]

This was Carson's first *cause célèbre* at the English Bar and "it fitted him as closely as an executioner's mask."[19] One of Wilde's letters to Queensberry's twenty-year-old son, Lord Alfred Douglas, was read in court:

> My own dear boy—Your sonnet is quite lovely and it is a marvel that those red roseleaf lips of yours should be made no less for the music of song than for the madness of kissing. Your slim gilt soul walks between passion and poetry. I know that Hyacinthus, whom Apollo loved so madly, was you in Greek days. Why are you alone in London, and when do you go to Salisbury? Do go there and cool your hands in the gray twilight of Gothic things, and come here whenever you like. It is a lovely place; it only lacks you, but go to Salisbury first. Always with undying love,
>
> Yours,
> Oscar.[20]

In the witness box Wilde stood "in a clumsy posture, clasping his hands nervously in front of him, over a pair of doeskin gloves he held, and occasionally wiping his forehead with his hand or with his handkerchief."[21]

The jury's verdict was in favor of Lord Queensberry as "having proved justification for the libel." Oscar Wilde was convicted under Section II of the Criminal Law Amendment Act, for acts of gross indecency between males. No charges were brought against Lord Alfred Douglas, the young man who shared Wilde's affections. Similarly, no charges had been brought six years before when a police raid found Lord Arthur Somerset, a friend of the Prince of Wales, in a homosexual brothel.[22] The difference was that Wilde had forced public notice of an ugly side of society, instead of keeping it discreetly quiet.

"The two great turning points of my life," Wilde said, "were when my father sent me to Oxford, and when society sent me to prison."[23] Two of his plays were then playing in London, and the management quickly covered his name on the billboards. The plays were soon suppressed, however, and his books were withdrawn from library lists. The ultimate insult came from Wilde's brother, who told George Bernard Shaw, "Oscar was not a man of bad character; you could trust him with a woman anywhere."[24]

It was a trial of fascination and horror for Jennie, as it was for all England. But for Jennie the trial would have a meaning far beyond her imagination. At that very same time, her own son Winston was enmeshed in a situation which would result in a charge that he had engaged in "acts of gross immorality of the Oscar Wilde type."

The scandal concerning Winston would not become public until a year later, in the spring of 1896. But the alleged incident on which the scandal was based was said to have taken place just before the Wilde affair.

The charge against Winston came from Alan Cameron Bruce-Pryce, a graduate of Oxford and a member of the Bar. His son, Alan George Cameron Bruce, had been a classmate of Winston's at Sandhurst and had gone into Winston's cavalry regiment, the Fourth Hussars. Early in March 1895, six subalterns of the Fourth Hussars invited Bruce to dine with them at the Nimrod Club. Winston Churchill apparently acted as the spokesman for the junior officers and "informed Mr. Bruce, almost in so many words, that he had been invited to the dinner in order to let him know that he was not wanted in the regiment." The primary reason given was that Bruce's allowance of £500 a year ($2500) was not sufficient to "go the pace" of the regiment. Oddly enough, Winston's own allowance was less than £300 a year.

According to one account, the young men intimated that "they had got rid of Hodge [Bruce's predecessor] and they would get rid of Bruce, too, adding that if the latter gentleman did not choose to make a graceful exit now, he would probably make a disgraceful one before very long."[25]

Hodge, who also apparently had had an "inadequate allowance," had been hauled from his bed to a horse trough, pushed under the bars, "dragged to the other end, and then hauled out, wet through, bruised and bleeding, and carried back to his room, his night clothing torn to shreds." They repeated the same action the next night, and shortly afterward Hodge resigned from the regiment.[26]

Despite all this, Bruce was determined to remain in the regiment, so a general social boycott against him was put into effect. Within a short time Bruce was called up on charges of forcing his way into the Sergeants' Mess, and he was asked to resign.

Bruce vehemently denied the allegation, but he did resign and nothing else was heard of the matter until almost a year later. At that time his father was negotiating with the new subaltern taking his son's place for the sale of some of Bruce's equipment. It was in a letter to this subaltern, Ian Hogg, in February 1896, that Bruce's father made the charge that led to the scandal.

Winston and his mother consulted their friends and solicitors and issued a writ:

STATEMENT OF CLAIM
In the High Court of Justice

QUEEN'S BENCH DIVISION
Writ issued 15 February 1896

Between WINSTON SPENCER CHURCHILL ...
Plaintiff

AND

A. C. BRUCE-PRYCE ... Defendant

1. —The Plaintiff is a lieutenant holding Her Majesty's commission in the 4th (Queen's Own) Hussars.

2. —On or about the 11th February 1896 the Defendant falsely and maliciously wrote and published to 2nd Lieutenant Hogg of the said regiment of and concerning the Plaintiff and of and concerning the Plaintiff in his said profession the words following that is to say:—

"His real offence however was that he was at Sandhurst with Mr. Churchill and that they had been rivals in shooting, fencing and riding throughout their career and incidentally that he knew too much about Mr Churchill.

"There was for instance one man whose initial is C, flogged publicly by a subaltern court-martial for acts of gross immorality of the Oscar Wilde type with Mr Churchill.

"I have not as yet ascertained what was done by the E Company to Mr Churchill, but as soon as I do I shall lay the statement before the War office."

3. –The Defendant meant and was understood to mean by the said words that the Plaintiff was a person of vile and disreputable character unworthy of associating with the officers of his regiment or any honourable men and unfit to hold Her Majesty's commission. That he had been guilty of gross acts of indecency with male persons and in particular had been detected and exposed in one flagrant case. That by reason of the premises the Plaintiff had been guilty of criminal offenses and was liable to be indicted under the Criminal Law Amendment Act 1885.

4.–By reason of the premises the Plaintiff has been grievously injured in his credit and reputation and in his said profession and in his position as officer in Her Majesty's Army and has been held up to hatred and contempt.

The Plaintiff claims 20,000 pounds damage.

W. Temple Franks

Delivered the 21st day of February 1896 by Messieurs LEWIS and LEWIS Ely Place, Holborn E.C. Solicitors for the Plaintiff.

The case was settled within a month for £500 and the withdrawal of the charges by Bruce-Pryce: "I unreservedly withdraw all and every imputation against your character complained of by you . . . and I hereby express my regret of having made the same."

Colonel Brabazon promply wrote Winston a letter expressing his "intense pleasure" at the outcome and his delight that the case had not come to trial:

> For altho you would have come out of it with flying colours & there could have been but one issue to the case, yet it is a thousand fold better that it should have terminated as it has, for one cannot touch pitch without soiling one's hands however clean they may have originally been, and the world is so ill natured & suspicious that there would always have been found some ill natured sneak or perhaps some d————d good natured friend to hem and ha! and wink over it— perhaps in years to come, when everyone even yourself had forgotten all about the disagreeable incident.[27]

The following week Brabazon wrote Winston that he had discussed the affair with Sir Redvers Buller, who was perfectly satisfied, "so we will consider the incident as closed for ever. Oddly enough Buller told me that he had on his table a letter from Lansdowne to Mr. B. P. [Bruce-Pryce] declining to reopen the racing case or to have anything more to do with him. He threatens to bring it before Parliament."[28]

The racing case was still another scandal in which Winston was involved, and this, too, occurred in March 1895.

Shortly before Jennie's mother died, Winston rode in a steeplechase race for the Fourth Hussar's Subaltern's Challenge Cup. He used the pseudonym of "Mr. Spencer," probably because he had promised his mother he would not ride in steeplechase races. The winning horse, at 6–1 odds, was "Surefoot." A year later, at the same time the Bruce scandal broke, the National Hunt Committee reported irregularities in the race. After an investigation, the race was declared null and void, and the horses which had taken part in it were disqualified from all future races run under National Hunt rules.

When Colonel Brabazon wrote Winston that the incident was "closed for ever," he was being hopeful but not realistic. *Truth,* a weekly magazine owned and edited by Henry Labouchere, had taken up the Bruce case as a cause. Labouchere, who was also a Member of Parliament from Northampton, demanded a full investigation by the Army and personally brought the matter up for debate in the House of Commons. In addition to raking up all the details of the Bruce case, Labouchere now combined it with the race scandal, observing that some of the same subalterns were involved in both affairs.

Labouchere asserted that the subalterns in the steeplechase race had substituted a superior horse for Surefoot as a last-minute "ringer" to collect on the heavy odds.[29]

The Army investigated the Bruce case and placed the fault on Bruce for not being proper regimental material. It also refused to reopen the racing case. Labouchere increased the pressure in his magazine and in Parliament, and Winston was worried. He urged his mother, ". . . what you do must be done from my point of view alone and not with reference to the regiment—who have no ideas beyond soldiering and care nothing for the opinion of those who are not their friends. I leave matters in your hands—but in my absence my dearest Mamma—you must be the guardian of my young reputation."[30] In his next letter, a week later, Winston again referred to the damage being done by the Labouchere articles, and added, "Therefore do muzzle him if you can."[31]

Jennie had already been busy making the necessary contacts. Brabazon was her confidant and strongest ally. The man who would make the final decision was Lord Joseph Garnet Wolseley, Commander in Chief of the Army. He had often dined at Jennie's home, as had Lord Henry Lansdowne, the Secretary of State for War. Sir Redvers Buller, the Commander at Aldershot, was an even closer friend of both Jennie and Brabazon. The Under Secretary of War, William St. John Brodrick, who defended the Army position in the House of Commons, was an old Churchill family friend. Jennie must certainly have been in touch with all of them, either personally or through Brabazon. Perhaps she also called on Labouchere himself, reminding him that he had once been a friend of her husband.

Labouchere described the growing pressure to drop the case:

> . . . The public must bear in mind that the young officer who assumed the part of ringleader in the conspiracy to eject Mr. Bruce from the 4th Hussars belongs to an influential family, and that all the influence at his back has been used to prevent a reopening of the case, as I can testify from my own experience.[32]

Soon afterwards, however, Labouchere finally dropped his attack.

In his letters to his mother Winston had seemed more concerned about the racing scandal than about the homosexual charges. It is likely, however, that Jennie had been more deeply troubled about the intimation of homosexuality.

When her own marriage disintegrated with the discovery of her husband's syphilis, Jennie sought other men. Lord Randolph, however, did not seek other women. It was as if he blamed all women for the syphilis which destroyed his brilliant political career. He increasingly took long trips with men friends, and there was some talk of his growing effeminacy.

Winston and Jack had never had the sort of close relationship with their father that is so important in encouraging the development of manliness in young boys. It was said of Jennie that she had invaded more of the man's world than any other woman of her time, but no woman can be a father to her sons. Jennie had toughness, but her sons' needs went beyond toughness, beyond strength, beyond love.

The relationship between father and son is an irreplaceable relationship, almost a spiritual kind of transference. It is a reaching and a giving of a unique kind. The mother-son feeling is usually soft, gentle, perhaps enveloping; but the father-son feeling is firmer and fuller. Winston and John had never had this.

This absence of a father-son relationship was not unusual in upper-class England during the nineteenth century, and it was probably part of the reason that homosexuality and sadism were so rampant in English boys' schools. All older public-school boys were catered to by younger "fags," who were often brutalized if they failed to give quick and proper service. Jennie's nephew, Shane Leslie, remembered one boy so brutalized that he attempted suicide by crawling up the pipe in the lavatory one night and chewing on the green copper which he believed was a deadly poison.[33]

Jennie might have been concerned that even though he was almost twenty-one, Winston showed little interest in girls and seldom dated. Perhaps the knowledge of his father's syphilis deterred him. "Ambitions I still have: I have always had them," said the hero in Winston's novel *Savrola,* "but love I am not to know, or to know it only to my vexation and despair."[34]

The only real love Winston had shown was for his mother. Filling his faithful flow of letters to her—at least once a week, for many years—was the kind of sentimental, romantic language a young man might write to the young woman he loves. There are many mothers who are possessive of their sons and flattered by such demonstrations of affection, but Jennie was not. She wanted his love, of course, but she also wanted him to be his own man.

Just before his death, Winston still had on his desk a hand molded in copper. It was a cast of his mother's hand, and his own hand was almost a replica of it.[35]

Nobody knew better than Jennie that what Winston needed most was the support of a strong man. With the Oscar Wilde scandal still stark in her mind, Jennie must have considered this deeply as she journeyed back to Paris in April 1895.

Twenty-Two

"P OOR DEAR MAMA. IT IS SO SAD. you and Winnie will have to pro- tect and take care of her now and make her happy. . . ."[1] The con- dolence note to Jack, after his father's death, was from his and Winston's childhood nurse, Mrs. Everest.

But far more than care and protection, Jennie needed the enduring love of a man. She seemed to find it in Paris with Bourke Cockran. If happiness in life consists of having something to do, someone to love, and something to hope for, then Jennie and Bourke must have been happy in Paris. The exceptional people are those who fit into no mold, but shape their lives ac- cording to the dictates of their own natures. How few are the people any- where at any time who really think, and how many fewer are those who really think for themselves.

Paris was a whirling world for Jennie and Bourke. It was always an- other restaurant, another party, another theater, another club. "It was a very lively life," remembered Jennie's nephew, who regarded his aunt as "picturesque, rather mysterious . . . something far more beautiful than any of the actresses we were called upon to admire. . . ."[2]

Bourke Cockran agreed. Jennie was filled with the joy of living, an enormous sense of gaiety and excitement, and Paris was the place for her. The night of the Grand Prix, the great race of the year, was the fête night of Paris. Richard Harding Davis wrote of it:

You will see on that night, and only on that night, the most celebrated women of Paris racing with linked arms about the asphalt pavement which circles around the bandstand. It is for them their one night of freedom in public, when they are permitted to conduct themselves as do their less prosperous sisters, when, instead of reclining in a victoria in the Bois, with eyes demurely fixed in front of them, they can throw off restraint and mix with all the men of Paris, and show their diamonds and romp and dance and chaff, and laugh as they did when they were not so famous.

The theme song of the Nineties was "The Man Who Broke the Bank at Monte Carlo," and the crowd of thousands sing and shout it in French and English, with a strut and swagger backgrounded by the clashing of cymbals and the big drums and the blaring of brass.

And when they reached the high note in the chorus, the musicians, carried away by the fever of the crowd, jumped upon the chairs, and held their instruments as high above their heads as they could without losing control of that note, all holding onto the highest note as long as their breath lasted. It was a triumphant, reckless yell of defiance and delight; it was the war cry of that class of Parisians about which one always reads and which one sees so seldom, which comes to the surface only at unusual intervals, and which, when it does appear, lives up to its reputation and does not disappoint you.[3]

At the Grand Prix of 1895, people still talked about the previous Grand Prix when the favorite was an English horse named Matchbox. So protective were the horse's owners that they had the horse escorted onto the track by eight gendarmes, seven detectives in plain clothes, two trainers, and the jockey. As one cynic put it, "Probably if they had been allowed to follow him round the course on bicycles he might have won, and no combination of French jockeys could have ridden him into the rail. . . ." Sophisticated Parisians claimed the sure way to win money at the Prix was to bet *against* any English horse.[4]

Jennie's house in Paris was a natural social center with a constant flow of people. The American news was that the heat along the Atlantic Coast was an unprecedented 96 degrees in the shade; that a soldier had bicycled from New York to Chicago in 13 days, 7 hours, and 45 minutes; and most importantly, that the New York State Senate had approved a resolution in favor of woman's suffrage.

The news from Britain was that Prime Minister Rosebery had won one race but lost another. His horse had won the Derby for the second year in succession, but Rosebery had resigned as Prime Minister.[5]

Friends brought news from other parts of the world. Revolution had spread throughout Cuba, and the insurgents had seized several towns. The Japanese had defeated the Chinese and declared a Kingdom of Korea. Sir Edgar Vincent had arrived from South Africa with news of increased friction there.[6] And Harry Cust, who had written delicate love poetry for Jennie and was now editor of the *Pall Mall Gazette,* arrived from Armenia with stories of turmoil and atrocities.

It was a humming household at 34 Avenue Kléber but it was well organized by Walden, who had been Lord Randolph's butler. He superintended a small staff of French servants, aided by Jennie's maid Gentry. Bourke fitted easily into this mélange of activity, completely accepted by both of Jennie's sisters as almost part of the family.

All three sisters had planned to accompany their mother's body back to Brooklyn for burial. A New York newspaper reported their plans, noting, "In their journey across the ocean, the three sisters will be under the care of Bourke Cockran."[7] But then Jennie decided not to go. The primary reason was that something had gone wrong in her relationship with Bourke.

What, and why? Religion? Bourke was a devout Catholic, an active worker and lecturer for the Catholic Church in New York. But was this difference insurmountable? Probably it was not. What else then? Kinsky? Was the "opium" of that romance still too strong, was he still too near, were they seeing each other again in Paris? Possibly. But was there another factor: If they were married, where would they make their home? A British reporter commented about Jennie, "She is allied to both [England and America] with bonds of steel. It is doubtful if she herself could tell to which she is closest."[8]

Jennie had lived most of her adult life in England. All of her dearest friends were there. Her sons belonged to it. She had absorbed its culture, its graces, its intellectual ferment, its very air. It was true that she retained her American accent, and proudly waved a small American flag when an American horse won the Derby. She was also the main American social focus in London, even more than the changing American Ambassador. But England now was as much a part of her blood and bone as America was. It would rip the whole fabric of her life to give it up. Bourke's roots were deep in America. It was not a matter for compromise; one of them would have to surrender.

That was probably the basic reason for the end of their affair: each of them was too big for surrender. Each was so remarkable a person, so strong a personality, that perhaps they found themselves competing with one another. A love affair can be intense, tempestuous, full of the fierceness and wonder of living, but marriage requires a long-range look. Ten years earlier, all their doubts and questions and logic would have been swept away by their emotions. But now they were both mature and toughened by the turmoil of their lives; they had learned how to look around all the corners. Their past and future marriages seem to demonstrate that, for a lifetime of living, each needed someone weaker. Each of them married noncompetitive mates whom they felt they could more easily control. Bourke and Jennie together were too much of a match.

Leonie was a confidante to both of them, and they both hinted to her of this sort of problem. Bourke told her that Jennie was so overcharged with energy that she wore him out, and Jennie said that it was exhausting to be alone with Bourke, that he really needed a table of guests for whom he could "show off."

The pity of it was that they could not face the challenge of each other. As it was, their parting regret must have been deeply felt, but there was no sharp break. Bourke continued to commute to London until he remarried, and it was not just to visit his sister and his niece. Jennie, in turn, depended on Bourke for a variety of advice and assistance. In fact they never stopped seeing each other or writing to each other, even after each remarried. Their letters became much more circumspect, of course, but whenever Jennie really needed Bourke, he never failed her.

When her sisters and Bourke went to America, Jennie went to Aix-les-Bains, a small, fashionable resort in southern France where the warm sulphur springs were said to give guests a new lease on life. For Jennie, however, it meant a lonely interval of solitary walks in the gardens, the baths, the brooding reflections among the Roman antiquities, with the future seeming more and more remote.

Her sons kept up a regular flow of mail. Winston had been to the races at Newmarket and wrote that "The Prince asked after you as did many others."[9] Another time Winston lunched at Government House. "The Prince was there and saw me. I had a long talk with Lord Roberts—who had just been made Field Marshal. Everyone of course asked after you. . . ."[10] Still another day, the Duke and Duchess of York (later King George V and Queen Mary) came to see a field day at the regiment and Winston was asked to have dinner with them. "The Colonel went there also and although everything was exceedingly formal I was very glad to have been asked. I had quite a long talk with the Duke of Connaught about the Election & of course everyone asked for you. . . ."[11]

Then came a sad letter. Their nanny, their childhood nurse Mrs. Everest, had died of peritonitis. "Everything that could be done was done," Winston wrote:

I engaged a nurse–but she only arrived for the end. It was very sad & her death was shocking to see–but I do not think she suffered much pain.

She was delighted to see me on Monday night and I think my coming made her die happy. Her last words were of Jack. . . . Please send a wire to Welldon to ask him to let Jack come up for the funeral–as he is very anxious to do so.

. . . Well my dearest Mummy . . . I feel very low–and find that I never realized how much poor old Woom [Mrs. Everest] was to me. I don't know what I should do without you.[12]

Winston's need for his mother was not only emotional (". . . How I wish I could secrete myself in the corner of the envelope and embrace you as soon as you tear it open"[13]), it was also intellectual. He discussed politics and people with her in great detail. Winston felt the new government of Prime Minister Salisbury was "too strong–too brilliant altogether. They are just the sort of government to split on the question of Protection. Like a huge ship with powerful engines they will require careful steering–because any collision means destruction."[14]

Taking office for the third time, Salisbury was then sixty-five years old, a bulky man, his shoulders more stooped than ever, his full curly beard more gray. He was a melancholy, unpredictable man who had a sharp, penetrating mind. Salisbury had distrusted Lord Randolph, but he had always been very appreciative of Jennie.[15] Winston had met Salisbury at his mother's dinner table.

When Jennie and Winston discussed politics, they usually had the advantage of discussing people they knew rather than remote names and abstract policies. In her letters to him, there was none of the condescension of a politically sophisticated woman to a son not quite old enough to vote. Jennie was careful to keep her correspondence on a level of equality, respecting the surprising maturity of her son's opinions and not hesitating to argue when she felt that he was wrong or uninformed. She always believed that his real future was in politics, and she was delighted when he wrote her of army life, "I do not think it is my *métier*." Later he commented, "It is a fine game to play–the game of politics–and it is well worth a good hand before really plunging."[16] He was counting on her, he said, to look out for the "good hand."

Her two sons were much different in their emotional makeup, their personalities, their abilities, their needs. Jack, not yet sixteen, was the quiet one. He was of medium height but would grow taller than Winston, and he was also the better looking of the two. He idolized his brother, who was everything that he was not–outgoing, adventurous, exuberant, although

Jack was very likely the better horseman. He also had more of his mother's elegance and charm, and certainly all of her musical ability. Winston was tone deaf.[17]

Jack's son, John Churchill, later wrote of his father,

> People sought his company, but frankly, he was not what I would call intelligent. Although he shared my passion for Wagner, he had no real understanding of art, and his love for his first-class library hardly went deeper than admiration for the covers and bindings, especially first editions; he seldom actually read the books.[18]

Despite John Churchill's assessment that his Uncle Winston had "pinched all the brains in the family,"[19] Jack Churchill did very well indeed at Harrow, even though he was the youngest boy in his class. The Reverend J. E. C. Welldon wrote to Jennie of him: "His conduct in the House is excellent; there is no better boy, and I think you may look with very great satisfaction upon his character."[20]

Jack was the kind of boy who kept a precise record of his expenses, studied hard enough to get top grades—particularly in English and History—and never had a school punishment. He was a loving boy, who adored his mother. Jennie, in turn, loved Jack as much as she did Winston, but in a different way because their needs were different. She was clearly more solicitous of Jack, more maternal, more concerned about his health. She called him "Darling Puss," urged him to go to bed early, chided him for his poor spelling,[21] and often wrote, "I miss you very much. I love you more!"

What worried Jennie most about Jack was that he lacked drive and direction. Unlike Winston, he did what she wanted him to do and seldom argued with her. But what he lacked in excitement, he made up for in dependability. When Jennie needed something done—especially in later years—she went to Jack, not Winston. Jennie was always doing things for Winston and Jack was always doing things for Jennie.

Jennie always reserved a large part of her life for herself, but whatever she gave to her sons, she gave with intensity and concentration. She let both of them know that she loved them deeply, and she proved it again and again. That, she felt, was giving them the strongest root of all. Everything else they could forgive.

"Jack and Winston have helped their mother in every way, even by not going to the University in order to work, and both absolutely adore her," Jennie's sister Leonie had told her son. "I have done everything and given my boys everything, but they don't seem to care for me at all."[22]

Both sons had joined Jennie in Paris for the short Easter holiday, and

Jack joined her again in August 1895 for a trip through Switzerland. Winston was unable to go, as he was laid up with a "sprung vein" caused by too much riding.

After returning from Switzerland, Jennie went on to the Isle of Wight for the Cowes Regatta. It was an event she never missed, as it was very social but in a relaxed kind of way. Yachting had been a love of her father's, and he had passed it on to his daughters.

The main rivalry this year was between the Prince of Wales and his nephew, Kaiser Wilhelm II of Germany. The Prince thoroughly disliked his nephew, and Princess Alexandra detested him. But even this did not spoil the light-hearted spirit of the event.

Strolling across the lawn of the Royal Yacht Squadron, the most exclusive yacht club in the world, Jennie was soon surrounded by her fashionable friends. Women's fashions had evolved toward the Gibson Girl figure—full-bosomed, full-bottomed, a tinier waist than ever before, and a flowing skirt. It suited Jennie well. The leg-o'-mutton sleeve, which had periodically shrunk and swelled, was at its zenith. Tall, tight collars covered most throats, and skirts again swept the floor.[23]

Hair was kept close to the head in a bun, although many women soon began to wear it fluffed out. During the "bun" period, a dignified nobleman complimented Jennie on her *"bum."* Suddenly realizing what he had said, he felt very embarrassed, but Jennie made light of it.[24] Also fashionable then were the wide-brimmed picture hats that seemed to float on top of the head and were called hatpin hats. Women skaters, however, had to be warned how to fall properly—"Falling on your back can drive your hatpin into your head."[25]

During Regatta Week at Cowes that August of 1895, everybody seemed to wear white: the men, white trousers and white shoes. Jennie and her sisters wore white serge sailor suits, with sailor hats that had been made fashionable by the Princess Alexandra.

One of the more sprightly but snobbish guests was Jennie's American cousin, Kitty Mott, a niece of her mother's. Kitty and her millionaire husband arrived on a luxurious three-masted schooner, the *Utoawana*. Jennie noted that the one thing that seemed to depress Kitty was the fact that her husband's iron works specialized in lavatories and his name was emblazoned on all of them.

Jennie and Leonie took time out to befriend a shy, teenage girl. "They saw me standing about, looking lost and bewildered, for I knew no one, so they came up and spoke to me in a gay, friendly way, transforming the day I had rather dreaded into a glorious episode of my hitherto quiet life. . . ."[26] The shy girl, who became the Duchess of Sermoneta, later considered the two sisters among her most intimate friends.

Jennie, however, did not spend all her time with Leonie and their friends. The Prince of Wales, who had left Cowes early, wrote to Jennie of a report he had heard that she was frequently seen in the company of Hugh Warrender. Mixing some jest with obvious jealousy, the Prince wondered "where your next loved victim is . . . ?"

Hugh Warrender seemed a likely candidate. A handsome, twenty-seven-year-old officer in the Grenadier Guards, he would periodically reappear in Jennie's life. Even her sons were conscious of the feeling between them and made references to Hugh in their letters. "Turn on the devoted Warrender," Winston wrote to his mother when he wanted more correspondents.[27]

Jennie's nephew mentions that his aunt seemed to have a particular attraction for young men. He remembered one who proposed marriage to her thirteen times but was always gently refused. He might have been Warrender.

Cowes Week over, Jennie went to London for some intensive house-hunting. During the summer, Winston had written, "I am longing for the day when you will be able to have a little house of your own and when I can really feel that there is such a thing as home. . . ." And while she and Jack were in Switzerland, he wrote, "I do look forward to having a house once more. It will be too delightful to ring the bell of one's own front door again. . . ."[28]

Jennie had been thinking the same thing. The gay, aimless, wandering life in which she had been free and easy for the first time was a tonic she had needed. But now she needed a home, not only for her sons, but for herself. She soon found what she wanted. It was not in fashionable May-fair, but on the wrong side of Oxford Street: a quiet, respectable address, 35A Great Cumberland Place, within sight of Marble Arch and only a few blocks away from Hyde Park. It was a handsome, seven-story Georgian house with a large library. Clara later sold her own large house opposite the Russian Embassy on Chesham Place and took a smaller one directly across the street from Jennie at Number 37. Leonie, too, soon moved nearby, to Number 10. At Number 4 there reportedly lived the phantom of a butler who had committed suicide. The ghost, it was said, still answered the doorbell in a most disconcerting manner—at least disconcerting enough for that house to have changed tenants ten times while Jennie lived at Great Cumberland Place. Much more alive was another neighbor, the celebrated Australian soprano Nellie Melba (originally Helen Porter Mitchell). Nellie and Jennie became friends, and they played piano duets and even sang together. But it was Jennie and her sisters who gave Great Cumberland Place its own social reputation, so much so that it came to be known as "Lower Jerome Terrace."[29]

Most of the socially important American residents of London lived within a mile of Hyde Park Corner. The more favored ones faced the park itself, as Jennie had when she lived at Connaught Place, several blocks away. Americans were moving into most of the gracious mansions. Lansdowne House, which had been a British institution of social grandeur, where the halls were filled with classical statues and where the concierge at the lodge gate wore a top hat, would soon be rented by William Waldorf Astor. And the magnificent Dorchester House, with its spectacular grand stairway, glass cases enclosing Shakespearian folios, and a splendid carriage drive laid down in ground red brick, would become the American Embassy.

"I shall go to Mintos for a few days," Jennie wrote Clara on October 3rd, "& then to London to look after '35A *Greater* Cumberland Place' as the boys call it—I hope to get into it the end of November; but you know how long it takes to do anything & I am going to have it all painted from top to toe, electric light, hot water etc. . . . How nice it will be when we are all together again on our 'owns'! The boys are so delighted at the thought of 'ringing their own front door' they can think of nothing else. . . ."

But Winston was thinking of other things, too:

> My dearest Mamma,
>
> I daresay you will find the content of this letter somewhat startling. The fact is that I have decided to go with a great friend of mine, one of the subalterns in the regiment, to America and the W. Indies. . . . We shall go to New York & after a stay there move in a steamer to the W. Indies—to Havana where all the Government troops are collecting to go up country and suppress the revolt that is still simmering on; after that back by Jamaica and Hayti to New York & so home. . . .
>
> Now I hope you won't mind my going my dear Mamma—as it will do me good to travel a bit with a delightful companion who is one of the senior subalterns. . . .[30]

Jennie was worried and tried to dampen the idea.

> You know I am always delighted if you can do anything which interests and amuses you—even if it be a sacrifice to me. I was rather looking forward to our being together & seeing something of you. Remember, I only have you and Jack to love me. You certainly have not the art of writing & putting everything in their best lights but I understand all right—& of course darling it is natural that you shd want to travel &

I won't throw cold water on yr little plans—*but* I'm very much afraid it will cost a good deal more than you think. N.Y. is fearfully expensive. . . .[31]

She made a strong point in her letter of saying, "I *must* know more about yr friend. What is his name? Not that I don't believe you are a good judge but still I shd like to be sure of him." Winston's friend was Reggie Barnes, the same young man who was involved in the Bruce case and the racing scandal.

Jennie also added a maternal criticism: "Considering that I provide the funds I think instead of saying 'I *have* decided to go,' it may have been nicer and perhaps wiser—to have begun by consulting me. But I suppose experience of life will in time teach you that tact is a very essential ingredient in all things."

At the end of her letter, however, she suddenly gave up the whole idea of being a careful and restraining mother and wrote, "P.S. I have had a talk with the Tweedmouths over yr plans & they can help you much in the way of letters to the Gov of Jamaica & in suggesting a tour. . . . Would you like me as a birthday pres to pay yr ticket?"[32]

The first of his mother's friends whom Winston contacted was Sir H. Drummond Wolff, Her Majesty's Ambassador in Madrid and one of Jennie's oldest admirers. She had met him at Cowes before her marriage and described him afterward as "the best of the company . . . with a pink-and-white complexion that a girl might have envied, and a merry twinkle which hid behind a pair of spectacles . . . a godsend if anything went wrong, and a joke from him saved many a situation." It was Wolff who had suggested starting The Primrose League, a political-social organization through which Conservatives could meet and work together, regardless of their social class. Jennie was part of the original group of twelve who helped organize it, until it became a working coalition of almost two million people. Wolff was cynical, flippant, and unflappable, but a man of great warmth who was very fond of Jennie. Winston wrote to him, and Wolff promptly replied:

After receiving yesterday your letter, I saw the Minister for Foreign Affairs [the Duke of Tetuan] & spoke to him about your wish to go to Cuba.

He said he would get you a letter from the Minister of War & give you one himself to Marshal Martinez Campos who is personally his great friend.[33]

Campos, who had been Minister of War and Prime Minister, was now the Captain-General of the Spanish Army. Wolff also asked about Jennie and sent her his love. He followed up with a very official letter from the Minister of War to Marshal Campos "which I hope will obtain for you the facilities you desire."[34]

Winston also got Colonel Brabazon's approval, and Brabazon sent him to see Lord Wolseley, who was then Commander-in-Chief of the Army and another friend of Jennie's. "He said he quite approved," Winston reported to his mother, "but rather hinted that it would have been better to go without asking leave at all." Wolseley, however, sent Winston to Military Intelligence for maps and background. "We are also requested to collect information and statistics on various points & particularly as to the effects of the new bullet—its penetration and striking power. This invests our mission with an almost official character & cannot fail to help one in the future."[35]

Now that the expedition to Cuba was settled, Winston was suddenly remorseful. "When are you coming to London?" he asked Jennie. "Do send me a wire to let me know. I must see a little of you before we go." He also remarked that he planned to bring back a great many Havana cigars "some of which can be 'laid down' in the cellars of 35 Great Cumberland Place." At the end of the letter he added, "Longing to see you."[36]

Only to her did he fully reveal himself. Only to her did he reveal his driving ambition. Only with Jennie was he always open and unabashed. She chided him for his conceit, but she believed in him. And for the rest of her life she would tap the men and open the doors to prepare the complicated pattern of stepping stones to his future.

Twenty-Three

$\mathscr{I}$T IS A RATHER EXTRAORDINARY WOMAN who can turn to a recently rejected lover and ask him to be host to her son. But Jennie scarcely hesitated. There was no need to. The love they had shared had enriched them both, and this favor would bring further mutual enrichment.

Bourke would never have a son of his own. His only child had been stillborn. This was a great lack in a man like Bourke Cockran, who had so much that he wanted to pass on. Now Jennie was giving Bourke a son for a time, just as she was giving Winston a father.

For Bourke, Winston must have seemed a double image. On the one hand, he had the courage, the intelligence, the ambition that Bourke himself had as a young man. And on the other, these qualities, in addition to the boy's remarkable self-confidence, no doubt reminded Bourke of Jennie.

For Winston, Bourke loomed not only as a father figure, but also as a man of enormous wisdom and experience, a great orator, a man of taste and style, much the model of the man he himself wanted to be. More than that, Bourke was much the model of the man Jennie wanted Winston to be.

Bourke was at the dock to meet Winston on his arrival in New York, and took him to his home. He had a spacious apartment at 763 Fifth Avenue, "beautifully furnished and fitted with every convenience."[1] The chairs were soft and deep, the library was large, and Bourke served the best brandy, the finest food, the longest cigars. It was one thing for Winston to weekend at the country homes of his mother's British friends; it was quite another to live in the apartment of a brilliant aggressive American, a man's man. "Mr. Cockran is one of the most charming hosts and interesting men I have met," Winston immediately wrote his mother.[2]

"I have never seen his like, or in some respects, his equal," he later added. "His conversation, in point, in pith, in rotundity, in antithesis and in comprehension exceeded anything I had ever heard."[3]

This was an extraordinary statement from a young man who had been in contact with the finest minds of England: Gladstone, Salisbury, Rosebery, Chamberlain, Balfour, and his own father. Bourke Cockran was not just a man with a fine mind and an eloquent tongue; he was also a superb listener. And with Winston, Bourke Cockran showed that he truly cared what the young man said, that he respected him.

They talked until very late almost every night. Bourke not only unwrapped the breadth of his experience and the depth of his mind, but he taught Winston how to use language. "What people really want to hear is the truth–it is the exciting thing–speak the simple truth."[4]

Avoid cant, he said, avoid mannerisms, invective, egotism. The two men analyzed their mutual admiration for the great English orator of a previous century, Edmund Burke. "Burke mastered the English language as a man masters the horse," Cockran said. "He was simple, direct, eloquent, yet there is a splendor in his phrases that even in cold type reveals how forcibly he must have enthralled his visitors. . . . How I should have loved to have heard him."[5]

Winston wanted to hear Cockran speak, and he persuaded him to read some of his speeches. What was so memorable to Winston was Cockran's titanic vigor, his poetic vision, the fire without frenzy. There were phrases of Cockran's that Winston never forgot. Many years later, he told an American audience:

> I remember when I first came over here, in 1895, I was a guest of your great lawyer and orator, Mr. Bourke Cockran. I was only a young cavalry subaltern, but he poured out all his wealth of mind and eloquence to me. Some of his sentences are deeply rooted in my mind. "The earth," he said, "is a generous mother. She will provide in plentiful abundance food for all her children, if they will but cultivate her soil in justice and peace." I used to repeat that so frequently on British platforms that my wife very strongly advised me to give it a holiday, which I have done for a good many years. But now, today, it seems to come back with new pregnancy

and force, for never was the choice between blessing and cursing more vehemently presented to the human race.

There was another thing Bourke Cockran used to say to me. I cannot remember his actual words, but they amounted to this: "In a society where there is democratic tolerance and freedom under the law, many kinds of evils will crop up, but give them a little time and they usually breed their own cure." Now, I do not see any reason to doubt the truth of that. There is no country in the world where the process of self-criticism and self-correction is more active than in the United States.

You must not—you must not indeed—think I am talking politics. I make it a rule never to meddle in internal or party politics of any friendly country. It's hard enough to understand the party politics of your own! Still, I remain, as I have said, a strong supporter of the principles which Mr. Bourke Cockran inculcated into me on my youthful visit before most of you were born.[6]

Winston Churchill even repeated Cockran's words in his historic Iron Curtain Speech at Fulton, Missouri:

> I have often used words which I learned fifty years ago from a great Irish-American orator, a friend of mine, Mr. Bourke Cockran. "There is enough for all. The earth is a generous mother; she will provide in plentiful abundance food for all her children if they will but cultivate her soil in justice and in peace."[7]

How remarkable to have retained whole sentences for half a century. But both men had amazingly retentive minds. Bourke explained to Winston how he prepared for his speeches: studying the subject in detail, storing in his memory material from a wide range of reading, trying to simplify the most abstruse questions with familiar, easily understandable illustrations, and then trusting to the inspiration of the moment for the phrasing of sentences.[8] Until then, everything Winston knew about oratory derived from his own analysis of what he himself had heard. Now for the first time he was learning basic techniques from an expert.

But it was more than technique, more than fine phrases that Winston absorbed. It was the spirit of oratory, something he already had within him but that was now suddenly made more exciting.

Jennie was delighted to get Winston's enthusiastic reports from New York. "I have great discussions with Mr. Cockran on every conceivable subject from Economics to yacht racing."[9] And in a later letter, he added, "We have made great friends."[10] No other man in Jennie's life could have given her son all that Bourke Cockran now gave him.

This was Winston's first trip to his mother's homeland, and there was much to do and see. Bourke planned a full itinerary. "We have engagements for every meal for the next few days about three deep . . . ," Winston wrote. "Last night we had a big dinner here to ten or 12 persons all of whom were on the Judiciary. Very interesting men–one particularly–a Supreme Court Judge–is trying a *cause célèbre* case here now. . . ."[11]

Winston sent further details about this to his brother:

> There is a great criminal trial going on now–of a man who shot a fellow who had seduced his sister. I met the judge at dinner the other night and he suggested my coming to hear the case. I went and sat on the bench by his side. Quite a strange experience and one which would be impossible in England. The Judge discussing the evidence as it was given with me and generally making himself socially agreeable–& all the while a pale miserable man was fighting for his life. This is a very great country my dear Jack. Not pretty or romantic but great and utilitarian. Everything is eminently practical and things are judged from a matter of fact standpoint. Take for instance the Courthouse. No robes or wigs or uniformed ushers. Nothing but a lot of men in black coats & tweed suits. . . . But they manage to hang a man all the same, and that after all is a great thing. . . .[12]

How Jennie must have laughed with pleasure at Winston's almost boyish excitement with everything he was seeing and doing in the United States. She had opposed his trip to Cuba because she had a mother's concern for her son's unnecessary exposure to combat. She had even expressed doubts about his enjoying New York. If he had been put into the hands of Jennie's elderly and very proper female cousin in America, Winston's enjoyment would indeed have been limited. Her decision to involve Bourke Cockran, however, had changed the whole tone of the trip.

"Mr. Cockran, who has great influence over here, procured us orders to visit the Forts of the Harbour and West Point–which is the American Sandhurst," Winston wrote to Jack.[13] And to his mother, Winston commented, "I was treated like a general."[14]

There was also the Horse Show, a trip on a tugboat, and the Fire Department:

The other night, Mr. Cockran got the Fire Commissioner to come with us and we alarmed four or five fire stations. This would have interested you very much. On the alarm bell sounding the horses at once rushed into the shafts—the harness fell onto them—the men slid half dressed down a pole from their sleeping room and in 5½ seconds the engine was galloping down the street to the scene of the fire. An interesting feat which seems incredible unless you have seen it.

What an extraordinary people the Americans are! Their hospitality is a revelation to me and they make you feel at home and at ease in a way that I have never before experienced.[15]

This was his mother's country, his mother's people, his mother's heritage, and therefore a part of his too. "I am a child of both worlds," he later said. But even as he wrote about his new world with wonder, he still could be critical. The comfort and convenience of elevated railways was "extraordinary" he noted, but the use of paper-dollar currency was "abominable"; and the essence of American journalism was "vulgarity divested of truth." American vulgarity, however, was not totally a bad thing, as he explained to Jack:

> I think mind you that vulgarity is a sign of strength. A great crude, strong young people are the Americans—like a boisterous healthy boy among enervated but well-bred ladies and gentlemen. . . .
>
> Picture to yourself the American people as a great lusty youth—who treads on all your sensibilities perpetrates every possible horror of ill manners—whom neither age nor just tradition inspire with reverence—but who moves about his affairs with a good-natured freshness which may well be the envy of older nations of the earth. Of course there are charming people who are just as refined and cultured as the best in any country in the world. . . .[16]

Some of the vulgarity that winter of 1895 was evidenced by the garish interiors of many of the mansions neighboring Cockran's apartment. One of them had a reception hall "conspicuously larger than the Supreme Court of the United States." Then there was Lillian Russell appearing in a white serge cycling costume with stylish leg-o'-mutton sleeves, riding a gold-plated bicycle with mother-of-pearl handlebars which bore her monogram in diamonds and emeralds, the hubs and spokes of its wheels also set in jewels.

However, there was also a growing informality to parallel the vulgarity. Young men were discarding frock coats, replacing "boiled shirts" with soft shirts with detachable starched cuffs and collars. Women were seen wearing the new "rainy-daisy" skirt that cleared the ground by a "scandalous" six inches.

Winston scarcely had time to examine much of this in detail. He and Reggie Barnes were soon en route to Cuba by way of Florida in a private stateroom thoughtfully arranged for by Bourke Cockran. "I hope in England to renew our discussions and I can never repay you for your kindness," Winston wrote him.[17]

While Winston was in the New World, Jennie, who was a part of both the New World and the Old, suddenly found that her identification with the United States took on a new dimension. In December 1895 President Grover Cleveland sent a message to Congress which was almost an ultimatum to Great Britain. It concerned the boundary between Venezuela and British Guiana. The United States had economic interests in Venezuela, and the Venezuelan government was laying claim to a large part of British Guiana. Negotiations had dragged on unsuccessfully, and now Cleveland informed Congress that he would appoint an American Commission to define the boundary and impose its decision on Great Britain—by war, if necessary—in the name of the Monroe Doctrine.

"Twisting the lion's tail" was then a popular political ploy, especially with a presidential election due the following year. Stocks were down but jingoism was up. An Anglo-American war not only seemed likely, but was quite an acceptable idea.

It is not difficult to imagine Jennie's reaction and that of her American friends in England. A few left for the countryside or the Continent or tried to become socially invisible. But Jennie, in her typical way, galvanized her closest friends in a quiet campaign behind the scenes. Their objective was to persuade government leaders and prominent editors that the war talk was manufactured by political propagandists and that it would soon disappear. This campaign consisted of small dinners, private parties, and seemingly casual encounters, but its calming effect was considerable.

Jennie and the other American women had a powerful base of influence. The British liaison in this crisis was Joseph Chamberlain, the new Secretary of State for the Colonies. Chamberlain's American wife was part of Jennie's circle, and the Secretary listened thoughtfully to Jennie, whom he had long admired. George Curzon, the Secretary of Foreign Affairs, who had known Jennie since he was a young man, had also married an American. He similarly needed little prodding to make his voice heard on this issue. There were no doors, official or unofficial, which were closed to these insistent women. And as always, Jennie had the ear of the Prince of Wales.

An American general in England returned to the United States and told the press that Lady Randolph Churchill was the active leader of ten American women,

> true daughters of the United States, who are working quietly and mightily to prevent war between the two countries that are looking at each other in a sinister way. For these women, the war means a thousand times as much as it does to other American women; and they have untold power of international arbitration. . . . These particular ten are so situated that they are in the midst of the greatest powers that rule England today. Their influence, thrown upon the scales, would turn it whichever way they bent themselves.[18]

Jennie's activity did not escape British notice either. "If there should come hard war talk," wrote one British correspondent, "Lady Randolph Churchill would set out lecturing, as she did when she elected her husband a few years ago. And her talks would put things straight in a short time. She has a clear and concise way of delivering them that robs them of the term 'lectures.' . . . And she would be convincing."[19]

"LADY CHURCHILL WAS U.S. 'BEST' AMBASSADOR," headlined a Boston newspaper.[20]

Jennie's influence in cooling the critical situation can, of course, be overestimated. Nevertheless, the intensity of her activity on this issue was important. She, too, was "a child of both worlds."

Just when one war threat was eased, another began to loom. The scene this time was the Transvaal, South Africa. Cecil Rhodes, whom Jennie knew well, was Prime Minister of the adjoining British Cape Colony. Rhodes had authorized Dr. Leander Jameson to organize an armed force in preparation for a rebellion by the Boers, settlers of Dutch ancestry, against the British government of the Transvaal. However, Dr. Jameson decided not to wait for the insurrection, and plunged in with his tiny force. The raid was a fizzle. Jameson's raiders were quickly captured by the Boers, and the incident made England an international laughing stock. But it was all a prelude to a bitter war that was slowly brewing, a war in which Jennie and her sons were fated to play important roles.

Jennie's immediate concern, however, was the war in Cuba and Winston's activity there. She had written Jack before Winston left that she thought the Cuban trip was "a foolish business." She turned out to be right, but for other reasons. From the standpoint of experience and excitement, Winston was delighted. It was almost as if every action in his life—even the mistakes—seemed to have some predestined purpose in his development. Some aspects of the Cuban War, however, did disappoint him:

> One conspicuous feature of this war is the fact that so few men are killed. There can be no question as to the immense amount of ammunition expended on both sides, but the surprising truth remains that ridiculously little execution is done. It has always been said, you know, that it takes 200 bullets to kill a soldier, but as applied to the Cuban War 200,000 shots would be closer to the mark.[21]

At the same time, Winston did find some action and he wrote his mother: "We advanced right across open ground under heavy fire." He recorded on the day of his twenty-first birthday that "for the first time I heard shots fired in anger and heard bullets strike flesh or whistle through the air."[22] He kept one bullet that struck and killed a Spanish soldier who was standing close to him.

Jennie was relieved when Winston finally returned to New York by mid-December, 1895. He again stayed at Bourke's apartment, although this time Cockran was in London with Jennie. Cockran had a long history of fighting for causes, and this romantic one was his own. Jennie had made up her mind, but what woman would not have been flattered by such persistent admiration? A firm friendship established with Winston, Bourke may have felt that he held stronger cards with Jennie. Indeed, he probably did. Winston wrote in his memoirs that after he was twenty-one his mother "never sought to exercise parental control."[23] The evidence shows otherwise, but the Cuban escapade at least illustrates how increasingly difficult it would be for Jennie to exercise such control. Winston did need Bourke. So did Jennie. But how could she go back to America now? She could fight for America, and she had. But go back? The bridge was too long.

Winston's return to England stirred up considerable resentment in the press against this young lieutenant who fought for Spain against the Cuban nationalists. Winston protested that he did not fight at all, that he simply observed. But the negative impressions remained. Jennie's intuition about the "foolish business" had proved correct.

Jennie also heard from her friend, Sir H. Drummond Wolff, the Ambassador to Spain, who sent her copies of letters from Winston to the Duke of Tetuan and Marshal Martinez Campos, wryly noting that they all called each other by their Christian names.[24] Winston, at twenty-one, might have felt an equality with these mature leaders because he had written his mother, "I am getting absurdly old." In a sense, he always had been.

Bourke Cockran had waited in England for Winston's arrival, and the two men now had more time together to deepen their relationship. Seeing this relationship grow before her eyes, Jennie had cause for further reflection. Who had the greater need, her son or herself? Every need had a price, but was the price right? She wanted and needed Bourke, but on her terms. So did Winston. They wanted and needed him in England.

Winston wrote and illustrated an article about his Cuban experience for the *Saturday Review*,[25] and Jennie sent copies to her most influential friends. A response came immediately from Joseph Chamberlain, who had played such a vital role in resolving the Venezuelan crisis. "It is the best short account I have seen of the problems with which the Spaniards have to deal, & agrees with my own conclusions."[26]

Winston, however, was more interested in the reaction of Bourke Cockran, who had returned to New York by the end of February. "I am much interested in the action of the United States as respecting Cuban belligerency. . . . I should very much like to know what your opinion is upon the whole question . . . ," he wrote to Cockran. "Of course I won't think of giving you away. . . . I hope the United States will not force Spain to give up Cuba. . . . Do write and tell me what you do think."[27]

Cockran completely disagreed with Winston about Cuba, as did most of the British and American people. Indeed, Cockran had addressed a mass meeting in New York protesting Spanish rule in Cuba. Perhaps his arguments influenced Winston, who later changed his views on the issue.

Their correspondence was not confined to the Cuban question; it ranged the world. Winston recommended books—". . . rather a good book . . . 'The Red Badge of Courage' . . . Believe me it is worth reading . . ."[28]—and Bourke sent him copies of his speeches, one of them on Irish Home Rule.

"It is one of the finest I have ever read," Winston replied. "You are indeed an orator. And of all the gifts there is none so rare and precious as that. Of course—my dear Cockran—you will understand that we approach the subject from different points of view and that your views on Ireland could never coincide with mine. . . ."[29]

About Irish Home Rule, which Cockran urged so strongly, Winston was certain that:

> the civilized world [will not] compel us as you suggest to a prompt settlement. How could they with justice? Does Russia give up Poland? Does Germany surrender Alsace and Lorraine? Does Austria give up Hungary? Does Turkey release Armenia—or Spain grant autonomy to Cuba? One more instance shd the United States accede to the demand for Confederate Independence? And one more argument. You may

approve of Home Rule in principle. But I defy you to produce a workable measure of it. He will be a bold man to rush
in where Mr. Gladstone failed.

Finally, let me say that when I read your speech I thought
that Ireland had not suffered in vain–since her woes have
provided a subject for your eloquence. Do write to me
again. . . .[30]

Cockran's answer was immediate:

. . . With your remarkable talent for lucid and attractive
expression you would be able to make great use of the information to be acquired by study of these two branches
[sociology and political economy]. Indeed I firmly believe
you would take a commanding position in public life at the
first opportunity which arose, and I have always felt that
true capacity either makes or finds its opportunity. I was so
profoundly impressed with the vigor of your language and
the breadth of your views as I read your criticisms of my
speech that I conceived a very high opinion of your future
career. . . .[31]

This was heady praise indeed for twenty-one-year-old Winston. Winston also mentioned to Bourke, "My mother has been rather ill and is
gone to Monte Carlo."[32] Cockran answered that he was immediately returning to Europe and would stop briefly in London on his way to
France. There he planned to see Jack, who was in Paris on holiday, and
then, surely, to go on to Monte Carlo. It was his third trip to Europe that
year.

Jennie had decided to go to Monte Carlo for a brief change of scene, as
well as for reasons of health–psychological as well as physical. Before she
left, she asked her friends to watch out for Winston, who was at Aldershot,
taking a signalling course. As a result, he was invited to a variety of dinners, and he wrote his mother about one at Mrs. Adair's:

Such an interesting party. Mr. Chamberlain-Lord Wolseley, Mr. Chaplin-Lord James, Sir Francis Jeune, and in fact
all the powers that be. Chamberlain was very nice to me
and I had quite a long talk with him on South Africa. . . .
Tonight I am dining with Lord James, who has the Duke of
Devonshire and a lot of "notables" so I hope to be quite
"au fait."[33]

It is difficult to exaggerate the value of such meetings for Winston's future. The political elite of London was a closed circle of small circumference. You were in or you were out. If you were in, the potential for leverage was great. Being "in" not only opened the necessary doors and warmed the welcomes, but it lit the cigar, poured the brandy, gave the knowing smile. It often meant the difference between getting something done and not getting something done.

Jennie made certain that Winston attended all the important parties while he was in London. And when she returned home that summer of 1896, she again made Great Cumberland Place a social center. "During this vivid summer my mother gathered constantly around her table politicians of both parties and leading figures in literature and art, together with the most lovely beings on whom the eye could beam," Winston wrote.

> On one occasion, however, she carried her catholicity too far. Sir John Willoughby, one of the Jameson raiders then on bail awaiting trial in London, was one of our oldest friends. In fact it was he who had first shown me how to arrange my toy cavalry soldiers in the proper formation of an advanced guard. Returning from Hounslow, I found him already arrived for luncheon. My mother was late. Suddenly the door opened and Mr. John Morley was announced.[34] I scented trouble; but boldly presented them to each other. Indeed, no other course was possible. John Morley drew himself up, and without extending his hand made a stiff little bow. Willoughby stared unconcernedly without acknowledging it. I squirmed inwardly and endeavored to make a pretense of conversation by asking commonplace questions of each alternately. Presently to my great relief, my mother arrived. She was not unequal to the occasion, which was a serious one. Before the meal was far advanced no uninformed person would have noticed that two out of the four gathered round the table never addressed one another directly. Towards the end it seemed to me they would not have minded doing so at all. But having taken their positions they had to stick to them. I suspected my mother of a design to mitigate the unusual asperities which gathered round this aspect of our affairs. She wanted to reduce the Raid to the level of ordinary politics. But blood had been shed; and that makes a different tale.[35]

Both of her sons were home often now, and both were delighted to be part of the social swirl. Winston knew the value of it and Jack enjoyed its pleasures. The activity at Great Cumberland Place now had a frenetic quality: parties, dinners, recitals, discussion groups. Shane Leslie remembered the homes of his mother and his two aunts as places that were

> full of servants all of whom looked as if they needed a holi-
> day by the seaside. Footmen seemed constantly harassed,
> cooks in a suicidal state tho cheering up when royalty con-
> sented to praise the soufflé, which had collapsed into a pan-
> cake on the stairs. The successive ladies' maids were as
> ambitious as their mistresses, but usually reached tearful
> state before the "Miss Jeromes" came out to an important
> dinner. One footman was so impressed by the frivolity that
> surrounded him that he fled the scene and, to his immense
> credit, took holy orders in the Church of England.[36]

It all cost money, however, a great deal of money, and Jennie's finances were always pinched. Her impulses and her far-ranging eye always exceeded her budget. She could no more change her style of living, though, than she could change her love of books or music or life.

Jennie was not the only one of the Jerome sisters with this problem. Leonie had the substantial financial resources of her husband's family to rely on, but Clara was often in critical need. "It was a common sight to see her running across the street to borrow a fiver from one of her sisters to pacify the butcher or candlestick maker."[37]

"Our finance is indeed involved!" Winston wrote his mother. "If I had not been so foolish as to pay a lot of bills I should have the money now." Rarely was a son so like his mother.[38]

Indeed it is difficult to understand how Jennie managed to keep afloat. All she really had was the $10,000 annual income from the rental of her father's house in New York. Since her mother had left her nothing and most of her husband's money was in trust funds for their sons, the upkeep of her new home was certainly beyond what she could afford. She must have been a marvelously adroit juggler of bank and insurance loans, but there must also have been a certain number of personal loans from friends, which were ultimately written off as gifts.

This need for money made Jennie especially vulnerable to a variety of get-rich-quick schemes. She again invested some money with her brother-in-law Moreton who "has just left on a journey, for the 500th time, to make a fortune." But it is one thing to lose money within the family; it is quite another to be suckered into a swindle. The man responsible for the latter was James Henry Cruikshank, who was introduced to the three sisters through the highest auspices—none other than the son of the highly respectable

Lord Cadogan. Cruikshank collected £4,000 from Jennie and her sisters and friends, promising that the money would be multiplied through some clever process. Instead, he simply spent it.[39] The loss was disastrous for Jennie.

There were few small secrets in London society, and Jennie's financial condition was not among them. Perhaps this was partly responsible for the many rumors of her imminent marriage.

To the Countess of Warwick Jennie wrote:

> . . . Dearest Daisy, I am *not* going to marry anyone. If a perfect darling with at least £40,000 a year wants me *very much* I might consider it. . . . [40]

There was one particular man who seemed to want her very much. He was not, perhaps, a *perfect darling,* but he did have much more than £40,000 a year. Furthermore, he and Jennie had known each other for many years. As an American magazine had noted, "Older New Yorkers recall the fact that Mr. Astor admired Lady Randolph before her marriage."[41] *The New York Times* had reported on its front page:

> The most interesting bit of society news which has been sent by cable from London of late is the engagement of Lady Randolph Churchill to William Waldorf Astor. This report will not occasion much surprise, for Mr. Astor's attentions to Lady Randolph Churchill have been so marked as to create no small amount of gossip. Letters received in New York by prominent people from friends in London from time to time, have contained hints of the probabilities of such an alliance. This announcement of the engagement will undoubtedly be received with enthusiasm by New York society. Although Lady Churchill who is a daughter of the late Leonard Jerome, and Mr. Astor, who is the son of the second John Jacob Astor, have lived a long time in England, they are thorough Americans. Had it not been for an unfortunate family jar,[42] several years ago, Mr. Astor might never have decided to make England his home. Lady Churchill, who is a cousin of Mrs. Clarence Gray Dinsmore, Mrs. David Thompson, and Mrs. Jordan L. Mott, is a most charming woman, and has been in the past somewhat of a power in English politics, her late husband owing much of his promotion to her influence, notwithstanding she is an American.[43]

"Wealthy Willie," as he was often called, reputedly had the largest fortune in America—a total of $200 million with an annual income of $6 million. A Frenchman visiting America wrote of him: "This man, this individual, who has only two arms and two legs, yes, and even a limit to his capacity for enjoyment, could stroll down Broadway or Fifth Avenue and stretch his arms hither and yon, saying, 'Mine! Mine! All mine!' "[44]

For all his money and property, Astor was a lonely and hated man, particularly in America.[45] When he moved to England, he referred to it as "a country where a gentleman might live."[46] Of America, Astor said, "Why travelled people of independent means should remain there more than a week, is not readily to be comprehended."[47]

In England, he had bought Cliveden, the great and lovely country estate noted for its spectacular views of the Thames. He furnished this Italian-style palace with exquisite paneling, magnificent tapestries, and the finest continental cooks. "The place is splendid," Jennie wrote her son Jack from Cliveden. "Mr. Astor has a great deal of taste."[48]

Jennie found much in Astor to appreciate besides his money and his good taste. A blue-eyed, ruggedly handsome man of firm character and great courage, he had a first-rate mind and a broad interest in history and languages. Besides having been Ambassador to Italy, he had also authored two novels.

There was little question that Astor wanted to marry Jennie. He had the reputation for being a cold man, so perhaps he needed her warmth. It hurt him to hear himself called a traitor in America, and Jennie's popularity could have enhanced his image. Moreover, Jennie's entrée would have been invaluable to him in his desire to be completely accepted in British society.

Astor's father had chosen his first wife for him, not even asking whether or not she was to his taste;[49] now he wanted to pick his own wife—the loveliest, brightest woman he could find. Jennie was a woman who could crumble any reserve, lighten any gloom, fill any emptiness.

What a fantastic temptation it must have been for Jennie! She had only to say "yes" and she would have been the richest woman in the world. All those niggling debts and piled up bills would be gone forever. She could have done anything within the realm of her creative imagination—writing, painting, operating a publishing company, supporting a whole movement of young authors, artists, musicians, creating her own theater, as her father once had—all this would have been possible for her. She could have been the hostess of the greatest literary and political salon of her time. She could have made herself and her husband a significant political force in England. She could have torn down the glass-topped wall around Cliveden's 300 acres and made it the social center of all Europe.

The challenge and the inclination probably would have been overpowering—for almost any other woman. Perhaps Jennie had the inclination, and assuredly she recognized the challenge, but she simply did not love Astor. She denied to the press the report of her engagement.

At the height of the rumors, the Prince of Wales was planning a house party in Scotland. He noticed William Waldorf Astor's name on the suggested guest list and crossed it off. "Not Mr. Astor," said the jealous Prince. "He bores me."

The Prince still saw a lot of Jennie. They were together at the Derby when the Prince's bay horse *Persimmon* won the race. "It was a very popular win and the crowd cheered tremendously," Jennie wrote Jack.[50] Her brother-in-law Moreton added in another letter, "As H.R.H. came down to lead *Persimmon* in, the Books shook hands with him and slapped him on the back, and one big Ringman roared out, 'Three cheers for the bloody crown!' "[51]

The Prince's victory lent an added gaiety to Cowes Week that year. The scent of mimosa seemed more pervasive than ever, and for Jennie there was a pride of admiring men trying to be more persuasive than ever. "What fun you must be having!" Winston wrote her. He said that his friend, "Bino" Stracey (Sir Edward Stracey) "had seen you there in great form—all over the place in a launch."[52]

After Cowes, the Prince of Wales was guest of honor at a weekend party at Deepdene to which Jennie secured an invitation for Winston. It was a great honor for a second lieutenant. Among the guests was his commanding officer Colonel Brabazon.

"I realized that I must be upon my best behavior: punctual, subdued, reserved, in short display all the qualities with which I am least endowed," Winston remarked. Unfortunately, he caught a delayed train that arrived even much later than scheduled. He expected to slip in unnoticed at the dinner table and to apologize afterward.

> When I arrived at Deepdene, I found the entire company assembled in the drawing room. The party it seemed without me would be thirteen. The prejudice of the Royal Family of those days against sitting down thirteen is well known. The Prince had refused point-blank to go in, and would not allow any rearrangement of tables to be made. He had, as was his custom, been punctual to the minute at half past eight. It was now twelve to nine. There, in this large room, stood the select and distinguished company in the worst of tempers, and there, on the other hand was I, a young boy asked as a special favor and a compliment. . . .

"Don't they teach you to be punctual in your regiment, Winston?" said the Prince in his most severe tone, and then looked acidly at Colonel Brabazon, who glowered. It was an awful moment![53]

His mother did not try to save him from that one. However, she did start to intervene for Winston in something more important. The Ninth Lancers were leaving shortly for South Africa and needed extra subaltern officers. Winston wanted to go.

My dear Mamma you cannot think how I would like to sail in a few days to scenes of adventure and excitement–to places where I could gain experience and derive advantage– rather than to the tedious land of India where I shall be equally out of the pleasures of peace and the chances of war. . . . I cannot believe that with all the influential friends you possess that I could not be allowed to go. . . . You really ought to leave no stone unturned to help me at such a period. . . . [54]

Winston was probably referring to the fact that Jennie had already tried to turn a few stones for him, with little success. Now he wanted her to try turning some more. Earlier that summer her requests for help from Lord Wolseley, Commander in Chief of the Army, and Lord Lansdowne, Secretary of State for War, had been fruitless. At that time the British Army was rigidly compartmentalized into areas of influence. Lord Lansdowne had made this clear when he answered Jennie, "The management of the operations in S. Africa is under Sir F. Carrington, & we are not in any way directing them, or interfering with the composition of his staff–I fear therefore that we can do nothing to find employment for Winston and I hope *you* may not be too much disappointed."[55]

Landsdowne had then offered some personal advice:

May I, as a friend, add this? I am not quite sure that in view of the enquiry which has been promised into the charges made recently against some of the officers of the 4th Hussars, it would be wise on Winston's part to leave England at this moment. There are plenty of ill-natured people about, and it is just conceivable that an attempt might be made to misrepresent his action.[56]

Truth Magazine had taken up the still-simmering racing scandal and the Bruce case in May; in June the charges made against some of the 4th Hussars were to be debated in the House of Commons.

Jennie accepted Lansdowne's advice and halted all her efforts to get Winston transferred to South Africa. For his part, Winston reconciled himself to the inevitable and wrote to Bourke Cockran, "I sail for India the 11th of September. I hope we shall meet again soon—if possible within a year. I may return to England via Japan after a little of India so perhaps I shall once more eat oysters and hominy with you in New York. Please send me press cuttings of your speeches."[57]

At about the time Winston would have arrived in India, Jennie wrote him, ". . . My darling, . . . take care of yrself & peer into that Bible sometimes, & love me very much. . . ."[58]

Twenty-Four

HE NEXT TWO YEARS WERE restless years for Jennie—restless and rootless. She had her own home, exquisitely refurnished, and she had made it a lively social center for her friends. Her friends reached into most strata of society, and she was spending more time visiting them all over England. She also spent an increasing amount of time at the Prince of Wales' country home at Sandringham. There were trips to France or Monte Carlo when she could afford it—and even when she couldn't. It was all very social, very time-filling, and yet very empty. Even though Winston was in India, her relationship with him seemed gradually to fill a large part of that emptiness. The regular correspondence between mother and son demonstrates how much they were in each other's thoughts at this time. The mail boat sailed once a week, and their letters seldom missed it. They were usually long, loving, revealing letters.

"The house is full of you—in every conceivable costume and style," Winston wrote her, soon after his arrival in India.

> My writing table is covered with photographs . . . my cigarette box that you brought me from Japan . . . my books . . .[1]
>
> I have thought of you so much, my darling boy . . . Darling Boy how I wish you were with me & that we cld have a good talk about everything. . . .[2]

> . . . Your letters . . . my dearest Mamma . . . I get none ex-
> cept yours. . . .[3]

Winston really had no one else. His brother Jack was barely seventeen
and still at Harrow. As much as Jack admired and idolized his older
brother, the distance between them—not simply the years, but their tastes
and temperaments as well—was always too great to cross easily. Bourke
Cockran's importance in Winston's life was growing, but he was of another
world. Winston's world was essentially England, and there he had no
close, personal friends. It would take unusual people to penetrate his ego
and his overwhelming self-confidence, to reach inside and find the troubled
human being.

Jennie therefore had to be everybody for Winston—mother, friend, sister, sweetheart. Her letters were packed with all the English news: politics,
books, social chitchat. Above all, they were personal letters, unsparing of
what was on her mind or in her heart. And his were the same. "I devote a
great deal of time and thought to my letters to you and endeavor to make
them not only worthy of the writer but even of the recipient. (Rather good
that!)" he wrote.[4]

Winston had quickly acclimated himself to all the comforts he could
find in India. Together with Reggie Barnes and another officer, he had
rented a palatial bungalow which Winston described as "all pink and
white, with heavy tiled roof and deep verandahs, sustained by white plaster
columns, wreathed in purple bougainvillea."[5] Land elsewhere was "bare as
a plate, hot as an oven,"[6] but Winston's two acres had 250 rose trees. "We
built a large tiled barn with mud walls containing stabling for thirty horses
and ponies. Our three butlers formed a triumvirate in which no internal
dissensions ever appeared. . . . Thus freed from mundane cares, we devoted ourselves to the serious purpose of life. . . ."[7]

This serious purpose was polo three times a week, butterfly collecting
("My garden is full of Purple Emperors, White Admirals and Swallow-
tails"[8]), and cutting three great basins of flowers every morning.

Jennie admonished him. "I hope you will find time for reading," she
wrote. "Think how you will regret the waste of time when you are in politics & will feel yr want of knowledge."[9]

Winston already had become sensitive to this lack in himself. He told
Jack, "I shall envy you the enjoyment of a liberal education, and of the
power to appreciate the classical works,"[10] and in his memoirs he noted,
"The desire for learning came over me. I began to feel myself wanting in
even the vaguest knowledge about many large spheres of thought."[11]

Jennie enthusiastically began to make her contribution. She sent him
the eight volumes of Gibbon's *Decline and Fall of the Roman Empire,* which had

so influenced the thinking and style of her husband. It had a similar impact on Winston:

> I was immediately dominated both by the story and the style. All through the long glistening hours of the Indian day, from when we quitted stables till the evening shadows proclaimed the hour of Polo, I devoured Gibbon. I rode triumphantly through it from end to end and enjoyed it all.[12]

Jennie also sent him twelve volumes of Macaulay—eight volumes of history and four of essays. He described his reading of it as embarking on a "splendid romance, and I voyaged with full sail in a strong wind." Winston described Gibbon as "stately and impressive" and Macaulay as "crisp and forcible. Both are fascinating. . . ."[13] The combination of Gibbon and Macaulay made a lasting impression on both his writing and speaking styles. It gave him, he said, "the feel for words fitting and falling into their places like pennies in the slot."[14]

Jennie continued to send him a selected library of books, mostly history and philosophy—Plato's *Republic,* Aristotle's *Politics,*[15] Darwin's *On the Origin of Species,* Malthus' *On Population,* Pascal's *Provincial Letters,* Adam Smith's *Wealth of Nations,* and the entire twenty-seven volume set of the *Annual Register.*

"The method I pursue with the Annual Register is [not] to read the debate until I have recorded my own opinion on paper of the subject—having regard only to general principles," Winston wrote her.

> After reading, I reconsider and finally write. I hope by a persevering continuance of this practice to build up a scaffolding of logical and consistent views which will perhaps tend to the creation of a logical and consistent mind.
>
> Of course the Annual Register is only valuable for its facts. A good knowledge of these would arm me with a sharp sword. Macaulay, Gibbon, Plato etc must train the muscles to wield that sword to the greatest effect.[16]

Jennie was absolutely delighted to play such a vital role in the development of her son. At his request she sent him "the detailed Parliamentary history (Debates, Divisions, Parties, cliques) . . . of the last 100 years. . . ."[17] Every book, every letter became a forum for discussion and cross-comment between mother and son. Of course in the process Jennie was stretching her own mind as well as Winston's. A later critic commented that she must have had an "inordinate belief in his capacity to digest" because she had sent him Lecky's work on the *Rise and Influence of Rationalism,* which was "stiff reading even for a well-educated man."[18] But Jennie knew the reach of her son's mind. Winston himself later characterized it as "an empty, hungry mind, and with fairly strong jaws; and what I got, I bit."[19]

Winston earlier had sent his mother a book, too, one entitled *Making Sketches,* "which interests me very much and which I am sure will please you still more–as you will have seen many of the scenes herein described."[20]

Jennie, meanwhile, maintained her customary maternal protectiveness, reminding him to be careful "of what you drink."[21] But she was particularly concerned about his horse racing in India. His American aunt, Duchess Lily, the widow of Randolph's brother the Duke of Marlborough, had given him a typewriter, a charger, and was now sending him a racing pony. "I want to talk to you very seriously about the racing pony," his mother wrote.

> It may be dead for all I know, but if it is not I want you to promise me to sell it. I had a long talk with the Prince . . . & he begged me to tell you that you ought not to race, only because it is not a good business in India–they are not square & the best of reputations get spoiled over it. *You* don't know but everyone else does that it is next to impossible to race in India & keep clean hands. It appears that Colonel Brab[azon] told the Prince that he wished you hadn't this pony. I am sure you will regret it if you don't [sell it].[22]

But Winston did not agree. ". . . When I see *all* those with whom I have to live and many whom I respect owning ponies–I must confess I do not see why you should expect me to deprive myself of a pleasure which they honourably and legitimately enjoy–or why you should distrust my ability to resist the temptation to resort to malpractice. . . ." As an obedient son, however, he added, ". . . If you still wish me to get rid of the pony–after you have considered what I have written here–I will do so . . . but . . . I beg you not to ask me. . . ."[23]

She answered, ". . . Do tell me in yr next that you have taken steps to sell the pony. You have no idea how it worries me. . . ."[24]

Winston then took another tack: ". . . Tell His Royal Highness–if he says anything further about racing in India–that I intend to be just as much an example to the Indian turf as he is to the English–as far as fair play goes."[25]

Jennie probably did not expect to win this contest of wills, and she later wrote Jack, "Of course I have given in about Winston's pony–and I hope he will sell it after it has won a race–if it ever does!"[26] The purpose of her exchange on this subject was to remind Winston of the scandal with which he had been associated only recently. Thanks to her well-placed friends in the Army and Government, the brush had tarred him only lightly. But it must not happen again. If ever he wanted to do anything in public life, he must be more than careful, he must be utterly irreproachable. Without saying any of this directly, Jennie had made her point.

Winston has described his daily life in India in a series of vivid pictures:

> Just before dawn, every morning, one was awakened by a dusky figure with a clammy hand adroitly lifting one's chin and applying a gleaming razor to a lathered and defenseless throat. By six o'clock the regiment was on parade, and we rode to a wide plain and there drilled and maneuvered for an hour and a half. We then returned to baths at the bungalow and breakfast in the Mess. Then at nine, stables and orderly room till about half-past ten; then home to the bungalow before the sun attained its fiercest ray. . . . Long before eleven o'clock all white men were in shelter. We nipped across to luncheon at half-past one in the blistering heat and then returned to sleep till five o'clock. Now the station begins to live again. It is the hour of Polo. It is the hour for which we have been living all day long. I was accustomed in those days to play every chukka I could get into. . . . I very seldom played less than eight and more often ten or twelve.
>
> As the shadows lengthened over the polo ground, we ambled back perspiring and exhausted to hot baths, rest, and an 8:30 dinner, to the strains of the regimental band and the clinking of ice in well-filled glasses. Thereafter those who were not so unlucky as to be caught by the Senior Officers to play a tiresome game then in vogue called "Whist" sat smoking in the moonlight till half-past ten or eleven at the latest signalled the "And so to bed." Such was the long, long Indian day. . . .[27]

"Life out here is stupid, dull and uninteresting," he wrote to his mother. ". . . This is an abominable country to live long in. Comfort you get— company you miss. I meet few people worth talking to. . . ."[28]

He had already had occasion to write, "I do wish, my dear Mama, you could come out . . . ,"[29] and he had invited Bourke Cockran, too. "You can't think how interesting this country is. . . . You must come out here—if only for a flying visit. . . ."[30]

His correspondence with Cockran dealt with a broad range of subjects. Winston, for example, expressed his disapproval of William Jennings

Bryan's demand for sweeping changes in currency. "Even if you prove to me that our present system is radically bad—my opinion is unaltered. . . . A man suffering from dyspepsia might pray for fresh intestines but he would fare badly while the alteration was being effected. . . . What Bryan has done is like an inebriate regulating a chronometer with a crowbar. . . ." He also congratulated Cockran on William McKinley's election to the Presidency and discussed the expense of presidential elections in America compared to the lesser cost in England. He then added, "Yours may be the government for gods, . . . ours at least is suitable for men."[31] His words, indeed, were falling into their proper places "like pennies into a slot."

In his letters to his mother, Winston was equally critical of British politicians:

> Among the leaders of the Tory Party are two whom I despise and detest as politicians above all others—Mr. Balfour & George Curzon. The one—a languid, lazy, lack-a-daisical cynic—the unmonumental figurehead of the Conservative Party; the other the spoiled darling of politics—blown with conceit—insolent from undeserved success—the typification of the superior Oxford prig.[32]

This letter must have jolted Jennie, for Balfour and Curzon were not only old and valued friends of hers, but they would prove to be of enormous help in advancing the career of her cynical son. Jennie, however, always had taught her sons to express their opinions about anybody or anything, and she would not counsel them differently now.

Jennie only wished that Jack had more of his brother's directness. "He is not given to strong opinions," Winston said of Jack, "and it is very difficult to get at what he really thinks."[33] Jennie earlier had suggested to Jack the possibility of a career in an infantry regiment, where her contacts were so firm that she felt he would be accepted despite his bad eye. When Jack demurred, she answered, "I do not wish to stand in your way if your heart is not on going into the Army."[34] Jack seemed to change his mind a year later, and Jennie answered, "Darling I don't want to make any tiresome remarks, but you must remember that your want of decision as regards your likes and dislikes and choice of a career has been a drawback to you—I have never heard you before really express a real desire to go into the Army. It is not too late. . . . Bless you, my child. Don't fret. All will come right for you, I am sure."[35]

Jack again changed his mind and now preferred the Bar, but despite his uncertainty about his career, the one thing of which he was certain was that he wanted no more of Harrow. Jennie was skeptical. "Your last report, just in, is very good and they seem to think you are doing well. Perhaps it would be a mistake to start a fresh place in the winter. Well! You must say what you want. If you are *very* keen to come away, I won't keep you there."[36]

Jennie went to Harrow to visit the Headmaster James Welldon, and she reported to Winston that Jack

> is too mature for school life—even Welldon thought so. . . .
>
> I have been very busy arranging things for Jack. I went to see Welldon and had a long talk with him as to his future. I am much against his going in the Army. I can't afford to put him in a smart cavalry regiment & in anything else he wld be lost & unhappy. Besides at the best it is a poor career. I think he might do [better] at the Bar. He has plenty of ability & common sense, a good presence, & with perseverance & influence he ought to get on. The City he hates. He is going to leave Harrow this term, spend a year or more in France & Germany, then study Greek for six months with a tutor & go to Oxford. He seems to like the idea. Meanwhile he is coming with me to Blenheim for Xmas."[37]

Taking up the issue with his brother, Winston told Jack:

> If you feel no desire to go into the Army, I should be the last person to press you to do so. . . . If you are not keen when you start you will never do any good in the Army. . . . But does this not apply with greater force to the Bar? . . . If you go to the Bar equipped only (as you put it) with "moderate work, little brains & lots of people to help you" you will inevitably end as a "briefless barrister." . . . You see, when people go to a lawyer—or when they go to a doctor—they don't ask—for good manners & lots of influence—what they want is a man who will win their cases or cure their diseases. . . . Don't think of drifting languidly and placidly—as your letter apparently suggests to the Bar. . . .
>
> I think you have great talents, Jack . . . but I *am* perfectly certain that unless you start full of enthusiasm and keenness, you will never develop your abilities. . . .[38]

To his mother, Winston wistfully observed, "What a strange inversion of fortune—that I should be a soldier and Jack at college."[39]

As Jennie had told Winston, Jack would spend Christmas with her at Blenheim. Christmas at Blenheim Palace, the Marlborough ancestral home, was a family tradition that could not be ignored, even though Jennie and her mother-in-law were at best only on polite terms with each other: ". . . Between you and I," Jennie told Winston, she [Frances, the Dowager Duchess of Marlborough] is not making herself pleasant to me & we have not exchanged a word—but I do not mind & perhaps it is as well. To the world we can appear friends, anything of the kind in private is impossible."[40]

The Dowager Duchess had never stopped grieving for her son Randolph, and she was bitter that Jennie was not similarly grieving. Her ill-will extended beyond Jennie to her grandsons, particularly to Winston. Thus when nineteen-year-old Consuelo Vanderbilt had become the Ninth Duchess of Marlborough the previous year, the Dowager Duchess had told her that "Your first duty is to have a child, and it must be a son, because it would be intolerable to have that little upstart Winston become Duke. Are you in the family way?"[41]

Consuelo and Jennie had quickly become very fond of each other, and despite the Dowager Duchess, Jennie's relations with the rest of the family were always mutually affectionate. Even Randolph's sisters were her friends. Of her sister-in-law Fanny, Lady Tweedmouth, Jennie said, "Without exception the noblest character I have ever met . . . her sympathy and advice were a tower of strength to all who came in contact with her."[42]

Even if there had been no such relationship with Randolph's sisters, Jennie would have maintained her link with the Marlborough family. Her own position in British society was solid enough so that she did not need the association for herself, but she did want to keep it intact for her sons. There is no question that Blenheim Palace and the historic Marlborough name were prestigious and influential factors in Great Britain.

Duchess Lily, the mother of the Ninth Duke of Marlborough, was also close to Jennie, not only because the Duchess was an American and had been widowed but because Jennie had been her social buffer in the early days. The Duchess was now married to Lord William Beresford, and it was to their home at Deepdene that Jennie went when, as in that winter of 1896, she wanted the quiet of the countryside. Her iron nerves had been upset by the persistent publicity of the scandal about Winston, the rumors of her engagement to Astor, and Cruikshank's swindle.

Winston was luckier that winter: he found the one thing Jennie lacked—romance. The young lady's name was Pamela Plowden. "The most beautiful girl I have ever seen—bar none," Winston wrote his mother.[43]

It might have made Jennie a little jealous to find her son so taken with the beauty of another woman, when he had so often written that there was no one more beautiful than his mother. On his twenty-second birthday, Jennie wrote, "I wish I cld give you a good kiss . . ."[44] Instead she sent him a check for £50, and made no reference to Pamela.

Jennie had met Pamela and knew her father, Sir Trevor John Chichele Chichele-Plowden, then British Resident to Hyderabad. Pamela was pretty enough to have been the object of many men's affections, and there was no indication how serious she felt about Winston. Jennie knew that Pamela could cope with Winston but she did not know if Winston could cope with Pamela.

Winston's feeling for Pamela, however, was obviously not overpowering enough to divert him from his main goal. He was determined to join Kitchener's army in Egypt in the advance up the Nile to reconquer the Sudan. "I should never forgive myself if an expedition started next year and I felt that it was my own fault I was not there . . . *Please do your best*," he wrote his mother.[45]

Jennie wrote directly to Kitchener, whom she knew rather well, but earlier she had explained to Winston:

> I am going to wire you today to write at once & apply to the War Office to be allowed to go to Egypt. . . . The chances of being taken are extremely remote as the competition is tremendous—but there is an outside chance of Sir H. Kitchener's personal influence being brought to bear & I am going to try it for you. Should it succeed you must know & remember that it means signing a paper to the effect that you will serve in the Egyptian Army for two years—& there will be no getting out of it if you don't like it—On the other hand should this fail you must not let it unsettle you & make you take a dislike to your work in India. Life is not always what one wants it to be, but to make the best of it as it is, is the only way of being happy—Of course the War Office will take no notice of yr application but as soon as you have applied I will write to Kitchener & if he asks for you you will probably be allowed to go. In my heart of hearts I have doubts as to whether it wd be the best thing for you—but Fate will decide.[46]

This was the kind of letter Jennie wrote to both her sons at every turning point in their lives. It was a way of training their point of view, giving direction to their attitudes, offering a method of analysis. They received this from no one else. Winston particularly needed someone to temper his youthful enthusiasm, sober his daydreams, clarify the alternatives.

For many Englishmen, Lord Horatio Herbert Kitchener was becoming the personification of the whole concept of British imperial expansion. The new Sirdar (Commander-in-Chief of the Egyptian Army) was a complex man. An intensely self-disciplined man who would not tolerate inefficiency or excuse failure, he was equally impatient of criticism or opposition. Margot Asquith had once written of him: ". . . He is either very stupid or very clever, and never gives himself away."[47]

Kitchener set the fashion of the strong, silent man, never in a hurry. Winston Churchill later said that Kitchener "will never be fettered by fear, and not very often by sympathy." And correspondent G. W. Steevens wrote of him, "Erect, six foot and more of flesh and bone, but mainly wire, tanned and mustached, yet with 'no body to carry his mind, no face to keep his brain behind.' "[48]

"I don't know how soon I may hear from the Sirdar," Jennie wrote Winston,

> but I will wire & if he takes you, you will have to square yr Colonel—but I don't suppose you wld join them until the end of March. In any case, when you receive this make enquiries & find out how much money you will want & answer by return—should you be taken—as I shld have to find it for you & it cannot be done in a moment.[49]

But a week later, Jennie said that she was beginning to think the situation "is more than doubtful, as I am told Kitchener won't take anyone under 27. . . ."[50]

"Well, my dearest Mummy," Winston replied on January 7, "I hope we may meet in Cairo but I begin to fear from your silence that the answer is adverse. Perhaps however as the Sirdar has been up at Dongala your letter will have been delayed."[51]

Winston was right. Kitchener was at Dongala, the first stage of his advance up the Nile, and Jennie finally received the note he had written to her on December 30 from his Frontier Force headquarters:

> My dear Lady Randolph,
>   I will note your son's name for special service and if he wishes to serve in the Egyptian Army he should send in his application through his Colonel to the A.G. [Adjutant General] Egyptian Army Cairo. I have however at present no vacancies in the cavalry but I will have his name put down on the list.[52]

Winston felt that meant there was still hope. "Keep pegging away about Egypt. I do not mind waiting and you will never make me believe there is anything which you could not in time achieve."[53] And again: "You will see that if I go to Egypt & if things turn out well, it might almost be worth my while to stick to soldiering. . . . I beg you to leave no stone unturned in your endeavor to obtain a vacancy for me."[54]

Jennie could not have been pleased to hear from Winston that he might "stick to soldiering," as she had already cautioned him:

> How little one hears of any of the Generals in time of peace. There is really very little honour & glory to be got out of the Army. A moderate MP gets better known in the country & has more chance of success than a really clever man in the Army.[55]

Earlier she had put it more plainly: "I am looking forward to the time when we shall live together again & all my political ambitions shall be centered in you."[56]

Consciously or subconsciously, she had more and more intertwined the ambitions of her son with her own ambitions. There was no limit to their combined drive, their combined determination. She had not been able to make her husband Prime Minister of England, but now she had a fresh chance with her son. It had been no idle whim when she refused to surrender her husband's robes of office after his resignation as Chancellor of the Exchequer. "I am saving them for my son," she had said.

Now it all became clear. How could she marry Bourke Cockran and go to the United States? Her son needed her in England. She could not desert his ambition because his ambition was now her own.

Twenty-Five

ARLY IN 1897 JENNIE HAD RETURNED to Paris, primarily to install Jack with a family in Versailles, where he could live for the year and study French. The persistently attentive Bourke Cockran synchronized his plans so as to be in Paris at the same time. Jennie also dined with the Breteuils, and she and Madame Breteuil, both Americans, must have scrutinized each other carefully. There was still another of Jennie's admirers in Paris, the legendary Cecil Rhodes, after whom the then British province of Rhodesia had been named.

The monumental blunder of the Jameson Raid in the Transvaal had forced Rhodes' resignation as Premier of the Cape Colony, but he was still a British colossus in South Africa and one of the richest and most powerful men in the world. He was also the kind of man who would and did go unarmed to meet the leaders of a native rebellion and persuade them to throw down their spears.

Rhodes' brother expressed the wish that Rhodes might marry Jennie. "Colonel Rhodes told me that he would sooner his brother married you—if you would have him—than any other woman in the world!"[1]

Rhodes had a passion for diamonds, power, and flattery. He had no use for sports or society or the ordinary amusements of rich men. He also was contemptuous of most women—Jennie being one of the few exceptions. Jennie, however, was not stirred by Rhodes: "He does not give the idea of a

clever man—a strong one, if you like, determined and dogged, but intellec-
tually weak."[2]

Jennie decided not to linger in rainy, muggy Paris, but to continue on to
Monte Carlo. Monsieur de Breteuil had told her he would be delighted to
invite Jack to his home whenever Jack was free, and Bourke had promised
to spend some time with him before leaving Paris. "I hated leaving you,
dear boy," Jennie wrote her son. "I am writing you a line before I go to bed
so that you may get it tomorrow & know that your Mama is thinking of
you. . . . Good night my darling Jack—work hard and don't get 'mopy.' Fill
you your life . . . & the time will fly. . . ."[3]

"Jack darling," she wrote afterward,

> the temptations of a big town are strong, I know; and you are
> very young, but you are sensible beyond your years and a
> great dear—and I am sure my confidence in you would not be
> displaced. Keep the good society and the friends I have intro-
> duced you to, and you would come to no harm. . . . Darling
> child, remember this year is the only one of your life you can
> give up entirely to French. Make the most of it—Do, like
> Winston, talk incessantly![4]

Jennie, though, had sharper words for Winston, who had overdrawn
his checking account, even after a warning from his bank:

> I *must* say I think it is *too* bad of you—indeed it is hardly
> honorable knowing as you do that you are dependent on me
> & that I give you the biggest allowance I *possibly can,* more
> than I can afford. I am very hard up & this has come at a very
> inopportune moment & puts me to much inconvenience. . . .
> I have paid it. But I have told them at Cox's not to apply to
> me in the future as you must manage yr own affairs. As for
> yr wild talk & scheme of coming home for a month, it is ab-
> solutely out of the question, not only on account of money,
> but for the sake of yr reputation. They will say & with some
> reason that you can't stick to anything. You have only been
> out 6 months & it is on the cards that you may be called to
> Egypt. There is plenty for you to do in India. I confess I am
> quite disheartened about you. You seem to have no real pur-
> pose in life & won't realize at the age of 22 that for a man life
> means work, & hard work if you mean to succeed. . . . It is
> useless my saying more—we have been over this ground
> before—it is not a pleasant one. I will only repeat that I cannot

help you any more & if you have any grit in you & are worth yr salt you will try & live within yr income & cut down yr expenses in order to do it. You cannot but feel ashamed of yrself under the present circumstances–I haven't the heart to write more.[5]

That was, of course, the kind of stern lecture that a father ordinarily would have given. It was comparatively easy for Jennie to be a surrogate father for an obedient son like Jack, but Winston had the same kind of stubborn, imperious nature she had. He, in turn, framed his answer coolly, discussing many other things first, and then bringing up the overdrawn account but blaming the bank. Jennie simply could not maintain her sternness. "Why an extraordinary boy you are as regards yr business affairs," she wrote.

You never say a word about them, & then spring things upon one. If you only told me when you were hard up–& why– perhaps I shd not be so angry. But I don't believe you ever know how you stand with yr account at the Bank. . . . Dearest this is the only subject on which we ever fall out. I do wish you wld try & reform–if you only realized how little I have, & how impossible it is for me to get any more. I have raised all I can, & I assure you unless something extraordinary turns up I see ruin staring me in the face.[6]

She then detailed her income and expenses:

Out of 2700 pounds a year 800 of it goes to you 2 boys, 410 for house rent and stables, which leaves me 1500 for everything–taxes, servants, stables, food, dress, travelling–& now I have to pay money in interest borrowed. I *really* fear for the future. I am telling you all this darling in order that you may see how impossible it is for me to help you–and how you *must* in future depend on yrself.[7]

Two weeks later she stressed the matter again:

. . . Darling I lay awake last night thinking about you & how much I wanted to help you–if only I had some money I wld do so. I am so proud of you & all yr great and enduring qualities. I feel sure that if you live you will make a name for yrself. But I know to do it you have to be made of stern stuff

376 ◆ RALPH G. MARTIN

> & not mind sacrifice & self denial. I feel I am reading you a
> lecture & you will vote my letters a bore–but you know that
> I do not mean it in that way. . . .[8]

How could Jennie lecture Winston on money, when she herself was so
much like him? Her own fantasy was that she would one day make a fortune at Monte Carlo. Newspapers played up the stories of those who did,
particularly one American who purportedly broke the bank several times,
winning the equivalent of $150,000.

Jennie had no such luck at Monte Carlo this time, but she did have a
visitor. "The Prince came over from Nice and dined with me," she wrote
Winston. "I told him of your wish to come home & he begged me to tell
you that he was very much against it & thought you ought to take the opportunity to go to the frontier & see something of the country."[9] To Jack,
Jennie added, "The Prince told me he had spoken to the Queen about him
[Winston]."[10]

There also had been other news of her sons. Bourke had detailed his
discussions and activities with Jack in Paris. And Brabazon had informed
her that he had made a special trip to a meeting of the Turf Club to successfully sponsor Winston for membership.[11] And "Bimbash" Stewart, a
friend of Kitchener's and Jennie's, had told her that Kitchener wanted Winston to have the first vacancy. "But you must take Bimbash's statement
with a grain of salt," Jennie had warned Winston.[12]

Winston, however, now had more immediate and exciting plans. On
April 21 he wrote to his mother: "I am afraid you will regard this letter
somewhat in the aspect of a bombshell." With the declaration of war by
Turkey on Greece, Winston wanted to serve again as a war correspondent.
But he was unsure which side to go on.

> This, my dearest Mamma, must depend on you. . . . If you
> can get me good letters to the Turks, to the Turks I will go.
> If to the Greeks–to the Greeks. . . . In thinking all this out it
> has occurred to me that Sir Edgar Vincent could probably
> do everything for me in Constantinople & could get me at-
> tached to some general's staff etc. as in Cuba. On the other
> hand, you know the King of Greece and could of course
> arrange matters in that quarter. . . . Of course nearly every
> paper has one [correspondent] there already, but I have no
> doubt you will find one to avail themselves of my ser-
> vices. . . . These arrangements I leave to you and I hope
> when I arrive at Brindisi I shall find the whole thing cut and
> dried. . . .

... Of course my dear Mamma–if you don't want me to go I won't.[13]

But as usual, Winston threw in his standard final plea, which nearly always worked: "I know you will not stand in my way in this matter."[14] Jennie considered it "a wild scheme," but consulted her friends at the Foreign Office and confided to Jack, "Luckily the war will be over by the time he gets home."[15] As she informed Winston, it was "like a damp firework."[16]

Bourke Cockran had returned to London and kept up his correspondence with Winston. Before his homecoming, Winston had written him, "I am looking forward to seeing you and hearing some account of your rhetorical successes, so much so that it makes me feel quite tired to wait."[17]

Jennie kept Jack informed about Winston. "You may imagine what talks Winston and I have been having," she wrote to him shortly after Winston's return. "He looks very well, I think, and is more quiet."[18] She also advised Jack that she was sending him copies of the *Daily Graphic*, some money for horseback riding and dancing lessons, and would contact him about a music teacher as soon as Breteuil had found one. "Politics are so interesting just now, and you must be *au fait*," she added.[19] She was also expecting him to join them soon in London.

In 1897 horses were still very much a part of the London scene. Young boys continued to chase in and out of traffic collecting horse dung to sell as fertilizer. For most people, the bells on the hansom cabs still sounded more romantic than the blare of the rare automobile horn. However, the science section of the *Annual Register* reported: "Prominent among the matters of general scientific interest has been a development of mechanical propulsion for road-carriages. In this country, the use of such carriages or 'motor-cars' is restricted by the act preventing any such vehicle exceeding a speed of more than four miles an hour. ..." The Mayor of Tunbridge Wells had put a number of horseless carriages on exhibition and one critic noted, "The new invention was generally derided. Besides, the law required that a man with a red flag should always precede a mechanically-driven vehicle on the road."

These new mechanical monsters did not acquire the seal of social approval until 1898 when the Prince of Wales took his first motorcar drive. There is a photograph of the occasion showing Prince Edward with three other passengers, one of them Jennie. "The motor-car will become a necessity for every English gentleman," the Prince announced.[20]

Maybe, but the bicycle was still enormously popular. "I went across Albert Bridge from Cheyne Court at 9:45," wrote one diarist.

> The Park Road was already full of bicyclists and many were already having coffee and rolls. I rode for a while with

General Sir Evelyn Wood and Sir Francis Jeune, the divorce judge. Colonel Brabazon, Mr. Claude Lowther, Mr. Sidney Greville, Lady Sykes, who rides a horse better than she does a bicycle, Mrs. Brown Potter, the actress, Lady Essex, Princess Dolgorouki, Mr. Lewis Waller, the actor, and so on. Mr. Henry Chaplin stood on the sidewalk looking on. He told me he prefers to ride an 18-hand-high horse that hasn't got wobbly wheels. . . .[21]

Jennie was a bicycle devotee and bought one to send to Jack: "I have got you a very good bicycle for 8 pounds. . . ."[22] She also reported, "I have been initiated into the mysteries of golf, and I like it . . . but I am quite sworn off poker which is a good thing—sixpenny bezique is now my form!"[23]

1897 was Diamond Jubilee Year, marking the fiftieth year of Queen Victoria's reign. The Queen had occasionally gone to Regent Street in an unpretentious open carriage, without even special traffic arrangements, but one day she was recognized near Hyde Park Corner. Someone called out, "It's the Queen! God bless her!" Suddenly all the traffic around her came to a halt as everyone stared at this little white-haired woman dressed completely in black.

And then an electric thrill seemed to go round. The passengers inside and outside the vehicles sprang up; the prim coachmen and footmen in their private carriages, usually as stolid as wax dolls, rose to their feet and shouted like schoolboys; the foot passengers swelled the cheering; such a cheer! It was a sight I would not have missed for worlds, that forest of waving hats and handkerchiefs, the faces of the people, startled for once out of their British reserve. Everyone in the crowd fixed eyes on the Queen as on a dearly-loved friend; everyone shouted that came near, "God bless you, Ma'am!" "How well she looks!! A long life to her! Hurrah!" As for the Queen, she burst into tears, and bowed right and left, making spasmodic attempts to dry her eyes with her black-bordered handkerchief, between the bows.[24]

For the formal Diamond Jubilee Procession from Buckingham Palace to St. Paul's Cathedral the Queen was in command of her dignity and carried a little sunshade. The weather had been misty and cold, the sky threatening, but just as Her Majesty left the palace, the sun broke through, bright and warm, to produce the proverbial "Queen's weather."

She seemed aged and fragile, still dressed in black, but now with cream-colored feathers in her bonnet. She rode in an open landau, drawn by eight cream-colored horses, and along the way the lampposts were decked with flowers.

"No one ever, I believe, has met with such an ovation as was given me," the Queen wrote in her Journal. "Every face seemed to be filled with real joy."

Jennie's nephew Shane Leslie described the occasion. "The slower the procession went, the more gorgeous it seemed. The Queen herself might have been playing her own part in a film of the future."[25] Leslie remembered overhearing someone say, "Imagine having seen a little lady whose Grandpa actually owned all America!"[26] The dome of St. Paul's Cathedral was floodlit by powerful searchlights and the streets were lined with colored lamps. There was the fine selection of British troops from all over the Empire, Field Marshal Roberts on his white charger, prime ministers from a dozen colonies, the German Emperor, and all sorts of potentates.

"There was a large tent in the garden at Buckingham Palace for the guests," one witness recalled.

> But, apparently, the question of ventilation for the guests had been overlooked. The result was that, when the tent was full, the heat was so great that many nearly fainted. Reggi Brett (afterwards Lord Esher) was at that time Secretary at the Office of Works, and therefore, everybody appealed to him. He said that obviously a current of air was necessary, and that if windows were cut in the canvas at each end of the tent, that would solve the difficulty. As there appeared to be no one capable of cutting holes in the canvas, he determined to do this himself. He was in Court dress and had a rapier at his side. This he drew, and at once thrust it through the canvas side of the tent. To his horror, there was a piercing yell, and it turned out that a housemaid was on the other side, looking through a crack. Mercifully, she was not hurt.[27]

Several weeks later the ball of the season was held at Devonshire House in Piccadilly. More than a ball, it was a spectacle. The guests were the most prominent people in England, including the Prince and Princess of Wales and assorted other royalty. "Everyone of note and interest was there representing the intellect, beauty and fashion of the day," Jennie wrote.[28] They had all been asked to come dressed as a famous person in history, and *Town Topics* reported that ". . . those who were present say that it was a sight . . . never to be equalled within living memory. . . ."[29]

Jennie described the frenzied thought and preparation that had gone into the costumes:

> ... Great were the confabulations and mysteries. With bated breath and solemn mien a fair dame would whisper to some few dozen or more that she was going to represent the Queen of Cyprus or Aspasia, Fredegonde or Petrarch's Laura, but the secret *must* be kept. Historical books were ransacked for inspirations, old pictures and engravings were studied, and people became learned in respect to past celebrities of whom they had never before heard.
>
> The men, oddly enough, were even more excited about their costumes than the women, and paid extravagant sums for them. There is no doubt that when a man begins to think about his appearance, he competes with women to some purpose, money, time and thought being of no account to him. On the night of the ball, the excitement rose to fever heat. Every coiffeur in London and Paris was requisitioned, and so busy were they that some of the poor victims actually had their locks tortured early in the morning, sitting all day in a rigid attitude or ... "walking delicately."[30]

The Prince of Wales came as the Grand Prior of the Order of St. John of Jerusalem, adorned with a dazzling diamond cross, and a carefully managed ruff to suit his short neck, looking "as if he had stepped off the stage of 'Les Huguenots.'" Princess Alexandra was Marguerite de Valois, attended by female nobility.[31]

The Duke of Devonshire was the Emperor Charles V, and the Duchess was Zenobia, Queen of Palmyra, "a dazzling vision of golden suns, jewels, peacock feathers, gems of all kinds, and a high crown with two startling horns, and a lovely pear-shaped pearl hung low on her lovely smooth brow."[32]

The Duke and Duchess "received on a raised dais at the end of the ballroom the endless procession who passed by, bowing, curtsying, or salaaming, according to the characters they represented."[33]

Princess Pless was the Queen of Sheba. Dressed in a blue silk gown covered with diamonds and turquoises, she "looked like a lily in a vase of purple and gold," and was "surrounded by a retinue in Oriental garb, some of whom so far sacrificed their appearance as to darken their faces."[34] One of the sacrificers was the Princess' younger brother, George Cornwallis-West, who would soon begin spending a significant part of his life with Jennie.

That evening, though, he left early, cursing the designer who had created his costume of "a multi-colored bed-quilt."

The woman who had loved Jennie's father, Mrs. Fanny Ronalds, represented Music as she had once before at a ball in New York, but this time her headdress was lit by electricity instead of gas. Lady Maud Warrender was most impressed by the two sisters who came as the "Furies" and "wore hairnets to keep their heads tidy!"[35]

Jennie also noted, perhaps a little cattily, that a certain Lady who had covered herself with priceless jewels was actually on the verge of bankruptcy. But she appreciated Lady Tweedmouth dressed as Queen Elizabeth "with eight gigantic guardsmen surrounding her, all dressed as yeomen of the guard." And she remarked upon the well-known baronet who "had been perfecting himself for weeks in the role of Napoleon, his face and figure lending themselves to the impersonation. But what was his dismay at finding in the vestibule a second victor of Austerlitz ever more lifelike and correct than himself. It was indeed a Waterloo for both of them."[36]

Jennie was dressed as the Byzantine Empress Theodora, a most interesting choice. For precedent there was, of course, "the divine Theodora," the leading character in Disraeli's novel *Lothair*, who wore a diamond star on her forehead, as Jennie did at one time. The similarity was not coincidental, as Disraeli had been a friend and admirer of Jennie's. The Empress Theodora was almost as multi-faceted as a diamond star. The daughter of an animal trainer, she had become an actress, a dancing girl, a courtesan, and finally the mistress and wife of the sixth-century Emperor Justinian I. Justinian was a man of considerable energy, but he was neither strong-willed nor profoundly intelligent. Theodora possessed many of the qualities he lacked. In addition to an imperious will and a piercing glance, she had intellectual brilliance and an extraordinary beauty. As Gibbon wrote in his *Decline and Fall of the Roman Empire* "Either love or adulation might proclaim that painting and poetry were incapable of delineating the matchless excellence of her form." Moreover, Gibbon added, "The prudence of Theodora is celebrated by Justinian himself; and his laws are attributed to the sage counsels of his most reverend wife, whom he had received as the gift of the Deity. Her courage was displayed amidst the tumult of the people and the terrors of the Court."

Justinian named Theodora as Empress of the Roman Empire, with ruling authority equal to his own. The governors of all the provinces had to swear an oath of allegiance to her, too, and together Justinian and Theodora were sole rulers of the entire Roman world. She was evidently an extraordinary person, "born to shine in any situation of life."

Jennie's costume was as flamboyant as the woman she portrayed. It was a heavily embroidered Byzantine robe, apparently copied from the mosaic portrait in the apse of the church in Ravenna. Ornate circular designs, worked in jewels and rich braids, were repeated throughout the gown. Encircling her forehead was a crown with pendants of pear-shaped pearls in the center and at her temples. Hanging from the crown was a filmy veil, and on her arms were veils of tulle and sparkling brilliants. Her neck was covered with pearl chokers, and her long black hair flowed forward over her shoulders almost to her waist. In one hand she held a giant lily and in the other the golden orb of power.

Her costume caused considerable comment in the press, and Winston later requested of her "some photos of you in Theodora costume—for my table."[37]

"She didn't need a costume to make her look like Theodora," her nephew accurately commented; "she *was* Theodora."[38]

All was not serene, however. "Towards the close of the ball," Jennie wrote, "two young men disputed over a certain fair lady. Both losing their tempers, they decided to settle the matter in the garden, and pulling out their weapons, they began making passes. But the combatants were unequally armed, one being a crusader, with a double-handed sword, and the other a Louis XV courtier, armed with his rapier only. He, as might be expected, got the worst of it, receiving a nasty cut on his silk stocking."[39]

Jennie did not mention that the courtier who got the cut was her son Jack. Winston had served as his brother's second in the duel.

It was strange that the calm, equable Jack was the one to fight the duel while his exuberant brother served as his second. Jack was only seventeen and it must have been a matter of high moment for him to find himself in the more dramatic position while his dashing brother watched from the sidelines. There were not many such moments in Jack's life.

Perhaps tempers were so short because it was too hot to dance, and besides, the weighty costumes made most kinds of dancing impossible. The Prince of Saxe-Coburg wore a heavy suit of armor with the visor down, but the heat soon forced him to open the visor so that he could breathe more freely. Jennie's sister Leonie also arrived helmeted, with sword and shield as well, rapresenting her favorite Wagnerian character, Brünnhilde.

Fortunately, the supper tent was built around the pond where it was cooler, and the area was lit by colored electric lamps hanging from the branches "like living jewels." Soon this would all be part of a vanished world, long before Devonshire House and its marvelous marble staircase would become an automobile showroom.

Within a week after that ball, Winston made his first public address, speaking at a meeting of the Primrose League of Conservative Party supporters. His mother, who had been one of the founders of the League, was still an active member. In deciding where to make his maiden effort, Winston surveyed the prospects "with the eye of an urchin looking through a pastrycook's window. Finally, we selected Bath."[40]

He spoke about the Workmen's Compensation Bill, which was then being debated before Parliament, having first discussed the speech in detail with his mother. Comments in the press about the speech were very favorable, one magazine dubbing it "an auspicious debut."

Jennie arranged a large party at her home afterward. Some of the guests were people whom Winston either did not know well enough or did not like well enough, such as Arthur James Balfour. The party was important for Winston, though, because he soon would need Balfour's help. Balfour was still in his late forties, the tall, handsome nephew of Prime Minister Salisbury, whom Jennie correctly believed he was destined to succeed. He had a nonchalant manner, but he was said to have "the finest brain that has been applied to politics in our time."[41] In 1895 he had published his second major work, *The Foundations of Belief,* which William James said he had read with "immense gusto." But to some, Balfour's soft, bland face made him seem mysterious. "No one could tell what banked fires burned behind it, or whether they burned, or even if they existed."[42]

Balfour was a wealthy bachelor, his blood as blue as his eyes, and he deeply admired Jennie's beauty and love of music. Their friendship dated from the early days when they worked in politics together, but there had never been any hint of romance between them.

It is not known what Winston and Balfour talked about at that party, but the importance of such parties is hard to overestimate. Upper-class British reserve often disappeared at such parties, and people were more easy and open with each other. Matters that might have lingered unresolved through a long correspondence often were settled with a few words. It was at such a dinner party a year before that Winston had gotten a promise from General Sir Bindon Blood that he could accompany him if he headed another expedition in India.

Winston and his mother were at Goodwood watching the races in lovely weather when reports arrived of a revolt of the Pathan tribesmen on the Indian frontier. The newspapers further announced that General Blood would head an expedition of three brigades to quell the revolt. Winston promptly telegraphed the General, reminding him of his promise, then kissed his mother good-bye and raced to catch the next boat to India.

It was at another such party that Jennie had spent a long evening discussing the British political situation with "Old Lawson"–Edward Lawson, owner of the *Daily Telegraph.* Therefore, when Winston wrote his mother that General Sir Bindon Blood had suggested that Winston join him "as a press correspondent,"[43] Jennie immediately telegraphed Lawson. Just as promptly, Lawson agreed, saying, "Tell him to post picturesque, forcible letters."[44]

"I have faith in my star," Winston wrote his mother.[45]

"I believe in your lucky star as I do in mine," Jennie answered.[46]

And then she wrote Jack, who by now had returned to France, "I shall feel very lonely without either of you."[47]

Twenty-Six

*L*OOK AFTER MAMMA," WINSTON wrote his brother, "and write often to her. I am afraid she will be worried about me. She certainly would if she were here."[1]

Yet Winston's own letters to Jennie spared her none of the grisly details of the war. This again revealed the multiple role she played in his life. She was not just his mother whom he wanted to shield from worry. She was his closest friend, the one he told about all his experiences. And she wanted to know. She shared with him a love of action, and she lived it with him through his letters. She shared his love of language and served as his best audience, so he left little to her imagination.

"It is a war without quarter. They kill and mutilate everyone they catch, and we do not hesitate to finish their wounded off."[2] Earlier he had told her about

> an awful rout in which the wounded were left to be cut up horridly by these wild beasts. I was close to both officers when they were hit almost simultaneously and fired my revolver at a man at 30 yards who tried to cut up poor Hughes' body. He dropped, but came on again. A subaltern—Bethune by name—and I carried a wounded Sepoy for some distance. . . . My pants are still stained with the man's blood. . . .

It was a horrible business. . . . Later on I used a rifle which a
wounded man dropped and fired 40 rounds with some effect
at close quarters. I cannot be certain, but I think I hit 4 men.
At any rate they fell.[3]

His attitude about performing such acts seemed to be summed up in a
later letter: "Bullets—to a philosopher, dear Mamma, are not worth considering. Besides, I am so conceited. I do not believe the gods would create so
potent a being as myself for so prosaic an ending."[4]

Jennie forwarded all of Winston's letters to Jack, but she reminded him
with each letter, "Mind you send it back at once." In one of her letters to
Jack, she remarked, "You may imagine how thankful I am to have received
a cable from him every day since the fighting, so that I know he is all
right."[5]

Winston had sent each of his columns for the *Daily Telegraph* to his
mother with such comments as, "Use your own discretion in editing it—as I
am too tired to write more now and then post it off."[6] ". . . Forgive this
scribble—and believe I love you. . . ."[7]

> Darling Winston
> . . . You may imagine how much I think of you, & how in
> my heart I shall be glad that the war will be over soon, & that
> I shall know you safely back at Bangalore—& yet I am more
> than glad for yr sake that you managed to get up there. . . .
> But I think of all the hardships you are going through & I feel
> for you darling. . . .
> . . . I read yr letters for the D.T. to Ld Minto who thought
> them excellent—but begged me not to sign yr name. He said
> it was very unusual & might get you into trouble. The 1st
> one appeared yesterday headed "Indian Frontier—by a young
> officer." The Editor wired to say they wld give 5 [pounds] a
> column. . . . I wrote to the Prince & told him to look out for
> yr letters. Also to lots of people. You will get plenty of kudos
> (can't spell it). I will see that you do darling boy. . . .[8]

Winston was displeased with the amount of payment, even more displeased that the columns did not have his name on them. ". . . Poor Winnie," Jennie wrote Jack. "He thinks his letters are not a success—*but they are!*"[9]

Despite his disappointment, Winston responded to his mother's suggestion about putting his columns together in a pamphlet. "Perhaps you will
have them put in a book," he wrote. "It would of course sell well and might
do me good."[10]

Winston never stopped reaching for recognition:

> I rode on my gray pony all along the skirmish line where
> everyone else was lying down in cover. Foolish perhaps, but I
> play for high stakes and given an audience there is no act too
> daring or too noble. Without the gallery things are differ-
> ent . . . quality not quantity is after all what we should strive
> for. Still I should like to come back and wear my medals at
> some big dinner or some other function. . . .[11]

Behind this public façade, with only his mother as audience, he could
reveal, "I am a little lonely here at times as I have never a friend to talk
to. . . ."[12]

On another occasion he cautioned her, "If I am to do anything in the
world, you will have to make up your mind for publicity, and also to my
doing 'unusual' things."[13]

Evidently Jennie was concerned about his penchant for self-promotion,
because during this period she wrote him:

> You have done more than well my darling boy & I am as
> always proud of you. Forgive a piece of advice—which may
> not be needed—but be modest. All yr feats of valour are sure
> to come out & people will know. Let it be from others & not
> from yrself. One must be tempted to talk of oneself in such a
> case—*but resist*. Let them *drag* things out.[14]

Neither was it really necessary for him to remind her, "You must get
people to do things for me,"[15] for she never stopped doing that. Colonel
Brabazon wrote her that Sir Bindon Blood was speaking "*very* highly of
our 'young officer,' "[16] and at the same time, Blood wrote to Jennie, "You
may depend on my looking after him if there is another opportunity for
him."[17]

Jennie remembered to send Winston the photos he requested of her "as
the wicked 'Theodora,' "[18] and she also asked him to give one to Kincaid-
Smith, a handsome Captain in Winston's outfit with whom she had been
corresponding. Winston knew about this correspondence and perhaps was
demonstrating a pang of jealousy when he deprecated Kincaid-Smith's polo
playing, which, he said, "has not got the dash of younger men."[19]

That November Winston was 23, and his mother cabled her congratulations to him. "I knew you would remember," he answered.[20] Jennie also
had written, ". . . if you don't go to Egypt . . . I will come and stay with you
next year. . . . We will have great fun. . . ."[21]

Winston later let his mother know just how much her letters meant to him:

". . . your letter is the central point of my week. If I thought mine could give you half as much pleasure, I should write all day."[22]

". . . when the mail comes in with no letter from you, I get in such a state of despondency & anger that I am not approachable by anyone and fly to my inkpot to let off steam."[23]

With the initial frontier action over, Winston wrote his mother that he had been under fire "for ten complete times," and observed that it was "quite a foundation for a political life." He added:

> . . . You must keep your eye on the political situation. Although I know & hear nothing out here, it is evident to me that a very marked reaction against the decision of the last general election has taken place. These numerous bye elections might, had I been in England, have given me my chance of getting in. However my experience out here has been of greater value and interest than anything else would be, or perhaps can ever be. Of course should a vacancy occur in Paddington—you must weigh in for me & I will come by the next ship. They would probably elect me even if I could not get back in time. I suppose Ld Salisbury's retirement is now only a matter of months. There might be sweeping changes after that."[24]

Winston still pressed his mother to renew her efforts to get him transferred to Egypt. "Indeed, my life here is not big enough to hold me. I want to be up and doing and cannot bear inaction or routine. . . ." He wanted her to "stimulate the Prince into writing to Kitchener."[25] He would later suggest she renew her own personal application on his behalf directly with the Sirdar: "Strike while the iron is hot & the ink wet."[26]

Jennie had other work to do for Winston. First she had to find a publisher for his book, *The Malakand Field Force.*

> Arthur Balfour . . . has been too nice about you. I told him all about yr book (the Campaign), & he is going to put me in the way of a good publisher and everything. You need only send me the MS & I will have it all done for you. A.B. said he had not read yr letters—but he had heard more than flattering things about them. The letters have been read & appreciated by the people who later on can be useful to you.[27]

It is easy to visualize Jennie doing all these things for her son—writing letters, persuading the Prince, cornering Balfour, arranging tête-à-têtes with prominent people. Of course, it wasn't only for her son. Her priorities would soon change somewhat, but at this time Jennie's life and future were integrated with Winston's. Moreover, she enjoyed working at it. How she reveled in persuading people to do something in which she deeply believed! There was an excitement, a challenge in it, a feeling of action and reaction, and, most of all, the satisfaction of tangible results. At a time in her life when the sequence of the social seasons seemed evermore repetitive and boring, she could gear her activity toward a specific goal. And there was no goal closer to her heart than Winston's future.

Perhaps, too, this was a way of compensating for guilt feelings about Winston's early years, when to some extent she had neglected him in favor, first, of her husband's ambitions, and then of his illness. In those days she could give Winston and Jack only whatever time she had left—which was not enough. Yet, somehow, they were never embittered by this period of neglect; on the contrary it seemed only to amplify their love for her. Winston wrote later that as a child he had loved her as "a fairy princess; a radiant being possessed of limitless riches and power. . . . She shone for me like the Evening Star. I loved her dearly—but at a distance."[28] Now that they were grown, the distance had been closed. But now Jennie had to determine how to divide her time between Winston and Jack according to their needs.

Winston was not shy about making his needs known. She had recognized his potential early and helped shape his direction. He knew where he was going and the roads to take, and he knew the vital part his mother had to play to help him get there. He demanded everything from his mother and got it.

Jack's need was different and in some ways stronger. He adored his mother, idolized his brother, and realized his own shortcomings in comparison to them. He did not have their dazzling kind of intellect, their drive, their ambition; and Jennie's attitude toward him was far more maternal and protective. During Jack's stay in Paris, Jennie's letters to him conveyed her worry about his ear infection, his spelling, his reading habits, his clothes—"I would send you the patterns & you cld choose & send me your measures." If he had an unplumbed potential, he did not know what it was at this time. He was eighteen and unsure of what he wanted or where he was going. (Jennie had thought of getting Jack into the Foreign Office ". . . if he cld pass the Exams—but I fear he is not clever enough.")[29]

To Jennie Jack was a good boy, a loving boy, who represented her own softer and more quiet side. She knew his want of her, but there was Winston as demanding as her husband had been. Jack did not really demand anything. How should she divide herself?

Jack had completed his year in Paris, and the question now was what he would do next. He had written Jennie a long letter:

> I can remember at Harrow one or two boys who had suddenly to change all their plans for their futures, but I don't think you could easily find one who changes every year! I have been "going to be" everything under the sun and as you know I have always had a great abhorrence of being a "something in the City," with the chance of becoming nothing. I have been "going into" the Army, the City, the Bar, the Foreign Office, or Diplomacy and now I am to change again to the City. Each time I have been told that I have lots of time, but I have no more. I am nearly 18 and must be settled.
>
> It is not wholly my fault that I have changed so; I am built heart & soul for the Army; but you asked me to give it up because it was expensive and not lucrative because it might leave you alone and because it was "no career." I am afraid that many are called & few chosen in anything.
>
> I began to like the idea of going to Oxford, of going where Winston had not been and even of plodding away at the Bar. But now you want me to go under the old gas lamp in the City. The life of a Cavalry Officer appeals to me more but I will do it if it is necessary & if you want me to.
>
> Your letter did not tell me much about your "serious financial crisis." Have things gone wrong in America? Or did they get muddled in England? Lord Vernon prophesied to me a year ago that you would either marry! or have a crisis in the next two years! . . .
>
> . . . The only part of your letter with which I agreed, was the wish that we should be more together. . . . If you could imagine how much I long to come home to you & Cumberland Place, you would realize that my only wish is to please you & to do whatever you wish.[30]

It was a rather extraordinary letter for Jack to write. He had matured in the preceding year, but his frustration of indecision must have been welling up within him for a long time before he could write about it. How revealing that one of the attractions of Oxford was that it was "where Winston had not been." Above all, he did not want to compete with Winston or with the image of Winston.

The further significance of this letter was its tone of freedom and intimacy. In most upper-class British families there was a chasm of reticence between generations which was surrounded by a framework of propriety. There were many unspoken rules about things one did not do and things one never said. It was remarkable that a son would write his mother of Lord Vernon's prophecy that "you would either marry! or have a crisis in the next two years!" That he was able to do so was the result of Jennie's consistent encouragement of her sons to say exactly what they thought and felt.

Jack could say almost anything to his mother—as could Winston—because all of them knew that the bond of love between them was indivisible. "How I long to come home to you," Jack wrote; "my only wish is to please you and to do whatever you wish."

On receiving this declaration from her son, Jennie answered somewhat defensively:

> Your last letter saddened me, but my darling boy, you can be certain of one thing, and that is that your happiness is the one thing I want above all others, and that I will make any sacrifice necessary to insure it. . . . Darling I don't want to make any tiresome remarks, but you must remember that your want of decision as regards your likes and dislikes and your choice of a career has been a drawback to you—I have never heard you before really express a real desire to go into the Army. . . . It is not too late—if you are content to have a small allowance and live on your pay—and be a Major at 45 on 600 a year! Bless you, my child. Don't fret. All will come right for you, I am sure.[31]

That December of 1897, as was customary, Jennie and Jack were invited to Blenheim for Christmas. The Churchill family had decided to put on an amateur play on behalf of charity, and the show would be open to the general public. "The whole of Oxford may turn up," Jennie wrote to Winston ". . . 10 [shillings] to see the Churchills playing the fool! . . ."[32] To Jack she added, "I am dying to see you, you darling. We go to Blenheim on Monday to begin rehearsing this terrible burlesque; but it cannot be helped. I am sending you the second act. You are a Chinaman."[33]

The playlet was called "An Idle Hour," and Jack was called Li-Down-Do, while Jennie was Mrs. Jubilee Junius, a newspaper reporter, and the Duke of Marlborough was another main character. Whoever wrote the piece managed to take some slaps at Jennie.

She was introduced in the play with the limerick:

> J is for Jennie and Jubilee June,
> She's bright and she's clever, but sings out of tune. . . .

Jennie herself sang:

> I'm called Mrs Jubilee "June"
> (Mrs Perkins is that the right tune?)
> A Lady Reporter
> Belle's Letters own daughter,
> The wife of the Man in the Moon.
>
> My life is a terrible hash
> From county to county I dash:
> To interview Mayors
> And Bishops and Players,
> I stir up the lot with my lash.[34]

The family theatrical seems to have received broad coverage, for Winston wrote to his mother: "I laughed a great deal reading the account of the Blenheim Theatricals, all of which the Indian Papers solemnly printed. Capital! I am so glad it went off well."[35]

Jack fully described to Winston his discussions with their mother about his future, and Winston wrote to Jennie about Jack's renewed interest in the Army. Then he added, quite perceptively:

> I do not gather that the idea of sending him into the City precludes his going to Oxford. I should be very sorry if it did & I hope you will try to send him there. His letters to me for some time have expressed much eagerness for a University education. Indeed I have rarely known him express such a decided opinion. Also I think his mind is *reflective* rather than *inventive*. If so he needs fuel & knowledge to work upon. This a University education would provide. I hope you will be able to secure one for him. If money prevents I could borrow a further £500 wh he might repay me when he came of age. I think he had set his heart on it. Perhaps the book may be a financial success. Mind you write and say nice things to me about it. Tell me what parts you like. I love praise.[36]

Winston also had mentioned the idea of Jack's joining the Army and Jennie answered:

> You talk glibly of Jack going into the Army–but you know he wld never pass the medical examination with his eye–& besides how could I give him an adequate allowance?

Everyone thinks my plan for him is the best. He will go to Germany for a year, learn bookkeeping(?) & German, & one of these days make a fortune. He is quite reconciled to it now. He has joined the Oxford Yeomanry & will have a month's drill at Aldershot & his 10 days before he goes to Berlin. It will set him up & give him a nice uniform for all requirements. How I am to pay for it I do not know![37]

To Jack, Winston now wrote: "The whole thing is your own fault for not expressing decided opinions. If you had made up your mind what you wanted—insisted upon it—no one would have stopped you. As it is you will probably be making £5,000 a year and playing polo at Hurlingham when I am struggling on a pittance—as a newspaper hack. I shall come down on you like a cartload of bricks."[38]

The money problem had become increasingly serious. Earlier Winston had written to Jennie, "Do not worry about money my dearest Mamma. If the worst comes to the worst you can let the house—and however annoying that might be you will always find lots of places glad to receive you while you remain the dearest & most beautiful woman in the world."[39]

But Jennie did worry about money, for early in 1898 she had to find 17,000 pounds, which she needed to "buy up all the loans I have made in different Insurance offices"[40] and also to clear up some pressing debts. Her security for the loan was to be the life-insurance policies on her life and on Winston's. Winston was now required to guarantee at least the premiums on these life-insurance policies, amounting to £700 per year, which would also cover the interest on the loans. Winston wrote his mother:

... Speaking quite frankly on the subject—there is no doubt that we are both, you & I equally thoughtless—spendthrift and extravagant. We both know what is good—and we both like to have it. Arrangements for paying are left to the future. My extravagances are on a smaller scale than yours. I take no credit to myself in this matter as you have kept up the house & have had to maintain a position in London. At the same time we shall vy soon come to the end of our tether—unless a considerable change comes over our fortunes and dispositions. As long as I am dead sure & certain of an ultimate £1,000 a year—I do not much care—as I could always make money on the press—and might marry. But at the same time there would be a limit.

... I sympathize with all your extravagances—even more than you do with mine—it seems just as suicidal to me when

you spend £200 on a ball dress as it does to you when I purchase a new polo pony for £100. And yet I feel that you
ought to have the dress & I the polo pony. The pinch of the
whole matter is that we are damned poor. . . .[41]

Writing to Jack about the loan, Winston noted: "I recognize that it is a
necessity for her to have the money. Indeed unless she has it—she could not
continue my allowance—or pay for your education."[42]

Arthur Balfour meanwhile had kept his word to Jennie, and sent her the
name of his literary agent, A. P. Watt. "I think you will find him invaluable
for the work you want. If he thinks such a course practicable I strongly recommend for Winston's sake a *royalty* on the sale, rather than any such
arrangement as either half profits, or a lump sum down. Watt will however
be a good adviser."[43]

Within a short time, Watt had arranged for a contract with the highly
respected firm of Longman. "I received yr book & rushed off to Watt's with
it," Jennie wrote Winston, and also informed him that another author was
preparing a book on the same subject. "I don't think you need mind—as I
hope yours will be out first."[44] The next morning, she wrote still another
letter:

I've received this morning Mr Watt's letter which I copy
for you—I am awfully sleepy still as we danced till 3. Everything very well done. I have to finish before breakfast in order to get it off by today's mail.
. . . I am going to show this to Mr Cassel & to Mr Lawson
who is here before wiring—but I have no doubt it is the best
that can be done. For Mr Balfour told me Watt was very
good at making a bargain & it is a great thing that yr first
book shld be published by such a good firm as Longman,
also that it shld be done at their cost.[45]

Winston had told his mother: "All financial arrangments in connection
with it—I shall leave entirely in your hands. But please have no false scruples or modesty about bargaining—as 'the labourer is worthy of his hire,'
and as I have quoted from Dr. Johnson to you before, 'No one but a block-
head ever wrote—except for money.' "[46]

In the same letter, he added, "I hope the book will please you. After all
it is your applause that I covet more than any other. Indeed I think that
would include all others."

Of course, Royal praise was also gratifying. "The Prince showed me yr
letter," Jennie told Winston. "He was very pleased with it."[47]

The Prince of Wales also wrote Winston:

> Accept my very best thanks for your letter of 4th which
> I have read with the greatest possible interest—as I did also
> your letters which appeared in the *Daily Telegraph.* You were
> very fortunate to have taken part in the campaign in the
> North West Frontier—& I only regret that you were not able
> to remain with Sir Bindon Blood. It does seem hard that
> when he applied for you to join him again that you were
> not allowed to do so. . . . Your mother & Jack are staying
> with us this week & she tells me that you are bringing out a
> book with an account of your recent campaign which I
> shall look forward to read—as you have great facility in
> writing. . . .[48]

Winston was still hoping to receive a transfer to Egypt in time for the
upcoming campaign. "You must work Egypt for me," he had pleaded to
Jennie in January. "You have so many lines of attack . . . Now I beg you—
have no scruples but worry right and left and take no refusal."[49] Then, a
few days later he had added, "Oh how I wish I could work you up over
Egypt! I know you could do it with all your influence—and all the people
you know. It is a pushing age and we must shove with the best."[50]

"I wrote to Sirdar 10 days ago," Jennie answered.

> Lady Jeune has written to Sir Evelyn [Wood], & Brab has
> been to the War Office & they promise to "note" your name.
> There is to be no advance until July or August so there is
> plenty of time. . . . bless you my darling don't fuss—we'll get
> you up there if it is possible. I may go to Cairo myself for a
> little, if I do I can perhaps work the Sirdar at nearer quarters
> with more chance of success.[51]

She also sent an extract of one of Winston's letters to Lord Roberts.
Roberts replied, "What a capital letter Winston writes. When he comes
home I must have a talk with him about the Frontier question. . . ."[52]
However, Lord Roberts had previously advised Jennie, "I would, with
the greatest pleasure, help your son, but it would be no use my commu-
nicating with General Lockhart as Sir George White is all powerful, and,
as he refused to allow Winston to join General Blood's Staff, after his
having previously served with that officer in the Malakand Field Force, I
feel sure he would not consent to his being sent with the Tirah Field
Force."[53]

Jennie earlier had written Winston:

> I had a letter from my Highlander friend Caryl Ramsden
> from Cairo. He said on his way out he heard Gen Getacre &
> a lot of military men talking of you—as the most "promising
> youngster out" but that you wrote too well to remain in the
> Army—where yr talents wld be wasted—& where yr writings
> wld sooner or later get you into trouble. Up to now however
> you have managed to be discreet.[54]

Major Ramsden, the "Highlander friend" Jennie mentioned, had made
a deep impression on her, and the two had been keeping up an intimate
correspondence. Fourteen years younger than Jennie, Caryl John Ramsden
was such a handsome ladies' man that he had earned the nickname of
"Beauty" Ramsden. Having spent a boring year with his battery in Malta
and Crete, he had just been ordered to rejoin his regiment for Kitchener's
campaign up the Nile, and Jennie decided to meet him in Cairo.

Jennie appeared to be specifically encouraging younger men. She was
still a striking beauty and the young men responded to her charms. "The
first time I saw her was at Ascot when I was on a coach belonging to the 1st
Life Guards," wrote young Lord Rossmore. "Suddenly my attention was
arrested by the appearance of a lady who was walking in my direction, and
who was accompanied by a half dozen men. I thought her the most beautiful creature imaginable and, dressed in white and wearing a big white hat,
she was perfectly delightful to look at, and I cried out impulsively, greatly
to the amusement of my brother officers, 'Good heavens! Who's that?' "

Rossmore went on to speak of her as "the loveliest woman I have ever
set my eyes on (my wife, of course, excepted)."[55]

As soon as she had decided to go to Egypt, Jennie wired Winston. He,
of course, assumed that she was going only for his sake, to further his cause
with Kitchener.

> Your telegram reached me on Saturday—and I can assure you
> I feel vy grateful indeed to you for going to Egypt—It is an ac-
> tion which—if ever I have a biographer—will certainly be ad-
> mired by others. I hope you may be successful. I feel almost
> certain you will. Your wit & tact & beauty—should overcome
> all obstacles.[56]

Staying with Ramsden at the Continental Hotel in Cairo, Jennie kept up
a steady stream of messages to Kitchener. "I have noted your son's name,"
Kitchener finally answered, "and I hope I may be able to employ him later

in the Sudan." Satisfied with this news she and Ramsden then took a trip on the riverboat *Dahabeyah* traveling up the Nile. Major Ramsden soon received orders to rejoin his unit at Wadi Halfa, and Jennie returned to Port Said to embark for London. There she was informed that her ship would be delayed for several days, so she hurried back to Cairo just in case Ramsden had not yet left.

He had not, but neither was he alone. Jennie entered his room without knocking, and there she found him embracing Lady Maxwell, wife of the Army Commander. Jennie's anger was unleashed loudly enough to be heard throughout the hotel.[57]

The echoes of that incident reached the Prince of Wales. "You had better have stuck to your old friends than gone on your Expedition of the Nile! Old friends are the Best!" he teasingly wrote.[58]

Jennie drafted a reply to him in London and read it aloud to her sister Leonie: "*So* grateful for your sympathy—as your Royal Highness knows exactly *how* it feels after being jilted by Lady Dudley!"[59] Leonie begged her sister not to mail the letter, as she was fearful the Prince would never speak to her again. But Jennie replied that she didn't care. In that case, Leonie said, she would mail the letter as she had to go to the post office for herself. Leonie went to the post office, but she never mailed the letter, and Jennie never knew.

The Prince, however, heard about Jennie's displeasure with his note and he answered: *"Ma chère Amie:* I must ask your pardon if my letter pained. I had no idea *'que c'était une affaire si sérieuse!'* "[60]

Apparently the Prince was anxious to be forgiven, as the next week he asked her to arrange a dinner at her home and then promptly expressed his gratitude: "I must write to thank you for your charming dinner of last night. . . . I thought your party was exceptionally successful." And perhaps to appease her further, he added, "I am delighted with Winston's book—admirably written and most interesting."[61]

The Prince followed this with a letter to Winston:

> I cannot resist writing a few lines to congratulate you on the success of your book! I have read it with the greatest possible interest, and I think the descriptions and the language generally excellent. Everybody is reading it, and I only hear it spoken of with praise.
>
> . . . You have plenty of time before you, and should certainly stick to the Army before adding MP to your name.[62]

The Prince's praise was undoubtedly sincere, for he also sent a copy of the book to his mother, Queen Victoria, saying that for having been "written by so young a man, [it] shows remarkable ability."

Winston quite openly appealed to his mother for her own reaction: "Write to me at great length about the book and be nice about it. Don't say what you think, but what I should like you to think. . . ."[63]

After reading the proofs, Jennie tried to buoy Winston's spirits: "I think [the book] is capital–most interesting & well written. It does you great credit & ought to be a gt success–but of course one cannot tell. I will 'boom it' judiciously."[64]

Her judicious booming included letters to G. C. Buckle, editor of the *London Times*, Frank Harris, editor of *The Saturday Review* and a close friend of her husband's, and Henry Norman, assistant editor of the *Daily Chronicle*, "asking them to review yr book favorably when it appears, which will be in a fortnight or so, *so* expeditious have Longman been."[65]

"I owe you a great deal for all the trouble you have taken," Winston answered, "and I feel *most* grateful for the spur which your interest and your applause give to my ambitions. . . ."[66]

As soon as the book was published, Jennie had copies sent to all her important friends who might be able to push it, particularly men in the military. Most of the critics were enthusiastic, as the sample from the *Athenaeum* indicates: "*The Story of the Malakand Field Force* (Longman) needs only a little correction of each page to make its second edition a military classic."[67]

The corrections probably were needed because Winston had asked Jennie to persuade his Uncle Moreton to correct the text of the book. That turned out to be a mistake. Frewen's copy editing left the book full of errors, and perfectionist Winston writhed when he read it. He realized that he would have done far better to have asked his mother to work on it, and he soon informed her: "If there is a second edition, I have told them to send them to you for revision."[68]

He also told her that he was sending her a short story, "wh I want you to sell, signed, to one of the magazines. I think the *Pall Mall* wd like it & would pay my price. You should not get less than £20 for it, as it is a very good story–in my opinion. So don't sell it without a good offer."[69]

Some months later he told her about a novel he was writing, a "political romance," that must "be entirely rewritten and polished, but I hope to send you the MS in about four weeks. . . ." He felt, though, that the manuscript had a major fault. ". . . you must help me with the woman in the novel," he wrote his mother. "She is my chief difficulty."[70]

Winston had three months' summer leave due to him in the spring of 1898, and he wrote Jennie that he planned to stop off at Cairo, then continue to England. Sir Evelyn Wood said that if he did get this leave, he himself "would see that I got to the front."[71] Winston also wrote to Sir Ian Hamilton, then a General, who was en route home with the manuscript of Winston's first novel, to be delivered to Jennie: "Please say nice things about me to everyone at home. If you would call on my mother—35A Gt Cumberland Place—she would be very grateful for news of me & to meet one who has shown me much kindness."[72] The next day, Winston wrote to his mother saying that he had asked General Hamilton to call on her. "He has been vy kind to me & I shall be very grateful if you will be amiable to him—should he call. He is a brilliant soldier and will one day be in high command."[73]

In his next letter, Winston was more specific: "Please be effusive. You will recognize him in a minute as his left hand was smashed to pieces by a bullet at Majuba Hill. . . . Were they to send another Brigade to Egypt he would vy likely get it. . . ."[74]

Of Jennie's own writing:

> When are you going to publish your Impressions of travel etc. We must talk about that when I come home. The Russian article might well be worked in. These things sell. And besides—if for no other reason—they amuse and interest others. So many people travel but so few observe—and of these a minority can express their thoughts & impressions.[75]

A week or so earlier he had told her:

> The desire to see England before again going to the wars was very strong upon me . . . Your letter of last week's mail decided me. . . . I shall be home on about July 2nd. . . . I hope I shall be able to see a good deal of you and that you will try and accept few invitations during my flying visit. . . .

He also listed several things he wanted her to do for him:

> (1) Sir B. Blood is . . . coming home by this ship and I want you to ask him to dinner and Lady B. (who is charming) and have some distinguished people—possibly the Prince—to meet him. . . .
> (2) I want to have at least two good public meetings during my flying visit. Can you not arrange one at Bradford. . . . I have the material for several speeches of some value ready and can easily bring it up to date & locality. . . . [76]
> You might arrange one or two dinners—and get me a few invitations. I want to see people and to get about. Try and get me a pleasant Sunday somewhere. I will go down to Deepdene for one day.

"*Au revoir*, my dearest Mamma. I am looking forward above all things to seeing you. If possible, let us dine alone together on the night I arrive—with Jack, of course."[77]

Jennie's income in 1898 had dropped to only 900 pounds—inclusive of her allowance to Winston and Jack. When she informed Winston how matters stood, he answered, "The situation as described by your letter is appalling. As you say it is of course impossible for you to live in London on such a pittance. I hate the idea of your marrying—but that of course would be a solution."[78]

Clearly, his feelings were ambivalent: he was jealous of any possibility of his mother's remarriage. As he had put it to her in a previous letter: "I have also to reckon on the possibility of your marrying again—perhaps some man I did not like—or did not get on with—and of troubles springing up—which might lessen your affections for me."[79] But now he had to recognize their need for money.

Jennie, meanwhile, was busy securing Jack's future. She consulted her longtime friend and financial confidant, Ernest Cassel, who promised to get Jack a position in the City. Cassel was a remarkable man. *The Times* of London described him as a person of "great wealth, a great heart, great influence . . . whose claim to rank among the outstanding figures of the last 20 years is indisputable."

Of German-Jewish descent, Ernest Cassel was several years older than Jennie, a widower who never remarried. He had been instrumental in financing the first Aswan Dam in Egypt, the Central Tube Railway in London, the Atchison, Topeka and Santa Fe Railway in the United States, as well as the economic structure of Argentina. He was also well known for his unstinting support of numerous charities, his love of horses and mountaineering, and his close friendship with the Prince of Wales.

Sir Sidney Lee records a story about the Prince of Wales inquiring of a friend whether he had seen the play, *The Importance of Being Earnest*. The friend replied, "No sir, but I have seen the importance of being Ernest Cassel."[80] Jack's career could not have been in better hands.

At the same time, Winston's career was coming under the influence of the Prince of Wales. The character of the Prince was changing perceptibly. The world thought of him as a pleasure-loving lightweight, and so perhaps he was. One of his friends, Margie Chandos Pole, had once taken him to a clairvoyant in Homburg, an old woman who seemed to know things about him that no one else knew. She predicted that he would not succeed to the throne, that Queen Victoria would outlive him. Some of his friends asserted that the Prince began to believe this prophecy, and that this might have contributed to his decision to lead a pleasure-seeking life.[81]

But now he was becoming increasingly serious about Great Britain's place in the world and he gathered about him men of vast experience in foreign affairs. He had the instinct for selecting the right people for the right information, but he was careful about whom he trusted and worked to develop a keener sense of discretion. Despite these personal reforms, he still adored beautiful women and, as Oscar Wilde had said of himself, he could "resist anything except temptation."

The Prince had kept a kind and sharp eye for the development of young Winston, and even made a friendly comment in one of his speeches about Winston's "Malakand" book. He also let it be known to Sir Evelyn Wood, then Adjutant General of the Army, that he personally favored Winston's placement on Kitchener's staff. Despite his efforts, however, Wood had to inform Jennie:

> Dear Jennie,
>   The Sirdar declines to take Mr. Churchill, and I wrote to show you the correspondence in order we may concert as to future measures–I will call tomorrow, either at 9 on my way home cycling–or about 10 on my way to the office.
>   Yours affect[.],
>   Evelyn Wood.[82]

General Wood also enclosed a copy of a telegram he had sent to Kitchener: "Personage asked me personally desires you take Churchill. . . . I strongly recommended Churchill as good value for you and Army."[83]

The day before, Kitchener had telegraphed Wood: ". . . do not want Churchill as no room."[84] Even Lord Salisbury, who was then Prime Minister, felt that he could not intervene. "The matter is absolutely in Kitchener's hands," he advised Winston, "and he may think that it is too late now to make any change on previous decisions. I shall greatly regret it, but like Sir Evelyn Wood, 'I can do no more.' "[85]

Winston meanwhile had written an article for a magazine and had asked Jennie to try to have it "printed in a July number so that I can see it when I arrive. Also the article which will reach you next week 'Ethics of Frontier Policy.' This goes to *U.S. Magazine* [*United Service's Magazine* in London] who know all about it. But I want the proofs of both revised & punctuated by some good scholar."[86]

As the time for the public meeting at Bradford approached, Winston became much more specific in his instructions to Jennie. "I want a real big meeting, at least 2,000 men," he wrote. "Compel them to come in. I am sure I can hold them."[87] Jennie knew Bradford well, as she had attended a great many political meetings there with her husband. Winston was quite satisfied with the arrangements and the reception he received. On July 15th, he wrote his mother from Bradford,

> The meeting was a complete success. The hall was not a vy large one—but it was closely packed. I was listened to with the greatest attention for 55 minutes at the end of which time there were loud & general cries of "Go on" . . . many people mounted their chairs and there was really a very great deal of enthusiasm.
>
> . . . The conclusions I form are these—with practice I shall obtain great power on a public platform. My impediment is no hindrance. My voice sufficiently powerful—and—this is vital—my ideas & modes of thought are pleasing to men.
>
> It may be perhaps the hand of Fate—which by a strange coincidence closed one line of advance and aspiration in the morning—and in the evening pointed out another with an encouraging gesture. At any rate—my decision to resign my commission is definite.
>
> P.S. They cheered you several times last night with great cordiality.
>
> You might drop a line to Oliver Borthwick and thank him for the vy excellent report in the M.P. [*Morning Post*]. He is also reporting my speech tonight at Heckmondwicke.[88]

Jennie received a message from R. V. Haldane, who had read the speech in the *Morning Post*. "I thought it very good—broad in tone—fresh & vigorous," Haldane wrote. "I hope he will soon be in the House, for there is in his voice something of the strong quality of one that is—alas—still—to the loss of all of us, & of you most of all."[89]

In the meanwhile, Jennie's persistent activity to get Winston assigned to Egypt caused considerable resentment on high official levels. Winston himself described this resentment:

> Who the devil is this fellow? How has he managed to get to these different campaigns? Why should he write for the papers and serve as an officer, at the same time? Why should a subaltern praise or criticize his senior officers? Why should Generals show him favour? How does he get so much leave from his Regiment? Look at all the hard-working men who have never stirred an inch from the daily round and common task. We've had quite enough of this—too much indeed. He is very young, and later on he may be all right; but now a long

period of discipline and routine is what 2nd Lt. Churchill requires.[90]

Others proceeded to be actually abusive, and the expressions, "Medal-Hunter," and "Self-Advertiser," were used from time to time in some high and some low military circles.

None of this deterred Jennie. She and Lady Jeune gingerly suggested to Sir Evelyn Wood that perhaps there was an alternate way to circumvent General Herbert Kitchener. Wood himself had said in Lady Jeune's presence at a dinner table conversation that Kitchener was going too far in picking and choosing among particular officers recommended by the War Office. Kitchener did have absolute power for his Egyptian Army but there were several regiments of an Expeditionary Force over which the War Office had complete control. Moreover, Winston had received the endorsements of the Prime Minister and the Prince of Wales.

Two days after this dinner table conversation, Winston S. Churchill was attached as "Supernumerary Lieutenant to the 21st Lancers for the Sudan Campaign":

> You are to report at once to the Abassiyeh Headquarters, Cairo. It is understood that you will proceed, at your own expense, and that, in the event of your being killed or wounded in the impending operations, or for any other reason, no charge of any kind will fall on the British Army funds.[91]

Jennie's two-year campaign had finally succeeded. As Winston later wrote, ". . . She left no wire unpulled, no stone unturned, no cutlet uncooked. . . ."[92] And now she again kissed her son goodbye as he went off to another war.

Twenty-Seven

W ITH WINSTON GONE AND JACK SETTLED, Jennie began seeing her friends more often. They swamped her with attention, affection, and invitations to weekend at their country homes.

The great country houses of England at the turn of the century served as a kind of pressure valve for the aristocracy. They provided a haven of tranquility and remoteness from the world. A few social commentators thought the British country home a kind of lounge and pleasure garden so comfortable and secure that it sapped the energy of the upper classes. Some even believed that this comfort made the British leaders incapable of matching the great achievements of the past.

Whether this was true or not, upper-class society felt the need for a refuge from the strictures of custom and convention. In London one traveled with footmen and left calling cards. There were so many functions at which attendance was obligatory. And one usually had the sense of being on a stage, subject to the critical examination of curious outsiders.

There was no such feeling during the four-night weekend at country houses. These estates were far away from city life and they were enormous. Chatsworth, belonging to the Duke and Duchess of Devonshire, accommodated almost five hundred guests.[1] Furthermore, the guests were all carefully selected, most of them so well known to each other that they needed no social pretenses, no strained courtliness, no polite hypocrisy.

Jennie was genuinely relaxed at these great country homes because they always provided an option: lose yourself in the laughter of a crowd, a game of bridge, the prattling talk, a walk in the woods, an amateur theatrical, a piano concert. Or find a confidante, charm a man.

There were numberless assignations among the guests. For some, they brought an ease from loneliness; for others, love. At this level of society, a great many marriages were arranged by parents and lawyers, and since they were marriages of convenience, divorce was usually out of the question. The number of "secret" affairs, therefore, was not so surprising. Every conscientious hostess knew exactly who was paired with whom:

> . . . The name of each guest would be neatly written on a card slipped into a tiny brass frame on the bedroom door. The question of disposition of bedrooms always gave the Duchess and her fellow hostesses cause for anxious thought. It was so necessary to be tactful, and at the same time, discreet.[2]

"It doesn't matter what you do in the bedroom," the great actress Mrs. Patrick Campbell wryly commented, "as long as you don't do it in the street and frighten the horses."[3]

There was always the tantalizing possibility of a new affair: eyes meeting across a dining-room table, a quick but meaningful pressure of a hand, an unexpected turn in the garden.

An example of the sort of thing that went on at these country weekends involved one of Lady Warwick's closest friends, the novelist Elinor Glyn. It was in the garden of Warwick Castle that Elinor Glyn found herself the unexpected object of amorous attention. The ardent pursurer was none other than her hostess' husband, whose former title was Lord Brooke. Elinor managed to struggle free. Later, while dressing for dinner, she told her own husband of the incident. Her husband gaped at her and said, "Did he, by Jove!" Then, smiling, he remarked, "Good old Brookie," and finished tying his tie.[4]

Lady Warwick was similarly unperturbed when she received an amusing note from Jennie with the postscript, "Tell Brookie I have designs on him. . . ."[5] Indeed, Lady Warwick, whom Jennie called "Daisy," had her own designs on some of the men in Jennie's life: Count Kinsky, William Waldorf Astor, and the Prince of Wales.[6] But the two friends usually did not compete for the same man at the same time.

Daisy claimed that she was descended on one side from Nell Gwyn, the mistress of Charles II, and on the other from Oliver Cromwell. Her genealogy actually showed, however, that the Cromwell was not the famous historical figure and that the Gwyn was one "Old Mother Gwyn" who had died drunk in a ditch near the site of Buckingham Palace. Daisy's husband, Lord Francis Brooke, had become the Fifth Earl of Warwick in 1895.[7]

Warwick Castle, with its battlemented walls and towers, stood on a rock rising sheer out of the River Avon and had been a Warwick family possession since the Middle Ages. Its interior was largely completed in 1604, when it was described as "the most princely seat within these midland parts of the realm." It had an approach which was cut through solid rock and wound from the porter's lodge to an outer court. Inside, there was a great hall overlooking the Avon, the galleries lined with portraits of Warwicks and royalty, by Rubens, Van Dyck, Holbein, and Lely. Daisy added two portraits of herself, one of which was by John Singer Sargent.[8]

Daisy had a party at Warwick Castle for the Prince of Wales in early July 1898.[9] As she usually did, Daisy invited Jennie, whom she described as "scintillating . . . a marvelous diamond—a host of facets seemed to sparkle at once. . . . She was as delightful to women as to men. . . . One never thought of giving a party without her. . . ."[10]

Any party for the Prince required enormous preparation. A full orchestra had to be hired and given specific instructions: the Prince did not like classical music and often got up and left when it was played. The Prince also made things difficult by bringing his own retinue of servants: two orderlies and two grooms, two valets, a gentleman-in-waiting, a couple of equerries, two loaders for the shooting, and his own footmen in royal livery to stand behind the table and serve his meals.

What is more, the Prince was most particular about his food. He was a gourmand as well as a gourmet—he liked the best, and lots of it—and best of all, he liked ptarmigan pie. In fact, J. B. Priestley, writing about the period when the Prince had become King Edward VII, observed that

> No Edwardian meal was complete without ptarmigan. Hot or cold.
>
> The Edwardian breakfast alone would make one of our Christmas dinners look meager. First-comers arrived about eight o'clock, latecomers finished eating about ten-thirty. There was porridge and cream. There were pots of coffee and of China and India tea, and various cold drinks. One large sideboard would offer a row of silver dishes, kept hot by spirit lamps, and here there would be poached or scrambled eggs, bacon, ham, sausages, devilled kidneys, haddock and other fish. On an even larger sideboard there would be a choice of cold meats—pressed beef, ham, tongue, galantines— and cold roast pheasant, grouse, partridge, and of course,

ptarmigan. A side table would be heaped with fruit—melons, peaches and nectarines, raspberries. And if anyone was hungry, there were always scones and toast and marmalade and honey and specially-imported jams.

This kept the guests going until luncheon, usually taken at 1:30, and it might consist of from 8 to 12 courses, some of them very rich, indeed. Then, after a walk in the park, it was time for tea, just to keep body and soul together until dinner. And there was no cup-and-a-biscuit nonsense about this tea: toast and brioches and hot scones and all the jams again; a fine choice of sandwiches; several kinds of rich, sticky cake. And if King Edward happened to be there at teatime, he would probably insist upon having his usual lobster salad. Dinner at 8:30: a dozen courses perhaps, with appropriate wines, and even richer food, probably including, if the chef were up to it, one of those quasi-Roman idiocies, in which birds of varying sizes were cooked one inside the other like nests of oriental boxes. And surely that is enough? But no, a fellow can feel peckish after a few rubbers of bridge; so 'round about midnight, in a neighboring room, he would help himself to sandwiches, devilled chicken or bones, the brandy and whiskey and soda; and then he could get through the night and be ready to welcome his early-morning tea and biscuits.[11]

One of the many other guests Lady Warwick invited to her July weekend party was a young lieutenant named George Cornwallis-West. A tall and darkly handsome man just two weeks older than Winston, he was the son of William Cornwallis-West of Ruthin Castle in North Wales, and although theirs was a family of important connections, they had little money.[12] George's mother was Jennie's age, and she, too, had shared the affections of the Prince of Wales. Both Jennie and Mary Cornwallis-West had been known as "PBs," professional beauties, whose photographs had sold in stores throughout the country.[13]

Mary Cornwallis-West had a more practical mind than Jennie, particularly in money matters. She later helped one of her daughters marry the very wealthy Duke of Westminster. Her other daughter, whom George greatly resembled, had married His Serene Highness, Prince Hans Heinrich of Pless. The Princess explained why:

I was never told I must marry rank or money but I think it must have been an understood thing, because, for our position and the scale on which we lived, we were poor.

> In Germany, every bride, whatever her rank, provides
> furniture, linen, trousseau, everything. . . . I could provide
> nothing; and my family could not even give me my
> trousseau on a fitting scale. Henry, knowing all this, dazzled
> me with descriptions of life in Silesia. I was to have hunters,
> jewels, castles, two ladies-in-waiting, visit England every
> year, and goodness knows what. It all sounded splendid and
> romantic. I did not realize it clearly at the time, but I was just
> being bought. . . .[14]

The Cornwallis-West family considered George a very eligible heir, and his parents fully expected him to select a bride from among the wealthiest, most noble young ladies in Britain.

A fellow officer in the First Battalion of the Scots Guards, John van der Weyer, described George as a "good-looking fellow; bit short on brains."[15] He had other qualities though: he played a good game of tennis, enjoyed yachting, was a superb shot and an excellent horseman. He was also a god-son of the Prince of Wales.

It was the latter that may have qualified him to be a guest at Daisy Warwick's weekend party for the Prince. George later said he was flabbergasted to receive the invitation. He was in the middle of a musketry course, and getting excused from it "was an almost unheard-of thing."

> On the other hand, an invitation to meet His Royal High-
> ness almost amounted to a command. I went up to see the
> Commandant, Colonel Hamilton, and he gave me leave.
> That visit to Warwick was a very eventful one for me, as it
> was there that I first met . . . Lady Randolph Churchill.
> Jennie, as she was always called by her friends—was then a
> women of 43, still beautiful, she did not look a day more
> than 30, and her charm and vivacity were on a par with her
> youthful appearance. I confess that I was flattered that so at-
> tractive a person should have paid any attention to me, but
> she did, and we became friends almost immediately.[16]

George and Jennie went out in a boat on the Avon, which might have reminded Jennie of her recent trip up the Nile with "Beauty" Ramsden. It must have deeply pleased Jennie's vanity that she could still attract some-one so young and attractive, for George was as good-looking as Ramsden, and even younger.

George was obviously overwhelmed. His experience had been mainly with the younger, more fragile, wide-eyed set. He was not easily flustered, but his memoirs indicate that with Jennie he felt as if he were accompanying a famous stage star, a living legend. She knew everyone, had been everywhere, seen everything, while he was just a poor, young lieutenant.

His first letter to Jennie—one of several hundred—was dated July 29, 1898, and decorated with hearts. In it he wrote, "I thought about you all yesterday & built castles in the air about you & I living together. . . ."[17] And Jennie was equally smitten. It was marvelous to be loved so completely.

It was a simple matter for Jennie to confide to her closest friends how pleased she would be if they invited George for country weekends when they invited her. They were delighted to oblige. Making their affair even more convenient was the transfer of George's Battalion of Scots Guards to London. Could Jennie have had a hand in that? It is entirely possible.

Jennie canceled most of her social appointments so that she could give George as much as possible of her time and attention, and she entertained him at her home in a way that he had never been entertained before. His letters rhapsodized about the soft, exquisite kimonos she wore, instead of the conventional whaleboned gowns.

"Of course, the glamour won't last forever," Jennie told a friend, "but why not take what you can, and not make yourself or anyone else unhappy when the next stage arrives?"[18]

She wrote her sons about George in the casual way she wrote them about everything. In return, Winston sent news of the front to George via Jennie. Winston and George probably had met, for they were of the same age, they had mutual friends, and their mothers had known each other well.

It is unlikely that Jennie was thinking seriously about George now—after all, he had been born the same year that she had married Lord Randolph Churchill. Her exact thoughts and feelings cannot be known, but she did something very revealing at this point. One of her closest friends and oldest admirers, George Nathaniel Curzon, had just been appointed Viceroy of India and was then assembling his staff. Jennie wrote him recommending George.

Going to India at this stage of their romance could scarcely have been George's idea. It must have been Jennie's. Was this her way of ending their affair before the inevitable family bitterness began? Or was she thinking of her brief fling with "Beauty" Ramsden—how it had ended on such a humiliating note? This time, perhaps, she wanted to be in control of the romance; this time, perhaps, she wanted to decide how and when it should end.

Curzon's answer, however, was cool and unresponsive:

> . . . You recommended young Cornwallis-West. He seemed
> a nice boy at Warwick but I don't suppose there is a chance of

my having room for him, as I fancy I can only take one English officer from here & I have 50 applications. . . .[19]

In addition to the practical difficulties of granting Jennie's request, Curzon
may in fact have been jealous of this handsome young man who had
achieved what he himself never could.

It was almost as if Curzon's refusal had lifted a veil of guilt from Jennie's conscience. She had tried to end the affair and had failed. Why
shouldn't she now enjoy this intense, fervid romance as long as it lasted?
Except for her relationship with Count Kinsky, she had seldom been as
happy. As for George, it would be torture for him to be turned away now.
Why shouldn't they enjoy their love for each other "until the next stage arrives," as Jennie put it?

That September Jennie and George were guests of Olive Guthrie, sister
of Jennie's brother-in-law John Leslie, at Duart Castle on the Isle of Mull.
"This is the most delightful place I've ever been in–too lovely," Jennie
wrote Winston.[20]

Jennie's twelve-year-old nephew Shane Leslie was also there, and
George took him fishing, "with myself to carry his net and fly. When I net-
ted a record trout for him, he gave me a gold piece."[21] Indeed, George's
passion for Jennie was almost equaled by his obsession with fishing and
hunting. Every letter to her, no matter how romantic, also contained detailed accounts of the pheasants he had shot or the fish he had caught or
the quality and range of his newest gun or fishing rod.

One day at Duart, George went out stalking deer on a nearby hill with
two men. After they had been away eight hours, Jennie put on her walking
shoes and set off toward the moors to meet them. ". . . I was elected to accompany Jennie in his pursuit," Shane Leslie wrote. "We missed our way
and Jennie broke an ankle. We had to crawl back and I half-carried her
home."[22]

The ankle was not actually broken, but it was badly sprained. "Fancy
what a bore for me," Jennie wrote to Jack, "–I have sprained my ankle and
can hardly put my foot to the ground. I was four miles from home when I
did it, and managed to hobble back–but today it is so swelled I have to
send for a doctor."[23]

The Prince of Wales consoled her: "I hope your ankle is better, but you
should be very careful. *Tout à vous.* A. E."[24] But from two Leslie great-aunts
Jennie received little sympathy. Jennie's great-niece gave the general verdict
as: "Chasing George–determined to get him–ruining the man's sport . . .
serves her right."[25]

Twenty-Eight

INSTON WAS NOW WITH KITCHENER'S 20,000-man force in the Sudan. Near Omdurman they awaited the charge of 60,000 fanatical Muslim Dervishes. With a religious fervor and fury that one would have imagined had disappeared after the Crusades, the Dervishes came like a tide, armed with spears and rifles and roaring their cheers for God, his Prophet, and his holy Khalifa. Against them, Kitchener threw the Camel Corps and his full force of modern artillery. Then he ordered the British 21st Lancers to charge. It was history's last great cavalry charge, and Winston was in it.

Immediately after the Battle of Omdurman, he cabled his mother: "ALL RIGHT WINSTON,"[1] and Caryl Ramsden sent her another cable: "BIG FIGHT. FINE SIGHT. WINSTON WELL."[2]

Soon afterward Winston described the battle to his mother:

> I fired 10 shots with my pistol—all necessary—and just got to the end of it as we cleared the crush. I never felt the slightest nervousness and felt as cool as I do now. I pulled up and reloaded within 30 yards of their mass, and then trotted after my troop who were then about 100 yards away. I am sorry to say I shot 5 men for certain and two doubtful. The pistol was the best thing in the world. . . . The Dervishes

showed no fear of cavalry, and would not move unless you knocked them over with the horse. They tried to hamstring the horses, to cut the bridles—reins—slashed and stabbed in all directions and fired rifles at a few feet range. Nothing touched me. I destroyed those who molested me and so passed out [of the battle] without any disturbance of body or mind.[3]

He told of friends who had been killed or slashed, and continued: "I speculated on the shoddiness of war. You cannot gild it. The raw comes through. . . . There are 7,000 bodies lying there. . . ."[4]

". . . I thought about you a great deal my dearest Mamma—before the action," he later wrote. ". . . I fear it must have been with a beating heart that you read the telegrams and looked down the casualty list."[5]

George Warrington Steevens, the brilliant special correspondent of the *Daily Mail,* who had observed the Battle of Obdurman and the twenty-four-year-old Winston Churchill, wrote an article entitled, "The Youngest Man in Europe":

In years, he is a boy; in temperament, he is also a boy; but in intention, in deliberate plan, purpose, adaptation of means to ends, he is already a man. . . .

He is what he is by breeding. From his father, he derives the hereditary aptitude for affairs, the grand style of entering upon them. From his American strain, he adds to this a keenness, a shrewdness, a half-cynical, personal ambition, a natural aptitude for advertisement and, happily, a sense of humor . . . qualities which might make him, almost at will, a great popular leader, a great journalist, or the founder of a great advertising business. . . .

. . . He is ambitious and he is calculating; yet he is not cold. He has a queer, shrewd sense of introspection . . . he has not studied to make himself a demagogue. He was born a demagogue and happens to know it.

. . . He has the 20th century in his marrow. . . .

What will he become, who shall say? At the rate he goes, there will hardly be room for him in Parliament at 30, or in England at 40.[5]

At the moment, however, Jennie was not pleased by Winston's continued friction with Kitchener. The Sirdar was furious with Sir Evelyn Wood for sending Winston to the Sudan and had told people that Winston was "only making a convenience" of the Army. Winston's opinion of Kitchener was no higher. "He may be a general–but never a gentleman," he commented to his mother.

Writing to Jack, Jennie remarked: "Of course, he talks like that about the sirdar, but only to me, I think–He wouldn't be so silly as to air his views in public. From the sirdar's point of view, I daresay he is right–I had hoped W wd. have made friends with him & that is the best way of clipping your enemy's claws. . . ."[6]

Winston soon would be returning to London, and the Prince of Wales invited him to "come & see me and tell me all about the recent campaign & about your future plans."

> I can well understand, [the Prince went on,] that it must be very difficult for you to make up your mind what to do, but I cannot help feeling that Parliamentary & literary life is what would suit you best as the monotony of military life in an Indian station can have no attraction for you–though fortunately some officers do put up with it or else we should have no Army at all![7]

In the meantime, Jennie had arranged two political meetings at which Winston was to speak, one at Bradford and the other Birmingham. By the simple expedient of inviting the editor to lunch with her, she also managed to have published in the *Morning Post* two letters to the editor which Winston had written to air some of his views about Egypt.

Jennie not only labored on behalf of Winston's career but also kept busy entertaining the stream of friends he kept sending to visit her while they were in London. Jennie made them all welcome, and no doubt enchanted them. But there were times during that winter of 1898 when she questioned the value of her ability to enchant.

Her romance with George was an affair of grand passion, but she seemed uncertain, dispirited, fearful. How long does beauty last? How long would this love last? What could she finally expect from life?

As always, Jennie sought advice from her friends. One was George Nathaniel Curzon, who had recently married Mary Leiter, one of the wealthiest women in America. People who did not know Curzon well compared him to German baroque architecture, "perhaps most admirable when viewed from a distance."[8] But Jennie knew that one reason for his cold, stiff appearance was a brace he wore on his back, and she remembered him with fondness as the witty young man who had once borrowed a nightgown from her during an unexpected overnight stay at Blenheim Palace.

Curzon was about to leave for India where he would serve as Viceroy, and at a farewell dinner for him given by the Duke and Duchess of Portland, Jennie was seated next to him and later described the conversation:

> . . . We got on the subject, which, without my knowing it at the time, was fraught with great importance for me. In a despondent mood, I bemoaned the empty life I was leading at the moment. Lord Curzon tried to console me by saying that a woman alone was a godsend in society, and that I might look forward to a long vista of country-house parties, dinners and balls. Thinking over our conversation later, I found myself wondering if this indeed was all that the remainder of my life held for me. I determined to do something, and cogitating for some time over what it should be, decided finally to start a Review.[9]

It was a spectacular idea, bold and to the point. Jennie needed to work at something to give her life direction. The fact that she then knew nothing about organizing and running a literary magazine did not deter her. She had an abiding interest in literature and a deep respect for writers. She knew many of the literary lions of the time and counted some of them among her intimates. Although she did not understand finance, she knew men who did; she had no knowledge of printing and other production matters, but she would find those who were experts. And although publishing was almost exclusively a man's world, Jennie moved easily among men.

But first she needed a clear concept.

"My ideas were of the vaguest, but they soon shaped themselves," she wrote. "I consulted my friend, Mrs. Craigie, whose acquaintance I had made . . . at the Curzons'."[10]

In fact, Jennie had known Pearl Craigie for several years, but their relationship had remained somewhat formal. Until February 1899, Mrs. Craigie's letters to Jennie always began with the salutation, "My dear Lady Randolph Churchill." Then this was changed to, "My dear Jennie, (since you insist!)," and several months later, it was "Dearest Jennie." Before the year was over Pearl Craigie became Jennie's closest friend.

At first glance, it seemed an odd association. Jennie was basically an extrovert; Pearl Craigie was usually reserved, distant, mysterious, full of "still deeps and silent pools."[11] She said of herself, "I not only think twice before I speak or move—but twenty times. If I could only be natural once, I should feel rested, but this eternal restraint, this unending, 'Shall I say this?' 'Is it wise to say that?' 'Is this wrong?' 'Will this be misunderstood?' 'Will this give a wrong impression?' tires me to death. . . . People scare me out of my wits. . . ."[12]

Yet, although Pearl Craigie was more than a dozen years younger than Jennie, the two women had a good deal in common. They were both Americans who had been brought to Europe as children, both loved music and were expert pianists, and both had had unhappy marriages.

Like Jennie, Pearl Craigie had married at nineteen; she was separated several years later and divorced in 1895. She had one child, John Churchill Craigie. (Could her admiration of Jennie have been responsible for her selecting that name?)

Beyond these similarities was Pearl Craigie's apparent adoration of Jennie. It was as if Jennie were the image of everything she herself wanted to be. She had written such things as,

> There is no woman who does not love to be loved.
> There is only one obligation in life, and that is courage. . . .
> Life is not what we find it, but what we make it. . . .
> People say, "Gather the roses while you may." I'd gather
> them fast enough, if I could see them. But where are they?
> When you find them, they have to be bought and paid for.[13]

Pearl Craigie must have seen in Jennie a woman who had the courage to love, to gather her roses, and what was most essential to the task of making of her life what she wanted it to be—an unshakable belief in herself. She also saw in Jennie the kind of striking beauty that made it easier to have those qualities. Pearl did not have that beauty. Gertrude Atherton described her as "a short, dark woman who would have been plain but for a pair of remarkably fine eyes."[14] But her large, attractive eyes often seemed sad, and her pale refined face with its tight narrow lips was softened only by a dimple in each cheek.

Her father, John Morgan Richards, a distant cousin of the Jerome family, had made a fortune in the patent medicine business[15] and moved his family from Boston to London when Pearl was a child. A man of magnetic personality, he loved books and wrote one himself about England. Pearl's neurotic, eccentric mother was a witty woman and an ardent advocate of peace. When war between the United States and Spain was imminent, she sent a cable: "ITALY, POPE, VATICAN, ROME. STOP WAR. RICHARDS."[16]

With her first book, Pearl decided on the *nom de plume* "John Oliver Hobbes." She chose John because it was the name of her father and her son, Oliver because of the warring Cromwell, and Hobbes because she liked the work by the philosopher of that name. Her first novel, *Some Emotions and a Moral,* was published when she was twenty-four and became an enormous success. It was essentially a satire on "Smart Society," rich in epigram and with implications that required careful reading to be perceived.[17] "You might as well flirt with the Ten Commandments as fall in love with your wife," she wrote.

Pearl Craigie wore "flowing Watteau gowns, lived in over-furnished rooms with stained glass lampshades" and spent much of her time in bed suffering from fatigue or vague illness. She was neither modest about her ability nor shy about her ambition, and perhaps, like Jennie, she envied the degree of freedom that men enjoyed. She most admired, she wrote, the fact that "if a man really wants a thing, he will ask for it." On the other hand, she felt that the clever women had to go in for "blimming." "Blimming," she explained, "is just talking and talking pleasant things, and saying nothing. This was a way to keep the world off. No one ever finds out that a blimming woman is cleverer than her husband. It's one of the great conservers of marital bliss."[18]

Pearl herself was expert at "blimming." Jennie called her, "a brilliant and clever conversationalist, she could hold her own with all manner of men, and yet in the more frivolous company, which she often frequented and thoroughly enjoyed, she never talked over people's heads. She had the art of drawing everyone out and making them appear at their best. So different to some clever woman writers I have met."[19]

Pearl Craigie's admiration of Jennie appeared boundless and Jennie surely found it flattering. Pearl was a celebrity, having written books, magazine articles, and a highly successful play. Important people catered to her, yet with her characteristic self-effacement, her early notes to Jennie were written as if she felt she were intruding on Jennie's time:

> Are you quite sure that there will be room for me this evening? . . . I should go in any case, solely for the pleasure of seeing you, and I would see you better when there were not a number of guests to claim your attention. . . .[20]

And another time: "I hope you will find a little moment to spare for me . . ."[21]

But Jennie also admired and appreciated Pearl. "On looking back at the early period of the Review," she wrote,

> I often wonder how I should have succeeded without Pearl Craigie's intelligent help and advice. A woman of great sympathies, her unselfishness has been realized by all who ever

came in contact with her, and her valuable time was always at the disposal of anyone she could help.[22]

In addition to the personal qualities which made it almost inevitable that these two talented women gravitate toward each other, there was the basic fact that they were two of the very few women on the London literary scene. Indeed, they were among the few women who dared to make a life for themselves outside of the home. Despite the growing freedom of the "Naughty Nineties," it was still a man's world. The Woman Suffrage Bill, introduced by Faithful Begg in 1897 and supported by 257,796 signatures, received only two readings in the House of Commons before its defeat by seventy-one votes. An unmarried mother was permitted to earn a living only if she gave up her child. And the child's father could escape legal responsibility for it with a payment of twenty pounds, which brought immunity from inspection for the boarding house that received his child. Moreover, in 1899 the law (*Regina v. Clarence*) held that "a husband could not be held guilty of committing rape on a wife who tried to refuse intercourse, even if he was suffering from a disease of which he was aware, though she was not."[23]

As Francis Power Cobbe wrote, men treated women "uniformly as minors." A significant breakthrough had occurred in 1892 when seven government departments hired some "typewriter girls." But a woman who tried to qualify in a profession was often told, "You surely don't imagine that men would ever put real confidence in one of your sex?"[24]

It was perfectly permissible for the Victorian woman to play the piano, sing, act on the stage, and write private poetry, but only a very few women had been able to make their mark on England's literary world—Jane Austen, early in the century; the Brontë sisters, Elizabeth Barrett Browning, George Eliot (Mary Ann Evans), and Pearl Craigie—but they were considered phenomena. For a woman to organize a literary magazine, making critical judgments and business decisions, must have caused a thousand British clubmen to cringe and curse. The kind of quarterly Jennie was considering was in itself unique, but her temerity in wanting to create it, to be editor and publisher, was outrageous.

But Jennie never had been fazed by "No" or denied by "Never." Challenge was the zest of her life. Not that she was unaware of the countless problems involved in the project, nor of her ignorance and inexperience; she knew she would need all the help she could get.

Among the most important men Jennie met at one of Pearl Craigie's many dinners was John Lane. A former railroad clerk, Lane had become one of the most successful publishers in Great Britain. His "Bodley Head" published a surprising amount of successful poetry and "daring novels," as well as high-level literary criticism by some of the youngest and most talented authors in England, which created new literary fashions and taste.

Lane's next move was to establish a literary quarterly. Probably more than in any other country, quarterlies have ebbed and flowed through the literary history of England. But in 1898 there was not yet a magazine that had successfully struck the modern note of the Nineties.

Yellow seemed to be the color of the Nineties. One of the most popular novels was *The Yellow Aster* and one of the most popular books of poetry was called, *Le Cahier Jaune (The Yellow Notebook)*. Cashing in on this trend, John Lane titled his literary quarterly *The Yellow Book*. "Its flaming cover of yellow, out of which the Aubrey Beardsley woman smirked at the public for the first time," made a powerful impact. Nothing like it had ever been seen before. "It was novelty naked and unashamed. People were puzzled and shocked and delighted."[25]

Aubrey Beardsley was a delicate, effeminate young man of great talent and enormous nervous energy. Oscar Wilde described him as having "a face like a silver hatchet, with grass-green hair." Lane had a nerve-wracking time with Beardsley's persistent attempts to slip some indecency into his cover drawing, and he had to spend considerable effort examining the covers, even submitting them to his friends for further checking before publication. Even so, one issue went to press before a particularly "audacious impropriety" was discovered, and Lane had to cancel the issue. Beardsley, like Wilde, was a doomed figure. He would die of tuberculosis at the age of twenty-five, a devout Catholic, begging his friends to destroy his "bawdy drawings."

Lane was in New York at the time of the Wilde scandal. A headline in one of the Sunday papers read: "ARREST OF OSCAR WILDE, YELLOW BOOK UNDER HIS ARM." "It killed The Yellow Book, and nearly killed me," Lane said.[26] Crowds threw stones at his windows, and six of Bodley Head's authors threatened not to let Lane publish any more of their books unless he suppressed Beardsley's work and eliminated Wilde from the catalogue. Lane surrendered; Beardsley left.[27]

Courage was not one of John Lane's prominent characteristics. A trend-setting magazine such as *The Yellow Book* needed audacity, but Lane brought to it an air of compromise. "Publisher John Lane had no objection against thin ice, provided he felt reasonably sure it would not let him through," wrote a critic of his *Yellow Book*.[28] He began to substitute more and more of the "safer," more established writers for the newer, bolder ones, and within two years *The Yellow Book* was dead.

The short, dandified Lane married a large, rich Bostonian, described as "an ice-covered Brunnhilde."[29] As an American, she soon found herself in Jennie's social circle and was an early supporter of Jennie's project. But it was not Jennie who had the first formal business meeting with Lane about the review; it was her son.

This was an eventful occasion in the changing relationship between Jennie and Winston. Until then, Jennie had always been doing things for him, and as long as she lived, she would be his advance guard. But now, gradually, Jennie and Winston acted more and more like a sister and brother. He was, of course, not only helping her but also asserting his own manhood.

Jennie was away for a weekend at Welbeck, the Duke and Duchess of Portland's estate, when Winston wrote her: "Lane lunches with me tomorrow. I will write you the results of our interview which should cover the whole ground. I have written to Mr. Cassel about the investment of the surplus loan I have raised."[30]

Two days later Winston wrote again:

> Mr. John Lane called on me yesterday, and after lunch we had a long talk. We agreed on nothing, but I cannot help thinking you will find him vy satisfactory. This, or something like this, should be the scheme. You would have to guarantee, say, £1000, the chance of loss on four numbers. £350 of this would be paid towards the first number. This will be your whole liability in the matter, and should the magazine show a balance profit, this would of course not be wanted, and you would not lose anything. Given the guarantee–Lane will produce the magazine on an agreed scale–paying the writers, printing, publishing, advertising, etcetera–on a scale previously fixed.
>
> In order to assist the production of the magazine he would do everything at cost price, and would take no profit until the enterprise was successful. Should it become successful you and he would divide profits. Lane thought these might amount to about £800 each. Harmsworth however said it would not be worth your while unless you had at least £2,000 out of it. I dissent. I think that even £800 for a beginning would enable you to live in the house–apart from the pleasure of influencing thought and opinion and becoming generally known as literary and artistic. I confess I do not think the ½ profit good enough. You had better get Moreton [Frewen] to go into that matter–or better still Harmsworth. I should much prefer a 25% on the total sales v.i.z., threepence in every shilling sold.
>
> However, these are, after all, details. The three features of the schemes are:

1. A guaranteed amount.
2. A Fixed scale of Production.
3. A division of Profits.

In what proportion these are to be fixed is a matter for bargain and contract—in which you must be represented by a clever man.

I think Lane has a considerable clientele of his own. He certainly has lots of ideas, and is full of enthusiasm. One of his ideas struck me as good. He is the great authority on bindings. He suggested that the magazine should come out each quarter—bound like some famous old book. This alone would command a public interested in bindings. All this you must talk to him about. I will leave his address, and you should write him at once—and arrange an early interview. He is a gentleman-like fellow, and would probably be willing to do a good deal.[31]

Jennie arranged her first business meeting with Lane on December 3, 1898. The formal note, still among Lane's papers, reads, "Lady Randolph Churchill presents her compliments to Mr. Lane, and in the absence of her son, who left for India last night—would like to know if it would be agreeable to him if she called between 11 and 12 o-c this morning."

Lane probably thought that he would be able to control Jennie and also handle the administration and finances of the project. Jennie, in turn, probably thought Lane would do all the production, reporting to her on the details. Neither one was correct.

By this time Jennie had decided exactly what kind of Review she wanted. It was to be unique, an international literary magazine that really would be international and really would be literary. She would get the best talent on both sides of the Atlantic. Everything about the magazine would be of high quality—the content, the art, the binding, and the paper. It would look like a book and be almost as expensive. No one had ever produced anything like it before. That was the kind of challenge Jennie relished.

Twenty-Nine

$\mathcal{T}$HE LAST YEAR OF THE CENTURY brought a fresh beginning for Jennie. Of all the envious women who watched her from the sidelines, a great number gladly would have taken that one year of Jennie's to fill the whole of their own lives.

Winston especially shared her excitement about the Review:

> ... you will have an occupation and an interest in life which will make up for all the silly social amusements you will cease to shine in as time goes on and which will give you in the latter part of your life as fine a position in the world of taste & thought as formerly & now in that of elegance & beauty. It is wide & philosophic. It may also be profitable. If you could make £1,000 a year out of it, I think that would be a little lift in the dark clouds.[1]

One of Jennie's acquaintances suggested that the Review was merely a means of further enveloping her "literary young man friend."[2] But George Cornwallis-West already was thoroughly enveloped. Besides, at that time George was more interested in sports than in sonnets. It was gratifying for Jennie to have such an ardent lover always available, but the new and growing excitement of a Review gave her a particular buoyancy.

The man she wanted to share this with was Bourke Cockran. Cockran was in London at the time, so the two met often. Bourke's maturity and wisdom were in strong contrast to the callow George. Jennie could talk to him about financial matters, such as the idea of forming a syndicate of six major contributors to supply the funds for the first year of publication. She could talk to him about the magazine's content—her desire for "lots of American talent to write for me . . ." She could talk to Bourke about all her hopes and dreams of finding fulfillment, of doing something important with her life.

George was more romantic and impressionable, a young reed whom Jennie could bend and turn at will; Bourke was a solid oak, a strong, mature man who had cultivated his individuality. "You were a tower of strength to me," Jennie wrote him after he left London, and then asked him to "find me a really clever man for my 'American Notes'—and oh! do find me a name for my magazine."[3]

When George came into her life, Jennie had relegated Bourke to a different level but had things changed again? Jennie was a woman of so many facets that it seemed she needed a variety of men to suit them. George's passion suited one need; Bourke's mature understanding and sensitivity suited another.

However insoluble the differences between her and Bourke must have seemed—her subconscious need to drive and dominate, the irreconcilable question of leaving England and her sons—deep within her Jennie still must have felt that Bourke was more the man for her, "Don't forget about me when you get home . . ." she had written him.[4]

The magazine, which Jennie and her friends called "Maggie," was now taking on its own life and making its own demands on Jennie's time. Finding a proper name for "Maggie" was one of the niggling problems. Jennie had asked Bourke to think of a title and she was now asking everyone. One friend had seriously suggested *The Mentor of Mayfair*. Other titles proposed were even worse. "It seemed as difficult to find an unappropriated title as though I were naming a racehorse, instead of a book," Jennie wrote.[5]

"I beg you not to be in a hurry," Winston had wisely written, "a bad name will damn any magazine." She should search for a title, he said, that would be "exquisite, rich, stately . . . something classical and opulent . . ."[6]

For an exquisite opulent title, Jennie asked an exquisite opulent man, one of her former lovers, Sir Edgar Vincent. He suggested *Anglo-Saxon*, and Jennie was enchanted. "How simple! It sounded strong, sensible and solid." She soon learned however, that someone else already had registered the same title, and Pearl Craigie, who had gotten the information at a party, warned Jennie that the owner "will wait, probably, till your circulars, advertisements [are out] . . . & then apply for an injunction, claiming damages and compensation . . ."⁷ Jennie had a simple solution: she merely added the word, "Review" and she had her title–*Anglo-Saxon Review*.

But that was an easy problem compared to the search for a basic concept and style. Jennie sought all those whose talents she most admired and asked them what *they* thought, what *they* wanted. She kept her questions sharp, her mind receptive, and tried to let her own imagination and ideas act as a filter for everything she heard. "Sometimes I became a little bewildered at the conflicting advice and suggestions I received."

> "Why don't you have three articles and three languages?"
> said one. "That would damn it at once," said another. "Mind
> you, have something startling in the first number–'new ideas
> on free love' or 'sidelights on Royal courts.'" "Be lofty in your
> ambitions; set up a poetical standard to the literary world."
> "Why not get a poem from the Poet Laureate?" "Or an essay
> on Bi-Metallism from Mr. Henry Chaplin?" "Aim at a glori-
> fied *Yellow Book*–that's the thing!" How amusing it all was!⁸

One of the less elegant suggestions was to emphasize the bond between England and the United States with a motto for the magazine: "Blood is thicker than water." Jennie told this to Winston and he exploded, saying that it should be "relegated to the pothouse Music Hall," that it "only needs the Union Jack & The Star-Spangled Banner to be suited to one of Harmsworth's cheap Imperialist productions. . . . People don't pay a guinea for such stuff . . . I confess I shivered when I read your letter."⁹ Jennie eliminated the motto. She wanted, after all, a deluxe magazine that might be read with interest and pleasure by educated people anywhere, a luxurious-looking magazine with writings of significance and artistry.

A guinea (approximately five dollars) a copy, furthermore, was enormously expensive. It greatly restricted her and made financial matters very delicate. Winston pleaded with her, therefore, to delay a final commitment until his return home as he felt he could more easily deal with John Lane than she could. He suggested that all agreements with Lane should be made on an annual basis only. He also wanted to make his own investment in the magazine, but he said, "I do not like Lane's 12½ percent of the gross profits. It is enormous!"¹⁰

Jennie agreed and wrote Lane, "I should like to know, and to have you explain to me, how you are entitled to so large a percentage–Of course, I only want what is fair between us . . ."¹¹

She soon made it plain to Lane that she was in charge, that he worked for her. Lane had printed a subscription form on which payment was to be made to his own bank. Jennie rejected that idea immediately. "I shall expect the order to be payable to my bank," she curtly said.[12]

Jennie had adopted Lane's idea of a quarterly, each issue bound, as Winston put it, "like some famous old book," and she prevailed upon Cyril Davenport of the British Museum to help her choose the most beautiful bindings from earlier periods. Then she wrote Lane that she hoped he was "*quite* satisfied" with the bindings, but she had already selected and decided on them.

To supervise other historical matters she went to Arthur Strong, librarian of the House of Lords, "and he will do all I want."[13] She also used Strong's support to get Lionel Cust of the National Portrait Gallery to be responsible for the illustrations.

But Jennie was beginning to have doubts about herself. What were her literary qualifications? She was well-educated for a woman of her time and her experience was broad and varied, but she was neither as educated nor as experienced as the men she was dealing with. She was essentially a dilettante. Her taste was excellent, but her judgments were instinctive. She knew nothing of being a professional editor. Cecil Rhodes tried to encourage her: "After all, women, remember, have great imagination and much more delicate instinct than my sex, who are rough and brutal. I think you should have a fair chance."[14]

In her pessimism, however, Jennie must have written an unhappy letter to Pearl Craigie, for she received this reply:

> Dearest Jennie, What do you mean by calling yourself uncultured, unliterary & old? You must be "going crazy"—to use our country's cheerful idiom. You are perfectly charming & your judgment in artistic matters is distinguished. These things you know in your heart, already, so I cannot be accused of flattering you.[15]

Winston agreed that she needed expert editorial assistance and volunteered his services. "I know I can help you in ways scarcely anyone else *can* and nobody else will."[16] He also saw in that prospect an opportunity of earning 200 pounds a year—"a very sensible addition to the advantages we derive from the venture."[17] However, Winston had to admit that he was probably no better qualified and no more experienced than Jennie, and that, in the initial stages, it was better to have an experienced man.

"I am quite prepared to do it alone," Jennie had written Lane, but she didn't really believe it.[18] Her great need, she thought, was for someone on whom she could rely to read manuscripts and to advise her on the selection of ideas for articles.

She found the ideal candidate one evening at a dinner party at Pearl Craigie's. He was Sidney Low, a slightly balding man with a very thick mustache and penetrating eyes.

The brilliant Sidney James Mark Low, three years younger than Jennie, had been the editor of the *St. James Gazette* (1888–97) and then the Literary Editor of the *Morning Standard*. The author of the *Dictionary of English History*, he was later co-author of *The Political History of England*. Even more significant for Jennie, Low had the reputation of having a keen eye for vital young talent. He was credited with having discovered a number of young writers, including Rudyard Kipling and James Barrie.[19]

John Lane and Sidney Low were vastly different men. Lane was a sharp businessman, whereas Low said his principal concern was with "spinning words."[20] Lane was a collector of things—books, pictures, furniture, old glass; Low was attracted to talented people—especially women—and the more celebrated they were, the more they fascinated him. For a literary man and serious scholar, Low had an unusual fondness for the social swirl. Few men more greatly appreciated the society of a beautiful, witty, and accomplished woman of the world. Jennie asked him to escort her to a succession of parties, which Low detailed in his diary. Of one, he wrote:

> Dined with Lady Randolph Churchill. Present: the Prince of Wales, Duke and Duchess of Devonshire, Cecil Rhodes, Countess of Warwick, Lady Gerard, Miss Plowden, Lord Hardwick, Sir Henry Burdett, Winston Churchill and his brother, and Mr. Ernest Cassel. Sat between Winston C. and the Duchess of Devonshire. Talked with Rhodes on South Africa. The Prince of Wales talked to me after dinner. Deplored imperfect knowledge of foreign languages by Englishmen. Spoke of the Dreyfus case and its scandals, and the state of France. Said he did not think there was any chance of an Orleanist restoration, and the Bonapartists were too lazy and unenterprising to do anything. Told me he had once met [French General Georges] Boulanger and thought him a poor creature. He also spoke of our hostess' venture, the *Anglo-Saxon Review*.[21]

As Low's biographer remarked, Jennie was "irresistible": she had "not only traditions of culture, but very great energy, and these allied to beauty, brilliance and wit . . ." Jennie had completely captivated Low. "She solicited his help, advice and contributions in support of her new Review, and freely he gave all these."[22]

Low personified a great deal of the literary substance of the Review, but Jennie was its soaring spirit. John Lane's file soon bulged with memoranda from her:

> After I have seen Mr. Wrightman's article, I shall better be able to judge, whether we can have it signed or not. I am glad you find him all I had heard of him . . . I shall write to W. D. Howells,–a story from him for September wd do well. We have enough fiction for the first no. I shall read with interest E[dith] Wharton's book. I hope you will like Robins' article on Lady M.M. I am glad that it is long, as we have so many pages to fill up. I have just returned from Paris, where I did considerable work, and have got a good many subscribers and some good contributors. I have come to the conclusion with Mr. Low, Mrs. Craigie and a few others that there is no harm in having one French contributor in each no.: even the first, [Paul] Bourget will write for the first, and he is as well-known here as in America and France. I must consider my foreign subscribers–besides, 250 pages takes a great deal of filling, and it will not be easy to find good contributors. . . . I will let you know about Prof. Waldstein–as it is for Sept., it can wait. Meanwhile, I have not heard one word from Prof. Thornton–and am trying to get an article on "Wireless Telegraphy" from Prof. Lodge, which will do well. . . . I am glad to hear of the interest the Review is awakening in the States–I have orders and cheques sent to me from there. . . . [23]
>
> I write a line to catch the post, to tell you that the first no. is now nearly completed, and I think it is very good–the J.F. cover is the greatest success. I saw Mr. Leighton this morning, and he, too, is very pleased with it. I shall see Mr. Davenport tomorrow. . . . The contributors are slow in sending in their stories, and it takes some reminding to get them![24]

Jennie was meticulous about detail, and a contemporary recalled the vision of her "on some of the numerous occasions when she called, maybe a bunch of proofs in her hand, to discuss . . . the format of the Anglo-Saxon Review . . ."[25] She was also highly critical of imperfection, and Lane bore the brunt of her anger.

> I am horrified in my old complete copy–the same mistake as to the word "received" . . . I thought you had settled it . . .[26]

I return to you the list and proposed proofs. You will see the center is missing from 16 to 40 . . .[27]

I am not going to be made ridiculous by publishing stuff which makes no sense. . . .[28]

As work on the Review progressed, Jennie became increasingly critical of Lane. She was unhappy that he had made both their names in the mast-head "a trifle large." Further, she had not received the prospectuses or the dummies she had asked for. And again: "I do not think you ought to get commissions on the subscriptions I get. . . ."[29] Worst of all, she was annoyed about his projected trip to America in May—with the first issue scheduled for publication on June 15th. "It is unfortunate that he absents himself at such a moment. . . ."[30]

Her memoranda to Lane came in a steady stream:

. . . I hope to send you next week articles by Mr. Whitelaw Reid [publisher of the *New York Tribune*], Lord Rosebery [former Prime Minister], two from Mr. Strong, Mr. Henry James, Prof. Thompson and Prof. Lodge. I have heard from Mr. Low this morning. He seems to think that unless you have all the copy by the first of May, the Review cannot appear this season. This need not be so, particularly as it need not be published until the end of June.[31]

I am expecting other MS. in a few days. The photogravures are in hand. Mr. Strong has been ill, and is at Versailles, but returns the 17th. . . . I have seen Mr. Cust about various matters, and Mr. Davenport. The latter has chosen two other bindings; therefore, with the 17th-Century French one we have, and the James I one we are having made, our year will be covered.[32]

. . . I will do what I can with regard to Mr. Bryce and the stories you mention, but they are not wanted for the first no. . . . I am going to ask Lord Shew Cecil to write something on the church; he is very clever and bold. Mrs. Craigie has sent me a drama in two acts, "Osbern and Ursyne," which I think is beautiful. It has not been published—and will not be for months, and will not be acted until July. . . . [33]

. . . I have written to Mr. Leighton to add the word "Review" to the designs for the back, and hope that he will be able to send me a rough sketch tomorrow. Then we can go ahead.[34]

. . . It will be necessary to have seven illustrations in the first no. . . . I shall consider the frontispiece, "The Queen," as

an extra for the first no. I have written to Miss Wharton, and
shall hope to see her. . . .[35]

Jennie kept her own list of the pieces for the first issue, with the author's
name, the length, and the price paid for each. The price paid ranged from
10 pounds to Charles Davenport for three bindings, to 50 pounds for the
Political Summary. Mrs. Craigie received 40 pounds for her play, which
ran thirty-three pages; Prof. Oliver Lodge 25 pounds for his article on
Wireless Telegraphy; Algernon Swinburne was paid 15 pounds for a poem;
Henry James 40 pounds for his twenty-five-page story. There was no price
listed for Lord Rosebery's article of twenty-three pages on Sir Robert Peel,
which may have been given to Jennie as a gesture of friendship. There were
also five letters from Lord Devonshire, for which he was paid 25 pounds.
Cecil Rhodes was to have been paid 5 pounds for an article which was apparently not received. And C. Robbins was paid 31 pounds 10 shillings for
a twenty-eight-page article called "A Modern Woman."

Heightening the frenzy of the beginnings of "Maggie" was the fact that
Lane was away for more than a month; Low was sick, and so was Strong
for part of the time. The full responsibility was on Jennie, but she had a decisive, organized mind and tremendous energy.

Through it all, she managed to maintain both a busy social schedule
and a heady romance; she even found time to perform at concerts. "I must
tell you that you were an angel," Pearl Craigie told her, "you played beautifully and I was immensely proud of you."[36] Jennie also persuaded Pearl to
play with her[37] and Mademoiselle Maria Janotha at another concert at
Queen's Hall. They played Bach's *Concerto in D Minor for three Pianos*, with an
orchestra from the Royal College of Music conducted by Sir Walter Par-
rott. Janotha, who had been Court pianist to the German Emperor, was a
great favorite of Queen Victoria. Before any performance at Court, she
knelt at the Queen's feet and presented her with some white heather. She
also kept a mascot on the piano while she played, to repel the evil eye.[38] It
must have worked, for their concert was a tremendous success and they received a rousing ovation. "This was the only time I ever remember enjoying playing in public," Jennie wrote.[39]

Pearl Craigie began to make herself more and more indispensable to
Jennie, both personally and professionally. She not only suggested stories
and contributors ("How about Anatole France?"), found her a secretary
("She is clever, industrious . . . can mind her business and be depended
on . . . not at all on the Woman Journalist lines . . ."), but she was also
watchful of Jennie's health and morale ("Do be careful & remember that
you are precious . . ." ". . . You are looking lovely . . .").[40]

It was extraordinary how rapidly their relationship had taken on new dimensions. At first Pearl had leaned heavily on Jennie; now the need was more mutual. They were regularly seeing one another, writing notes, exchanging ideas.

Despite her involvement with the Review, Jennie gave a lot of time and thought to Pearl's play, which was then being readied for production.[41] During a country weekend she wrote her a long letter explaining why she thought a certain actor would be ideal for the lead. Jennie's love of the theater was another bond between her and Pearl.

A major element in their friendship was the fact that, unlike almost everyone else, Pearl Craigie asked little of Jennie. She seemed to get great satisfaction from just being her friend, a part of her work and her life. As for Jennie, she could ask almost anything of Pearl, and Pearl was quick to oblige. When Jennie asked her to play with her in the concert, she hesitated only because she had not performed for a long time. But she put herself to the task, taking a dozen lessons from one of the best teachers in London, Signor Bisaccia, who commented that "She plays with her brain."

Pearl Craigie seemed to depend upon her brain in all aspects of her life, usually keeping her emotions strictly contained. After her divorce she revealed herself to few people other than Jennie, and that was part of her misfortune. Jennie understood Pearl's problems, her longings, her unhappiness, and her great gifts. She accepted her effusive attachment and returned to her some peace and love.

But as the pressures increased, Jennie had less time for her personal life. "Maggie" was not yet in print, but already it had became an irresistible target for cartoonists, satirists, columnists, rumor-mongers, and society wags. Some of their comments were genuinely funny, and Jennie laughed along with them, as was the case with this poem, which Jennie enjoyed reciting for her friends:

> Have you heard of the wonderful Magazine
> Lady Randolph's to edit, with help from the Queen?
> It's a guinea a number, too little by half,
> For the Crowned Heads of Europe are all on the staff;
> And everyone writing verse, fiction, or views—
> The best blue-blood ink must exclusively use;
> While (paper so little distinction achieves)
> 'Twill wholly be printed on strawberry leaves;
> And lest the effusions, so dazzlingly bright
> And brilliantly witty, should injure the sight,
> A pair of smoked glasses (of ducal design)
> Will go with each copy to shelter the eyne.
> The articles promised already, or written,

Suggest what a treat is preparing for Britain.
The Princess of———will describe a new bonnet;
The Spanish Queen Mother has offered a sonnet,
Provided that all whom its scansion may beat
Will refrain from indelicate mention of feet;
And the Duchess of———has accepted the section
Devoted to "Babies, their Tricks and Correction."
The Czar will contribute a fable for geese,
"On Breaking up China and Keeping the Peace";
The Porte sends a batch of seraglio tales,
And our Prince will review "Mr. Bullen on Whales."
Mr. Primrose, who also has thoughts of the sea,
Addresses the captains of every degree.
A treatise profound, yet delectable, too,
On "How to be a Father-in-Law to a Crew(e)";
While William of Potsdam, the ablest of men,
Will fill every gap with one stroke of his pen,
And, lest art be slighted 'midst hurry and rush,
Will illustrate all with one flirt of his brush.

Such, such is the hint of the new Magazine
Lady Randolph will edit, with help from the Queen.[42]

The London correspondent of a New York magazine offered some kindly opinions: "Lady Randy is sure to have a clever magazine, for she is so clever, brilliant, keen of wit. She is highly educated, observing, and has as varied a knowledge of the world and society as it is possible for a woman to have. . . . Lady Randy's acquaintance is limited only by the confines of the earth. . . ." The same correspondent later reported seeing "Black Jennie" almost every evening in the House of Commons, lobbying for articles and subscriptions. "Poor Arthur Balfour, who is intensely lazy, has promised to write an article for the first number, but according to my latest intelligence, he has not come up in time. Viscount Peel, the ex-Speaker, has promised to write an article on the licensing question, and Emperor William was to write on yachting. . . . H.R.H. [the Prince of Wales] has even been induced to put his pen to paper for the fascinating Jennie. . . ." And he pointed out that Whitelaw Reid, publisher of the *New York Tribune* and a former Ambassador to France, had written a revealing article not for his *Tribune* but for the *Anglo-Saxon Review*.[43]

"I think Lady Randolph made a great mistake in not calling her publication, *The Transatlantic*," the American correspondent continued. That title he said, had been awarded the prize at a dinner at Arthur Balfour's house where the question was supposed to have been decided. "*Anglo-Saxon,* as I have said before, will not succeed in this country."[44]

This was an ominous note from a friendly commentator, and some of the other comments were more discouraging—enough so that Pearl Craigie felt it necessary to try to boost Jennie's morale:

> As for criticism, if one gives work to the general public, one has to accept the fate of an Aunt Sally, so far as the journalists are in question. They detest every educated influence. . . . They fear the brightening of the average intelligence—for in the imbecility of the mob (well-dressed and otherwise) is the hack journalist's strength. But the times are changing rapidly. The mob—as a mob—is becoming well-read, even philosophical, the Press in England has less power, and the country more power every day.[45]

In the meantime, Winston had returned home, having resigned his commission in the Army. "I can live cheaper and earn more as a writer," he explained.[46] Jennie put him to work on the Review, and the two of them worked on the Preface for the initial issue—their first literary collaboration.[47] (The quotation from Samuel Johnson in the second paragraph was a favorite of Winston's; he had used it twice in letters to his mother.)

> The explanation of the production of another Review will be found in the number of those already in flourishing existence: the excuse must be looked for in these pages. Yet a few words of introduction are needed by this newcomer, who comes into the crowded world thus late in the day, lest, in spite of his fine coat, he be thought an unmannerly intruder. I desire to say something of his purpose, of his aspirations, of his nature, in the hope that, if these seem admirable, good friends, instead of jostling, will help him through the press, and aid him somewhat in his journey towards the golden temple of literary excellence.
>
> The first object of every publication is commercial. "No one but a blockhead," says Dr. Johnson, "ever wrote except for money"; and the *Anglo-Saxon* is not disposed to think lightly of his wares, or set low value on his effort, for otherwise his green-and-gold brocade would soon be threadbare. But after the vulgar necessities of life are thus provided for, reviews, and sometimes reviewers, look to other and perhaps higher ideals. It is of those that I would write, for are they not

the credentials which must carry the ambitious stranger on his way?

Formerly, little was written, but much of that little was preserved. The pamphlets, the satires, the lampoons, the disquisitions—above all, the private letters—of the 18th Century, have been carefully stored for the delight of succeeding generations. Now, the daily production of printed words in incalculably vast. Miles of newspapers, tons of magazine articles, mountains of periodicals, are distributed daily between sunrise and sunset. They are printed; they are read; they are forgotten. Little remains. And yet there is no reason why the best products of an age of universal education should not be as worthy of preservation as those of a less-cultivated era. The literary excellence of the modern review is high. How many articles, full of solid thought and acute criticism, of wit and learning, are born for a purely ephemeral existence, to be read one day and cast into the wastepaper basket the next? The most miserable lampoons of the reign of Queen Anne are still extant. Some of the finest and cleverest productions of the reign of Queen Victoria are almost as difficult to find as ancient manuscripts. The newspapers of today light the fires of tomorrow. The magazine may have a little longer life. It rests on the writing-table for perhaps a month, and thereafter shares the fate of much that is good in an age that, at least in art and literature, takes little thought for the future. The sure knowledge that their work will perish must exert a demoralizing effect on the writers of the present day. Newspapers and periodicals become cheaper and cheaper. To satisfy the loud demand of the enormous and growing reading public, with a minimum of effort, is the modern temptation.

I do not imagine that the *Anglo-Saxon Review* will arrest these tendencies. But its influence may have some useful effect. This book is published at a price which will ensure its respectful treatment at the hands of those who buy it. It will not be cast aside after a hurried perusal. It appears, too, in a guise which fits it for a better fate. After a brief, though not perchance unhonoured, stay on the writing-table, it may be taken up into that Valhalla of printed things—the library. More than this, that it may have company, another of similar character but different design, will follow at an interval of three months, until a long row of volumes—similar but not alike—may not only adorn the book-shelves, and recall the elegant bindings of former times, but may also preserve in a permanent form something of the transient brilliancy of the age.

It is with such hopes that I send the first volume out into the world—an adventurous pioneer. Yet he bears a name which may sustain him even in the hardest of struggles, and of which he will at all times endeavor to be worthy—a name under which just laws, high purpose, civilizing influence, and a fine language have been spread to the remotest regions.

Lastly, I would in this brief note express my sincere thanks to all those who have helped to fit the *Anglo-Saxon* for the battle of life—not only to those who have, as subscribers, furnished him with his costly habit, but also to those who, like the fairy godmother in the child's story, have given him something of their energy, their wisdom, and their brains.[48]

Jennie gave a luncheon to introduce the *Review.* Its fate was then up to the critics and the public. Lady Warwick called it "a thing of splendor . . . its contents almost equalled its binding."[49] The *Saturday Review,* however, said that it was a swindle to charge a guinea for a copy which was not in real leather and not tooled by hand. But to do that, Jennie said, it would have cost at least a hundred pounds to produce a copy. Another critic thought it "*The Yellow Book* in court dress and bedroom slippers . . ." and the New York *World* commented: "You pay five dollars for this magazine. It may be good, but you can buy the *World* for a cent." The *Pall Mall Gazette* provided the most careful and perceptive review:

Why should not an effort be made to preserve some, at least, of the best work of the day? Lady Randolph Churchill has set herself to answer that question, and she has done so in an eminently practical way. She has realized—and this is the distinctive feature of her venture—that there is no better method of insuring respectful treatment for any article offered for sale than to make the purchaser pay handsomely for it. Provided that good value be given for good money, there is, we most firmly believe, no surer way to commercial success. And certainly the *Anglo-Saxon Review* bids fair to perform that condition alike in the material form and the literary substance of its production. Let us proceed "from without inwards," as the anatomists say, and begin with what is the special feature of the Review—the binding, paper, and print.

To say that the cover alone is worth the money—
considering that the money is a whole golden guinea—would,
no doubt, be an exaggeration. But it is clear that no one who
loves books well enough to pay that price will likely throw
away a volume bound in green calf, richly-tooled in gold, according to a design which is a facsimile of a binding executed
for King James I. That sapient monarch, "the most learned
fool in Christendom," as Sully called him, was a considerable
connoisseur in book-binding, as Mr. Cyril Davenport shows
in a scholarly note on the binding of this volume. . . . And
this beautiful binding encloses paper and print which are a
joy to the senses of touch and sight. Selecting her contributors, Lady Randolph Churchill, as might be expected from
the title of the Review, has gone to American as well as to English sources. The United States is represented by Mr.
Whitelaw Reid, Mr. Henry James, and Miss Elizabeth
Robins. The most interesting contributions, however, and
those which may give that abiding interest to the number
which the editor desiderates, are those of Lord Rosebery and
Mr. Algernon Swinburne. Lord Rosebery's appreciation of
the life and character of Sir Robert Peel not only helps to
throw new light on the personality of that statesman, but also
affords the ex-Premier the opportunity of expressing his own
views on the functions and the position of an English Prime
Minister. They are well worth consideration. Mr. Swinburne's lines on the Centenary of the Battle of the Nile have
an intense earnestness of patriotism, albeit something lacking
in the lyric "surge and thunder" one is accustomed to expect
from the poet. Dr. Sir Rudolph Slatin writes of the Soudan
with his unique experience, and the Duchess of Devonshire
contributes some amusing unpublished letters of the beautiful Duchess Georgiana. A word of praise is due, likewise, to
the seven charming photogravures with which the Review is
illustrated. In short, there is nothing but good to be said of
this unprecedented venture in periodical literature.[50]

"Maggie" was launched. "I am perfectly delighted and congratulate you
with all my heart," wrote Pearl Craigie.[51] To Lane, Jennie wrote: "The
book had a great success, and so it ought!"[52]

The dilettante had become a professional. She had created something
unique. Although she had received a great deal of advice and technical

help, it would not have been born without her. The *Anglo-Saxon Review* was a publication of quality and substance. It had imagination and style. What its fate would be was another question, but the overwhelming fact of its birth could be credited only to Jennie.

There was little time for Jennie to revel in success. The second volume was waiting.

Thirty

ᴮOTH OF JENNIE'S SONS WERE in London in the summer of 1899.
Jack was with a brokerage firm in the "City"–London's financial district–and doing well; and Winston, pursuing "the larger ends of life," had finished his new book, *The River War*, and was looking out for a politcial opportunity.

The opportunity came unexpectedly. He had been invited to speak at a public meeting of the Oldham Conservatives, and two days before the meeting, Oldham's senior Member of Parliament died. Winston was asked to be the Conservative Party candidate.

"Everything is going capitally–" he wrote his mother.

> Owing to the appearance of a Tory Labour Candidate it is quite possible we shall win. There is no meeting Monday but on Tuesday night I make my big opening address. I would like you to come down for that. There is no hotel but this house is very comfortable, and Wittaker [Chairman of the local Conservative Association and former Mayor of Oldham] is a very nice fellow. He will be delighted to put you up. Come if you can, by the 12 o'clock train (look it up.) You can return early the next morning.

There is practically no local society—only multitudes of workers.

My speech last night at the club produced great enthusiasm and there is no doubt that if anyone can win this seat I can. . . . Find out if Pamela would like to come down—and wire me. Send me a box of good cigarettes—Jack knows the sort—and let me have all my letters to this address. Write every day. . . . Good luck to the Magazine.[1]

The next day Winston wrote again telling his mother that the women of the local Primrose League wanted her to attend a reception they were to hold at the Conservative Club. Then, after discussing the time of her arrival, he went on to say: "If you bring *Pamela* with you there will not be room for your maid nor for her's so that if you cannot conveniently do without your maid for one night it would be necessary to tell *Pamela* that there is no accommodation *and put her off.*"[2]

Apparently his romance was not going smoothly. Winston had little experience with young women. He could talk interestingly and write endearing letters, but Pamela had often protested that he was not demonstrative enough. She was more experienced than he and knew how much attention she was entitled to expect from a young man who presumably loved and wanted to marry her. However, the pattern of love and marriage preeminent in Winston's mind was undoubtedly that of his parents. By the time he understood anything of their relationship, the romance was dead and his father was distant and harsh with him. Winston therefore came into his first courtship awkward and unsure. Although he had invited Pamela to attend this meeting, which he fully expected would be significant to his career, he was obviously relieved when she declined. "I quite understand your not coming:" he wrote, "it would perhaps have been a mistake."[3]

Jennie knew Oldham well. She had campaigned there for her husband and still had friends in the borough. And now she moved with more than her usual zest. She had long been urging Winston to leave the Army and enter politics, and now that he had done it, it was up to her to help in any way she could, despite any other work she had to do. But it was fun for her, too, and after the frenzy of starting "Maggie" this was a refreshing change of pace. It brought back pleasant memories of the days when she had conducted Randolph's campaigns.

Winston, of course, realized the political importance of his mother's presence in Oldham. The *Oldham Daily Standard* on Tuesday, June 27, 1899, announced:

TONIGHT'S MEETING
LADY RANDOLPH CHURCHILL
EXPECTED

Oldham Conservatives will learn with the greatest satisfaction that Lady Randolph Churchill will attend tonight's meeting at the Theatre Royal, at which her son, Mr. Winston Churchill, and Mr. James Mawdsley will deliver their first public speeches in support of their joint candidature. Lady Churchill, talented mother of a talented son, is naturally deeply interested in this election, and she may be certain that not only for her late husband's and her son's sake, but for her own, she will receive a most cordial welcome to Oldham. There are thousands of true hearts in this constituency, which have a warm corner for Lady Randolph Churchill.

The next day, the same newspaper reported on the meeting and noted:

Lady Randolph Churchill had a most enthusiastic reception, as she accompanied Alderman Wittaker on the platform. Her charming and graceful presence gave an added interest to the proceedings. She listened intently to the speeches, and seemed especially pleased and amused with Mr. Bottomley's vigorous and humorous address.

Jennie went with Winston everywhere: the mass meetings at the big halls, the open-air meetings, the small gatherings at individual homes. She bowed, she smiled, she made brief speeches. She was proud and she showed it. One news report said:

Lady Randolph Churchill had a most enthusiastic reception at the co-operative Hall meeting, and repeatedly during the evening had she to gracefully bow her acknowledgments to the hearty cheering.

On the same day the *Standard* reported:

A gathering of the lady members of the Oldham Habitation of the Primrose League took place on Tuesday evening at the Central Conservative Club, Union Street, when about 200 Dames attended. Alderman Woddington introduced Lady

Churchill to the meeting, and she was most cordially greeted by the assembly. Her Ladyship addressed a few words to the gathering, and stated she had no idea there would be so large and representative an audience in attendance. She was delighted in the interest that was shown in the cause which they had all so much at heart, and she hoped they would do everything in their power to further it by returning the two Conservative candidatures at the head of the poll. (Applause). Lady Churchill then retired, and subsequently accompanied her son to an open-air meeting at Glodwick.

Before his mother's arrival in Oldham, however, Winston, who had always consulted her about his political strategy, went out on a limb of his own choosing. He announced that he would not support the Government position on the Clerical Tithes Bill, a controversial measure intended to benefit the clergy of the Church of England and the Church schools. This put him in opposition to his own Party on an important issue.

In American politics, where party lines are crossed every day, such a decision would be a trifling matter, but in England a Member of Parliament—and especially a candidate—is expected to show firm party loyalty. As Sir Ivor Jennings has written,[4] members of a British political party "realize that their chance of office depends upon maintaining the unity of the party . . . The unity of the party implies . . . the loyalty of party members to their leaders. . . . 'Our men' must rally round their leaders because party divisions tend to 'let the other fellows in.' "

Labour candidates, therefore, proceeded to taunt the Conservative government that their own candidate had repudiated them. The *Manchester Evening News* was moved to say of Winston that "as a politician, he hardly is out of his swaddling clothes."

This was something Jennie could not undo, but she put up a brave front on polling day in Oldham. ". . . dressed entirely in blue . . . [she] arrived in a landau and pair with gaily-ribboned and rosetted postillions. . . ." She was with Winston when he received the news of his defeat. "Lady Randolph Churchill, who had listened to the results with a tinge of regret, bore herself proudly as she retired from the room with her talented son," the *Oldham Daily Standard* reported.

Jennie wasted no time in writing to all her friends in politics, emphasizing that Winston had lost by fewer than 1500 votes against a very popular opponent and that his defeat was only a slight blemish, not a stain. She appealed for their declarations of support in the future.

Their replies were prompt:

Arthur Balfour: "Never mind—it will all come right; and this small reverse will have no permanent ill effect on your political fortunes. . . ."[5]

H. H. Asquith: ". . . Winston's good fight at Oldham gives him his spurs, & perhaps (as you hint) there are more desirable constituencies to be found. . . ."[6]

The Prime Minister, Lord Salisbury: "Winston made a splendid fight . . ."[7]

Winston answered Salisbury: ". . . I take the opportunity of making my excuses for my ill success at Oldham and of thanking you for the lenient allusion you made to the contest in a letter which you recently wrote to my mother. . . ."[8]

Winston was so buoyed by the encouraging responses to his mother's letters that he asked her to plan ". . . my little political dinner on Thursday, only 6 or 7. They will all be in town on account of Parliament."[9] He also sought further advice from another of his mother's close friends, Joseph Chamberlain, then Colonial Secretary.

He was most forthcoming, and at the same time, startlingly candid and direct. His conversation was a practical political education in itself. He knew every detail, every turn and twist of the game, and understood deeply the moving forces at work in both the great parties, of whose most aggressive aspirations he had in turn been the champion. . . . South Africa had begun again to be a growing topic. The negotiations with President Kruger about the delicate, deadly question of suzerainty were gradually engaging national, and indeed, world attention. The reader may be sure that I was keen that strong lines should be taken, and I remember Mr. Chamberlain saying, "It is no use blowing the trumpet for the charge, & then looking around to find nobody following." Later, we passed an old man, seated upright in his chair on the lawn on the brink of the river. Lady Jeune said, "Look, there is [Liberal Party leader Henry] Labouchere." "A bundle of old rags!" was Mr. Chamberlain's comment, as he turned his head away from his venomous political opponent. I was struck by the expression of disdain and dislike which passed swiftly but with intensity across his face. . . .[10]

Henry du Pré Labouchère was not only a bitter opponent of Chamberlain's in Parliament, but as editor of *Truth Magazine* he had persistently attacked Winston on the scandalous allegations of homosexuality and race-fixing. The damage such a man could do to a political career had already come home to Winston.

Whereas earlier Jennie had cautioned her son to avoid notoriety, it was now his turn to be concerned about her activities. Jennie had gone to Goodwood for the annual races and Winston wrote:

> . . . I also beg you not to bet or play cards. You have so much to make life interesting that there is no excuse or sense or reason for taking refuge in the desperate forms of excitement which the brainless butterflies of the world long for. I feel a little worried about this because I know you played and gambled last year vy high at Goodwood: and it can if repeated only end in bringing the most terrible misery upon us all. Already we feel the sting sharply. Forgive my lecture. It is an appeal.[11]

Gambling was one of Jennie's vices. Her father had been one of the great gamblers of his day—the New York stock market, horse races, cards—and her husband had had a similar appetite. The Prince of Wales loved to gamble; indeed, most of the men she knew well were gamblers. She probably acquired the taste for it from them, but gambling was also compatible with her own personality. It offered excitement and challenge. And with her finances frequently ebbing toward disaster, gambling provided hope of a sudden recoup. E. F. Benson remembered playing cards with Jennie. "And after a hectic hour's hard work," he wrote, "she won exactly a shilling. She greedily seized it. 'Is this all mine?' she asked. 'Someone will now want to marry me for my money.' "[12]

George was with Jennie at Goodwood that weekend, as he was with her almost every weekend. During the week he was stationed at a nearby camp, but wrote her almost daily. They were most unusual love letters. He coupled his intense ardor for her with detailed discourses on the quality of his guns, the number of birds or animals he had shot, why there was too much wind for fishing on a particular day, and so forth. Had Jennie been less in love, all this probably would have been unbearably tedious.

Apparently George still tried to shroud their relationship with some degree of subterfuge. When at the end of one weekend Jennie went with him to the station, someone saw them together, and George later told his fellow officers that Jennie was his sister. "They believed me," he told her. "Some day soon, I hope to be able to say wife instead of sister."[13]

Their affair already had lasted a year and there seemed to be no abatement. George's parents, who had tried to ignore the situation, now decided to try another tactic. They were entertaining the Prince of Wales at Ruthin Castle one weekend, and they invited Jennie.

That weekend at Ruthin Castle must have been a severe test for Jennie. The Cornwallis-Wests certainly would have been polite, but hardly warm. Other members of George's family must have stared and gossiped. The Prince of Wales would not have treated her cordially. Jennie's courage had survived colder receptions than this, but there could be little question that the situation was trying and unpleasant. There was general agreement, however, that Jennie and George looked "smashing" together.

Jennie then returned the favor. She took George and Winston for a weekend at Blenheim Palace. This was still another turning point of social acceptance. "Sunny," the young Duke of Marlborough, had always deeply admired his aunt Jennie, and Consuelo, his Duchess, considered Jennie one of her closest confidantes. Nevertheless, this visit would not have been possible except for the fact that Jennie's mother-in-law, the Dowager Duchess of Marlborough, had died the preceding month.

This rotund, dowdily-gowned Duchess who always traveled with cages of birds and Blenheim spaniels, this disagreeable, embittered woman had so idolized her son Randolph that no daughter-in-law could ever have been good enough. But Jennie had also had the disadvantages of being an American, of being stronger than the Duchess' son, and of being more beautiful and talented than her daughters. Yet despite the enmity between them, these two unusual women had had a grudging respect for each other.

Blenheim Palace with its giant trees and beautiful grounds was full of memories for Jennie. She had first come here as a nineteen-year-old bride, and the townspeople had unhitched the horses of the Churchill carriage so that they themselves might pull the young couple to the palace. How overwhelmed she had been: the ornamental lake, the miles and miles of magnificent park, the hundreds of rooms, the gold dinner plate, the unrelenting formality. And her handsome, brilliant husband Lord Randolph—what would he have thought of George?

Seeing Winston and George together at Blenheim must have made Jennie contemplative: two young men of the same age, one her son, the other her lover. There was no question that Winston was the more brilliant, the more ambitious, the more energetic, but George was more attractive.

It does not seem unfair to suggest that Winston was jealous of George's relationship with his mother and that George was jealous of Winston's accomplishments. Their relationship was most proper, but there were subtle references in letters, occasional demeaning criticisms: "I saw Winston today in St. James Str," George wrote Jennie. "Don't tell him I said so, but he looked just like a young dissenting parson, hat brushed the wrong way, and at the back of head, awful old black coat and tie, he is a good fellow, but very untidy . . ."[14] Winston, in turn, did not keep from his mother his strong reservations about the possibility of her marrying George.

Such a possibility however, was still distant in Jennie's mind. More immediate was the *Review*. Part of Jennie's job was extracting from authors the articles they had promised to write. Cecil Rhodes was difficult: "I will come and see you, if you will let me, on my return in about three weeks. . . . I will try to write something for you on board ship, but do not announce it."[15]

George Bernard Shaw was more punctual in producing an article called, "A Word More about Verdi." But when Jennie invited him to a luncheon, he responded by telegram: "Certainly not! What have I done to provoke such an attack on my well-known habits?"[16]

Jennie replied in another telegram: "Know nothing of your habits; hope they are not as bad as your manners."[17]

Then she received the following letter from Shaw:

> . . . Be reasonable. What can I do? If I refuse an invitation in conventional terms, I am understood as repudiating the acquaintance of my hostess. If I make the usual excuses, and convince her that I am desolated by some other engagement, she will ask me again. And when I have excused myself six times running, she will conclude that I personally dislike her. Of course, there is the alternative of accepting; but then I shall endure acute discomfort and starvation. I shall not have the pleasure of really meeting her and talking to her any more than if we happened to lunch at the Savoy on the same day by chance. I shall get no lunch, because I do not eat the unfortunate dead animals and things which she has to provide for other people. Of these other people, half will abuse the occasion to ask me to luncheons and dinners, and the other half, having already spread that net for me in vain, will be offended because I have done for you what I would not do for them. I shall have to dress myself very carefully and behave properly, both of which are contrary to my nature.
>
> Therefore I am compelled to do the simple thing, and, when you say, "Come to lunch with a lot of people," reply flatly, "Won't." If you propose anything pleasant to me, I shall reply with equal flatness, "I will." But lunching with a lot of people—carnivorous people—is not pleasant. Besides, it cuts down my morning's work. I won't lunch with you; I won't dine with you; I won't call on you; I won't take the

smallest part of your social routine. And I won't ever know you, except on the most special and privileged terms, to the utter exclusion of that "lot of other people" whose appetites you offered me as an entertainment. Only if I can be of any real service at anytime, that is what I exist for; so you may command me.[18]

Jennie found it more and more enjoyable to be associated professionally with so many literary celebrities. She had met most of them before at parties, dinners, teas, and some of them she knew very well. There was, however, a monumental difference between knowing them as an admiring woman and as a demanding editor. The distinguishing factor was power. She had exerted social power before and political power, but this was her first experience with literary power, and she liked it very much indeed. Her feeling of power filled her memoranda to John Lane:

> . . . I suppose you are *"en retraite"* enjoying your holiday. You have not let me know . . . your opinion as to Mr. Leighton's letter in reference to the bindings–I have decided not to have the better leather until the magazine is more established. But I have written to Mr. Leighton that I will have the end papers and tooled gold lines inside the boards, which will add sixpence to the cost of every vol.: I think this is necessary, as the book looks unfinished as it now stands. . . . No. 2 fills up slowly. I am to have an article on the 20th by Mr. Gorst, the financial advisor to the Khedive–he writes well, and is much thought of–Sir Henry Wolff is trying to get me an article from some prominent Spaniard on the situation in Spain, and I have one or two other "irons in the fire." You will be glad to hear that Mr. [George] Meredith has promised me his next work. I wish I could have got that poem "Cruisers" from Mr. Kipling–but I dare say the *Morning Post* paid him 200 pounds for it. I can't say I admired it much– so rough and informal. . . . I hope early next week to hand to the printers the order in which they can make the ten pages up to date. . . . No. 2 . . . will be a very readable number, perhaps more so than Volume 1. But nothing brilliant or startling. . . . It has been very difficult to get any prominent politicians. They all want to enjoy their holidays. I admire Mr. Phillip's poem very much, and have written to tell him so. It is exceedingly fine. . . . Am waiting to hear from America. . . .[19]

At each week's end, Jennie was transformed from a tough editor to a tender woman. However, her absences during the week served to strengthen George's resolve to marry her. But she was reluctant. "Jennie and I had discussed it many a time," George later wrote, "and she had always said that the difference in our ages made marriage out of the question."[20]

It is one thing, however, to understand a fact with your mind, and it is quite another to accept it with your heart. Jennie was forty-five years old, but she looked and felt much younger. She wanted to keep feeling young, and George could help her do that. To her, her spirit still seemed as young as his.

Meanwhile, as George noted: "people began to talk." The popular magazine *Gentlewoman* remarked that "a handsome American woman is to marry a handsome young man about the age of her son. . . ." Often the talk was snide and cruel. Winston told his mother about one clipping he had seen which compared the expected marriage to that of "Lobengula [a Zulu king] with a white woman." "I tore it up," he said, "and I don't know why I waste my time in repeating such trash. . . ."[21]

Nevertheless, Jennie and George already had decided to announce their engagement. The announcement would be made during Cowes Week, the first week in August, on the Isle of Wight. The choice of time and place could not have been mere coincidence. It was from the Isle of Wight that the first Jerome had sailed to America in 1710. But more significant, it was on the Isle of Wight that Jennie had first met and fallen in love with Lord Randolph Churchill, and it was there, during Cowes Week that he had proposed marriage and she had accepted. Why did she now choose that place and that time to become formally engaged again? Was it another attempt at cutting across time? Was it her singular way of defying society? Or was it the longing of a romanticist to return to one of the most unequivocal feelings she had known?

The headline in *The New York Times* read:

LADY CHURCHILL TO WED
Lord Randolph's Widow Engaged
to Lieut. Cornwallis-West
BRITISH SOCIETY ASTONISHED[22]

British Society was more than astonished; it was incensed. For a woman of Jennie's position to dally with a young man might raise a few eyebrows, but for her to actually marry him was downright scandalous. She was the leader of Anglo-American society in Great Britain, a member of the Royal circle, an intimate of some of the very important people of the world. She could have chosen a husband from among many of the mighty men of her time. And whom did she pick?—a callow young man who was also plainly improvident.

Pressures against the marriage mounted immediately and one of the most forceful was wielded by the Prince of Wales. George later wrote:

> ... I had been invited on board the Brittannia at Cowes, and the Prince of Wales took the opportunity of taking me aside and pointing out to me the inadvisability of my marrying a woman so much my senior. He admitted that this was the only argument against our engagement, told me that no one could possibly say what might happen within the next three months, and begged me to do nothing in a hurry. "If there *is* war," he added, "you are sure to go out. There'll be time enough to consider it when you come back."[23]

Perhaps the Prince was thinking more of himself than of George. Jennie was one of the favorite women in his life, and he counted on her in many particular ways, as he did on very few others. He liked her to be available to arrange parties, dinners, entertainments; he relied on her for sympathy, understanding, confidence. It was not that he minded Jennie's getting married—he might even have preferred it. A marriage of convenience simplified matters because it kept the woman in his orbit, giving her some protective social coloration. But a marriage of love meant that the woman was no longer available. To that the Prince objected—and he objected vehemently.

Of course George also heard from his father as well as the rest of his family and friends. In view of their disapproval of the relationship, it is not unlikely that Colonel West told his son to expect no future income from him, and he may even have threatened disinheritance. Next George's commanding officer, Colonel Arthur Paget, also became involved; he requested "a verbal understanding that I would not marry or become engaged before leaving" for South Africa.[24] The Colonel was a good friend of Jennie's, but he was a better friend of the Prince of Wales.

How reminiscent the whole scene must have seemed to Jennie: The Duke and Duchess of Marlborough had made similar attempts to stop her marriage to their son. George West, however, was not a Lord Randolph. He was an anxious young man very much in love but overwhelmed by the concerted pressures against him. He buckled.

On the front page of *The New York Times* the day after the engagement announcement appeared the following report:

SAYS THEY ARE NOT ENGAGED
Lady Randolph Churchill's Son Denies
That His Mother Will Marry Young Cornwallis-West.

COWES, Isle of Wight, August 4–Lieut. Winston Leonard Spencer-Churchill, the son of Lady Randolph Churchill, asked the Associated Press to deny the reported engagement of his mother to Lieut. G. F. M. Cornwallis-West, brother of Princess Henry of Pless.

The matter continued to be the subject of much conversation among their friends. Neither Lady Randolph Churchill nor Lieut. Cornwallis-West has been seen about since the engagement was reported.[25]

How delighted Winston must have been to be the one to deny that his mother would marry George.

Jennie left immediately afterward for her favorite watering-place, Aix-les-Bains, France. Jennie had a great deal to think about as she soaked in the hot baths. Several months before, Caryl Ramsden had come to say goodbye before returning to Cairo. Jennie, who concealed little from her sons, then wrote Winston, "I told him I did not think England . . . would feel any colder for his absence. He has too many irons in the fire to be able to concentrate. . . ."[26] To Jack she remarked:

"Who knows what a butterfly like him thinks of, and shall I add, Who cares!"[27]

But this sad merry-go-round with George was a more serious matter, and she did care.

A letter from Winston followed immediately. "I do hope the cure will do you good and that you will not find the time hanging heavy on your hands. I am afraid so. I wish I could have come with you—no humbug. The book alone prevented me. . . ."[28]

Knowing that the marriage plans were forestalled but not abandoned, George's father, Colonel West, now wrote to Winston and forcefully declared the inadvisability of any future relationship between his son and Winston's mother. He asked for Winston's support in thwarting the relationship.

However much Winston agreed with the Colonel, his loyalty to his mother was unswerving. He forwarded the Colonel's letter to Jennie and asserted: "I don't want to be dragged into their [Cornwallis–West] family cabal. Whatever you may do or wish to do, I shall support you in every way. But reflect most seriously on all the aspects of the question. . . . Fine sentiments & empty stomachs do not accord."[29]

On September 3, Winston wrote to his mother from Blenheim:

I have had a second letter from Colonel West, which since he has not marked it *Private*–I send you, but you must destroy it and not tell anyone that I showed it to you, as I rather think he meant it to be looked on as private. There is not much in it and I did not think it necessary to answer. It is for George to settle with his family: for you to consult your own happiness.

At the end of his letter Winston added, "Please send me a telegram when you get this letter to say that you love me and will write the same sentiment at a greater length." And in a postscript, he remarked, "After all I don't believe you will marry. My idea is that the family pressure will crush George."[30]

Winston was nearly proved right. The family pressure could have crushed George, as his and Jennie's economic circumstances were even more critcal than the difference in their ages. They had little money and, what's more, no friendly support. They had their love, and it was strong enough for Jennie, but was it strong enough for George? He did not have Jennie's fiber. It seemed, then, as if the romance had run dry, the last chapter finished. But unexpectedly, there would come news that would change everything. Within two months Great Britain would be at war with the Boers in South Africa.

Thirty-One

B Y THE TURN OF THE CENTURY, Britain's foreign policy had changed from "splendid isolation" to "swaggering imperialism," from an era of conspicuous peace to a time of turmoil. The poet and critic Wilfred Blunt wrote:

> Of the new century, I prophecy nothing except that it will see the decline of the British Empire. Other worse empires will rise perhaps in its place, but I shall not live to see the day. . . . For a hundred years we have done good in the world, for a hundred, we shall have done evil, and then the world will hear of us no more.[1]

Rudyard Kipling had written his famous poem, "The Recessional" for the Diamond Jubilee two years before, ending on the note:

> *Lord God of Hosts, be with us yet,*
> *Lest we forget—lest we forget.*

But pessimism and humility were not the mood of the British people in the autumn of 1899. Sensationalism was the mood. Jingoism was the mood. War was the mood.

The excitement of the Jameson Raid into the Transvaal and the gory drama of the Battle of Omdurman seemed to have whetted a national appetite. The young Lord Alfred Harmsworth, publisher of the *Daily Mail,* commented that what his readers wanted most and what his newspaper supplied best was "a good hate."[2]

Since the abortive Jameson Raid three years earlier, the Transvaal had been rearming heavily. The Transvaal was one of three Republics bordering the British Cape Colony, which constituted the southern part of South Africa. The British had once annexed the Transvaal, but the Boers of the Transvaal had beaten them at Majuba Hill and asserted their independence in 1861. South Africans of Dutch descent, the Boers (meaning "farmers") were rugged and fiercely individualistic.

With the discovery of gold in 1866, the Transvaal rapidly became the most industrialized and wealthiest land on the African continent. Gold also brought an influx of "outlanders," mostly British, and this became the point of international tension. President Kruger of the Transvaal refused to grant outlanders the right to vote. Jennie's good friend, Sir Alfred Milner, the new High Commissioner of the Cape Colony, became the most ardent advocate of the outlanders. He wrote to Colonial Secretary Joseph Chamberlain, saying:

> The spectacle of thousands of British subjects permanently in a position of helots, constantly chafing under undoubted grievances and calling vainly to Her Majesty's Government for redress does steadily undermine the influence and reputation of Great Britain and the respect for the British Government within the Queen's dominions.

After unsuccessful negotiations with President Kruger, Milner reported back to the Colonial Secretary, "There is no way out of the political troubles of South Africa except reform in the Transvaal or war."[3]

Shortly afterward, Chamberlain and Jennie were weekend guests at Chatsworth. "One night at dinner," Jennie said, "we discussed the situation, and he frankly told me he considered [war] inevitable."

Joseph Chamberlain was the dominant figure in Lord Salisbury's Conservative Government. Once opposed to Imperialism, Chamberlain not only had learned to "think imperially," but had placed himself at the crest of the rising imperialist wave. This elegant man with his monocle on a black ribbon was now known to the public as "Pushful Joe," and when war came many called it "Joe's War."[4]

Jennie's own views were mixed. She had friends in both camps. She feared, as almost twenty years before her husband had, that "the final triumph of the British arms, mainly by brute force, would have permanently and hopelessly alienated it [the Transvaal] from Great Britain."[5]

Winston, however, was completely one with the new mood. "Imperial aid must redress the wrongs of the Outlanders", he had written in 1897. "Imperial troops must curb the insolence of the Boers. There must be no half measures. The forces employed must be strong enough to beat down all opposition from the Transvaal and the Free State; and at the same time win over all sympathizers in Cape Colony. . . . For the sake of our Empire, for the sake of our honour, for the sake of the race, we must fight the Boers."[6]

Much of the press was fanning this jingo imperialism into a patriotic fury. Historian R. C. K. Ensor later noted:

> . . . It is often said that distemper caused the war; and it may be true, though not in the most obvious sense. . . . If the Boers became united by the mistaken conviction that a British Government wanted their blood, it was largely because they heard a British public calling for it.[7]

In early October 1899, President Kruger of the Transvaal sent an ultimatum to Great Britain: withdraw British troops massing along his frontiers and stop any further reinforcements. There was a three-day deadline for a reply, after which war was inevitable.

The Boers had 50,000 troops,[8] twice as many as the available British force. They were ready for guerrilla war and the British were not.[9] Soon en route with reinforcements was British Commander-in-Chief General Sir Redvers Buller, and aboard his ship was the war correspondent for the *Morning Post,* Winston Churchill.[10] Jennie had made some of the preliminary contacts and Winston had made the final arrangements.

The Prince of Wales, meanwhile, had not forgotten his conversation with George West about Jennie. "I was told by my C.O.," George wrote, "that Lord Methuen had applied for a junior officer from his old regiment to go as his Aide-de-Camp, that it must be someone who could ride, and that my name had been sent in. It came as a surprise to me, as I had done nothing to bring it about. The explanation was soon forthcoming, however, as I found a note from the Prince of Wales awaiting me when I went home:

> My dear George West,
>   I had the opportunity of speaking to Lord Methuen at the station yesterday when I took leave of Sir Redvers Buller, and strongly urged him to take you on his staff, so I hope it may be all satisfactorily settled. I envy you going out on

active service with so fine a battalion, and wish you good luck and a safe return home.

Yrs. very sincerely,
Albert Edward.[11]

The arm of the Prince of Wales was long and his friends had expedited his wishes. He may have thought, as George's parents did, that an enforced separation would cool the couple's ardor. Nearly twenty-five years before, the Duke and Duchess of Marlborough had mistakenly thought the same thing about Lord Randolph and Jennie.

For the short time remaining, Jennie canceled all her appointments so that she could be with George as much as possible. She even excused herself from one of the season's prized social events, the annual country house party given by Lord and Lady Wolverton for the Prince of Wales.

Formerly, George and Jennie had been reasonably judicious about being seen together in London, but now they appeared to flaunt their relationship. Jennie also accompanied George on his extensive shopping tours, and it was rather mockingly reported that they were seen together at a play called *Elixir of Youth*.

The Boer War was one of the last of the so-called "gentlemanly wars." Officers going to the front were permitted to bring with them some of their favorite foods, liquors, guns, horses, clothing. Fortnum and Mason instituted a special "South African War Service," and other well-known stores followed suit. "They brought their own dressing cases, with silver or gold fittings; they brought their splendid shotguns by Purdy or Westley-Richards; their magnificent hunters saddled by such masters as Gordon of Curzon Street. They brought their valets, coachmen, grooms and hunt-servants."[12] The Prince of Wales made his final inspection of George's regiment before its departure. "I shall never forget our march from Chelsea Barracks to Waterloo Station at about five o'clock on a dark autumn morning," George later wrote.

There was a slight fog and, comparatively speaking, the streets were badly lighted in those days. A good many wives and sweethearts accompanied the men from the Barracks and linked arms, and naturally nothing was done to prevent them. . . . Over Westminster Bridge, our ranks almost degenerated into a rabble, so great was the crush of civilians. . . . Some of the scenes were particularly heartrending. . . . [13]

The regiment embarked from Southampton on a small ship called *The Nubia*. The British correspondent for a New York magazine reported:

When Mr. West started for South Africa, the tears were
rolling down his face, while Lady Randolph, who was more
or less in hiding at the hotel, as so many of his own relatives
had come to see him off—was quite prostrated with grief. . . .
Lady Randolph herself told a friend that she had promised
George not to touch either port or champagne until they met
again. . . . [14]

Twenty-four hours after *The Nubia* had sailed, a London newspaper reported with blaring placards that the ship had sunk with all hands on
board. When the fog lifted, however, *The Nubia* was found steaming dead
slow not more than a half mile from shore. The false news about the ship
only intensified Jennie's anxiety. How she must have regretted her obstinacy in refusing to marry George so many months before. It would have
been different if they themselves had decided to end their relationship, but
George's going to war gave the situation an aura of drama and foreboding.

Winston tried to ease her mind. He assured her that he would look up
George in South Africa, and he said he expected that George would probably be back in England in time for that year's Derby.

Jennie tried to divert her mind to the *Anglo-Saxon Review,* but her early
enthusiasm took an emotional downturn. She had assigned and collected
copy for Volume III, and when the second issue appeared it, too, received
critical praise. Its green cover was tooled in gold, and its contents included
articles on subjects ranging from the Dreyfus Case to the Marlborough
Gems.

Just at this time, Jennie received a visit from Mrs. A. A. Blow, the American wife of the manager of one of South Africa's richest mining syndicates.
Mrs. Blow was very excited about an idea she had, but it was one that
would never be realized, she said, unless Jennie took it over. The idea was to
provide an American hospital ship to care for the wounded in South Africa.

At first Jennie was hesitant. No American group in England had ever
done anything like that before. The practical part of her mind foresaw giant
tangles of international red tape. Furthermore, a major part of the American
public was pro-Boer, seeing in the Transvaal a small country fighting for its
independence against the mighty British Empire. Indeed, a large segment
within England itself, led by Jennie's friend John Morley, was similarly
against this war. But Jennie discussed the idea with another friend, Sir
William Garstin, who strongly urged her to take up the project. "Believe me,"
he said, "you will be making history, apart from the excellence of the work." [15]

"Then and there," Jennie said, "I made up my mind to do it." [16]

Florence Nightingale, who had organized a unit of nurses for the
Crimean War in 1854, had written an article entitled "Cassandra" in which

she posed the question, "Why have women passion, intellect, moral activity—these three—and a place in society where no one of these can be exercised?"

> Some women [she continued] have an intention like a battering ram, which, slowly brought to bear, can work upon a subject for any length of time. They can work for ten hours just as well as two, upon the same thing. . . . What do you suffer—even physically—for the want of such work, no one can tell. The accumulation of nervous energy, which has nothing to do during the day, makes them feel every night when they go to bed as if they were going mad; and they are obliged to lie long in bed in the morning, to let it evaporate and keep it down.[17]

Jennie's thinking on these matters followed the same lines, and she had arrived at similar conclusions about the role and abilities of women. On October 25, 1899, the first committee meeting for the organization of a hospital ship was held at Jennie's home. Mrs. A. A. Blow was elected Honorary Secretary; Fanny Ronalds, Treasurer; Mrs. Cornelia Adair, Vice-Chairman; and Jennie, Chairman.[18]

"A large and influential general committee was formed." Jennie wrote.

> All worked with zeal and enthusiasm, and soon the whole thing was well in train. There was a general impression that the war would be short and sharp. Hospitals of all kinds were greatly needed, and we hurried with feverish activity. Funds and the ship—those were the two great and immediate preoccupations. No stone was left unturned to procure money—much money—and it had to be all American money. It is useless to deny here that the war was viewed with disfavor by my countrymen. They had a fellow-feeling for the Boer, fighting, as they thought, for his independence. But the plea of humanity overran their political opinions, and the fund once started, money poured in. A resolution carried at the meeting of the Executive Committee was embodied in our appeal to the public:
> "That whereas Great Britain is now involved in a war affecting the rights and liberties of the Anglo-Saxon people in South Africa, and has under arms 70,000 troops to maintain its rights and liberties;
> "And whereas the people of Great Britain have, by their sympathy and moral support, materially aided the people of

the United States of America in the war in Cuba and the Philippine Islands, *it is therefore resolved*:

"That the American women in Great Britain, whilst deploring the necessity for war, shall endeavor to raise, among their compatriots in America, a fund for the relief of the sick and wounded soldiers and refugees in South Africa. It is proposed to dispatch immediately a suitable Hospital Ship, fully equipped with medical stores and provisions, to accommodate 200 people, with a staff of four doctors, five nurses, and 40 commissioned officers and orderlies.

"To carry the above resolution into effect, the sum of $150,000 (£30,000) will be required."[19]

There were fund-raising concerts, matinees, and entertainments of all sorts. Large firms contributed so many medical supplies that the committee found some difficulty in storing them. Checks and donations, from a few shillings to a thousand pounds, poured in. On the other hand, there also were some rebuffs. Jennie cabled a New York millionaire asking for a contribution. He replied that he had "no knowledge of the scheme," and Jennie cabled back, "Read the papers."[20]

A British paper remarked upon the intensified feeling of kinship between the two nations in times of trouble and crisis. It went on to praise "our American cousins" for their independence, their capacity, their methods, "and, we may add, their strong sense of humour." Discussing the generosity of the American women in Britain and their offer of a hospital ship, it commented: "It is noticeable that they have formed a strong committee, with Lady Randolph Churchill as its head. It is to be supposed, therefore, that the result will be a great success . . ."[21]

Winston later wrote that his mother "raised a fund, captivated an American millionaire, obtained a ship . . ."[22]

This was true. She had wanted an American ship and cabled her distant cousin, Theodore Roosevelt, then Governor of New York, to ask if he could help. Unfortunately he had no suggestions to make. It was then that she found the American millionaire: forty-five-year-old Bernard Nadel Baker. Founder of the Atlantic Transport Company in Baltimore, Baker had spent all of his adult life in the shipping business. At a special meeting of his Board of Directors, on December 12, 1899, Baker reported that without an opportunity to consult the Board as a whole, he had taken the responsibility of tendering to the British Government the use of one of the company's transport ships for the duration of the war in the Transvaal.

It was an unusual gift, particularly since Baker had offered that the hospital ship as well as the crew would be maintained at his company's expense. This represented a gift of some 3000 to 4000 pounds a month ($20,000).

The ship was called the *Maine* after the vessel that had been sunk in Havana Harbor before the start of the Spanish-American war. Unfortunately, she was an old cattle boat.[23] How does one convert such a ship into a floating hospital? Jennie asked experts in the Army and the Red Cross, but they were of little help. There was no precedent for this kind of conversion and no existing plans or procedure, so Jennie and her group had to find people to draw up plans and procedures.

What about doctors, surgeons, and nurses? Jennie wanted most of them to be American. She remembered that Mrs. Whitelaw Reid had provided nurses for the Spanish-American War from the Mills School of Nursing, which her father had founded. Jennie knew the Reids well, and Whitelaw Reid had written an article for the first issue of the Review. Mrs. Reid was pleased to accept the responsibility of providing an American medical staff.

The next task Jennie set for herself was to get the *Maine* officially designated a military hospital ship. She went directly to Lord Lansdowne, the Secretary of War, and Lord Goschen, the First Lord of the Admiralty, as she had known both men on a first-name basis for a long time. The *Maine* got its military designation as well as Lt. Col. Hensmen, a surgeon from the Second Life Guards, and some men from the St. John Ambulance Brigade.

During October and November, the committee met almost daily. A series of defeats in South Africa had caused gloom and depression in Britain, but for Jennie it was one of the most absorbing times of her life. She urged and badgered the War Office and the Admiralty. "Would they supply us with this? Would they guarantee us that? We would not take No for an answer," Jennie recalled.

At the first meeting of the General Committee, Jennie reminded them:

> A little more than a fortnight ago, the scheme was not in existence. Today we have a ship, we have a magnificent staff, and, what is even more important, we have £15,000, hundreds of donations and our fellow countrymen are working for us in all parts of the world. We may differ as to the policy which necessitates the sending of so many gallant soldiers to the front. It is always easy to criticize, but as a gifted compatriot wrote to me, "The wounded are the wounded, irrespective of creed and nationality." And, indeed, we can have but one mind in this matter: If we can alleviate sufferings and at the same time comfort the many aching and anxious hearts at home, shall we not be fulfilling our greatest mission in life?

These are "Women's Rights" in the best sense of the word. We need no others. We have heard of the friendship between England and America. These are better than words, and we greatly hope that the hospital-ship *Maine* may do more to cement that friendship than years of flag-waving and pleasant amenities.[24]

The New York Times revealed further news about the project:

The possibility of Lady Randolph Churchill accompanying the American hospital-ship *Maine* to the Cape of Good Hope has aroused much interest here. Her ladyship said today:

"The question of my going is dependent upon several contingencies. It is quite possible that I may go, but the matter has not yet been fully determined."

Lady Randolph Churchill has taken the most active part in the scheme to fit out the *Maine,* obtaining privileges from the War Office, which otherwise would have been impossible, in favor of the American nurses, and her friends are now anxious that she should see the matter through personally.[25]

It was finally decided that she would go, and several days later, Jennie was quoted as saying:

The *Maine* is to be essentially an American women's ship. We are not only to aid the wounded, but are to show the world that American women can do the good work better than anyone else can do it. I am going to the Cape in the *Maine,* not because my son is there, for he will be a thousand miles away, but because I want the generous efforts of American contributors to be carried out under the personal supervision of a member of the Executive Committee.

I am going because I think I may prevent any kind of friction between the American nurses whom Mrs. Whitelaw Reid is sending out on Saturday, and the British officials, in case such friction should arise. I contribute that much time and service gladly.[26]

The value of what she was doing, however, could not still the voices of the gossip-mongers. One magazine remarked: "Everyone in London is wondering what Lady Randolph will do when she arrives in South Africa.

It is well known that her one object in going out with the *Maine* was to follow Mr. George West. . . ."[27]

Similarly, Consuelo Vanderbilt Marlborough, who was working closely with Jennie in outfitting the hospital ship, wrote in her memoirs "that everybody knew that Lady Randolph was going out on the ship, to join her son Winston. We knew that she was equally anxious to see young George Cornwallis-West."[28]

The Sunday Sketch even quoted punsters saying that Jennie was going to South Africa to remove George West "from the field of danger by *Maine* force. . . ."[29]

Jennie took no public notice of such comments, and in a newspaper interview, she clarified her role:

> . . . I am not going to do any amateur nursing, because I
> don't believe in it; it really is not at all fair to the patients. . . .
> I shall superintend the correspondence, which is certain to be
> heavy, and I am taking a secretary to assist me. For the rest, I
> have no doubt that I shall find plenty of work to do—in fact,
> I mean to help in any way I can. . . . Where we shall go first,
> I have no idea. We are entirely in the hands of the Govern-
> ment, and they will naturally send us where we shall be of
> most use. When shall I be back? How can I tell you how
> long the war will last, and I certainly mean to see it
> through.[30]

Queen Victoria met the American staff on the ship and told them how much she appreciated their kindness "in coming over to take care of my men." Two days later, Jennie was invited to "dine and sleep" at Windsor, and had a long conversation with the Queen about the war and the *Maine*. The Queen remarked, "I think the surgeons look very young." Whereupon Jennie answered: "All the more energetic therefore."[31]

The royal blessing later helped resolve a teapot-tempest at a *Maine* fund-raising function in New York. The celebrated actress, Lily Langtry[32]—who had once captured the varied hearts of the Prince of Wales[33] and Jennie's father and brother-in-law Moreton Frewen, among others—was appearing on the New York stage and Jennie drafted her to help. Lily announced a concert and tea at Sherry's featuring a variety of entertainment, as well as an "American Bar." She told the press that the program would be sponsored by New York's leading Society women, and that she herself would invade Wall Street to sell tickets.[34]

Word soon circulated that prominent actresses and society women would serve as barmaids in short skirts. The Women's Christian Temperance

Union organized full opposition, saying that the "spectacle would be degrading, . . . a blot on the reputation of the women of this city . . . and a violation of State laws . . ." The *New York Journal* printed an editorial about the tea, under the headline, "Should Good, Pure Women Associate with Mrs. Langtry, Even for the Sake of Charity?"[35]

Reinforcement was forthcoming from the Society for Political Study, which claimed that "the women belonging to The 400 who are taking part in this tea are no more representative American women than the submerged tenth. . . . They represent money and society, but not the brains. We clubwomen represent the brains."[36]

New York Society leader Mrs. William Backhouse Astor served notice that she would not attend the tea, and advised her friends to do likewise. Lily cabled Jennie: "Cold shoulder. What's to be done?"

Jennie knew exactly what to do. The best weapon against snobbery is snobbery, so she appealed to the Prince of Wales. Through the appropriate channels, the Prince immediately let it be known that unless Mrs. Astor changed her mind and attended the tea, he would see that her daughter in England would not be in Royal favor.

What would *the* Mrs. Astor do? Would she continue to assert her prerogatives and her principles? Could she possibly demean herself to associate with that notorious actress for such a questionable project? Indeed she could, and did. And trooping along with her went the rest of New York Society's leaders.

The tea was a smashing success; it raised more than $5,000 for the *Maine*. As part of the entertainment, a strongman demonstrated muscle-developers and sold them on behalf of the fund. Lily Langtry, wearing a gown of lace and ermine, recited Rudyard Kipling's "The Absent-Minded Beggar."[37] A detective wearing a light-check sack coat, red shirt, and lavender trousers was "secretly" present to make sure there were no short-skirted barmaids. The Earl of Yarmouth was the amateur bartender, wearing a white apron over his velvet-collared coat and unblushingly accepting tips "that would even make a Waldorf-Astoria waiter lose his presence of mind." *The Times* quoted the Earl as having said that his role in the affair "may make a bit of a stench here, but it will do me a lot of good with the Prince."

Jennie had no such problems with her final fund-raising party at Claridge's in London. Sir Arthur Sullivan had arranged for the ground floor of the hotel, and Jennie and her friends had it converted into a garden of chrysanthemums, roses, and multicolored lights. A large contingent of British Royalty arrived, accompanied by an escort of the Life Guards in their brilliant white-and-scarlet uniforms, drummers and drum-majors, and Scots Guards in tartans. The casts and orchestras of two musical shows,

Belle of New York and *El Capitan*, also had been corralled, and the featured singer was Mrs. Brown Potter, one of the Prince's favorites.

Describing the event in great detail, the London correspondent of *The New York Times* noted:

> Lady Randolph Churchill looked in for a few minutes, but was deeply distressed, owing to her anxiety as to the fate of her son, Winston Churchill, believed to be a prisoner in the hands of the Boers, and left before the guests arrived. The absence of the leading spirit in the movement, due to the uncertainty as to the death or capture of her son, gave a tragic tone to the gathering.[38]

The Boers had ambushed an overturned armoured train in which Winston was a passenger. Walden, who had been Lord Randolph's valet and now served his son, wrote to Jennie:

> . . . The driver [of the train] was one of the first wounded, and he said to Mr. Winston: "I am finished." So Mr. Winston said to him, "Buck up a bit, I will stick to you," and he threw off his revolver and field-glasses and helped the driver pick 20 wounded up and put them on the tender of the engine. . . . He [the driver] says there is not a braver gentleman in the Army. . . ."[39]

Telegrams of concern arrived from the Prince of Wales ("pray he may be safe and sound . . ."), Empress Eugénie, who had lost her only son in the Zulu War; and George West ("How anxious you will be, my poor darling. How I wish I could help you . . .").[40] But the message that warmed her most was a telegram from her son Jack: "Don't be frightened. I will be here when you come home."[41]

Jennie had been away for the weekend when she first heard the news, and she rushed back to London where Jack was indeed waiting. Her relationship with Winston had reached a turning point some months before and now so did her relationship with Jack. At this time, she needed him as a man whose strength she could lean upon.

Good news soon arrived—a letter from Winston. He was uninjured but was being held in a Boer prison camp in Pretoria. "You need not be anxious in any way but I trust you will do all in your power to procure my release."[42] To Bourke Cockran, Winston wrote: "I am 25 today—it is terrible to think how little time remains!"[43]

Jennie called upon all her influential friends and asked them to exert their leverage to get her son released from prison. He was, after all, officially a newspaper correspondent and not a soldier.

George, too, had been in the thick of the war. He had wired her after a battle saying that he was safe and asking her to forward the news to his mother. "It's been a very stiff fight," he wrote, "and thank God so far I am unhurt." In his next letter, he said that he had been involved in the

> hardest fight that has taken place in any part of the colony . . . 13 hours' hard fighting was the time the Battle of Modder River lasted. I can tell you it was a near shave. . . .
>
> The men started without breakfast and went the whole day without food, and water, having finished their water long before noon. It was a terribly hard day, and the heat was terrific. I was knocked over by sunstroke at 3 P.M. and don't remember anything till the evening, when I found myself in the hospital . . . four days' tomorrow. . . . I am sick of this war, three big battles in six days is enough for any man, and I think most of us think the same. . . . How busy you must be with your ship, which appears to be a great success, and *Maggie*. I do hope this number will be a success. . . . [44]

Jennie, however, spent little time with the daily workings of the Review, and Sidney Low capably carried on for her during the time of her intense activity for the *Maine*. Now there was added impetus to hurry the conversion of the cattle-boat. *The Nursing Record & Hospital World* inspected the result and called the *Maine* "the most complete and comfortable hospital ship that has ever been constructed."[45]

Then one day in mid-December, Jennie received a call from *The Morning Post:* "All I could hear," she recalled, "was, 'Hurrah! Hurrah!' repeated by different voices, as one after the other seized the instrument in their kind wish to congratulate me."[46]

CHURCHILL ESCAPED

was the headline carried by the *Post.*
Winston later described the feat:

> Now or never! I stood on the ledge, seized the top of the wall with my hands, and drew myself up. Twice I let myself down again in sickly hesitation, and then with a third resolve scrambled up and over. My waistcoat got entangled with the ornamental metal-work on the top. I had to pause for an

appreciable moment to extricate myself. In this posture I had one parting glimpse of the sentries still talking with their backs turned fifteen yards away. One of them was lighting his cigarette, and I remember the glow on the inside of his hands as a distinct impression which my mind recorded. Then I lowered myself lightly down into the adjoining garden and crouched among the shrubs. I was free![47]

The Boers offered 25 pounds for Winston's recapture and gave this description in a circular:

He is about five foot eight or nine inches, blond with light, thin, small mustache, walks with slight stoop, cannot speak any Dutch, during long conversations he occasionally makes a rattling noise in his throat. . . . Speaks through his nose, cannot pronounce the letter "s" . . . [48]

Winston had escaped, but he was still three hundred miles from the frontier. He walked, ran, hid in ravines, jumped onto a train, and finally, by the sheerest of luck, stumbled into friendly hands. "Thank God you have come here," the man said. "It is the only house for twenty miles where you would not have been handed over. But we are all British here, and we will see you through."[49]

Jennie was relieved, proud, exultant. Now she made final plans for the launching of the *Maine*. She wanted the ship to fly the flags of the United States and Great Britain. Queen Victoria was pleased to agree and promised to send a British flag to the ceremony with her son, the Duke of Connaught. President William McKinley, however, did not agree with Jennie's contention that "it would carry no political significance." Americans were predominantly pro-Boer, and there would be a presidential election in less than a year. McKinley's refusal to personally send an American flag placed Jennie in an awkward position at the ceremony. "Under the circumstances," she wrote, "I thought the best policy was to preserve a judicious silence."

The Duke of Connaught presented the flag on behalf of the Queen and, after thanking the "large number of American ladies," said:

Never has a ship sailed under the combined flags of the Union Jack and the Stars and Stripes; and it marks, I hope, an occasion which brings out that feeling of generosity and affection that the two countries have for each other. . . . Therefore, I ask Lady Randolph Churchill to accept, in the name of all those who have worked with her, the thanks both of the Sovereign of our country and of all Englishmen and women in this splendid present which has been made in aid of our wounded soldiers in South Africa.

Jennie herself made a short speech, in which she said, ". . . All who have been interested in this work have made it a labor of love. We hope that the *Maine* will be more than useful on her errand of mercy, and that our charity will be as widespread as possible, irrespective of nationality."

The Duke hoisted the British flag to the mainmast as the Scots Guard band played "Rule Britannia." The music changed to "The Star-Spangled Banner" as the Stars and Stripes were run up the mizzen, and the Red Cross flag to the foremast. "Add to these the Admiralty's transport flag at the helm, and it is not surprising that we felt much beflagged and bedecked," Jennie said. "It was a great moment for us all, and I confess I felt a lump in my throat."[50]

The ship was in a state of chaos. Ten thousand people had visited her the previous Sunday, leaving the decks covered with mud and the paint no longer clean. What is more, the reconstruction itself had not yet been completed; painters, carpenters, plumbers, and engineers were still to be seen in every nook and corner; the wards were littered with wood shavings, paintpots, ropes, scaffoldings, and debris.

On that final hectic day of the sailing, a small crisis developed when three male nurses left the ship because Colonel Hensman had told them to serve his five-man staff. They said they would serve themselves and the wounded, but not Hensman's men. Hensman was nominally the officer in charge, and Major Julian M. Cabell of the U.S. Army Medical Department, who had been granted a special leave of absence by the Secretary of War, was the senior American surgeon on board. Cabell let it be known before sailing that he was "virtually head and is to do all the work." This conflict in command made Jennie's presence during the voyage essential for easing tension between the British and Americans.

Jennie's sister Clara had been ill with a cold, but came to the sailing anyway with her two sons, Hugh and Oswald. Neither was Jennie without an admiring man to help her—he was Allison Vincent Armour, a member of the Chicago meatpacking family, whom Jennie kept busy getting last-minute supplies at the Army & Navy stores.[51]

Jack was also there and planned to stay aboard after everyone else left. But the rolling of the ship made him ill, and he left with his Aunt Clara.

Even though everyone else at the dock was jubilant, cheering and waving, Jennie, as Clara wrote afterward to Leonie, "seemed depressed. . . ." She had just received a cable:

INVALIDED. PROBABLY RETURNING HOME ALMOST
IMMEDIATELY. REPEAT TO MOTHER. GEORGE.[52]

In a letter that reached her too late, he asked her to postpone her departure until he arrived, or they would miss each other, "which would be too awful."

As the *Maine* moved out from the dock, "the fog was so thick one could not see an inch." Jennie stood on deck listening to cheers.[53] She probably had anticipated this moment as one of elation but her mood now matched the sad bleating song of the foghorn.

Thirty-Two

ON CHRISTMAS DAY 1899 the *Maine* sailed into a full gale in the Bay of Biscay.[1] Jennie had been on many ships in many gales during her trip around the world, but this was the worst.[2] It lasted six days—into the new year and the new century.

". . . no fiddles can restrain your soup from being shot into your lap, or the contents of your glass into your face," Jennie wrote. ". . . I never realized before how one can suffer by color. The green of my attractive little cabin, which I had thought so reposeful, became a source of acute suffering. . . . The sound of the waves breaking on the deck with the report of cannon-balls . . . and I remember thinking, as I rolled in sleepless wretchedness, that if we went to the bottom, at least we should be counted as victims of the war."[3]

She told Leonie that the gale often made sleep impossible and so she "sat up in a secure chair & read." And in a postscript she added, "Look after Jack and George. Write to me all he says. . . ."[4] George West had left Africa for England at just about the time that Jennie had left England, their ships probably crossing somewhere in the ocean. There was no knowing when she would see him again. She was committed to the purpose of this trip and she could not desert that purpose. As Winston told her in a letter, "Your name will be long remembered with affection by many poor broken creatures. Besides, it is the right thing to do, which is the great point."[5]

Late in the evening on the second of January, the *Maine* anchored off Las Palmas, in the Canary Islands. The air was soft and balmy, and the low verandahs of the houses were covered with bougainvillea of varying shades. Jennie was reminded of Monterey, California: "the same square pink houses, with green shutters and center court or patio, tropical vegetation, and the sea at the door." For Jennie, Las Palmas was merely pretty, "whereas Monterey, with its 17-mile drive, unparalleled gardens, and unique, storm-swept cypress-groves overlooking the ocean, is probably one of the most beautiful spots in the world."

> We returned to the ship laden with spoils—birds, parrots, fruit, plants, coffee-pots, and Heaven knows what else. I had an opportunity of judging the appearance of the Maine as we came alongside. Alas! The brilliant green stripe, denoting our status as a military hospital ship, was a thing of shreds and patches, many of our stanchions were bent and twisted, and our would-be immaculate white paint a foggy grey.[6]

In the letter in which Winston had praised Jennie for doing her duty, he had gone on to inform her:

> I have another piece of [news] that will surprise you. . . . Jack sailed from England on the 5th, and I have obtained him a lieutenancy in the S.A. Light Horse [Brigade], too. I feel the responsibility heavily, but I knew he would be longing to come and I think everyone should do something for the country in these times of trouble & crisis. I particularly stipulated that Cassel should agree, and I hope you will not mind.[7]

Jennie minded very much indeed. Jack was nineteen, barely old enough to grow a mustache, and his vision in one eye was so poor it could be a hazard in battle. Then, too, such was Jack's adoration of his brother that a need to prove his courage might make him foolhardy. "This adds to my worries," Jennie wrote to Clara.[8]

Adding even more to her worries was the news from Winston that General Buller had given him a lieutenancy with the South African Light Horse, while still permitting him to retain his correspondent's status. "There is a great battle—the greatest yet fought—impending here . . . ," Winston said. "If I come through alive, I shall try to run down to Cape Town—or perhaps you will come to fetch the wounded from Durban."[9]

The phrase "if I come through alive" must have acted upon Jennie's ready imagination. Now the lives of both her sons were in danger.

Soon the *Maine* was at sea again and her decks were busy. There was much to do on the seventeen-day voyage to Capetown. There had been no time to batten down the mass of articles brought on board at the last minute, and the gangways and hold were in complete disarray. "... The filth and dirt ... something awful ...," Jennie wrote.

In addition, there was a continuing clash of ideas, methods, and personalities between the British and the Americans on board. Some of the personnel assigned to specific wards, for example, would order others not to walk through their wards, or someone would say, "Be good enough to keep your wet feet off my clean [mat] ..."[10] Jennie also felt that some of the men were acting like priggish young medical students, not mature doctors. "I may change my mind," she said. "I hope I will ..."[11] As head of the Hospital Committee and its representative, she had final authority, but she reserved its use. Instead, she called upon all her charm, tact, and firmness to engender a sense of camaraderie.

One of the personal problems was particularly acute:

> ... I am sorry to tell you that Sister Barbara is a great thorn in our side. ... I have tried to befriend her but honestly, everyone in the ship thinks she is rather mad—She has fought with everyone from the Captain to the Stewards—The Ship's Officers went in a body and said they would dine in their rooms, she insulted them so—She and Mrs. Hancock [wife of the Medical Officer] fight all day. Hibbard [Superintendent of Nurses] isn't on speaking terms with her. ... I have begged her to be less antagonistic to everyone. I told her how suicidal such a course was to her—She alternately tries to flirt with the men on board—or insults them. ... I will try to get one of the transports to take her back—Poor wretch, she hasn't a penny, I suppose I shall have to give her some.[12]

With the British Colonel and the American Major both jealous of their prerogatives, Jennie's presence was often required to smooth differences and calm tempers. She had two strong allies on the ship: one a personal confidante, the other a professional medical worker.

The professional was Superintendent of Nurses Mary Eugenie Hibbard. She had been in charge of the Grace Hospital and Nursing School in Detroit, and was to later become Chief Nurse of the U.S. General Hospital at Savannah, Georgia. Mary Hibbard was tall and dignified, with attractive gray hair rolled back from her brow. She had a soft, well-modulated voice and a keen mind. It was perhaps inevitable that she and Jennie would clash over the prerogatives that went with her nursing activities, but at the outset their working relationship was correct and efficient.[13]

Jennie's other ally was Eleanor Warrender, her companion, secretary, and librarian, who did "a thousand things. . . ." She was a pale, quiet girl, the older sister of Jennie's persevering admirer, Hugh Warrender. Hugh and his family had decided that Eleanor needed a change of scene and had persuaded Jennie to take her along. Jennie called her "a capital girl . . . she and I understand each other perfectly. She is intelligent, and a lady—and the whole ship swears by her. . . . I think she is quite happy."[14]

But Jennie was not happy, even though the *Maine* celebrated her birthday on January 9th by "dressing" the ship, all flags flying. She was forty-six years old, not an age she especially wanted to accept. The man she loved seemed more remote than ever. And the great achievement and adventure of the hospital ship had been diminished by petty squabbles. Later she would remember star-gazing at the Southern Cross one evening and gloomily observing, "I thought its beauty a delusion."[15] The single happy note was that Jack would join her at Capetown.

Two weeks later, the *Maine* slowly sailed into Capetown's bay, the sun rising through the breaking clouds above nearby Table Mountain. For the first time Jennie felt the immediacy of war. Filling the bay was a forest of ships' masts—the transports were disembarking troops and supplies at a furious pace.

The Governor of the Cape Colony, Sir Alfred Milner, who had known Jennie for many years, organized a reception for her at the Mount Nelson Hotel.[16] They ate strawberries in a pretty garden, but Jennie kept thinking of the streets filled with soldiers. Jack had not yet arrived and the war news from Winston was bad. General Redvers Buller was in retreat, and critics were already calling him "Reverse" Buller.

For Great Britain, there already had been Black Week: three serious defeats with the loss of several thousand men.[17] One of them was the only son of Lord Roberts, who was now appointed to supersede Buller as commander, with Lord Kitchener as his Chief of Staff.[18]

"Swaggering down the highway of the world," Great Britain had been beaten by an untrained army. Queen Victoria, however, set the tone of British resoluteness when she told Arthur Balfour, "Please understand that there is no one depressed in *this* house; we are not interested in the possibilities of defeat; they do not exist."[19] Reinforcements comprising the entire British Army outside India, were already en route to South Africa, as were volunteer forces from England and the colonies.

On the day the *Maine* arrived in Capetown, Jennie received a change in orders from Capetown's chief medical officer. He felt that the current war situation called for an alteration in priorities, and he gave the *Maine* a new mission: proceed directly to Durban, take on the wounded, and return immediately to England.

Another woman might have been overjoyed. Here was the chance to return to an anxious lover waiting in England. Moreover, the decision was not hers—she was being *ordered* back, so no one could fault her.

But Jennie was infuriated. The *Maine* was not a transport for patients; it was designed as a floating hospital with a staff of superior surgeons and nurses and the latest operating room and X-ray facilities. Its purpose was to stay close to the war and the wounded, a symbol of international concern and good will. That mission was more important than the wishes of any individual. Jennie made it clear that she would appeal the medical officer's decision at Durban. Jack arrived just before the *Maine* sailed. "No time to write, off to Durban," Jennie wrote Clara. "Best love. Jack with me."[20]

Jack wore a dashing sombrero hat—one side up, the other down. But for Jennie he must have been an unsettling sight, this handsome young man with a thin mustache, equipped with revolver, rifle, bayonet, yet looking so young and vulnerable. The idea of Winston as a soldier was already familiar, but to Jennie seeing Jack must have given her a feeling of dread. Jack had tried to explain why he wanted to go to war:

> . . . I should be a fool not to accept a chance of going & doing what I have longed to do so often. . . . I am afraid I am in for a rough time but I am sure I shall like it. . . . [21]

Before setting off, they cabled Winston to try to meet them at Durban for a family reunion—"After all," Winston had written Jennie earlier, ". . . there are only us three in the whole world. . . ."[22]

Jennie has provided us with a description of the voyage.

> And we emerged to bask in the sun like lizards. I gazed for hours through my glasses at the shore, which was only three or four miles distant. The soft green hills and bright sandy beaches, with kraals dotted here and there, gave it such a cultivated appearance that one could hardly realize that this was "Savage South Africa." As we approached Durban, the wind began to blow, and an ominous bank of gray cloud came up, with lightning flashing on the horizon. I shall never forget the astonishing storm which suddenly burst upon us. The electric barometer in my cabin dropped perpendicularly. Torrents of hailstones beat down on us as large as small plums; the wind increased to a hurricane, and was so violent that the ship stood still, although we had been going at 10 knots. The

awning aft was violently blown into the sea, carrying with it all its rafters and stanchions, smashing one of the big ventilators, and only just missing some of the sisters, who were crouching on the deck. The sea, meanwhile, presented a most curious appearance, being covered with millions of little jets about a foot high, due to the force with which the hailstones fell, and as they floated for awhile, it was quite white in a few minutes.

Inside my deck-cabin, the din was terrific, the noise of the hailstones striking the skylight and windows, sounding like bullets. It was impossible to speak. One window was smashed, and the water and ice poured in everywhere. The hailstones were solid lumps of ice, each with a pattern like an agate. With the decks covered with ice, the thermometer at 82 degrees seemed an anomaly, and reminded one of the Scotsman who, during a rainstorm, threw out his rising barometer, shouting after it: "Go and see for yourself!" Luckily, the storm did not last long, and we were soon able to emerge and look at the damage.[23]

Waiting for them at Durban was the port's British medical officer, who was equally determined that the *Maine* immediately fill up with wounded and set forth for England. Within the next few days, Jennie used her power of persuasion with "the government of Natal, Sir Redvers Buller, and other influential friends" in Durban and successfully frustrated three attempts to make the *Maine* a transport.

Winston was waiting for her in Durban. The reunion was a moving one. "And so we three met all together again, about 7,000 miles from where we expected each other to be," Jack wrote.[24] Jennie and her sons had two days for themselves, and the Governor of Natal, Sir Walter Hely-Hutchinson, invited them to go to Pietermaritzburg. It was a lovely trip on a twisting railway through hills of ever-changing colors. For two days, in this peaceful place, they all tried to push from their minds the impending bloody battles for the relief of Ladysmith. But all too soon the boys left to join their brigades. "It was hard to say goodbye to my sons. . . ."[25]

Frederic Villiers, the noted war correspondent, and Captain Percy Scott of the H.M.S. *Terrible* met Winston and Jack while all of them were en route to the front. "Winston introduced his brother to me," said Villiers, "who at once told me that he had heard me lecture before the boys when he was at Harrow, and said he especially remembered that I threw a portrait of his mother on the screen in the act of firing a revolver."

Villiers had taken the photograph in 1894 aboard the *Empress of China,* on which Jennie and Lord Randolph were traveling to Manchuria. To help pass the time, Villiers and some Japanese officers were practicing with their revolvers, shooting at empty beer bottles slung over the stern of the ship. Jennie, who was a good shot, joined them.

Villiers told Jack and Winston that he had flashed that same photograph of their mother onto a screen during a lecture at the University Club in Madison Square, New York. "To my surprise," he said, "the whole room stood up and cheered with great enthusiasm, and it was some time before I could proceed with my lecture." Later he learned that the mansion that housed the University Club had been built by Jennie's father for his young family, that he had given it to Jennie as her dowry, and that the present lecture hall had once been Leonard Jerome's private theater. "Why, Lady Randolph used to act on that very platform!" one of the members said.[26] Winston and Jack were most amused by the story.

The conversation later shifted to the war. They were arguing a point about Kitchener's campaign in the Sudan when Winston said, "I know I'm right, for I put it in my book."

> He reached for his grip-sack on the rack, and produced his book on Khartoum, from which he immediately quoted, and, I must admit, his view was a very sound one. He went on reading till we were all nearly asleep. Presently I roused to a decided opinion on another point. I was about to clinch it at once by waking Winston, who was by now fast asleep, when his brother said–
>
> "For heavens sake, don't wake him, or we shan't have any rest at all tonight! He's got another volume of that book up in the rack!"[27]

The wounded from Spion Kop were already en route to the *Maine*, moving along by day in their jolting wagons and lying all night on the hillside. When the first ambulance train arrived near the dock, Jennie and the staff of the *Maine* were ready. The *Central News of Durban* reported: "Lady Randolph superintended their reception, personally directed berthing, and flitted among the injured as an 'angel of mercy.'"[28]

Of the typical soldier Jennie said, "Out of his uniform he is a big child, and wants to be kept in order, and not too much spoilt. I am afraid we were inclined to do this!"[29] "I had long and frequent talks with many of them."

Jennie also wrote letters for them, and if they paused, finding it difficult to think of anything else to dictate, she would suggest things. "Won't you send your love to anyone?" she asked one wounded soldier. He gave her a reproving look and answered "Not out of the family."

One very gallant Tommy, who lay with a patch over his eye, and inflamed cheek and the broken arm, asked me to add to his letter: "The sister which is a-writing of this is very nice."[30]

All the nurses wore simple uniforms consisting of a long white skirt and a short white jacket, a brassard with *Maine* and a Red Cross embossed on it, and a white cap that peaked in the middle. Jennie wore the uniform too, and many of the men called her "Sister Jennie."

One of the first wounded officers to arrive carried a note that was to be delivered to Jennie. It was from Chieveley Camp, in Natal, and it began, "My dearest Mama." It was, of course, from Winston. "It is a coincidence," he said wryly,

> that one of the first patients on board the Maine should be your own son. Jack, who brings you this letter, will tell you all about the skirmish and the other action he took part in. He behaved very well and pluckily and the Adjutant, the Colonel and his squadron leader speak highly of his conduct. There was for ten minutes quite a hot fire. And we had about ten men hit. Jack's wound is slight though not officially classed as such. The doctors tell me that he will take a month to recover and I advise you not to allow him to go back before he is quite well. He is unhappy at being taken off the boards so early in the game and of course it is a great nuisance, but you may be glad with me that he is out of harm's way for a month. There will be a great battle in a few days, and his presence–though I would not lift a finger to prevent him–adds much to my anxiety when there is fighting.[31]

Later Winston would write:

> It was a great joy to me to have my brother Jack with me, and I looked forward to showing him round and doing for him the honours of war. This pleasure was, however, soon cut short. On February 12, we made a reconnaissance six or seven miles to the east of the railway line, and occupied for some hours a large, wooded eminence known to the Army as Hussar Hill.
>
> After quitting Hussar Hill and putting at a gallop a mile between us and the enemy, our squadrons reined in into a walk and rode slowly homewards up a long, smooth grass

slope. On this occasion, as I looked back over my shoulder . . . I remarked to my companion, "We are still much too near those fellows." The words were hardly out of my mouth when a shot rang out, followed by the rattle of magazine fire from two or three hundred Mauser rifles. We leapt off our horses, threw ourselves on the grass, and returned the fire with an answering roar and rattle. Jack was lying by my side. All of a sudden he jumped and wriggled back a yard or two from the line. He had been shot in the calf, in this, his very first skirmish, by a bullet which must have passed uncommonly near his head.[32]

Jack described the conclusion of the incident in a letter to his Aunt Clara:

> Thank goodness it had turned out to be nothing, but it hurt a good deal at the time. I mounted again as the squadron continued to retire, but after going about a mile, Winston made me get into an ambulance; and so my military career ended rather abruptly. It was very bad luck being hit the first time I was under fire. But I saw a very good day, and while it lasted, I heard as many bullets whiz past as I ever want to.
>
> I went straight onto the *Maine,* and there I remained until she sailed for the Cape. . . . [33]

Listening to Jack's dramatic account of the fighting only increased Jennie's desire to visit the war zone. She wrote Winston to this effect, and he answered: ". . . I can easily arrange for you to come to Chieveley–if the fighting stops . . ."[34]

Winston soon managed a few days' leave and again visited his mother and brother aboard the *Maine,* which was still lying at anchor. Helping Jennie entertain her sons was her new friend and protector, the commanding officer of Durban Captain Percy Scott of the *H.M.S. Terrible.* Captain Scott, whom Winston called "the greatest swell in Durban," was an inventor as well as a sailor.[35] He had invented, among other things, a gun carriage which enabled the 4.7 naval gun to be taken up country to the front. Captain Scott lavished every courtesy on Winston and Jack. He showed them all the wonders of his armoured cruiser, one of the two largest warships afloat, and displayed the 4.7 gun which he had named *Lady Randolph Churchill*–Jennie fired the test round before the weapon was shipped to the front.

The *Maine* was now almost filled with wounded soldiers. "We were busy from morn to night. Indeed, one never seemed to have a moment to write or read: the one difficulty on board ship at any time, and more particularly on a hospital ship, is to be alone, and when alone, to be able to concentrate."[36]

Jennie was particularly bothered by the fact that a number of sick and wounded men sent to the *Maine* from other hospitals arrived still wearing the tattered garments in which they had been taken from the battlefield. She wrote of some wounded being taken aboard the Maine from a tug, "one man wearing only shreds of some khaki trousers, another still with only a pocket handkerchief tied around his wounded leg." There were many like that, some of whom already had been transferred from several hospitals, always sent out again in the same rags they had worn on arrival.[37]

The medical situation during the Boer War was described in a book by W. L. Burdett-Coutts as "hopelessly insufficient." He told of patients "dying like flies for want of attention. . . . Three doctors for 300 patients, and no nurses, few trained orderlies . . . Not enough beds, stretchers on the ground . . . Delirious patients wandering in the wards at night . . . The hospital death rate almost 8% . . . and at one hospital, a 21% death rate . . . Robberies by orderlies . . ."[38]

Jennie wanted to visit the front and see conditions in the hospitals at first hand. With the backing of Captain Scott, she got permission to go to Chieveley Camp, along with Eleanor Warrender and Colonel Hensman. Scott had planned to escort them, but emergency duty delayed him at the last moment and he sent his coxswain instead.

Jennie described the trip: "The train was full of officers and men returning to the front. Although we were traveling at night, I was kept awake by the thought that I was going to pass all those well-known, and, to me, peculiarly interesting places. . . ."

In the middle of the night, the train was searched for spies.

> Every pass was then minutely examined, every face scanned, and I saw with keen interest two individuals dragged out of the next compartment. . . . Both were marched off—to what fate, one wonders!
>
> I was asleep when we reached Frere at five a.m. A vigorous tap on the window awoke me. "Lady Randolph Churchill, are you there?" "Yes, very much so," I answered, as I dropped the shutter and put my head out, finding an officer of the Seaforth Highlanders on the platform. "I knew you were coming up, and thought you would like a cup of

coffee," he said—"If you will accept the hospitality of my tin hut, 50 yards from here; you won't get anything more for a long time." In my eagerness, I was proceeding to jump down, when he remarked that I had no shoes on, and, with a glance at my dishevelled locks, suggested a hat. As I walked to the hut, dawn was just breaking. A long orange-red streak outlined the distant brown hills; through the haze of dust showing on the skyline, trains of mule-carts were crawling along, and in the plain, little groups of soldiers and horsemen were moving about, emerging from every tent. My host seated me on a stool in the tiny verandah, and gave me an excellent cup of coffee. He was so delighted to have someone to speak to that the words and questions came tumbling out, waiting for no answers. In one breath, he told me how he had been there for months, broiling with heaps of uncongenial work to do, all responsibilities and anxiety, and no excitement or danger. He lived in daily hopes of getting some fighting. Meanwhile, "Someone has to do the dirty work, and there it is."[39]

When the train was underway again, a guard rushed to tell Jennie that they were passing the place of the armored-train disaster where Winston had been taken prisoner. The train was still lying on its side, a mangled and battered wreck. A few yards away was a grave with a cross.

Finally, they reached the camp at Chieveley and Jennie observed the weather-beaten and in many cases haggard men, with soiled, worn uniforms hanging on their spare figures; the horses, picketed in lines or singly covered with canvas torn in strips to keep off the buzzing, plaguing flies; the khaki-painted guns; the ambulance-wagons with their trains of mules; and above all, the dull booming of "Long Tom." . . . She also saw the gun that Captain Scott had named after her, and the gun crew gave her an empty shell as a souvenir.

Having briefly borrowed the General's tent, Jennie was scribbling a note to her sons when a rider galloped up, calling out in a cheery voice: "General! Are you there?" "His look of blank astonishment when he caught sight of me was most amusing. A woman in the camp, and in the General's tent! I explained, and after a few laughing remarks, he rode off."[40]

Jennie took time to visit an area where two thousand horses were resting before being sent to the front. Hundreds of them had just arrived from South America. Jennie, who loved horses, could not help visualizing the trip they had endured: penned up for days on a rolling ship, then crammed into an open truck under a blazing sun, to be taken out, stiff, sore, and dazed. With two days' rest, they were to be sent up to the front, only to be fodder for Boer bullets.

When Jennie returned to the hospital ship, the soldiers wanted to know what she had learned of the war. "Any news?" "Ladysmith?–Nothing?" "What, back again at Chieveley Camp? That Buller, he's unlucky." In one of the wards, she hung a large framed map with flag pins that represented the military situation. But every day a few more Boer flags were found stuck in the frame, their places taken by Union Jacks. Whenever there was a victory, "a grand cheer went up from the men; lights were flashed, messages heliographed from Captain Percy Scott's electric shutter on board the *Terrible* to all ships in the harbor, the band played itself out, the men sang themselves hoarse, and at last, after a bouquet of fireworks, we went to bed."

Jennie was dining with Captain Scott aboard the *Terrible* on March 29th when news came of the relief of Ladysmith.[41] The city of Durban "went mad." Jennie described the demonstration at which the cheering was so continuous that none of the speakers could be heard. In London, crowds massed in the streets and sang "Soldiers of the Queen," strangers embraced each other, poured water on each other, drank toasts together, and fireworks went off everywhere.[42] Robert Browning's lines fit well:

> How bad and sad and mad it was,
> But, Lord! how it was sweet!

The time had come for the *Maine* to take its patients to England. While the ship was being prepared for the voyage Jennie, Winston, and a Captain Thorp, who was one of her discharged patients, went to Ladysmith on a special pass from General Buller. They saw the carcasses of horses, the masses of spent shells, the newly made graves. At one point, they crossed a small sandbagged bridge over which British soldiers had run single-file under a barrage of fire from three hills. The dust of the battle area was up to their ankles, the sun was scorching, misery and desolation were everywhere. On their way into the town, they got a ride atop a pile of gripsacks on a Scottish mule cart. Jennie thought they made a strange sight "but no one noticed us." The faces of the townspeople were "empty and resigned."[43]

Jennie borrowed a wild horse which had never before been in harness and she rode with Winston and Thorp to the camp of the South African Light Horse Brigade "where we had some tea out of bottles and tin mugs. By this time, I was too tired to take in any more, and the hazardous drive back in the semi-darkness quite finished me."[44] The next day she returned to the *Maine* on a Red Cross train filled with wounded men.

She had come a long way from the savoring of strawberries in the garden of the Mount Nelson hotel. She had seen war as it was: the mangled bodies, the eyes of despair, the unmitigated desolation.

George now seemed remote from her, their love affair was part of another world. She had written to him, but she had little time to yearn for him. But on her return to the ship, she found a letter from George waiting for her. He had written from his father's home:

> I have just received your wire, re-directed—saying you are going to remain at Durban a month—I thought and hoped that, once you had arrived at Durban and got things started on board the *Maine,* you would think of returning. . . . I am alone with my father, who never misses an opportunity of dropping hints about financial difficulties, and how easily they could be overcome if I married an heiress. . . . [45]

Such a letter might have worried her more at another time, but now the *Maine* was ready to set sail from Durban and Jennie would soon be back in England. The other crews in the harbor cheered them as they moved out to sea. In a column as dispassionate as could be expected, war correspondent Winston Churchill reported:

> The Maine left yesterday for Cape Town with 12 officers and 175 soldiers, mostly serious cases.
> During the two months the ship had been at Durban, more than 300 cases have been treated, and many difficult operations have been performed successfully.
> Lady Randolph Churchill has been untiring in her attention to the management, and I impartially think that her influence has been of real value to all on board. . . ."[46]

From the ship, Jennie wrote to her "Darling boys," telling them she was anxious to get the war news so that she could figure out, even indirectly "where you two boys are." "One more week, and then home," she added. "I shall find all my work cut out for me there."[47]

When the *Maine* arrived at Capetown, Jennie learned to her dismay that there were orders for the ship to unload the wounded and wait for other patients.[48] Aboard ship the wounded men, filling every berth and still dreaming of home, were thrown into despair by the news. Jennie hurried ashore, found the Medical Officer, and declared that it was her intention that the *Maine* would leave at daybreak the next morning, as previously arranged, "and that I was cabling to the Minister of War to back me up . . ."[49]

That evening, the Minister of War, Lord Lansdowne, did back her up, and at daybreak the *Maine* sailed for home.

The weather was perfect, and the men who were well enough sat on deck. They talked about their hopes and their plans, they sang, and sometimes Jennie sang with them. These men had become a part of her life. As she had written the Prince of Wales: "I am satisfied with the Mission the Maine has fulfilled—& if I may say so my connection with it. It has been hard work & sometimes the temptation has been great to fly off in a mail steamer for home—but I am glad I resisted . . ."[50]

It had been four months and a day since the *Maine* left England. Jennie had been depressed then. Now as the ship docked at Southhampton, she stood on deck radiant in a white straw hat with a blue ribbon on which were embossed the British and American flags. On her blue serge dress, she wore the *Maine* badge over the left breast, and on her red cravat was a Red Cross pin.[51]

As her friends crowded aboard ship, they told her how wonderfully healthy she looked, at least fifteen years younger. Someone gave her a large bouquet of roses.

And then she saw George.

Thirty-Three

COLONEL CORNWALLIS-WEST had discovered a telegram Leonie had sent to George informing him of the time of Jennie's arrival in Southhampton. The Colonel bitterly accused Leonie of assisting Jennie "in her insane infatuation for my son."[1]

The Colonel was wrong if he thought Jennie was simply infatuated with George; she loved him. Yet she had been changed by the war and was no longer certain what she wanted. She was, after all, what some thought of as "an older woman." The Empress Eugénie, whom Jennie loved, had said that a woman over forty "begins to dissolve, loses color, grows dark like a cloud." And Emilie du Chatelet, mistress of Louis XV, had written in her "Treatise on Happiness" that the older woman has only three pleasures left: gambling, study, and gourmandizing at the dinner table.[2]

Jennie's life, however, contradicted both of them. At forty-six she was in her prime. She had kept pace with the world in a rather remarkable way. Those who were envious often accused her of having "a man's mind." How else, they said, could she have so successfully invaded the private preserves of Power? First, politics; then, publishing; and now, war.

Her political power had been exercised indirectly, maneuvering and campaigning for her husband and then her son. Her publishing power was a real literary force. But her successful organization of the *Maine* represented a maximum of administrative efficiency and dedicated purpose. Never had she felt more effective, more vital.

"I hate leaving the ship," she wrote Winston. "People are gradually understanding the work I have done, and in any case, I have my own consciousness of something accomplished. . . . The H.R.H. and everyone seems to take it for granted that I am not going again and that I shall have done enough."[3] But she herself felt that she had not done enough, and she talked of going back to the *Maine*. As late as May 26, she told Winston, "I shall probably go out on the third voyage."

This resolve naturally made a difference in her personal relations, and her new attitude about marriage to George was reflected in a letter to Winston: ". . . There are so many things against my doing it–that I doubt it's ever coming off. . . ."[4]

George was even more changed than Jennie. He had come home from the war to recuperate at his father's home. His family combined pampering of their only son, with steady and less than subtle pressure. They maligned the marriage he hoped to make as "ill-assorted" and "doomed." The Colonel had let it be known that "if this marriage takes place it will estrange the whole of my family from my son and so I have told him."[5] George particularly resented the continuous inference that if only he would choose a young heiress, he could replenish the family fortune. His father pointedly stressed their need for money to restore Ruthin Castle and to keep alive the heritage of the Cornwallis-Wests.

None of this impressed George. He was no longer the callow, impressionable young man, "the spoiled darling." The father he had admired now disappointed him, and he had never liked his mother, who had given her love to many men, but seldom to her son. In fact, so strong was his hostility toward his mother that he insisted that he did not want to be buried near her. He was close with his two sisters, but at this point he was confiding in almost no one.

George's growing maturity was largely the product of his brief but vivid contact with war. He had come home depressed about the carnage on the battlefield, which had only been emphasized for him by the ghastly work of burying the dead after they had been spoiling under a blazing sun.

> A magnificent specimen of an old Dutchman, lying dead, with a look of marvelous calm upon his face, very like Rembrandt's picture of Joseph Trip in the National Gallery. For the first time, it struck me that we were fighting against men of a splendid type, whose sole idea was to protect their own country from invasion.[6]

The change in Jennie did not mean that she no longer cared for George, although her ardor had been tempered by the companionship of the brave, dashing, brilliant Captain Percy Scott of the H.M.S. *Terrible*. Captain Scott had offered the wisdom of a more mature man, and Jennie had had that contrast to consider, too. But her love for George had lasted for more than a year, and it was not a relationship she could easily dismiss. Cooled passions can start smoldering again, and romance was an art George knew.

George had recovered enough so that he was sent to Pirbright as a musketry instructor for recruits and reservists. While there he stayed with Consuelo, Duchess of Manchester, who had taken a house near Windsor that year. Consuelo was one of those friends on whom Jennie could always depend for love and laughter. The other Consuelo, the young Duchess of Marlborough, had written that Jennie had a fund of risque stories which she told with a twinkle in her eye. Most of these had first been told to Jennie by the older Consuelo.

The Duchess of Manchester had been born Consuelo Iznaga. Her father was Cuban and her mother American. Before moving to England, they had lived on a Louisiana cotton plantation and in New York. Consuelo's husband, the Duke of Manchester, had died in 1892. Besides her husband's estate, she had inherited her brother's property valued at over two million dollars, which she generously shared with her sisters.[7]

Consuelo had a graceful figure, golden hair, large dark eyes, and an angelic expression. Yet she was the kind of woman who, while riding in a carriage to a Court Ball, decided that her stays were too tight and that she was going to remove her corset. And so she did, twisting and wrenching it out over her breast, much to the astonishment of her escort.

Consuelo was probably also the "American Duchess" who upon returning from Ireland was asked whether she had seen the Blarney Stone. "Yes, certainly I have," the Duchess replied.

"Well," the man said with a smile, "they do say that the virtues of the Blarney Stone can be conveyed to another by a kiss."

"I guess that may be," she answered, "but I don't know anything about it, because I sat on it."

Jennie, of course, was also at Consuelo's house near Windsor for weekends when George was there. George used to "hack a pony over every morning so as to arrive at Pirbright in time for parade," and then return in the afternoon.[8]

Many years later, Jennie wrote:

> If people sufficiently prominent for one reason or another
> succeed in surrounding themselves with an atmosphere of

mystery, the interest of the public is aroused. . . . There are men and women we well know who can, through their personality, live down scandals, whereas the less-favored go under, emphasizing the old saying that, "One may steal a horse while another may not look over the wall."[9]

Jennie was certainly one of those people who aroused "the interest of the public." Reporting on the on-again, off-again marriage rumors, *The New York Times* stated, "Mr. Cornwallis-West's family . . . have cut Lady Randolph Churchill dead. . . ."

Other press reports indicated the wide variety of rumor:

> The engagement of Lady Randolph Churchill and young Cornwallis-West is absolutely broken. They have both promised to give up the idea of ever becoming man and wife. . . .

> The engagement . . . has been reported so many times and contradicted so often, that people are inclined to believe that the interesting rumor—probably on account of its vitality—has a good deal of truth in it. . . . [10]

Dr. Samuel Johnson had said: "I believe marriages would in general be as happy, and probably more so, if they were all made by the Lord Chancellor, upon a due consideration of characters and circumstances, without the parties having any choice in the matter."[11] It is not difficult to predict what the Lord Chancellor would have said about Jennie and George.

Jennie truly did not know what she wanted. Her letters were full of indecision, questions, and longings. Complicating matters for her were additional problems: her two sons were still in combat in South Africa and she knew more intimately now what a bullet or shell could do to a human body; her sister Leonie was expecting another baby soon, "and as she has not had one for 11 years, it is always rather bad. . . . She is counting on me . . .";[12] and the *Anglo-Saxon Review* needed Jennie's complete attention to save it from an early death. The financing she had gotten had been only for the first year, and now she had to scurry for more funds.

Jennie sent George a note apologizing for being "snappy and tired," but she had good reason to be. Her irritating relationship with John Lane was becoming more turbulent. Earlier, she had complained to Lane about a new prospectus which he had issued

> without telling me anything about it—and that my name figures in it in such microscopic type, I wonder you put it on at

all! Considering that I am the proprietor and the editor, and you merely the publisher, it is rather audacious—I must say I am exceedingly surprised at the line you are taking, and considering the circumstances of the case, my patience is very nearly exhausted. . . . Also, Mr. Thompson is to see that all sums to the credit of the *Anglo-Saxon Review* . . . at the office are to be paid over to the Second National Bank, as agreed upon between you and Mr. Thompson. I really cannot see how we are to get on if you are to go back on your word like this and not to be counted on. . . . [13]

Lane had answered: ". . . I really don't know what 'line' it is that surprised you, or what I am doing to exhaust your patience. . . ."[14] He then went into great detail about the new prospectuses and the quality of his sales force in both America and England.

Jennie was angered because she felt he was printing too many copies of the *Review,* not notifying subscribers about renewals, and not informing booksellers that back issues were available. She was also curt in her comment on some articles he suggested: "I do not like them."

Sales of the early issues had been below expectations, particularly in America. The interest there seemed to have been more snobbish than literary. Perhaps if there had been no Boer War and no relationship with George, Jennie would have gone to the United States on a promotion tour for "Maggie." A survey of publications of the time, though, indicates that this kind of magazine was generally short-lived and seldom a viable proposition. Such people as Ernest Cassel and Bourke Cockran had invested in the *Review* with no great expectations of profit. They had put in their money more as a personal matter than as a financial one, and even Jennie knew the limit of their responses.

Jennie's subeditors had ably carried on in her absence, particularly Sidney Low. Low had sent an issue of the *Review* to the editor of the popular magazine *Sphere:* "I hope you may find time to cast a glance at it. I am interested in the magazine. I look after it during Lady Randolph's absence. . . ."[15] But neither Low nor any of the other editors had Jennie's persuasive powers for getting contributions from well-known authors and celebrities. When Jennie set herself on an assignment, few could refuse her. One potential contributor who had failed to come through was her son Winston, but he was most apologetic: "I have never had a moment either to write your Anglo-Saxon article, nor to write the three American articles for which I was offered £300."[16]

Winston had no qualms, however, about making more demands on his mother.

I have very nearly made up my mind to stand again for Oldham. They have implored me not to desert them.

Mind you send me all the reviews on my new book on this war, and I do hope you will realize the importance of making the very best terms you can for me, both as a writer and lecturer.[17]

And again:

I do hope you will have been able to arrange good terms for me to lecture in the United States, probably during December, January and February, and we can consider the desirability of my undertaking to lecture in England during the autumn when I come home. . . . [18]

"I am doing all the things you want," she had written. She had seen his publisher, Longman, to complete financial arrangements for his new book; she had checked into the American lecture bureau of Major Pond and found it highly reputable. ("I believe he *is* the man.") She was also sending him a fat collection of reviews of his book. ("I trust they will satisfy your greed.")[19]

And then she continued:

. . . Pamela spoke to me about your idea of a play, but I discourage it. Honestly, it would not do. People would not stand any war play. . . . It would be thought bad taste. Even a year after the Civil War, nothing could be given at that time, of that kind. . . . You will find plenty to write about without it. . . ."[20]

Jennie convinced him.

Then, in a reminiscent mood, Winston wrote to Leonie:

I have had many adventures, and I shall be glad of a little peace and security. I have been under fire now in 40 separate affairs in this country alone, and one cannot help wondering how long good luck will hold. But I stand the wear and tear pretty well. Indeed, my health, nerve and spirits were never better than now, at the end of seven months of war. I saw Jack for a day in Cape Town, on his way to Beira. He will have a very interesting position on Carrington's staff, and should not, under ordinary circumstances, run into much danger. Don't worry. . . . [21]

Jennie, meanwhile, was worrying about Jack.

> Of course, I have been following Buller's advance, and
> have had some bad moments, thinking of you, but have
> trusted you for the best, and think you capable of looking af-
> ter your skin as well as most. I am glad to think that the end
> is approaching, and that the war must soon be over now. I
> am also glad that you are moving, anything is better than
> stagnation in an unhealthy camp. How fit you must be, as
> riding suits you, I know. I am much more frightened of fever
> than of bullets, so don't be rash as regards water, etc. I have
> a long letter from Winston today, from Bloemfontein, dated
> March 1st. He seems to have had a narrow escape at Dewets-
> dorp, from falling into Boers' hands, as an advance party met
> the enemy, Winston's saddle turned, and I understand his
> horse galloped away, but luckily, his own people turned back
> for him. He did not give me this account himself. I suppose I
> shall see it in the papers. Meanwhile, Pamela had heard it
> from someone and told me. I am sure that you, like him, are
> heartily sick of the whole thing. Everyone is; and all longing
> for peace and home.[22]

Jennie was careful not to mention George in her letter to Jack. She knew
that both of her sons were unhappy about the possibility of her marrying,
but that Jack was particularly sensitive to it. Winston had a carefully patterned future and a romantic interest in Pamela. Though he still needed his
mother for important things, Jack needed her for nearly everything. He
had had no career until his mother mapped one out for him. Jack's initia-
tion into war was the only thing he could call his own, and even that was,
at least, in part a way of competing with his brother. He was a young man
in search of an anchor and a frame of life.

The war in South Africa was still raging, but in May Mafeking was relieved. For 216 days the small British garrison there had held out against
continuous bombardment, starvation, and fever. Lord Roberts had promised to end the Boers' siege by May 18th, and on that date the Lord Mayor
of London proclaimed that the siege had been lifted.

Mafeking had become the British symbol of stubborn courage. When
the Boers first surrounded the garrison and asked the commanding officer
to surrender to avoid bloodshed, his answer was: "When does the bloodshed begin?" Now London went wild. Men draped themselves with the
large posters announcing the news. Performers stopped their shows to sing
the national anthem. People spontaneously formed processions and marched

through the city in every direction. Strangers hugged and kissed each other. The fears and tensions of war were momentarily overcome by joy.[23]

But Jennie's personal life was still in turmoil. Her inner debate about marrying George was revealed in a letter to Winston:

> . . . added to the reasons in favor of it, is his extraordinary devotion to me through all these trying times, and my absence–Also, the fact that it is possible for him to help me in a money way in the future, if not at present. There is no doubt that you will never settle down until you have a home of your own, and in the four years that I have had this house, you have spent about 3 months in all in it–I mention this to show you why I do not feel that I would be breaking up our home if I should marry.
>
> . . . You know what you are to me, and how you can *now* and *always* count on me–I am intensely proud of you, and apart from this, my heart goes out to you and understands you as no other woman ever will–Pamela is devoted to you, and if your love has grown as hers–I have no doubt that it's only a question of time for you to marry–What a comfort it will be to you, to settle down in comparative comfort–I am sure you are sick of the war and its horrors–You will be able to make a decent living out of your writing, and your political career will lead you to big things–Probably, if you married an heiress, you would not work half so well–but you may have a chance in America–tho I do not urge you to try–You know I am not mercenary, either for myself or you boys–More's the pity![24]

Finally the question was resolved. The persistent and loving George at last persuaded Jennie to let him announce their engagement.

The Prince of Wales had talked to Jennie at length about the subject and she was quoted as saying that "she knew her own mind a great deal better than the Prince." He also expressed his views in a letter which she angrily tore up and answered in blistering terms. The Prince responded, almost sadly:

> It has been my privilege to enjoy your friendship for upwards of a quarter of a century–therefore, why do you think it necessary to write me a rude letter–simply because I have expressed my regret at the marriage you are about to make? I have said nothing behind your back that I have not said to

your face—You know the world so well that I presume you are the best judge of your own happiness—but at the same time, you should think twice before you abuse your friends and well-wishers for not congratulating you on the serious step you are going to make! I can only hope that we shall all be mistaken.[25]

George, too, was pressured further:

On the Thursday morning of that week my engagement was announced in the *Daily Telegraph,* and I received a peremptory order from the officer commanding my battalion, Colonel Dalrymple Hamilton, to go up and see him. He told me at the interview that if I married Lady Randolph, I should have to leave the regiment. Considering that she had a host of friends, including himself, and was liked by everybody, and that there was no rule in the regiment against subalterns marrying, I considered such an ultimatum outrageous and saw red. If I had had any doubts as to the wisdom of what I was about to do, they were blown to the four winds by what I considered nothing less than a piece of unwarrantable interference, and it made me obstinate. I dashed off in a hansom to the War Office and sent in my name to the Adjutant-General, who was then Sir Evelyn Wood, whom I just knew. A few minutes later, I caught him going out of his office, and he said: "I've no time at the moment unless you can go with me in a cab to where I am lunching, and tell me what I can do for you."

On our way down Piccadilly, I told him what had happened, and asked whether it was in accordance with Queen's Regulations that an officer should be told to leave his regiment because he wished to marry a woman admittedly older than himself, but of whom nothing else could be said except in her favor. Sir Evelyn reassured me, and promised to do what he could to help me.[26]

Shortly afterward George was ordered to report to the regimental orderly room, to see Colonel Fludyer, who commanded the regiment.

[Fludyer] poured out the vials of his wrath upon me for having dared to go to a man whom he described as "the enemy of the Brigade of Guards." Why, heaven knows! He made it quite clear to me that my presence in the regiment would no longer be desired or expected. I felt more angry than ever, and after consultation with Jennie, wrote to the Prince of Wales, asking if I might have an interview. When I saw him and told him all about it, he came to the point at once: "Is it your intention to make soldiering your profession for the rest of your life?" he said. "If it is, then I advise you to sit tight. If, however, it is not, why make enemies of men who have been your friends and who probably will continue to be your friends after all this has blown over? My advice to you is to go on half-pay for six months or a year, look around and see if you can find something else to do, and then make up your mind at the expiration of the time."[27]

Jennie would not simply wait quietly. She had made her choice. This was the man she wanted. For her, that meant that she would fight for him in every way she could. She went directly to Secretary of War Lord Lansdowne, and later that day Lansdowne advised her:

I have spoken to the Commander in Chief, who was very sympathetic.

It is clear that Mr. West could not be required to leave the regiment except by the military authorities, with the concurrence of the Commander in Chief. Until, therefore, an attempt has actually been made to bring about his removal, you can afford to disregard vague threats such as those which you mentioned to me this morning.

I would venture to urge you strongly to adopt this line, and not to gratify the busybodies by taking serious notice of the incident which you described to me.

May I as an old friend tell you how sincerely I wish you all possible happiness. . . . [28]

George followed the Prince's advice to him and applied for half-pay duty, determined to seek another way to make a living.

Now Jennie's main concern was to reconcile her sons to the marriage. "It is rather hard on me not to have a word from either of you boys," she wrote Jack.[29] Winston accepted the situation, but apparently without enthusiasm. He had long ago said he would quit the war only after Pretoria had been retaken. That having been accomplished, he now agreed to come home for his mother's wedding. She accordingly scheduled the wedding to coincide with his return at the end of July.

Next she had to persuade Jack to come home, too:

> I hope this will find you with your face more or less
> turned towards home. I dined with Cassel last night, and he
> said that he thought that now that the war was almost over,
> you had done your duty by your country, and that you
> ought to come home and attend to your business.[30]

Jennie asked Winston to try to influence Jack, and Winston urged him:

> Please telegraph Mamma what you propose to do. It is all
> very well being consistently loyal to the South African Light
> Horse, but at the same time, when the war becomes merely
> an affair of guerillas, I think you would do much better to
> come home to the quills of the city and the arms of the
> ladies.[31]

Jack answered:

> I envy you going home, and was much tempted when I
> received your wire to "chuck" the regiment and catch you at
> Cape Town. However, although I am very sick of all this
> here, I should feel unhappy if I were home before it is over.
> The quills of the city can I think wait a little while and so can
> the arms of the ladies. . . . [32]

It was natural for Jennie to want Jack to attend her wedding, but she
also wanted him home so that she could try to reconcile him to the marriage. But Jack was resistant, and his worst fears may have been realized
when he received her letter of June 23rd:

> Now listen, darling boy, I have thought over everything
> and have come to the conclusion that, for many reasons, it
> would be unwise for either you or Winston to live with us,
> once we are married. Knowing how fond I am of you both,
> you will believe that I have not come to this conclusion
> hastily. It seems hard, and it gives me a pang every time I
> think of it, but I know it is the nicest plan. I should like you
> and Winston to have rooms together, which I would furnish
> for you, and arrange, and your life, as far as your material
> comfort goes, to the best of my ability. I need hardly say you
> will always be more than welcome here. You can both look

upon it as your home for everything but sleeping. George is helping me in every way possible, to make my income larger by putting my affairs straight. As I wrote to Winston, I hope to make you both independent of me by giving you a certain amount of capital. Of course, this would have to be worked out when you come of age, next year. Meanwhile, if all goes well, George and I propose getting married very quietly (but not at the Registry Office) on the 28th of July. Have many things to settle and arrange–I shall go to Paris and then to Aix, and after that, here. God bless you, my darling boy. . . . You must stand by me. I have, & will, always stand by you . . .

Your loving mother.[33]

Jennie must have recognized that her words had been neither very motherly nor very tactful, as she wrote again in a different tone a week later:

My darling Jack:

Surely, darling boy, you would not stay out much longer? You will find Cassel ready to receive you–and your "Mommer" with open arms. Winston will be here in time for my wedding, if all goes well–It will be very quiet–No breakfast–except for the family. But I won't do it in a "hole-and-corner" fashion, as if I was ashamed of it. I pray from the bottom of my heart that it would not make you unhappy. You know how dearly I love you both, and the thought that it may hurt you, is the one cloud on my happiness. But you won't grudge me the latter? Nothing could exceed George's goodness and devotion, and I think we shall be very happy. Everything I can do for you, I will. Meanwhile, my real friends are most kind, and have given me charming presents; and they all like him so much that they are reconciled. . . . [34]

Then, on the very day of her marriage, she again wrote Jack:

I am more than distressed to think that my letters, with the exception of one, have not reached you. You must know that your "Mommer" would not forget you. I wired you and Winston that I was going to marry George, and here am I, actually at the day. I would give much if you were here and could give me a big fat kiss. I could assure you with my own lips what you already know, and that is that I love you and Winston dearly, and that *no one* can ever come in between us. I shall always remain yours, your best friend, and do everything in the world for you. You both can count on me. I am glad to think you know & like George. He has behaved like a brick. By the next mail, I shall write and tell you all about the wedding. Sunny [her nephew, the Duke of Marlborough] is giving me away; and I am well supported by the Churchill family. People here have been most kind. . . . I want you to come home as soon as you decently can. Both Winston and I hate to have you away. I have all sorts of plans for you, and I want to make your life as pleasant as possible. God bless you, *my darling boy*. . . . [35]

The New York Times carried a detailed account of the wedding:

LADY RANDOLPH
WEDS LIEUT. WEST

Many Notables Attend the Nuptials in London

QUIET WEDDING BREAKFAST

Marlborough Gives the Bride Away–
Many Rich and Handsome Gifts
Received.

LONDON, July 28.–Lady Randolph Churchill (née Jerome) was today married to Lieut. George Cornwallis West at St. Paul's Church, Knightsbridge. The church was thronged with handsomely dressed women. There was no restriction upon the number admitted to the church to witness the ceremony, but only relatives and intimate friends were bidden to the subsequent wedding breakfast, and no reception was held.

The usually quiet neighborhood of Witten Place, where St. Paul's Church is located, was this morning early astir with excitement. Before 9 o'clock crowds had collected outside the church gates. The scenes which ensued gave some idea of the interest or curiosity the public took in the wedding. By 10:15 o'clock the crowds had swelled to large proportions. The late opening of the church doors caused great inconvenience to early guests. When the gates were opened, a rush was made for the doors, the crowds fighting and push-ing to enter the church. It was only with the aid of policemen that they were in any way controlled.

The Duke of Marlborough, who gave the bride away, ar-rived in Summerlike attire—a gray suit and blue shirt—and wore a crimson flower in his buttonhole. Directly after he had performed his official duties, he took a seat near his young American wife, who was one of the first to arrive. She was dressed in pale gray, with a fashionable bolero, a waist belt of two shades of rose color, and a small black toque. The next most interesting guests were Lady Georgiana Curzon, Lady Sarah Wilson, and Winston Churchill, a son of the bride.

Lady Randolph's attire was quite up to date, and she looked as if just from Paris, instead of the South African veldt. Lady Tweedmouth, another sister-in-law of Lady Ran-dolph's was present. Lady Blandford, mother of the Duke of Marlborough, brought Lady Norah Churchill. Mrs. Jack Leslie, sister of the bride, whose child was christened yester-day, arrived with Lady Randolph. Mrs. Moreton Frewen, an-other of the bride's sisters, was attired in a soft black and white gown, with hat to match. She brought her little girl, while Moreton Frewen acted as usher.

A great many Americans were present, among others, Ambassador Choate and several attachés of the Embassy. Mme. von André, in white muslin and a black and white hat, sat near the front of the church. Mrs. Dudley Leigh wore a pink and white liberty satin gown and a white hat, wreathed with roses. Mrs. Arthur Paget came dressed in a pretty black and white muslin gown, carrying pink roses. Mrs. Ronalds wore a mauve and white muslin dress and a toque of rose leaves. She was accompanied by Mrs. Blow, who had on a gown of pale pink and white. Mrs. Adair wore dark gray, a white tulle boa, and a pale-blue toque, with pink mal-maisons.

Among other important people present were M. de Soveral, Lord and Lady Londonderry, Lady de Grey, Lady Granby, Lady de Trafford, Count Albert Menadorff, Baron and Baroness Eckhardstein, Lady Limerick, and Mrs. Willie Grenfell.

The arrival of Lady Randolph Churchill with the Duke of Marlborough was the signal for a general rush of enthusiasts outside the church, all eager to catch a glimpse of the bride as she walked slowly up the path. There was some little delay at the church door, and the Duke, who was carrying a large umbrella, handed it, with great ceremony, to a friend, before proceeding to give his arm to Lady Randolph. His Grace was very serious, almost severe, as was Lady Randolph, as they walked up the aisle. The bride was wonderfully handsome and young-looking in a gown of pale blue chiffon, with real lace and ostrich feathers in her toque.

The register was signed by Mrs. Moreton Frewen, the Duke of Marlborough, Winston Churchill, and the best man, Lieut. H. C. Elwes, a brother officer of Lieut. West in the Scots Guards. Directly they entered the vestry Winston Churchill gave his mother a tremendous hug and then spoke to Lieut. West. Afterward, as they came down the aisle, Lady Randolph looked radiant, as did the young bridegroom, who was smiling and nodding to friends.

After the ceremony, the wedding party repaired to the residence of the bride's sister, Mrs. Moreton Frewen, where the wedding breakfast was served to fifteen people, at six small tables decorated with roses. Mr. Frewen proposed the bride's health, and the bridegroom in responding, said:

"Jennie's friends are my friends. I thank you all from the bottom of my heart and the bottom of Jennie's heart for all of your good wishes."

After the breakfast the bride and bridegroom started for Broughton Castle, which Lady A. G. Lennox has placed at their disposal for the honeymoon.

Lady Randolph's going-away dress was a pale blue batiste. Lieut. West was attired in a flannel suit. Showers of rice were thrown after the couple as they departed. The Prince of Wales called on Lady Randolph Churchill yesterday and bade her good-bye. He also sent a present.

Among the presents received by Lady Randolph was an exquisite pearl and diamond tiara, the joint gift of A. J. Balfour, the Duke and Duchess of Devonshire, Lord and Lady Londonderry, the Marquis and Marchioness of Lansdowne, Lily, Dowager Duchess of Marlborough, Lady Georgiana Curzon, Henry White, Mrs. Arthur Paget, Mrs. George Cavendish-Bentinck, the Countesses of Crewe and Essex, and many others. Another gift was a splendid jug of beaten

silver and two massive tankards from the officers of the Scots
Guards, comrades of the bridegroom. Lieut. West's gift was
a beautiful pearl and diamond necklace. Sir Ernest Cassel
gave a pearl and diamond aigrette. There was a great deal of
plate and some handsome gold boxes.[36]

It was a lovely wedding, and even the weather had turned fine. The day
before, it had been stormy, but on Saturday the sun came out.[37]

Lady Dorothy Nevill, who had recently contributed an article for Jennie's *Review,* also contributed an acrid comment on the marriage. Strolling
among the children in Hyde Park, the distinguished eighty-year-old matri-
arch of London Society was asked what she was doing there. "Well," she
answered, "if you want to know, my dear, I am searching in the perambu-
lators for *my* future husband."[38]

A newspaper account of the wedding described George as "a fair young
man, rather like his sister, Princess Pless. He is very good at lawn tennis."

Daisy, the Princess of Pless, was not exactly forthright in her comment
on the occasion: "In spite of the disparity in their ages," she said, "we were
all pleased with the marriage, and hoped it would bring about lasting happiness to them both."[39] Not a single member of the Cornwallis-West family
was present at the wedding. Colonel and Mrs. Cornwallis-West left for Ireland the day before.

Winston described the wedding to his brother:

> Mama was married to George West on Saturday, and
> everything went off very well. The whole of the Churchill
> family, from Sunny downwards, was drawn in a solid pha-
> lanx, and their approval ratified the business. The wedding
> was very pretty, and George looked supremely happy at hav-
> ing at length obtained his heart's desire. As we already know
> each other's views on the subject, I need not pursue it.[40]

Despite the disapprovals and the open criticism, Jennie's mail was full of
messages from well-wishers in all parts of the world. There was one card,
however, that must have made her tremble as she opened it. It was from the
Chancellor of the Austro-Hungarian Embassy in St. Petersburg. The card
had a black border, and on it was the simple inscription in French: *"Toujours
en deuil"* ("Always in mourning").

It was from Count Charles Kinsky. Theirs had been the kind of love
that not even the happiest marriage would obliterate. It had been a chapter
in Jennie's life that she had closed but could never end.

Thirty-Four

30 July, 1900   Broughton Castle
                                                        Banbury

My dear Winston,

... This is an ideal place for any couple to come to, honey-moon or otherwise, we are most comfortable, the best of food, drink and everything, besides a most delightful old, rambling, weatherbeaten, stone-roofed house of the 14th century.

My dear Winston, I cannot impress upon you how much I appreciate the line you have taken as regards my marriage to your mother. I have always liked and admired you, but I do so ten times more now. I only wish, as I wrote and told my father, that my family could have taken a leaf out of your book. Nothing could have exceeded the sympathy and kindness which you, and all the Churchills have shown me. I hope always, as now, to be a real true friend to you, and never to come in between yourself and your mother. If I ever do, which God forbid, you can always refer me to this letter, which is a record of the feelings I have in the bottom of my heart towards you and yours. We arrive tomorrow at 2.15.

Will you order lunch for three unless you have another coming. *A demain,* my dear friend.

Always *your sincere friend,*
George C-W.[1]

As much as anything else, Jennie and George wanted acceptance of their
marriage. Although they did not expect it from the Cornwallis-West family
for some time, they did hope to get at least grudging approval from Winston and Jack. George's letter to Winston was a preliminary approach.

As time passed, George would realize more and more the varied facets
of his wife's personality. Even on their honeymoon Jennie's zealous mind
never stopped working. George later smilingly told Shane Leslie that Jennie
had brought along hampers of correspondence and articles for the *Anglo-
Saxon Review.* She even brought a pile of unpaid bills, explaining to George
the need to be "businesslike."

"Of course, I was eager to put her affairs in order," George said, "but I
found it a bit thick when I was expected to pay for Lord Randolph
Churchill's barouche, purchased in the 80's."[2]

All her life Jennie complained of "trying to cope with bills and bores."
This was not an uncommon condition for women in her situation. Society
widows, pinched for funds, paid only their most pressing debts and learned
how to juggle the others. It was customary for the new husband to settle
whatever claims he could. Fortunately for George, his father did not disin-
herit him; he continued to get a small allowance from his family, and he
had some money of his own. Jennie also continued to receive the annual
rental from her New York home. She and George, therefore, had enough
money to take a prolonged honeymoon trip to Belgium and France, with
the last few weeks spent in Scotland.

Winston intruded on his mother's honeymoon to tell her, ". . . Indeed I
require a brand-new outfit of socks & pocket handkerchief, etc. I send you
a specimen sock for a pattern and I know you will know best what to order." Winston also made it clear that he intended his letter to her to be private: "I hope you will always understand that these letters are written for
your eye alone, and I could not write with any freedom if I felt they were
ever to be read by anyone else. Not that there is anything very intimate in
this." He signed the letter, "Good-bye, my dearest."[3] In his first letter after
her marriage, he had not even mentioned George. A week later, however,
he did close a letter with "Best love to George."

Winston had moved to an apartment in London made available to him
by his cousin Sunny. There was another election scheduled at Oldham, and
Winston was ready to try again, this time with greater hope of success.

He wrote to his mother in Scotland and asked her to contact a number of her friends, such as Lord Rosebery and Lord Wolseley, and request that they serve as chairmen at several of his lectures. Rosebery was the first to agree,[4] and writing to thank him Winston commented, ". . . I would have written to you myself, but I felt such a request would come better from my mother. . . ."[5]

This election was so important to Winston that he felt it necessary to ask his mother to cut short her honeymoon. "I hope that you and George will be able to come down here [from Scotland] and stay at the Queen's Hotel, Manchester, for the last four or five days of the Election. It is thought that your presence here would do good, and if George takes any interest in electioneering, he will have plenty of opportunities of watching or of participating in it as much as he likes during the next fortnight. . . ."[6]

The very next day, he made his invitation more urgent.

> I write again to impress upon you how very useful your presence will be down here, providing you really felt equal to coming down and doing some work. Mr. Crisp, the other candidate, has brought his wife down and she is indefatigable, going about trying to secure voters and generally keeping the thing going. I know how many calls there are on your time, and from a point of view of pleasure I cannot recommend you to exchange the tranquil air of Scotland for the smoky tumult here, but I think it will be worth your while to see the close of this contest. . . . They have spoken to me several times, have the committee, as to whether you would be likely to come down. I need not say that it would be very pleasing to me to see a little more of you in that way. . . .
>
> . . . Give my love to George. If he comes to Manchester with you, I suggest your stopping at the Queen's Hotel, that being more comfortable than here. I shall easily find lots of work for him if he will do it, either in speaking or in organization.[7]

Jennie came, but without George. She had also asked Joseph Chamberlain to come to Oldham to speak on behalf of Winston. After the meeting Chamberlain wrote her: "I was delighted to speak for your son. . . . He has so much ability that he must succeed–& he is so young that he can afford not to hurry too much."[8]

This time Winston won a sweeping victory at Oldham. He shared the happy news with Bourke Cockran, to whom he announced:

> . . . I have suddenly become one of the two or three most popular speakers in this election, and am now engaged on a fighting tour, of the kind you know—great audiences (five and six thousand people) twice & even three times a day, bands, crowds, and enthusiasm of all kinds. . . . [9]

Bourke's almost fatherly pride could not compare with Jennie's sweeping enthusiasm. Her son was now truly started on the political career she had long ago predicted and had tried so hard to promote. Of course, she knew that there is no road more uncertain than the political road, so she continued writing to the Prince about Winston, forwarding his replies to her son. She also set up small luncheons and dinners for Winston with political leaders.

Winston scheduled his first public lecture in London on October 30, 1900, and Jennie asked for a lot of tickets for influential friends. "Mamma dear, tickets herewith. Don't give away more than dozen or so; for the space is limited and others may crop up."[10]

Jennie received an enticing invitation from J. B. Pond, head of the lecture bureau in New York, with whom she had corresponded about Winston's tour:

> Have you any idea how green your memory is here in New York City? I would suggest that you accompany your son on the voyage and witness his reception here. It seems to me it would be a very proud day for you, and your friends here would appreciate it, and I need not add it would doubly enhance the value of the lecture.[11]

Normally Jennie might have been tempted by such an offer. It would have been a matter of great pride to escort her son to the United States, to share in his success. She was not simply an American—she was an enthusiastic American, and she would have reveled in touring the country with her son.

But she could not leave George. He now needed her more than Winston did. He had made a most romantic decision and now had to face the hard economic facts of living. He needed to find work, and his qualifications were few. He could hunt, fish, play lawn tennis and bridge, but none of these could earn him an annual income to support an expensive way of life. Even more than money, he needed the dignity of being the man in the house. If he failed at this, his only future would be as a handsome lapdog for an extraordinary wife. Jennie knew this, and she confided her concern to her steadfast friend, Sir Ernest Cassel, who soon took advantage of an opportunity to broach the subject with George.

"Now that I had practically left the Army, and had only a small income, it became necessary for me to seek a new profession," George later wrote.

> The question was: Which? Soon after I returned, I met Sir Ernest Cassel at Lady Lister Kaye's house, and found myself next to him after dinner. It was he who broached the subject and asked me what I thought of doing with myself. I told him that the administrative side of an electrical engineering concern rather appealed to me. "Not the City?" he asked. I replied that the prospect of going on a half-commission basis to a firm of stockbrokers and touting for orders from my friends had no allurements for me. He thought a moment and said: "There are many young men of your class who should never go east of Temple Bar [in central London]. Perhaps you are one of them."[12]

Cassel suggested that George might benefit from some technical knowledge. He mentioned the fact that he had some interest in the Central London Railway, which was then nearing completion, and he offered to put George in touch with the Managing Director of the British Thomson-Houston Company, contractors for the line. Soon afterward, George became one of the nonpaid members of the company's staff in Glasgow.

> I lived at Troon—I couldn't stand Glasgow—and went in every day. Looking back, I am convinced that Cassel's idea of sending me there was to find out whether I really meant to take up a business career seriously or not. Perhaps he thought that if I could stick putting on overalls and acting as sort of unpaid plumber's mate to the highly-paid experts who were building this vast power unit, I might be worthy of help. He had been through the mill himself, and I imagine he felt that nobody could be of use unless he had some sort of similar experience.[13]

After George learned something about the technical side of commercial electricity, he was sent to the company's Managing Director for an interview.

> He was prepared to find in me a useless sprig of aristocracy, out of a job, and not particularly wanting one, who at the same time wished his friends to consider that he was "something in the city." . . .

"Good morning. Sit down," he greeted me. "I know . . . what you have come about. The best thing I can do is to offer you a seat on the board of the Potteries Electric Traction Company, which operates the tramways at Stoke-on-Trent and the Potteries towns. It is one of our biggest concerns, but the fees are only £50 a year. Good bye."

I was taken aback and replied, "It isn't a question of money. . . . I want to learn something about the business. Attending a board meeting once a month would teach me nothing. I want an office in this building. Can it be arranged?"

His whole manner changed, and he at once became sympathetic. In three months' time, I was Chairman of the company and of several others, and was also elected a member of the Advisory Committee, and a director of the parent company itself a few years later.[14]

It was an unexpected beginning for their marriage: George working near Glasgow; Jennie in London, busy with the *Anglo-Saxon Review*. They met on weekends, either at her London house or in the country. It was almost as if they were still courting.

But an item in *Truth* magazine pointed out that Jennie's situation had changed; "Lady Randolph Churchill loses her precedence as widow of the younger son of a Duke, by her second marriage, and also the privilege of the entrée which was granted to her by the Queen as widow of a Cabinet Minister."

Yet she still had the privilege of retaining the name of Lady Randolph Churchill; indeed, her sister-in-law, the Dowager Duchess of Marlborough, had set a family precedent by keeping her title despite a second marriage. Jennie received a letter on that very question from George Curzon, now Viceroy of India:

> I have absolutely no idea what to call you. I suppose you are not Lady Randolph or Lady Jennie. I cannot identify you as Mrs. West—"Dear Mrs. West"—no, that will never do. On the other hand I dare not essay the bold flight of Jenny, for I think I remember trying it, without success, about 18 years ago. In this, there is something rather touching.[15]

Jennie did not leave people in doubt for long. She put a notice in *The Times,* and a limerick soon circulated about it:

The papers give this information
At Lady Randolph's own request,

That now her proper designation
Is Mrs. George Cornwallis-West.[16]

Life for Mrs. George Cornwallis-West was no less exciting than life for
Lady Randolph Churchill had been. Jennie was still Jennie. Discussing her
marriage with a friend while they were out motoring, Jennie said, "I suppose you think I'm very foolish." Her friend was evasive, and Jennie said,
"But it's worth it. I'm having such fun." Jennie's kind of fun was quite new
for George, and he enjoyed it all thoroughly. Their weekends were filled
with a never-ending series of parties. He wrote:

> Another delightful place to which we used to go for
> weekend parties was Reigate Priory, which was at that time
> leased to Mr. and Mrs. Ronnie Greville. Their parties were
> always amusing, as they contained a leaven of interesting
> and intellectual people, as well as those who moved in Ed-
> wardian society. One of the most entertaining of them,
> though I doubt very much whether the guests looked upon
> him as such, was Mrs. Greville's father, old Mr. McEwan,
> Scottish millionaire. A frail old gentleman with a beard, he
> gave one the impression that his one idea was to obliterate
> himself, although it was indirectly through him that such
> luxury as one experienced there was possible. I liked the old
> man immensely, and often used to go for walks with him.
> One day, I was explaining to him that my sole motive for
> having gone into business, apart from having something to
> do, was to endeavor to make sufficient money to pay off the
> mortgages on my family estates. He stopped in his walk and
> looked at me with his head on one side, and, with the Scot-
> tish accent which was natural to him, he said: "A most
> praiseworthy object, young man. I hope ye'll succeed, but I
> doot ye will."
> "Why?" I asked.
> "Some men are born to make money, it just comes natu-
> ral to them; others never will. Maybe ye're one of the latter."
> "I've worked hard all my life," he went on, "but it's been
> an easy thing for me to become rich, I just couldn't help it;
> and the only pleasure it gives me is the thought that I'm able
> to give pleasure to others. But money doesn't necessarily
> come from hard work."
> I thought of Cassel's remark about men who should
> never go east of Temple Bar, and thought how strange it was
> that two millionaires should have said practically the same

thing. I realized now how true it is that in order for a man to make money, he must have a natural *flair* for it.[17]

For the June 1900 issue of the *Anglo-Saxon Review,* Jennie's friend, the Countess of Warwick, contributed an article which began: "Love and Misery proverbially go together. There is a popular notion . . . that a lover could not get along without a little misery . . ." But Jennie's miseries that year concerned "Maggie," not love. In fact, George, among many others, urged her to sever all connections with John Lane, whose responsibilities to the *Review* did not seem to preclude his being anywhere in the world except England. Lane had been in America for an extended period, most of the time ill with typhoid and nervous prostration. When matters came to a head between him and Jennie it was from Italy that he wrote to her.

> Mr. Jenkins informs me that you are giving notice of your intention to take away the A.S.R. . . . I am writing to know the grounds of your complaint & to beg of you, under all the circumstances of my absence through illness, to refer the matter to arbitration if there is any serious difference.
>
> I hope you will reconsider your proposal, at any rate, I hope you will not do anything in the matter until I return— certainly within three weeks.[18]

Jennie, however, had made up her mind, and in his next letter Lane took a more practical approach.

> After very carefully considering the matter of your dissatisfaction with my publishing the ASR, I have decided not to offer any opposition to your withdrawing it from me, but I will offer you my advice, which is simply to stop the Review at once, or most certainly at the end of two years. This is the view I took when I saw Mr. Crisp & he certainly was of my opinion & he then encouraged me to tell you exactly what I felt.
>
> I was in America when the first 4 vols were completed & I had much trouble in getting subscribers to renew their subscriptions in most cases. The people only renewed under the impression that it could not last beyond the second year & that sets in consequence would become rare & even valuable. I am convinced that is the only way you will get your money back by stopping with vol. 8 & selling the remainder in sets as a "limited edition." But in event of your stopping it with vol. 8,

no one here or in America could handle it as well as myself. I know that particular market & let me urge on you the old proverb that it is bad to change horses in crossing the stream. If you will close Vol. VIII, I believe that I could sell a sufficient no. of the Review to clear you *of all loss at least*. . . .

I shall be in town on Wednesday for the day & I would come to see you if you are free & care to discuss the matter with me. I think I could get someone to purchase the title & conduct it on a different line as a 2/6 quarterly, if you decide to stop it. I enclose two poems by Mr. Theodore Peters, which seem to me good, though short. I think £21 would satisfy him for either of them.[19]

Jennie answered Lane immediately:

I am in receipt of your letter of the 13th inst., which I have read with much care. I note that you have decided not to offer any opposition to my withdrawing the *Anglo-Saxon* from you. Whilst thanking you for your advice concerning it, I have other views at present. I would only like to remind you that it was a pity that you did not let me know at the end of the first year the conclusions which you had come to, and which you put out at length in your letter. I would be much obliged to you if you would give up the stock you have in hand of the Anglo-Saxon Review to the representatives of Mr. John Macqueen, who will call for it on my behalf on Wednesday. Mr. Yeatman will see you as to the matter of winding up our various accounts, etc. both here and in America.

I am going out of town today, and shall not be back until the end of the holidays, so should not be able to see you at present, but will make an appointment with you later.

Yrs. sincerely,
Jennie Cornwallis-West.[20]

The December 1900 issue of the *Anglo-Saxon Review* listed Mrs. George Cornwallis-West as the new publisher, replacing John Lane. She may have felt that it would confuse her readers if she substituted Mrs. Cornwallis-West for Lady Randolph Spencer Churchill as Editor, so she used both names, putting the West name in parenthesis under the Churchill name.

She now had several editors helping her. Besides Sidney Low, there were William Earl Hodgson, former editor of the *National Review* and *Realm;*

and Charles Whibley, a distinguished author of political portraits. Lady Cynthia Asquith referred to Whibley in her Diaries as her "literary mentor," but described him as having "frivolity without humor and cleverness without intelligence."[21] Whibley's English was characterized as "so flawless that it makes one ache with the presumptuousness of daring to put pen to paper."[22]

With the backing of such an editorial team, Jennie could now spend more time searching for money and contributors. Pearl Craigie wrote her, "All right. Will prepare essay for March number."[23] On the lists of authors that Jennie kept, she had placed question marks after the names of those from whom she had expected articles but who had not come through. They included her distant cousin Theodore Roosevelt, then Governor of New York, Sir Bindon Blood, H. H. Asquith, Eleonora Duse, and Stephen Crane.

Roosevelt had an excuse; he had been busy getting elected Vice President of the United States; and Stephen Crane finally came through, producing an article for her entitled "War Memories." The famous young author of *The Red Badge of Courage* finished the piece just before his death at the age of twenty-nine. ". . . War is neither magnificent nor squalid," he wrote, "it is simply life, and an expression of life can always evade us."

Crane and his common-law wife had rented Brede Place in Sussex, the huge, wind-swept house that Clara Frewen had fallen in love with and bought with her husband several years before.[24] Brede Place was a remnant of medieval England, a feudal home built in 1350 that had a chapel, a great hall, straw on the stone floors, a double-sided fireplace that consumed whole tree-trunks, a solarium, timbered inner walls, outhouses, and ghosts. The ghosts were so real that when the Cranes gave a party, the local cook had to "be bribed to function in the evening, with a bottle of brandy."[25]

Jennie and her sisters remembered a three-day party that Stephen Crane gave for sixty guests, including Henry James, Joseph Conrad, H. Rider Haggard, and H. G. Wells. Wells invented a game of racing on broomsticks over the polished floors, and the guests reveled until dawn.

H. G. Wells' home in Worcester Park became the site of another literary scene. Jennie's friends had decided that they had discovered the worst novel of the decade, *Irene Iddesleigh,* and they met at Wells' home to read parts of it aloud. One of the choice passages concerned the heroine's first quarrel with her husband: "Irene, if I may use such familiarity–" begins Sir Hugh, who ends his tirade, "Speak, Wife. Woman! Do not sit in silence, and allow the blood that now boils in my veins to ooze through the cavities of unrestrained passion, and trickle down to drench me with its crimson hue!" Sir Hugh's suspicions that his wife has another lover are confirmed, and he locks her up in her room for a year. But at the end of the year a trusty maid helps her escape, to run off with her lover. Sir Hugh expunges Irene's name from his will. "With the pen of persuasion dipped into the ink of revenge, he blanked the intolerable words that referred to the woman who, he was now convinced, had braved the bridge of bigamy."[26]

Jennie loved the spirited fun of the literary world, so different from the formality of the society world. She particularly enjoyed meeting visiting American authors and repeated with glee a story about her friend Mark Twain. At a London gathering he asked Mrs. J. Comyns-Carr, "You *are* an American, aren't you?" Mrs. Carr explained that she was of English stock and had been brought up in Italy. "Ah, that's it," Twain answered. "It's your complexity of background that makes you seem American. We are rather a mixture, of course. But I can pay you no higher compliment than to mistake you for a countryman of mine."[27]

Several months later, Mark Twain would introduce Winston to an American audience, saying:

> I think that England sinned when she got herself into a war with South Africa, which she could have avoided, just as we have sinned in getting into a similar war in the Philippines. Mr. Churchill, by his father, is an Englishman; by mother, he is an American, no doubt a blend that makes the perfect man. England and America; we are kin. And now that we are also kin in sin, there is nothing more to be desired. The harmony is perfect—like Mr. Churchilll himself, whom I now have the honor to present to you.

On arriving in America for his lecture tours, Winston had been quoted in the *New York Evening Journal* as having said, "I am not here to marry anybody. I am not going to get married, and I would like to have that stated positively." Waiting for him was an invitation to dine with Theodore Roosevelt, and from Boston he wrote his mother:

> I stayed with Bourke Cockran in New York, who worked indefatigably to make the lecture a success and who gave a large dinner party at the Waldorf before it.
>
> I should like you to write him a line if you have time because he has treated me in a most friendly way, and that in spite of his strong Boer sympathies.[29]

Winston had Christmas dinner in Ottawa with another of his mother's admirers, the Earl of Minto, Governor General of Canada. Pamela Plowden was also there. His romance with Pamela had ended months before when he discovered that she was promised to two other young men. After Christmas dinner, Winston wrote of Pamela to his mother: "We had no painful discussions, but there is no doubt in my mind that she is the only woman I could ever live happily with."[30]

The lecture tour had not been as profitable for Winston as he had expected. "I have decided to come home on the 2nd of Feb.," he wrote in mid January. "As you know, my tour has not been the success I had hoped. I shall, I think, clear £1600, which though no mean sum, is nothing to what I had anticipated, and I think an inadequate return for all that I have had to go through."[31] Indeed, his finances were in such poor shape that, even though Ernest Cassel was successfully investing what money Winston had, he had found it necessary to write Jennie:

> I hope my dearest Mamma to be able to provide for myself in the future—at any rate until things are better with you. If you can arrange to relieve me of this loan, with the interest of which I am heavily burdened—£300 per annum—I will not ask for any allowance whatever from you, until old Papa West decides to give you and G. more to live on. Jack in a few years should be self-supporting too. . . .[32]

At least as far as his brother was concerned, Winston's prediction may have been unduly optimistic. Jack had returned from the war still unsure of what he wanted, and Jennie invited him to live with her and George. Jack's commanding officer had written Jennie a note, saying,

> I cannot let Jack go without sending you a line to say how well he has done. Of course I always knew he would. . . . Since Ladysmith, the regt. has always been at it—with scarcely a week's rest anywhere . . . and had some exceedingly hard work and heavy losses—Jack has always done his share with the greatest keenness—He is most gallant in action, and most trustworthy and hard-working in camp. In fact I am very sorry to lose him. . . .[33]

He was still the same quiet, affectionate young man. There was an initial awkwardness in having him and George in the same household, but George was not often home. He traveled a great deal on business, and it was a comfort for Jennie to have one of her sons home.

Jennie had received an invitation to accompany her nephew, Sunny, the Duke of Marlborough, on a visit to the Curzons in India. At first she had written Jack, "You and George will have to look after each other and keep out of mischief in my absence."[34] But perhaps she then reflected on something Winston had mentioned about Jack in a letter to George. ". . . He is not yet really grown up; though he seems so old in some things."[35] At any rate, she decided to stay.

Curzon was disappointed.

> Well, I have two things to say. First, we are very much distressed at not seeing you here when we counted upon you to conjure a little vivacity & colour into our humdrum processional lives. I suppose that a too uxorious spouse has kept you at home. Second—I got some time ago from Burma an old silver Burmese bowl, which we meant to offer you as a wedding gift. Our chance having gone, I have had no alternative but to send it to Gt. Cumberland Place, where it should arrive some day.[36]

Jennie's decision to have Jack live in her home seemed to be what he needed. He soon resettled himself in his job in the City, and wrote Winston a bright letter about it. In a letter to his mother, Winston remarked that Jack had sent him ". . . an interesting account of his life on the stock exchange. He writes so well, and if he practised with his pen would I am sure be able to make his name much better known than it is at present, and moreover to add to his interest in life and the balance at the banks."[37]

Winston also asked Jennie to select some watches for the men and a brooch for the woman who had helped him escape from the Boers: "I am sure you will choose much better than I shall. . . ."[38]

There was some talk of a dissolution of Parliament, which would have meant another General Election and another campaign battle at Oldham for Winston, "which I really do not think I should have had the strength to fight. . . ." But Jennie cabled Winston that as yet there was no substance to the report.

Jennie probably was right at the time, but within a matter of days the situation was suddenly reversed. On January 22, 1901, at 6:30 P.M., Queen Victoria died. Soon after he heard about it Winston wrote his mother:

> So the Queen is dead. The news reached us at Winnipeg, and this city far away among the snows—one thousand four hundred miles from any British town of importance—began to hang its head and hoist half-masted flags. A great and solemn event: but I am curious to know about the King [until then, Albert Edward, the Prince of Wales]. Will it entirely revolutionise his way of life? Will he sell his horses. . . . Will

he become desperately serious? . . . Will the Keppel[39] be appointed first lady of the Bedchamber? . . . Will he continue to be friendly to you?

I contemplated sending a letter of condolence and congratulations mixed, but I am uncertain how to address it and also whether such procedure would be etiquette. You must tell me. I am most interested and feel rather vulgar about the matter. I should like to know an Emperor and a King. Edward VIIth–gadzooks, what a long way that seems to take one back! I am glad he has got his innings at last, and am most interested to watch how he plays it.

P.S. I have been reading, "An English Woman's Love Letters." Are all Mothers the same?[40]

Queen Victoria had become critically ill in mid-January. "When the Prince of Wales went in to see the Queen," wrote Sir Frederick Ponsonby, "she gained consciousness for a moment and recognized him. She put out her arms and said, 'Bertie,' whereupon he embraced her and broke down completely."[41] Another time, during a moment of consciousness, she sent for her dog, a little white one, and called it by its name.

"It was three o'clock before the bells began tolling," Shane Leslie remembered,

and the one-and-eighty guns thundered salute to the dead. In time, there appeared a very small coffin, surmounted by sceptre and crown, and slowly hauled by bluejackets in their straw hats at the slope. A bunch of Kings and Emperors followed. Grim fates, exiles, dethronements and assassinations were awaiting them. How unimportant they all seemed, the kings of the earth, compared to the little packet of ashes they were honoring with bowed heads and shuffling tread. A cortege of diplomats passed like so many resplendent lackeys. . . .

Lord Roberts passed in tears, looking tiny in his big boots and cocked hat. And the Kaiser was obviously suffering from nerves, for compared to the solemnity of others, he was chafing and twisting round. He had rushed loyally to the funeral, and whispers said he had offered to lift his grandmother into her coffin, but that the Queen's surviving sons had interposed, and lifted her reverently. . . . Incredible how light she was . . . as though some last ray of departing glory had stricken her to a handful of ashes. . . .

On the following Sunday, the Queen still lay in state in St. George's Chapel before internment at Frogmore. The body lay in state suffocated by a carnage of flowers. The sweet and sickly air smelt like laughing-gas, and the soldiers toppled over, from time to time, under the fumes.

London was plunged in fog and crepe. Every shop window was streaked by a mourning shutter. The women, old and young, were draped with veils, and most touching was the mourning worn by the prostitutes, in whose existence the old Queen had always refused to believe. Even the crossing sweepers carried crepe on their brooms. Old men were already boasting that they had lived in three reigns. My grandmother prepared to go into perpetual mourning. It seemed as though the keystone had fallen out of the arch of heaven.[42]

Albert Edward, Prince of Wales, had become King Edward VII, and a new era was beginning.

Thirty-Five

My dearest Mamma,

   I enclose a cheque for £300. In a certain sense, it belongs to you; for I could never have earned it had you not transmitted to me the wit and energy which are necessary.[1]

It was a touching tribute from a grateful son.

Four days later, on February 18, 1901, three weeks into the reign of King Edward VII, Winston Churchill rose in Parliament to make his maiden speech. Although he defended the war vigorously, he expressed his respect for the Boers: "If I were a Boer—fighting in the field—and if I were a Boer, I hope I should be fighting in the field. . . ." But he called it a war of duty and hoped the Boers would not "remain deaf to the voice of reason" and "refuse all overtures, disdain all terms."[2]

Listening intently in the gallery, as she had so often listened to Lord Randolph Churchill, was Jennie Cornwallis-West. Before her was her twenty-six-year-old son with the same hand-on-hip stance as his father, the same slight lisp, the same nervousness that Lord Randolph had suffered during his own maiden speech in Parliament. But he spoke with more frankness, more incisiveness, more flashes of humor than his father had done.

Jennie knew what Winston was going to say, as she had been his audience and critic while he rehearsed the speech. As she sat there, proud and anxious, she may have remembered sitting in the same gallery, many years before, with the worried wife of another new Member who literally mouthed every word her husband spoke.

A few of Jennie's friends were worried that the strains of the preceding year had taken their toll on her and that she was not looking as well as she might. Pearl Craigie wrote her:

> Do not forget to keep quiet. You look as fresh & bright as possible, but you must not tax your brain. Read boring books & the daily papers; your mind is too active in the particular circumstances. Later on, you can do as you please. Just now, however & for some months you ought to emulate the milch cow!!
>
> Your new plans are most interesting. Winston, nevertheless, must not tire you. . . . [3]

Pearl Craigie might better have sent that letter to Winston, as he was, in fact, taking a great deal of his mother's time. His requests of her were constant: surely she could find him a new secretary; he wanted a painting for a particular space on his wall; wouldn't she please ask the Duke of Portland to preside over one of the meetings at which he was scheduled to speak? And he needed a hostess to help him greet guests at the White Friars Club Annual Banquet. "Please telegraph me if you could care to help me. . . ."[4]

Of course, he was appreciative. And he was thoughtful, too, about helping her when he could. "I have seen Gen. Ian Hamilton, who will make it his business to see that the *Maine* and its mainstay receive a complimentary allusion in Lord Roberts' concluding dispatch. You may regard this, I think, as settled."[5]

Later that year, he advised his lawyers, Lumley & Lumley:

> While my mother's position remains unchanged, I recognize that it is difficult for her to make me or my brother any allowance, and I feel it my duty, on the other hand, to assist her in any manner possible without seriously prejudicing my reversionary interests. I therefore forego the allowance of £500 a year she and my father had always intended to give me. So I also defray the expenses of the loan of £3500 I contracted at her suggestion for my brother's allowance and my own from 1897–1900, amounting to £305 per annum.
>
> I view the question of the £1100 in the same light, and will raise no objection to its dissipation as proposed.

What I desire in my brother's interest, as in my own, is that there should be a clear understanding necessarily not of a legal nature, that in the event of Mr. George Cornwallis-West being at some future time in a superior financial position, my mother will make suitable provision for her children out of her own income; in other words, that she will reciprocate the attitude I am now adopting.[6]

Jennie paid close attention to Jack, too, even when she was away on short holidays. ". . . Make Walden [her butler] get you a bottle of the hairwash from Floris's—Ask for Col. Clayton's Hairwash, and tell Walden to pay for it. You must use it with a little sponge. Now, do this—Otherwise, you won't have a hair on your head. Poor old boy, I think of you so much. . . ."[7]

On August 10, 1901, the signature of Jennie Cornwallis-West appeared for the first time in the Blenheim Palace Guest Book. Arthur Balfour was also there that evening. Within a year, Balfour, who had long been a political force in England, would succeed his uncle, Lord Salisbury, as Prime Minister of England.

Balfour was not the Prime Minister that the new monarch would have wished. He was an aloof, unbending man,[8] and Edward VII was a man of warmth and laughter. The Edwardian Age was the era of "Good old Bertie," "the first amiable king since Charles II."[9] Edward was a king who enjoyed being King, and the British people took pleasure in his enjoyment. They loved him, as Lord Granville said, "because he has all the faults of which the Englishman is accused."[10]

Edward was fifty-nine years old, portly, bearded, and jovial. He was a polished, sophisticated man who relished pomp and pleasure,[11] "sweet women and dry champagne." In contrast with the somber Queen Victoria, always in mourning and withdrawn, King Edward loved bright uniforms, medals and decorations, and ceremonial occasions of all kinds; instead of quaint, quiet Court Drawing Room receptions, there were now loud, lavish Court Balls; instead of peaceful, carefully paced carriage rides in the park, there were horse races, yacht regattas, and automobiles.

> *For to him above all was life good,*
> *Above all he commanded her abundance full-handed,*
> *The peculiar treasure of kings was his for the taking;*
> *All that men come to in dreams, he inherited waking.*[12]

It was still an age of kings in Europe. Edward's niece was Empress of all the Russias, another niece Queen of Spain, his daughter was Queen of

Norway, the German Emperor was his nephew, and the Kings of Denmark and Greece were his brothers-in-law.

In England the Edwardian Age was a time of opulence, extravagance, and peace. The Boer War may have tarnished the British lion, but the British pound was the most solid and respected currency in the world. Despite this, a third of the British people still knew what hunger meant—they were overworked and underpaid and lived in wretched slums. The average workman earned only a pound a week. Yet the general public mood of gloom was gone. Education offered hope, universal male suffrage promised change. It was a time of less boredom, less pretense, and increased freedom. As for the rich, "more money was spent on clothes, more food was consumed, more horses were raced, more infidelity was committed, more birds were shot, more yachts were commissioned, more late hours were kept than ever before."[13]

King Edward's Danish-born Queen, the lovely and gracious Alexandra, adjusted easily to the new informality of Court. At a ball at Chatsworth, Alexandra and George's sister, Daisy, took off their shoes "to see what difference it made in our height. The Queen took, or rather, kicked hers off, and then got into everyone else's, even into Willie Grenfell's old pumps. I never saw her so free and cheerful—but always graceful in everything she does."[14]

The King wanted informal, honest friends around him, rather than flattering courtiers. He had long ago forgiven Jennie what he felt was a mistaken marriage and had taken the initiative in writing her. In a letter to Jack from Cowes that year, Jennie wrote: "I had a very nice letter from the King, nicest I've had from him since I married. . . ."[15]

So Jennie was again absorbed into the inner circle, and with her, George.

> My wife had a host of friends in London, whom I soon got to know and who were exceedingly kind to me; and thus I became an Edwardian, in the sense that I was a member of that particular set in society with which King Edward associated himself, a set with which a young officer in the Guards or the son of a country gentleman living in the country was not likely in the ordinary course of events, to become particularly intimate.[16]

George called these "the wonderful days."

> I worked hard all the week, and every Saturday Jennie and I used to go somewhere. . . . Estates which had been for

centuries in one family were still intact. . . . Taxation and the
cost of living were low; money was freely spent and wealth
was everywhere in evidence . . . I doubt whether in any period of history of the modern world . . . has there been such
a display of wealth and luxury as during King Edward's
reign. . . . Dinners were Gargantuan affairs . . . champagne,
port and old brandy were the order of the day, or rather,
night. . . . Women's dresses at dinner parties were very elaborate, and quantities of jewelry were worn. Those were the
days of tiaras and stomachers. The blaze of jewels displayed
at the opera was really amazing. . . . [17]

It was a time of self-indulgence. Not only did women go to extremes in
adorning themselves, but standards of comfort and convenience were exaggerated. Everything was more than lavish. Every estate had multitudes of
servants who were themselves stratified within a rigid hierarchy. There
were "upper" servants and "under" servants. Upper servants included the
housekeeper, the cook, the head housemaid, the butler, the lady's maids,
the steward. They usually enjoyed many of the upper-class comforts: the
choice of the dining-room food, sofas and armchairs in their sitting rooms,
coal-fires in their bedrooms. The under servants slept in basements, in at-
tics, or on folding-beds in the pantries. They worked long hours and slept
little. Teen-age scullerymaids often were washing up the kitchens until one
in the morning and then had to be up a few hours later to help prepare the
enormous breakfasts. Fires crackled often without anyone having seen their
being lighted. Curtains were drawn and breakfast brought up without the
guests being awakened. By eight in the morning lawns were rolled, dead
leaves removed, and fresh flowers placed in vases. Servants were silent and
invisible. They made possible a rarefied way of life for the British aristocracy, but the Frenchman E. D. Gramont remarked that "this majestic silence got on my nerves. Those great mute corridors, those never-raised
voices made me homesick for the Latin hurly-burly; servants shouting,
banging pots and pans, slamming doors. . . ."[18]

A few months after Queen Victoria's death, Grand Duke Michael of
Russia gave a weekend party at Keele Hall for King Edward. The guests arrived in "the deepest mourning" and returned to London on a special train.
Since it was soon after the King's accession, the train slowed at the major
stations en route so that the people could see their new Sovereign. "It was a
very hot afternoon," George wrote,

and we were all perspiring freely; and one lady as we neared
London produced some *papiers poudres* and began to whiten

her nose and generally clean up her face. The King asked what it was she was using, and, on being shown, took two leaves himself and proceeded to powder his nose. The result was comic, but was duly rectified before he stepped out of the train at Euston.[19]

George played a rubber of bridge with Edward and won thirty pounds from His Majesty, "who produced an enormous roll of notes from his pocket from which to pay me. I had always understood that kings never carried money, which shows how mistaken one can be."[20]

Where the King went, Jennie and George usually went, too. Races, tennis, bridge, amateur theatricals, long walks, elaborate teas, sumptuous luncheons, enormous dinners. One host had his own private circus, at which he acted as ringmaster. Another provided small carriages drawn by ponies for ladies too tired to walk. And there was always music in the evenings: private orchestras, celebrated singers and musicians in intimate recitals. George remembered a recital by the recently married Fritz Kreisler, who had brought his bride. "He seemed to play for her alone. To him there might not have been anyone else in the room; and she, on her part, appeared hypnotized by his playing. Her eyes closed and her whole body swayed as if she were about to faint."[21]

When this social whirl was too much for them, the country home of Lord and Lady Tweedmouth provided Jennie and George with an ideal summer haven. They were there one night when former Prime Minister Lord Rosebery was also a guest, and George wrote of an incident that characterized Rosebery well. Rosebery had just commented on something with a marvelous epigram, when another guest, a youth of seventeen, offered that he had noticed Lord Rosebery studying Marcus Aurelius before dinner. Rosebery stared at the young man "with those curious cod-fish blue eyes of his" and said, "All my life I've loved a womanly woman and admired a manly man, but I never could stand a boily boy."[22]

If Rosebery had been younger, King Edward would much have preferred him as his Prime Minister. Balfour was correct but cold and too intellectual for the King. In contrast, Rosebery and Edward spoke the same language, shared many of the same interests.[23] Rosebery was no less an intellectual than Balfour, but he knew when not to show it.

Jennie and Winston were seeing less and less of each other and were moving in different directions now. But when Jennie complained to him about it, Winston replied:

No, my dear, I do not forget you. But we are both of us busy people, absorbed in our own affairs, and at present independent. Naturally, we see little of each other. Naturally, that makes no difference to our feelings. I remain always,

Your loving son,
Winston S.C.[24]

Winston was now twenty-eight, and Jennie wanted to see him married and settled. But he had no grace with young women.[25] He could write romantic letters, but he had little patience for small talk. After his unfulfilled romance with Pamela two other young ladies refused his proposals of marriage: the wealthy Muriel Wilson and the strikingly beautiful young American actress, Ethel Barrymore. The Blenheim guest book of July 13, 1902, shows that Miss Barrymore had been present along with Jennie and her family.

Winston was busy writing, asking Jennie's advice for help with research, borrowing her secretary. His notes to her often ended with a date and the question, "Dinner?"

King Edward's Coronation had been delayed by the Boer War and by a sudden operation the King had to have.[26] It was finally scheduled for August 9, 1902.

We'll be merry
Drinking whiskey, wine and sherry,
Let's all be merry
On Co-ro-nation Day.[27]

On Coronation Day, Westminster Abbey admits only royalty, the dukes and duchesses, the lords and their ladies, and some of the lesser rank. In the King's Box, however, sat a small group of beautiful women whose love and favors had meant much to the King. Among others, they included his current mistress, Mrs. George Keppel, and Jennie and her mother-in-law, both wearing diamond tiaras which they had "begged, borrowed or stolen."[28] The King's close friend, the Marquis de Soveral, was overheard to remark about them: "What that lot doesn't know about King Edward . . ."[29]

Alice Keppel had replaced Lady Warwick in the King's affections. Daisy Pless confided in her diary that she had met Mrs. Keppel for the first time at a luncheon. "Three or four of the women present had several lovers, and did not mind saying so. Alice is fascinating."[30]

A story was told of a bridge game in which the King and Mrs. Keppel were partners. Mrs. Keppel bid No Trumps, and was left to play it out. Edward as dummy put down his cards, and there was hardly a trick in them. Mrs. Keppel glanced at her hand again, and then at Edward, and said, "All

I can say, Sire, is, 'God save the King and preserve Mrs. Keppel!!' " King Edward roared with laughter.[31]

Mrs. Keppel's husband was Lieutenant-Colonel George Keppel, the younger son of the Earl of Albemarle. The couple had two children, and the younger one, Sonia, remembers Edward well. She called him "Kingy" and was particularly delighted by his "kind, deep voice" and his "plump, be-ringed hands."[32]

> He would lend me his leg, on which I used to start two bits of bread and butter (butter side down), side by side. Then bets of a penny each were made (my bet provided by Mamma), and the winning piece of bread and butter depended, of course, on which was the more buttery. The excitement was intense while the contest was on. Sometimes he won, sometimes I did.[33]

Alice Keppel and Jennie were good friends, and it was Jennie's brother-in-law, John Leslie, who had first introduced Alice Keppel to the King. She was a lovely woman, with a natural hour-glass figure, large turquoise eyes, and light chestnut hair. Soft-spoken and graceful, she was also unusually quick at repartee. Margot Asquith said of her: "She is a plucky woman of fashion; human, adventurous and gay, who in spite of doing what she liked all her life has never made an enemy."[34] One of the reasons she didn't was that she never flaunted her influence.[35]

The Coronation was commemorated in Volume VIII of Jennie's *Anglo-Saxon Review* which paid tribute to the new sovereign with a frontispiece portrait and a lead article by Frederick Greenwood entitled "Monarchy and the King." "The Queen dies," Greenwood observed, "and immediately it is as if we marched with our backs to a completed past and our faces to a future of which we see nothing."

This issue also featured articles by George Bernard Shaw, "John Oliver Hobbes" (Pearl Craigie), Winston Churchill, and Jennie's brother-in-law, Moreton Frewen, who wrote about conservation of fish—half a century ahead of his time. Winston's long-promised article was about the British Cavalry. There was also a piece on "Decorative Domestic Art" by the editor and publisher, who signed herself "Lady Randolph Churchill" rather than "Mrs. George Cornwallis-West." Jennie's article began,

> Taste and common sense, with a desire for knowledge, allied to a limited purse, will go farther nowadays to please the eyes and the senses, than the riches of a South African millionaire, spent for him by upholsterers. . . . The rich man

often orders hastily and repents at leisure; because he has leisure to repent in. . . .

She was delighted, she said, to see the disappearance of "the heavy uncomfortable monstrosities of the early Victorian epoch. . . ." And it was important to England, she believed, "that some of our best artists do not think it beneath their dignity to give designs for the homeliest objects (such as wallpapers and table-linen)." Moreover, she agreed with the current tendency "to approve everything which pleases the eye, without regard to orthodoxy."[36]

The article concluded with a warning against snobbishness:

> Because a thing is old, its value should not be necessarily enhanced, unless it had beauty or an historical interest attached to it; and most people will prefer a good, solid, well-made copy of a fine model to a rickety, worm-eaten original, with only its antiquity to recommend it.

The *Review's* next two issues featured articles on everything from the American Revolution to the American athlete, from the Great Seals of England to snuffboxes, from "The Absurdity of the Criticism of Music" to "Celebrated Women of Recent Times." This was perhaps both the charm and the major fault of the *Review:* it had too much range and no focus.

An article entitled "The Next Government" was a last-minute substitution made after Jennie had thought the issue was closed, and she had gone off to Scotland for a holiday with George. The article was extremely critical of Lord Rosebery, the former Prime Minister who was one of her friends and a contributor to the first issue of the *Review.* Jennie wrote Rosebery an apologetic note, explaining how grieved she was that anything even approaching criticism of him should have appeared in the *Review.* She received the following characteristic answer:

> It was very good of you to write me. . . . Frankly, I think the introduction of politics into the Anglo-Saxon a great mistake. But you are a better judge of this than I am.

As for the article, he said, "I think it very unlikely that I shall ever see it, and I am quite sure that, if I do, it will not trouble me. But I tender my humble and hearty thanks to the Editress."[37]

The *Review* could be hard-hitting. In a regular column called "Impressions and Opinions," there had been an editorial comment on the Boer War:

The South African War still drags its weary course along. He would be a bold man who should predict that it will be over when this or even the next number of the Anglo-Saxon Review is in print. Never was there a campaign which has seemed so often on the very verge of extinction and then has suddenly blazed up again. . . . The fight is not for victory but for conquest. We do not ask for our beaten foes to make terms; we require an unconditional submission and the surrender of their territory. There is no question of treating for peace. . . . We ought not to be surprised if, amid the circumstances, the struggle is slow and desperate.

There was then this added note: "But whatever is done, the British nation is in the last resort responsible. . . . Nothing can be more cowardly than to say to a general: 'Do what you think proper. Burn farms, starve women, lay waste land, shoot, hang and plunder. But for Heaven's sake don't tell *us* anything about it. . . .'"[38]

That had not only been Jennie's feeling about the Boer War, but the growing feeling among the British people. It was not until May 1902 that a peace treaty with the Boers was finally signed.

The future of the *Anglo-Saxon Review* still looked uncertain. Pearl Craigie at first thought that Jennie ought to "stick to the A.S.R. on its present lines; it is an exotic perhaps—but that is in its favour.—I hope myself that it will prosper, flourish and proceed!"[39]

Pearl's hope notwithstanding, the possibility of proceeding began to look less likely, and the two women talked about a variety of alternatives. They thought of making the *Review* a monthly magazine. "Do you think that a monthly Review would be as successful as a good weekly?" Craigie wrote. "You might work up one of those already in existence." Jennie mentioned buying the *St. James Gazette,* and Craigie replied: "The St. James Gazette is excellent—at a proper price . . . ," and she recommended a staff member of *Punch* Magazine as a first-rate editor. But *Punch* publisher Agnew promptly promoted him. "The Agnews I believe were put on their mettle at once when they heard you had him for the A. S. Review. . . ." Craigie also informed Jennie that her father, an astute businessman, "thinks *very* well of your new Review scheme. . . ."[40]

Pearl's father, John Morgan Richards, was not representative of the many men Jennie approached for money.[41] They all liked and admired her, but this was more a matter of giving good money to go the way of bad money, and they discouraged her in as kindly a way as they could.

Reluctantly, Jennie made the tenth issue the last, and quietly folded the

Review.[42] It must have been very difficult for her to make the formal arrangements and write the necessary letters:

> *Anglo-Saxon Review*
>
> Dear Sir:
>
> Will you please be good enough to instruct your agent in New York to give Messrs. Putnams Sons, full particular of stock in your possession, *viz*–of volumes bound, quires, cases, plates, etc., and hand the whole or any part thereof to them on their written order.

Trying to buoy up her spirit, King Edward gave Jennie new royal honors. In 1901 he had made her Lady of Grace of St. John of Jerusalem. Now, in recognition of her services on the *Maine,* he invested her with the Order of the Royal Red Cross. He was also increasingly considerate of Winston, who wrote his mother from Balmoral Castle in September 1902:

> I have been vy kindly treated here by the King, who has gone out of his way to be nice to me. It has been most pleasant & easy going & today the stalking was excellent, tho I missed my stags.
>
> You will see the King on Weds when he comes to Invercauld; mind you gush to him about my having written to you saying how much etc etc I had enjoyed myself here.[43]

But the death of the *Anglo-Saxon Review* was a jolt for Jennie. She did not like defeat. It drained her of some of her energetic optimism. She felt tired and would have loved a change of scene and mood. Sir Ernest Cassel offered her just that in the form of a cruise on his yacht up the Nile to the Aswan Dam with a small group of friends, including Winston and Mrs. Keppel. But George could not leave his work and Jennie would not leave him.

She had Jack to consider, too. Winston had written her from Egypt, "I often think of you and Jack: and feel vy anxious about him. Please concentrate your attention on him. He is rather untamed & forlorn."[44] Jennie did not need Winston's warning, even though Jack seemed to be flourishing on the stock exchange. A quiet, likeable young man, he had an easier way with women than Winston, but he, too, seemed reluctant about marriage. Jennie and Jack were a frequent twosome that season at concerts, the opera, and the theater.

Jennie had a more difficult case in transforming her niece, Clare, from a provincial wallflower to a London debutante. She was Clara's daughter, the only female child of all three Jerome daughters. Clare had had a sad childhood, an education at a French convent, and a lonely interval at her father's ancestral home in Ireland. Winston had advised her to "cultivate a philosophical disposition. . . . it is something after all, to be fed and clothed and sheltered. . . ."[45]

But Clare was an awkward, gangly sixteen-year-old who needed love. Under Jennie's tutelage she blossomed.

> I grew to love Jennie, as soon as I got over being intimidated by her. One had to admire her; she was resplendent. Jennie's advice was generally worldly, my mother's was sentimental, Leonie's was ethical. . . . My Aunt Jennie became my second mother. . . .
>
> Jennie looked at me in kind of an overhauling way, and said I must pull in my waist and put up my hair. I was still growing, so my dresses had to have big, turned-up hems. It was the fashion for them to touch the ground and for the collars to be kept up by whalebones that dug into one's neck. Veils were worn—it was like being in a cage. I was a wild animal being tamed. The taming process outlasted the London Season.[46]

The three sisters still lived together in their cluster of houses on Great Cumberland Place, and Jennie had Clare come across the street every morning and read the *Times'* leading editorial while she breakfasted. "After that I had to practice how to do my hair, for I did it, she said, abominably." Above all, Jennie told her, she had to try to talk and to smile and not look bored whenever anyone else was introduced. "Remember that you are not invited for your own amusement, but to contribute to the party."[47]

Jennie practiced what she preached. Her own house was perfect for lunches, intimate soirees, and small dinners, but not large enough for the old-fashioned grand salon. Such a salon would have required her to spend more time at home, which would have put her in a restricting social frame. She was too restless for that. She liked to visit. She liked to travel. She presided at flower shows, played at concerts, began writing a book and a play, and became an automobile enthusiast.

Just as Jennie had had the first home in London to be lit by electric light, she and George were the first in their social set to own a motor-car. "Although we never went at more than twenty-five miles an hour, I thought it was a thrilling experience," she wrote.[48]

Driving a turn-of-the-century automobile was a rather uncomfortable and hazardous operation. There were no tarred roads and the thick dust whitened women's hair and lashes despite swathes of chiffon. Men wore goggles and more protective hats, but because there were neither windscreens nor side doors, men and women alike took to wearing long canvas coats and other kinds of clothing to help keep them warm. Jennie wrote Jack of a trip "in the motor—156 miles, and did it in under six hours. Too fast, I have a head[ache] in consequence. . . ."[49]

For night driving, courageous motorists took along acetylene torches, which often worked rather badly. Jennie and George were returning from a dinner date one evening when one of their acetylene torches burst into flames—"fortunately," George wrote, "without setting fire to the car"—and the other soon followed suit.

> We had nothing left but a very small electric torch, with which Jennie, with arm extended in front of her, did her best to throw a feeble light on the road. All went well until we came to a corner which we ought to have turned but didn't, and instead went up a small bank. Fortunately we were going very slowly, but I shall never forget my feelings when I saw my wife fall slowly out, the car remaining perfectly upright—there was, of course, no side door to hold her in. However, she was not hurt; we reversed and arrived home about two in the morning.[50]

Their marriage had started off with surprising success, and even the Cornwallis-West family gradually adjusted to it. George was a very happy man. He had a business position of dignity and growing importance; he mingled among people of wealth and splendor; and his wife was one of the most beautiful, desirable, and important women of their world. His single criticism of her was her attitude toward money.

> In money matters she was without any sense of proportion. The value of money meant nothing to her: what counted with her were the things she got for money, not the amount she had to pay for them. If something of beauty attracted her, she just had to have it; it never entered her head to stop and think how she was going to pay for it. During all the years we lived together the only serious misunderstandings which ever took place between us were over money matters. Her extravagance was her only fault, and, with her nature, the most understandable, and therefore, the most forgivable.[51]

But George himself was not without extravagance. Soon after his election to his company's Advisory Committee, he was "motoring up" from a visit with Cassel to attend his first meeting. Along the way his car broke down; fortunately, he was near a railroad station: "So I did the only possible thing—chartered a special train."[52] It cost him about twenty-five percent of all the fees he would have collected from the company that year.

Certainly Jennie was having fun, and as Pearl Craigie wrote, she was "looking beautiful and happy." She was the star attraction of a costume party she attended which had as its theme "British Society Beauties Dressed as Famous Men in History." George's mother went dressed as Hamlet, his sister Daisy as Romeo, Lady Sarah Wilson as Bonnie Prince Charlie. But as the New York *Journal* reported:

> Historically, the success of the evening was Mrs. George Cornwallis-West, formerly Lady Randolph Churchill, who came as a roistering Spanish cavalier. She wore black silk tights, doublet and hose, a dark velvet cloak trimmed with gold; had a sword, a great diamond blazing in her black sombrero, with its drooping feathers; diamond buckles on her pretty shoes, and a black mustache, waxed and ferociously curled, like the Kaiser's.[53]

It was a relatively carefree time for Jennie and George, and Jennie was delighted by George's enthusiasm for people and interesting parties. Even Pearl Craigie, who was the slowest among Jennie's close friends to accept George, now wrote her, "I particularly want Mr. Cornwallis-West to come also."[54] But she would never call him "George."

Pearl Craigie was probably jealous of George. Because of him, Jennie was giving Pearl proportionately less of her time. Pearl had a possessive nature, and her affection for Jennie was deep. Even when she went to India for a long stay, she wrote Jennie: "My dearest Jennie: I have wished for you every moment since I came out. . . ."[55] And from Paris three months later: "Dying to see you! . . . I missed you every second. . . ."[56] She even named the leading character in one of her novels "Jennie." She loved the name so much, she said, that "I gave it to someone who was beautiful and charming. . . ."[57]

On her return from Paris, Pearl urged Jennie to join her in organizing a social and professional woman's club. ". . . You are the one woman who can get it going and maintain it. . . ."[58] A new club was not the most exciting of prospects for Jennie, but this was a time in her life when she was not searching for excitement—and so she did join.

The world surrounding her was searching for peace and quiet, too. France had been hostile toward England for a number of years, but as Jennie's nephew, Shane Leslie, described it, Edward VII's courage and charm dissipated this national bitterness. On a visit to France, King Edward signed his name in French, complimented a French actress on being symbolic of the spirit of France, and did a dozen small things that were favorably publicized in the press. Soon crowds formed wherever he went and turned into rallies. "The cry of *Vive le Roi* was raised, shouted down, and raised again till it conquered. *La Ville lumière* had become Royalist."[59] Shortly afterward an Anglo-French treaty was signed.

King Edward was perhaps less able and industrious than his mother had been, but he had a better understanding of the democratic forces of the new century. He advised Prime Minister Balfour that if a tax on food was pushed through Parliament, he would use the rarely exercised Royal veto.

At the time, the major political issue in the country was the old question of Free Trade versus Protectionism. Balfour's Conservative Party favored Protectionism, the Liberal Party stood for Free Trade. Winston was in a quandary: he was a Conservative who believed in Free Trade. Jennie, who was in a similar dilemma, had her own views of the issue. She sent a sharp letter to the Randolph Churchill Habitation of the Primrose League:

> I understand, from the notice sent to me, that at the General Annual Meeting of the Randolph Churchill Habitation of Primrose League, which is to be held on December 1st, Mr. J. Ratcliffe Cousins, Secretary of the Tariff Reform League, is to address the meeting in favor of Tariff Reform. Under these circumstances, I am afraid I cannot see my way to preside that evening. In the first place, I am not a Protectionist, and do not desire to associate myself in any way with this retrograde movement, and secondly, I should like to enter my protest against the Randolph Churchill Habitation giving its countenance to views which go far beyond those of the Government and of the Prime Minister. I can quite understand the Habitation desiring to enlighten itself on the great question which is filling all minds at the present moment, but that only one side of the case should be stated is unworthy of the Primrose League, which has always been open-minded on all questions outside the terms of its Constitution. As one of the Vice-Presidents of the Executive Committee, and one among the first twelve members of the League, I cannot identify myself with such proceedings. Had you arranged for the views of Mr. Balfour and the Unionist Party to be explained at the same time, I should have been very glad to have attended the meeting. But, under existing circumstances, I must reluctantly decline.
>
> Believe me, Yours Faithfully,
> [signed] Jennie Cornwallis-West.[60]

While Winston was traveling, Jennie cared for his political chores:

> It was very kind of you to open the Bazaar & I am sure those people were vy pleased at your going. I don't know what I should have done if you had failed me. They were already put out at my absence . . .[61]

And now he kept her informed of his political activities:

> I send you another crop of newspaper cuttings. I daresay they will amuse you.
>
> I have had eight small meetings in Oldham, of 200 apiece, and have been extremely well received, as you will see from the papers. . . . There are of course a lot of Protectionists and Fair Traders in the party there, and there is no doubt that everything will have to be handled very carefully; but they are all quite agreed in recognizing that I am the only person that has got the slightest chance of winning the Election for the Tory Party there, and in consequence, they are prepared to give me very wide liberty. In addition to this, there is a great deal of personal enthusiasm, and I find that the working classes are very much attracted by the idea of a representative whose name they read frequently in the newspapers, and who as they think, confers distinction on the town. . . . We must try to see something of each other in Scotland. . . . I hope your cure has been satisfactory. I find myself in very good health, but I shall be glad to lead a quiet, regular, temperate life, for a month. I shall do my exercises every day.[62]

When they later missed each other in Scotland, he wrote:

> I am indeed sorry to miss you here: but we shall see each other often in the autumn & I may need you often in Oldham, if you have time & inclination.
>
> The situation is most interesting & I fancy a smash must come in a few days. Mr. Balfour is coming to Balmoral on Saturday. Is he going to resign or reconstruct? If he resigns, will the King send for Spencer or Devonshire? If for either, will he succeed in forming a govt & what kind of government? If he reconstructs—will it be a Protectionist reconstruction of a cabinet wh does not contain the Free Trade

Ministers, or a Free Trade reconstruction of a cabinet? . . .
All these things are possible.[63]

Bourke Cockran had strongly influenced Winston's thinking. The two
men originally had disagreed on the Boer War, but Winston gradually
grew more sympathetic toward the Boers.[64] On the Free Trade question
Winston and Bourke were of like mind and exchanged many long letters
on the subject. In 1896 Bourke had differed so strongly with his own
Democratic Party leadership on this single issue that he had crossed over to
the Republicans to campaign for William McKinley for President.[65]

Winston in England was now prepared to cross over to the Liberals on
the same issue. At the end of May 1904, he entered the House of Commons, stared for a moment at the Government benches, then at the Opposition benches, and walked quickly to the Liberal side, taking a seat
alongside Lloyd George. It was a place where his father had once sat.

Seymour Leslie remembered being with his Aunt Jennie that night in
her library. She was glaringly angry and told him: "Haven't you heard?
The moment Winston crossed the floor to the Liberal benches and rose to
speak, that detestable Arthur Balfour and his entire party got up and
walked out of the House! What an insult from a Prime Minister. . . . I'll
never speak to him again. . . ."[66]

Thirty-Six

*J*ENNIE WAS FIFTY YEARS OLD IN 1904. A British author considered this the time of life when the American woman ". . . is filled with unrealizable ideals . . . her life frustrated, [so] she turns to religion or bridge, becomes either a colorless individual or a fanatic. . . ."[1]

Jennie, however, had achieved much in her life and now wanted little. Her handsome young husband continued to be adoring and was doing surprisingly well in business. Her sons had accepted George more readily than she could have hoped. She had come to terms with most of her husband's family, and although there was little warmth, there was a grudging acceptance of her. George's father, however, still kept his distance, and Winston gave Jennie encouragement:

> I thought a good deal over all you said to me about yourself & I feel sure you are right to concentrate on and take pains with the few people you really are about. But I have no doubt that when papa G. [Conwallis-West] is at length gathered to Abraham, you will be able to renew your youth like the eagle. . . . [2]

Jennie otherwise felt a sense of fulfillment and peace. The marvelous thing about her, too, was that she was still handsome woman. George's sister, Daisy, who had become outwardly cordial to Jennie but was privately catty; confided to her diary that Jennie was "wearing lovely clothes . . . looking very well, but *so* fat. . . ."[3] A lengthy magazine profile, however, said of Jennie that her figure

> has an almost girlish slightness . . . that definite seductiveness of outline announced irresistibly by erectness of carriage, correctness of proportion from bust to waist and from waist to hip, and that serpentine slope of the neck into shoulder which has been referred to by sculptors as the most maddening line in art. The taper of no waist in the world has more roundness, the freshness of no complexion in London entices with such genuineness. . . .
>
> . . . Mrs. Cornwallis-West is neither slim nor plump, neither young nor old, but to quote the words of *Truth,* "just herself." She has neither that mincing accent which has become so common nor the weird almost simian antics—for example, the shoulder-high handshake—nor the falsetto voice which go with the character she is made to play. . . . She has been praised . . . for spreading the spirit of graciousness about her, and for giving to human intercourse at social functions a new reality. It is not that she cultivates what the English call "charm," but that fate has bestowed upon her, in addition to her enduring beauty of face and figure and perfect elegance of deportment, an instinct for courtesy. She avoids giving offense. She is stately without stiffness. There is no condescension in her distinguished air, which compels respect by an unconscious dignity of its own. One never detects in Mrs. Cornwallis-West that studied indifference, approaching insolence, which, according to the French, buries the good manners of the English at their great social functions. . . . Time has not robbed her of the American accent in which she carries on her conversations with brilliant Englishmen, or diminished the brightness of a pair of eyes of which the late Grand Duke Sergius once said that they were the most beautiful in all Europe.[4]

Capping its admiration, the article discussed Jennie's new home at Salisbury Hall and quoted a British newspaper as saying of her, "She is the only hostess of genius in the United Kingdom."

Salisbury Hall was not a stately home. It was comfortable and quiet, and a haven for friends and family. It was a lovely old manor house near

St. Albans, on the site of a thirteenth-century castle, and there was still a moat surrounding it and an Elizabethan hall with carved stone plaques on the walls. The house also had a beautifully carved staircase, superb fireplaces, wood-paneled rooms, several adjoining cottages, and an elaborate servants' wing. King Charles II had used it as "a home away from home" for his mistress, Nell Gwyn.[5] It was said that her ghost still haunted the place.

George, who believed in spiritualism and reincarnation and claimed to be psychic, insisted that he had seen "the figure of a youngish and beautiful woman with a blue *fichu* round her shoulders. She looked intently at me, and then turned and disappeared through a door into the passage. I followed and found nothing."[6] He later identified the apparition as the ghost of Nell Gwyn.

Jennie was different at Salisbury Hall, much more relaxed than in London. And she never before had had a home with enough land for a proper garden. She loved color and she loved flowers. Winston helped her to decide which ones to have and where to plant them, and the two of them spent one day getting the duckweed out of the moat. The more practical Jack advised on the bathroom renovation, and George supervised the installation of electric lights. George now even had his own place for pheasant shoots.

Jennie no longer rode horses as much as she once did, but she and George played a lot of golf together and she was getting good at it. Their marriage was now four years old, and life was sweet and serene for them.

"George and Jennie have made this little house delightful," said Daisy Pless; "it is full of pretty things, and the garden will be very nice."[7] "SH," as Jennie called it, was not really "a little house." However, it had one drawback which became apparent when King Edward made one of his frequent visits, forcing Jennie to demonstrate some of her "genius" as a hostess. The King had become very stout, and it was not comfortable for him to climb stairs. Jennie, therefore, had to create a suite downstairs, where there were no bedrooms. She did this by hanging green silk in the paneled drawing room to make it more intimate and by converting the gentleman's cloakroom into a private bathroom. Walden served meals on the refectory table in the Tudor Hall. How simple all this was compared, for example, to the King's reception at Chatsworth, where the Duke and Duchess of Devonshire posted two lines of torchbearers from the railroad station to their mansion, the whole area lit with thousands of colored lamps and the marble staircase lined with footmen in powdered wigs.[8]

Daisy envied Jennie's easy relationship with Edward VII, and she probably was not pleased that when Emperor Wilhelm II of Germany visited at her Prussian castle, he reminisced warmly about the beautiful, charming

Lady Randolph Churchill.[9] Moreover, for Daisy, royalty had been a bad bargain. Her marriage with the Prince of Pless was cold and unhappy, and she remarked in her *Diary*: "Royalties are very nice to meet occasionally, but difficult to live with."[10]

But Daisy was especially jealous of Jennie's relationship with the Marquis Luis de Soveral. As one of King Edward's three closest friends, Soveral was usually invited wherever His Majesty was invited. He was the Portuguese Ambassador to Great Britain, and few were better informed on European politics; indeed it was said that "had he wished he could have become one of Europe's leading statesmen. . . ." But Soveral preferred to remain in England, "where he made love to all the most beautiful women and where all the nicest men were his friends. . . ."

Soveral had long been one of Jennie's most unfailing admirers. He was a genial, charming, and tactful bachelor, with a fund of risqué stories. Always dressed in the height of fashion, he usually wore immaculate, white gloves and a white flower in his buttonhole. He had a swarthy complexion and wore a fashionable mustache, and the press often referred to him as "The Adonis of Diplomacy."[12] His collection of Court ladies was referred to by one woman as a "harem."

Initially Daisy was contemptuous of Soveral, even virulent. She called him

> the oddest character in English Society: he imagines himself
> to be a great intellectual and political force and the wise ad-
> viser of all the heads of the government and, of course, the
> greatest danger to women! He is so swarthy that he is nick-
> named the "Blue Monkey" and I imagine that even those
> stupid people who believe that every man who talks to a
> woman must be her lover, could not take his Don Juanesque
> pretensions seriously. Yet I am told that all women do not
> judge him so severely and some even find him *très séduisant.*
> How disgusting![13]

As the following letter to the Marquis reveals, however, Daisy's disgust was only part of her complex attitude toward him:

> It says in the Bible—"Put not your trust in Princes." I say
> put not your trust in foreign ministers—you knew I wanted to
> go home and you simply went home without me after telling
> me you did not want to go so soon, for like Jenny you
> wished to dance some more dances. . . . You are simply get-
> ting bored with me and that's the truth. . . . No my dear, I am

not going to be taken up one moment & dropped the next. . . .

Now that I have said all that I feel better. Let me know tomorrow if you are coming for lunch or not.

Yours,
Daisy.[14]

Jennie's relationship with Soveral was much more secure. He seems to have destroyed any correspondence between them, but he did save one note that was signed: "forever Jennie."[15]

Soveral also became a good friend of Winston's and occasionally acted as his friend in Court when Winston began to differ with the King on some issues. One such issue was Free Trade.

Toward the end of 1904 Jennie wrote to Winston from Sandringham:

My dearest Winston,

I read your speech at Glasgow with such interest—I did *not* discuss it with the King, you will be surprised to hear. I think it was rather a pity your Chairman attacked A B [Arthur Balfour] the way he did. I see the audience resented it—at least so the papers make out. Henri de Breteuil tells me that in France they look upon you as the coming man. Here I am in a hotbed of protectionists. You have probably seen the party in the papers. We have been asked to stay on till Monday. It has been most pleasant nice weather—pleasant people & excellent sport. George shot very well & [we] are both seen in good favor—so *that* is all right. Where shall you be next week? Salisbury Hall is at your disposal if you want to come. By the way, I have been so ill ever since I ate those oysters with you—I had to see the doctor here, & he told me I had been poisoned. I am all right now.—We are thinking of going to Paris for Xmas. Why don't you come? The Breteuils would put you up—Now good-bye.

Yr loving
mother.[16]

Winston visited often at Salisbury Hall now. He had an "aerial summerhouse" built in an old lime tree, and there he would practice his speeches to an audience of sky and leaves. He had also begun writing a biography of his father and he prodded Jennie constantly to remember things that she perhaps would rather have forgotten: ". . . how you first began in Charles Street . . . then the row, I suppose in 1877, then Ireland. . . ."[17]

Jennie still maintained relations with many members of her first husband's family. In the early years of her marriage to Randolph, Jennie and Randolph's sister Fanny (Lady Tweedmouth) had politely detested each other. But gradually their friendship grew so close and warm that Jennie called Fanny "without exception the noblest character I have ever met. . . ."[18]

George and Jennie were guests at a ball given by Lady Tweedmouth, "and when we came away," George recalled, "Jennie was terribly depressed, almost in tears. I asked her the reason, and she told me that her hostess had confided to her that she had received her death warrant from the doctor that afternoon, and could not live more than three months. . . . She had been the life and soul of the evening, and nobody would have guessed that this terrible sentence was hanging over her. . . ."[19]

Jennie had lost other friends within the past few years: Cecil Rhodes, Baron Hirsch, Oscar Wilde. And now Mary Leiter Curzon was also seriously ill.[20]

When her husband was first made Viceroy of India, Mary told Jennie: ". . . I feel like a ship in full sail on the high seas of dignity! . . ." And on another occasion she added: "There is no happiness so great to a woman as the admiration she can feel to the depths of her heart for her Belovedest."

Most of her letters to Jennie, however, indicated a longing to return to England. And finally she and Lord Curzon did, in 1905 after Curzon clashed unsuccessfully with his Commander-in-Chief Horatio Kitchener. Unfortunately, Mary's health continued to fail, and a short time later Mary Leiter Curzon died. Jennie felt deeply the loss of her tall, stately friend with the soft voice and the radiant smile.[21]

There was further sadness for Jennie that year. Since her marriage to George, she had seen little of Pearl Craigie. Pearl was always somewhere else: a long stay in India with the Curzons, a spring visit to Spain, a long summer with her son on the Isle of Wight, and then a tour of the United States for a series of lectures on "The Science of Life." The tour proved too tiring for her and she found herself unable to complete it. In February 1906 she wrote: "I don't believe I shall live much longer. There is nothing organically wrong with me, but I flag, the pulse stops." And then she added, "Please don't think I want a long illness and horrors. I want to die in harness and at work. . . ."[22]

Pearl's final request of Jennie was a strange one for her: she wanted to be presented at Court. In Queen Victoria's time she had been barred from Court by the stigma of her divorce. But she had been the innocent party and her former husband had now remarried.

Providing Jennie with family background for the presentation, Pearl observed that her cousin, Admiral Cowles, had married Theodore Roosevelt's sister. Since Jennie also had a distant family relationship with President Roosevelt, she and Pearl could claim kinship. Their kinship, however, was far closer than that of cousins. Indeed, their relationship was all the more remarkable because Pearl had so few women friends. She often said that she never really understood women.

> My mother was at one time very fond of telling how, when I was a very little girl, she left me alone one day with my dolls, to whose mute companionship she commended me for a short hour. On her return, she found a long row of sawdust puppets hanging by their necks, and me contemplating their dangling bodies in silent pleasure, and they were all women dolls, too. . . . [23]

"Jennie," the heroine of Pearl Craigie's novel *The Vineyard,* was an idealistic, intelligent woman in love with a handsome but morally weak man. In the novel, the dying father tells Jennie, "If I fall asleep, take care of the candle."[24] Earlier Pearl had written of herself that doctors "told me some years ago that I should go out like a candle: my heart was broken with grief long ago. . . ."[25] In August 1906 Pearl Mary-Teresa Craigie died in her sleep, her rosary in her hand.

If Pearl Craigie had intended the handsome, morally weak man in *The Vineyard* to represent George Cornwallis-West, that descriptive arrow seemed now to be wide of the mark. George had matured through the years. He still loved his hunting, fishing, and motoring, and kept careful count of the results of the shoot, the weight of the fish, and the miles traveled per hour ("averaged 31 miles an hour the whole way"). But by now he had also spent four years with the British Electric Traction Company, earning a good income from directorships and various other fees.

1906 had started off as a smashing year for him. He and a friend had established their own brokerage firm, "Wheater, Cornwallis-West & Co." George had made use of many of Jennie's contacts, and the company's earnings in 1905 were £23,000. By 1906, they had expanded, holding large interests in steel companies and copper mines, and George was traveling more than ever. One of the men he met was a quiet, capable engineer—then not interested in politics—named Herbert Hoover.[26]

For Winston the beginning of that year had been even better. In 1904 his cross-over from the Conservatives to the Liberals on the Free Trade issue had brought a worried letter from Bourke Cockran, who had been disturbed by a cartoon in the *Pall Mall Gazette.*

It represented you as a mosquito or a fly or a wasp or some variety of winged irritant perched on the coach of Sir Henry Campbell-Bannerman whose repose you have evidently disturbed and are plainly striving to ruin. Under it is the paragraph to which I have referred and which states in substance that Mr. Winston Churchill will not be given a place in the Liberal Cabinet if one should be formed after the next election. . . .

Now this conception of your attitude presents you in rather a sordid character. . . . Of course we must realise that where a man changes sides, however lofty the motives which actually govern him, he is very likely to be accused by those whom he has left of being actuated by the very basest desires and ambitions. . . . Why not confound the hostile and surprise the indifferent by declaring now that you won't seek or even accept membership in a Liberal Government if one is to be formed with the new parliament? Such a declaration would be in the nature of a bomb whose explosion would resound throughout the whole Empire but whose fragments would damage none but your critics. . . . [27]

Winston, however, clearly expected to be offered a cabinet post in the new Liberal government, and he fully intended to accept it. Balfour had resigned in December 1905 and Liberal leader Herbert Campbell-Bannerman had become Prime Minister. A seventy-year-old man who had led the public fight against the Boer War,[28] "C-B" was "easygoing to the point of laziness," liked French novels, had few enemies and fewer intimate friends, but a core of fundamental honesty. He offered Winston the Cabinet post of Undersecretary of State for the Colonies.

Winston accepted, but a member of the government still had to represent a constituency. The election Winston had to fight for and win was at Manchester.[29] Jennie was there with him. One of the issues against the Conservative Party was their support of expensive coal, and Jennie told a crowd, "The Conservatives give you dear coal, I give you dear Winston. . . ."

To Leonie, Jennie wrote: "The election is most exciting—they say it will be a close thing. The female suffrage women are too odious. Every night they make a disturbance and shriek and rant. They damage their own cause hopelessly . . ."[30] At another time, Jennie told a crowd of suffragettes that "they ought to be forcibly fed with common sense."[31]

Jennie was at Town Hall while the votes were being counted and afterward at the Reform Club "where the scene," she said, "was indescribable. . . . I have been to lots of elections, but I never saw such excitement. . . .

Winston told me two days before that he thought there would be a clean sweep. . . ."[32]

Jennie also took advantage of this opportunity to chide Leonie who had been miffed by Winston's switch from the Conservatives:

> I am amused by what you say about turncoats–I suppose that is a dig at Winston for going to the other side. There is no doubt it takes a big man to change his mind. You might have quoted Dizzy [Disraeli], Gladstone, and last but not least, Chamberlain. As for Arthur Balfour, his mind is never made up, so he has none to change. . . .[33]

This had been an important time for Winston: his biography of his father had been published and was an enormous success;[34] the Cabinet post was just what he wanted; and now his overwhelming victory in Manchester topped it all off. Jennie immediately set herself to work on another job she loved: decorating a house she had rented for Winston on Bolton Street. "It will be charming," she confidently told Leonie.

Winston also hired a new private secretary, a young friend of Leonie's whom he had met at a party. His name was Edward Marsh, and Leonie strongly recommended him. Edward Marsh would become one of Winston's most intimate lifelong friends. Marsh wrote to Leonie:

> Such an excitement. I *must* tell you. Your nephew has asked me to be his private secretary for 6 months or so. It will be the most interesting thing I have ever done but I'm most terribly afraid of not being the right person and turning out a failure. I am sure it's your doing. When you come back in May I'll tell you whether I bless you or curse you! You'll find me a gray-haired skeleton in either case as he means to work me to death. It's funny that just after we were discussing the problem of what I should do to age myself, this easy solution should have dashed forth. I've just dined alone with Winston. He was most perfectly charming to me, but made it quite clear what he would expect in the way of help and I almost *know* I can't do it–its [*sic*] awful! . . .[35]

Through the years, Marsh also became very close with Jennie and wrote of her:

> It was at Blenheim that I first met Lady Randolph Churchill, who soon became one of my dearest friends.

> She was an incredible and most delightful compound of fla-
> grant worldliness and eternal childhood, in thrall to fashion
> and luxury (life didn't begin for her on the basis of less than
> 40 pairs of shoes) yet never sacrificing one human quality of
> warmheartedness, humor, loyalty, sincerity, or steadfast and
> pugnacious courage.[36]

After their first meeting, Jennie said she thought Marsh "very pleasant,"
but she could not refrain from adding, "I think it is a pity he has such a
squeaky voice. . . ."[37]

As much as Jennie came to like Marsh, she may have had some reservations about his being secretary to her son. This had nothing to do with
Marsh's qualifications—he was loyal, sincere, warmhearted, sensitive, and
hardworking. But he was also homosexual. Indeed, as the year passed,
Marsh—who became Sir Edward Marsh—was recognized as "the center of a
large homosexual artistic colony" in England.[38] There was never any scandal about it, but Jennie could hardly forget how an alleged homosexual association had jeopardized Winston's military career. A similar smear might
have had an even more crippling effect on the career of a young politician.

The year which had begun so bright finally brought trouble. The worst
of it was for George. The promising capitalist, booming in every direction,
suddenly was in financial trouble. He had been swindled by a glib lawyer
who left him 8,000 pounds in debt. The Duke of Westminster wrote to
Winston on August 19, 1906:

> . . . I hear you & your brother Jack have between you come
> to his aid. I would have helped before I left if there hadn't
> been some misunderstanding between us. I send you en-
> closed cheque to be used on condition that George should
> not know of this transaction till I choose, if ever, to let him
> know. I think it very hard that you & Jack should bear the
> brunt, when it should have come on me, as his brother-in-
> law.[39]

Winston immediately sent a confidential letter to George:

> My dear George,
>   I send you herewith a cheque for £3000 to be devoted to
> the repayment of the sums of wh you were robbed by your
> solicitor, & wh I understand you have now borrowed from
> Cox's Bank. The transaction is personal between us & the
> money is a loan to be repaid at any time at three months

notice on my request. Meanwhile you should pay interest at 21/2% per annum into my account at Cox's. Perhaps you will write me a letter confirming this in precise detail.[40]

And George answered:

... I thank you also, my dear Winston, for your great kindness of heart. . . . [41]

George was not the only one who had trouble. He mentioned to Winston that Consuelo, Duchess of Marlborough, had come to Salisbury Hall at Jennie's invitation:

Poor little Consuelo . . . I do pity her with all my heart, what a tragedy. The whole thing reminds me of Hogarth's series of satyr [sic], "Marriage à la Mode." Take my advice & if ever you do marry, do it from motives of affection & none other. No riches in the world can compensate for anything else.

Do come down here soon; I am sure you want a rest, or soon will.[42]

The week before, in a letter marked SECRET, Winston had written his mother:

Sunny has definitely separated from Consuelo, who is in London at Sunderland House. Her father returns to Paris on Monday. I have suggested to her that you would be vy willing to go and stay with her for a while, as I cannot bear to think of her being all alone during these dark days. If she should send for you, I hope you will put aside other things & go to her. I know how you always are a prop to lean on in bad times.[43]

But Jennie now needed a prop for herself. George's financial disaster had caused him to become edgy, irritable, and increasingly argumentative. They quarreled more, most often about George's wandering eye, which was perhaps partly his way of bolstering his ego. Both Jennie and George, however, were quick to regret their battles.

Jennie had gone to Cannes, and George wrote her: "I'm awfully worried as I find you thought I chased you away. You know I didn't and that I'd sooner see you than all the others. . . ." And Jennie wrote Jack, "Please tell Walden to send me by post George's photograph on my mantel-piece. He is to take it out of the frame. . . ."[45]

Part of the time she was away, Jennie stayed with George's sister Daisy, who had rented a villa nearby. When Jennie arrived there on April 14, 1907, Daisy, with her usual bite, commented in her diary:

> We are all going on a motor trip—Jennie, my sister-in-law—who married George and still loves him immensely poor dear; she is uncommonly nice and still very handsome, but of course the difference in age is a sad and terrible draw-back (no babies possible); well, she is coming with us. The Duke of Marlborough, her cousin by marriage . . . also comes. . . . [46]

Daisy also mentioned an attempt Sunny made to move the picnic table. It was loaded with food "and down the whole thing went. . . . The Duke was miserable; by the way he looked at the debris one might have thought he was peering at his own life, which at the present moment is in much the same state. . . ."[47]

While Daisy suffered the young Duke politely, she actively disliked Winston. When Jennie and George were married, Daisy had noted, "It made Winston Churchill a connection of ours, a prospect we viewed with somewhat mixed feelings. I cannot honestly say I ever cared for him very much. . . ."[48]

So closely intertwined was international society that it was perhaps not surprising for Jennie to discover that Daisy was related by marriage to none other than Charles Kinsky. Daisy was also a close friend of Kinsky's wife Lily, which might have helped determine her attitude toward Jennie.

With the death of his father, Count Kinsky had become Prince Kinsky. He had left the diplomatic service and become Privy Counselor and Chamberlain to the Emperor of Austria. He was also a Major in the Army Reserve, and an hereditary member of the Austrian House of Lords. When one of Jennie's young friends, the brilliant pianist-composer Ethel Smyth,[49] wanted to study and work in Vienna, Jennie wrote Kinsky to ask his help for her. Miss Smyth described the incident in her memoirs:

> Dear Lady Randolph Churchill, who had the beautiful faculty of keeping the friendship of those who were said to have loved her in her youth, had written to one of these, a perfectly delightful man, and a great power in Vienna—who at once promised to do all he could to influence his friend Count Montenuovo in my behalf. Count Montenuovo was

the son of Marie Louise, and the Emperor Francis Joseph
had created for him some very dignified post connected with
the Opera. . . . Lady Randolph's friend had worked up the
feeble Montenuovo to a pitch of zeal. . . .

"I wish she had married Kinsky," Ethel Smyth later remarked, ". . . he
was so delightful. . . ."[50]

Kinsky and his wife came to England at least once a year to see the
Grand National, and it is conceivable that he and Jennie might have attended some of the same parties. It is unlikely, however, that they ever
wrote to each other. But they had mutual friends and were not ignorant of
each other's lives. How delighted the hypocritical Daisy Pless would have
been to tell Jennie any happy news about the Kinskys—and how careful Jennie would have been not to give her the satisfaction of a reaction.

Jennie now received news of another former lover. Bourke Cockran
had remarried. The headline in the *Sunday World* read:

She, Pretty and Popular;
He, Famous and Wealthy.[51]

She was Anne Ide, daughter of the Governor General of the Philippines.[52] She and Bourke and Alice Roosevelt and Nicholas Longworth all
had traveled together to the Philippines on a government-sponsored inspection tour. The trip resulted in both couples' marrying. And again, in
the constant interweaving of upper-class society, Anne Ide's sister later married Jennie's nephew, Shane Leslie, with the ceremony taking place on
Bourke Cockran's estate at Sands Point, New York.[53]

Shortly before her marriage, Alice Roosevelt had journeyed to England,
where she met Jennie. Jennie invited her to stay with her at Salisbury Hall.
"I got the feeling," Alice Roosevelt Longworth remembered, "that she was
terribly lonely, and that she was grasping at me as if I were a sturdy
straw."[54]

It was a time when George was traveling a good deal, when Winston
was kept busy by the Colonial Office, and Jack was preoccupied with a
stock-market panic. Clara had moved to Brede Place in Sussex, and
Leonie alternated between Ireland and London. "The fact is when I go to
London, there are only two people I ever try to see, one is Winston, the
other you," Jennie wrote Leonie from Salisbury Hall. "Both are aforesaid
disappointments. One is on account of work, the other on account of pleasure. I may go away feeling sore at heart. I snatch a few minutes of Winston's society by driving him to the Colonial Office, and the most you can
afford are a few words uncomfortably (for me) on the telephone." But then

she added, "You know I love you and that when you want me, I am to be found."[55]

It is hard to imagine Jennie being lonely. She was so vibrant, she had so many friends, so many interests. But this was a loneliness that only a husband or family could fill.

There was never any rift among the three sisters, but there was no longer the physical closeness provided by their clustered houses on Great Cumberland Place. Clara's husband, Moreton Frewen, that year traveled between Africa, where he planned to buy forest land, and Prince Rupert, Canada, where he planned to create a great port city. Both projects failed. Clara was often alone, and Jennie made frequent visits to Brede Place. Compared to the fine, logical minds of her sisters, Clara was almost a fey creature, easily abstracted. Her nephew, Seymour Leslie, recalled her greeting him at the end of his school term: "Why you *Dear Thing!* how perfectly *lovely* to see you back from school! I can't *wait* to hear your news of it! Tell me *all* about it, sit on the sofa there and don't leave anything out!"

"Whereupon," said Seymour, "she turned to continue her correspondence."[56]

Yet this was a woman of penetrating passion, and her love letters to her husband reveal a woman few people ever knew.

Clara shared Jennie's disregard for money: she spent it, often when she didn't have it. The renovation of beautiful, historic Brede Place created a drain of thousands of pounds.[57] She built dams and rose gardens and had outdoor sculpture done by the American Augustus Saint-Gaudens, while her artistic daughter Clare[58] modeled cement swans around the lily pond. Clara's most inexpensive innovation was to establish a tradition of having trees planted by visiting celebrities–King Edward, Rudyard Kipling, Clemenceau, Queen Marie of Rumania, and even her nephew Winston.

Winston and his lovely cousin Clare were good friends, and years later, the two posed for each other–Clare sculpting while Winston painted. In 1907 Winston also agreed to find an administrative job in Nigeria for Hugh Frewen, Clare's brother, who wanted to spend some time there.

Late that year, Winston went on a four-months' trip around Europe with Eddie Marsh, and Jennie wrote Marsh: "Bless you, dear Eddie . . . Look after my Winston–he is very precious to me."[59]

Before leaving, Winston had asked his mother to sublet his house, find work for his secretary, and take care of a number of other things. "I do rely upon you dear Mamma to help me in arranging these affairs; for wh I am not at all suited by disposition or knowledge."[60]

She was happy to oblige. She advised him of what she planned to do and told him, "Don't worry about it. . . ." Then she went on to say:

. . . I have followed the H of C debates and Eddie wrote to me of your all-night sitting. You will be glad to get away from speeches–I thought the Govt wd have to practically drop the Scotch Bill–I hear nothing but abuse of it. I don't pretend to know anything about it–but that dual ownership business has been tried in Ireland and has been found more than wanting! I liked yr Transvaal speech, and quite agree with you. . . .

Do try and read my chapters at SH. The 3 will only take you an hour–if as much–I want you to add to the 5th chapt that story of yr father and Goschen and the Exchequer. If told at all it must be well told–and I feel diffident–also, make a little note in the 4th as to where I can get some Irish data– that chap is too short. . . .

. . . I hate to think of your going off for so long–and that I shall not see you again before your departure. But you will enjoy it, and it will be a great rest and change. . . . Mind you get Trevelyan's *Garibaldi* to read en route–also, *Memories and Impressions* of George Brodrick. . . .[61]

The chapters Jennie wanted Winston to read were from her *Reminiscences*. "I am struggling with this book," she said. "My feelings fluctuate about it. Sometimes I think it is going to be splendid, and then again I am most depressed. . . ."[62]

Winston tried to advise her:

You have a great chance of making a charming woman's book about the last 30 years, & do, I beg you, lavish trouble upon it, & banish ruthlessly anything that will hurt other people's feelings. It is well worthwhile.[63]

She did exactly that. She ended her reminiscences with the time just before her marriage to George West and refrained from including anything that might make anyone unhappy. The tone was not apologetic, but neither was the book very revealing. As she said in the Preface, ". . . there may be some to whom these Reminiscences will be interesting chiefly in virtue of what is left unsaid."[64]

Although Winston himself was sensitive to criticism, his mother's response to some of his remarks indicates that he took a different attitude toward her work:

. . . We are still in Scotland, as you see. . . . It is very mild up here, but I like the outdoor life, & have taken to fishing, which I enjoy. I write all the mornings & have got on with the book. I received the chapters. You were a bit scathing about Chap. V, but I did not mind, as I ought to have told you that V was *quite* in the rough—merely a lot of notes put together which Miss Anning typed in order that you might see them. In any case, I shd never have sent the chapter to the *Century* as you saw it. I have added a lot to Chapt 4 & lead up to Ireland. The *Century* have now 4 chapters & I hope they will leave me in peace for a little. . . . In the memoirs of Mme. de Boigne, she gives an account of a conversation she had with Napoleon. I have copied it out for you, as I know yr keen interest in him. Bless you, darling. Thank you so much for looking at my chapters & I forgive you for saying 'Fie!' to your loving

Mother.[65]

Faced with this reaction, Winston took a tactful approach: "You must not regard my criticisms as personal. Literary judgments are not worth much—but they are worth nothing unless they are at once impartial & impersonal."[66]

A few months later Winston received startling news from Jack:

I am writing to tell you that a very wonderful thing has happened. Goonie [Lady Gwendeline Bertie] loves me. I have loved her for a long time—but I have always attempted to put thoughts of that kind out of my mind—because I thought that I had nothing to give her—and also chiefly because I never for one moment imagined that she would ever care for me.

This is absolutely secret. Only my mother and George know about it. Her parents know nothing. Nor must they—*until I can come with some proposition. . . .*[67]

Winston may have wondered about Jack's reference to "my mother." "You understand all this?" Jack continued.

I wish you were here. You were in love really once—and you know what that meant. But you had other things to think of. Your career and your future filled more than half your life. I love the same way you did—but I have no other thoughts. All dreams of the future—my career and everything else, are wrapped up in one person. Nothing else matters to me in the least. I suppose that sounds very silly–but the only people who think it so are those who have never been able to feel these things themselves.

Write to Goonie–But I impress on you, keep our *secret absolutely*. If her family suspected now–her life at Wytham would be unbearable. . . .

I am going through a mixture of happiness and fear, that is not enviable.[68]

Winston later wrote about the contrast between his brother and himself:

He is quite different from me, understanding women thoroughly, getting into touch with them at once, & absolutely dependent upon feminine influence of some kind for the peace & harmony of his soul. Whereas I am stupid & clumsy in that relation, and naturally quite self-reliant & self-contained. Yet by such different paths we both arrive at loneliness.[69]

Winston had known "Goonie" well. Discussing Jack's news, Jennie commented to Winston, "I sometimes thought you had designs in that quarter. . . ."[70] Indeed, Goonie's earlier letters to Winston had seemed edged with anticipation. Clearly, however, Winston had had other ideas. Now he only wanted to help his brother. "Poor dear–We must manage to drive that through for him," he wrote his mother. "How happy he must be & how glad he must be & how glad I am he had not married some beastly woman for money. . . ."[71]

Goonie wrote Winston about a lunch she had had with Jennie, ". . . a very wonderful woman & so philosophical. . . . In spite of everything her spirit and vitality are wonderful. She never gives in–not for a single moment. . . ."[72] A financial panic in New York in 1907 had compounded the losses George had suffered in the swindle. As Jennie told Winston, "George hasn't been able to draw one penny from his business this year–so we have no nest egg to fall back on. . . . It preys dreadfully on poor George, who is getting quite ill over it all. . . ."[73]

Jennie could bear the crisis, but George couldn't. A few months later Jack reported to his brother:

. . . things seem to be going pretty badly in the home ménage. Poor George who has little stamina, has knuckled under to bad times and is in a bad way. I am trying to make him "buck up" against the bad times–but it is hard work.[74]

Jennie described their situation:

> George has been so seedy these last 4 weeks with a cold
> that the doctors have ordered him off to St Moritz to recoup.
> Unfortunately owing to the expense I have not been able to
> go with him—which is depressing for both—as he feels ill & is
> lonely—& I hate being away from him as you know. How-
> ever, there it is![75]

She was so short of money that she apologized to Winston for not sending him a cable on his birthday. She didn't have his address, she said, but
she also "thought it might be expensive. 'Strange fit of economy,' you will
say. . . ."[76]

However, anxiety about money did not prevent her from keeping active
and from keeping Winston posted on some of the latest news: The Prime
Minister was seriously ill, and a change in Government was expected soon;
she had dined with Cassel, who sent regards; Leonie had met the German
Emperor who "asked a great deal after me";[77] Consuelo was looking very
well "& quite fat for her . . ."; she had opened an Exhibition of Books on
Bond Street:

> All the publishers and authors were there—& I made a
> speech & Mr. John Murray proposed a vote of thanks to me.
> He is very deaf & made a "fuddly" speech—said, "Mrs.
> Cornwallis—who is an authoress & the mother of an au-
> thoress!" Shrieks from the Audience . . .[78]

The Times recorded that in her speech Jennie had described herself as "neither bookish nor literary," and added, "Publishers are as important to authors as Cabinet Ministers to suffragettes."[79]

In an effort to economize, Jennie and George decided to move back to
London. The good thing about their return, she wrote Winston, "is that I
shall see more of you. . . ."[80] But after referring to Jack's engagement, in another note to Winston, she remarked, wistfully, "I suppose you will be next
to 'pop off'; it is always so in a family. . . ."[81]

Goonie also wrote to Winston. She told him that Jennie had read her
parts of a recent letter from him, and she chided him—"how cruel you
are"—about his criticism of his mother's "little 'potions & histories.'—A
forbidding-looking 'no!' on the margin."[82]

Jennie had still another duty to perform on behalf of Winston, this one
particularly difficult. His long-time servant Scrivings had died, and Winston asked Jennie to break the news to Scrivings' wife. Then she had to find

another servant for Winston, as he would soon be returning from his four-month trip. Winston wrote Jack the details:

> . . . On my return I think I shall go to the Ritz Hotel, & please ask Mamma to engage me a bedroom, a bathroom, & a comfortable sitting room, & to make the vy best terms she can with the Manager. She should tell them that if they make me comfortable & do not charge me too much I will in all probability stay a month, but if they overcharge me I will clear out at once & tell everybody what robbers they are. . . . P.S. Show this to Mamma with my best love.[83]

Jennie answered:

> I came here on Sat, Jack being here & George still abroad. . . . How I wish you cd have taken George with you. He needs an open-air life. This City grind is very hard for him. . . . I am longing to get you back—but it is cold & gray here. Stay away as long as you can is my advice. . . .[84]

George returned from St. Moritz "a little better," but he needed an operation on his nose. "Poor fellow, he never seems to be out of the hospital," Jennie wrote.[85] Jennie herself was not in the best of health. "I feel like a boiled gooseberry," she wrote Winston in January 1908. "How I wish I could have gone to Paris to meet you!"[86] And, five days later: "Do telegraph . . . the actual day & hour you arrive that your 'Mommer' may be there. . . ."[87]

In the spring of 1908, not many months after Winston's return, Prime Minister Campbell-Bannerman did have to resign because of ill health. His successor was H. H. Asquith, a shrewd, unimaginative stubborn Yorkshireman, who could also be genial and tactful when he wanted. His wife was the brilliant Margot Asquith, a friend of Jennie and Winston. The new Asquith Cabinet included Winston as President of the Board of Trade. New Ministers, however, were then required by law to stand again in a by-election.

The weekend of his appointment, Winston attended a party his mother gave at Salisbury Hall. One of the guests was Clementine Hozier. Clementine's father had been Sir Henry Montague Hozier, a flamboyant, brilliant military man who had died the previous year. He had separated from his wife so many years before that he hadn't even listed his marriage in *Who's Who*. His wife, Lady Blanche, had known Jennie in earlier years,[88] and Jennie's brother-in-law John Leslie was Clementine's godfather.

Winston had first seen Clementine when she was nineteen. They were at a dance at Lady Crewe's in 1904, and Winston asked his mother if she knew the girl. Jennie said she didn't but would find out about her. It was then that she discovered Clementine was the daughter of her old friend, "whom I haven't seen for years."[89]

Jennie then introduced Winston to Clementine. "Winston just stared," Clementine later said. "He never uttered one word, and was very gauche– He never asked me for a dance, he never asked me to have supper with him. I had of course heard a great deal about him–nothing but ill. I had been told he was stuck-up, objectionable, etc. And on this occasion he just stood and stared."[90]

Two years before, Winston had demonstrated his gaucherie with another young woman, Violet Asquith. After a long silence, he suddenly asked her how old she was. She replied that she was nineteen. Almost despairingly, Winston said that he was already thirty-two–"Younger than anyone else who *counts,* though." And then he added, "We are all worms, but I do believe I am a glow-worm."[91]

The next time Winston met Clementine was in March 1908 at a party given by her great-aunt, Lady St. Helier. On this occasion Winston did speak to her, asking if she had read his recent biography of his father. She had not. "If I send you the book tomorrow, will you read it?" She said she would. But he never sent the book, and that, too, made a less than favorable impression.[92]

Now on April 12th, at Salisbury Hall, here was Clementine again. Four days later he wrote her:

> I am back here for a night and a day in order to "kiss hands" on appointment, & I seize this fleeting hour of leisure to write & tell you how much I liked our long talk on Sunday and what a comfort & pleasure it was to me to meet a girl with so much intellectual quality & such strong reserves of noble sentiment. I hope we shall meet again and come to know each other better and like each other more: and I see no reason why this should not be so. Time passes quickly and the six weeks you are to be abroad will soon be over. Write therefore and tell me what your plans are, how your days are occupied, & above all when you are coming home. Meanwhile I will let you know from time to time how I am getting on here in the storm; and we may lay the foundations of a frank and clear-eyed friendship which I certainly should value and cherish with many serious feelings of respect.

So far the Manchester contest has been quite Napoleonic
in its openings & development. The three days I have been in
the city have produced a most happy change in the spirits of
my friends. . . .[93]

Despite his "Napoleonic" campaign, Winston was defeated in the Manchester election[94] and had to run again for a safer seat, the working-class
district of Dundee. He won overwhelmingly. He had openly attacked the
Conservative Party, saying, "It is filled with old, doddering peers, cute financial magnates, clever wire-pullers, big brewers with bulbous noses. All
the enemies of progress are there—weaklings, sleek, smug, comfortable, self-
important individuals."[95] He also presented his views of the virtues of Liberalism in contrast with Socialism:

Socialism wants to pull down wealth. Liberalism seeks to
raise up poverty. Socialism would destroy private interests—
Liberalism would preserve them in the only way they could
justly be preserved, by reconciling them with public right. . . .
Socialism attacks capital, Liberalism attacks monopoly.[96]

Jack also had good news. His firm had guaranteed him a sufficient income to allow him to make marriage plans, and on August 7, 1908, Winston wrote Clementine:

Jack has been married today—*civilly*. The service is tomorrow at Oxford; but we all swooped down in motor-cars upon
the little town of Abingdon and did the deed before the
Registrar—for all the world as if it was an elopement—with
irate parents panting on the path. Afterwards we were shown
over the Town Hall & its relics and treasures—quite considerable for so small a place—& then back go bride & bridegroom
to their respective homes until tomorrow. Both were "entirely
composed" & the business was despatched with a celerity &
ease that was almost appalling.[97]

On the next day, again from Abingdon, Winston wrote:

My Dear,
I have just come back from throwing an old slipper into
Jack's departing motor car. It was a vy pretty wedding. No
swarms of London fly-catchers. No one came who did not really care, & the only spectators were tenants & country-folk.

> Only children for bridesmaids & Yeomanry with crossed swords for pomp. The bride looked lovely & her father & mother were sad indeed to lose her. But the triumphant Jack bore her off amid showers of rice & pursuing cheers—let us pray—to happiness & honour all her life.[98]

As Jennie had predicted, Winston would be "the next to pop off." He lost little time in coming to his decision and planned to propose to Clementine at Blenheim Palace, his birthplace.

> Let us all go to Blenheim for Monday & Tuesday & then go on Wednesday to Salisbury Hall. Sunny wants us all to come & my mother will look after you—and so will I. I want so much to show you that beautiful place & in its gardens we shall find lots of places to talk in, & lots of things to talk about. My mother will have already wired you. . . .[99]

At first Clementine was reluctant to go, but finally she did. Her mother did not accompany her, so Jennie was the chaperone. Winston took Clementine for a walk in the late afternoon. It started to rain and they took shelter in an ornamental temple overlooking the lake. There he proposed, and she accepted.

Jennie confided the secret to her friend Mary Crichton, saying, "You see my Winston is not *easy*; he is very difficult indeed and she is just right."[100]

A short time later Jennie received a letter from Clementine's grandmother, Countess of Airlie, who said, "I thank you for your loving welcome to her. I hope she will be all you can desire as a wife for your son. . . . Blanche is an old friend of yours. So she will not be quite among strangers. . . ."[101] And to Winston, Countess Airlie wrote, ". . . Your mother has welcomed her so heartily, this will add to her happiness and she will learn much from her. . . ." And then she added a thoughtful note: ". . . A good son is a good husband. . . ."[102]

Winston later wrote: "We were married on Sept. 12, 1908—and lived happily ever afterwards."[103]

The wedding took place at St. Margaret's Church in London. The bride wore a lovely veil of point de Venise lace that Jennie had worn at her own wedding.[104]

Jennie was gowned in "golden beaver-colored satin charmeuse, made in the exacting princess style that is so merciless to the hips of middle-aged women. The gown was finished with the widest of metal embroideries. The hat was of satin antique of the same color, with large velvet and satinpetaled lilies in metallesque coloring with bronze and silver centres, around the brim."[105]

> As the widow of "Randy" and the mother of "Winny" swept up the aisle on the arm of her strapping son John there was a murmur of admiration among the crowded pews which the appearance of the bride herself quite failed to evoke.
>
> It seems too cruel to say, [but] his mother seemed the junior of the bride by at least two years. . . .[106]

It was a gratifying compliment for the fifty-four-year-old Jennie. The day after the wedding, she received another compliment, this one from Winston at Blenheim:

> Dearest Mamma,
>
> Everything is vy comfortable & satisfactory in every way down here, & Clemmie vy happy & beautiful. The weather a little austere, with gleams of sunshine; we shall long for warm Italian suns. There is no need for any anxiety. She tells me she is writing you a letter. Best of love, my dearest Mamma. You were a great comfort & support to me at a critical period in my emotional development.
>
> We have never been so near together so often in a short time. God bless you.
>
> What a relief to have got that ceremony over! & so happily.
>
> Your loving son,
> W.
>
> P.S. I open this letter again to tell you that George said he could wish me no better wife or happier days than he had found in you.
>
> W.[107]

Thirty-Seven

*J*ENNIE BECAME A GRANDMOTHER TWICE IN 1909: a boy for Jack and Goonie in May, and a girl for Winston and Clemmie six weeks later. But she neither felt nor looked like a grandmother.

For a while the quiet country life had agreed with her, but her energy and imagination could not long be confined to the peace of flowers and fireplaces. Soon she found herself again at the storm center of international society. Mrs. William Astor had expressed her views on New York Society for the press and Jennie's reply in the New York *World* was splashed on the front page:

> Modern society, and what is vulgarly dubbed the "smart set," both in New York and in London, are constantly being arraigned, criticized and judged before tribunals which often are obliged to form opinions of their merits or demerits from the outside–perhaps, if the truth were known, secretly envying their *"joie de vivre"* and their so-called wicked ways. . . .
>
> The best society does not necessarily mean the "smart set." It certainly does not in London, and lately in an interview which has aroused much interest on both sides of the Atlantic, Mrs. William Astor tells us that the women who have the greatest influence and who give New York Society

its tone are almost unknown outside their own circle. Her views are expressed most freely as to the iniquities of certain would-be fashionable women whose empty lives and ostentatious, not to say vulgar, entertainments are naturally condemned by all sensible and right-thinking people. The glorified and detailed accounts of some of these senseless festivities, as given by the press, although probably exaggerated, have brought blushes to the cheeks of their compatriots abroad, who have been mercilessly chaffed on the "strange doings" of their country people. We read of pink luncheons and violet teas, pale-blue dinners where the sauces match the hostess' gowns (shades of Lucullus!), and where everything is blue except the conversation, red suppers and freak dinners where the guests are invited to sit on horses and imagine they are in the hunting field, or in a gondola and fancy themselves in Venice. . . .

. . . No one likes to have their shortcomings pointed out to them, and on social matters, we Americans are proverbially sensitive. If we are too proud to be led by anyone, our good sense ought to help us to know that we are not infallible, and that there is nothing derogatory in learning. Of all nationalities, Americans are the best in adapting themselves. With them, to see is to know—and to know is to conquer.

We are told that the most refined and cultured in New York Society find exclusiveness an absolute necessity. There is no doubt where there is no recognized authority—no "fountainhead," so to speak—Society tends to break up into different sets, each a law unto itself, and looking down on the others as vastly inferior. This is the case in Paris, where since the Republic there has been no recognized head. New York Society is so small compared to the great numbers which comprise that of London, it seems incredible that those women, who, by their assured position and knowledge of the world would have the right to speak, should not be able to wield some authority on matters of taste.

Perhaps, if they opened their doors a little wider, their influence, not to say example, might be felt. In England, Society is easier of access than in any other place in the world, being built on broader and more solid foundations, and a long-established order of things has made people less apprehensive of having their privileges encroached upon or their position shaken, and can afford to receive whom they please, and, be it said to their credit, in the most exclusive of charmed circles, individual merit is more appreciated than rank or fortunes. Beauty and charm in a woman, and brains and good fellowship in a man will take them where dull duchesses and rich bores seek in vain to enter. You may be a princess or the richest woman in the world, but you cannot be more than a lady, and surely, this ought to be a passport all over the world.

In the interview already quoted, exception is taken to the manners of some of the United States Senators and Representatives who are so uncouth, it is averred, that they could not possibly be received in the best houses. Of these, I am not in a position to speak. In the older country, brains cover a multitude of sins, and those possessing them are received everywhere, in spite sometimes of their lack of manners. Nature's "gentleman" is quite in the ascendant today, and people forgive want of knowledge of customs and usages, which, after all, are but conventionalities, if the man who has made his way is clever and has what the French so admirably described as a *"politesse du coeur."* . . .

Taking modern society of the present day as a whole, . . . although undoubtedly in many ways deserving of criticism and even censure, is it really more pleasure-seeking and extravagant than that of other generations? I do not think so. One has but to study history to realize that in many respects this generation compares very favorably with the eccentricities and wild extravagances of past generations. It will not be denied that the majority of women are better educated than formerly, and that a larger view of life is open to them. In England, the most frivolous of social butterflies has her earnest and serious occupations, even if they be few and far between, and most are imbued with a certain desire to appear *au fait,* of the questions of the day. In this, she is better off than her cousin across the sea, to whom politics are a sealed letter, and who is restricted in rationally spending her money by having fewer outlets.

In concluding these remarks, which with diffidence I have ventured to make, I feel it may be said that my long absence from my own country incapacitated me from being a fair critic. But I have followed with the keenest interest any controversy affecting American women. I am sure that if, on this social question, some are making mistakes, it is only a passing phase which, with their good sense of the fitness of things and proverbial intelligence, can soon be put right.[1]

The *World* article aroused a rage of protest in America. New York Society matrons accused Jennie of "talking through her millinery." Mrs. Oliver Hazard Perry Belmont, the mother of the Duchess of Marlborough, said she would give Jennie's comments "the notice we would give some autumn leaf which tries, as it flutters to the earth, to attract attention."[2] And Mr. John B. Baker, an American millionaire who had spent forty years abroad, called Jennie's criticism "distinctly un-American, not to say unpatriotic."[3]

Jennie thoroughly enjoyed the fuss, but she was thankful that comments she received about her *Reminiscences* were less caustic. It was a pleasant, unpretentious book. She had written nothing about her love life, her frustrations, her relationship with her sons. But it was a successful book and went through several editions, both in England and the United States.

Her success spurred her on to playwriting. Her love of the theater was an old love, and she had written and acted in a dozen amateur theatricals at her friends' country houses, from Sandringham to Blenheim.

She had started writing her first full-length play in August 1903. She was staying at Blenheim while George went shooting in Wales, and he wrote her: "I am glad you are working at your play. Stick to it." But apparently she did not do much on it at that time, because, in July 1909, she told a reporter:

> Whatever be the play's fault, and I am quite prepared to hear that they are many, it is, at any rate, my first dramatic effort. It was written in a single week, in the country, some two years ago. For one reason or another—partly because I was called away to write my book of reminiscences—it has been left lying idle in the meantime. But in that one week, it was undeniably written.[4]

Perhaps. However, Jennie had often complained that she wrote slowly, almost painfully. But regardless of the time it took, it was a venture that required courage. No less a literary lion than Henry James had met disaster with his first play[5]—it had been well acted, spendidly mounted, but a stupendous failure. When the leading man took his bow, he was hooted and jeered. He told the audience how pained he was at the rebuff, how hard the company had worked to do justice to the play. "T'aint your fault, Guv'nor," called a voice in the gallery, "It's the rotten play."[6]

The Victorian Age, generally, had been a stagnant period for English theater. Although it had produced a score of great novelists and poets, it had not produced a playwright of distinction until the early Shaw.[7] In contrast, the Edwardian period produced the best work of Sir Arthur Wing Pinero, George Bernard Shaw, John Galsworthy; and the Irish theater yielded many writers of talent, including J. M. Synge. Furthermore, repertory theater in the provinces was in its full flower. ". . . Since the beginning of the century, a great number and a greater variety of plays have been produced in the English language than in any other," wrote theater historian William Archer.[8]

Despite the variety, it was generally an age of "teacup-and-saucer" plays, frivolous and witty. It usually took four acts for a gentleman, having triumphed over his rivals, to be accepted by the lady.

"The theaters are abominable," wrote Daisy, Princess of Pless.

> No theater is prosperous, or a play complete, unless there is a bedroom scene in the second act; the hero is always in bed with his wife or his *vieille amie,* his *ancienne cocotte*; and then they get out of bed and dress on the stage; he puts on his trousers, she her drawers and stockings; one cannot help laughing, but the "tone" of the whole thing is horrible.[9]

Pearl Craigie had had a different view: "The British public does not care about verbal wit, and must have emotion and intensity and action."[10] But her own plays were successful,[11] and so were the serious plays of Shaw,[12] Galsworthy, Synge, and Maugham. Somerset Maugham's *Smith,* was described by a critic as "In many ways, the best of his plays, although the fact that his central character is a servant somewhat lowers the standard of his comedy."[13] Clerks and greengrocers, artists and landladies could figure in farce, perhaps, and provide "comic relief" in melodrama, but were not thought worthy to appear as main characters in drawing-room comedy. In *Smith,* Maugham allowed an honest, hardworking parlormaid to win the love of a pioneer returned from Rhodesia.

The Edwardian period was exceptionally distinguished for its acting. Much of it, no doubt, was what we might now consider "hammy." An actor let himself go, spoke his words with a relish, and used all kinds of flourishing gestures.

"Mrs. Pat"—Beatrice Stella Campbell—was one of the great theatrical stars of the Edwardian era, together with Sarah Bernhardt, Eleanora Duse,[14] and Ellen Terry.[15] She was a sultry, striking beauty and an actress with perfect diction and dramatic intensity. She acquired sudden fame with her role in Pinero's *The Second Mrs. Tanqueray* in 1893, and throughout the rest of her career played every major part from Juliet to Lady Macbeth. A high-strung woman herself, she preferred playing women who were high-strung, complex, fascinating, magnificent, and she played them with "a glorious flamboyance." "The rich drift of the black hair, the movements in the full-skirted costume, feline in their grace. And the husky voice . . . infinitely suggestive of nervous strain within, and yet soothing in its sheer beauty. . . ."[16]

She was known to startle her leading men on stage by sticking pins into them; she smoked long cigars, and George Bernard Shaw, along with a host of other men, was in love with her.[17]

Her husband, Patrick Campbell, had been killed in the Boer War, leaving Mrs. Pat with two children. Her daughter was old enough to share the stage with her, and in 1908 they had a highly successful American tour together. They had also appeared with Dublin's renowned Abbey Theater players in William Butler Yeats's *Deirdre*. Mrs. Campbell admitted to being forty-four years old in 1909—eleven years younger than Jennie. She and Jennie had much in common: their attitudes, their beauty, their aura of excitement, their way of life. And it may well have been George who recommended to Jennie that she engage Mrs. Pat as actress-manager.

In his memoirs, George claims to have first met Mrs. Patrick Campbell in the winter of 1909, when she "became a constant visitor to the house." "Besides being a very beautiful woman," he said, "she was a brilliant conversationalist, and had a keen sense of humour and a ready wit."[18] But in a letter to her husband several years earlier, Clara Frewen had written: ". . . Leonie says Jennie seems so happy and contented, so I do hope George's little flirt with Mrs. Pat Campbell means nothing. . . ."[19]

Jennie told Mrs. Pat about her play, *His Borrowed Plumes*, at a luncheon party.[20] "She read the play to me," Mrs. Pat said.

> It had certain points of cleverness, and I considered that, with ingenious production and good actors, it could be pulled together, and perhaps made into a success.
>
> Feeling it would be a friendly act and an amusing piece of work for me, I offered to produce it for her.
>
> So it was eventually arranged.[21]

There is a play within a play in *His Borrowed Plumes*. The heroine, Fabia Sumner (Mrs. Campbell) has written the scenario of a novel. The "other woman," Angela Cranfield, steals it and hopes to steal Fabia's husband, Major Percival Sumner, too. Angela gives Fabia's manuscript to the Major (he does not suspect its source), and he uses it as the basis of a play of his own. The last act takes place in the ante-room of the National Theatre. Through a door leading into a stage-box, we get a view of the auditorium, and hear the actors declaiming and the audience cheering and calling for the author. Before he faces the audience, the Major makes his peace with his wife. Then he announces to the theater audience that his wife, and not he, is the real author of the play, and that he has been masquerading "in borrowed plumes."

"My adventuress [Angela Cranfield] is not quite the cut-and-dried villainess that she seems to have appeared to some people," Jennie told a reporter.

> She is not supposed to steal the manuscripts in cold blood. It was a sort of half-accidental deed, done without full intention, in a moment of outraged pride. She is just such a woman as is to be found again and again in London Society.[22]
>
> It is these little refinements of temperament that are so difficult to express unerringly, definitely, obviously, on the stage. But that, again, is what gives writing for the stage its fascination. It is so tempting to try the most difficult thing possible.
>
> As to sheer facts, perhaps, the best answer to anyone who disagrees with them is that the story, in its main details, happens to be a true one. Some of my scenes I know are more melodramatic than the vogue is, but I admit being old-fashioned in these matters. I myself have grown rather tired of plays that are all talk. Personally, I like something to happen, so I just did my best to be dramatic in the old-fashioned way.
>
> . . . In drama it is more difficult than in almost any other art to express exactly what one means to express. There are so many things in between one's own mind and that of the audience.[23]

Friends found it interesting to speculate how much of George was in Major Sumner, and how much of Jennie in Fabia.

> *Fabia:* . . . I'm always leaving my work to fly about after him. (*After a pause*): Better if I did it more often. He does love Society.
>
> *Basil:* I'm not surprised, he's so popular.
>
> *Fabia:* But you see, he doesn't realize how slowly I write, how easily I lose the thread of my ideas. It takes time to start the machine again.
>
> *Fabia (collecting notes):* Oh dear, I have intended writing such a lot this week, but these parties upset one's train of thought.
>
> *Basil:* You wonder you are handicapped, leading this ridiculous life, trying to write in a hotel, with people in and

out all day, expeditions, river parties, and near enough to London to have a crowd today? . . . How can you work? You ought never to have come.

Fabia: It amuses Percival. I couldn't let him come alone.

And then, later:

Fabia: But am I not the one to blame? I feel I don't enter into Percival's plans and amusements half enough.

Jane: But how can you, with your work? He has more time for frivolities. He doesn't write half as much as you do.

Fabia: Ah, that's just it! I believe my writing so much bores him. And if it does, what's it all worth to me?

Jane: I don't think he's bored—but jealous.

Fabia (impetuously): My dear Jane, what nonsense you talk! Percival jealous! Your affection for me makes you unjust. How could he be jealous? To begin with, our work is so different.

Jane (sulkily): The real difference in this case is that you are successful, and he isn't.

Discussing Fabia's husband, two men say:

Walter: . . . He is gay and light-hearted.

Martin: Large-hearted, you mean.

Walter: And very generous to the fair sex, I am told. You must own, physically he is a fine type of a man.

Martin (shakes head): . . . Insists on being the center figure, wherever he is. Must have the first place, and the prettiest woman to talk to. Look at him now.

(Percival in the background, surrounded by several of the ladies.)

Mrs. Cranfield (to Fabia): If I had your brains, I too would not indulge in frivolity. When you can command all the cleverest people in London to come to you, why should you seek them in a crowd? *(She goes on.)*

How I envy your position. I mean, your supreme independence. You can do without Society. If you had half a dozen lovers, and tomorrow elected to run away with one of them, all your clever world would rally around you—They are tolerant, understanding and open-minded—"Natural selection— affinity of souls," they would say. You'd find no difference.

Mrs. Cranfield: I take my happiness where I find it—stolen or otherwise.

Basil tells Fabia that Mrs. Cranfield is just a passing fancy for Percival.

Fabia: Perhaps so, but he may think he cares, which comes to the same thing. She is clever and unscrupulous, and her influence is already altering him.
Basil: Altering him? How?
Fabia: He has become restless and anxious, and what is worse, to ease his conscience, I suppose, he likes to dwell on my shortcomings. . . .
Basil: But remember, a man ends by hating the woman who he thinks has found him out.

Somebody asks Martin how Percival and Fabia get on.

Martin: I fancy as well as most married couples who have lived together for ten years. If you can stand that strain, it ought to last forever. . . .
Alma: I rather suspect her of being in love with him.
Martin: Her own husband? Monstrous! What a selfish woman!
Fabia (discussing a visiting actress): You think that she and my husband are too much together?
Jane: You're so occupied you don't see what all your world does. Among snakes, that woman is a puff-adder.
Fabia (with a bitter laugh): Are you so sure that I do not see—that I don't know?[24]

If Jennie did know, she didn't show it. ". . . The rehearsals are getting on," she wrote Leonie,

and this week there are to be two daily. Mrs. Pat has really been an angel, and the Play would not exist without her. . . . I can't understand why I feel so calmly about the Play. Bernstein tells me he's *dans les trances* for weeks beforehand. Perhaps I do not know the horrors before me! I gave a supper party at the Ritz last Friday, too successful for words. . . . Kitty, Ann, Consuelo, Juliette, Violet Rutland, and Mrs. Pat, Stella [her daughter], Muriel Wilson, Henry Ainley, Yates, Hugh Cecil, Bernstein, Martha Bibesco, Maurice Baring, Milwood (my

leading gentleman), Clare [Frewen], Winston and Jack, etc.,
We kept it up till 2:30 AM. A hundred wild dances and fan-
dangos . . . everyone taking the floor . . . [25]

However much Mrs. Pat may have enjoyed the party and Jennie's
appreciation of her, she afterward expressed a colder view of the situation:

> An exaggerated importance gradually grew around the
> production, owing to Royalty and many distinguished peo-
> ple being interested in it.
> Serious work became difficult—but was most mandatory
> to hold the play together—some of the actors started calling
> the play, "Sorrowing Blooms"—a dangerous sign.
> Jennie, I fancy, imagined producing her own play would
> be of some social advantage to all of us: I was intolerant of
> what I thought nonsense, and showed it quickly.[26]

Nonetheless, Mrs. Pat let Jennie design one of the scenes in the play—
the ante-room behind the Royal Box at the National Theatre. It was a room
Jennie knew well. She herself supplied the Elizabethan furniture and decorations.

The opening matinee at Hicks' Theatre in London on July 6, 1909 was in
the old tradition of splendor, "one of the most brilliant audiences of the season." Winston Churchill, President of the Board of Trade, "looking profoundly nervous," sat in a box with his mother and his stepfather, Mr. George
Cornwallis-West.[27] There was no mention of Jack, but he surely was there.

In the opposite box was the Dowager Duchess of Manchester, and
among the audience were Prince Francis of Teck, Grand Duke Michael of
Russia, the Duchesses of Marlborough, Rutland, and Roxburghe, Earl
Howe, Lord Elcho, Lord Charles Beresford, Mrs. Asquith, and a score of
other celebrities and well-known peeresses—complete with their tall wide-
brimmed hats and their Directoire gowns. Mr. Walkley, in *The Times* was
amusing about the hats:

> When mundane ladies—if the Gallicism may pass—when
> mundane ladies produce original, modern comedies out of
> their own original, modern, and quite charming heads, all of
> the other mundane ladies who have written original, modern
> comedies themselves, or might have done so if they had cho-
> sen, or are intending to do so the very next wet afternoon,
> come and look on. These are the occasions that reconcile one
> to the theatre. For a sudden feminine glory invades it and

transfigures it, so that it becomes an exhibition of beauty and elegance; the very latest dialogue on the stage is accompanied by a *frou-frou* of the very latest Paris fashions in the stalls. An especially pleasing detail is the air of sweet resignation—Is it the firm composure of the martyr or the serene smile of the seraph?—with which the ladies remove the wide-brimmed and very high-crowned hats of the present fashion from their heads and pose them very delicately upon their knees. It is with an effort you avert your gaze from this fascinating spectacle to the proceedings on the stage. But this is only to exchange one pleasure for another of the same sort. On the stage you have a bevy of ladies supporting—beautiful caryatides that they are!—the same remarkable hats, with the privilege of not having to remove them. In the presence of so many, and so beautifully complicated hats, it is, of course, impossible to think of them as mere coverings for the head. They really fulfill the really important office of creating an illusion about life, like the poetry of Shelley or the music of Debussy. With their exaggerated brims and monstrous crowns they completely shut out the dull, the workaday, and the disagreeable. Everything you feel is for the best, and looking its best, and wearing its best in the best of all Directoire worlds.

And yet, by a sort of paradox, what was perhaps the most beautiful thing, but was certainly the most suave and distinguished thing in the Hicks' Theatre yesterday afternoon—we mean, of course, Mrs. Patrick Campbell—wore no hat. . . .

Some of the performers had not properly adjusted their voices to the theater's acoustics, and several times they were loudly commanded by the audience to "speak up." Mr. Dawson Milward, in the role of an amateur dramatist, had to make a derogatory remark concerning his actors. "They speak so naturally," he said, "that not a word gets over the footlights." The audience roared with laughter. But at the end, they called "author, author" and Jennie took her bow "amid much cheering."

By and large, the critics also enjoyed themselves. One wrote:

> . . . a new dramatist's first play is terribly like the curate's first sermon—very portentous and self-conscious, laden with long-bottled message to mankind at large. "His Borrowed Plumes" has proved so entirely different, so free and light-hearted, that it has seemed in some ways difficult to believe that it could be a first play at all.[28]

He went on to praise "the unburdened brightness of its dialogue and the undercurrent of cheery satire upon the foibles of either sex that lies beneath the dramatic scenes . . ."

In *The Era* the reviewer wrote:

> Mrs. Cornwallis-West's play opened badly, owing to an accident of acoustics; but it was soon evident that she has a real gift and instinct as a dramatist, and "His Borrowed Plumes" took a firm hold on the interest of the audience, and maintained it to the close of the performance.[29]

Plays are meant to be seen, not read. Much of what Jennie wrote, and the manner in which she wrote it, seems dated, almost archaic, now. But one can sense the characters—they are not cardboard. And the parallel to Jennie's life gives the play an added dimension.

The most perceptive review came from the distinguished Max Beerbohm:

> Now, from the standpoint of the average simple play-goer, "His Borrowed Plumes" is a very good entertainment. From the standpoint of the purely technical critic, it is a very good piece of work: a story conceived and set forth clearly, without halting, with a thorough grasp of dramatic form. From the standpoint of a critic who desires an illusion of real life, it does not pass muster. The characters have been sacrificed to the story. Now and again, as in the scene between the two jealous women, the characters emerge and are natural, real and moving. There is much that rings true in the relations of Mrs. Cranfield and the Major. But, for the rest, Mrs. Cornwallis-West has let herself be led into the temptation that awaits everyone who essays dramaturgy for the first time—the temptation to write not as a seer of life, but as a playgoer who knows all about the theater. I conjure her not to bother, henceforth, about what she thinks is needed to make a good play, but rather to let her characters do just as they would in real life. Having, as she evidently has, an instinct for dramatic form, she need not fear for the result of this process. . . . [30]

Jennie seemed exhilarated by the reaction. "Criticism is exactly what I want, and the more candid the better," she told a reporter. "Although this is my first play, I am not by any means determined that it shall be my last. . . . [31]

In those days, even a good play often ran only a couple of weeks. *Hedda Gabler* and *Electra,* and even *Deirdre,* with the splendid Mrs. Campbell, only played a few special matinees. *His Borrowed Plumes* lasted almost a fortnight.

Jennie's young nephew, Seymour Leslie, later admitted that he had seen the play five times, but the only line he remembered was: "Mary has had a *fausse-couche.*"[32] There were, however, a number of trenchant lines that were given wide circulation:

> "We could all dress well if we could afford not to wear our failures."

> "Is there so much difference between politicians and actors? Both are equally eager for popular applause, both equally doubtful whether they will get it."

> "All natures are in nature."

> "What is love without passion?–A garden without flowers, a hat without feathers, tobogganing without snow."

> "Italians love–sun, sin and spaghetti."

> "Those sincere women are generally very sly."

She would later remember some of those lines with pain. Her attitude now, though, was just short of smug. "After all," she wrote Leonie, "and I say this without conceit but as a fact, if I were to die tomorrow, of all the 'Souls' lot, I am the only woman who should have a record behind her. The Primrose League, the Maine hospital ship, the Anglo-Saxon Review, my book, my play!"[33]

Her record soon would be longer than that.

Thirty-Eight

*I*N 1909, COLONEL LOUIS BLERIOT had made the first airplane flight across the English Channel. The automobile was rapidly replacing the horse-drawn carriage. More homes and factories were being lit by electricity instead of gas. Increased industrialization had given trade unions pivotal political strength, maintaining the Liberals in power, and pushing new social and tax reforms. When the House of Lords threatened to use its veto on the proposed budget the Liberals urged a reduction of the power of the Lords. "The House of Lords is not the watchdog of the Constitution," said Lloyd George, "it is Mr. Balfour's poodle." "The House of Lords represent nobody but themselves," added Augustine Birrell.[1]

One of the loudest voices against the Lords was the new Home Secretary,[2] Winston S. Churchill, who had been appointed to the post in February 1910. Winston warned that "the whole machinery of representative government had been brought to a standstill," and that "the Tory party regard themselves as the ruling class, exercising by right a Divine superior authority over the whole nation." He demanded "a fair and equal Constitution," which could only be possible when "the harsh and cruel veto," of the Upper House had been shattered into fragments, "so that they were dust upon the ground."[3]

Conservatives bitterly attacked Churchill as "a traitor to his class." A new general election in 1910—the second in twelve months—returned the

Liberals to government control but by a greatly reduced margin. They were now dependent for political survival on the support of the Irish Nationalist vote in Parliament.

Jennie earlier had written to her nephew Shane Leslie, who was deeply involved in Irish politics: "Two Sundays ago, Lord Crewe, Mr. Lloyd George, Mr. Birrell and Winston came down . . . quite a Cabinet council! In fact, they did hold an informal one on the Irish question. I wish you had been here. . . ."[4]

Besides the Lords, the Irish question, the threat of strikes, and the suffragettes, the political situation was also troubled by the specter of a powerful Germany and the renewed threat of war. But the popular song said:

> There'll be no wo'ar
> As long as there's a King like Good King Edward.
> There'll be no wo'ar
> For 'e 'ates that sort of thing.
> Mothers need not worry,
> As long as we've a King like Good King Edward.
> Peace with 'onour
> Is his motter,
> So God Save the King.

Edward paid his usual Spring visit to Biarritz that year, but a short while after his return, he became critically ill. He told his equerry, Frederick Ponsonby, "I can't sleep. I can't eat. They really must do something for me." Then as Ponsonby left, the King said, "In case I don't see you again, goodbye."[5] By the next day he had died.

When the King was dying, Queen Alexandra sent a brougham to fetch Mrs. Alice Keppel, and Alexandra herself waited to take her up to Edward's bedroom. She left her alone with him for a long time.[6]

Jennie grieved for him, too. King Edward had been her supporter, an early love, and one of her oldest friends. His approval had eased Jennie's entry into British society when she was one of the first of the American brides of prominent Englishmen. And although he had strongly opposed it, it was he who had hastened the acceptance of Jennie's marriage to George. Even when Winston embittered the King by denouncing the House of Lords, Edward kept his friendship with Jennie intact. Moreover, Jennie's relationship with the King was responsible for her lifelong closeness with Sir Ernest Cassel—and it was Cassel who was instrumental in furthering Jack's career, who helped George get started in business, and who acted as financial advisor for Winston.

Circulating among the people in the streets were broadsheets announcing King Edward's death:

> Greatest Sorrow England Ever Had
> When Death Took Away Our Dear Dad;
> A King Was He from Head to Sole,
> Loved by his People, One and All.

"With King Edward's passing, we lost a lovable, wayward and human monarch," Sir Frederick Ponsonby wrote.

> He was one who came to decisions by instinct and not by logic, and rarely made a mistake in his judgment of men. On the whole, he preferred the society of the female sex, and was never happier than in the company of pretty women. He always thought a men's dinner party was tiresome and dull. I remember one Ascot Week, after the death of the King of Denmark, when it was decided to have a men's party, as Queen Alexandra was in mourning, and I happened to be with him when the list of guests was sent in to him on his arrival at Windsor. He looked at it and said with a sigh, "What tiresome evenings we shall have!"[7]

For three days the body of Edward VII lay on a raised catafalque in Westminster Hall, and at times the queue stretched unbroken for six miles. Every class of people was represented among the 250,000 mourners who filed past. The King's women friends made their final curtsies, the young Kings of Portugal and Spain knelt for a long time. Kaiser Wilhelm II came, preceded by an enormous wreath.[8]

In the funeral procession the King's saddle-horse was led behind the gun-carriage, and his dog Caesar was led by a valet.[9] At the head of the procession rode the new King, George V, in a field marshall's uniform, baton in hand.[10] Then came the King of Norway, the King of Greece, the King of Spain, followed by the Tsar of Bulgaria, the King of Denmark, the King of Portugal. The King of the Belgians rode behind the King of Denmark and between Archduke Ferdinand and the heir-apparent of the Ottoman Empire. Former President Theodore Roosevelt arrived just in time to represent the United States. (There had been some concern, because the American Ambassador was afraid that Roosevelt might wish to ride in the uniform of Colonel of the Rough Riders alongside the nine Kings who were to follow the coffin.)

The tribute that Edward VII would have appreciated most occurred at Ascot Week in July 1910, afterward referred to as the "Black Ascot."

> All the ladies admitted to the Royal Enclosure wore black feathers and ribbons in place of the usual flowers and gauzes. Their tall and slender figures, surmounted by enormous hats, were like weird blooms springing from the bright green lawns. It was on this race-course that the peace-loving King had won some of his greatest victories and passed the happiest hours. . . . The grandees of the Edwardian Era exchanged the latest items of news: "Mrs. Keppel has gone to China . . . ," "Queen Alexandra refuses to leave the palace . . . ," "Soveral has gone back to Portugal . . . ," "Lily Langtry has been ruined by racing debts. . . ."[11]

They might also have mentioned that Jennie Cornwallis-West had bought, redecorated, and sold another house.[12] It was her one sure way of making money. Her last venture along these lines had been so profitable that it drew high praise from Winston:

> I am so glad to hear of your excellent stroke of business. The utility of most things can be measured in terms of money. I do not believe in writing books which do not sell, or plays which do not pay. The only exceptions to the rule are productions which can really claim to be high art, appreciated only by the very few. Apart from that, money value is a great test. And I think it very creditable indeed that you should be able after two or three months' work, which you greatly enjoyed, to turn over as large a sum of money as a Cabinet Minister can earn in a year. There is no reason why the experiment should not be repeated. There are lots of other houses in London, and you will have learned a great deal more than you knew before of the latest methods of furnishing. I really think it would be well worth your while to look about for another venture of the same kind. Your knowledge and taste are so good and your eye for comfort and elegance so well trained, that with a little capital you ought to be able to make a lot of money, and if you sell a few more houses, you will be able, very nearly, to afford to produce another play. I am sure George admires your great cleverness over this house as much as I do.[13]

Through her interest in the theater Jennie was able to help Winston in an unexpected way. As Home Secretary, he was profoundly concerned with prison reform. Having seen John Galsworthy's play *Justice,* he told his mother how much he admired it, and Jennie arranged a small dinner party for Galsworthy and Winston, at which the two men could meet informally and talk at leisure. Churchill later said that Galsworthy's views deeply influenced his own action on prison reform.

Whether she could afford it or not, Jennie was thinking seriously about her second play. A newspaper announced that she planned to go to America to arrange for the production of a new play which dealt with "the uplifting of humanity" at the expense of personal domesticity. It added: "There is a possibility that Mrs. West may be induced to appear on a lecture platform in America, dealing with her own experiences in Society."

The announcement, it turned out, was premature. Jennie had a larger theatrical project in mind—the creation of a national theater. "As things are in London," she said, "the establishment even of a permanent repertory theater is really next-door to impossible without official and national status. . . . The more I see of our theaters, the more I am convinced of the need for the National School of Acting. . . ."[14]

Jennie helped organize a National Theatre Committee, coauthored a detailed report, "The National Theatre, Scheme and Estimate," and was largely responsible for raising most of the £30,000 ($150,000) to buy a site opposite the Victoria and Albert Museum. Then, when the National Theatre Committee merged with the Committee for a Shakespeare Memorial Theatre, the combined group turned to Jennie to act as Chairman of the new Executive Committee. She held their first meeting at Leonie's house.[15]

Quickly immersing herself in the cause, Jennie realized that the greatest and most immediate need was for funds, and her imagination conceived an idea: a Shakespearean Memorial National Theatre Ball at which all six hundred guests would be dressed in either Shakespearean or Tudor costume. Jennie decided to be Olivia from *Twelfth Night.*

The place: Royal Albert Hall. The date: June 20, 1911.

"It will rank with the Eglinton Tournament and the most famous masques of earlier ages," wrote H. Hamilton Fyfe.

> Those who were fortunate enough to see it have something to recollect all their lives. . . . For a few all-too-brief hours the magnificence of Tudor England was revived. Here were no tawdry stage costumes, no mere imitations of reality. Here was the real thing.
>
> Real satins and ermines, real silks and brocades, real gold and silver embroideries, real lace of the finest periods, were

cunningly employed to set off the beauty of the fairest
women in England. They made the Albert Hall glow with
rich color; they lent the scene a beauty which defied description. And among the sheen of wonderful stuffs, there was the
sparkle of jewels, real jewels, priceless heirlooms, glittering in
the hair of fair possessors, rising and falling on their bosoms,
clasping them with glittering girdles, or flashing from Elizabethan "stomachers" of a value beyond belief. . . .

. . . In 48 hours, the Albert Hall was transformed from its
habitual sombre Early Victorianism into an Italian garden. . . .

. . . The blue sky which hid the roof was a positive inspiration. It struck the note at once of gaiety and freedom from
care. It made everyone light-hearted and sunny-tempered.
People came in looking doubtful about enjoying themselves,
worried about their costumes perhaps, uncertain whether
late hours (dancing was from 11:00 to 5:30 A.M.) were not
a mistake. When they had recovered from the pleasant
shock of finding themselves in such a delightful place, they
had forgotten all their doubts and anxieties. They caught
the spirit of their surroundings. They dropped their self-
consciousness. They were infected with the Southern atmosphere. . . .

. . . The first tier of boxes . . . resembled bowers in the tall
hedge of clipped yew, with quaintly-fashioned birds topping
them, after the manner of old-world gardeners.

Over the next tier there appeared to be growing a noble
grapevine, above that the boxes were made to look as if they
formed part of a marble terrace. Then came slopes of green
turf, and on top of all a balcony, where supper was laid.

All round the hall, at the height of the balcony, a very fine
impression was made by tall, dark cypresses, standing erect
and dignified. . . .

The guests arrived with more than usual punctuality. By
a quarter to eleven, there was a string of carriages half a mile
long. . . .

. . . While the throng that covered the floor moved slowly
round and about between the dances, as if stirred by some gigantic, invisible spoon, the color effects were delicious. . . .

. . . Then, when a dreamy waltz began, or a lively two-
step, the whole arena broke into movement at once. The
kaleidoscope, which had been revolving slowly, slowly, was

given a brisker turn. The scene became more and more fascinating. The whirl of colors kept one simply breathless with delight.

And then, when the pageant of the Court of Queen Elizabeth began! The signal for clearing the hall was given by bugles. Upon a platform in front of the hidden organ, the Tudor Queen and her courtiers took up their places. Applause greeted Mrs. Arthur James [costumed as Queen Elizabeth] as she bowed with infinite dignity and condescension. Nearly all her Court were either direct descendants or the wives of direct descendants of the historical characters they played. They made a very splendid show as they ranged themselves round their Sovereign and settled down to watch the quadrilles and the procession of all the dancers, each group taking parts from one particular play, with additional companies of Amazons and Lovers, and a special quadrille of the famous people of Tudor times.

This is the period of the ball which will linger longest in the memory. It was like a dream of fair women. With graceful swayings and rhythmical steps, they went through the figures of their dance. There was a hush of admiration and delight. Alas! It was over too soon.

. . . It never could happen again. . . . Such a company of masqueraders could not be assembled twice. Such an array of spectators—boxes filled with royal persons, with the aristocracies of birth and brains and wealth; rows of great ladies glittering with diamonds of priceless worth—could not be twice drawn together in an age. . . . this age has shot its bolt. And whatever the future may conceal of splendour and beauty, it will certainly not outdo this.[16]

The date of the Ball had been synchronized with the coronation of George V, which took place on June 22nd. Clementine Churchill was a guest in the Royal box, but Jennie was not. London was ablaze with flares and fireworks, and the next night Jennie dined with Frederick Edwin Smith, later Earl of Birkenhead, "and walked out into the dark streets to see the gushing flares outside the clubs in Pall Mall."[17] Then Jennie and some friends motored down to Exbury for the Naval Review the following day.

During that summer of 1911, there were more rumbles of possible war with Germany, and in September Prime Minister Asquith easily persuaded Winston to switch Cabinet posts and become First Lord of the Admiralty.

Jennie meanwhile conceived another spectacular idea that would make her Shakespeare Ball seem just a prelude. The limitations of the Ball were that it had been evanescent–it had lived only for a single night–and it had been necessarily restricted to a small segment of the people, the titled and the rich. Why not create something more lasting and universal?

Her idea, simply, was to convert a section of London into an Elizabethan town. People would walk straight out of the twentieth century into the sixteenth. Jennie enlisted the help of Sir Edwin Lutyens, who had redesigned Albert Hall for the Ball, to ensure that the Elizabethan buildings would be authentic. Many of them would be reproductions of houses, churches, and town halls which were still in existence.

But the exposition would be more than buildings. There was to be the same kind of street life and street incidents that Shakespeare might have seen and from which he got so many ideas for incidents in his plays. Every trade was to be represented at work, as it might have been then. A model of the Globe Theatre would be built. A company of players would give performances daily, as in Shakespeare's time, except that the women's parts would be played by women, not by boys. There would even be "gallants" on the stage of the Globe and "groundlings" making comments from the pit. There also was to be a Fortune Playhouse for concerts of sixteenth-century music with sixteenth-century instruments. There would be open spaces for country dancing, and halls for the more formal Assembly Balls. And there would be sideshows, pageants, singing, and games. It would be called "Shakespeare's England."

The site selected was Earl's Court, a dilapidated part of London close to the Thames consisting of rundown houses and old theaters. Jennie's plan was to redecorate those existent buildings still usable and then build whatever else was needed.

To finance the vast project she wheedled an initial £40,000 from Cox's Bank, which was augmented by contributions wangled from her wealthy friends. "Another fifteen thousand pounds was necessary," George West later wrote, "and Jennie asked me to approach Mrs. W. B. Leeds, a great friend of mine and the widow of an American millionaire, who had left her everything he possessed. . . . I was loath to do so . . . however, I thought it over, studied the figures carefully, and came to the conclusion that, although there was an undoubted risk, if it was good enough for the bank . . . she might be justified in assisting my wife. . . ."[18]

George went to see Mrs. Leeds in Paris, and returned with the money. Mrs. Leeds' scarcely-concealed love for George was generally recognized in London society.

The London *Daily Mail* referred to Jennie now as "the busiest woman in London":

She has always been energetic. It is in her American blood. When she first came to England, as Lady Randolph Churchill, she gave London Society a fillip. Never has she been content to travel in a groove. But just now, she has in hand a scheme which is by far the biggest she has ever evolved.[19]

A few months later the *Daily Express* wrote:

A handsome, fashionably-dressed lady, with striking dark eyes and a notably strong chin, is standing in a hall the size of a railway station with half a dozen men. The lady is talking. The men are listening. She asks them questions, terse, straight to the point, and the answers are given equally directly.

She is Mrs. Cornwallis-West, the originator and tireless director of the "Shakespeare's England" Exhibition at Earl's Court. There is nothing amateurish about Mrs. West's management of this great Exhibition. There is nothing casual. Her staff are all experts, but she directs.

The features of the exhibition—the Globe Theatre, the "Revenge" and the rest—were her ideas. . . . She knows exactly what she wants, and she has a very shrewd idea how it is to be done. The big . . . hall, where an "Express" representative found her was the old Empress Theatre, the scene of "Savage South Africa" and many other famous shows, and Mrs. West was intent on arranging for a series of six-penny popular dances, which are to combine the staid joys of Elizabethan Morris dances with the wilder thrills of the 20th-century "Turkey Hug." The floor, the sitting-out accommodations, the refreshments, were all discussed. Mrs. West is nothing if not thorough.

How tireless she is may be gathered from the fact that she is at Earl's Court every morning at eleven, and that she stays there until late in the evening. She has a charming Tudor house in the grounds, and, for the moment, Earl's Court is her home.

As one talked with her and realized the enthusiasm with which she has approached her work and the complete grasp that she has of all of the details, one began to understand how very much Mr. Winston Churchill is the son of his mother. He may have inherited his political genius from his father, but he certainly owes to his American mother the superb energy and thoroughness with which he astounded the Board of Trade, appalled the Home Office, and is delighting the best elements at the Admiralty. [He had been appointed First Lord of the Admiralty in October 1911.] . . .

. . . Dances and tournaments in the Empress Hall do not monopolize Mrs. West's attention. There is the Globe Theatre to be considered, and here, among the "coming events" is an amateur performance of "The Midsummer Night's Dream," with Lady Lytton as Titania.

There is not a detail of the show that escapes her notice. The signs outside the Tudor shops are a particular hobby of hers. . . .

Mrs. West is an admirable example of the "idle rich." Earl's Court was practically derelict. She has revivified it, and, incidentally, is not only giving London a distinctive pleasure ground, but is finding employment for hundreds of workers. All this is done, not for profit or for popularity (Mrs. West's position is far too assured and distinguished for that), but from interest in a fine scheme, and also from the pure love of getting about and doing things.

Mrs. West is the friend of queens and empresses. She has been on intimate terms with most of the famous men and women of her generation. Her reminiscences are a sort of inside history of our own times. And she is spending her days walking about Earl's Court Exhibition, concerned with pleasure-planning and the proper observance of trifles.

It is all very wonderful, and, in a way, very inspiring.

How this masterful lady succeeds in looking after everything, in approaching just the right people, in carrying through all her thousand-and-one plans, is a little difficult to understand. But her chin is very strong, and she has the cool "nothing-will-flutter-me" aspect of the born organizer. Moreover, no time is wasted in unnecessary discussions and chatter.

She herself is the committee—assisted by subcommittees.

Mrs. West is not the least anxious to talk about her work. She is just keen to make the thing a memorable success, and success without work is impossible—and there is no more to be said. It is a new Earl's Court that she has called into being, and there is a new spirit in the place.[20]

The *Revenge* mentioned in the article was a full-size reproduction of one of the prize galleons in Sir Francis Drake's fleet, which defeated the Spanish

Armada in 1588. To prevent the *Revenge* from looking stagy, Jennie enlisted an historian who made sure that the ship's armor was copied from existing pieces, that sailors' breeches were fastened to their coats by hooks, and that the ship's interior was as accurate as its exterior—an expert had to be sent to Amsterdam and Nuremberg to copy the drawings of the interior.[21] To add further reality, the ship basin smelled of tar and there were fish stalls where real fish could be bought.

Jennie's idea of a jousting tourney, although not historically related to Elizabethan England, turned out to be the most fascinating of them all. Such a tourney was something that the English had not seen since the Ivanhoe period. The great Empress Hall was transformed into a replica of the courtyard of Warwick Castle, and Jennie persuaded a variety of Dukes and other nobility to squeeze into their family armor—or rent some—and play the parts of knights of old in jousts of combat.[22] They were to charge at each other with fourteen-foot-long wooden lances, and points were to be awarded according to where opponents were hit and whether they were unhorsed. Then there was to be a melee in which a dozen knights would go at each other with swords in an attempt to slice the plumes from each other's helmets.

To celebrate the opening of "Shakespeare's England," Jennie gave a series of parties at the Mermaid Tavern for groups of friends and European royalty.

Her guest book one night contained a surprise. The signature read simply: "C. Kinsky." His wife had died the year before. Not only was Kinsky a guest, but he also had agreed to be part of the entourage for the Princess Errant pageant. The Princess Errant was Daisy of Pless, George's sister. George, of course, was also at the party, and it must have been a most interesting evening for Jennie. It is easy to imagine her sparkling in the company; it is not so easy to conjure up her thoughts as her eyes wandered from George to Kinsky.

For the past few years George had not been a model husband. The affair with the ardent Mrs. Leeds had been but one among many. Much more serious was his persistent attention to Mrs. Campbell. As "Mrs. Pat" put it, "Then, in the unexpected way things sometimes happen in the world, George Cornwallis-West was seriously attracted by me. . . . I believed his life was unhappy, and warmly gave him my friendship and affection. . . . This caused gossip, misjudgment, and pain that cannot be gone into here. . . ."[23]

Shane Leslie had quoted from Stendahl, saying that "in France women watch each other, in Italy they watch the men." And, he might have added, in England they do both. Jennie herself said cynically to a friend, afterward, "No woman ever loved a good man."

Mrs. Pat may have been "a troubling enchanting enigma," as one theater critic said,[24] but she made George feel enormously important. Jennie was so immersed in her Shakespeare's England Exposition that George found himself filling only the odd corners of her life. There is little question that he resented her preeminence. In his novel *Two Wives,* one of the women is described:

> Everyone knew Lady Carsteen by name; as one of the few remaining Edwardian beauties, her photograph was often in the weekly illustrated press—Lady Carsteen at Newmarket; as chairman of the committee of some charity ball; or even selling flags in the foyer of the Cosmopolitan Hotel. . . . Like most silly people who arrive in a position in life which they have always hoped for but never expected, she had an exaggerated idea of her own importance. If she happened to find herself thwarted in some petty way by persons in an inferior position to her own, who were unacquainted with her, she had a habit of saying, "You don't appear to know who I am." . . .[25]

Jennie and George often quarreled bitterly now.

"He had fallen, in the first instance, to her physical charms," *Two Wives* explained, "and, when these became stale, had come positively to dislike his wife. He loathed rows and she loved them. Now, in middle age, he tolerated her. All he wanted was peace and quiet, and to be allowed to collect stamps without hindrance."[26]

George's stamps were guns, fishing equipment, and women, and for these he traveled far and often.[27] His and Jennie's absences from each other had become more frequent and prolonged. The Shakespeare exposition was the breaking point. In Jennie's guest book at the Mermaid Tavern someone had written, "Oh, lady Fortune, stand you auspicious . . . ," but it was, unfortunately, a fanciful hope. Shakespeare's England was a historical success but a financial failure. The pageant was splendid, the tournament was stirring, but the costs were too heavy to be recouped. C. B. Cochran, a successful theatrical producer who had worked with Jennie, said: "Her ideas were wonderful. It was money that perplexed her. She threw it around like water."[28] Cochran brought in more sideshows, a scenic railway, an international circus, and Jennie gave a harpsichord recital, but at the end the exposition still lost money.[29]

George West often remarked that his major arguments with Jennie were about money. In his novel, the hero tells his wife:

We hadn't been in this house six months before I told you that we could not possibly afford to entertain on the scale you appeared to think necessary! and not the slightest notice has been taken, or ever is taken, of anything I say, and now I find myself in a very serious position.

. . . Lady Carsteen was aghast. Her husband was actually standing up to her and displaying a trait of sarcasm which she had finally imagined she had long ago successfully suppressed, if not entirely obliterated. . . .[30]

The marriage was over. For George, the love was gone. Envy had replaced it. He now felt he could never be a man in Jennie's house. He could never be as important as she was. Cassel was right about him: he was not meant for moneymaking, and yet money was his measure of success. Jack Churchill was also right about him: he couldn't stand the strain.

George now had his own ideas—fostered by Mrs. Campbell—of becoming a famous playwright and novelist. But they were illusions without substance. Jennie was fifty-eight and he was thirty-seven, but she was younger than he was. Not only did he not have her fire of youth, but he had little of her talent and almost none of her quality.

Nor did he have her sense of dignity, of grace, of style: On December 24, 1912, Jennie wrote:

Dearest George,

I am glad that I was prepared for your letter—the blow falls hard enough as it is—But if this thing is to take place, it can't be done too quickly now—and we shall both be happier when it is over—Thank God I have the physical and mental strength and courage enough to fight my own battle in life.

George answered on January 2, 1913:

Dearest Jennie,

Thanks for your nice letter. I have been on the verge of ringing you up once or twice but honestly don't think I could bear the sound of your dear old voice just now. . . .

The petition for divorce was filed by Jennie on January 20, 1913. The next legal step was an order against her husband for restitution of conjugal rights. This was handed down on March 3, 1913. The case was noted on the Court calendar as "West vs. West."

"What is the nature of the desertion?" asked the President of the Court, Sir Samuel Evans.

"The Respondent [George Cornwallis-West]," said Lord Tiverton, "left the house where they had been living in Norfolk-street. Certain correspondence took place at the end of December and the beginning of January, in which the Respondent, after having been requested to do so, refused to come back."

"Mrs. West," called the usher, and Jennie, who had only at the moment entered the court, went into the box.

> She looked strikingly handsome. There was something stately about her figure, dressed in black velvet, in exquisite taste. Magnificent sables drooped from her shoulders; a black toque crowned her rich black hair, and a large sable muff hid one hand, from which a dainty purse of chain-gold dangled. She took the oath.
>
> She was evidently suffering from a severe cold. She answered the questions that were put to her in a quiet, low voice that had a trace of huskiness in it.
>
> "Are you the Petitioner in this case?" asked Lord Tiverton.
>
> "I am," replied Mrs. West.
>
> "Were you married to your husband on July 28, 1900?"
>
> "I was."
>
> "After which you cohabited with him in various places, and latterly in Norfolk-street?"
>
> Mrs. West signified in affirmative with a nod of her head.
>
> "On December 23rd last, did the Respondent leave Norfolk-street?"
>
> "He did."
>
> "On December 29th, did you get a letter which was exposed in your affidavit before Milord?"
>
> "I did," said Mrs. West, in a businesslike voice.
>
> "Did you reply on December 31st?"
>
> "Yes."
>
> "Did you further reply to him on January 3rd last?"
>
> "That is so."
>
> "Has he come back to you since?"
>
> "No."
>
> There was a slight pause, while the judge looked at the correspondence that had passed between the husband and wife. The letters were not read.
>
> "Is the Respondent in this country?" asked Sir Samuel Evans.

"I am not sure," replied Mr. Harvey Murphy [the counsel].

The usual order of restitution of conjugal rights was made, and Mrs. Cornwallis-West left the court as quietly as she had entered it.[31]

The British correspondent of *The North American* Magazine noted:

> Mrs. Cornwallis-West is extremely anxious that the court proceedings should be as quiet as possible, and that there should be no scandal. She has no desire to drag in anybody unless it is absolutely unavoidable.
>
> Mrs. West's two sons, Winston and John, are anxious that their mother should get the divorce. . . .[32]

The divorce had several further stages to go through, and the legal process would take another year. In the interim, Jennie had another project to consume her time and attention—her second play. She had written a synopsis of it three years before and had been working on it intermittently for almost a year. Alfred Wareing now felt that it was ready for production at his Glasgow Repertory Theatre.

The Bill was a political play. Jennie described it to a reporter as "a play about politicians . . . neither a propagandist play nor a controversial play. It is just a comedy with a political situation, a certain amount of lovemaking, the necessary dash of intrigue, a contrast in temperament between a father and his son, and just a little touch of villainy."[33]

The critics gave it a rousing reception:

> "An oustanding feature of Mr. Wareing's season . . ."
>
> ". . . excellently written throughout . . ."
>
> ". . . Many of the speeches are brilliant, while the shrewd incisive hits at all political parties and many of our social conventions are delightful. . . ."
>
> ". . . Mrs. Cornwallis-West has succeeded perfectly . . . the characters of modern politicians are real flesh-and-blood people. . . ."
>
> ". . . one of the most powerful comedies ever written . . ."

Jennie was not swept away by the favorable reception. She was seen in the prompter's wings the first few nights, taking notes of the production and the audiences' reaction to it.[34]

The Bill concerns universal suffrage and the political maneuvering by women to help gain power for their husbands or lovers. "So cleverly and naturally did the discussion seem last night that many members of the audience forgot their surroundings and gave vent to a chorus of 'Hear! Hear!' and other evidences of approval or dissent."[35]

One of the wives in the play reminds her husband: "You had no ambition. I persuaded you to take office." Then there is this exchange:

> *Sir George:* You must allow for the fact that, taking her all around, she is the stronger animal of the two.
>
> *Vernon:* 'Pon my soul, I believe you're right and she has the advantage of being utterly unscrupulous.
>
> *John:* Men have made women unscrupulous.[36]

Later the leading lady remarks to "Sir George," "We don't elope nowaways, and we don't divorce, except out of kindness."

The divorce proceedings against George West were proceeding without complication. He and Mrs. Pat were now together more openly. Jennie's comment on the two of them: "Well, George evidently has a penchant for brunettes. I'm always taken for a gypsy, but as for Mrs. Pat—why she's nothing more or less than an ink bottle!"

Mrs. Campbell was still in the midst of her love affair in letters with George Bernard Shaw. Shaw, who was married but had never consummated his marriage, was fifty-seven years old and convinced that he was passionately in love with Mrs. Pat. But she had written to him that "George is more precious to me than my bones."

Shaw answered her, calling her, "Ever blessedest darling," and saying:

> I want to implore you not to arouse the family solicitor by talking of marrying George. . . . No sooner do you mention George than I see with a frightful lucidity all the worldly reasons why you should marry him. . . . Therefore, though I like George (we have the same taste) I say he is young and I am old; so let him wait until I am tired of you. . . . And about you, I am a mass of illusions. It is impossible that I should not tire soon; nothing so wonderful could last. You cannot really be what you are to me; you are a figure from the dreams of my boyhood—all romance. . . . I promise to tire of you as soon as I can leave you free. . . .[37]

Shaw was writing *Pygmalion* at the time, primarily for Mrs. Pat, and she continued to cultivate him. But when he planned a visit with the intention of making love to her, she told him not to come. He answered:

Very well, go; the loss of a woman is not the end of the world. The sun shines: It is pleasant to swim: it is good to work: my soul can stand alone. But I am deeply, deeply wounded. . . . I have treated you far too well, idolized, thrown my heart and mind to you (as I throw them to all the world) to make what you could of: and what you make of them is to run away. Go then: The Shavian oxygen burns up your little lungs: seek some stuffiness that suits you. You will not marry George! At the last moment, you will funk him, or be ousted by a bolder soul. You have wounded my vanity: an inconceivable audacity and an unpardonable crime. Farewell, wretch, that I love. G.B.S.[38]

Some years later Shaw was quoted as having said of Mrs. Campbell, "She was not a great actress, but she was a great enchantress, how or why I don't know; but if she wanted to capture you, you might as well go quietly; for she was irresistible."[39]

Shortly after Jennie had filed her first claim in the divorce suit, Winston and Clemmie offered her a change of scene:

It wd do you a gt deal of good to get away from England, worry & expense for three weeks & to bask a little in Mediterranean & Adriatic sunshine. Why will you not come with us on the 8th & be delivered safely . . . back on the first or second of June. We start from Venice & go round by the Dalmatian coast to Malta, Sicily, Ajaccio & Marseilles (perhaps Athens). The Asquiths are coming; so that you wd have to make up your mind to get on with Margot & the PM. But again, why not?

Otherwise, we are only Admiralty and Admirable. It wd be so nice if you cd come, & Clemmie and I wd so greatly enjoy it.

It wd cost nothing or next to nothing.

Answer please in the affirmative.

> Always your loving son,
> W.[40]

Jennie agreed to go, but before leaving she sent a wire about her play to Alfred Wareing in Glasgow: "Don't let them overact when they get familiar with the roles."

The next step in the divorce suit came on July 15, 1913. Jennie's lawyers had petitioned unsuccessfully for the case to be heard *in camera*.

They were able, however, to arrange for the case to be placed near the top of the court calendar, although it had originally been last.

"As she stood in the witness-box yesterday," the newspaper reported,

> she was seen to be a woman of no ordinary appearance. . . . Her second son, Mr. John Churchill, accompanied Mrs. Cornwallis-West to court. They and their solicitor stood chatting in the thronged lobby for ten minutes, while the President finished off for the day the Moosbrugger suit. Then, at four o'clock, the men and women interested in the fortunes of the Moosbruggers, swarmed out of court, and a dozen husbands and wives with "undefended" petitions to be heard, filed in and filled the vacated seats.
>
> Mrs. Cornwallis-West entered and took a seat near the witness-box.[41]

The background facts were repeated, this time with the addition "that Mr. George Cornwallis-West stayed, from March 28th to March 31st, at the Great Western Railway Hotel at Paddington, with 'a woman unknown.' "

Asked whether her husband had complied with the order of the court for restitution of conjugal rights, Jennie replied: "He did not, My Lord." The court testimony continued:

> Mr. Drew, Private-Inquiry Agent and Ex-Chief Inspector of Scotland Yard, whitehaired, a "Sherlock," told the President of the inquiries he made at Paddington, and of the identification of a photograph of Mr. Cornwallis-West by one of the chamber-maids. Louisa Mintern, the chamber-maid, gave evidence of the stay of "Captain and Mrs. West" at the Great Western Railway Hotel from March 28th to March 31st. She knew their name from the luggage, she said, with a smile, and she had seen Mr. Cornwallis-West at Mr. Russell's office.
>
> Miss Mintern was leaving the witness-box when Mr. Smith stopped her.
>
> "One more question," he said. "Was the lady you saw at the hotel, the lady sitting below you?"
>
> The chamber-maid looked down. Mrs. George Cornwallis-West looked up. They glanced in each other's faces, and the maid said, "No."
>
> There ended the story, and the President granted decree.

Jennie had obtained a *decree nisi* for the dissolution of her marriage, but it would take nine months for the decree to be made final. George and his sister Daisy went on a trip to South America that summer. Jennie did some traveling, too, mostly on the Continent.

That winter, Winston, as First Lord of the Admiralty, asked his mother to christen a new battleship, the *Benbow*.[42] She was told she would only have to name it and wish it Godspeed.

"With a light heart, I went off to Glasgow," she later wrote, "where the launch was to take place. I beamed on the crowds at the docks, I accepted bouquets. . . ." She said her "Godspeed" and her words were "drowned by the crashing sound of the breaking of timbers and snapping of ropes as the giant ship glided slowly down the slips."

"Now for the luncheon," said the Chairman. "We've got a splendid crowd—at least 500, and they are all looking forward to your speech."

Jennie explained that she had been specifically told that she would not have to make a speech. But someone whispered to her that they were going to present her with a handsome gift, "a Louis XVI gold chatelaine, I believe," and the Chairman added that as the mother of the First Lord of the Admiralty, she must know all about naval matters. "Surely, your son tells you everything? No? Well, you can always fall back on 'Our Cousins Across the Seas' for a topic."

"Oh! That miserable, untasted luncheon!" Jennie confided afterward.

> What should I say? My mind was a blank, and the fatal moment was approaching. A brilliant thought struck me. I would draw a comparison between the delicate, antique beauty of the old Louis XVI chatelaine, which was to be given me, and the modern, awe-inspiring, formidable iron monster I had just christened and launched. I was comforted—that would be a beginning, and for the rest, I trusted to Providence.
>
> I was on my feet, receiving with many smiles and grateful thanks a velvet box, which I proceeded to open for the expectant and admiring company to see—Lo! and behold, a very modern diamond brooch![43]
>
> Alas! For my opening remarks, where were they? My dismay was so great that I burst into speech and threw myself at their mercy. . . .[44]

The audience was kind and sympathetic and Jennie's brief, informal talk was received much better than a more formal, well-prepared one might have been.

As the date of the final divorce decree approached, Daisy decided that Jennie was preferable to a notorious actress as a sister-in-law and she cabled: "Wired you twice. Don't make decree absolute."

But on April 14, 1914, Jennie wrote:

> My dear George,
>
> Mr. Wheeler brought me your message. The d.n. [*decree nisi*] will be made absolute on Monday, and I understand that you are going to be married on Tues. You need not fear what I may say, for I will not willingly speak of you. And we are not likely ever to meet. This is the *real* parting of the ways. But for the sake of some of the happy days we had together—should you ever be in trouble and wanted to knock at my door, it would not be shut to you. I am returning you my engagement and wedding rings—I say good-bye—a long, long good-bye.
>
> Jennie.[45]

Moreton Frewen was less gentle: "So that beauty George West is to be married on Tuesday to Mrs. Pat Campbell—the decree absolute is Monday. Full Fathom Five they dive to a joint folly."[46]

On April 16, 1914, within an hour after the decree was made final, George West and Mrs. Patrick Campbell were married. The ceremony was performed in a Registry Office, and only two friends were present as witnesses. "Mrs. Campbell's wedding dress was of black silk, and she was wearing a black hat. She gave her age in the register as 47, and Mr. Cornwallis-West as eight years her junior."[47]

Mrs. Campbell had left her house in Kensington Square after lunch, and motored to the Registry House; all that was known at the house was that she was going to be married and that she would be away for a couple of days. She was to appear in Shaw's *Pygmalion,* at His Majesty's Theatre on Saturday night, "rehearsals for which are now proceeding."

Very few people had been in on the secret. ". . . Immediately after the ceremony, Mr. and Mrs. Cornwallis-West drove away in the car; and it is understood that they are staying in the country."

Mrs. Pat was later quoted as saying, "Ah, the peace of the double bed after the hurly-burly of the *chaise longue.*"

In the Classified Notices section of the *Times* on April 7, 1914 there appeared this notice:

> I, Jennie Spencer-Churchill, commonly called Lady Randolph Churchill, hereinbefore called by the name of Jennie

Cornwallis-West, of 32, Dover-street, in the County of London, hereby give public notice that on the first day of April, One-thousand-nine-hundred-and-fourteen, I formally and absolutely RENOUNCED, relinquished, and abandoned the use of my said surname of CORNWALLIS-WEST, and then ASSUMED, adopted, and determined thenceforth on all occasions whatsoever to use and subscribe the name of SPENCER-CHURCHILL instead of the said name of Cornwallis-West.

Thirty-Nine

THE NEXT CHAPTER OF JENNIE'S LIFE was filled with surprises. Hers was not a life that could slowly unwind. She was constantly renewing herself, her energy, her love of life.

Leonie told of a visit her sister made to her on a bleak afternoon in early 1914. Still smarting from the divorce and George's swift remarriage, she let the hurt show that day. She also bemoaned her financial insecurity and the forever accumulating bills. And now her sons had their own lives with their families, and her friends were dying or scattering. Jennie herself was sixty years old. After unburdening her anxieties and distress, she left. The loving Leonie had planned to attend a ball that night, but Jennie's talk had so depressed her that she decided not to go. The next day a friend telephoned her to describe the splendid evening. And who had been the belle of the ball, looking absolutely wonderful? Why, Jennie, of course.

Clara's son, Hugh Frewen, was being married in Rome to the daughter of the Duke of Mignano, and Jennie decided to attend. She stayed with her young friend, Vittoria, the Duchess of Sermoneta, at her *palazzo*. It was peaceful and lovely, with its avenue of tall plane trees, the entrance gate flanked by carved stone bears, the inner court garden with its seven splashing fountains, the formal patterns of flower beds, the delicious fragrance of tangerine trees.

The wedding party was held at the Grand Hotel. Hugh introduced Jennie to a friend of his, Montagu Porch, a young man serving with him in the Colonial Service in Nigeria. He was very handsome, gloriously mustached, had a slim figure and prematurely white hair.

"I can remember still the first moment I saw her. . . . She was sitting with some friends. She wore a green dress. Was it long or short? Don't remember. But she looked very beautiful." Porch asked her to dance. Jennie smiled and said: "I think you better go and dance with some of the younger girls."[1] Porch was thirty-seven, three years younger than Winston.

Not many weeks before, Leonie had had a dinner party for Jennie's sixtieth birthday. After the party, Jennie went to Leonie's room, sat despondently on her bed, and reminisced. How intoxicating it always had been to sweep into a room and know that every man would turn his head to stare at her; how unhappy she was that it was no longer true. Yet here was this very young, very handsome man who obviously found her very attractive. Her nephew Shane Leslie later said of her: "She could have married young men until she was a hundred. . . ."[2]

For a certain kind of young man, Jennie was not just a beautiful woman, she was an overwhelming adventure into a new world. It was true of George West and Montagu Porch and a dozen others. They must also have seen in her something of a surrogate mother. She had the drive, determination, and strength they did not have, and by comparison they were insecure and dependent.

But when she bared her soul to Leonie, her strength had ebbed:

> I wish we could see more of each other. Life is so short and we are both so down the wrong side of the ladder! The fact is that we are both "Marthas" instead of "Marys" and allow things which do not really count to take up our time and to keep us apart. We pander to the world which is callous, and it only wants you if you can smile and be hypocritical. One is forever throwing away substance for shadows. To live for others sounds all right—you do, darling—but what is the result? You are a very unhappy woman all around! As for me every effort I make to get out of my selfishness meets with a rebuff. My sons love me from afar and give me no companionship even when it comes their way. The fault is undoubtedly with me. Every day I become more solitary and prone to introspection, which is fatal.[3]

Such self-indulgence for Jennie never lasted very long. She always found someone or something more important than her own problems.

Most threatening now was the rapidly looming war in Europe. Jennie had spoken with Winston about it and wrote to Leonie: ". . . He seemed to think the worst of the European situation and thought war inevitable. . . . As I am writing, the fate of the Government is hanging in the balance. . . ." Later, after a lunch with Winston, she again wrote to Leonie: "Winston is really so 'big!' " Discussing a political question, she had told him: "If that happens you will have the other side saying they have won the day."

"What would that matter," answered Winston, "if good came of it. . . ."[4]

And, again, on August 1st: "Only a line to tell you that Winston tells us [French President Raymond] Poincairé has written an impassioned letter to the King imploring his aid. The fleet will be mobilized today probably. . . ."[5]

That same evening Winston was dining with a friend at Admiralty House when an aide brought in a dispatch box. Winston opened it with a key and found a single sentence: "Germany has declared war against Russia. . . ."

"There is one thing they cannot take away from you," Kitchener later told Winston. "The fleet was ready."

The assassination of the Archduke Francis Ferdinand, heir apparent to the crowns of Austria and Hungary, had activated a chain of treaties that soon divided Europe into two camps. The murder plot had been hatched in Serbia, and the German Kaiser supported the Austrian attack on its ancient enemy. Russia mobilized. Britain suggested a conference. Germany asked that Britain remain neutral if a conflict were to develop. Britain refused to make such a pledge. Germany declared war on Russia on August 2nd, and the next day declared war on France. Britain asked Germany and France if they would respect Belgian neutrality. France agreed. Germany refused, and German troops invaded Belgium.

Britain sent an ultimatum to Berlin that required Germany to agree to withdraw from Belgium by midnight of August 4th. The day before, on August 3, in the office of the Foreign Minister Viscount Grey: "We were standing at a window of my room. . . . It was getting dark, and the lamps were being lit in the space below on which we were looking." Viscount Grey said to his guest: "The lamps are going out all over Europe; we shall not see them lit again in our life-time."[6] World War I had begun.

It was a time of drama and personal despair for Jennie and her sisters. Each soon had a son at the front: Jack Churchill, Hugh Frewen, Norman Leslie. Norman was killed early in the war.

Deep in grief over the loss of her son and determined to help the war effort in some way, Leonie took a job washing dishes at a soldier's canteen. One night she saw a familiar face. It was George Cornwallis-West, again an officer. "The day of my divorce was the saddest of my life," he told her. "Perhaps the happiest in my sister's," Leonie answered sharply.[7]

George West had found that he could not be the head of the household with his second wife either. When Mrs. Pat toured in *Pygmalion,* George played the dustman.[8] He discovered, too, that his second wife was no less extravagant than his first, and he soon faced bankruptcy.

Prince Charles Kinsky had come quietly back into Jennie's life. After his wife's death, he and Jennie had seen each other intermittently. He had taken part in her Shakespeare's England, and he always retained his apartment on Clarges Street, only a few blocks from her home.[9] If they had any thought of marriage, the war made it impossible; as a Reserve Officer in the Austro-Hungarian Army, Kinsky was recalled to duty.

"I said goodbye to him at the end of Goodwood Week in July 1914," remembered Kinsky's close friend, George Lambton, "when he left to go fight for his own country, on the side of the Germans, a nation he had always hated. He loved England and the English."[10] Rumors had circulated that Kinsky had ordered that his English racing horses be destroyed rather than serve the British Army. But the truth was that Kinsky had asked Lambton to have his horses distributed among his many friends in the English Army, and Lambton had done so.[11]

In order not to have to fight against his British friends, Kinsky requested assignment to the Russian front. His nephew, Prince Clary, told of meeting his uncle on the Russian front in 1915. "I found him sitting on a bench in the garden, reading the *Times.* His first remark to me was—in English!—'How odd, old X is taking a very strong line against racing during the War. . . .' "

A Major in a regiment of Hussars, Kinsky was an aide to the commanding general of an Army corps. "When the Russians retreated in October 1914," Prince Clary wrote,

> some cossack detachments were left behind to hide in the big forests. They were dressed in civilian clothes to do spy-work and sabotage and take prisoners whenever they could. As, the roads were impracticable for cars, and the telephone did not exist or had often been interrupted, the message from any headquarters to another had to be carried by ADC's [aides-de-camp] on horseback. These aides usually took an escort with them. Not so Charles Kinsky. I remember seeing him arrive one day, quite alone, and when asked by the General why he had not taken an escort, he answered that he would be quite capable of dealing alone with a few cossacks. On his way back he was stopped by two of them, but, pulling out his revolver, he shouted at them in Russian that they were his prisoners. The cossacks were so taken aback by this

reaction and the old major's language that they let themselves be taken to headquarters.[12]

Kinsky kept in occasional contact with his butler in England, who still took care of his Clarges Street flat. One note from the butler said: "Yesterday I saw Lady R.C., she told me to let you know that I saw her, and that she is well. . . ."[13]

In fact, Jennie was not well; she was often depressed. Her nephew Oswald's diary noted, "Lady Maud Warrender came over and took Pa and Ma and Aunt Jane (she's very much out of the picture) off to lunch."[14] But she didn't stay out of the picture very long. She and Lady Maud toured the camps and the hospitals, Jennie playing the piano and Maud Warrender singing, with Jennie joining in. Lady Maud remembered that Jennie was "always full of good stories . . . a staunch friend with a lively sense of humor, the best company. . . ." One story she recalled Jennie telling was about an American Senator she had entertained at dinner. The Senator arrived very late, without his wife, and blurted out: "Please excuse me, Lady Churchill. I regret to say that my wife is unable to accompany me here tonight; she is suffering from womb worries."[15]

Jennie soon found herself organizing buffets for thousands of soldiers at railroad stations, helping her sister-in-law start a convalescent home in the country for wounded soldiers, and raising money and acquiring space and staff for an American Women's War Hospital at Paignton in South Devon, for which she was chairman of the Executive Committee.

Jennie wrote of the courage of the wounded: "A man shot through the face will smile crookedly and wink his one eye . . ."; of the incredulous civilians who said when the first wounded arrived in their town on troop trains: ". . . then there really is a war going on . . ."; of the stories some of the men told about opposing trenches at the front so close together that the German and the English soldiers could hear each others' singing; and of the plea of the newly arrived wounded, "Please, Sister, let us sleep . . ."[16]

Few things angered Jennie more than the pseudo-benevolence of some of the society ladies who took wounded soldiers out for drives. They asked at the Paignton Hospital for "those with the most conspicuous bandages please. The last lot of officers you gave us might not have been wounded at all, for all anyone could see. . . ."[17] In contrast, Jennie told of her young friend, Eleanor Warrender, youngest daughter of Lady Maud Warrender, who had worked with her on the *Maine* and now served at French frontline hospitals, where she was ". . . shelled at Furnes and Dunkirk, sleeping all night in cellars full of rats. . . ."[18]

Jennie also became an "Olympian head matron" of a hospital at Lancaster Gate, and Lady Maud Warrender recalled how hard Jennie worked and how she "never spared herself."[19] In fact, Jennie was genuinely grateful for the chance to serve: "We might have been pottering out our little hum-drum lives, eating our chickens and going through our daily routine in comfort and smug complacency. . . ."[20]

Jack's son Peregrine Churchill remembers the time his grandmother took him to the Lancaster Gate Hospital where she was then spending most of her time. Jennie wanted her young grandson to balance his heroic view of war by seeing some of the casualties. He remembered, too, that she continu-ally corrected his pronunciation of "Ypres," the town in Belgium where a number of bloody battles had taken place. And the only time Peregrine ever saw his grandmother angry enough to hit anyone was during their hospital visit. A Boy Scout who had been assigned to act as a watchman was instead lounging elsewhere eating oranges, and Jennie boxed his ears.[21]

Jennie was a devoted grandmother. She gave her grandchildren not only love, but an education and a heritage as well. The devotion to music that she had shared with her son Jack had been passed on to Jack's son Peregrine. He remembered an occasion when he was perhaps five years old. His grandmother was attending a luncheon, and Peregrine was in an-other room pecking out a tune on the piano. Jennie left the luncheon party to sit alongside her grandson at the piano and tell him the story of the opera from which the tune he was playing came. It was *Siegfried,* and she played the main themes for him, including the music representing the warn-ing of the bird. Then she told him about a performance she had seen in which the bird song was sung by "a great big fat soprano," and Jennie puffed her cheeks to indicate how fat the soprano was.

She went on to tell him that since the soprano was too fat to climb into a tree on stage, she stood on a box behind the cardboard tree, just pretend-ing. But all that didn't matter, Jennie told him, because the soprano had a beautiful voice. "You mustn't mind singers being fat," she said, "just listen and use your imagination."

Peregrine Churchill never forgot that incident. It wasn't only the story, it was the way his grandmother talked to him—as if he were not a child but a young man.[22]

The grandchildren called her "Granny" or "B.M." (*"Bonne Mère"*), and they were always delighted to see her "because she always brought us pres-ents. . . ."[23] They enjoyed her because she obviously enjoyed them. When her sons were young, she was the wife of an important political figure who demanded her constant attention; now her time was her own. She took her grandchildren on visits, picnics, automobile rides, to the theater, to con-certs, parties.[24]

Once she took Winston and Clemmie's son Randolph to the birthday party of another child. Part of the entertainment was a magician whom young Randolph was obviously not enjoying. Suddenly he jumped onto his chair and exclaimed: "Man, stop! Band, play!" And the man did stop and the band did play. How like Winston, Jennie must have thought.[25]

Jennie was also very attentive to her large number of nieces and nephews. "She was always leading; we all followed," said Shane Leslie.[26]

The diary of Oswald Frewen recorded: "Lunch at Aunt Jane's . . . took us to the war pictures at the Sculos . . . very large-hearted of Aunt Jane. . . ." Later he added that she "bore me off to the Admiralty to see Winston. He, however, was at a Cabinet meeting. . . ."[27]

In 1915 Winston suffered a major defeat over the Dardanelles. Earlier, he had gone to Antwerp, and had volunteered to resign from the Admiralty if Prime Minister Asquith would allow him to command the defense of that city. Asquith refused. Next Winston proffered a grand plan to help end the war more quickly: an intricate scheme to invade and open the Dardanelles, detaching Turkey from the Central powers. This would win control over the Balkan states and prepare the way for a sweeping British victory in the East. It would be a back-door attack on the enemy. Winston's friend and ally, Lord Fisher,[28] at first supported the plan, then opposed it, but Winston forced the plan through.

The official British Government history of the war records, "The Turkish gun crews were demoralized and even the German officers present had, apparently, little hope of successful resistance if the Fleet attacked next day." However, three British ships were blown up in a minefield and the admiral in charge broke off the action. Lord Fisher refused to overrule him.

After the war, the German General at the Dardanelles, Liman von Sanders, said, "If the orders at that moment had been carried out, the course of the world war would have changed after the spring of 1915, and Germany and Austria would have been constrained to continue the fight alone."[29]

Instead, when the British infantry did attack nearby Gallipoli several months later, they found a refreshed enemy, more deeply entrenched and better prepared. The result was a disaster in which British casualties reached over 200,000. The defeat caused a political crisis in England and the formation of a new coalition government—without Winston Churchill.

On June 10, 1915, war correspondent E. Ashmead Bartlett noted in his diary:

> This evening I dined with Lady Randolph Churchill to meet Winston. . . . I am much surprised at the change in Winston Churchill. He looks years older, his face is pale, he seems very depressed and he feels keenly his retirement from the Admiralty. . . . He has no one but himself to blame for his

misfortunes. He held the most important post in the Cabinet at the outbreak of the war, and he had only to curb his impetuosity and direct its labours, guided by his advisers, and he would still be First Lord. But his nature rebelled at the prospect of sitting in an arm-chair directing naval strategy when others were actually fighting. He was torn between conflicting emotions, the demands of his great office, and his paramount desire to take an active part in the war itself. . . .

At dinner, the conversation was more or less general, nothing was said about the Dardanelles and Winston was very quiet. It was only towards the very end that he suddenly burst forth into a tremendous discourse on the Expedition and what might have been, addressed directly across the table in the form of a lecture to his mother, who listened most attentively. . . .[30]

"This slow and supine government are now beginning to realize what Winston has preached for the last six months," Jennie wrote to Leonie. "If they had made the Dardanelles policy a certainty, which they could have done in the beginning, Constantinople would have been in our hands ages ago. *In confidence,* it is astounding how Winston foresaw it all. . . ."[31]

Earlier Jennie had expressed her concern about Winston to Clara:

I'm afraid Winston is very sad at having nothing to do. When you have had your hand at the helm for four years it seems stagnation to take a back place, and for why? No fault can be found with his work at the Admiralty and they give him the sack whereas a gigantic mistake is made at the War Office [Kitchener at Gallipoli] and the man responsible for it is screened and given the Garter. It makes my blood boil. . . .[32]

Winston has given us a vivid picture of this period of enforced inactivity:

The change from the intense executive activities of each day's work at the Admiralty to the narrowly measured duties of a counsellor left me gasping. Like a sea-beast fished up from the depths, or a diver too suddenly hoisted, my veins threatened to burst from the fall in pressure. . . . I had long hours of utterly unwonted leisure . . . at a moment when every fibre of my being was inflamed to action. . . .[33]

Winston and his mother were guests at a dinner party, whose host overheard a conversation between them that he recorded in his memoirs. Jennie suggested to her son that he should do some painting. "It sounded like an innocent wife, offering to read to her husband, while he was vainly hacking a golf ball out of a bunker."[34] But in the country the following Sunday Winston experimented with a children's paint-box, and the next morning he bought a complete set of oils and an easel. It was not a new activity for him. When he was a little boy, he had accompanied his mother to her painting lessons with Mrs. E. M. Ward, and painting was one of the few subjects at school that he had really liked and excelled in. He had written his mother from school about his "drawing little landscapes and bridges," and had illustrated many of his letters with drawings.

Now his mother's suggestion seemed exactly the right thing for him. "Just to paint is great fun," he later wrote. "The colours are lovely to look at and delicious to squeeze out. Matching them, however crudely, with what you see is fascinating and absolutely absorbing. . . . I know of nothing which, without exhausting the body, more entirely absorbs the mind. . . ."[35]

Indeed, after watching Winston painting, Lady Violet Bonham Carter said, ". . . it was the only occupation I had ever seen him practice in silence. . . ."[36]

"His last paintings are very good," Jennie later wrote Leonie. "Lavery says that if Winston cared to take painting up as a profession he could, but of course he uses it as an opiate."[37]

The war had become the bloodiest one in history, involving some thirty countries. Casualty lists kept getting longer and longer, and there seemed to be no end to it. A great many of Jennie's friends had suffered personal losses. Conversation was muted and often grim, parties were few. Jennie concentrated more and more on her family, especially after Clara's daughter Clare—who was married to Wilfred Sheridan and the mother of two children—learned that her husband was missing in action and presumed dead. Jennie, who had contacts in the War Department, was the first to receive the news.

It came as a shock to learn that Winston had asked to rejoin his old Regiment at the front in France. He was then staying in his brother's house on Cromwell Road. F. E. Smith recalled after a visit, that the house was soon "upside down while the soldier statesman was buckling on his sword. Downstairs, Mr. 'Eddie' Marsh, his faithful secretary, was in tears. . . . Upstairs, Lady Randolph was in a state of despair at the thought of her brilliant son being relegated to the trenches. . . ."[38]

Many times before, Jennie had bid her sons good-bye as they had gone off to war, but this time everything seemed more ominous. She had seen so many wounded soldiers at the hospital; and she had personally known many of the dead and missing. She also knew Winston's fearlessness, his need to be in the frontline fighting. "Please be sensible," she warned him. "I think you ought to take the trenches in small doses, after 10 years of more or less sedentary life—but I'm sure you won't 'play the fool'—Remember you are destined for greater things. . . . I am a great believer in your star. . . ."[39] Beyond that, she could do little more than pray for him.

She saw more of her daughters-in-law now, with Clementine and "Goonie" sharing the house on Cromwell Road. Clementine went to work in a munitions factory and Jennie spent more time with her grandchildren. Her relations with Clemmie and Goonie were what one might expect—close but not intimate. The young women sensed her overpowering presence and were naturally jealous about maintaining their own independent lives. They did not resist, however, when Jennie offered to contribute regularly toward their housekeeping expenses and pocket money while their husbands were away.

Jennie was able to help her daughters-in-law with money she was getting from *Pearson's* Magazine for a series of articles which would later be collected into a book entitled *Small Talks on Big Subjects*.

Her first article appeared in the September 1915 issue. Called "Mars and Cupid," it concerned marriage in wartime. Jennie inserted her own thrust at marriage, recalling the cynic who said he didn't know that there was much difference between marriage and war. She also quoted the remark, "Marriage is a field of battle, not a bed of roses. . . ." And she commented rather acidly, "Your castle in Spain has no foundation, that is why it is so easily built. . . ."

Jennie was equally well qualified to write the next month's essay on "Extravagance." As much as she endorsed wartime thrift, she made the wistful point, ". . . we owe something to extravagance, for thrift and adventure seldom go hand in hand. . . ." She might also have said that had it not been for a lifetime of extravagance, she might never have been able to move in the social circles she did and accomplish as much as she had. And if she had not done that, she would not have been able to ease the entry of her sons Winston and Jack into the positions they held.

Jennie's other essays covered a variety of subjects. Her views on suffragettes had been modified through the years, and she now believed that their cause "must ultimately lead to victory." She applauded their strategic switch from fierce agitation to peaceful demonstration. She was delighted with the new model of the Englishwoman. "The girl of today, in whatever class of society, is not content to emulate her American cousin, she wants to go 'one better.' . . ." Independence, however, can go too far, she wrote, because a man "is not inclined to feel very tenderly towards a girl who has just beaten him severely on his own ground at lawn-tennis or golf. . . ."

But she refused to fall into the trap of comparing generations, "for we live in such different conditions." She sympathized with the girl who wanted to emancipate herself from a dull home, "but when she got her freedom, she often found bachelordom very dull without a bachelor boy to play with. . . ."

Jennie defined sins as "exaggerated inclinations."

All of her essays were enriched by her memories. What does success owe to failure? "Everything," an artist had told her. "I am built on the failures of others. If their paintings were not so bad, mine would not be thought so good."

"Another friend of mine," she wrote, "attributed all the disasters of his life to the fact of having had, at his first venture, the luck to buy a horse that won everything. . . . Thinking he could at any time buy more winners of the same type, [he] became too confident and was ultimately ruined. . . ." In contrast, she told of her friend Disraeli, who had been mocked on his first speech in the House of Commons and said, "I sit down now, but the time will come when you will hear me. . . ."

She wrote about friendship: "Treat your friends as you do your pictures, and place them in their best light." And she tried to describe the perfect friend: warm, glowing, sensitive. "I had such a friend once," she wrote, thinking of Pearl Craigie.

> It was impossible to know her and not love her. She was so human, so sympathetic and her brilliant and delicious mind so deep a well to draw from.
>
> I remember a day we spent together in the country. We went for a walk. It was one of those days the English climate never wearies of giving—gray, raw, damp, odious. But we became so interested in our talk that it was some time before we noticed that we had wandered into a ploughed field. To me, it seemed, listening to her, that the field was enamelled with flowers, and that a warm sun beamed on us. She had the rare faculty of making you feel at peace with yourself, and inspiring you with unfailing hope. Her own life lacked much of the brightness she gave others, but she was happy in her work and overflowing interests, and notwithstanding her rather frail physique, her enthusiasm made her a true optimist.

The year 1916 began badly for Jennie. She had always had a special vanity about her lovely legs and dainty feet, but one toe had become badly infected and had to be amputated. To add to her miseries, her home was robbed.

LADY RANDOLPH CHURCHILL ROBBED
ROYAL GIFTS STOLEN

Early yesterday morning, at 72 Brook Street, Hanover Square, West, the residence of Lady Randolph Churchill was entered by burglars. Jewelry and articles of great personal value were stolen. Among them were a gold seal, with jade and ruby top, and a gold papercutter, both bearing an inscription, "From King Edward to Lady Randolph Churchill"; a large chagreen box, inscribed "Presented by Queen Alexandra," a heart-shaped gold box with cat's head, with emerald eyes, "From George to Pussie," engraved underneath; a yellow enamel frame, ivory box, portrait of Col. Winston Churchill as a child, wearing a bead necklace; gold metal [locket] bearing faces of Winston and John Churchill, at 17 and 20 years of age; and a small round, gold box, with blue-enamel round edges, and the portraits of King Edward and Queen Alexandra in the center.

Of the store of trinkets carried off by the thieves, one, a flat, gold box, dated back to the Queen Anne period, and bore a bust of the First Duke of Marlborough in the center, supported by Hercules and Mars. Also missing is an oval miniature, at least a hundred years old, mounted with seed pearls, showing the bust of a middle-aged woman, with hair dressed and powdered. The thieves appeared to have forced one of the windows of the drawing-room.[40]

There was more unpleasantness to come. In her *Diaries,* Lady Cynthia Asquith described a dinner party that took place on August 8, 1916:

Conversation was mainly general and very agreeable. I felt in good form. Cowans [General Sir John Cowans, Quartermaster General of the Army] came on the block. There is an Enquiry Commission sitting on him, on account of the following ugly story: Lady Randolph Churchill (Black Jane [41]) fell in love with a private and, at her instance, General Cowans gave the man a commission. Either another woman entered the lists and captured this man, or in any case he did not respond to Jane's passion, and spleen and pique made her induce Cowans to degrade the man to the ranks again.... Cowans, poor man, has the reputation of jobbery, owing to his susceptibility to "ladies," but this story sounds quite incredible.... [42]

It was. It was not incredible that Jennie might take a liking to some handsome soldier and try to help him, as she had many times before. When Winston was First Lord of the Admiralty she had asked him to help a young man named Crundal, but Winston was unable to oblige. "I am very sorry about Crundal (whom I know). But the promotion of lieutenants is merciless. . . . It is cruel. The only thing that would make it crueler would be favoritism. . . ."[43]

The unlikely part of the Asquith story was the suggestion that Jennie would turn on the man and try to have him stripped of the commission. That would have been out of character. She might have thrown something, laughed bitterly, cursed her folly, but there was no meanness in her. Revenge was not her style.

The truth of the story was quite different. An article in *The Times* was headlined:

Army Inquiry

YOUNG OFFICER'S ORDEAL

A WOMAN CENSURED

The article named a sergeant in the Royal Welsh Fusiliers who had been made a second lieutenant and described his attempted removal, which "followed a letter of remonstrance to Mrs. Cornwallis-West." It seemed that the newly appointed lieutenant had "consistently failed to respond" to "a more than ordinary interest" which she had taken in him. At the Court of Inquiry, the officer was vindicated and Mrs. West "was found to have acted in a highly discreditable manner and have given untruthful evidence." She was also accused of "injudicious boasting of power she wielded at the War Office. . . . The lady's conduct [was] highly discreditable in her vindictive attempts to injure him."[44]

The catch was that the woman was not Jennie. Mrs. Cornwallis-West was identified as the wife of Colonel William Cornwallis-West of Ruthin Castle—Jennie's former mother-in-law!

The public confusion was not surprising. Not only had their names been similar, but both were beautiful women and both had had a similar reputation for favoring young men.

This reputation made Jennie particularly fascinating to her teen-age niece.

"She was my heroine," said the Baroness Cedestrom, the daughter of Lord Randolph's sister.

> She was the only person I ever knew who could physically light up a room by entering it. It wasn't just her beauty, it was her charm, it was her voice. I knew she was "naughty."

I overheard my family talk about her being "free and easy with the gentlemen," and I was naive enough to ask them what they meant. I asked Jennie one day how it felt to be run after by all these young men, and she said quietly, "I love people. I love the world. I love life."[45]

"We used to talk music all the time," the Baroness continued.

We both loved Wagner. We used to play piano duets. I wanted to be a concert pianist–I had all the training and teaching. But my parents thought it was common to play in public, and Aunt Jennie took my side and told them how cruel it was of them to prevent me. She would always ask for me when she came for a visit.

If it was a short visit, I'd wait until she finished talking to my parents, then I'd run to her and she would say, "Let's walk around the block and talk." . . . How I wished she was my mother. . . . [46]

Lady Betty Cartwright, whose sister was married to Jack, remembered: "I was a young girl when Jennie took me to the opera and parties. I hadn't had my coming-out yet, and so it was my only chance to go. She was so fascinating to talk to because she knew everybody and had been everywhere."[47]

She had, indeed. But now a new Jennie was gradually emerging. She had decided that she would not try to keep her youth by fighting Time. Her youth was within her. Oswald Frewen had noted in his diary the first trace of white in his aunt's hair. The striking "Black Jane" was no longer black. Edward Marsh, who visited her often, wrote: ". . . She suddenly decided to let hair, waist and complexion, and everything go, and became, in a day, one of the most beautiful human beings I have ever seen. . . ."[48]

But she was still lonely. "When I go to the theater, I often have to go with my maid, because no one else will go with me," she told Oswald.[49] It was an exaggeration, but there were fewer men knocking at her door.

One who came calling late that year was Montagu Porch, the attractive young man she had met in Rome. Montagu Phippen Porch resembled George Cornwallis-West only in that they were both very handsome. But Porch was a much less forceful man, and he did not have George's talent for aggressive gallantry with women. His background was that of a country squire in Glastonbury. His neighbors there described him as "nature's own gentleman," "a quiet man and a kind man," "a man of old-fashioned courtesy." "You never knew what he was really thinking and he seldom told you. . . ." ". . . At a meeting he would always agree with the majority." "He was a very dapper man—the kind of a man you would expect to wear spats, although he never did."[50]

Porch was a member of the landed gentry, and his family represented the most solid social substance. Their wealth had originally come from Australian sheep. The family had a general reputation for being "tight and meanfisted" with money, but no family was more active in community affairs. A Porch-Porch was the first Mayor of Glastonbury.

Glastonbury nestles among the green, rolling hills not far from the Bristol Channel. It is said that in 60 A.D. St. Joseph went there with the chalice from the Last Supper and that when Joseph stuck his legendary staff into the ground it became a "holy thorn" that bloomed on Christmas Day. Glastonbury is also the site of the most ancient Christian Church in England, an abbey of which two piers are still standing. The legend is, too, that King Arthur is buried there.[51]

Montagu Porch loved Glastonbury and eventually returned, but he was away for a long time. There had been a family scandal in which one of his sisters had been convicted of poisoning her husband in China. Her life sentence was later commuted and she returned to live in nearby Bath, where her mother joined her.

Porch was a graduate of Oxford and had served in the Boer War. After the war he went on an archaeological expedition, crossing the Sinai Desert by camel, to collect ancient stone implements.[52] He was a young man at loose ends, still not wanting to go home. In the British Colonial Service it was said that traditionally the first-class young men went to India (as Montagu's father had done), and the second-class men settled for Africa.

When his period of service was over, Porch returned to London, "and it was Winston, oddly enough, who gave me my next job." That was in 1906, when Winston was Undersecretary of the Colonial Office. It was his secretary, Edward Marsh, who interviewed Porch, and he was assigned to Nigeria as a Third-Class Resident.

> I remember him [Marsh] asking me: "Do you ride?" I had done quite a bit with the Taunton Vale Foxhounds. That's how I came to get a job in Northern Nigeria. I built the first town of Kaduna there—a few mud and straw huts for the engineers building the railroad to Kano.[53]

While he was in Nigeria, the Lagos *Standard* reported: "The Third Class Resident had two clerks tied and flogged because they did not prostrate themselves to the ground before him. All clerks must prostrate on the ground when meeting him."[54] The name of the Resident was not mentioned, but since there were only a few British officials in Nigeria, some may have thought it was Porch. The man must have been another Third Class Resident, as such actions do not fit in with the mild manner and character of Montagu Porch. Porch was concerned with introducing peanuts and cotton in the agricultural economy and keeping pet leopards off the streets.[55]

As a friend of Hugh Frewen's, he had taken time off to attend Hugh's wedding in Rome. When Jennie refused to dance with him, he did not persist. But the following day, the Duchess of Sermoneta invited him to lunch at her *palazzo,* and Jennie, of course, was there.

"We met again," he remembered. "We met a lot, though she was only there a fortnight. We looked at monuments a lot, talked a lot."

They both loved music, and both played the piano.

"You look as though you've got snow on your hair," she told him.

"It was true," Porch recalled, smiling. "It's a family thing."[56]

On the eve of World War I, Jennie had written him what he said was "a wonderful letter." Since then he had become a lieutenant in the Nigerian Regiment of the Cameroons Expeditionary Force, and now he was back in England on leave. Jennie was not in the mood to discourage him, and they saw a great deal of each other in a short time. After Porch returned to his Regiment, Jennie wrote Leonie: "I've met a young man I shall probably marry."[57]

But there were soon other young men on the scene, as well as people she cultivated in order to help further Winston's career while he was away at war. J. L. Garvin, a gaunt, young man with "intense eyes" and "a lovable nature," was a frequent visitor. Garvin was the brilliant editor of *The Observer,* and Jennie persuaded him to promote Winston as a political figure whose talents were urgently needed. Garvin regretfully informed her later that William Waldorf Astor had vetoed the plan. Astor, "tho personally friendly to Winston, does not want *The Observer* to run him politically just now. . . ."[58]

Jennie also dined with Lord Frazer, who "writes nearly all the leaders in *The Times.* . . . I thought he was a good person to 'hot up.' " There was also a long evening with her good friend Prime Minister Asquith, and Jennie sent Winston an account of it.

During this period Jennie told a friend, Colonel Court Repington, that she had had the pleasure of seeing both her husband and her son leading the House of Commons—"Winston once did so for a fortnight—'and the pain of hearing them both make speeches when they resigned.' " Repington also remembered how energetically Jennie went about trying to convert Winston's enemies. At a luncheon she met "Austin Harrison, who is one of Winston's most bitter opponents, and she took him away with her afterwards. . . ."[59] She also kept in close touch with Winston's political friends, always urging them to pull him out of the war and back into the government. Among them was Lloyd George, who had succeeded Kitchener as Minister of War.

In December 1916, Lloyd George became Prime Minister,[60] heading a Coalition Government. One of his early acts was to invite Winston to become Minister of Munitions, and Winston accepted.

Winston was back in England, but his job was demanding and he spent most of his free time with his wife and children. The same was true of Jack. Jennie complained to Clara "that her children never come near her."[61] But her nephew Oswald recalled that she seemed well supplied with other male escorts: Norman Forbes Robertson, a man named Simon, an Italian gentleman called Casati and a soldier named "Taylor, who has sung in public," among others.

She also translated a French book into English for a relief fund of the French Parliamentary Committee. It was called *My Return to Paris* and contained contributions by some of the prominent authors of the time. In addition, she edited and wrote the preface for a book entitled *Women's War Work,* a collection of articles telling of work performed by women in different countries to aid the war effort. She also organized a series of luncheon conferences under the auspices of *Outlook* magazine, in which leading French statesmen, including Clemenceau, spoke about the French effort in the war. These luncheons were held at the Ritz ballroom, and the tickets were always quickly sold.[62]

In her free time she called upon Society women in an effort to collect a chorus of singers to be featured in Mrs. Lloyd George's Welsh Memorial Matinee in December 1917; she also spent more time with her sister Clara, whose husband Moreton was seriously ill; organized a small dinner party for Winston so that he could meet the composer of "Keep The Home Fires Burning," a song he especially admired, and talked to theatrical producers about adapting some French plays.[63]

Jennie had sold her house on Brook Street, again turning a handsome profit. Winston had complimented her on the sale of a previous house because she did not have a fixation about staying in any particular home. "Not being a snail," he told her, "you can get on quite well without it." She now bought a home at 8 Westbourne Street in the Hyde Park section. Most of the houses she had bought and sold were in the same small area. This one was a four-story house with two columns at the entrance and a small garden. Each large window on the upper floors opened onto a small balcony. Within sight was an old church with a beautiful stained-glass window in the tower. A few minutes' walk away was Kensington Gardens.

The interior of the house did not have much to recommend it when she moved in, but Jennie soon gave it life and color. "She was an original when it came to interior decorating," recalled her niece excitedly, as if she were recreating the scene. "She was the first to use yellow curtains to catch the sunlight. . . . It was lovely. She transformed that house."[64]

She made door handles out of old silver watch cases; used tinted electric bulbs to provide a softer and more flattering light; papered the drawing room with an artificial wall paneling which "you can sponge . . . after the fogs"; and often used placemats instead of tablecloths on the gleaming mahogany tables. The furnishings and artwork were English (Queen Anne), French, Italian, Chinese, and Japanese.

But Jennie did not stop with renovating the house. Her long-time servant Walden had pleaded to be allowed to serve in the war in some way, and Winston found him a position at headquarters. Instead of replacing him with another man, Jennie created a sensation by using her maids as footmen and waiters. To make them look more impressive, she designed a hybrid uniform. They wore tight-fitting black cloth jackets with lapels, but cut off above the hips. Under the jackets the maids wore white starched collars, black bowties and waistcoats. Completing the uniform was a plain black skirt. Jennie classified her new servant as a "foot-maid."[65] Eddie Marsh remembered a dinner at Jennie's house during which Lord Rosebery spent much of the time examining the foot-maids.

Increasing zeppelin raids made dinner parties unpredictable. Lady Diana Cooper described a house being hit, the kitchen-maids screaming, the wounded brought to the basement. "Later . . . arrived Jennie Churchill and Maud Cunard, both a little tipsy, dancing and talking wildly. They had been walking and got scared, and had stopped for a drink." They were going to the opera because "it being raid-night, the public required example."[66]

Maud Cunard was another of Jennie's old American friends and had helped raise money for the *Maine*.[67] A short, slight figure with a receding chin and a high, piercing voice, she always wore a profusion of jewels and rings and called herself "Emerald." Her Grosvenor Square house was always open to the amusing, the important, the attractive. Maud Cunard could be malicious, but she was never dull. Beneath her excitability and her jewels was a pathetic, disillusioned woman. Jennie was a good listener.

Jennie also had listened to Winston's complaints about the government's inability to share his enthusiasm for tanks as a weapon of war. He had first urged their development when he was at the Admiralty, and after a time as Minister of Munitions he was able to do something about it. Later he had the satisfaction of being proved a prophet. At the end of 1917, when there was a successful Allied tank attack, Jennie wrote Leonie:

Do you see how successful Winston's caterpillars have
been and how disgusting the *Daily Mail* is today? Winston

worked at those things, scratching the money for them. . . .
Two years ago he went to France to "boom" them and Haig
sent for him when he was at the Admiralty to explain them.
Of course Winston did not invent them but they would not
exist today . . . had it not been for his foresight and push, and
now they want to take away from him the credit for them. It
makes my blood boil—the injustice and meanness with which
he is treated.[68]

Jennie often visited Leonie at her castle in Ireland, occasionally combining business with pleasure. The London *Daily Chronicle* assigned her to write several political articles. She wrote with loving memory of Isaac Butt, "that broad-minded and far-seeing man" who had "invented Home Rule," and expressed hope for the recently-convened Irish Convention, "fiercest of enemies . . . but there they all are, meeting under the same roof to discuss for once in amity, the problem of Ireland." [69]

She detailed the political problems in Ireland, analyzed the varied positions, and wrote of the general mood: the lighted streets, the absence of air-raids, the remoteness of war. "These men evidently do not understand or realize that, if the war is lost, their benighted country, under the iron rule of the Prussian mailed-fist, will cease to exist. . . ." But the Irish problem would not be solved, she concluded, "by trying to make good Irishmen into bad Englishmen."[70]

It was about this time that Jennie heard of the death of two of her earliest admirers, the Marquis Henri de Breteuil and Harry Cust. She was sixty-four now, still a remarkably handsome woman, her face smooth and unwrinkled, her eyes bright and eager. But she must have felt very mortal, even though she told her friends that she planned to live to be ninety. With her energy almost undiminished, they did not doubt her. Yet projects and social life could not satisfy her restlessness.

"She had been very lonely in her new house on Westbourne Street," her nephew Seymour Leslie remembered. She often telephoned him to come over to dine and play the piano with her. "I would find her in tears," he said.[71]

She had her moments of cynicism, too. She and some friends were listening to one man in their group praising his "adored one" effusively. Her virtue, he said, "above rubies."[72]

"Try diamonds," Jennie retorted.

Montagu Porch was home on leave again in 1918. He had had two more years to think about Jennie and to decide that he still wanted to marry her. "I don't think I remember proposing," Porch said. He and Jennie had been invited to visit Leonie at her castle in Ireland, and "by the time we got to the castle, there was an understanding."[73] Jennie later confessed to him, "You know I could never marry a man of my own age." They stayed there two weeks, deep in the peace of the Monaghan forests, overlooking the silent lake, and Leonie told them, "You look like a very happy and comfortable couple."[74]

Winston, according to Porch, was "very surprised." His reaction certainly must have been stronger than that—he was then forty-four years old and Porch was only forty-one.

There were other questions: Would Winston be politically embarrassed? What was the likelihood of success for a marriage based on equal proportions of loneliness and love?

Colonel Court Repington lunched with them, and recorded in his diary: "Lady R. charming about her future. Mr. Porch quite good-looking and intelligent. They get married tomorrow and go to Windsor for the weekend. Winston says that he hopes marriage won't become the vogue among ladies of his mother's age. . . ."[75]

The wedding on June 1, 1918, was unheralded and simple. They arrived at the Registry Office on Harrow-road quite unnoticed. Porch remembered exactly what Jennie wore: "a gray coat and skirt and a light-green toque. She looked very beautiful."[76]

Winston was the first to sign the register as a witness, and then he told Montagu, "I know you'll never regret you married her."

"I never did," Porch said many years later.[77]

Forty

$\mathscr{H}$E HAS A FUTURE AND I HAVE A PAST," JENNIE TOLD HER friend Lady Adele Essex, "so we should be all right."[1]

At dinner the night of Jennie's wedding, the novelist George Moore ". . . was rather funny about Lady Randolph. I suggested," Lady Cynthia Asquith recalled, "that perhaps she liked the idea of being known as the 'one white woman in Nigeria' instead of the one black one in London. He said he could only account for how they would spend the evenings by a re-application of the principle of the Arabian Nights, she regaling him with the recital of one of her amours (Moore claimed 200 lovers for her) nightly—and the collection would be known as the Nigerian Nights."[2]

Such acrid remarks soon spread all over the London dinner party circuit, and even Jennie joked to Porch about it: "I think people are saying that Miss Jerome went up the Church Hill, to the West, into the Porch. . . ." But Jennie's favorite motto was: "They say. What *do* they say? *Let* them say!"

At one dinner she attended, a woman was mentioned during the conversation, and another of the guests, a waspish lady, completely dissected her character, "practically casting her fragments on the dinner table." The room quieted for an awkward moment, because everyone else there knew that the woman in question was a good friend of Jennie's. Leaning across the table, "with that curiously quick uplift of her flashing eyes which never lost its charm," Jennie retorted, "It's a wise virgin who looks after her own lamp."[3]

When asked long afterward, "Didn't you care about the social censure?" Montagu Porch looked somewhat astonished. "Care?" he said, "I was in love."[4]

Porch wrote Winston that he found it incredible that he should be allowed so much happiness when the world was in anguish. He regarded this marriage as the most important step in his life and it "is not taken in the dark."

"I love your mother," he said. "I can make her happy–Her difficulties and obligations from henceforth will be shared by me–so willingly."[5]

Before returning to Nigeria, Porch took Jennie to Bath to meet his mother, who had not attended the wedding. Her son was the last of his line, and now she could expect no heir. The meeting was polite and brief.

Jennie was not allowed to accompany her husband to Africa. Civilian travel was restricted for the duration of the war, and the government did not even permit Porch to make an official request to have Jennie go with him. A West African newspaper urged that Jennie be permitted a passport, saying that Nigeria needed Jennie's "brains and push" to help right some of the country's injustices.[6]

"Poor Porchey is very lonely," Jennie wrote her sister, and Clara read to Jennie part of a letter from her son Oswald saying that Jennie ought to join "Montie" that fall "as it was the custom in England for married people to live together as much as possible." Jennie was not amused.[7]

Reporters observed that Jennie spent "many hours trying to persuade authorities to give her a passport," although an influential friend had told her that it was hopeless. "I feel so powerless to do anything," she wrote Leonie, "but I must try." But then she added, "Life is so short, and I have had a good share already. . . ."[8]

There were those who felt that Jennie was not really making the greatest effort to get permission to go. "She kept promising she would come to Nigeria, but she never came," said Mrs. Hadley Hucker, who became Porch's closest companion and friend in his later years. "She was too old to stand the heat probably."[9] Heat or no heat, the suspicion lingers that if it had been Kinsky or George in Nigeria, Jennie would have found a way to get there.

"My marriage will not in any way interfere with my war work," Jennie told the press. "I shall go on just as before, but I do not want to say what my plans are."[10] In truth, she really didn't know what her plans were. One thing about which she was certain was that she did not want to be known as Mrs. Montagu Porch. Her change of name to Mrs. George Cornwallis-West had ended in a battered pride, and she did not want that to happen again. On a visit to Blenheim after her new marriage, she signed her name, "Lady Randolph Churchill." She had "no snobbish feeling about it," she said, but she did want that name restored to her legally. "My boys asked me to," she added.[11]

London was a somber city: few cars in sight, people grim and worried, Lancaster Gate hospital where Jennie worked filled with "poor gassed soldiers." There had been four long years of casualty lists, rationing, and small hope. Then the military tide turned. There was a series of big battles and major victories. Suddenly—unbelievably—it was all over.

The Armistice of November 1918 allowed all the pent-up frustration and fear to explode into delirium. In London strangers marched down the streets arm-in-arm singing at the top of their voices; girls climbed onto tops of taxis and waved flags; people in automobiles kept up a steady blare of horns. That night Eddie Marsh collected playwright John Drinkwater and poet Siegfried Sassoon (who had been a patient at Lancaster Gate hospital) and took them to a party at Jennie's house. "The riotous celebrations were still in full swing . . . ," he later wrote.

King Edward's death had brought one era to a close for Jennie; now with the end of World War I another was rounded. Jennie was sixty-four years old and most of her contemporaries had slipped into social retirement. They had neither the inclination nor the servants for any more entertaining in the grand style. There was a new tone to the times. Graciousness was being supplanted by speed. Cars were being driven faster and faster. Dinners had fewer courses. More entertaining was being done in restaurants. Younger people danced the Turkey Trot, migrated in an evening from one nightclub to another, laughed louder and more easily. Jennie was one of the younger people.

She was, in fact, much younger-spirited than her old-fashioned husband. He had come from the quiet countryside, and was accustomed to a more fixed and orderly world. At the end of the war he resigned from the Nigerian Civil Service, returned to London and decided that he wanted more of Jennie's life. He sold some of his Glastonbury land, and Jennie bought a house in Berkeley Square as an investment. She redecorated it and then sold it for £17,000 ($80,000), making an excellent profit. "But she went through it like that," said Mrs. Hucker, snapping her fingers.[12]

Of course she did. She was not likely to change the style of a lifetime, nor did Porch want her to. Years afterward, he said, "I just want you to know that we had a very happy life together. There was never a dull moment. . . ."[13]

They traveled through France. Jennie's friends there were still flourishing, and there were new and exciting people at the parties—Stravinsky, Picasso, Ravel, Proust, James Joyce. Some of them later visited Jennie and Montie in London. Jennie still invited old friends such as Queen Alexandra, too—when the Queen came, Porch had to "telephone for a constable to be outside"[14]–but now she had more of the younger people. It was at her house that Zelda and F. Scott Fitzgerald met Winston, whom they found at first "so hard to talk to," until he later "turned out to be so pleasant."[15]

Shane Leslie remembered how exhilarated Porch was, as if he had come out of a cocoon into a new world. "Oh, Porchey, Porchey," said Leslie, with warmth and affection, as if he could still visualize the young man's wide-eyed wonder.[16]

In the midst of all this, Jennie was sharply recalled to old memories. Prince Charles Rudolf Andreas Kinsky died in Austria on December 11, 1919. His friend George Lambton wrote, "If ever a man died of a broken heart, Charles Kinsky did. . . ."[17]

It was not a shock that Jennie could share with Porch, but never was she more grateful to have him. More than ever now she needed a man who needed her. She still arranged small dinners for Winston to meet certain people, but Clementine did most of the entertaining his career required. And she still wrote Jack frequent notes about business contacts, but Jack now had his own contacts. Porch, however, depended on her completely.

After a year of fun and interesting people, he now wanted to take on some work of his own. Moreover, he and Jennie needed money. Jennie sought Jack's advice, as she did more often now. Winston was still in the Government, and in 1919 he was made Secretary of State for War as well as Air Minister, so he was usually inaccessible. Jack advised his mother on investments, listened to her complaints, adored her as always.

Porch's qualifications for a career were few. His only real knowledge was of Nigeria. But for a man who had knowledge of it, Nigeria was full of potentially profitable investment opportunities. Jack and Winston decided to finance his exploratory trip there.

Porch left London for Nigeria early in 1921. He had become increasingly resentful of the snubs and sneers. "I prefer the bullets of the Boer War or the flies of the Gold Coast," he said, "to the stings of the snobs in a London drawing room."[18]

Shortly after he left Jennie wrote him a note that he always treasured:

> My darling,
> Bless you and *au revoir* and I love you better than anything in the world and shall try to do all those things you want me to in your absence.
> Your loving wife,
> J

PS Love me and think of me.[19]

"My second marriage was romantic, but not successful," Jennie later said. "My third marriage was successful, but not romantic."

She was now sixty-seven years old and again alone. What could she do with herself?

She could try flying. At a party she met a jovial monocled man who was in the Royal Air Force, and soon she found herself sitting in a small wicker chair in his airplane flying at ninety miles an hour. "An extraordinary experience. Right above the clouds in a little coupe."[20]

She could act in a movie. During a dinner party with a group of young people, a film director suggested they all go out to his set and improvise a film for charity. Everyone there was forty years younger than Jennie, ". . . but we never gave it a thought," said Lady Altrincham. "She was just one of us. Jennie *was* young."[21]

She could take an interest in a young singer. A Welsh singer named Foster was making her debut. Just before her appearance she was trembling with nervousness, but an older woman "with extraordinary eyes" approached her without introduction and calmed her. That was Jennie.[22]

She could be controversial. "LADY RANDOLPH CHURCHILL DESCRIBES AMERICAN EDICT AS ABSURD." A Philadelphia clergyman had preached that for a gown to be "moral" it must not be cut more than three inches below the neck or seven and a half inches above the ground. Jennie told the press: "There is no such thing as a moral dress. . . . It's people who are moral or immoral. . . ."[23]

She could help her family. The American Embassy had mysteriously refused to permit her niece, Clare Sheridan, to enter the United States. Clare had been to Russia sculpting busts of Lenin and Trotsky, and Jennie discovered that there was a "dossier" on her in England. Checking the dossier, she learned that detectives had observed a newspaper editor going into Clare's apartment and often staying late. The newspaper was considered too friendly to Moscow, so the government suspected a plot. Jennie called on the American Consul to explain that Clare had been sculpting a bust of the editor, and Clare got her visa.

Jennie accompanied Clare to the station, urging her to come back quickly if she wasn't happy there. "She looked so beautiful that morning," remembered Clare, "and wistful. . . ."[24]

Her loveliness retained a contemporary quality. She wore her white hair "not like an elderly lady but in the Marquis style of the Louis XV days, when white frothy curls were affected by sprightly belles. . . ."[25]

Her list of activities still included everything from the Shakespeare Union to the YWCA. There were no new dances which she did not dance expertly. There were few good contemporary books she did not read. "I wept when I came to the end," she said of one, "and from such an emotionally hardened sinner, it meant a great deal. . . ." Her wit was still sharp. Describing an amorous gentleman, she observed that he had "more buzz than biz."

Her many friends pressed invitations on her, asking her to stay with them as long as she wished. In the spring of 1921 she accepted one from Vittoria, the Duchess of Sermoneta. From Florence, Jennie wrote to Leonie:

> I shall come home as good and sweet-tempered as a cherubim [sic]. How wonderful is this place! and what fun I am having! It seems positively selfish to be having such a good time and you in Ireland amidst a civil war.
>
> Winston, Clementine and I stayed with the Laverys at Cap d'Ail and he painted some delightful pictures. Vittoria met me in her car and I found Rome very gay, races, dances, *antiquaries*. Her palazzo charming but not grand like the Colonna palace where I lunched—such magnificence!
>
> They all play bridge *madly* and for very high stakes. I had to stop, you know how badly I play and the Romans are ra-pacious to a degree!
>
> . . . I have bought some lovely things. . . .[26]

Jennie had bought "some dainty slippers at the best Roman shoe-makers." The Duchess later observed that Jennie had the prettiest feet imaginable.[27]

"We did a good deal of sightseeing," the Duchess also recalled.

> We ransacked all the old curiosity shops and Jennie bought profusely; her zest in spending money was one of her charms. She was still a handsome woman, her dark eyes had lost none of their sparkle with the passing of years and the shape of her face was always admirable. Sargent's drawing of her was an excellent likeness; her beauty was of a dark southern type.[28]

The Duchess also remembered how much Jennie spoke of Winston and her "unswerving faith in his capacities." Jennie had said, "Winston's shoul-ders are broad enough to bear any burden." The Duchess also remarked that Jennie was "absolutely certain" that everything Winston did "was right."[29]

After her lively trip to Rome, Jennie accepted an invitation from Lady Frances Horner to visit at Mells Manor in Somerset, only a short distance from her husband's ancestral home in Glastonbury.[30] The home of "little Jack Horner" stood high on a rock and had a broad terrace overlooking the lakes below. Mells Manor was a gay house, with light pouring in through its Georgian windows. Outside there were shimmering masses of primroses and bluebells; inside were old-fashioned furnishings, enormous and comfortable.

At teatime, Jennie put on her new Italian shoes and hurried down the well-worn stairway. Three steps from the landing, she fell.[31] "I did not actually see what happened," Lady Horner recalled, "but I heard her fall and cry out . . . she could not rise. I propped her up with cushions under her back and feet and telephoned for the doctor from Frome. He came in a quarter of an hour and said it was a bad fracture of the left leg near the ankle."[32]

The bones were set, and two days later she was taken in an ambulance with a doctor and nurse to her home in London. The doctor diagnosed the injury as a simple fracture of both bones directly above the ankle. There was very little displacement, but there was considerable swelling of the ankle and foot. Progress was satisfactory at first, but within two weeks a portion of the skin blackened and gangrene set in. When her fever became dangerously high, Winston was called.

"In spite of the late hour, and with a characteristic promptness, he called in a surgeon at once, with the result that an operation was decided upon without delay, and actually performed within two hours."[33] When the doctor told her that her leg was to be amputated, Jennie calmly asked him to please make sure he cut high enough.[34] The amputation was done above the knee.

Oswald Frewen described the day in his diary on June 14, 1921:

> She (Mom) habitually looks at the worst side of things, and if poor little Jane is suffering physically, its nervous reflection on Mumkin is intensified. And I long ago discovered it is fatal to sympathize with her over everything: she only uses the sympathy as fuel to add fire to her torments. Ma sits next to the hall at Westbourne Street, conjuring up a vision of an amputated leg all the time, and fearful lest she not be sufficiently miserable to prove her love for her sister. Aunt Leonie came in while I was there. If Ma was 75% distraught, Leonie was most certainly 95% prostrate. . . . She was gray, white, and far beyond scenes or hysterics, and like a spent wave on a level beach. . . .
>
> Jack (the only unperturbable sanity in the place) motioned me to escort him home, as he was manifestly distraught. As we set out, he said hollowly, "I knew there was death in the house, I had a presentiment of it. I only did not

know who it would be. I thought it was your father. And of course it has come.[35]

But Jennie rallied wonderfully after the operation. She had good health, strength, and determination. When Eleanor Warrender came to visit, Jennie greeted her by saying, "You see, I have put my best foot forward to meet you. . . ."[36]

On June 28th, two weeks after the operation, Oswald brought a bouquet of lilies to Westbourne Street.

> I sent up to ask if she would see me, and she *did!*
>
> Aunt Leonie there. She [Jennie] looked her old self, and asked of every individual member of my family, and was very sweet, but kept grimacing with pain. She said she never realized in her hospital what the men were suffering, and she said, "The more it hurts, the more those devils of doctors like it. They say it's healing."
>
> Leonie said, quite low, "You mustn't stay too long," and Jennie overheard and said, "Oh no, I like to hear you two pussies talking." . . .[37]

The mail was arriving in a flood. Among the letters was a moving note from a legless soldier, wishing that Lady Randolph might be tended as she had once tended him.

Still in Nigeria, Porch finally received the news and immediately prepared to return to London.

On the morning of June 29th, Jennie awakened feeling fine. Her spirits were high, and she inquired about Leonie's daughter-in-law, who was due to have a baby that very morning. Then she ate a good breakfast. Suddenly, without warning, the main artery in the thigh of the amputated leg hemorrhaged. "Nurse, nurse," she called, "I'm pouring blood." Before the nurse could rush in to apply a tourniquet there was a heavy loss of blood.

Quite by chance, Bourke Cockran and his wife were in London at the time.[38] Bourke drove Leonie to Jennie's house where they learned that she was in a coma. Jack had arrived and so had Winston, still in his pajamas.

Later in the day, Oswald Frewen telephoned Leonie's son Shane Leslie. Shane asked him, "Have you heard the news?"

"No, what news?" asked Frewen.

"About Aunt Jennie . . ."

"I just got a telegram from Ma, saying she's worse."

"She's dead."

Oswald was told to break the news to his mother Clara, but she had been in Trafalgar Square and already had seen the headline on news posters: "DEATH OF LADY RANDOLPH CHURCHILL." Another had a black border and simple said, "LADY RANDY."[39]

"They put Aunt Jennie in her coffin at three, and were to close it down at eight," Frewen wrote in his diary on June 29, 1921.

> Ma went up with me and Aunt Leonie. First time I had ever seen anyone laid out. . . . I didn't want to go up, but accompanied Ma. . . . I got no sort of psychic reaction from Jennie herself and her body, in death, was as unlike herself as Lord Jellicoe is from Evelyn Laye. I had never seen her before without puckers round her mouth, and powder on her nose and flashing eyes, full of vivacity. Here the mouth had set, not in a Cupid's bow, but in a crescent, corners drooping, grim as a warrior-chief, the nose emerged aquiline, the wax-like complexion was sallow, the brow noble. It might have been the body of a Roman emperor, or a red-skinned chief; the only woman it called to my mind was my formidable grandmother, who died in 1896. We all saw the likeness. Ma, Aunt Leonie, Winston. . . .[40]

On July 1 Winston wrote a perceptive letter to Lady Islington:

> . . . But anyhow, she suffers no more pain; nor will she ever know old age, decrepitude, loneliness. Jack & I will miss her vy much: but for herself I do not know whether she has lost much. A long ordeal lay before her, at the end of wh there cd only be a partial & a limited respite.
>
> . . . I wish you could have seen her as she lay at rest—after all the sunshine & storm of life was over. Very beautiful & splendid she looked. Since the morning with its pangs, thirty years have fallen from her brow.
>
> She recalled to me the countenance I had admired as a child when she was in her heyday and the old brilliant world of the eighties & nineties seemed to come back. . . .

On July 2 the family traveled to Oxford in a reserved Victorian coach that had been attached to the train at Paddington Station. The blinds were half-drawn to keep out the blazing sun. It was a small and silent group: two sons, two sisters, three nephews, her butler Walden, a few friends, a representative of Queen Alexandra. Seymour Leslie remembered Winston saying to him, "You, too, loved her very much. . . ."

At Oxford they went by car the last eight dusty miles over the parched landscape to the church at Bladon, where the funeral was held. It was a quiet, country church that seemed almost tucked away from the rest of the world. Simultaneously there was a Memorial Service in London at St. Margaret's Church.[41]

"She was laid out amid a wealth of wonderful flowers," Shane Leslie wrote.

> I supplied two altar lights which burnt all night and Sir John Lavery painted the beautiful scene on canvas placing a crucifix between the lights to point the whole, and indeed the great suffering of her last days made her deathbed not unworthy of the crucifix. . . . Her sons and sisters were affected almost beyond the grief that is claimed by ties of flesh and blood. . . . Winston was bowed as under the greatest grief of his life. . . . We all threw roses into her grave. . . .[42]

Adjoining the small cemetery was a children's playground—Jennie would have liked that. She was buried in the Churchill family plot, alongside Lord Randolph. This was the cemetery where their two sons would one day join them.

There was a wreath of flowers from George West. Montagu Porch was still on a ship en route from Nigeria.[43]

Jennie's influence on Winston and the help she gave him would have justified her place in the history of our time. But the meaning of her life encompassed much more. More than the devotion of a King of England or of the many other men who had loved her. More than politics or an international literary review or a hospital ship or books and plays or war work.

Jennie was part of the action and passion of her world, and no woman of her era played a greater part in its history than she did. In doing so, she established her own frontiers and made her own rules. She had courage to match her beauty, an excitement to match her intelligence, energy to match her imagination.

Reminiscing with a friend, Jennie had agreed that if they could begin again from the age of seventeen, they would do the same as they had done, only more so. "Then we decided that we could not have done more so if we had tried."[44]

Prime Minister Asquith said of her: "She lived every inch of her life up to the edge."[45]

That could have been her epitaph.

Notes

Prologue

[1] This was the title of a magazine article about Jennie in *Current Literature* (December 1908).

[2] In Spain, bullfighters breed the courage of a bull not from the bull, but from the cow. In Ireland, horse trainers trace the spirit of a foal from its mare. And when Winston Churchill was born, a racing friend of the family commented to Mrs. Clara Jerome, "Interesting breeding, stamina goes through the dam and pace through the sire." Anita Leslie quotes this in her book *The Fabulous Mr. Jerome* (New York, Henry Holt, 1954).

[3] Jennie was fifty-four when her son Winston was married in 1908, and in its December issue that year, *Current Literature* commented, "It seems cruel to say that, at the recent marriage of her illustrious son, his mother seemed the junior of the bride by at least two years."

[4] From *The Autobiography of Margot Asquith,* (London, Thornton Butterworth, 1920). Her husband Herbert Asquith became Prime Minister in 1908.

Chapter 1

[1] Jerome maintained a financial interest in *The New York Times* Newspaper Establishment from 1858. During the Civil War period, he had fifteen to twenty of the hundred shares, each of $1,000 par value. Meyer Berger, *The Story of The New York Times* (New York, Simon and Schuster, 1951).

[2] Jerome family scrapbook of Mrs. John Sloane, New York.

[3] Mrs. Sloane's Jerome family records estimate his total estate value at £7,000 ($35,000), a fortune in those days.

[4] A copy of the inventory, filed with the county clerk in Wallingford, Connecticut, appears in Ralph G. Martin and Richard Harrity, *Man of the Century: Churchill* (New York: Duell, Sloan and Pearce, 1962).

[5] Leonard Jerome wrote a letter to his wife, May 6, 1889 in which he explained: "My grandfather, Aaron Jerome, in 1786, married Betsy Ball, daughter of Major Stebbings Ball, of the Army of the Revolution, and granddaughter of Rev. Eliphalet Ball, of Ballstown Spa, Saratoga County, who was an own cousin of Mary Ball,

Washington's mother. Washington had no lineal descendent. Consequently, we are the nearest of kin!!"

[6] The activity of his American ancestors in the Revolutionary War made Sir Winston Churchill an honorary member of the Sons of the American Revolution. Martin and Harrity, *op. cit.*

[7] The Isaac Jeromes lived to celebrate their Golden Anniversary in 1857, three years after Jennie was born.

[8] Professor T. J. Wertenbaker, historian of Princeton University, has written the full story of the incident in the *Princeton Alumni Weekly* (November 19, 1943).

[9] From *Princeton Faculty Minutes* (July 10, 1838).

[10] In a letter to Princeton, Jerome amplified his offer, "I think that the most pressing necessity of young America just now is, we have plenty of science and are pretty well up . . . in art, but our manners, I must say, are rather rough. The character of a gentleman I consider within the capacity of all—at least, it requires no extraordinary intellect. A due regard for the feelings of others is, in my judgment, its foundation."

[11] Cornelius Mann, in "Two Famous Descendents of John Cooke and Sarah Warren," *New York Genealogical and Biographical Record,* LXXIII: 3 (July 1942), 159–66, details the fact that Winston Churchill and Franklin Delano Roosevelt were eighth cousins, once removed.

[12] There are no genealogical facts to support any Indian ancestry in the Jerome family. Most of the genealogical lines of the Jeromes are carried back to the seventeenth century, with the exception of the Anna Baker line. She was Jennie's maternal grandmother. In his biography of his father, *Winston S. Churchill* (Boston, Houghton Mifflin, 1967), I, 15–16, Randolph S. Churchill notes that Anna Baker's mother's maiden name is not recorded in the genealogies and "is believed to have been an Iriquois Indian." However, Anna Baker and her mother came from Nova Scotia, and there were then no Iriquois Indians in Nova Scotia. Furthermore, intermarriage between whites and Indians were then very rare. Gladys E. Caffyn, in *Fragments in the Life of Ambrose Hall,* (Palmyra, N. Y., 1956), pp. 135–36, discounts the whole Indian claim as a myth. However, the physical fact of the marked Indian features of Clara Jerome and her sisters and their children lends credence to the possibility that Anna Baker may have been raped by an Indian, and that Clarissa Willcox may have been a half-caste. Certainly it was a Jerome family legend. Anita Leslie, in *The Remarkable Mr. Jerome* (New York, Henry Holt, 1954), quotes her grandmother, Leonie Leslie, remarking on her energy as saying, "That's my Indian blood—only don't let Mama know I told you." Leonie's son, Sir Shane Leslie, despite his Scottish kilts, has strong Indian facial features.

[13] These descriptions come from Moreton Frewen's letters in Allen Andrews, ed., *The Splendid Pauper* (Philadelphia, Lippincott, 1968), from Shane Leslie's *American Wonderland* (London, Michael Joseph, 1936), and from Mrs. John Sloane's Jerome family scrapbook.

[14] The daughter of Samuel Wilder. Dr. Blake McKelvey, in *Genesee County Scrapbook,* III: 1 (Spring 1952), notes that the Jerome brothers published a sprightly

pamphlet called *The Fancy Party,* about an elaborate costume party at the home of Mrs. William H. Greenough.

[15] Abraham Lincoln said this of *Uncle Tom's Cabin.*

[16] Stephen Fiske, *Offhand Portraits of Prominent New Yorkers* (New York, Lockwood & Sons, 1884).

[17] Reported in the New York *Herald,* March 5, 1891, a story of reminiscence on Jerome's death.

[18] The family joke was that Clara was the only woman Leonard Jerome had ever dated more than once who couldn't sing a single note.

[19] One of Clara's most persistent courtiers was Baron William Teggethoff, of whom she wrote, "he seemed to be, though one should not say it, rather taken." Jerome family letters.

[20] Twenty thousand New Yorkers waited until midnight outside Jenny Lind's apartment while three hundred red-shirted volunteer firemen, with flaming torches, came to serenade her. Seats to her concerts sold at auction for as high as $225.

[21] Jennie's actual birthdate has long been in question. Brooklyn kept no birth records at that time. The city eventually set a plaque on the house on Henry Street indicating that Jennie Jerome was born there in January 1850 (no day given). This corresponds to Jennie's own imagined recollection in her memoirs of being in Trieste when her father was Consul. But Jennie was never there. Leonard Jerome's first letter to the State Department from Trieste on May 1, 1852 (filed in the *Consular Dispatches,* Trieste, Vol. IV), mentions his wife "and child"—not "children." This is further substantiated by the Manifest of Passengers of *Baltic,* preserved in the National Archives in Washington D.C. (Roll 133, List 1146, November 13, 1853, lists Clara Jerome, aged two years, six months, as the only child of Mr. and Mrs. Jerome to arrive with them in New York.)

This also clearly indicates that Jennie was born after that date. The date recorded in the family Bible, although put in some years later, was made by Leonard Jerome's cousin, Margaret Middleton, an historian for the Daughters of the American Revolution and an accomplished genealogist. She unquestionably checked her facts with the immediate family. Further confirmation of the 1854 birth-date comes from a letter Jennie wrote to her husband on January 8, 1883, thanking him for a present: "Just in time for my birthday tomorrow—29 my dear! but I shall not acknowledge it to the world, 26 is quite enough."

Randolph S. Churchill in his biography, *Winston S. Churchill* (Boston, Houghton Mifflin, 1967), adds the further evidence of Jennie's christening mug which was engraved *"Jennie Jerome 1854."*

For a time there was even confusion as to whether Jennie was born in Brooklyn or Rochester. In 1941, in a speech at the University of Rochester, Winston Churchill said, "As you tell me, my mother was born in Rochester." And, later, touring the Henry Street home in Brooklyn, Churchill was overheard by his accompanying guide, James Kelly, historian of Brooklyn, to mumble, "But I thought it was Rochester?" However, even Dr. Blake McKelvey, city historian of Rochester, has firmly eliminated Rochester as Jennie's birthplace.

²² Cornelius Vanderbilt Jr., in *The Vanderbilt Feud* (London, Hutchinson, 1957), also adds that the top floors contained rooms for thirty-three servants. Vanderbilt noted that his grandparents spent five million dollars to build The Breakers at a time when a dollar represented a daily wage for an average worker.

²³ During a hectic period of partnership, Jerome told Vanderbilt, "My God, Commodore, if we keep on, we'll break every house on The Street!"

"My God, Commodore," became a Wall Street watchword. This anecdote appears in D. H. Smith, *Life of Commodore Vanderbilt* (McBride, 1927).

²⁴ *Ibid.*

²⁵ Lloyd Morris, *Incredible New York* (New York, Random House, 1951), adds that the seven-story Fifth Avenue Hotel, built by Amos Eno, was called "Eno's Folly" because it was said to be too far uptown to be profitable, and that its main business would be as a summer resort.

²⁶ New York City Landmarks Preservation Commission (November 23, 1965, Calendar No. 2, LP–0015) lists the Jerome house as the "first of New York City's 'private palaces.'" It added that it "represented one of the finest manifestations of that carefree architecture which transcended the miles of timid brick and correct but gloomy brownstones with a new gaiety." Its architect was Thomas R. Jackson.

²⁷ From Morris, *op. cit.*; also, Allen Nevins and Milton Halsey, eds., *The Diary of George Templeton Strong, 1835–1875* (New York, Macmillan, 1952). Both note that Jerome built the stables first.

²⁸ Stephen Birmingham, *Our Crowd* (New York, Harper, 1967). Belmont later became financial advisor to the Democratic Party. His wife's father, Commodore Matthew Perry, lived for a while with the Belmonts.

²⁹ Louise Chanler (whose mother was married to an Astor), lived nearby and was a childhood friend of Jennie's, remembering her as "a madcap," who caused her no end of trouble. Another mutual friend and neighbor was Consuelo Yznaga, who later became the Duchess of Manchester. Julie Chanler, *From Gaslight to Dawn* (New York, Pacific Printing Co., 1956). Several blocks away from Jennie lived a distant cousin of hers, four years younger, a boy named Theodore Roosevelt. He later became a close friend of Jennie's brother-in-law, Moreton Frewen.

³⁰ All of Jennie's comments in this chapter come from her *Reminiscences of Lady Randolph Churchill* (New York, Century, 1908).

³¹ In 1865, when the Atlantic cable was reported broken, Jerome offered his yacht to take the engineer Everett to repair the break. A New York newspaper reported, "This liberality on the part of Mr. Jerome will not only prevent any delay in the transmission of cable messages but will enable the Telegraph Company to meet the expedition with a vessel of which not only the American yachtsmen but every man in the country may be proud." Anita Leslie, *op. cit.*

³² Anita Leslie, *op. cit.*

³³ Minnie Hauk, *Memories of a Singer* (M. Philpot & Co., 1925). Miss Hauk also remembered how Mr. Jerome would take her and his daughters on dog-cart rides almost every Saturday.

[34] On December 31, 1862, President Lincoln approved a contract to resettle these 5,000 Negroes on Haiti, at the cost of fifty dollars apiece. Jerome's original involvement was to handle 450 of them.

[35] Sir Shane Leslie had an old Princeton College magazine clipping (no date) which said, "The United States owe more than is generally known to such men as . . . Leonard Jerome. Mr. Jerome gave at this period literally many hundreds of thousands of dollars for the preservation of the Union. . . ."

[36] Best sources of this are the files of the newspapers, particularly *The New York Times,* the New York *Tribune,* and the New York *Herald.*

[37] Lloyd Morris, *op. cit.* Morris notes that Wall Street speculator Jim Fisk later outshone Jerome with a coach; using three pairs of black and white horses, gold-plated harnesses, two Negro postillions in white livery on the leaders, and two white footmen in black livery on the back. Upholstery was of gold cloth.

[38] Widely quoted was Travers' remark to his wife, after returning late from carousing with the Jerome brothers:

"Is that you, Bill?" his wife asked.

"Ye-yes. Wh-why—yes," he stammered. "Who-who did you expect?"

It was also Travers, attending a yacht race with fellow stockbrokers, who asked, "B-but, wh-where are the customer's yachts?"

[39] From Shane Leslie, *op. cit.* Leslie records that his grandfather used some of his betting profits from that race to build a magnificent six-horse sleigh, painted in red, blue, and gold.

[40] Jerome had arranged for a competition of dinners between him, Belmont and Travers. The goal was the most perfect dinner ever achieved in Society. Lorenzo Delmonico, who made them all, called them "The Silver, Gold and Diamond Dinners." The competition was generally regarded as a tie. The menu for Jerome's dinner included "Aspic de Canvasback, salad of stringbeans with truffles and a truffled ice cream." (*Incredible New York,* Lloyd Morris.)

[41] Anita Leslie, *op. cit.,* quoting a member of the Belmont family.

Chapter 2

[1] Napoleon III was the third son of Louis Bonaparte, King of Holland and brother of Napoleon I. The two other sons had died leaving no children.

[2] From A. Forbes, *Life of Napoleon III* (New York, Dodd, Mead, 1897); Encyclopedia Brittanica (Chicago, 1960).

[3] G. P. Gooch in *The Second Empire* (London, Longmans, 1960), describes the features of the exhibition: the steam locomotive, the first aluminum, the new American rocking chair. The prizewinner, however, was a huge gun exhibited by Herr Friedrich Krupp of Essen. Gooch also wrote, "Paris has gone quite mad for the divine Patti when she sang 'Lucia . . .' "

[4] Jennie's comments in this chapter are quoted from *Reminiscences of Lady Randolph Churchill* (New York, Century, 1908), unless specifically attributed to letters.

[5] From Anita Leslie, *The Remarkable Mr. Jerome* (New York, Henry Holt, 1954).

[6] March 14, 1891.

[7] Stephen Fiske, in *Offhand Portraits of Prominent New Yorkers* (New York, G. R. Lockwood, 1884), describes Jerome's status just before this time: "He led the street now to the exclusion of everyone . . . was the pet as well as the king . . . almost worshipped as well as watched and imitated."

[8] His fortune has been estimated at $10 million, but it was probably never more than half of that.

[9] From Anita Leslie, *op. cit.*

[10] From Philip Guedalla, *The Second Empire* (New York, Putnam's, 1922).

[11] Guedalla quotes British Ambassador Lord Cowley: "To hear the way men and women talk of their future Empress is astounding . . . She has played her game so well that he can get her in no other way but marriage, and it is to gratify his passions that he married her. People are already speculating on their divorce."

[12] Empress Eugénie's doctors informed her that a second pregnancy might be fatal. After that she told a friend, "There is no longer any Eugénie. There is only the Empress." Simone André Maurois, *Miss Howard and the Emperor* (New York, Knopf, 1957).

[13] *Ibid.*

[14] Gooch, *op. cit.* Gooch also quoted Princess Mathilde as saying, "He is never angry. His strongest expression is 'Absurd.'"

[15] From Theodore Aronson, *The Golden Bees* (Greenwich, Conn., New York Graphic Society, 1964). Aronson quotes Carolyn Murat, "Oh, the boredom of these gatherings which lacked gaiety and life, which were absolutely devoid of witty conversation. There was no thought, save as to who should have precedence—a struggle which was renewed every Monday during the 52 weeks of the year!"

[16] *Ibid.* Aronson reports that at the age of seventy, Princess Mathilde discovered that her young lover Claude Popelin had been deceiving her. Mathilde and Popelin had been lovers for twenty years.

[17] Harold Kurtz, *The Empress Eugénie* (Boston, Houghton Mifflin, 1964). Pauline's husband, Prince Richard Metternich, was the son of the famous Chancellor. Pauline was not only his wife, but his niece. Dr. Bartens, who recorded the singing incident, later noted that he afterward had met the Princess in her home, where she seemed "the most accomplished great lady, serious in her manner, and wrapped up in her home and children."

[18] T. A. B. Corley, *Democratic Despot* (New York, Clarkson N. Potter, 1961).

[19] July 30, 1892. A. J. P. Taylor, *Bismarck* (New York, Knopf, 1955). Bismarck's general, Mottke, said years before the war: "Nothing could be more welcome to us than to have *now* the war we must have."

[20] From Philip Guedalla, *op. cit.* Empress Eugénie, however, denied that she had said "It is only a little war."

[21] Winston S. Churchill, *A History of the English Speaking Peoples* (New York, Dodd, Mead, 1956).

[22] From Mrs. Elizabeth Latimer, *France in the 19th Century* (Chicago, A. C. McClurg, 1892).

[23] The London *Spectator* published this poem about the incident:

> How jolly, Papa! How funny!
> How the blue men tumble about!
> Huzza! There's a fellow's head off—
> How the dark red blood spouts out!
> And look, what a jolly bonfire!
> Wants nothing but colored light!
> Oh, papa, burn a lot of cities,
> And burn the next one at night!

[24] On reading the news, Empress Eugénie was described as saying, "No, the Emperor has not capitulated. A Napoleon never capitulates. He is dead! . . . Listen to me: I say he is dead and they are trying to keep it from me!" Afterward she said, "Why didn't he get himself killed? Why isn't he buried under the walls of Sedan? . . . Had he no feeling that he was dishonoring himself? What a name to leave to his son!" "Lettres de Napoleon III," *Revue des Deux-Mondes* (September 1, 1930), p. 8.

[25] Henri Rochefort in *La Lanterne* at the time wrote his celebrated *bon mot*, "France has thirty-six million subjects, not counting the subjects of discontent." T. A. B. Corley, *op. cit.*

[26] The yacht belonged to Sir John Burgoyne, grandson of the General Burgoyne who surrendered his British Army to the Americans at Saratoga. It was only a small yacht with a crew of six.

Chapter 3

[1] Dec. 31, 1870. From Philip Guedalla, *The Second Empire* (New York, Putnam's, 1922).

[2] Brown's was a fashionable hotel, "a dingy looking building on a narrow street, frowsy-looking rooms with a bewildering variety of the 'rubbish of centuries.' Rigid armchairs had lace antimacassars; comfortless couches stood stiffly against the wall. . . . A chandelier with gas flares hung over a large round table on which was spread *The Times,* the *Morning Post,* a copy of *Punch* and the fashionable weekly, *The World.* Over the window hung heavy plush curtains, and the meager light was still further dimmed by the heavy lace window curtains." Consuelo Vanderbilt Balsan, *The Glitter and the Gold* (New York, Harper, 1952).

[3] There was also a pigeon postal service. From Elizabeth Latimer, *France in the 19th Century* (Chicago, A. C. McClurg, 1892).

[4] From Andre Simone Maurois, *Miss Howard and the Emperor* (New York, Knopf, 1957). It later became the clubhouse of the Chislehurst Golf Course.

[5] *Ibid.*

[6] From Latimer, *op. cit.*

[7] Theodore Aronson, *The Golden Bees* (Greenwich, Conn., New York Graphic Society, 1964). Charles Joseph Bonaparte was a grandson of Jerome Bonaparte and his American wife, Elizabeth Patterson of Baltimore. The young Bonaparte was then only twenty; he later graduated Harvard Law School and afterward became U.S. Attorney General in President Theodore Roosevelt's Administration.

[8] From Robert Baldick, *The Siege of Paris* (New York, Macmillan, 1964).

[9] From Werner Richter, *Bismarck* (New York, Putnam's, 1965).

[10] From Latimer, *op. cit.*

[11] E. B. Washburne, *Recollections of a Minister to France* (New York, Scribner's, 1887). "Amid all these sad scenes, the French will have their fun," wrote Washburne. "One of the illustrated papers exhibits the danger of eating rats, by the picture of a cat which has jumped down a man's throat after the rat, leaving only the hind legs and tail sticking out of his throat."

[12] Many Frenchmen directed their emotions toward vilifying Napoleon and Empress Eugénie. Obscene caricatures of Eugénie were sold in the streets showing her in the nude being fondled by several men. Melvin Kranzberg, *The Siege of Paris* (Ithaca, N.Y., Cornell University Press, 1950).

[13] From Philip Guedalla, *The Hundred Years* (Garden City, N. Y., Doubleday, 1936).

[14] From Anita Leslie, *The Remarkable Mr. Jerome* (New York, Henry Holt, 1954).

[15] From Elizabeth Longford, *Queen Victoria* (New York, Harper, 1965).

[16] From Alan Bott and Irene Clephane, *Our Mothers* (London, Gollancz, 1932). Bott and Clephane add that Queen Victoria served no refreshments at Palace receptions, and permitted no smoking.

[17] From R. C. K. Ensor, *England: 1870–1914* (London, Oxford University Press, 1936). Ensor also quotes a poem from a play *Dipsychus* (Scene V) by Arthur Hugh Clough, which typified the Victorian Age:

> Staid Englishmen, who toil and slave
> From your first childhood to your grave
> And seldom spend and always save–
> And do your duty all your life
> By your young family and wife.

[18] From Bott and Clephane, *op. cit.*

[19] From George Du Maurier, *From Punch: Society Pictures* (London, Bradbury, Agnew, n.d.).

[20] From Bott and Clephane, *op. cit.*

[21] From Frances, Countess of Warwick, *Life's Ebb and Flow* (New York, Morrow, 1929).

[22] From Virginia Cowles, *Edward VII and His Circle* (London, Hamish Hamilton, 1956).

[23] Max Beerbohm. *Things New and Old* (London, Heinemann, 1923). The caption under the cartoon reads, "The rare, the rather awful visits of Albert Edward, Prince of Wales, to Windsor Castle."

[24] From Cowles, *op. cit.*

[25] From Frances, Countess of Warwick, *Discretions* (New York, Scribner's, 1931). The Countess also added, "We considered the heads of historic houses who read serious works, encouraged scientists and the like, very, very dull. . . . We wished to know as little of them as possible, and our wishes were law."

[26] From Cowles, *op. cit.*

[27] From Jerome Hamilton Buckley, *The Victorian Temper* (Cambridge, Mass., Harvard University Press, 1951).

[28] From Guedalla, *The Second Empire*. Guedalla quotes Napoleon III as saying that armies do not follow ill men in carriages.

[29] From *Reminiscences of Lady Randolph Churchill.*

[30] From Bott and Clephane, *op. cit.*

[31] From Anita Leslie, *op. cit.*

[32] *Ibid.*

Chapter 4

[1] Jennie's own account of her first meeting with Randolph and his subsequent proposal is in a private memorandum in the family archives in the Muniments Room at Blenheim Palace.

[2] Anita Leslie, *The Remarkable Mr. Jerome* (New York, Henry Holt, 1954).

[3] Ralph Nevill ed., *Leaves from the Notebooks of Lady Dorothy Nevill* (London, Macmillan, 1907). Lady Nevill afterward commented that, "I think the influx of the American element into English society has done good, rather than harm, whilst there are many old families which, in mind and pocket, have been completely revivified by prudent marriages with American brides."

[4] *Reminiscences of Lady Randolph Churchill.*

[5] Anon., *Kings, Courts and Society* (London, Jarrolds, n.d.).

[6] The term "fag" in England does not have the American slang connotation of homosexual; it simply means a new student.

[7] Winston S. Churchill, *Lord Randolph Churchill,* (London, Macmillan, 1906).

[8] Merton College at the time had about seventy students and teachers. The best rooms went to the students who had the most money because one paid rent for the rooms. Randolph's room later became part of the college library, but before it did, it was used by Max Beerbohm, who found the name "Lord Randolph Churchill" carved on the table.

[9] He was also a member of the Debating Club.

[10] Anonymous, *Reminiscences of an Oxogenarian* (London, n.d.) describes the author's memory of his first day at Oxford, seeing young Randolph Churchill throwing oranges at a fellow classmate's open window, and saying to his compatriot, "More oranges."

[11] Frank Harris, *My Life and Loves* (New York, Grove Press, 1963).

[12] Robert Rhodes James, *Lord Randolph Churchill* (New York, A. S. Barnes, 1960). Rhodes James notes that parliamentary critic H. W. Lucy tested Churchill's ability to memorize a page of Gibbon in the 1880's, and Randolph recited it perfectly.

[13] Most of the letters referred to in this chapter are in the family archives at Blenheim Palace.

[14] Winston S. Churchill, *Marlborough: His Life and Times,* 4 vols. (London, Harrap, 1934).

[15] Duchess Sarah would have liked Jennie; they were much of a kind. Both were beautiful women who loved love, and yet both would have made mighty men. Each was exciting, furiously outspoken, and always conscious of her power. Much could be made of the parallel of their lives. Sarah was almost nineteen when she married

John Churchill. If she loved him, he wrote her, "it would make me immortal." John Churchill had strength and ambition, but it was Sarah who did help make him immortal. She and Jennie were both tempestuous women of courage and common sense.

[16] A. L. Rowse, *The Early Churchills* (New York, Harper, 1958) also noted that the fourth Duke of Marlborough had a passion for astronomy, while the fifth Duke preferred botany.

[17] The *Dictionary of National Biography,* which also describes him as "a sensible, honorable and industrious public man."

[18] Stephen Fiske, *Offhand Portraits of Prominent New Yorkers* (New York, Lockwood & Sons, 1884).

[19] According to the head librarian at Oxford, Brodrick also wrote lead editorials for *The Times,* and later served as Warden of Merton College. He ran three times for office in Woodstock, and lost each time.

[20] Sir Edward Clarke, *The Story of My Life* (London, John Murray, 1918).

[21] This was the same Herbert Asquith who later became Prime Minister. J. A. Spender and Cyril Asquith, *Life of Herbert Henry Asquith, Lord Oxford and Asquith* (London, Hutchinson, 1932), Vol. I, note that Asquith "spent two or three hours a day sailing on the upper river and some of the residue of his time in speaking for Mr. Brodrick against Lord Randolph Churchill at the Wood-stock election."

[22] Anita Leslie, *op. cit.*

[23] Rowse, *op. cit.*

[24] Jerome, in that same letter, also added, "My daughter, although not a Russian princess, is an American and ranks precisely the same. And you have no doubt seen that the Russian settlement recently published claims *everything* for the bride." Jerome was referring to Czar Alexander II's daughter, who had been married earlier that year to Queen Victoria's son, the Duke of Edinburgh. The bride was given about a million dollars, the income from it for her "exclusive use and enjoyment."

[25] A letter from the British Ambassador in Paris, Lord Lyons, to British Foreign Secretary Lord Derby, dated April 15, 1874 (Public Record Office, F.O. 146, Book No. 1745, No. 380), reads: "My Lord: I have the honor to transmit herewith, under flying seal, a letterhead which I have addressed to the Secretary of the Bishop of London's Registry Office, containing the certificate of a marriage solemnized at this Embassy, between Lord Randolph Henry Spencer Churchill, bachelor, and Jennie Jerome, spinster.

"Together with the usual declaration and customary fee of one pound for the due registry of the same."

In the pouch from Paris on that same day were letters about the French Vice Admiral's plans for an International Geographical Congress in Paris the next year.

[26] Anita Leslie, *op. cit.*

Chapter 5

[1] Letter from Winston Churchill to Edward Marsh, April 30, 1937. (The Papers of Sir Edward Marsh, in possession of the Marquess of Bath, unpublished.)

[2] Jennie wrote her mother on July 1, 1874, that the Duke of Marlborough paid ten thousand pounds ($50,000) for the lease. "Randolph had no settlements made on him when he married," Jennie added, "and this, of course, makes a settlement. If anything was to happen to him, this house comes to me."

[3] During an election campaign, Winston Churchill spoke at Blenheim before a huge crowd. Before his speech, he walked through the palace with Gerald O'Brien, and then suddenly asked "O'Brien, has this old ruin got bathroom facilities for all these people?" (Ralph G. Martin and Richard Harrity, *Man of the Century: Churchill,* New York, Duell, Sloan & Pearce, 1962.)

[4] Consuelo Vanderbilt Balsan, *The Glitter and the Gold* (New York, Harper, 1952). The author was a former Duchess of Marlborough.

[5] Part of the epitaph for Blenheim's architect, Sir John Vanbrugh, was:

> Lie heavy on him, earth, for he
> Laid many a heavy loan on thee.

[6] A different view comes from *Blenheim* (Oxford, Henry Slatter, n.d.) quoting the *Travels of Mirza Abu Taleb Khan, 1799–1803*: "This place is without comparison superior to any thing I ever beheld. The beauties of Windsor Park faded before it, and every other place I had visited was effaced from my collection, on viewing its magnificence."

[7] *Reminiscences of Lady Randolph Churchill.*

[8] M. J. Gifford, ed., *Pages from the Diary of an Oxford Lady* (London, n.d.).

[9] Earl of Ronaldshay, *Life of Lord Curzon* (New York, Boni & Liverwright, 1927).

[10] Jennie remembered how the blood from the wounded pigeons often stained the gowns of the watching women. Lady Warwick noted in *Discretions* (New York, Scribner's, 1931), "I saw two birds, one with a broken wing and one with a broken leg, come painfully to rest on the green. That was enough! I vowed I would never go there again. . . ."

[11] Anon., *Kings, Courts and Society* (London, Jarrolds, n.d.).

[12] Virginia Cowles, *Edward VII and His Circle* (London, Hamish Hamilton, 1956).

[13] Margot Tennant, who later became Margot Asquith, the wife of the Prime Minister, described the Prince of Wales as "a professional lovemaker." After a single meeting with Tennant, the Prince sent her a gold sharkskin cigarette case with a diamond and sapphire clasp. Virginia Cowles, *op. cit.* Rudyard Kipling called Prince Edward "that corpulent voluptuary." A cartoon of the time showed a pretty girl getting dressed for an evening out. Beside her looking glass was an invitation to Buckingham Palace; the cartoon caption said, "She Stoops To Conquer." (Theo Lang, *The Darling Daisy Affair,* New York, Atheneum, 1966.)

[14] Interview with Sir Shane Leslie.

[15] Consuelo's marriage had the greatest social prestige, since there were only twenty-seven Dukes in the whole United Kingdom. When the Duke arrived in the United States to court Consuelo, the New York *World* ran a headline, "Attention American Heiresses, What Will You Bid?" and then went on to say, "Manchester is the poorest Duke in Burke's Peerage, financially and in morals." Consuelo's father was a Cuban who had settled in Louisiana and become a rich cotton plantation owner.

Consuelo, like Jennie, was beautiful, witty, and soon very unhappy. Elizabeth Eliot, *They All Married Well* (London, Cassell, 1960).

[16] Sir George Arthur, *Concerning Winston Spencer Churchill* (London, Heinemann, 1940).

[17] Anita Leslie, *The Remarkable Mr. Jerome* (New York, Henry Holt, 1954).

[18] Lady St. Hélier, *Memories of Fifty Years*. (London, E. Arnold, 1909).

[19] Quoted in Robert Rhodes James, *Lord Randolph Churchill* (New York, A. S. Barnes, 1960).

[20] H. W. Lucy, *Speeches of the Rt. Hon. Lord Randolph Churchill, with a sketch of his life* (London, 1885). Lucy described him then as "a well-groomed young man with protuberant eyes, pale face and a ponderous mustache." Lucy himself was described as "absolutely unique ... the only individual in the world who can amusingly describe the proceedings of that dismal, make-believe assemblage, the modern House of Commons."

[21] Rhodes James, *op. cit.*

[22] W. F. Monypenny and G. E. Buckle, *The Life of Benjamin Disraeli* (London, John Murray, 1929), Vol. II.

[23] Shane Leslie, *Men Were Different* (London, Michael Joseph, 1937). Sir Shane also reports that the Churchill family shield is inscribed with the Spanish words, "Fiel Pero Desdicado" ("Faithful but Unfortunate").

[24] Lady St. Hélier, *op. cit.*

[25] *Reminiscences of Lady Randolph Churchill.* Lady Randolph regarded Gladstone and Lord Salisbury as two of the pleasantest companions at dinner "of all the statesmen I have met. Both had the happy knack of seeming vastly interested in one's conversation, no matter what the subject ... there was no condescension or 'Tempering of the wind to the shorn lamb' about it. ..."

[26] Anita Leslie, *op. cit.*

[27] *Leaves from the Notebooks of Lady Dorothy Nevill,* ed. Ralph Nevill (London, Macmillan, 1907). "Here Lady Nevill reiterated Lady Cowper's formula: To make a ball successful, three men should always be asked to every lady—one to dance, one to eat and one to stare—that makes everything go off well."

[28] Winston S. Churchill, *Savrola* (New York, Random House, 1956), pp. 32–33.

[29] Virginia Peacock, *Famous American Belles of the Nineteenth Century* (Philadelphia, Lippincott, 1901). Peacock adds, "One of the first American women before whom these latter-day barriers of social prejudice gave way, was Jennie Jerome of New York. She penetrated the innermost recesses of British society, opening the way more than any other woman to the position her countrywomen occupy there at the end of the century, and holding herself a place second to no other American woman in Europe."

[30] A. L. Baron, *Man Against Germs* (New York, Dutton, 1957); Judson Bennett Gilbert, *Disease and Destiny* (Los Angeles, Dawson's, 1962). *Medical Annual* (District of Columbia, 1955) also lists a number of other prominent people who supposedly had syphilis: King Francis I, Ivan the Terrible, Pope Alexander VI, Pope Julius II, Guy de Maupassant, Frederick the Great, Benvenuto Cellini, Beethoven,

Schubert, and Heinrich Heine. The researcher at the *Wellcome British Medical Library* also adds Goya, Lenin, Rabelais, Oscar Wilde, Edouard Manet, and Woodrow Wilson.

[31] A. L. Rowse, *The Early Churchills* (New York, Harper, 1958).

Chapter 6

[1] Philip Guedalla, *The Hundred Years* (Garden City, N. Y., Doubleday, 1936).

[2] *Ibid.*

[3] James Truslow Adams, in *Empire on the Seven Seas* (New York, Scribner's, 1940), adds that the Queen objected to conversation with the respectful but blunt Gladstone "as tho she were a public meeting," but that she enjoyed talking to Disraeli. Winston S. Churchill, in *A History of the English Speaking Peoples* (New York, Dodd, Mead, 1956), Vol. IV, quotes Gladstone as saying, "The Queen is enough to kill any man." The Queen's preference for Disraeli was based on the fact that he not only bought control of the Suez Canal after he came into power, but he also made the Queen the Empress of India.

[4] W. F. Monypenny and G. E. Buckle, *The Life of Benjamin Disraeli* (London, John Murray, 1929), Vol. II. The letter was addressed to Lady Bradford and dated April 4, 1876.

[5] A. L. Rowse, *The Early Churchills* (New York, Harper, 1958).

[6] Randolph S. Churchill, *Winston S. Churchill* (Boston, Houghton Mifflin, 1967), I, 29.

[7] *Ibid.,* Supplement Number II (April 21, 1876).

[8] Anita Leslie, *The Remarkable Mr. Jerome* (New York, Henry Holt, 1954).

[9] Extract from letter dated March 10, 1876, the Royal Archives, published in Randolph S. Churchill, *op. cit.,* I, 29.

[10] George W. Smalley, *Anglo-American Memories* (New York, Putnam's, 1912). Smalley was a noted American editor and a good friend of the Churchill's, Lady Jeune, and Lady Nevill. However, it seems that these were not the only copies of the letters. See Randolph Churchill, *op. cit.*

For an excellent description of Hartington, see Barbara Tuchman, *The Proud Tower,* (New York, Macmillan, 1965).

[11] Robert Rhodes James, *Lord Randolph Churchill* (New York, A. S. Barnes, 1960). Randolph S. Churchill gives the most complete account of the incident in the first volume of his *Winston S. Churchill,* although he does not have the details of Lord Hartington's intervention, as described by G. W. Smalley.

[12] *Reminiscences of Lady Randolph Churchill.*

[13] Winston S. Churchill, *Lord Randolph Churchill* (London, Macmillan, 1906).

[14] Randolph S. Churchill, *op. cit.* Letter dated April 20, 1876.

[15] Harry Tyrwhitt-Wilson was better known to his close friends as "The Smiler." He was the eldest son of Sir Henry Thomas Tyrwhitt and the Baroness Berners, and assumed the name of Wilson by royal license in 1876. He was also a good friend of Lord Rosebery's and an equerry to the Prince of Wales.

[16] Lloyd Morris, *Incredible New York* (New York, Random House, 1951).

[17] Lawrence Jerome was the sixth of eight sons of Isaac Jerome, and younger than Leonard. He and Leonard had married the Hall sisters, Clara and Catherine. This made Lawrence's son, William Travers Jerome a double first cousin of Jennie. Jennie wrote of the Philadelphia trip with her Uncle Larry, "He kept us in transports of laughter."

Chapter 7

[1] *Reminiscences of Lady Randolph Churchill.*

[2] Winston S. Churchill, *My Early Life* (New York, Scribner's, 1930).

[3] Viscount D'Abernon, *Portraits and Appreciations* (London, Hodder & Stoughton, n.d.).

[4] Randolph S. Churchill, *Winston S. Churchill* (Boston, Houghton Mifflin, 1967), I, 35.

[5] R. Barry O'Brien, *The Life of Charles Stewart Parnell* (London, Smith, Elder, 1898). O'Brien noted, "Parnell liked few men; above all, he liked few Englishmen. Yet he regarded Lord Randolph Churchill with no unfriendly feelings. He thought that the young Tory Democrat possessed generous instincts, entertained kindly feelings toward the Irish, and was full of originality, resource and courage."

[6] Louis J. Jennings, ed., *Speeches of Lord Randolph Churchill* (London, Longmans, 1889).

[7] Winston S. Churchill, *Lord Randolph Churchill* (London, Macmillan, 1906). Churchill also quotes the rest of the Duke's letter, which expressed amazement and annoyance and encouraged a public rebuke of his son's views.

[8] Randolph S. Churchill, *op. cit.,* I, 35–36.

[9] Winston S. Churchill, *My Early Life.*

[10] This, of course, may also explain Jennie's supposed paucity of maternal feeling for Winston in his early years. Perhaps she, too, saw in her son the early fruit that had forced the marriage.

[11] Joan Haslit, *The Lonely Empress* (Cleveland, World, 1965), and Count Egon Corti, *Elizabeth, Empress of Austria* (New Haven, Yale University Press, 1936). Haslit also quotes the Empress as saying of Ireland: "The great advantage of Ireland is that it has no Royal Highnesses. . . . Here at last I feel free and at my ease. . . ."

[12] Winston S. Churchill, *My Early Life.*

[13] Mabell, Countess of Airlie, *With the Guards We Shall Go* (London, Hodder & Stoughton, 1933). In 1880 Strange Jocelyn became the Earl of Roden.

[14] John Spencer-Churchill.

Chapter 8

[1] From W. J. Reader, *Life in Victorian England* (New York, Putnam's, 1964): "Authority, except in the special case of the Queen, nearly always meant male authority. . . . women, because they were weaker, should be protected rather than exploited."

[2] From R. C. K. Ensor, *England: 1870–1914* (London, Oxford University Press, 1936).

[3] Frances, Countess of Warwick, *Discretions* (New York, Scribner's, 1931). She added, "Nobody felt quite safe—How could we, recognizing that, in the feverish search for pleasure, any woman might lose her lover, any man's mistress might be lured away!"

[4] Anon., *Uncensored Recollections* (Philadelphia, Lippincott, 1924): "The illness that first seized him during his Oxford days, began ere long to cause trouble, and although he was always willing, nay glad enough to consult any specialist, he never would follow the treatment recommended." He would say, "All right," and do nothing. The author told of taking Randolph to see a famous specialist in Paris. "When we got to the doctor's, he wanted to back out and I had to take him to the Hotel Chatham bar and refresh him with a brandy cocktail before he would go any further." The author tells of tipping the manservant to get immediate access to the doctor without waiting. "When I returned triumphant . . . I found that Randolph had bolted down the *escalier de service!* I rushed after him, dragged him back; the doctor saw him at once, prescribed for him and warned him. But all in vain. . . ."

[5] They had sublet their Charles Street home while in Ireland.

[6] Twenty-seven contributors to *The Times, Fifty Years: 1882–1930* (London, Thornton Butterworth, 1932).

[7] Winston S. Churchill, *My Early Life* (New York, Scribner's, 1930).

[8] Winston S. Churchill, *Lord Randolph Churchill* (London, Macmillan, 1906).

[9] Shane Leslie, *Long Shadows* (London, John Murray, 1966). Other games Leslie remembers Jennie playing that night with Winston included "Hunt the Thimble" and "Hunt the Slipper." By 2 A.M., Shane Leslie quotes Jennie as saying, "Winston, you are impossible." Leslie notes that this occasion marked the first time Mrs. Everest had gone on holiday in five years.

[10] This letter is reproduced, without a date, in Anita Leslie, *The Remarkable Mr. Jerome* (New York, Henry Holt, 1954). Randolph S. Churchill in *Winston S. Churchill* (Boston, Houghton Mifflin, 1967) reproduces another letter dated Jan. 4, 1882, which he regards as Winston's first letter.

[11] Winston S. Churchill, *My Early Life*.

[12] Shane Leslie, *op. cit.*

[13] *Reminiscences of Lady Randolph Churchill*.

[14] G. W. E. Russell, *Portraits of the Seventies* (London, Fisher Unwin, 1960).

[15] *Reminiscences of Lady Randolph Churchill*.

[16] Barbara Tuchman, *The Proud Tower* (New York, Macmillan, 1965). The author quotes Lord Hartington as saying of Balfour, "Of all the statesmen I have known [he was] the most persuasive speaker."

[17] John Morley, *Life of William Ewart Gladstone* (London, Macmillan, 1932).

[18] R. Barry O'Brien, *The Life of Charles Stewart Parnell* (London, Smith, Elder, 1898). O'Brien adds that Parnell "also had the shrewd suspicion that there was nothing which this rattling young Tory would relish more keenly than 'dishing' the Whigs—except perhaps 'dishing' the Tories."

[19] Sir Henry Lucy, *Diary of a Journalist* (London, John Murray, 1920). Lucy suggests the origin of the Fourth Party name came when a Member of the House said in debate that there were two great political parties in the State. Parnell then called out, "Three," and Randolph stood up and yelled, "Four." But Lucy also says that Frank Hugh O'Donnell already had referred to the Irish Nationalists as the Third Party.

[20] *Ibid.*

[21] *Reminiscences of Lady Randolph Churchill.*

[22] Robert Rhodes James, *Lord Randolph Churchill* (New York, A. S. Barnes, 1960).

[23] Winston S. Churchill, *My Early Life.*

[24] Rhodes James, *op. cit.*

[25] Moreton Frewen, *Melton Mowbray & Other Memories* (London, Herbert Jenkins, 1924). Frewen described his father-in-law's conversational dinners: "I doubt if, on the earth's surface, did such a far-flung group of men ever collect round a single table. What a poem was the table itself! It was a slab of Honduras mahogany, lacquered with age and care."

[26] *Ibid.* Frewen later listed Jennie as one of three "really beautiful Americans" in England.

[27] Virginia Cowles, *Edward VII and His Circle* (London, Hamish Hamilton, 1956). Cowles writes that Frewen was one of Langtry's earliest admirers.

[28] Lady St. Hélier (Mary Jeune), *Memories of Fifty Years* (London, E. Arnold, 1909). Lady Jeune notes that the one unchanging quality in his unpredictable nature was his deep feeling for his mother.

[29] Jerome family letters.

[30] *Ibid.*

[31] Lloyd Morris, *Incredible New York* (New York, Random House, 1951).

[32] *Ibid.*

[33] *Reminiscences of Lady Randolph Churchill.*

Chapter 9

[1] Jennie also noted in her *Reminiscences* that the dynamo in her basement for the electric power, made so much noise that "it greatly excited all the horses as they approached our door."

[2] The Victorian slogan, however, was "Have nothing in your house except what you know to be useful or believe to be beautiful." R. C. K. Ensor, *England: 1870–1914* (London, Oxford University Press, 1936).

[3] An article in the *Evening News,* October 15, 1921, describing a sale of Lady Randolph Churchill's furniture and belongings, mentioned a catalogue of objects and art from at least five countries. The anonymous author also noted, "I remember once seeing in one of her houses, a tall, slender cupboard, lined with silk, and glass-fronted, which contained nothing but brocaded evening shoes, shelf upon shelf of them, with their old paste buckles glistening through the glass. I remember her saying that she never threw away her evening shoes, and that some of them, she had had for twenty years. . . . Lady Randolph's feet were exceptionally small

and beautifully formed, so that her shoes kept their shape and always looked nice, to the end of their days. Consequently, this array of tiny shoes was most effective and pretty."

[4] "My father was over five feet nine and a half inches—quite a passable stature," wrote Winston Churchill in *Thoughts and Adventures* (New York, Scribner's, 1932), "but because he was pictured in conflict with Mr. Gladstone, he was always represented as a midget." Churchill added that he continually got letters from people asking of his father, "Is it really true he was no more than five feet high?"

[5] Robert Rhodes James, *Lord Randolph Churchill* (New York, A. S. Barnes, 1960).

[6] Colonel Burnaby of the Royal Horse Guards served as a war correspondent for *The Times,* took a solo balloon flight from Dover to Normandy, and captured national attention in 1875 with his ride from London to Khiva—Russian protests stopped his riding on to Samarkand in Central Asia. He was killed in 1885, "sword in hand, while resisting the desperate charge of the Arabs at the battle of Abu Klea."

[7] *Leaves from the Notebooks of Lady Dorothy Nevill,* ed. Ralph Nevill (London, Macmillan, 1907). In *Under Five Reigns,* also edited by her son (London, Methuen, 1910), Lady Nevill quoted the comment, often repeated, "I have seen women so delicate that they were afraid to ride, for fear of the horse running away; afraid to sail, for fear the boat might upset; afraid to walk, for fear that the dew might fall; but I never saw one afraid to be married!"

[8] *The Daily Telegraph* in London, July 3, 1963, quoted the New York State Supreme Court ruling that it was "an inalienable right" to have one's body tattooed, regardless of the contention that it might cause hepatitis. The article said, "Lady Randolph Churchill, mother of Sir Winston Churchill, was tattooed for ornamental purposes as were King Frederick IX of Denmark, King George V, Edward VII, Alfonso XII of Spain, Viscount Montgomery, and countless other distinguished members of society."

[9] In Randolph Churchill's biography of his father, and in the supplemental volumes, which is the definitive collection of Churchill letters, there are very few letters from Randolph to Winston.

[10] Von Josef Erwin Folkmann, *Die Gefürstete Linie des Uralten und Etlen Geschlechtes Kinsky* (Prague, 1861), traces the Kinsky family back to the year 1209.

[11] George Lambton, *Men and Horses I Have Known* (London, Thornton Butterworth, 1924), relates the story of Kinsky's first experience in London society, a dinner by Sir Horace Farquhar. A drunk cabman had taken Kinsky all over London before bringing him to the Farquhar home, at which time the dinner there was half over. Kinsky was explaining all this to his host with such furious gestures that he knocked a plate of soup into Lady Castlereagh's lap. Kinsky was so handsome and such a hero that Lady Castlereagh "continued her conversation with him as if nothing had happened."

[12] Blandford was quoted as saying, "Mistress, yes; but future Duchess of Marlborough, *never!*"

[13] Curzon was five years younger than Jennie. There is a family story that Jennie once loaned Curzon her nightgown when he unexpectedly decided to spend the night at Blenheim and had no pajamas.

Chapter 10

[1] Her membership card number was 12.

[2] John Hadfield, ed., *The Saturday Book—25* (London, Hutchinson, 1965). Hadfield refers to this Victorian period as "the Sober Eighties," as compared with the oncoming "Naughty Nineties." He quotes the poet William Butler Yeats as saying, "Everybody got down off his stilts; henceforth, nobody drank absinthe with his black coffee; nobody went mad; nobody committed suicide . . . or if they did, I have forgotten."

[3] Shane Leslie, *The End of a Chapter* (New York, Scribner's, 1917).

[4] *Reminiscences of Lady Randolph Churchill.*

[5] January 24, 1884. Winston S. Churchill, *Lord Randolph Churchill* (London, Macmillan, 1906).

[6] George W. Smalley, *Anglo-American Memories* (New York, Putnam's, 1912). Smalley adds, "The Duchess of Marlborough was a woman who may always be adduced in support of the theory that qualities of mind and character descend from mother to son."

[7] *Ibid.*

[8] The man was Lord Hartington. Randolph later told Jennie, "This is the sort of remark that overturns a coach." Robert Rhodes James, *Lord Randolph Churchill* (New York, A. S. Barnes, 1960).

[9] *Reminiscences of Lady Randolph Churchill.*

[10] R. C. K. Ensor, *England: 1870–1914* (London, Oxford University Press, 1936); see also Stephen Gwynn, *The Life of the Rt. Hon. Sir Charles Dilke, Bart., M.P.,* completed and edited by Gertrude M. Tuckwell (London, John Murray, 1917). Dilke's public downfall came when he refused to testify in the divorce case listing him as a corespondent.

[11] Lady Randolph Churchill, *Small Talks on Big Subjects* (London, Pearson, 1916). She also added, "If people sufficiently prominent for one reason or another succeed in surrounding themselves with an atmosphere of mystery, the interest of the public is aroused, for the possibilities of the 'dark horse' are always attractive."

[12] Leonie, in a letter to Clara, commented on the rumor of Randolph and Lady de Grey, and said that "Randolph is not in the least devoted to Gladys de Grey . . . only as she [Jennie] has no flirtation on hand, she suddenly notices his coldness. It has been like that for years. . . . *Chacun à son gout.*"

[13] Rhodes James, *op. cit.*

[14] Elliott O'Donnell, ed., *Mrs. E. M. Ward's Reminiscences* (New York, Pitman, 1911). Mrs. Ward added, "Lady Randolph Churchill showed a decided talent for painting. . . . She brought her father to see my studio, and on more than one occasion, was accompanied by her son Winston, a delightful little boy in short trousers. It was at her house that I first saw cigarettes handed to a lady, a departure which seemed to me then a matter for wonder, rather, I think, than of annoyance."

[15] *Punch* Magazine ran a series of cartoons on Professional Beauties. The caption to one of them read:

Gwendolyn: "Uncle George says every woman ought to have a profession, and I think he's quite right."

Mama: "Indeed! And what profession do you mean to choose?"

Gwendolyn: "I mean to be a Professional Beauty."

[16] Frances, Countess of Warwick, *Discretions* (New York, Scribner's, 1931). Virginia Cowles, in *Edward VII and His Circle* (London, Hamish Hamilton, 1956), records that Randolph Churchill, years before, had written Jennie, "I dined with Lord Wharncliffe last night and took in to dinner a Mrs. Langtry, a most beautiful creature, quite unknown, very poor, and they say she has but one black dress." In her *Reminiscences,* Jennie commented, "Mrs. Langtry owned one dinner dress, not because of poverty, but because, until now, she had only needed one."

[17] Sir Shane Leslie's private papers. Sir Shane noted, "Poor Leonard Jerome must have read those figures with an ashen heart." The newspapers reported "elegantly appointed equipages" blocking the streets near Grace Church, and that "Solomon's concubines in their glory could hardly have equaled" the clothes of the attending society women. Sir Shane also remembered that the Leslie family in Ireland regarded the wedding day as a tragic day for fasting. The date was October 2, 1884.

[18] Frank Harris, *My Life and Loves* (New York, Grove Press, 1963). Harris noted after the incident that he remonstrated with Randolph that he should not have done that in front of him because "your wife will always hate me for having been the witness of her humiliation." Harris added, "Ever afterwards Lady Randolph missed no opportunity of showing me that she disliked me cordially. . . . She showed her worst side to me almost always and was either imperious or indifferent."

Chapter 11

[1] *Reminiscences of Lady Randolph Churchill.*

[2] Frances, Countess of Warwick, *Discretions* (New York, Scribner's, 1931). Lady Warwick, also known to her friends and to the Prince as "Daisy," was later to be involved in a scandal concerning a personal file of love letters sent to her by the Prince. She wanted a large sum of money from the Crown after Edward VII's death, or else, she threatened, she would print the letters in a book. The letters were never printed. Lady Warwick later became a Socialist.

[3] Moreton Frewen, *Melton Mowbray & Other Memories* (London, Herbert Jenkins, 1924). Frewen also makes reference to the Hungarian band that Kinsky often brought along with him to entertain guests.

[4] Leonie's letters that year are full of references to Jennie and Kinsky. Telling about a visit to the House of Lords on June 18, 1884, Leonie noted, "Jennie, with Kinsky, came in after. . . ."

[5] Lady Leslie had considered herself a good friend of both Dickens and Thackeray.

[6] Clare Sheridan, *Naked Truth* (New York, Harper, 1928). Clare Sheridan, who became a prominent sculptress, was the daughter of Clara and Moreton Frewen. She tells the story of her father arriving home on one of his infrequent visits. "I tried to get close to him by climbing onto the arm of his chair. Suddenly his smile faded. He turned to me severely: 'Don't be clumsy, child! You've stepped on my varnished shoes.'"

[7] Interview with Sir Shane Leslie.

[8] Despite an inheritance of some 30,000 acres, Lady Warwick also wore her mother's cast-off clothes.

[9] Frances, Countess of Warwick, *op. cit.*

[10] Alan Bott and Irene Clephane, *Our Mothers* (London, Gollancz, 1932). The bustle finally faded into oblivion by 1890.

[11] *Ibid.*

[12] Frances, Countess of Warwick, *Afterthoughts* (London, Cassell, 1931).

[13] Winston S. Churchill, *Lord Randolph Churchill.* (London, Macmillan, 1906).

[14] Lord Rosebery described Randolph's humor as "burlesque conception, set off by an artificial pomp of style; a sort of bombastic irony, such as we occasionally taste with relish in an after-dinner speech." Quoted in Philip Guedalla, *Mr. Churchill: A Portrait* (London, Hodder & Stoughton, 1941).

[15] Barbara Tuchman, *The Proud Tower* (New York, Macmillan, 1965). Mrs. Tuchman also said of Salisbury that he cared nothing for sport and little for people, and added, "His aloofness was enhanced by shortsightedness so intense that he once failed to recognize a member of his own Cabinet, and once his own butler."

[16] Robert Rhodes James, *Lord Randolph Churchill* (New York, A. S. Barnes, 1960).

[17] Winston Churchill, *op. cit.*

[18] *Ibid.*

[19] *Reminiscences of Lady Randolph Churchill.*

[20] *Ibid.*

[21] "It was the tandem that did it," wrote Sir Henry Drummond Wolff in *Rambling Recollections* (London, Macmillan, 1908).

[22] The many suitors for the hand and fortune of the Baroness included King Leopold of Belgium, but in 1880 she had married a 27-year-old American. She was then sixty-eight, and a smirking comment in a gossip magazine said: "AN ARITH-METICAL PROBLEM: How many times does 27 go into 68 and what is there over?"

Campaigning for Coutts, Jennie was told by one male voter, "If I could get the same price as was once paid by the Duchess of Devonshire for a vote, I think I could promise." The Duchess had kissed him, he said. "Thank you very much," Jennie said, "I'll let the Baroness Burdett-Coutts know at once." The Baroness' young husband was later cut at the Clubs because of his snide comments about his aging wife. He was quoted as saying aloud at a charity bazaar, "By Jove, I must go and look after my grandmother."

[23] Across the street from where Jennie later lived on Great Cumberland Road, there is a plaque on a house which reads: "Elizabeth Garrett Anderson, 1836–1917. The first woman to qualify as a doctor lived here."

[24] George W. Smalley, *Anglo-American Memories* (New York, Putnam's, 1912).

[25] Another Birmingham butcher asked her how late Lord Randolph slept in the morning. When she said he slept until eleven, the butcher said he would not vote for any man "what lies abed" that late. As she was walking out, he asked her name and she answered: "I am Lady Randolph Churchill." The butcher stared at her appreciatively, then said, "I'll vote for him. He doesn't get up until eleven, eh? Well, by Gad, Mum, it's a wonder to me now he gets up at all!"

Jennie told her friends of knocking on another Birmingham door. A big strapping woman answered the door and Jennie asked, "Is your husband home?"

The woman held her arms akimbo, stared, sneered, and said sarcastically, "And what, in goodness' name, do *you* want with *my* husband?"

[26] John, Viscount Morley, *Recollections* (New York, Macmillan, 1917).

Chapter 12

[1] *Reminiscences of Lady Randolph Churchill.*

[2] G. E. Buckle, ed., *Letters and Journals of Queen Victoria* (London, John Murray, 1930).

[3] *Ibid.*

[4] The illness is described in detail in Randolph S. Churchill's biography of his father, *Winston S. Churchill* (Boston, Houghton Mifflin, 1967), Vol. I and in Part 2 of the companion volume.

[5] Allen Andrews, *The Splendid Pauper* (Philadelphia, Lippincott, 1968).

[6] Papers at Blenheim Palace.

[7] Medical records at Wellcome British Medical Library in London.

[8] Robson Roose, *The Waste and Repair in Modern Life* (London, John Murray, 1897), Chap. 1, "The Wear and Tear of London Life."

[9] T. H. S. Escott, *Randolph Spencer-Churchill* (London, Hutchinson, 1895).

[10] Frank Harris, *My Life and Loves* (New York, Grove Press, 1963).

[11] John Morley, *Life of William Ewart Gladstone* (London, Macmillan, 1932).

[12] Winston S. Churchill, *Lord Randolph Churchill.* In his speech, Randolph also referred to Gladstone's "senile vanity." Even hard-hitting Joseph Chamberlain called the speech "rather strong." The date of the speech was June 20, 1886.

[13] Buchan's added comment was that Balfour's gift was that he could pull the most out of other people and in conversation pull up the quality of discussion without monopolizing it. Barbara Tuchman, *The Proud Tower* (New York, Macmillan, 1965).

[14] Jennie's style of speech was clear and concise. See Elizabeth Eliot, *They All Married Well* (London, Cassell, 1960).

[15] The critic was Hugh Martin, quoted in A. G. S. Norris, *A Very Great Soul* (New York, International, 1957).

[16] Randolph made only two speeches in that General Election of 1886.

[17] A letter dated July 29, 1886, published in Sir Arthur Hardinge, *The Fourth Earl of Carnarvon* (London, Oxford University Press, 1925), Vol. III, quotes the Earl as saying, "I cannot forget my last conversation with R. Churchill—which was, on his side, as mad a one as I ever listened to from mortal lips."

[18] Lady St. Hélier, *Memories of Fifty Years* (London, E. Arnold, 1909).

[19] Winston S. Churchill, *op. cit.*

[20] The Rt. Hon. Earl of Ronaldshay, *The Life of Lord Curzon* (London, Ernest Benn, 1927).

[21] Lady Randolph Churchill, *Small Talks on Big Subjects* (London, 1916).

[22] Roose, *op. cit.*

[23] Ralph Nevill, ed., *Leaves from the Notebooks of Lady Dorothy Nevill* (London, Macmillan, 1907). Lady Nevill also said of Randolph Churchill that he "would never allow the tone of the conversation to degenerate into familiarity, and would be quick to resent any approach to it. He always seemed to be, to me, a man who was secretly conscious that he must make his mark quickly. Who can tell that some foreboding of his premature end did not loom before him?"

[24] Daphne Fielding, *The Duchess of Jermyn Street* (London, Eyre & Spottiswoode, 1964). Rosa Lewis, the subject of this biography, was Lady Churchill's cook. She noted that the Prince liked plain broad beans, ptarmigan game pie, and Carlsbad plums.

[25] *Ibid.*

[26] Winston would later write on the same subject to his younger brother Jack. Discussing the flowing style of letters of the past, and how much better they were, Winston wrote, "In those times pains were taken to avoid slang, to write good English, to spell well and cultivate style. . . . I try to imitate their virtues." Randolph S. Churchill, *op. cit.,* companion Volume I, Part 1.

[27] Winston S. Churchill, *My Early Life* (New York, Scribner's, 1930).

[28] She did, however, send him a book for his twelfth birthday on November 30, 1886, "To Winston S. Churchill, from his loving mother JSC." The book was entitled *The Young Carthaginian.*

[29] *Letters and Journals of Queen Victoria.*

[30] It was in a speech to the House on some coal mining statistics that Winston Churchill said, "Neither I nor my father was ever any good at figures."

[31] George W. Smalley, *Anglo-American Memories* (New York, Putnam, 1912).

[32] Escott, *op. cit.*

[33] Earl of Ronaldshay, *op. cit.*

[34] Robert Rhodes James, *Lord Randolph Churchill* (New York, A. S. Barnes, 1960).

[35] *Reminiscences of Lady Randolph Churchill.*

[36] Robert Rhodes James reports both versions in *Lord Randolph Churchill.*

[37] In a letter to Sir A. Godley, January 31, 1901, George Curzon wrote, "I was at Hatfield that night; and I remember the thanksgivings and hosannas that went up. . . . He [Randolph] did not know that [Salisbury] would be only too pleased to get rid of him." Curzon called it "a thundercloud from the clear sky."

[38] *The Times,* December 23, 1886. The editorial added, "The resignation of Lord Randolph Churchill has, beyond all question, deprived the government of its ablest member, if we except the Prime Minister himself."

[39] *Letters and Journals of Queen Victoria.*

[40] Hardinge, *op. cit.* Lord Carnovan wrote of the resignation, "The color is taken out of the body; but I should fancy that there is no help for it, and that Randolph's temper was so imperious that they had little option."

[41] There has been a small historical argument as to whether Lord Randolph ever said that. However, Lady Dorothy Nevill wrote that Conservative Party leader Walter Long was with Randolph in the smoking-room of the Carleton Club when he was informed that Goschen, who was not a Member of Parliament, had accepted the

Chancellorship of the Exchequer. Long quoted Randolph as saying, "All great men make mistakes. Napoleon forgot Blücher, I forgot Goschen."

In a letter to *The Times,* December 11, 1949, Sir Clive Morrison Bell, B. T., remembered that when he was an Ensign of the Queen's Guard several years after Randolph's resignation, he was a dinner guest of Lord Annaly, as was Randolph Churchill. After dinner, during the coffee and cigars, Lord Randolph reminisced about the incident. "It was then that he used those very words," Bell wrote. "The next day I wrote a long account of the evening to my father, including, of course, this historic sentence."

[42] A clipping from a New York magazine (source unclear), dated February 10, 1887, reported, "Lady Randolph will accompany her father back to New York in April or May. Lord Randolph will not be in the party."

[43] The robes were black, braided with gold.

Chapter 13

[1] *Reminiscences of Lady Randolph Churchill.* Unless otherwise stated, all quotations attributed to Jennie in this chapter are from this source.

[2] The magazine went on to say, "Jennie had converted Randolph Churchill from a *flaneur* [wastrel] into a hard-working man of affairs."

[3] *Private Diaries of Sir Algernon West* (London, John Murray, 1922). Sir Algernon also quoted Lady Randolph as saying, "Instead of 'the woman who hesitates is lost'—'the woman who does not hesitate is lost.' "

[4] Margot Asquith in her *Autobiography* (Boston, Daran, 1920–22) records that she later told Randolph Churchill at a dinner party, "I am afraid you resigned more out of temper than conviction." To this, he replied, "Confound your cheek! What do you know about me and my convictions! I hate Salisbury! He jumped at my resignation like a dog at a bone! The Tories are ungrateful, shortsighted beasts!" And she also remembers his saying of Salisbury "something I could not catch about Salisbury lying dead at his feet," and then he added, "I wish to God I had *never* known him!"

[5] Extract from Queen's Journal, Buckingham Palace, June 20, 1887, published in G. E. Buckle, ed., *Letters and Journals of Queen Victoria* (London, John Murray, 1930). Of the day, Queen Victoria also recorded another feminine note: "I wore a dress with the rose, thistle and shamrock embroidered in silver on it, and my large diamonds."

[6] By the age of fourteen he supposedly had read Rider Haggard's *King Solomon's Mines* fourteen times.

[7] Abbess was by Trappist out of Festive, and Randolph Churchill bought her for three hundred guineas in September 1887. Between 1889 and 1891, Abbess won ten races with prizes totaling more than $50,000 (£10,050).

[8] Breteuil was a member of the Chamber of Deputies from 1877 to 1892.

[9] Blenheim Palace Papers.

[10] Lady Warwick, in *Discretions* (New York, Scribner's, 1931), also remembered the Czarina as a girl, Princess Alix of Hesse, "a wholesome, thoroughly normal

person ... loved to laugh and joke, and there were certainly no indications of any mystic leanings in her nature. . . . Court life had turned her into a nervous wreck. . . ."

[11] Jennie also visited a Russian museum where she recognized one of the furniture exhibits—an Italian cabinet that had once been at Blenheim.

[12] *The Times* of London reported on January 3, 1888, that the Russians hoped that they had convinced Randolph Churchill of the peaceful and harmless character of their people, so that he would try to convince other Cabinet members to resign as he did from a government which they regarded as the traditional enemy of Russia.

[13] When Kinsky was stationed at the Foreign Office in Vienna and returned to London for one of his many short trips, Leonie wrote a letter to her husband noting that Randolph and Jennie were thinking of returning with Kinsky to Vienna for Whitsuntide.

[14] The strange note is that while there is frequent mention of Jennie's men friends being entertained at the Churchill home, there is rarely any mention of Trafford or Tyrwhitt as guests.

Chapter 14

[1] Extract of letter from Marquis of Salisbury to Queen Victoria, February 13, 1888. G. E. Buckle, ed., *Letters and Journals of Queen Victoria,* (London, John Murray, 1930). An extract from the Queen's Journal on January 13, 1887, notes: "Lord Salisbury considers Lord Randolph Churchill as a most selfish statesman, not caring for the good of the country. . . ."

[2] Barbara Tuchman, *The Proud Tower* (New York, Macmillan, 1965), notes that the men of The Souls all followed political careers, and nearly all were Junior Ministers in Lord Salisbury's Government.

[3] Lady Warwick, in *Discretions* (New York, Scribner's, 1931), called Curzon "one of the most tragically misunderstood of men. . . . I never lost my affection for a personality that was both warmhearted and lovable beneath a cold and rather hard surface."

[4] *Op. cit.*

[5] There is an unpublished story passed on by a woman who knew Lord D'Abernon, and would rather not be quoted: she and Lord D'Abernon accompanied a friend of hers who had decided to buy a bed. In a shop on Bond Street they saw a magnificent bed with four posters which came together at the top in a cupola and crown. Her excited friend loved it and decided to buy it. But Lord D'Abernon paled. "I would not buy it if I were you. It is very unlucky," he said. Her friend asked D'Abernon why he thought so. "It belonged to Lady Randolph," he said. Her friend later smilingly commented, "I suppose D'Abernon had slept in that bed many times."

[6] Tuchman, *op. cit.,* writes that Cust's "fatal self indulgence with regard to women" hurt his political career, which never fulfilled its promise.

[7] D'Abernon, *op. cit.,* described The Souls as being "intellectual without being highbrow or pretentious; critical without envy; unprejudiced but not unprincipled;

emancipated but not aggressive; literary but athletic; free from the narrowness of clique, yet bound together in reciprocal appreciation and affection." He also admitted, however, that they were brilliant without being profound.

[8] From *Culture and Anarchy* (London, 1869).

[9] Lady Warwick, *op. cit.* Lady Warwick, who later became a Socialist, wrote that her friends felt it was necessary to "keep servants in their place." The dockworkers, incidentally, won that strike when the Australian dockworkers cabled thirty thousand pounds to support them. James Truslow Adams, *Empire on the Seven Seas* (New York, Scribner's, 1940).

[10] *Letters and Journals of Queen Victoria.*

[11] Winston S. Churchill, *My Early Life* (New York, Scribner's, 1930).

[12] Frank Harris, *My Life and Loves* (New York, Grove Press, 1963).

[13] Frances, Countess Warwick, *Afterthoughts* (London, Cassell, 1931).

[14] Randolph S. Churchill, *Winston S. Churchill* (Boston, Houghton Mifflin, 1967).

[15] In her book, *Small Talks on Big Subjects* (London, Pearson, 1916), Lady Randolph Churchill later wrote: "Indiscretion is not a crime. It is not even a vice. In the earlier Victorian days, the word had more meaning and more censure, wrecked plans and broke up homes. If a woman's behavior was called indiscreet, it was 'equivalent to social ruin.' But in the changing times, the word applied in the same sense does not represent anything so serious."

[16] A New York newspaper also reported how the Duke created a sensation by being arrested for "scorching" (fast and reckless driving on his bicycle) on Riverside Drive.

[17] Moreton Frewen, *Melton Mowbray & Other Memories* (London, Herbert Jenkins, 1924).

[18] Lady Dorothy Nevill, *Under Five Reigns* (London, Metheun, 1910). Lady Nevill said this to Joseph Chamberlain in 1888, before he married an American. Chamberlain answered, "I am ready to give up the lobster, so you must be prepared to like the girl."

[19] Blenheim Palace Papers.

[20] Leonie was the only one of the three Jerome sisters to celebrate a golden wedding anniversary. The Leslie family motto was "Grip fast." (That's what the original Leslie supposedly told Queen Margaret during a storm at sea.) The Leslie family had been founded in England by an Hungarian nobleman who escorted Margaret to Scotland in 1067.

[21] Allen Andrews, *The Splendid Pauper* (Philadelphia, Lippincott, 1968).

[22] Frewen mainly wanted to persuade Salar to "an open mind whether all India might, in the fulness of time, drape her vast docile and elephantine bulk with those same Federal trappings, but subject to a white Mahout." Shane Leslie, *Studies in Sublime Failure* (London, Ernest Benn, 1932).

[23] Frewen, *op. cit.*

[24] After his brother's three daughters married into aristocratic English families, Lawrence Jerome began a speech before the American Jockey Club by saying, "Many years ago, before I had any blue blood in my veins . . ."

[25] Leonard Jerome wrote his wife that Travers "fought a great Tammany leader on a brutal assault, and got him convicted and sentenced to a one-year imprisonment and a $500 fine." Richard O'Connor, *Courtroom Warrior* (Boston, Little, Brown, 1963).

[26] King Milan, next to the last of the Obrenovitch dynasty, divorced his wife Queen Natalie in 1888 and abdicated his throne a year later in favor of his son.

[27] Clare Sheridan, *Naked Truth* (New York, Harper, 1928). "He was a big, gentle, tender 'savage,' and talked to me in a soft melodious voice. I loved him."

[28] Count Kinsky had been transferred to the Austro-Hungarian Embassy in London from Berlin in March 1888 and then transferred to Paris less than a year later. Wherever he was, he made frequent trips to be with Jennie.

[29] Baron Hirsch's biggest project was building a railway from Vienna to Constantinople. He also shared the Churchills' love of horses and racing.

Chapter 15

[1] *Town Topics.*

[2] In a retrospective article about Randolph Churchill, the *Review of Reviews* (March 1895), wrote, "Lord Randolph made a special point of assembling round his table distinguished foreigners and eminent Americans. In this respect, his work was materially assisted by the fact that he married an American lady."

[3] Lady Dorothy Nevill, *Under Five Reigns* (London, 1910). Lady Nevill added that "nobody ever came to his estate unless they were invited, even his children."

[4] *Ibid.* He also told Lady Nevill, "I don't like your English aristocracy. They are not educated, they are not serious; but they do interest me. I want to find out all about them; I should like to be able to explain them to myself. I don't think anybody understands them and I want to do so."

[5] On December 22, 1888, Randolph Churchill had added a codicil to his will bequeathing all his private papers, letters, and documents to his brother-in-law, Viscount Curzon, and his friend Louis Jennings, "In trust to publish, retain all or any of them, as they in their absolute discretion think proper."

[6] Margot Asquith, in her *Autobiography* (Boston, Doran, 1920–22), wrote of Chamberlain, "He encouraged in himself such scrupulous economy of gesture, movement and color that, after hearing him many times, I came to the definite conclusion that Chamberlain's opponents were snowed under by his accumulated moderation."

[7] *Punch* critic Henry Lucy remembered that day of decision and its physical effect on Randolph: "He was so altered in personal appearance that for a moment I did not know him. Instead of his usual alert, swinging pace, with head erect and swift, glancing eyes, he walked with slow, weary tread, his head hanging down, and a look on his face as if tears had been coursing down it. No one who knew him only in public life would have imagined him capable of such emotion." *Later Peeps at Parliament* (London, Newnes, 1905).

[8] *Reminiscences of Lady Randolph Churchill.*

[9] June 2, 1889.

[10] *Reminiscences of Lady Randolph Churchill.*

[11] *Lord Randolph Churchill* (New York, A. S. Barnes, 1960).

[12] *Reminiscences of Lady Randolph Churchill.*

[13] The letter later turned out to be a forgery by another Irishman.

[14] Kitty O'Shea had inherited 144,000 pounds from her aunt, but the will was contested, and none of the money available.

[15] Parnell's lawyer, Sir George Lewis, urged Parnell to contest the divorce suit because he strongly believed it could not be pressed after cross-examination. Parnell refused, answering, "My first duty is to the lady." (Shane Leslie was told this by Lady Lewis, and he reported it in *The End of a Chapter,* (New York, Scribner's, 1916.)

[16] *Punch* showed Gladstone as an old pilgrim with a sword, advancing along a narrow ridge called Home Rule, with a bog of Irish nationalism on one side, and a last ditch of Orange Resistance on the other.

[17] Lord Rosebery, *Lord Randolph Churchill* (New York, Harper, 1906).

[18] Arthur James Balfour, *Chapters of Autobiography*, ed. Mrs. Edgar Dugdale (London, Cassell, 1930), noted that Randolph Churchill had recited these lines to him. Six years before, Balfour also remembered, Randolph had recommended to him a new book entitled *Treasure Island.*

[19] But he was still embittered by his father's resignation. Shane Leslie, *op. cit.,* quotes him as replying to someone who noted a tear in the elbow of his jacket, "How should I not be out of elbows when my father is out of office?"

[20] Winston S. Churchill, *My Early Life* (New York, Scribner's 1930).

[21] Violet Bonham Carter, *Winston Churchill: An Intimate Portrait* (New York, Harcourt, Brace & World, 1965), a good friend of Winston Churchill's, quotes him as saying of himself that he was "a child of both worlds."

[22] The Sheffield *Telegraph* on April 14, 1891, reports: "Lord Randolph's high-flown reference to his going forth on a mission to seek homes for the overcrowded masses of the mother country has excited a titter among those who are acquainted with the real purpose of his journey. This is the plain truth. Fortune does not smile on Lord Randolph at home. He wants money, and like the bold adventurers who have planted the British flag all over the world he is going forth to search for it. If he can combine the acquisition of wealth for himself with the provision of homes for our surplus population, so much the better for all parties."

[23] Allen Andrews *The Splendid Pauper* (Philadelphia, Lippincott, 1968).

Chapter 16

[1] Kinsky had been transferred from the Paris Embassy to London in June 1890.

[2] "I have known Charles Kinsky all my life," Prince Clary added, in a letter to author, "as he was not only a cousin, but also a very dear and close friend of my mother's, who was born Countess Thérèse Kinsky. When my father, who was an Austro-Hungarian diplomat, was sent to London in 1895 as Chancellor of the Embassy, my mother was received in the most friendly way by Lady Randolph and I remember having seen her several times in my parents' house in Lowndes Square. It was only much later, of course, that I heard of my uncle's great romance with Lady Randolph."

³ Count Kinsky also caught the measles from Winston.

⁴ Shane Leslie, *The End of a Chapter* (New York, Scribner's, 1917), and interviews with the author.

⁵ Daphne Fielding, *Duchess of Jermyn Street* (London, Eyre & Spottiswoode, 1964).

⁶ Jennie also wrote him, "How I long for you to be back with sacks of gold."

⁷ Allen Andrews, *The Splendid Pauper* (Philadelphia, Lippincott, 1968). Frewen also added that Mrs. Jerome had managed her money so well that she had paid off most of the debt on the Madison Square house in New York, part rental of which still came to Jennie in quarterly payments.

⁸ Randolph Churchill's columns were collected in a book called *Men, Mines and Animals in South Africa* (New York, Appleton, 1892).

⁹ Blenheim Palace Papers.

¹⁰ This printed rumor served as an interesting point for those who had previously claimed that Jennie had much more to do with the writing of Randolph's speeches than most people had imagined.

¹¹ The incident was reported by Rhys H. Price in a letter to the editor of *The Times* in London, August 6, 1926.

¹² Such was Jennie's love of music that even a severe toothache didn't prevent her attendance at all the Wagner performances; she borrowed some cocaine from a woman seated behind her to help ease the pain.

¹³ Paderewski arrived in London with a letter of introduction to Jennie from a mutual friend. Her Connaught home, of course, was a haven for musicians arriving from all over Europe.

¹⁴ Shane Leslie, interview with the author.

¹⁵ *Reminiscences of Lady Randolph Churchill.*

¹⁶ Count Kinsky had written Princess Metternich about Jennie's concert program and she sent Jennie a long letter advising her about the setting of one of the scenes.

¹⁷ A cartoon in *Punch* showed Jennie at the piano, with the caption, "Her piano was forte."

¹⁸ *Reminiscences of Lady Randolph Churchill.*

¹⁹ *Ibid.*

²⁰ Randolph S. Churchill, *Winston S. Churchill* (Boston, Houghton Mifflin, 1967).

²¹ Peregrine Churchill collection.

²² Jennie also wrote, "I saw poor Harry Tyrwhitt at Ascot. He does look so ill, poor fellow, but seemed in fairly good spirits. He asked me much about you, and I told him how grateful you would be if he could find time to write you a line. I think he will do this." Within a few months Tyrwhitt was dead.

²³ Shane Leslie, *Film of Memory* (London, Michael Joseph, 1938).

²⁴ Seymour Leslie, son of Leonie and John, in *The Jerome Connexion* (London, John Murray, 1964), says of his uncle Randolph that he was "rude and arrogant" to his servants and "aloof in manner to his two boys—Leonie, it is clear, did not like her brother-in-law."

²⁵ Andrews, *op. cit.*

²⁶ Dr. Keith had written several books on the subject, including, *Contributions to Surgical Treatment of Tumors in the Abdomen.* He was also a Honorary Fellow of

Gynecology in the United States. His son George Elphinston Keith was a gynecologist like his father, and the two had co-authored several books.

[27] Frank Harris, *My Life and Loves* (New York, Grove Press, 1963).

[28] Winston Churchill, *My Early Life* (New York, Scribner's, 1930).

[29] Andrews, *op. cit.*

[30] Kinsky's friendship with the Archduke, as well as his family position, accounted for the ease with which he managed to be transferred from one embassy to another. In his diaries, *Tagebuch meiner Reise um die Erde* (Vienna, 1895), the Archduke describes Kinsky as "an excellent traveling companion" who had "helped make the journey such a success."

[31] Winston Churchill, *op. cit.*

[32] Frances, Countess of Warwick; *Discretions* (New York, Scribner's, 1931). Another frequent guest was the American correspondent for the New York *Tribune,* George Smalley, who echoed Lady Warwick's observations.

[33] Winston Churchill, *op. cit.*

[34] Frank Harris, *Contemporary Portraits* (New York, Brentanos, 1920).

[35] Henry Lucy, *Diary of a Journalist* (London, John Murray, 1920). Lucy was a close friend of Randolph's, and broke with him about this time, but later renewed his friendship, as few others did. Lucy later reported Randolph's closest supporter and friend, Louis Jennings, as having said to him, "It's an odd thing Randolph has just as many friends today as he had a week ago. He has regained you and he has lost me."

[36] Carson afterward asked Winston what he thought of his (Carson's) speech that day in Parliament. "I concluded from it, sir, that the ship of state is struggling in heavy seas," Winston answered.

[37] Winston Churchill, *op. cit.*

[38] Blenheim Palace Papers.

[39] A. J. P. Taylor gives a good account of this period in *Bismarck* (New York, Knopf, 1955). Shortly after this time, Prince Otto Von Bismarck was confined to a carriage, then to a wheelchair. He had told Sir Charles Dilke, "The rule of kings is the rule of women; the bad women are bad and the good are worse." His son Herbert's involvement in the divorce scandal had seriously crimped his career.

[40] *Reminiscences of Lady Randolph Churchill.*

[41] In *Thoughts and Adventures* (New York, Scribner's, 1932), Winston Churchill wrote: "I suppose if I were to relive my life, I ought to eschew the habit of smoking. Look at all the money I've wasted on tobacco. Think of it all invested and mounting up in compound interest, year after year. I remember my father, in his most sparkling mood, his eyes gleaming through the haze of his cigarette, saying, 'Why begin? If you want to have an eye that is true and a hand that does not quiver, if you are never to ask yourself a question as you ride at a fence, don't smoke.'"

[42] Interview with Peregrine Churchill.

[43] She worried about Winston's blood being out of order and the boils on his back, wrote him details about political campaigns, and refused invitations elsewhere for weekends when Winston was home.

[44] Winston Churchill, *op. cit.*

[45] John, Viscount Morley, *Recollections* (New York, Macmillan, 1917). The exact date was March 13, 1894.

[46] Lord Rosebery, *Lord Randolph Churchill* (New York, Harper, 1906).

[47] Interview with Sir Shane Leslie.

[48] Harris, *My Life and Loves.* Guy de Maupassant also died of syphilis, with madness in the final stages.

[49] Wilfred Scawen Blunt, *My Diaries: Being a Personal Narrative of Events, 1888–1914* (London, Martin Seeker, 1919), Part One, 1888–1900.

Chapter 17

[1] Buzzard Papers. Dr. Thomas Buzzard, was brought in by Dr. Robson Roose as the new consultant on Lord Randolph's case. Dr. Buzzard, a specialist in diseases of the nervous system, was the consulting physician to London's National Hospital for the Paralyzed and Epileptic. He and Dr. Roose advised both Lord and Lady Randolph that they had reassessed the case and decided that a trip through the United States would be too hot in June, and a prolonged trip, in any case, was inadvisable. Instead, they suggested a fishing trip to Norway. Randolph refused to change his plans.

[2] Dr. George E. Keith, the son of Dr. Thomas Keith (Lady Randolph's doctor), had just returned from New York where he had been house surgeon at the Women's Hospital. He was ten years older than Lady Randolph.

[3] In 1907 Lady Randolph saw Land League, a grandson of Abbess, win the big race at Cambridgeshire.

[4] Winston Churchill, *My Early Life* (New York, Scribner's, 1930).

[5] Frank Harris, *My Life and Loves* (New York, Grove Press, 1963).

[6] Mrs. John Sloane reported this as one of the anecdotes passed down in the Travers and Jerome families.

[7] *The New York Times* many years later recorded that during her visit to New York, Lady Randolph Churchill "created and named" the Manhattan cocktail. "She conceived the notion of blending bourbon with a lesser portion of herb-piqued wine [sweet vermouth] and aromatic bitters."

[8] The magazine from which the clipping came is unclear, but the date is July 21, 1894. The article referred to Lord Randolph as "the Clemenceau of the English House of Commons" and goes on to say, "In point of beauty, Lady Churchill, who accompanies her husband here, has long been acknowledged one of the fairest women in America. Only as long ago as the April drawing room, London correspondents described her as one of the most beautiful and distinguished women to make their bows to the Queen. . . . The charming suavity of her manner and a generous fund of tact and diplomacy have won for her the highest respect of all Englishwomen, who have unconsciously grown to consider her an Englishwoman to the manner born. . . . By a clever and ingenious method of pulling the political wires, [she] contrives to make herself of invaluable service to His Lordship."

[9] They traveled by private railroad car, which they first thought was a generous gesture of the Canadian railroad owner, but which they soon discovered they had to pay for.

¹⁰ *Reminiscences of Lady Randolph Churchill.* Unless otherwise stated, all quotations in this chapter attributed to Jennie are from this source.

¹¹ In coming years, Winston Churchill repeatedly said he expected to "peg out early" and probably die before his thirties. A family friend remarked that Churchill probably said this because he felt he had somehow inherited his father's disease.

¹² Winston Churchill's knowledge of his father's syphilis deeply strengthened his future relationship with his mother, because he now saw her in terms of the innocent victim. The specter of syphilis conceivably explains a possible leery attitude toward sex and the fact that he did not marry until he was thirty-three years old.

¹³ Lady Randolph reported that King Thebaw at Rangoon presented three princesses—two pretty ones, completely covered and the third, old and ugly, hardly wearing any clothes at all. The princesses presented Lady Randolph with some cheroots which they hoped she would smoke.

¹⁴ Dr. A. L. Baron, in *Man Against Germs* (New York, Dutton, 1957), writes, "When the brain is invaded by the germs, the last act of syphilis may be ended suddenly, or it may drag on for many dreary years. The fragile blood vessels of the brain are eroded, eventually the blood will spurt out and the fatal apoplectic stroke will terminate syphilis."

¹⁵ The coffin was lead-lined to prevent the deterioration of the body in the tropical heat.

¹⁶ His fiancée was 21-year-old Countess Elisabeth Wolff Metternich zur Gracht, a cousin of the Empress of Austria.

¹⁷ E. T. Raymond, in *Uncensored Celebrities* (London, T. Fisher Unwin, 1918), makes the point that Winston Churchill's "extra touch of recklessness" and "an unbridled tendency to naked 'bossing' of any 'show'" might well have been a characteristic inherited from his American mother.

¹⁸ A. G. Gardiner, *The Life of Sir William Harcourt* (London, Constable, 1923), Vol. II, notes somebody saying to Harcourt of Randolph Churchill, "Why, he isn't even an educated man."

"No," answered Harcourt pleasantly. "If he were educated, he would be spoiled."

¹⁹ Allen Andrews, *The Splendid Pauper* (Philadelphia, Lippincott, 1968).

²⁰ Blenheim Palace Papers.

²¹ Shane Leslie, *Salutation to Five* (London, Hollis & Carter, 1951).

²² Describing her lying in bed, Sir Shane remembered vividly, "Her black, brushed hair and pallor of death reflected in her own face—with those eyes, needing no jewels—the most beautiful vision of a woman I had ever seen."

Chapter 18

¹ Ralph G. Martin, *Jennie: The Life of Lady Randolph Churchill, the Romantic Years–1854–1895* (Englewood Cliffs, N. J., Prentice-Hall, Inc., 1969), Volume I.

² Letter from Clara to her husband, Moreton Frewen, January 19, 1895, Manuscript Room, Library of Congress.

[3] *Ibid.*

[4] The will was probated on February 28, 1895, filed at Somerset House in London.

[5] Letter from Clara, January 19, 1895.

[6] Interview with Sir Shane Leslie.

[7] Excerpt from letter dated February 27, 1895. Randolph S. Churchill, *Winston S. Churchill,* Companion Volume No. I, Part 1, 1874–1896 (Boston, Houghton Mifflin, 1967).

[8] Correspondence with Prince Clary, a nephew of Count Kinsky, in Venice; interview with Countess Kinsky in London.

[9] Letter of May 18, 1903, from the Viceroy's Camp. *The Reminiscences of Lady Randolph Churchill* (New York, The Century Co., 1908).

[10] Speech at Harrow, October 29, 1941.

[11] The house was rented as a club, first the University Club and then the Manhattan Club. Jennie continued to get her annual payments until the time of her death. At that time, the *New York Tribune* of November 16, 1921, headlined a story: "250,000-Dollar Churchill Trust Fund Goes to Two Sons. Court Signs Order Cancelling Mortgage on Manhattan Club Property." For a fuller description of the house, see Martin, *op. cit.*

[12] Interview with Lady Altrincham.

[13] *Scots Pictorial,* July 16, 1921.

[14] The phrase is Walter Bagehot's from an article written in 1872, quoted in Anthony Sampson, *Anatomy of Britain* (New York, Harper & Row, 1962).

[15] Ivor Jennings, *Parliament* (Cambridge, Macmillan, 1939).

[16] Sampson, *op. cit.*

[17] Ralph Waldo Emerson, *English Traits* (New York, 1888).

[18] The Rt. Hon. H. H. Asquith, *Some Aspects of the Victorian Age* (Oxford, at the Clarendon Press, 1918). (This was part of the Romanes Lecture, delivered in the Sheldonian Theatre, on June 8, 1918.)

[19] James Truslow Adams, *Empire on the Seven Seas* (New York, Scribner's, 1940).

[20] Allan Bott and Irene Clephane, *Our Mothers* (London, Victor Gollancz, 1932).

[21] *Ibid.*; also, R. M. Titmuss, *Essays on the Welfare State* (London, G. Allen, 1958).

[22] Excerpt from speech of Sir Henry Campbell-Bannerman at Perth, reported in *The* [London] *Times,* June 6, 1903. Campbell-Bannerman was then leader of the Liberal Party, and later became Prime Minister.

[23] Margot Asquith, *Autobiography* (London, Thornton Butterworth, 1920).

[24] Depew had made a private railroad car available to Jennie and her sick husband, Lord Randolph, when they traveled across Canada and the United States on their trip around the world. Depew had been the first U.S. Minister to Japan (1866). He was President of the New York Central Railroad (1885–98) and a U.S. Senator from New York (1899–1911).

[25] E. T. Raymond, *Portraits of the Nineties* (New York, Scribner's, 1921).

[26] Richard Le Gallienne, *The Romantic Nineties* (New York, Doubleday, Page, 1925).

[27] Holbrook Jackson, *The Eighteen-Nineties* (New York, Knopf, 1922).

[28] *Town Topics,* January 17, 1895.

[29] By 1895 almost a hundred towns in England had their own electric supply stations.

[30] George Bernard Shaw was a friend of Jennie's and later wrote for her magazine.

[31] Interview with Sir Shane Leslie.

[32] Margot Asquith, quoted in Virginia Cowles, *Edward VII* (London, Hamish Hamilton, 1956).

[33] Frances, Countess of Warwick, *Discretions* (New York, Scribner's, 1931).

[34] Shane Leslie Papers, Letter from Queen Alexandra to Lady Leslie, July 3, 1921.

[35] The Princess's eldest son, the Duke of Clarence, seems to have been smitten by Jennie. *Town Topics* reported that "Young 'Collars and Cuffs' has been dogging her [Lady Randolph] about for months. He haunted her at her house, he stuck to her like wax at other people's houses, and was by her side everywhere in public. He is a ridiculous young creature, and the American lady's evident enjoyment of his devotion was the occasion for many a laugh, it was so evident a worship of the shadow of greatness." The same Duke of Clarence was mentioned in the London *Sunday Times* in November 1970 as possibly having been the sensational Jack the Ripper. Jack the Ripper was the brutal murderer of five prostitutes in the Fall of 1888, four of whom he disemboweled. The *Times'* allegation came in response to a hint from the eminent author and physician, Dr. Thomas E. A. Stowell, who had been accumulating evidence for fifty years. Dr. Stowell said that Jack the Ripper was a young man of royal blood who contracted syphilis during a World Tour just after his sixteenth birthday, and had been treated by the royal doctor, Sir William Gull. The Duke of Clarence died of syphilis at the age of twenty-eight.

[36] Winston S. Churchill, *My Early Life* (London, Odhams Press, 1930).

[37] *Ibid.*

[38] *Ibid.*

[39] *Ibid.*

[40] *Vanity Fair,* May 29, 1886, p. 201.

[41] The Duke of Portland, *Men, Women and Things* (London, Faber & Faber, 1938).

[42] Randolph S. Churchill, *op. cit.*

[43] *Ibid.*

[44] Winston S. Churchill, *op. cit.*

[45] *Ibid.*

[46] Bott and Clephane, *op. cit.*

[47] *Annual Register,* Volume 137 (London; Longman, Green, 1896).

Chapter 19

[1] See Ralph G. Martin, *Jennie: The Life of Lady Randolph Churchill, the Romantic Years, 1854–1895* (Englewood Cliffs, N.J., Prentice-Hall, Inc., 1969), Volume I.

[2] Richard Harding Davis, *About Paris* (New York, Harper, 1895).

[3] *Ibid.*

[4] This was particularly true of the salon of Mrs. Richard Haight in the Place Vendôme, directly opposite where the Ritz Hotel now stands. The drawing rooms of Mrs. Ridgeway, in the Rue François I, were also as exclusive as any in Paris.

[5] *New York Herald*, Paris Edition, February 26, 1895.

[6] *The New York Times*, December 6, 1964.

[7] *Town Topics*, February 21, 1895.

[8] Some sources (*e.g.*, *The New York Times*, December 10, 1964) suggest that the total dowry might have reached $20,000,000. At one time, Consuelo and her husband each received $100,000 a year from her father. Consuelo was the eldest of the three children of William Kissam Vanderbilt and the former Alva Smith. Consuelo's grandfather, Commodore Cornelius Vanderbilt, was the founder of the New York Central Railroad.

[9] See Martin, *op. cit.*

[10] *New York Herald*, Paris Edition, March 5, 1895.

[11] *New York Journal Magazine*, undated clipping.

[12] *Town Topics* also quoted Henry Labouchere, editor of *Truth*, saying, "I confess to a contempt for Americans who come over here with apparently the sole object of working by means of their dollars into English fashionable society, as though society in their own country was not good enough for them." March 25, 1897.

The New York *Journal* on October 24, 1909 had a story entitled "How Titled Foreigners Catch American Heiresses." It listed forty marriages, itemizing the amount of the fortune and the final result of the marriage. Most of them had ended badly.

[13] *The New York Herald*, Paris Edition, June 27, 1896.

[14] Winston S. Churchill, *My Early Life* (London, Odhams Press, 1930); interview with Sir Shane Leslie.

[15] Interview with Sir Shane Leslie.

[16] Seymour Leslie, *The Jerome Connexion* (New York, Macmillan, 1964).

[17] March 2, 1895. Randolph S. Churchill, *Winston S. Churchill,* Companion Volume No. I, Part 1, 1874–1896 (Boston, Houghton Mifflin, 1967).

Clara Frewen's daughter Clare gave this description of her aunt Leonie in *The Naked Truth* (New York, Harper, 1928):

"Alone with me, she was almost a sage, disguised; she gave me direction and saved me from drifting along the path of doubt and cynicism. Her advice was profound. I thought she might have been a very great woman, had she the chance, or had she trusted herself. The world had either buffeted her too much, or perhaps not enough. She had led a strangely repressed life, but she was too proud to resent it, and had too much humor for self-pity. She hid behind her wit as completely as any Oriental woman behind her yashmak. Few people have known the face of Leonie, and Providence even dimmed her eyes, so that they should not reveal the intensity of her soul."

[18] Shane Leslie, *Long Shadows* (London, Hollis & Carter, 1951).

[19] Anonymous, *Uncensored Recollections* (New York, Lippincott, 1924).

[20] See Martin, *op. cit.*

[21] Jennie had wired her father to find out more about the finances of the Garner girls. Her father wrote, "There is no doubt they are very rich girls, but as to the

incomes, I can't get at it with any certainty as yet." It was obviously more than enough. Mr. Garner had been the largest producer of cotton prints in the world, and had inherited a fortune of some $20,000,000. The three Garner girls became orphans when their parents' yacht overturned—it had been the largest sailing yacht in the world.

[22] Marcel Proust, *Remembrance of Things Past* (New York, Random House, 1934). Volume I.

[23] *The Notebooks of Henry James* (London, Oxford University Press, 1947).

[24] See Martin, *op. cit.*

[25] *New York World*, Paris Edition, March 20.

Chapter 20

[1] Randolph S. Churchill, *Winston S. Churchill*, Volume I: *Youth, 1874–1900* (Boston, Houghton Mifflin, 1966), p. 272.

[2] New York Public Library, Manuscript Room, Bourke Cockran Papers.

[3] The passport is dated, "This 19th day of March, A.D. 1895, in the 119th year of the independence of the United States."

[4] Interview with Alice Roosevelt Longworth.

[5] James McGurrin, *Bourke Cockran, A Free Lance in American Politics* (New York, Scribner's, 1948).

[6] From a published interview in *T. P. O'Connor's Weekly*, 1903, cited in McGurrin, *op. cit.*

[7] Bourke Cockran would in later years become the defense attorney of his own celebrated case, defending Labor Leader Tom Mooney. Mooney was convicted as a participant in the bomb killings of the San Francisco Preparedness Day Parade of 1916 and condemned to death. The sentence was commuted to life imprisonment, and Mooney was finally pardoned in 1938.

[8] Extract from a speech in New York, given in honor of a visiting priest from the County of Sligo. New York Public Library, Manuscript Room, Bourke Cockran Papers. Cockran's love of his home county was indicated by his gift of £10,000 ($50,000) to County Sligo for the benefit of helping local industry.

[9] Cockran had been sent to Ireland by the *New York Herald* to report the events marking the celebration of the centennial of the birth of Daniel O'Connell. On his return to New York, he was offered a position on the *Herald's* Foreign News desk, which he declined.

[10] Cockran's clients represented railroads, banks, bus companies, tobacco companies, public utilities, and steamship lines. In later years, he also acted as special counsel for the Long Island Railroad. His net income in 1895 was estimated at $100,000.

[11] Bourke's father "was a cultured gentleman, well-versed in the classics." His mother's kin included a gifted poet and dramatist, and a former Chief Justice of the United States, Edward Douglas White. Ambrose Kennedy, *Bourke Cockran, American Orator: His Life & Politics* (Boston, Bruce Humphreys, 1948). Bourke Cockran, however, had little love for his father, who had often beaten him. Bourke's father was

twenty-three years old when he married Bourke's mother, who was then thirty-six. His mother was a convert to Catholicism, and wanted young Bourke to become a priest.

[12] See Martin, *op. cit.*

[13] *The Splendid Pauper* is the title of an excellent biography of Moreton Frewen by Allan Andrews (Philadelphia and New York, Lippincott, 1968).

[14] Shane Leslie also added: "It was impossible for a third party to speak while they were locked in conflicting phrase and paragraph, but it was equally impossible to eat or drink during the time, or to feel that anything could be more satisfying than the schemes of one, or more intoxicating than the critical eloquence of the other." With regard to the silver question, Cockran's strong stand on this issue resulted in his political break with the Democratic presidential candidate William Jennings Bryan in the 1896 election. Shane Leslie, *American Wonderland* (London, Michael Joseph, Ltd., 1936).

[15] The quote is from a Boston newspaper, undated, quoted in a book by Mrs. T. P. O'Connor, *I, Myself* (London, Methuen & Co., 1910). The other two women named in the article were the Baroness Burdett-Coutts and Mrs. T. P. O'Connor. Like Jennie, Mrs. O'Connor was an American, and the Baroness was married to an American.

[16] William Travers Jerome was actually a double-cousin of Jennie's; his father was the brother of Jennie's father, and his mother was the sister of Jennie's mother.

[17] Despite his pious front, "Honest John" Kelly still managed to leave an estate of $500,000. Ralph G. Martin, *The Bosses* (New York, Putnam, 1964).

[18] McGurrin, *op. cit.*

[19] Martin, *The Bosses.*

[20] Unidentified clipping.

[21] Cockran was also quoted as saying "All bosses look alike to me. I do not believe that Bossism is an essential feature of democratic government. On the contrary, I have never known it to flourish except where democratic government has been abolished." Kennedy, *op. cit.*

[22] Amos Cummings, *The New York Sun,* June 26, 1892.

[23] Quoted in Arthur Wallace Dunn, *From Harrison to Harding* (New York, Putnam's, 1922).

[24] The Governor's full name was Roswell Pettibone Flower.

[25] *Philadelphia Press,* May 7, 1893.

[26] *Toledo Sunday Journal,* Toledo, Ohio, June 26, 1892.

[27] *The New York Herald,* undated clipping. New York Public Library, Manuscript Room, Bourke Cockran Papers.

[28] *Toledo Sunday Journal,* Toledo, Ohio, June 26, 1892.

[29] *Ibid.*

[30] Senator Champ Clark, *My Quarter-Century of American Politics* (New York, Kraus Reprint Co., 1969.)

Paxton Hibben, in his biography of William Jennings Bryan, *The Peerless Leader* (New York, Russell and Russell, 1967), told how a younger William Jennings Bryan had been similarly impressed:

"He listened enraptured to the type of oratory he'd never heard before—a diction, a phrasing, an eloquence, a passion that might have belonged to Pitt or Fox, as distinct as day and night from the stodgy pedantism of Daniel Webster and Henry Clay, in which young Bryan had been steeped. . . ." Bryan, who later became a Democratic presidential candidate in three different elections, strongly disagreed with Cockran on the gold-versus-silver basis of our currency. It was William Jennings Bryan who made the historic speech in which he said, "You cannot crucify mankind on a cross of gold."

Theodore Roosevelt, in introducing Cockran to a New York audience in 1910, said, "I will introduce to you now a great orator, one of the greatest of all time. . . ." And later, Roosevelt told his friend, Archie Butt, "Archie, . . . I believe Cockran is the greatest orator using the English language today . . ." (*The Intimate Letters of Archie Butt,* New York, 1930, Doubleday) (Quoted in *Letter to the Editor,* New York Times, January 3, 1953, by James McGurrin.)

[31] Shane Leslie, *Long Shadows* (London, Hollis & Carter, 1951).

[32] New York Public Library, Manuscript Room, Bourke Cockran Papers.

[33] Lincoln Springfield, in *Some Piquant People,* (London, T. Fischer Unwin, 1924) wrote this verse about Sir John Hibbert's opinion of the divided skirt:

> Let laws and commerce, wit and learning die;
> We'll even scrap our old nobility;
> Our Church may promptly disestablished be—
> But leave us still the ladies' *lingerie.*
> A disunited kingdom will not hurt—
> But do not, prithee, e'er divide the skirt.

[34] Undated letter, Peregrine Churchill Papers.

[35] *New York Times,* March 4, 1895.

[36] Cornelia Otis-Skinner, *Madame Sarah* (Boston, Houghton Mifflin, 1967).

[37] Shane Leslie, *op. cit.*

[38] *Ibid.*

[39] The Duke of Portland, *Men, Women and Things* (London, Faber & Faber, 1938).

[40] *New York Herald,* Paris Edition, March 11, 1895.

[41] Davis, *op. cit.*

[42] Mrs. T. P. O'Connor, *op. cit.*

[43] Davis, *op. cit.*

[44] *New York Herald,* Paris Edition, March 22, 1895.

[45] E. De Gramont, *Pomp and Circumstance* (London, Jonathan Cape and Harrison Smith, 1929).

[46] Shane Leslie, *Film of Memory* (London, Michael Joseph, 1938).

[47] March 1, 1895. The text of this letter, as of all letters quoted here unless otherwise noted, is to be found in Randolph S. Churchill, *Winston S. Churchill,* Companion Volume No. I, Part 1, 1874–1896 (Boston, Houghton Mifflin, 1967).

[48] March 2, 1895.

[49] March 1, 1895.

[50] March 28, 1895.

Chapter 21

[1] Clare Sheridan, *To the Four Winds* (London, Andre Deutsch, 1955).

[2] Library of Congress, Manuscript Room, Moreton Frewen Papers.

[3] Letter dated April 16, 1895.

[4] Electrozone was basically a deodorant obtained by the electrolysis of sea water, which freed chlorine with small quantities of iodine and bromine. However, it had a terrible odor. "Just before that, Moreton Frewen was involved in something called the Ashcroft Process for treatment of sulphide ores, a process for separating zinc from lead and silver, and even from gold, by the electrolytic treatment of sulphide ores, whereby even the residue was saleable as crude sulphur. The exploration company, however, discovered Moreton Frewen's option was not entirely correct in its legal form, and disclaimed him and repudiated its agreement. The firm made a fortune in the next twenty years, dividends totaling 2500 percent per share—but not to Moreton Frewen." Allan Andrews, *The Splendid Pauper* (New York and Philadelphia, Lippincott, 1968).

[5] E. T. Raymond, *Portrait of the New Century* (New York, Doubleday, Doran, 1928).

[6] *Ibid.*

[7] Holbrook Jackson, *The Eighteen-Nineties* (New York, Knopf, 1922).

[8] *Time Was: The Reminiscences of W. Graham Robertson* (London, Hamish Hamilton, 1931).

[9] Hesketh Pearson, *The Pilgrim Daughters* (London, Heinemann, 1961).

[10] Mrs. George Cornwallis-West, *The Reminiscences of Lady Randolph Churchill.* (New York, The Century Co., 1908).

[11] Jackson, *op. cit.*

[12] *New York Herald,* Paris Edition, April 4, 1895.

[13] Richard Le Gallienne, *The Romantic Nineties* (New York, Doubleday, Page & Co., 1925).

[14] Barbara W. Tuchman, *The Proud Tower* (New York, MacMillan, 1965).

[15] Lincoln Springfield, *Some Piquant People* (London, T. Fisher Unwin, 1924).

[16] E. F. Benson, *As We Were* (London, Longman, 1930).

[17] Comment by Fannie Hurst, quoted in Springfield, *op. cit.*

[18] E. T. Raymond, *Portraits of the Nineties* (New York, Scribner's, 1921).

[19] Springfield, *op. cit.*

[20] *The New York Herald,* Paris Edition, April 4, 1895.

[21] *Ibid.*

[22] Tuchman, *op. cit.*

[23] E. T. Raymond, *Portrait of the Nineties* (New York, Scribner's, 1921).

[24] Pearson, *op. cit.*

[25] Randolph S. Churchill, *Winston S. Churchill,* Companion Volume No. I, Part 1, 1874–1896 (Boston, Houghton Mifflin, 1967).

[26] *Ibid.*

[27] March 9, 1896.

[28] March 20, 1896.

[29] Extract from *Truth,* June 25, 1896.

[30] Letter dated November 12, 1896, from Randolph S. Churchill, *Winston S. Churchill*, Vol. I: *Youth, 1874–1900* (Boston, Houghton Mifflin, 1966), p. 242.

[31] *Ibid.*

[32] *Truth,* October 8, 1896.

[33] Interview with Sir Shane Leslie.

[34] Winston S. Churchill, *Savrola* (New York, Random House, 1956).

[35] Lord Moran, *Churchill: Taken from the Diaries of Lord Moran, The Struggle for Survival, 1940–1965* (Boston, Houghton Mifflin, 1966).

Chapter 22

[1] Undated letter signed, "Your loving old Woom," from "St. George's Vickerage, Bellow in Furness, Thursday." Peregrine Churchill Papers.

[2] Interview with Sir Shane Leslie.

[3] Richard Harding Davis, *About Paris* (New York, Harper, 1895).

[4] *Ibid.*

[5] The Liberal Government of Lord Rosebery was succeeded by a Coalition Government headed by Conservative Lord Salisbury with a group of former members of the Liberal Party who had disapproved of Home Rule for Ireland.

[6] Sir Edgar Vincent (1857–1941) was made the first Viscount D'Abernon in 1926. He had been Governor of the Imperial Ottoman Bank from 1889 to 1897. He would later serve as a Conservative M. P. for Exeter, 1899–1906, and British Ambassador in Berlin, 1920–26.

[7] *The New York Herald,* July 7, 1895. The headline was: "THESE ARE THREE FAMOUS SISTERS." The story added that it would be the first time that Clara had been back in the United States in fifteen years, and the first time in eight years for Leonie. Jennie, of course, had been in the States on her world tour with her husband the previous year. The story also noted that the Madison Avenue home of Leonard Jerome had become the Union Club, and in 1895 the University Club.

[8] *The New York Journal,* undated article in 1895, quoted in Elizabeth Elliot, *They All Married Well* (London, Cassell, 1960). The article is dated from London.

[9] Letter dated May 2, 1895. Randolph S. Churchill, *Winston S. Churchill,* Companion Volume No. I, Part 1, 1874–1896 (Boston, Houghton Mifflin, 1967). (Unless otherwise cited, all letters are from this source.) Among the "many others" mentioned in the letter, Winston notes "the Wolvertons." Prior to his marriage that year, Lord Wolverton's name had often been coupled with Jennie's in the gossip press. He was a prominent racehorse owner and all-around sportsman, especially interested in yachting and big-game hunting. It is interesting to note that Wolverton and Sir Edgar Vincent later joined together to buy the Stanley house stable. Wolverton was ten years younger than Jennie.

[10] June 6, 1895. In this letter Winston also wrote that he had been selected as the officer to attend on and to escort the Duke of Cambridge, a distinct honor for a young officer. However, it also meant seven hours on horseback without dismounting.

[11] July 24, 1895.

[12] July 3, 1895. Winston personally went to Harrow to tell Jack the news of Mrs. Everest's death, "as I did not want to telegraph the news. He was awfully shocked, but tried not to show it."

[13] August 31, 1895.

[14] August 3, 1895.

[15] For his part, Lord Randolph Churchill had detested Lord Salisbury, and confided to Margot Tennant that he wished he had never met him.

[16] August 16, 1895.

[17] Interview with Peregrine Churchill. Peregrine and John Churchill were the two sons of Jack Churchill. Jack Churchill also had a daughter who later became Lady Avon. Lord Avon is the former Sir Anthony Eden.

[18] John Spencer Churchill, *A Churchill Canvas* (Boston, Little, Brown, 1961).

[19] *Ibid.*

[20] November 27, 1894.

[21] In one letter she pointed out to him that he had written "I *here,*" instead of "hear." Letter dated February 26, no year, Peregrine Churchill Papers.

[22] Shane Leslie, *Long Shadows* (London, John Murray, 1966).

[23] Allan Bott and Irene Clephane, *Our Mothers* (London, Victor Gollancz, 1932).

[24] Leslie, *op. cit.*

[25] Bott and Clephane, *op. cit.*

[26] The Duchess of Sermoneta, *Sparkle Distant Worlds* (London, Hutchinson, 1947).

[27] On February 5, 1897, Jennie wrote Winston: "Both Jack and Warrender . . . have written to you today. . . . They can tell you more than I can, as I am in the throes of 24 to dinner tonight."

[28] August 31, 1895.

[29] Shane Leslie, *op. cit.*

[30] October 4, 1895.

[31] October 11, 1895.

[32] *Ibid.*

[33] October 8, 1895.

[34] *Ibid.*

[35] October 19, 1895.

[36] October 21, 1895.

Chapter 23

[1] Letters from Winston to his mother, November 10, 1895. (All letters unless otherwise noted, are from Randolph S. Churchill, *Winston S. Churchill,* Companion Volume No. I, Part 1, 1874–1896 [Boston, Houghton Mifflin, 1967].)

[2] *Ibid.*

[3] Winston S. Churchill, *Thoughts & Adventures* (New York, Scribner's, 1932).

[4] New York Public Library, Manuscript Room, Bourke Cockran Papers.

[5] *Ibid.*

[6] Speech at the University of Rochester, New York, reported in *The Times* of London, April 10, 1954.

[7] Speech at Westminster College, in Fulton, Missouri, March 5, 1946. The title of the speech was "The Sinews of Peace."

[8] In one of his speeches, Bourke Cockran said: "I have a farm on Long Island. I require plows. I am told if I don't have protection against foreign plows, they'll be dumped on me. If that means I'll get plows cheaper than my country can produce them, cheaper even than the country of my origin can produce them, I say, 'Dump on, dump on,' and damned be he who first cries, 'Hold, enough!'"

[9] November 10, 1895.

[10] November 12, 1895.

[11] November 10, 1895.

[12] November 15, 1895.

[13] *Ibid.*

[14] November 10, 1895.

[15] Letter to Jack, November 15, 1895; letter dated November 10, 1895.

[16] Letter to Jack, November 15, 1895. In this same letter, Winston also wrote of American journalism: "Their best papers write for a class of snotty housemaids and footmen, & even the nicest people here have so much. . . ."

[17] November 20, 1895.

[18] *New York Journal,* undated clipping. Quoted in Elizabeth Eliot, *They All Married Well* (London, Cassell, 1960).

[19] *Ibid.*

[20] *Ibid.*

[21] Interview in the *New York Herald,* December 19, 1895.

[22] *Ibid.*

[23] Winston S. Churchill, *My Early Life* (London, Odhams Press, 1930).

[24] December 25, 1895.

[25] Issue dated February 15, 1896.

[26] March 3, 1896.

[27] February 29, 1896.

[28] *Ibid.*

[29] April 12, 1896.

[30] *Ibid.*

[31] April 27, 1896.

[32] April 12, 1896.

[33] May 1, 1896. At this time Chamberlain was Colonial Secretary; Lord Wolseley, Commander-in-Chief of the British Army; Henry Chaplin, President of the Local Government Board; Lord James of Hereford, Chancellor of the Duchy of Lancaster; Sir Francis Jeune, President of the Probate Division and Judge Advocate General; and the 8th Duke of Devonshire was Lord President of the Council. Mrs. Cornelia Adair was the sister of Mrs. Arthur Post, who became Lady Barrymore. Mrs. Adair was originally a Wadsworth from Rochester, New York. The wife of Senator Stuart Symington of Missouri was related to her.

[34] John Morley had been an old friend of Lord Randolph Churchill's, and a close friend of Jennie's. He was a Liberal M.P. and a bitter critic of the Jameson Raid.

[35] *My Early Life.*

[36] Shane Leslie, *Long Shadows* (London, Hollis & Carter, 1951).

Clara Frewen did not move to Great Cumberland Place until about 1902. She did, however, live nearby on Chesham Place, and was a constant visitor at the homes of her two sisters.

[37] Interview with Sir Shane Leslie.

[38] May 1, 1896.

[39] Cruikshank testified that he had spent most of the money on travel. He was sentenced to eight years in jail.

[40] Undated letter, from Frances, Countess of Warwick, *Life's Ebb and Flow* (New York, William Morrow, 1929).

[41] *Town Topics,* March 12, 1896.

[42] "The family jar" had been a social war between William Waldorf Astor's wife and his aunt over which one was *"the"* Mrs. Astor. It was a dispute so bitter that when William Waldorf Astor's wife died in 1894, and he brought her body back to America for burial, there was no member of the American Astor family to receive the body at the pier. And on the night of the funeral, *"the"* Mrs. Astor had a large party.

[43] *The New York Times,* February 21, 1896.

[44] Quoted in Harvey O'Connor, *The Astors* (New York, Knopf, 1941).

[45] When Astor later renounced his American citizenship in 1899 and became a British citizen, a hooting, jeering crowd burned his effigy in Times Square.

[46] To improve his image, Astor invented his own genealogy and published it. In it, he connected himself with Spanish and French nobility. Recognized genealogists, however, soon discovered a variety of errors and there was no justification for most of his claims. Genealogist Lathrop Withington pointed out that John Jacob Astor probably had French Huguenot ancestors, but there was nothing which positively indicated noble descent, and certainly no authenticity in the account which found the family origin among the Spanish nobility (*New York Sun,* July 30, 1899, article entitled, "Astor Pedigree Upset"). From a two-volume biography by Kenneth Wiggins Porter, *John Jacob Astor* (Cambridge, Harvard University Press, 1931). The incident became an international joke, and some members of the press suggested that a more fitting family coat-of-arms for Astor should be "a butcher's block with a cleaver," in memory of John Jacob Astor's humble origin in Germany.

[47] George Smalley, *Anglo-American Memories* (New York, Putnam's, 1912), however, said: "The truth is, Mr. William Waldorf Astor has remained, in spite of his British naturalization, an American. Nobody could take him for anything else: in appearance, in manner, in speech. He has the American abruptness, quickness, decision. He has been in close contact with three civilizations, American, British and Italian, but it is the American which has left its stamp on him; an ineffaceable hallmark."

[48] Undated letter, Peregrine Churchill Papers.

[49] Conversation between William Waldorf Astor and the Countess of Warwick. "My father was the hardest man I have ever known, and I strive to follow in his footsteps." Astor told the Countess: "He was a law unto himself, and a law unto me. He even chose my wife without asking me whether the lady was to my taste or not." Frances, Countess of Warwick, *Discretions* (New York, Scribner's, 1931).

[50] Undated letter, Peregrine Churchill Papers, from "The Deepdene, Dorking."

[51] Moreton Frewen Papers, Manuscript Room, Library of Congress, Washington, D.C.

[52] August 4, 1896.

[53] *My Early Life.*

[54] August 4, 1896.

[55] July 3, 1896.

[56] *Ibid.*

[57] August 31, 1896.

[58] October 1, 1896.

Chapter 24

[1] October 14, 1896. Unless otherwise noted, all letters are from Randolph S. Churchill, *Winston S. Churchill,* Companion Volume No. I, Part 2 (Boston, Houghton Mifflin, 1967).

[2] December 24, 1896.

[3] November 12, 1896.

[4] December 8, 1896.

[5] Winston S. Churchill, *My Early Life* (London, Odhams Press, 1930).

[6] January 21, 1897. Jennie had written him earlier: "You are like me in not minding heat—I simply loved it!" (October 1, 1896).

[7] *My Early Life.*

[8] October 15, 1896. Winston asked his mother to send his butterfly net and mounting equipment. He soon had a collection of sixty-five different butterflies, which was later "destroyed by the malevolence of a rat who crawled into the cabinet and devoured all the specimens" (December 2, 1896).

[9] December 24, 1896.

[10] January 7, 1897.

[11] *My Early Life.*

[12] *Ibid.*

[13] January 21, 1897.

[14] *My Early Life.*

[15] *Ibid.* The *Politics* of Aristotle was edited by James Welldon, Winston's former headmaster at Harrow.

[16] March 31, 1897.

[17] February 4, 1897.

[18] Francis Neilson, *The Churchill Legend* (London, Nelson, 1954).

[19] *My Early Life.*

[20] July 24, 1895. Randolph S. Churchill, *Winston S. Churchill,* Companion Volume No. I, Part 1.

[21] September 23, 1896.

[22] *Ibid.*

[23] October 14, 1896.

[24] October 1, 1896.

[25] October 21, 1896.

[26] Undated letter, Peregrine Churchill Papers.

[27] *My Early Life.*

[28] November 4, 1896. A "godless land of snobs and bores," Winston had said of India (October 26, 1896).

[29] October 14, 1896.

[30] November 5, 1896. Winston had also written his mother, "Bourke Cockran writes me a long letter—describing his campaign against Bryan & is very pleased with himself indeed. He has had great audiences & much enthusiasm. He has received the volume I sent him, and is delighted. I shall endeavor to lure him out here; India to an American would be the most interesting experience possible to a human being" (October 26, 1896).

[31] November 5, 1896.

[32] February 25, 1897.

[33] Letter to Jennie, November 18, 1896.

[34] October 8, 1895.

[35] Undated letter, Peregrine Churchill Papers.

[36] Undated letter, Peregrine Churchill Papers.

[37] December 11, 1896.

[38] January 7, 1897. Winston also advised his brother: "Find something *congenial* at all costs."

[39] January 14, 1897.

[40] December 24, 1896.

[41] Consuelo Vanderbilt, *The Glitter and the Gold* (New York, Harper, 1952).

[42] *Reminiscences of Lady Randolph Churchill* (New York, Century, 1908).

[43] November 4, 1896.

[44] November 19, 1896.

[45] December 16, 1896.

[46] November 27, 1896.

[47] Margot Asquith, *More Memories* (London, Cassell, 1933).

[48] George Steevens was a correspondent for the *Daily Mail.* E. T. Raymond, *Portrait of the New Century* (New York, Doubleday, Doran, 1928).

[49] December 17, 1896.

[50] December 24, 1896.

[51] January 7, 1897.

[52] December 30, 1896.

[53] January 21, 1897.

[54] February 18, 1897.

[55] January 29, 1897.

[56] December 24, 1896.

Chapter 25

[1] Undated letter from Mrs. Pearl Craigie to Jennie, from "Cliveden, Maidenhead. Monday."

[2] Letter to Winston dated February 12, 1897, from the Hotel Bristol in Paris. Jennie had first met Cecil Rhodes in the early 1880s. She described him by saying, "Although not a literary man, he could speak clearly and with great authority on his own particular subjects. He was then a handsome young man with a delicate chest, and was just starting for South Africa, where he hoped the wonderful air would cure him. This it did, for although he died at a comparatively early age, it was not from consumption. I remember once having a most interesting conversation with him over his aims and ambitions. His whole soul was bound up in the future and progress of South Africa, and although he was not a self-seeker in any way, he was justly proud of having the immense province of Rhodesia named after him. In his heart of hearts, he wanted his name to be handed down to posterity in this indelible manner, and he would have been bitterly disappointed had any other been chosen. When I questioned him as to this, he admitted it quite frankly. He was, I think, a very happy man, for he never allowed small things to worry him, and his mind was not encumbered with the subtleties with which so many are hampered. A man of big ideas, he knew what he wanted, and made for his goal. He was singularly outspoken. On one occasion, discussing a sculptor, he said, looking at me critically: 'Why don't you let the fellow do you? You've got a good square face.'" *Reminiscences of Lady Randolph Churchill* (New York, The Century Co., 1908).

[3] Undated letter, Peregrine Churchill Papers.

[4] Undated letter, Peregrine Churchill Papers.

[5] Letter to Winston, dated February 26, 1897. She wrote to Jack the same day, "I have written him a very stiff letter which I fear hurt me more to write than it will him to receive."

[6] Letter dated March 5, 1897, to Winston.

[7] *Ibid.*

[8] Letter to Winston, dated March 18, 1897.

[9] Letter to Winston, April 2, 1897.

[10] Undated letter, Peregrine Churchill Papers.

[11] Letter from Colonel J. P. Brabazon to Jennie on Saturday, February 6, 1897.

[12] Letter to Winston, March 11, 1897.

[13] April 21, 1897, from Bangalore.

[14] *Ibid.*

[15] Undated letter, Peregrine Churchill Papers.

[16] Letter to Jennie from Winston, May 26, 1897, the *S.S. Caledonia* off Brindisi.

[17] June 10, 1897.

[18] Letter dated Monday, the 7th, 1897.

[19] Letter dated Tuesday, 1897, Great Cumberland Place.

[20] Ethel Raglan, *Memories of Three Reigns* (London, Nash & Grayson, 1928).

[21] R. D. Blumenfeld, *R.D.B.'s Diary* (London, Heinemann, 1930).

The latest style fad among lady cyclists was to wear gold and jeweled anklets showing beneath their knickers or short skirts. The new fashion for lady cyclists included a short Eton jacket, closing over the bosom with two buttons. Also popular was a coat buttoned high at the throat, single-breasted with short coattails. Bloomers were considered absolutely essential "for sanitary reasons."

[22] Letter to Jack from Halton, Tring, dated Monday the 7th, 1897.

[23] Undated letter from Ness Castle, Inverness, Peregrine Churchill Papers.

[24] *Town Topics,* August 13, 1896.

[25] Shane Leslie, *The Film of Memory* (London, Michael Joseph, 1938).

[26] *Ibid.*

[27] Sir Frederic Ponsonby, *Recollections of Three Reigns* (London, Eyre & Spottiswoode, 1951).

[28] *Reminiscences of Lady Randolph Churchill.*

[29] *Town Topics,* July 22, 1897.

[30] *Reminiscences of Lady Randolph Churchill.*

[31] *Ibid.*

[32] *Town Topics,* July 22, 1897.

[33] *Reminiscences of Lady Randolph Churchill.*

[34] *Ibid.*

[35] Lady Maud Warrender, *My First Sixty Years* (London, Cassell, 1933).

[36] *Reminiscences of Lady Randolph Churchill.*

[37] Letter dated August 17, 1897.

[38] Interview with Sir Shane Leslie.

[39] *Reminiscences of Lady Randolph Churchill.*

[40] Winston S. Churchill: *My Early Life* (London, Odhams Press, 1930).

[41] Barbara Tuchman, *The Proud Tower* (New York, Macmillan, 1965. Tuchman quotes *Punch's* parliamentary correspondent.

[42] Margot Asquith, when she was still Margot Tennant, "moved heaven and earth," according to Lady Jebb, to marry him. Queried on the rumor of this marriage, Balfour replied, "No, that is not so. I rather think of having a career of my own." Lady Jebb said of him, "Arthur was the best in a family all of whom are best . . . a man that almost everyone loves." However, she thought his nature was "emotionally cold," and that his one attempt at love, with May Lyttleton, sister of a Cambridge friend and Gladstone's niece, had "exhausted his powers in that direction." May Lyttleton died when she was twenty-five. (Balfour was then twenty-seven.) Tuchman, *op. cit.* Mrs. Tuchman believes it was not so much that Balfour was emotionally cold as that he was warmly attached to his freedom to do as he pleased.

[43] Letter dated August 29, 1897.

[44] Letter to Winston from Jennie, dated September 9, 1897.

[45] September 5, 1897.

[46] September 21, 1897, written from Langwell, Berriedale, R.S.O. Caithness.

[47] Letter dated "Friday, Great Cumberland Place."

Chapter 26

[1] Letter dated October 2, 1897, from the 31st Punjab Infantry.

[2] Letter dated October 2, 1897.

[3] Letter dated September 19, 1897.

[4] Letter dated December 22, 1897.

[5] Letter dated October 17, 1897.

[6] September 12, 1897

[7] September 19, 1897.

[8] October 7, 1897.

[9] Undated letter, Tuesday, 1897, from King Lynn.

[10] October 25, 1897.

[11] September 19, 1897.

[12] *Ibid.*

[13] December 22, 1897.

[14] November 4, 1897.

[15] November 2, 1897.

[16] November 1, 1897.

[17] November 3, 1897.

[18] November 4, 1897.

[19] December 2, 1897.

[20] December 2, 1897.

[21] December 24, 1897.

[22] April 13, 1898.

[23] May 16, 1898.

[24] November 17, 1897. During the coming Christmas recess, and early in 1898, there were a number of by-elections, which suggests that the Government's popularity was declining. Lord Salisbury, however, fought and won another General Election, and did not retire until July 1902.

[25] October 25, 1897.

[26] December 9, 1897.

[27] December 16, 1897.

[28] Winston S. Churchill, *My Early Life* (London, Odhams Press, 1930).

[29] Letter to Winston, September 30, 1897.

[30] Undated letter from Presles, Peregrine Churchill Papers.

[31] Undated letter from Lambton Castle, Peregrine Churchill Papers.

[32] Letter to Winston, December 10, 1897.

[33] Undated letter from Great Cumberland Place, "Saturday," Peregrine Churchill Papers.

[34] Randolph S. Churchill, *Winston S. Churchill,* Companion Volume I, Part 2 (Boston, Houghton Mifflin, 1967).

[35] January 19, 1898.

[36] January 10, 1898.

[37] January 13, 1898.

[38] January 19, 1898.

[39] November 17, 1897.

[40] January 23, 1898.

[41] January 28, 1898.

[42] January 30, 1898.

[43] December 24, 1897.

[44] January 20, 1898.

[45] January 21, 1898.

[46] January 26, 1898.

[47] January 27, 1898.

[48] January 27, 1898, from Sandringham.

[49] January 6, 1898.

[50] January 10, 1898.

[51] January 21, 1898.

[52] February 13, 1898.

[53] February 9, 1898.

[54] January 27, 1898. "General Getacre" was William Forbes Getacre, who had gone to Egypt to command the newly formed brigade being sent from Cairo to take part in the advance on Khartoum.

[55] Lord Rossmore, *Things I Can Tell* (London, Eveleigh Nash, 1912).

[56] February 16, 1898.

[57] Incident reported by Jennie's great-niece, Anita Leslie, *Lady Randolph Churchill* (New York, Scribner's, 1969).

[58] *Ibid.*

[59] *Ibid.*

[60] *Ibid.*

[61] *Ibid.*

[62] April 22, 1898.

[63] January 19, 1898.

[64] January 27, 1898.

[65] *Ibid.*

[66] March 18, 1898.

[67] In a letter dated April 13, 1898, in *The Athenaeum*.

[68] April 13, 1898.

[69] *Ibid.*

[70] November 17, 1897. Winston's literary ambitions were almost unlimited at this time in his life. He mentioned at various times his interest in writing a short history of the American Civil War, a life of Garibaldi, a volume of short stories called "The Correspondence of a New York Examiner," and later, a book on the Marlboroughs. About the Marlborough book, he said, "I think it would do something that would ring like a trumpet call."

[71] April 18, 1898.

[72] April 18, 1898, Bangalore.

[73] April 19, 1898.

[74] May 10, 1898.

[75] Letter dated June, 1898, from the Fourth Hussars, India.

[76] May 22, 1898.

[77] June (1898).

[78] April 25, 1898.

[79] March 27, 1898. Cyrus Adler, *Jacob H. Schiff*, Vol. II (London, Heinemann, 1929).

[80] *The Times* of London described Cassel as a person of "great wealth, a great heart, great influence . . . whose claim to rank among the outstanding figures of the last 20 years is indisputable." Margot Asquith saw him as "dignified, autocratic and wise; with the power of loving those he cared for." Cassel cared very much for Jennie. Whenever Jennie's finances became critical, she went to Cassel. But theirs was a close friendship, not a romance.

[81] "A well-known physiognomist has formulated the axiom that full, blue eyes [such as the Prince had] are generally associated with a cheerful and happy disposition; that they evidence a candid and generous nature, and belong to those who make the best of unpleasant circumstances . . . and that they hint of strong feelings, love of children, and a general fondness for pleasure." James Laver, *Edwardian Promenade* (Boston, Houghton Mifflin, 1958).

[82] July 10, 1898.

[83] July 10, 1898.

[84] July 9, 1898.

[85] Letter from Lord Salisbury to Winston, July 19, 1898.

[86] June 1, 1898.

[87] Undated letter.

[88] July 15, 1898.

[89] July 15, 1898.

[90] Churchill, *My Early Life.*

[91] *Ibid.*

[92] *Ibid.*

Chapter 27

[1] Frances, Countess of Warwick, *Afterthoughts* (London, Cassell, 1931). Lady Warwick also reported that Earl Fitzwilliam's house had about three hundred bedrooms. "It is a very Vatican of country houses, ugly and uncomfortable, noteworthy only because of its useless size. . . . The labor of running country houses, where the light is made on the premises, and the water comes from your own wells—with no running water in the bedrooms, and one bathroom to each floor—makes the use of these old-time places out of the question." Lady Warwick also observed that Wellbeck Abbey, which belonged to the Duke of Portland, had a riding school on the grounds.

[2] J. B. Priestley, *The Edwardians* (New York, Harper & Row, 1970).

[3] Theo Lang, *The Darling Daisy Affair* (New York, Atheneum, 1966).

[4] *Ibid.* Elinor Glynn used some of her Warwick Castle experience in a novel called, *The Reflections of Ambrosine.* She showed Lady Warwick the manuscript of another novel, *Three Weeks,* and Lady Warwick warned her not to publish it. If she did, said Lady Warwick, none of her noble friends would ever speak to her again; one might *do* such things, but one should not even talk—let alone write—about one's own or one's friends' love affairs.

[5] Frances, Countess of Warwick, *Life's Ebb & Flow* (New York, William Morrow, 1929).

[6] *Ibid.* Lady Warwick wrote in her *Memoirs:* "Prince Charles Kinsky was a sharer of my horsey adventures!"

[7] Lang, *op. cit.*

[8] *Ibid.*

[9] The Prince of Wales had signed the marriage register in 1881 when Frances married Lord Brooke, who later became the Earl of Warwick. The Prince's love affair with Lady Warwick began seven years after her marriage.

[10] Frances, Countess of Warwick, *Afterthoughts.*

[11] J. B. Priestley, *op. cit.* See Ralph G. Martin, *Jennie: The Life of Lady Randolph Churchill,* Vol. I: The *Romantic Years, 1854–1895* (Englewood Cliffs, N.J., Prentice-Hall, Inc., 1969), p. 163, for more details about country-house entertainment.

[12] William Cornwallis Cornwallis-West, Honorary Colonel of the First Volunteer Battalion, Royal Welsh Fusiliers, and holder of the Volunteer Decoration, was a grandson of the Second Earl de la Warr, Lord of the Bedchamber to George I, and Governor and Captain-General of New York. "West," the additional surname of Cornwallis, was not "officially" assumed by deed poll until 1895, though it had been in use for decades before that. George's mother, Mary Cornwallis-West, was a grand-daughter of the Second Marquis de Headfort, in the peerage of Ireland. (Michael Harrison, *Lord of London: A Biography of the Second Duke of Westminster* [London, W. H. Allen, 1966]) William Cornwallis-West was also the Lord-Lieutenant of Denbighshire, and Member of Parliament for that county from 1885 to 1892.

[13] The music halls in London were full of skits and songs about the professional beauties. One of the most popular songs was:

> I have been photographed like this,
> I have been photographed like that,
> But I have never been photoed as a raving maniac.

Virginia Cowles, *Edward VII and His Circle* (London, Hamish Hamilton, 1956).

[14] *Daisy, Princess of Pless, by Herself* (New York, Dutton, 1929).

[15] Harrison, *op. cit.*

[16] George Cornwallis-West, *Edwardian Hey-Days* (New York, Putnam, 1930).

[17] Anita Leslie, *Lady Randolph Churchill* (New York, Scribner's, 1970).

[18] Ethel Smyth, *What Happened Next* (London, Longman, 1940).

[19] September 7, 1898.

[20] Undated letter, Peregrine Churchill Papers.

[21] Shane Leslie, *Long Shadows* (London, Hollis & Carter, 1951).

[22] *Ibid.*

[23] Letter dated Tuesday, the 20th.

[24] (September 19, 1898?) From the Bachelor's Club, Piccadilly, W.

[25] Anita Leslie, *op. cit.*

Chapter 28

[1] September 3, 1898.

[2] September 5, 1898.

[3] September 4, 1898. All letters, unless otherwise noted, are from Randolph S. Churchill, *Winston S. Churchill* (Boston, Houghton Mifflin, 1967), Companion Volume I, Part 2, 1896–1900.

[4] *Ibid.*

[5] Reprinted in *Churchill by his Contemporaries,* edited by Charles Eade (New York, Simon and Schuster, 1954). Steevens had represented the *Daily Mail* in the United States and also at the Dreyfus trial. He died of enteric fever in the Transvaal in 1900. Winston Churchill called him "the most brilliant man in journalism I have ever met."

[6] Undated letter.

[7] October 6, 1898.

[8] Daisy, Princess of Pless, *What I Left Unsaid* (London, Cassell, 1936).

[9] *Reminiscences of Lady Randolph Churchill* (New York, The Century Co., 1908).

[10] *Ibid.*

[11] Earl Curzon of Kedleston, *Subjects of the Day* (London, Allen & Unwin, 1915).

[12] Conversation with author George Moore. Moore later said of her: "When a man has collaborated with a woman it is the same as if he had slept with her. She has no secrets left to reveal." Vineta Colby, *The Singular Anomaly* (New York, New York University Press, 1971).

[13] Unidentified clipping dated March 21, 1904.

[14] Gertrude Atherton, *Adventures of a Novelist* (New York, Liveright, 1932).

[15] Included among his products was Carter's Little Liver Pills.

[16] Mrs. T. P. O'Connor, *I, Myself* (London, Methuen, 1910).

[17] A verse circulated about her epigrams:

> John Oliver Hobbes, with your spasms and throbs,
> How does your novel grow?
> With cynical sneers at young Love and his tears,
> And epigrams all in a row.
>
> *Bookbuyer,* (April 1894), 127.

[18] Interview in *New York Herald,* November 16, 1905.

[19] *Reminiscences of Lady Randolph Churchill* (New York, The Century Co., 1908).

[20] Letter from 56, Lancaster Gate. W., dated July 19.

[21] Letter from Guildford, dated Sunday.

[22] *Reminiscences of Lady Randolph Churchill.*

[23] Vera Brittain, *Lady Into Woman* (London, Andrew Dakars, 1953).

[24] Francis Power Cobbe, *The Duties of Women* (New York, Swan Sonnenschein, 1905).

[25] Richard Le Gallienne, *The Romantic Nineties* (New York, Doubleday, Page, 1925).

[26] James Lewis May, *John Lane & The Nineties* (London, John Lane, 1936).

[27] Beardsley went to work for another new literary quarterly, *The Savoy,* which survived only for a year. The artist Whistler, who had been critical of Beardsley's work, told him, "Aubrey, I have made a very great mistake—you are a very great artist . . . I mean it—I mean it—I mean it . . ." May, *op. cit.*

[28] *Ibid.*

[29] Anna Eichberg was the daughter of a distinguished American musician, Julius Eichberg, who became Director of the Boston Conservatory of Music. At the age of sixteen she wrote the words to "America."

[30] November 29, 1898.

[31] December 1, 1898.

Chapter 29

[1] January 1, 1899. (All letters, unless otherwise noted, are from Randolph S. Churchill, *Winston S. Churchill* [Boston, Houghton Mifflin, 1967], Companion Volume I, Part 2, 1896–1900.) In that same letter, Winston told his mother that he did not think she should allow the full investment in the magazine to be made by outsiders, that she should guarantee some of her own money.

[2] Frances, Countess of Warwick, *Life's Ebb and Flow* (New York, William Morrow, 1929).

[3] Undated letter from Blenheim Palace. In it she also said she would need about 1500 pounds for the first year.

[4] *Ibid.*

[5] Undated letter.

[6] February 16, 1899. In his letter Winston dismissed other suggested titles such as *The Arena* and *The International Quarterly,* among others.

[7] Letter dated March 24, 1899.

[8] *Reminiscences of Lady Randolph Churchill* (New York, The Century Co., 1908).

[9] March 2, 1899.

[10] March 30, 1899. In the same letter Winston suggested that he and Jack should put 250 pounds into the guarantee for the Review.

[11] Undated letter from Great Cumberland Place.

[12] Undated letter from Great Cumberland Place.

[13] Undated letter from Great Cumberland Place.

[14] *Reminiscences of Lady Randolph Churchill.*

[15] March 22, 1899.

[16] February 23, 1899.

[17] January 1, 1899.

[18] Undated letter.

[19] A number of other people claimed to have "discovered" Kipling, including Moreton Frewen.

[20] Major Desmond Chapman-Huston, *Lost Historian* (London, John Murray, 1936). Huston also quoted Low as saying, "Journalism is the grave of genius." Low was knighted in 1918.

[21] *Ibid.*

[22] *Ibid.*

[23] April 19, 1899.

[24] April 26, 1899.

[25] George G. Harrap, *Some Memories* (London, Harrap & Co., 1935).

[26] Undated letter from Great Cumberland Place.

[27] Letter dated "Saturday."

[28] Undated letter from Great Cumberland Place.

[29] June 23, 1899.

[30] Letter to "Mr. Chapman" dated May 26.

[31] May 12, 1899.

[32] Undated letter.

[33] March 22, 1899.

[34] Undated letter.

[35] May 31, 1899.

[36] February 13, 1899. In the same letter Pearl also wrote: "I wish you could have heard Sir Evelyn's praise of your boy. He has the highest hopes for him." (Sir Evelyn Wood was then Commander-in-Chief of the Army.)

[37] Like Jennie, Pearl had studied music in Paris.

[38] Sir Frederick Ponsonby, *Recollections of Three Reigns* (London, Eyre and Spottiswoode, 1951).

[39] *Reminiscences of Lady Randolph Churchill.*

[40] Undated letters.

[41] Her first play was produced in 1894, a one-act play called *Journey's End in Lovers Meeting*, with Ellen Terry in the lead. She had three other plays produced by Sir George Alexander between 1898 and 1900. The most successful of these was *The Ambassador*, produced in 1898. Jennie was publishing her most recent play, *Osbern*, in her *Anglo-Saxon Review* before its London production.

[42] The poem was written by E. V. Lucas.

[43] *Town Topics*, February 9, 1899. Whitelaw Reid had served as attorney on the Paris Treaty Commission. Reid had explained the action of the United States in giving Spain $20 million for islands that were already theirs by force of arms. He said it was compensation "solely in recognition of the principle that debts attaching to a territory, and incurred for its benefit, should be transferred with its sovereignty."

[44] *Ibid.*

[45] March 22, 1899.

[46] Letter to Dowager Duchess of Marlborough, March 26, 1899.

[47] Winston had written earlier (March 30, 1899), "The preface to the first number, I should like to write, but we can talk about this when I get home. . . ." The final product was signed by Jennie.

[48] Quoted in *Reminiscences of Lady Randolph Churchill.*

[49] Frances, Countess of Warwick, *op. cit.* The Countess also had written, "Nobody, even the most literary, could have lived up to such a grand binding in a mere review." Jennie had sent her a scribbled outline of the Review's expected contents, including an article about his childhood and youth by the Prince of Wales— which she never received. She also asked her friend Daisy to send her "the recipe for your Cumberland sauce for the Wench of my kitchen. . . ."

[50] *Pall Mall Gazette*, undated clipping.

[51] June 20, 1899.

[52] Dated "Sunday," from Great Cumberland Place.

Chapter 30

[1] June 25, 1899.

[2] June 26, 1899. Aside from the words in italics, the letter was written by Winston's secretary. In the same letter he also asked his mother to bring some medicated spray for his inflamed tonsil.

[3] June 28, 1899.

[4] Sir Ivor Jennings, *The British Constitution,* 5th ed. (Cambridge, at the University Press, 1966).

[5] July 6, 1899. But earlier in the campaign, when Winston had denounced the Clerical Bill that Balfour had introduced, Balfour had said to him: "I thought he was a young man of promise, but it appears he's a young man of promises."

[6] July 14, 1899.

[7] July 20, 1899.

[8] August 9, 1899.

[9] July 23, 1899.

[10] Winston S. Churchill, *My Early Life* (London, Odhams Press, 1930).

[11] July 23, 1899. Winston, like his mother, enjoyed gambling—both at the races and at Monte Carlo.

[12] E. F. Benson, *As We Were* (London, Longman, 1930).

[13] Anita Leslie, *Lady Randolph Churchill* (New York, Scribner's, 1970).

[14] October 6, 1899. In England the term "dissenting" refers to Protestants who are not members of the Church of England. As used by George here, the term connotes low social class and a kind of grubby Puritanism.

[15] Letter dated from Burlington Hotel. W. *Reminiscences of Lady Randolph Churchill* (New York, The Century Co., 1908).

[16] *Ibid.*

[17] *Ibid.*

[18] *Ibid.*

[19] August 17, 1899.

[20] Cornwallis-West, *Edwardian Hey-Days* (New York, Putnam, 1930). In his memoirs, George West also said of Jennie: "Like many well-bred American women, she had the will and the power to adapt herself to her immediate surroundings. She was equally at home having a serious conversation with a distinguished statesman, or playing on a golf-course. A great reader, she remembered much of what she had read, and that made her a brilliant conversationalist, but although gifted with extreme intelligence, she was not brilliant in the deepest sense of the word. She was not a genius."

[21] August 13, 1899.

[22] August 4, 1899.

[23] Cornwallis-West, *op. cit.*

[24] *Ibid.*

[25] August 5, 1899.

[26] Undated letter.

[27] Undated letter, Peregrine Churchill Papers.

[28] August 13, 1899.

[29] August 22, 1899.

[30] September 3, 1899.

Chapter 31

[1] Shane Leslie, *Men Were Different* (London, Michael Joseph, 1937).

[2] The *Daily Mail* was patterned after the sensational American "yellow press." It used fewer words and bigger headlines than other newspapers in England. Harmsworth used to say that other papers served their news raw, but the *Mail* served it cooked. Lord Salisbury derided the paper, saying it was "written by office boys for office boys." Its circulation at that time had jumped to 200,000 copies a day, twice as many as any other daily newspaper in England. Harmsworth later became Lord Northcliffe.

[3] Cecil Hedlam, ed., *The Milner Papers,* Volume 1 (London, Cassell, 1931).

[4] Joseph Chamberlain was then sixty-three years old. His explanation for his vigor was: "No exercise and smoke all day." At fifty-one he had married a twenty-three-year-old American girl from Cleveland, Ohio, Mary Endicott. J. L. Garvin, *The Life of Joseph Chamberlain,* Vol. II (London, Macmillan, 1933).

[5] *Reminiscences of Lady Randolph Churchill* (New York, The Century Co., 1908).

[6] Randolph S. Churchill, *Winston S. Churchill,* Vol. I: *Youth, 1874–1900* (Boston, Houghton Mifflin, 1966).

[7] R. C. K. Ensor: *England: 1870–1914* (London, Oxford University Press, 1936).

[8] This represented the combined forces of Transvaal and the Orange Free State. There were about a million Boers scattered throughout South Africa.

[9] In a Letter to the editor of *The Times,* a Boer wrote that the British were a decaying race with its children born weak, diseased, and deformed, that the major proportion of British people consisted of females, cripples, epileptics, consumptives, cancerous people, and lunatics of all kinds, who were carefully nourished and preserved. Quentin Crewe, *Frontiers of Privilege* (London, Stevens Press, 1961).

[10] Winston had written his mother from the ship, "Sir R. Buller is vy amiable, and I do not doubt that he is well disposed towards me. . . ."

[11] George Cornwallis-West, *Edwardian Hey-Days* (New York, Putnam, 1930). The letter was dated October 15, 1899.

[12] Michael Harrison, *Lord of London: A Biography of the Second Duke of Westminster* (London, W. H. Allen, 1966).

[13] George Cornwallis-West, *op. cit.*

[14] *Town Topics,* January 25, 1900.

[15] *Reminiscences of Lady Randolph Churchill.* Sir W. E. Garstin had been a senior British official in Egypt, responsible for several vital irrigation schemes. He would later (January 19, 1900) write her: "I often think of that evening at the Van Andres [M. and Mme. Edouard von André, a stockbroker friend of Jennie's and his wife, who was a portrait painter] when you were talking over the scheme before it had definitely taken shape or form. You have done more than most people, towards drawing the bonds closer between the two countries. They must always be made

of sympathy & what you & other American ladies have done makes every Englishman's heart beat a bit faster."

[16] *Ibid.*

[17] H. J. and Hugh Massingham, *The Great Victorians* (New York, Doubleday,
Doran, 1932). Florence Nightingale, in that article, also wrote, "And marriage being
their only outlet in life, many women spend their lives in asking men to marry
them, in their refined way. . . ." Florence Nightingale went into nursing at the age of
thirty-four, and her first organizational activity was to set up a hospital for women
in Harley Street in London.

[18] Mrs. Fanny Ronalds had been an old romance of Jennie's father, Leonard
Jerome. She was then in love with Sir Arthur Sullivan, of Gilbert and Sullivan, who
helped considerably in the fund-raising for the hospital ship. Mrs. Cornelia Adair
had been one of the reigning beauties of Newport Society when Jennie was a girl.
Her husband was John Adair; he owned vast ranches in Texas and was a good
friend of Jennie's brother-in-law Moreton Frewen.

[19] *Reminiscences of Lady Randolph Churchill.*

[20] *Ibid.*

[21] *The Nursing Record and Hospital World,* November 4, 1899.

[22] Winston S. Churchill, *My Early Life* (London, Odhams Press, 1930).

[23] The cattle boat had been engaged in transatlantic trade between London
and Philadelphia. It was an iron-screw steamer of 2,228 tons, with a speed of $11\frac{1}{2}$
knots.

[24] *The Nursing Record and Hospital World,* November 18, 1899.

[25] November 5, 1899.

[26] *The New York Times,* November 9, 1899. In the same article Jennie was also
quoted as saying that "It is especially the province of American women to promote
this cause, but it is a woman's function to foster and nourish the suffering.
American women are more adept at it, we believe, than any others."

[27] *Town Topics,* January 25, 1900.

[28] Consuelo Vanderbilt Balsan, *The Glitter and the Gold* (New York, Harper,
1952).

[29] January 7, 1900.

[30] Interview in London *Daily Mail,* as reported in Oldham *Daily Standard,*
November 9, 1899.

[31] *Reminiscences of Lady Randolph Churchill.*

[32] For New York Society, she was "Mrs. Hugo de Bathe."

[33] The Prince had given her a silver turtle to be used as an inkstand.

[34] She sold a ticket to John Pierpont Morgan, Sr., by walking directly into his
office.

[35] Pierre Sichel, *The Jersey Lily* (Englewood Cliffs, N.J., Prentice-Hall, 1958).

[36] *The New York Times,* undated clipping.

[37] Kipling himself donated 20 pounds and some books for the *Maine* fund-
raising. Kipling's wife was an American, Carolyn Belestier, and they lived for a
while in Brattleboro, Vermont. His "Absent-Minded Beggar" was set to music by
Sir Arthur Sullivan and played on barrel-organs all over England. Kipling donated

the income from it to a variety of charities, which resulted in the offer of a knight-hood for Kipling–but he declined it.

[38] November 19, 1899.

[39] Letter from Walden to Lady Randolph, dated November 17, 1899, printed in the Oldham *Daily Standard,* Dec. 14, 1899.

[40] *Reminiscences of Lady Randolph Churchill.*

[41] Telegram, November 17, 1899.

[42] November 18, 1899.

[43] November 30, 1899.

[44] December 3, 1899. Anita Leslie, *Lady Randolph Churchill* (New York, Scribner's, 1970).

[45] November 18, 1899. The British Medical Journal of the same date also described the ship's facilities: "The ship has four large wards and one small isola-tion ward, providing accommodation altogether for 218 patients on two decks. . . . The operating room has been fitted up on the saloon deck, and is provided with an enamelled iron operating table with plate-glass top, instrument cupboards, steriliz-ers etc., and also an X-Ray installation." The operating room was described as "the most remarkable yet designed for South African service."

[46] *Reminiscences of Lady Randolph Churchill.*

[47] Winston S. Churchill, *My Early Life.*

[48] *Ibid.*

[49] *Ibid.*

[50] *Reminiscences of Lady Randolph Churchill.* Discussing the legal question of a ship sailing under two flags, *Truth* (December 21, 1899) wrote: "The ladies in com-mand possibly are not aware that a ship sailing under the flags of any two nations, is, by international law, a pirate." *The United Services Gazette* (December 9, 1899) had noted the rules for hospital ships: "They are to afford relief and assistance to all wounded belligerents, irrespective of nationality. During and after an engage-ment, they run at their own risk–though by International Law, they are absolute-ly neutralized. The belligerents have the right to visit them and control their movements."

[51] The Army & Navy Stores was at the time a unique British institution. The stores themselves were almost clubs. Members were usually recognized by name by the sales staff and doormen, and there were writing and reading rooms where mem-bers often arranged to meet. The stores had their own factories to produce gro-ceries, confectionaries, cigars, shirts, watches, guns, golf clubs, perfume. They offered all kinds of special services, from home repairs, decoration, and removals to auction rooms and catering. They bottled and shipped their own wine, and their catalogue included everything from elephant's feet (made into liqueur sets) to big game trophy-stuffing. A catalogue of 1907 offered fifty-six different designs of bedroom-toilet services, as well as "sculpture by corsetry" that promised a swan sil-houette. There were also leather dress protectors for hems which swept the pave-ments. And there were two whole pages on dinner gongs. The store also had a list-ing of entertainers for hire for parties, from Mystery Men in Native Costume to a White Viennese Band. The catering department offered everything from a wedding

breakfast to a thirteen-course dinner. (*The Very Best English Goods,* 1969. Introduction by Alison Adburgham. Army & Navy Store Catalogue of 1907).

[52] There had been a large party at the Carleton Hotel that night before the *Maine* sailed. The woman who organized the party was Lady Arthur Paget. Her husband was Colonel Arthur Paget, George West's commanding officer, who had decided to send George home. The doctors believed that his severe case of sunstroke might have affected his heart.

[53] *The New York Times,* December 24, 1899, reported: "As the *Maine* moved into the river, three cheers were given for the ship, then for Lady Churchill, and finally, for the United States."

Chapter 32

[1] Jennie told a reporter, "I know of no better way to spend Christmas than on an American hospital ship bound for South Africa. . . . Wherever the ship goes, I go. . . ." *The New York Times,* December 24, 1899.

[2] Jennie wrote her sister Clara that "the ship is not built for the big seas." January 3, 1900.

[3] *Reminiscences of Lady Randolph Churchill* (New York, The Century Co., 1908). *The* [London] *Times* (December 18, 1899) had written that the *Maine* "is the first vessel which any nation has ever dispatched to succour the wounded forces of another state."

[4] Letter from Las Palmas, January 2, 1900. In the same letter Jennie noted that the gale was so strong that the ship had to "lie to" for forty-eight hours.

[5] January 6, 1900.

[6] *Reminiscences of Lady Randolph Churchill.*

[7] January 6, 1900. Randolph S. Churchill, *Winston S. Churchill* Companion Volume I, Part 2 (Boston, Houghton Mifflin, 1969). Unless otherwise indicated, all letters quoted in this chapter are from this source.

[8] Undated letter, Peregrine Churchill Papers.

[9] January 6, 1900.

[10] *Reminiscences of Lady Randolph Churchill.*

[11] Undated letter, Peregrine Churchill Papers.

[12] *Ibid.*

[13] Miss Hibbard was Canadian-born, a member of the American Society of Superintendents of Training Schools for Nurses, and also a member of the Daughters of the American Revolution. Her great grandfather was a chaplain in the Revolutionary Army and also one of the earliest graduates of Dartmouth College. Miss Hibbard later became a leader in the development of nursing in Cuba, where she established seven schools of nursing and became Inspector General of Nurses. She also spent four years in the Panama Canal Zone. At the Gorgas Hospital in Ancon there is a bronze plaque which honors her as "Nurse, patriot, gentlewoman, humanitarian, friend, who rendered outstanding service to the development of better health in the tropics." Mary M. Roberts, *American Nursing: History and Interpretation* (New York, Macmillan, 1930).

[14] Undated letter, Peregrine Churchill Papers.

[15] *Reminiscences of Lady Randolph Churchill.*

[16] Jennie and Sir Alfred Milner had both been members of The Souls, that small social group of intellectuals who had become politically powerful in England. Two of them became Prime Ministers; Balfour and Asquith; Haldane became Lord Chancellor; Curzon, the Viceroy of India, and, later, Secretary of State for Foreign Affairs; Alfred Lyttleton became Secretary of State for War and George Wyndham Chief Secretary for Ireland. They had met mostly at George Wyndham's house near Salisbury, called "The Clouds." In July 1899, Wyndham had written to Milner, "The country has settled down to a stolid view that we must vindicate our supremacy, and that you must guide us as to how to do it. Wyndham regarded Milner as the coming man of the nineteenth century. Milner was the one man to whom Joseph Chamberlain had written a letter of introduction for Winston Churchill when he first went to South Africa, and Chamberlain had told Winston, "You will not need any other letter." Milner had been in love with Margot Tennant, who then married Henry Herbert Asquith. Michael Harrison, *Lord of London* (London, W. H. Allen, 1966).

[17] Winston had written "I cannot begin to criticize–for I should never stop. . . ." January 10, 1900.

[18] When the Boer War broke out Lord Roberts returned to England after forty-one years in India. Lord Lansdowne, who had been Viceroy of India when Roberts was there, appointed Roberts Supreme Commander in South Africa. Roberts, who had been one-eyed since infancy and was of considerably less than average height, was often called "Little Bobs." An orphan of Irish descent, he had made his way on sheer ability. He was a neat, precise man, quick and nervous in his movements, direct in his conversation. He was amiable, able, courageous, and devoted to duty. In contrast, Kitchener was complex and secretive. E. T. Raymond, *Portraits of the Nineties* (New York, Scribner's, 1921); Sir John Fortescue, *The Post-Victorians* (London, Ivor Nicholson and Watson, 1933).

[19] Lady G. Cecil, *Life of Robert, Marquis of Salisbury* (London, Hodder, 1931), Volume III.

[20] Undated letter, Peregrine Churchill Papers.

[21] Letter to Leonie, January 5, 1900. In that letter he had also written, "I trust Winston and he would never make me go 7,000 miles on a wild goose chase. . . . I look too beautiful in my big sombrero hat . . . I have becoming tummy bands and revolvers and belts and bayonettes and rifles and all the necessary implements of war, including a chain round my neck and a few charms. . . ." Randolph S. Churchill, *Winston S. Churchill* (Boston, Houghton Mifflin, 1969), Companion Volume I, Part 2.

[22] March 27, 1898.

[23] *Reminiscences of Lady Randolph Churchill.*

[24] Undated letter, Peregrine Churchill Papers.

[25] *Reminiscences of Lady Randolph Churchill.*

[26] Frederic Villiers, *Peaceful Personalities and Warriors Bold* (New York, Harper, 1907).

[27] *Ibid.*

[28] February 10, 1900.

[29] *Reminiscences of Lady Randolph Churchill.*

[30] *Ibid.*

[31] February 13, 1900.

[32] Winston S. Churchill, *My Early Life* (London, Odhams Press, 1930).

[33] March 27, 1900.

[34] February 18, 1900.

[35] Captain Percy Moreton Scott (who later became an Admiral) was a year younger than Jennie. His ship was diverted from a trip to China so that Scott could bring his heavy 4.7 naval guns to the defense of Ladysmith. He afterward went on to China, where he was active in putting down the Boxer Rebellion. By 1910 Scott had received £10,000 in reward for his various inventions. At the beginning of World War I, he was responsible for the creation of the anti-aircraft corps, and the anti-aircraft defense of London.

[36] *Reminiscences of Lady Randolph Churchill.*

[37] *Ibid.*

[38] W. L. Burdett-Coutts, *The Sick and Wounded in South Africa* (London, Cassell, 1900).

[39] *Reminiscences of Lady Randolph Churchill.*

[40] *Ibid.*

[41] *Ibid.* Sir Percy Scott, *Fifty Years In The Royal Navy* (New York, Doran, 1919). In his book of memoirs, Scott wrote, "I ordered the main brace to be spliced (for which I subsequently got hauled over the coals by the Admiralty). Every one in the town who could get a firework, let it off . . ."

[42] W. Pett Ridge, *I Like To Remember* (London, Hodder & Stoughton, n.d.).

[43] *Reminiscences of Lady Randolph Churchill.*

[44] *Ibid.*

[45] Anita Leslie, *Lady Randolph Churchill* (New York, Scribner's, 1970).

[46] Undated clipping.

[47] Undated letter, Peregrine Churchill Papers.

[48] To Jennie, the elegant clothing and the babble of both the men and the women in Capetown were "bewildering, and seemed under the circumstances rather out of place. . . ." *Reminiscences of Lady Randolph Churchill.*

[49] *Ibid.*

[50] March 10, 1900. The Prince of Wales had been critical to Countess Warwick "of some of the silly Society women who went to South Africa in the Boer War ostensibly to nurse the wounded, but actually to have as good a time as they could." His main reference was to the women who "walk the streets of Capetown, dressed as though they were at Ascot or Monte Carlo. One would suppose that, if they were not prevented by a sense of fitness of things, at least they would be deterred by a sense of humor." Frances, Countess of Warwick, *Afterthoughts* (London, Cassell, 1931).

[51] *The Daily Mail,* April 24, 1900. The reporter quoted Jennie as saying, "I have never had an idle moment all the time I've been away." She also now owned a chameleon which she called "George." "It hates a chilly day," she said.

Chapter 33

[1] Anita Leslie, *Lady Randolph Churchill* (New York, Scribner's, 1970).

[2] Samuel Edwards, *The Divine Mistress* (New York, David McKay, 1971). Madame Emilie du Chatelet also said she saw no virtue in repentance, "for despair only destroys one's appetite for life; besides, if the purpose of repentance is to avoid making the same mistake again, the precaution is useless, for nothing in life happens the same way twice. If a woman finds herself depressed, let her get herself a new gown or some new furniture." Voltaire said of Madame du Chatelet, "She was a great man whose only fault was in being a woman. . . ."

[3] Letter dated April 17, 1900.

[4] Undated letter, Peregrine Churchill Papers.

[5] Leslie, *op. cit.*

[6] George Cornwallis-West, *Edwardian Hey-Days* (New York, Putnam, 1930).

[7] Hesketh Pearson, *The Pilgrim Daughters* (London, Heinemann, 1961). Consuelo's eldest child, Kim, became the Ninth Duke of Manchester and married Helena Zimmerman, daughter of a Cincinnati millionaire. Before he died, Consuelo's husband had led "a disgraceful career—which included a shameful appearance in the police court and eventually sank absolutely into the gutter." *New York Journal,* quoted in Elizabeth Eliot, *They All Married Well* (London, Cassell, 1959).

[8] Cornwallis-West, *op. cit.*

[9] *Reminiscences of Lady Randolph Churchill* (New York, The Century Co., 1908).

[10] Undated clippings.

[11] Quoted in Pearson, *op. cit.*

[12] Undated letter to Jack, Peregrine Churchill Papers.

[13] Undated letter from the Isle of Mull, Duart Castle, Peregrine Churchill Papers.

[14] Cornwallis-West, *op. cit.*

[15] Letter to Clement King Shorter, January 27, 1900. Berg Collection, New York Public Library.

[16] June 9, 1900.

[17] May 1, 1900.

[18] June 9, 1900.

[19] May 12, 1900.

[20] *Ibid.* Jennie also wrote in that letter that she was finishing an article about the hospital ship, was consulting Cassel about some investments, and had seen the Queen, who "was most gracious."

[21] Letter to Leonie Leslie, May 15, 1900. His aunt had asked him to be the godfather to her expected child.

[22] Undated letter, Peregrine Churchill Papers.

[23] Lincoln Springfield, *Some Piquant People* (London, T. Fisher Unwin, 1924). W. Pett Ridge also wrote of the event: "Anyone in uniform was cheered and honored. I saw a railway porter near Charing Cross being carried along triumphantly, much as though he were Baden-Powell himself. Cordiality between the sexes was helped by the tickling of necks with feathers. There was the sale, too, at the curbs, of less agreeable articles—ladies' tormentors, which sprayed water in your face, and

that ridiculous toy that was being drawn down the back of a coat or blouse, making the sound of a tearing garment. Illuminations appeared at nearly every shop, every house, and any exception was resented. Hats went into the air, and nobody seemed to mind whether or not they came back to their owners." *I Like to Remember* (London, Hodder & Stoughton, n.d.).

[24] May 26, 1900.

[25] Anita Leslie, *op. cit.*

[26] Cornwallis-West, *op. cit.*

[27] *Ibid.*

[28] June 20, 1900.

[29] Undated letter, Peregrine Churchill Papers.

[30] June 23, 1900.

[31] June 17, 1900.

[32] July 10, 1900.

[33] June 23, 1900.

[34] June 30, 1900. In the same letter she also told him that Leonie had given birth to a son, and also asked him whether he was short of clothing.

[35] July 28, 1900.

[36] An undated clipping from a British newspaper (no source) noted: "Though the name of the Prince of Wales did not appear in Lady Randolph Churchill's present list, lest he should seem to abet a marriage of which his judgment disapproved, the Prince did not forget his friend, but personally gave to the bridge, the day before the wedding, a little gold pig, set in jewels." Jennie collected replicas of pigs.

[37] The *Northern Whig* (August 6, 1900) estimated the crowd outside the church at several thousand. The *Yorkshire Herald* (August 4, 1900) observed that Jennie, being a widow, "had no bridesmaids." And, an undated clipping (no source) reported that the bridge's dress was designed by Madame Hayward of New Bond Street and that the groom looked "splendidly tall and handsome, well-built, and with a charmingly good expression to boot."

[38] Lady Maud Warrender, *My First Sixty Years* (London, Cassell, 1933).

[39] Daisy, Princess of Pless, *From the Private Diaries,* ed. M. D. Chapman-Huston (London, John Murray, 1950).

[40] July 31, 1900.

Chapter 34

[1] Randolph S. Churchill, *Winston S. Churchill* (Boston, Houghton Mifflin, 1967), Companion Volume II, Part 2. (Unless otherwise indicated, all letters quoted in this chapter are from this source.)

[2] Interview with Sir Shane Leslie, and quoted in Anita Leslie, *Lady Randolph Churchill* (New York, Scribner's, 1970).

[3] August 12, 1900.

[4] Lord Rosebery earlier had written to Winston advising him to take elocution lessons. In a letter of July 31, 1900, Winston said he would take the advice "though I fear I shall never learn to pronounce an 'S' properly."

[5] September 18, 1900.

[6] September 20, 1900.

[7] September 21, 1900.

[8] October 12, 1900.

[9] October 7, 1900. Winston also told Bourke in that letter that he was particularly proud of having reversed the 1500-vote loss recorded against him there a year before.

[10] October 16, 1900.

[11] November 2, 1900.

[12] George Cornwallis-West, *Edwardian Hey-Days* (New York, Putnam, 1930).

[13] *Ibid.*

[14] *Ibid.*

[15] December 25, 1900.

[16] Daisy, Princess of Pless, *From the Private Diaries,* ed. M. D. Chapman-Huston (London, John Murray, 1950).

[17] G. Cornwallis-West, *op. cit.* Some years later, George took Jennie's nephew Seymour Leslie for his first real ride in an automobile and told him, "Go in for electricity or motor-cars . . . The coming thing, dont-you-know!" Seymour Leslie, *The Jerome Connexion* (London, John Murray, 1964).

[18] Letter from the Moreton Frewen Papers, written on notepaper from a hotel in Milan, Italy, and dated November 9, 1900.

[19] Letter from the Moreton Frewen Papers, written from Torquay, England, December 14, 1900.

[20] December 15, 1900.

[21] Lady Cynthia Asquith, *Diaries: 1915–1918* (New York, Knopf, 1969). Whibley was very enamored of Lady Asquith.

[22] Lincoln Springfield, *Some Piquant People* (London, T. Fisher Unwin, 1924).

[23] December 12, 1900. In the same letter Pearl Craigie told Jennie she had given up trying to produce her play in Egypt because the actors were terrified by the "gang" in the gallery. "No English actor or actress can perform unless they have their 'receptions.'"

[24] Stephen Crane spent most of his dying days at Brede Place. He had asked that he might be taken to die in the Black Forest, and this was done. His death came on June 5, 1900, and Moreton Frewen organized a fund to pay Crane's debts. Rudyard Kipling was asked to complete Crane's unfinished work, but he said, ". . . a man's work is personal to him and should remain as he made or left it." Allen Andrews, *The Splendid Pauper* (Philadelphia, Lippincott, 1968).

[25] The ghost of Brede Place was supposed to be that of Sir Goddard Oxenbridge, whose family had lived there from 1395. It was said that he had had the habit of devouring babies. According to legend, the children of Sussex plied him with beer until he was drunk, then laid an enormous wooden saw on him and see-sawed him to death, cutting him in half. "Many people have reported ghostly manifestations at Brede Place." *Ibid.*

[26] W. Pett Ridge, *I Like To Remember* (London, Hodder & Stoughton, n.d.).

[27] Eve Adam, *Mrs. J. Comyns Carr's Reminiscences.* London, Hutchinson, 1925).

[28] Randolph S. Churchill, *op. cit.,* Companion Volume I, Part 2, p. 1222n.

[29] *Ibid.,* letter from Boston, December 21, 1900.

[30] January 1, 1901. He also wrote, "I am vy proud that there is not one person in a million who at my age [he was then twenty-five] could have earned £10,000 without any capital in less than two years." Several months earlier Colonel Brabazon had written Jennie how pleased he was that Winston was not marrying Pamela. "She ought to be a rich man's wife."

[31] Letter to George from Chicago, January 16, 1901.

[32] January 1, 1901.

[33] July 31, 1900.

[34] Undated letter.

[35] Letter from Chicago, January 16, 1901.

[36] December 25, 1900.

[37] January 9, 1901.

[38] *Ibid.*

[39] *I.e.,* Mrs. Alice Frederica Keppel, the Prince's mistress.

[40] January 22, 1901.

[41] Sir Frederick Ponsonby, *Recollections of Three Reigns* (London, Eyre & Spottiswoode, 1951).

[42] Shane Leslie, *The Film of Memory* (London, Michael Joseph, 1938).

Chapter 35

[1] February 14, 1901. Randolph S. Churchill, *Winston S. Churchill,* Companion Volume II, Part 1, 1901–7 (Boston, Houghton Mifflin, 1969). Unless otherwise noted, all letters quoted here are from this source.

[2] Cecil Rhodes, whose promising career had been broken by the Boer War, also warned those British who talked only of revenge: "You think you have beaten the Dutch; but it is not so. The Dutch are not beaten; what is beaten is Krugerism, a corrupt and evil government no more Dutch in essence than English. No, the Dutch are as vigorous and unconquered today as they have ever been; the country is still as much theirs as it is yours, and you will have to live and work with them hereafter as in the past." Arthur Bryant, *English Saga* (London, Collins, 1940).

[3] February 1, 1901.

[4] March 26, 1901.

[5] February 20, 1901. General Sir Ian Hamilton was happy to do this for Winston and Jennie. Winston earlier had asked Hamilton to visit Jennie. "She would be very grateful for news of me, and to meet one who has shown me much kindness." Hamilton also remembered in his memoirs that Winston had given him a copy of the completed manuscript of Winston's novel, *Savrola,* and that he had "handed it over to his mother, Lady Randolph Churchill." General Sir Ian Hamilton, *Listening for the Drums* (London, Faber & Faber, 1944).

[6] December 17, 1901.

[7] Undated letter.

[8] Margot Asquith (later, Margot Oxford when her husband became Lord Oxford) wrote in her memoirs: "Arthur Balfour was born with perfect equilibrium,

and an admirable temper and iron nerves. I have often seen him masterful, cool, and collected in debates which aroused prolonged party fury in the House of Commons. I have sat by his side on several occasions when his motor skidded down dangerous slopes, and one day when it went with a crash against a lorry in the dark. He never moved in his seat, and we continued our conversation as if nothing had occurred." Margot Oxford, *More Memories* (London, Cassell, 1933). In 1904, the King's lack of enthusiasm for Balfour was to turn into resentment when Balfour stripped away the King's royal power to see the Territories without consent of Parliament.

[9] "The King dearly loved a joke, indeed only a man or woman who could keep him amused or interested was sure of ready welcome." Frances, Countess of Warwick, *Discretions* (New York, Scribner's, 1931).

[10] King Edward smoked cigars incessantly, against his doctor's advice. He ate what he pleased, but he was always temperate in his use of alcohol. *Ibid.*

[11] The King was also very superstitious. His hostesses had to be certain that knives were not crossed on the table, mattresses were not turned on Fridays, and, of course, that she never sat thirteen down to dinner. Virginia Cowles, *Edward VII & His Circle* (London, Hamish Hamilton, 1956).

[12] Poem by Rudyard Kipling.

[13] Cowles, *op. cit.*

[14] Daisy, Princess of Pless, *From the Private Diaries,* ed. M. D. Chapman-Huston (London, John Murray, 1950).

[15] Undated letter.

[16] G. Cornwallis-West, *Edwardian Hey-Days* (New York, Putnam, 1930).

[17] *Ibid.*

[18] E. D. Gramont, *Pomp and Circumstance* (London, Jonathan Cape & Harrison Smith, 1929).

[19] G. Cornwallis-West, *op. cit.*

[20] *Ibid.*

[21] *Ibid.* At one of these parties, Jennie sat next to the Ambassador from Japan. Jennie had been to Japan and loved it, and had brought back prints and other antiques for her house. She and the Ambassador discussed proverbs and Jennie wondered whether there was a Japanese equivalent for, "Penny wise and pound foolish." The Japanese Ambassador hesitated thoughtfully, then answered, "The literal translation of the Japanese equivalent is: 'The man who goes to bed early to save candles gets twins.'"

[22] *Ibid.*

[23] Both King Edward and Lord Rosebery owned horses which won the Derby.

[24] December 13, 1901.

[25] In his novel *Savrola,* published the previous year (1900). Winston had great difficulty portraying women. One reviewer wrote, "His love scenes are shirked as far as possible."

[26] People were so partisan about the Boer War that there were still riots when pro-Boer speakers held rallies. Some 40,000 people surrounded Town Hall where Lloyd George was scheduled to make a pro-Boer speech. They broke all the windows of the

Hall and Lloyd George had to be smuggled out disguised as a policeman. Gramont, *op. cit.*

The coronation originally had been scheduled for June 26, 1902, eighteen months after his accession, but recovery from the operation took almost a month.

[27] J. B. Priestley, *The Edwardians* (New York, Harper & Row, 1970).

[28] Anita Leslie, *Lady Randolph Churchill* (New York, Scribner's, 1970).

[29] *Ibid.*

[30] Daisy, Princess of Pless, *op. cit.*

[31] Some years later, there was a popular ballad, which included the verses,

> There is peace within the palace
> At a little word from Alice.
> *Send for Mrs. Keppel!*
> She alone can keep the King from dumps,
> Once she's shown him how to play his trumps.
> *Send for Mrs. Keppel!*

Shane Leslie, *Long Shadows* (London, John Murray, 1966).

[32] Sonia Keppel, *Edwardian Daughter* (New York, British Book Center, 1959).

[33] *Ibid.*

[34] Margot (Asquith) Oxford, *op. cit.*

[35] "When some people, jealous at not being in such high favor themselves with King Edward as she was, made ill-natured remarks about her, she never retaliated; and although her influence with the King was so great that, had she chosen to exercise it, she could have gotten the scandal-mongers into serious hot water, she never attempted to make use of her power in the smallest degree. Her magnanimity, which, while commanding my deepest admiration, makes me regard her as a truly remarkable, if not unique, woman." The Duke of Manchester, *My Candid Recollections* (London, Grayson & Grayson, 1932).

[36] Jennie told in her article that when Catherine of Medici became a widow she had her bedroom hung with black velvet embroidered with pearls forming crescents and suns. She also described Madame de Lafayette's bed of crimson satin, but noted that her bedroom also had "a chest of drawers, a small bookcase containing two hundred volumes, eight tapestry chairs, white cotton curtains, a spinet, a picture representing the demolition of the Bastille, a card table and two maps." Marie Antoinette's bedroom featured a domed Imperial bed, fourteen-and-a-half feet high draped with silver brocade and two enormous chandeliers of rock crystal.

[37] Anita Leslie, *op. cit.*

[38] So intense was the feeling on the Boer War that the owner of the London *Chronicle* forced his pro-Boer editor to resign and launched a pro-war policy. On the other hand, Lloyd George formed a syndicate to buy *The Daily News* and oust its anti-Boer editor to reverse its editorial policy.

[39] August 19, 1901.

[40] Undated letters, Peregrine Churchill Papers.

[41] John Morgan Richards had lived for thirty years in London, had a keen interest in literary matters, wrote a book called *With John Bull and Jonathan,* and even

owned for a while a magazine called *The Academy*. He was a rich, popular American with a soft, gentle voice.

[42] Mr. Michael Rhodes, a respected British historian who has deeply researched the turn-of-the-century English literary magazines and is currently writing a book about John Lane, feels that the first four issues were the best written, the best edited, and the most interesting. Jennie's involvement with the hospital ship, the Boer War, and her marriage diverted much of her time thereafter. Rhodes also feels that *The Anglo-Saxon Review* was not fated to last much longer because although the reading audience for such things had broadened vastly, the Review's price was prohibitive. But he added, "The Anglo-Saxon Review even now, is unique. There has never been any other journal quite like it, an international literary review of high quality that really was international and literary." Interview by the author.

[43] September 27, 1902.

[44] December, 1902.

[45] Clare Sheridan, *The Naked Truth* (New York, Harper, 1928).

[46] *Ibid.*

[47] *Ibid.* On a typical week of the Debutante Season, Clare's social calendar read:

Monday 29th	(Go to *castle* concert)
Tues., 1st	(Royal Hospital Ball)
Wed., 2d	(Castle Ball)
Thurs., 3	(Dance)
Fri., 4	(Royal H. Dinner and Dance)

She also had a list of necessary clothes:

Court train for best ball gown

3 evening or ball-gowns

3 tidy silk shirts, to come down to breakfast in, with tweed skirts

3 ordinary shirts, to wear with short skirt

3 nice shooting caps

1 smart feather hat

1 hat to drive to meets, etc.

[48] Undated letter to Jack, Peregrine Churchill Papers.

[49] Undated letter, Peregrine Churchill Papers.

[50] G. Cornwallis-West, *op. cit.*

[51] *Ibid.*

[52] *Ibid.*

[53] Elizabeth Eliot, *They All Married Well* (London, Cassell, 1959).

[54] Undated letter, Peregrine Churchill Papers.

[55] January 29, 1903.

[56] March 9, 1903.

[57] January 28, 1904. The novel with "Jennie" in it was *The Vineyard*.

[58] January 11, 1904. Jennie joined two clubs: The Atheneum and the Ladies Automobile Club.

[59] Shane Leslie also had written that after the King's visit "the English royal family had a spiritual home on the Seine." Shane Leslie, *Long Shadows* (London, Hollis & Carter, 1951).

[60] *The* [London] *Times,* November 30, 1903.

[61] December 19, 1902.

[62] August 12, 1903.

[63] September 18, 1903.

[64] During the Boer War, Bourke Cockran had addressed pro-Boer rallies in New York, Chicago, and Boston, and called it "one of the most barbarous wars in all the dreary annals of aggression." He said Joseph Chamberlain had generously consented to give the Boers a choice between subjugation and conquest, "which was very much the same as if a man should invite another to commit suicide, in order to save the trouble and risk of murder. . . . This is a war of the London Smart Set, the stock exchange gamblers and the street mobs. It has never been approved by the sober judgment of the English people; it is abhorrent to the conscience of the American people. It is a fashionable war on both sides of the Atlantic; it is a popular war on neither side."

[65] At Bourke Cockran's death in 1923, Winston Churchill said of him: "All of his convictions were of one piece. To him, the brittle loyalties of party were unimportant, compared with fidelity to principles."

[66] Seymour Leslie, *The Jerome Connexion* (London, John Murray, 1964).

Chapter 36

[1] Mary Borden also wrote in the London *Spectator* that the American woman "lives at great speed with high intensity, acts quickly on her beliefs, dashes into every adventure." She also regarded them as being "very ignorant and very emotional. . . ." An article in *Review of Reviews,* April 1902, entitled "Do Americans Live Too Fast?" said: ". . . Americans are developing their brains and nerves at expense of their bodies. This is especially the case with women." It recommended more fresh air, dumb bells, Indian clubs, and chest weights. It also said that the morning newspaper "devours a large part of the nervous force which ought to be derived from breakfast."

[2] August 22, 1904.

[3] Daisy, Princess of Pless, *From the Private Diaries,* ed. M. D. Chapman-Huston. (London, John Murray, 1950). Daisy, who was then thirty, admitted in this same diary, "I would be much plumper if I did not wear long and well-made French corsets."

[4] "The Most Influential Anglo-Saxon Woman in the World," *Current Literature,* December, 1908.

[5] Nell Gwynne (or Gwyn) had been an orange seller at the Theater Royal and made her debut as an actress at the Drury Lane in 1665. She was best in comic roles. She became the mistress of Charles II in 1669 and bore him two sons, one of whom became the Duke of St. Albans.

[6] George Cornwallis-West, *Edwardian Hey-Days* (New York, Putnam, 1930).

[7] Daisy, Princess of Pless, *op. cit.*

[8] The Duchess of Devonshire wore a formidable iron corset to keep her rigid, "and although she took an hour to climb the stairs, she led in all respects the life of

a very young woman. Balls, dinners, races, the Opera, the social gatherings, charity committees—she presided over and managed everything. . . . her age vanished between the aids of art; a wig made up of little fair curls framed the petal-pinkest of faces . . ." E. D. Gramont, *Pomp and Circumstance* (London, Jonathan Cape & Harrison Smith, 1929). Gramont added: "Animal spirits in England are more impetuous than in France. It has been demonstrated that English legs move with greater velocity than ours. And this world carries even the ancient with it. Evening functions in London are a mass of venerable reliquaries, bewigged and covered in jewels. They go on showing themselves at an age when French women softly cling to the fireside and lock up their jewels in the vaults . . ."

[9] Kaiser Wilhelm had known Jennie since the time she had first visited Berlin with Lord Randolph. See Ralph G. Martin, *Jennie: The Life of Lady Randolph Churchill,* Vol. I: *The Romantic Years, 1854–1895* (Englewood Cliffs, N.J.: Prentice-Hall, Inc., 1969).

[10] Daisy, Princess of Pless, *op. cit.*

[11] Sir Frederick Ponsonby, *Recollections of Three Reigns* (London, Eyre and Spottiswoode, 1951).

[12] *Sheffield Daily Telegraph,* October 29, 1909.

[13] Daisy, Princess of Pless, *op. cit.*

[14] Marquis de Soveral Private Papers, courtesy of Viscountess de Soveral. Undated letter from Vice Regal Lodge, Dublin.

[15] *Ibid.*

[16] November 12, 1904.

[17] February 9, 1905.

[18] *Reminiscenses of Lady Randolph Churchill* (New York: The Century Co., 1908).

[19] Cornwallis-West, *op. cit.*

[20] In India, Mary Leiter Curzon was called "The Leiter of Asia." She was a lovely woman with deep, dark eyes and black hair.

[21] Lord Curzon, the man so many considered cold and stiff, wrote a poem about his wife which began:

> I would have torn the stars from the Heavens for your necklace,
>
> I would have stripped the rose-leaves for your couch from all the trees. . . .

[22] Vineta Colby, *The Singular Anomaly* (New York, New York University Press, 1970).

[23] Untitled newspaper clipping dated February 3, 1903. Signed "W. F. B."

[24] Colby, *op. cit.*

[25] *Ibid.*

[26] Cornwallis-West, *op. cit.*

[27] June 12, 1905.

[28] "C-B" once said of the Boer War: "When is a war not a war? When it is carried on by the methods of barbarism in South Africa." He received a letter from an indignant clergyman who called him "a cad, a coward and a murderer." E. T. Raymond: *Portraits of the New Century* (New York, Doubleday, 1928).

[29] The Duke of Devonshire appeared with Winston at a Free Trade meeting in Manchester and asked him whether he felt nervous before he made a speech.

Winston said yes. "I used to," said the Duke, "but now whenever I get up on a plat-form, I take a good look around, and as I sit down, I say, 'I never saw such a lot of damned fools in my life,' and then I feel better." Barbara Tuchman, *The Proud Tower* (New York, Macmillan, 1965).

[30] Undated letter to Leonie, Moreton Frewen Papers.

[31] Lord Riddell quoting Jennie in Jack Fishman's, *My Darling Clementine* (New York, Avon, 1963).

[32] Undated letter to Leonie, Moreton Frewen Papers.

[33] *Ibid.*

[34] Literary editor Frank Harris, a good friend of Lord Randolph's, served as Winston's literary agent on this book. Winston had asked Harris to do this, telling him, in a letter, that he thought Harris had written (in a book) the best short biography of Lord Randolph that he had ever read.

[35] Undated letter in 1905, Shane Leslie papers. Randolph S. Churchill, *Winston S. Churchill*, Companion Vol. II, Part I, 1901–7 (Boston, Houghton Mifflin, 1969). Marsh later quoted Pamela Plowden (who became Lady Lytton) as saying, "The first time you meet Winston, you see all his faults, and the rest of your life you spend in dis-covering his virtues." Christopher Hassall, *Edward Marsh* (London, Longman, 1959).

[36] *Ibid.*

[37] Letter to Leonie, January 6, 1906.

[38] Douglas Plummer, *Queer People* (London, W. H. Allen, 1963).

[39] Randolph S. Churchill, *op. cit.* The young Duke of Westminster had married George's sister Shelagh in 1901. He was one of the richest men in Britain. Besides estates in Cheshire and Scotland, he owned 600 acres of rich property in London, and an estate in Flintshire that covered 30,000 acres. His home there was one of the great houses in England. When his bride first saw it, she said, "It's not a house; it's a town." Shelagh and the Duke were separated in 1910, but the Duke maintained a pension for the Cornwallis-West family. Michael Harrison, *Lord of London* (London, W. H. Allen, 1966).

[40] October 18, 1906.

[41] October 20, 1906.

[42] *Ibid.*

[43] October 13, 1906.

[44] Anita Leslie, *Lady Randolph Churchill* (New York, Scribner's, 1970).

[45] Undated letter. Jack, not Winston, acted as the peacemaker in Jennie's fights with George.

[46] Daisy, Princess of Pless, *op. cit.*

[47] *Ibid.*

[48] *Ibid.* Jennie and George often visited Daisy at her palace in Furstenstein where George had every kind of hunting and fishing facility. Winston once asked George to get him an invitation to visit there.

[49] Ethel Smyth, *What Happened Next* (London, Longman, 1940). Ethel Smyth, *Streaks of Life* (London, Longman, 1921). Ethel Smyth's brother served in the same regiment with Winston at the Battle of Omdurman. Her brother wrote her: "Winston taught us a new game called bridge, which comes from Constantinople,

and is like whist, but more of a gamble." Her brother also said of Winston, "If he lives, he'll be a big man some day." Miss Smyth also became an ardent suffragist, and from a jail cell window she once used her toothbrush to direct the singing of a chorus of sympathizers.

[50] Smyth, *What Happened Next.*

[51] Undated clipping.

[52] She was born on Christmas Day and received much publicity when Robert Louis Stevenson publicly offered her his birthday as her own. He gave his birthday (November 13) to her in the form of a legal document. The document stated that the birthday should be celebrated by feasting and singing, and, if this was not done, then the birthday would be taken away from Miss Ide and given to whoever was President of the United States at that time.

[53] They were married in 1912.

[54] Interview with Alice Roosevelt Longworth.

[55] Anita Leslie, *op. cit.*

[56] Seymour Leslie, *The Jerome Connexion* (London, John Murray, 1964).

[57] Within a year the bailiffs moved into Brede Place and auctioned off all the furniture which Mrs. Jerome had saved through the Paris Commune. Jennie was there to bid for and buy a few things that Clara really wanted to save. Clare wrote of her mother: "Poor old Mumkin, she made her choice, she chose her husband and sacrificed her children, she must abide by her choice." Allen Andrews, *The Splendid Pauper* (Philadelphia, Lippincott, 1968).

[58] Jennie and her niece Clare were so close that even back in February 1904, Clare wrote her mother, "Tell Auntie J. that the chief reason I want to come to London is to see her." Letter from Moreton Frewen Papers, Manuscript Room, Library of Congress. And another time, "Give my tenderest love to Aunt Jennie. . . ." Andrews, *op. cit.*

[59] Undated letter; Hassall, *op. cit.*

[60] August 21, 1907.

[61] August 22, 1907.

[62] August 30, 1907.

[63] September 26, 1907; Randolph S. Churchill, *Winston S. Churchill,* Companion Volume II, Part 2 (Boston, Houghton Mifflin, 1969).

[64] *Reminiscences of Lady Randolph Churchill.*

[65] September 17, 1907.

[66] September 26, 1907; Randolph S. Churchill, *op. cit.,* Companion Volume I, Part 2.

[67] November 14, 1907.

[68] *Ibid.*

[69] August 8, 1908.

[70] November 21, 1907.

[71] January 3, 1908.

[72] November 26, 1907.

[73] November 21, 1907.

[74] January 2, 1908.

[75] December 13, 1907.

[76] December 5, 1907.

[77] December 13, 1907.

[78] November 21, 1907.

[79] *The* [London] *Times,* November 22, 1907.

[80] November 21, 1907.

[81] December 5, 1907.

[82] December 16, 1907.

[83] December 28, 1907.

[84] December 30, 1907.

[85] January 3, 1908. Letter on Ladies Automobile Club stationery from Claridge's Hotel, Moreton Frewen Papers.

[86] January 7, 1908.

[87] January 12, 1908.

[88] On January 4, 1882, Jennie had recorded, "Went out and breakfasted with Blanche Hozier."

[89] Randolph S. Churchill, *Winston S. Churchill: Young Statesman,* 1901–14 (Boston, Houghton Mifflin, 1967).

[90] *Ibid.*

[91] *Ibid.*

[92] *Ibid.*

[93] April 16, 1908.

[94] After the loss at Manchester, Austen Chamberlain, son of Joseph Chamberlain, wrote his stepmother (Chamberlain's third wife): "Have you heard the stock exchange telegram to Winston on the morrow of his defeat? . . . It ran: 'To Winston Churchill, Manchester: "What's the use of a W.C. without a seat?"' " (A "w.c.," which stands for "water closet," is the British term for a toilet.) Randolph S. Churchill, *Winston S. Churchill: Young Statesman.*

[95] Randolph S. Churchill, *Winston S. Churchill: Young Statesman.*

[96] *Ibid.*

[97] August 7, 1908.

[98] August 8, 1908.

[99] August 7, 1908.

[100] Anita Leslie, *op. cit.*

[101] August 17, 1908.

[102] August 20, 1908.

[103] The wedding account in *The New York Times,* September 13, 1908, mentioned that ". . . the list of wedding presents fills two columns of small type." The presents included some duplicates: twenty-five candlesticks, twenty-one inkstands, twenty silver bowls, fifteen vases, fourteen silver trays, eight sets of salt cellars, and ten cigarette cases. Ralph G. Martin and Richard Harrity, *Man of the Century* (New York, Duell, Sloan & Pearce, 1962).

[104] *Ibid.*

[105] *Current Literature,* December, 1908.

[106] *Ibid.*

[107] September 13, 1908. In his only novel, *Savrola* (New York, Random House, 1956), Winston had this dialogue between his hero and heroine:

"Do you despise me very much?" she asked.

"No," he replied, "I would not marry a goddess."

"Nor I," she said, "a philosopher."

Then they kissed each other, and thenceforth their relationship was simple.

Chapter 37

[1] October 13, 1908. Also on the front page was a three-column picture of Jennie. She signed the article "Jennie Cornwallis-West."

[2] Mrs. Belmont's comments were sent in a telegram to the Paris *Herald.*

[3] Quoted in the London *Express,* October 21, 1908.

[4] London *Daily Chronicle,* July 8, 1909.

[5] The play was *Guy Domville,* and had opened on January 6, 1895.

[6] *The New York Times,* January 6, 1895.

[7] George Bernard Shaw's first play, *Widowers' Houses,* opened in 1892. Shaw also had the experience at one of his early plays of hearing some booing. During a curtain call after an opening performance, in response to a solitary loud boo, he said, "Personally, I agree with my friend in the gallery, but what can we two do against an audience of such a different opinion."

[8] William Archer, *The Old Drama and the New* (New York, Dodd, Mead, 1923).

[9] Daisy, Princess of Pless, *From My Private Diary* (London, John Murray, 1931), entry on April 28, 1904.

[10] In conversation with Sidney Low, as reported by Major Desmond Chapman-Huston, *The Lost Historian* (London, John Murray, 1936).

[11] However, her last play, *The Flute of Pan,* was a financial failure and it cost her £1,000 a week to keep it going. It also had been booed on its opening night. "When, on the first night, I heard that discordant note, I resolved to go on. It simply fired my resolve. I had no tears at that moment. But when I had finished, and the audience applauded; when the audience took it off my shoulders upon theirs—then I broke down." Unidentified article, dated November 19, 1904.

[12] *The Era,* July 3, 1909, reported that Shaw's new play, *The Showing Up of Blanco Posnet,* had been forbidden by the censor, probably because the leading character too closely imitated a living person. Shaw's letter of protest said that he himself was so successfully imitated on stage that a near relative actually believed the actor to be Mr. Shaw himself. The reference was to John Tanner in *Man and Superman,* in which Shaw represented himself as a Don Juan, with all the women running after him. But in his stage directions, he described the character as a megalomaniac. In July 1909 Shaw also wrote a skit called *Press Cuttings,* for a private performance, in which he had the Prime Minister disguised as a suffragette shrieking, "Votes For Women!"—in order to get from Downing Street to the War Office.

[13] A. E. Wilson, *Edwardian Theater* (London, Arthur Baker, 1951).

[14] Duse was a guest of Jennie's at Salisbury Hall one weekend. In his memoirs George Cornwallis-West recalled that Duse had just broken with her lover, the

Italian writer and soldier Gabriele D'Annunzio, and she arrived in tears. Jennie took her to the drawing room "where she remained the whole day, visited at intervals by the lady members of our party." Neither George nor any of the male guests ever got to speak to her.

[15] Ellen Terry remembered a dinner at the Beef Steak Room where Jennie arrived "wearing a dress embroidered with green beetles' wings." That dress was the origin of the idea for Lady Macbeth's robe that Ellen Terry later wore. Roger Manvell, *Ellen Terry* (New York, Putnam, 1968).

[16] Ernest Short, *Sixty Years of Theater* (London, Eyre & Spottiswoode, 1951).

[17] Although their correspondence became a part of literary history, George Bernard Shaw never consummated his love affair with Mrs. Pat.

[18] George Cornwallis-West, *Edwardian Hey-Days* (New York, Putnam, 1930).

[19] Anita Leslie, *Lady Randolph Churchill* (New York, Scribner's, 1970).

[20] Winston also read his mother's play and wrote her: "... The last half is the best. There are many criticisms I could make on detail and structure. But I will keep these until the business of production has actually been undertaken. Then I will give any assistance in my power. ..." May 14, 1909.

[21] Mrs. Patrick Campbell, *My Life & Some Letters* (New York, Dodd, Mead, 1922).

[22] Jennie's play might well have been inspired by the legal brouhaha of Mrs. W. K. Clifford, a well-known author who had written a play called *The Likeness of the Night*, which Jennie had published in the *Anglo-Saxon Review*. A year after its publication in the *Review*, the play was scheduled for London production. However, just then another play was produced which had an astonishing resemblance to her own. The main difference between the two plays was that in one play the former mistress commits suicide by poison, and in the other play, the wife does so by drowning. Mrs. Clifford, a woman of social distinction, refused to sue for plagiarism and still produced her own play. Both plays were successful. A. E. W. Mason, *Sir George Alexander and The St. James Theater* (London, Macmillan, 1935).

[23] Interview in London *Daily Chronicle,* July 8, 1909.

[24] Play filed as No. 34 in Lord Chamberlain's Office; date of license, July 12, 1909.

[25] Letter to Leonie, June 27, 1909; Anita Leslie, *op. cit.*

[26] Mrs. Patrick Campbell, *op. cit.*

[27] Unidentified clipping, dated July 7, 1909.

[28] Unidentified clipping, undated.

[29] July 10, 1909.

[30] Max Beerbohm, *Around Theaters* (New York, Simon & Schuster, 1954). Beerbohm was not only one of the foremost critics of his time, but he was also a noted essayist and caricaturist. He succeeded George Bernard Shaw as dramatic critic for the *Saturday Review*. His most famous book was *uleika Dobson,* a satiric fantasy about Oxford.

[31] London *Daily Chronicle,* July 8, 1909.

[32] Seymour Leslie, *The Jerome Connexion* (London, John Murray, 1964).

[33] June 1910.

Chapter 38

[1] Quoted in J. B. Priestley, *The Edwardians* (New York, Harper & Row, 1970).

[2] The office of Home Secretary concerned itself with everything from strikes to prison reform.

[3] E. T. Raymond, *Uncensored Celebrities* (London, T. Fisher, Unwin, 1918), wrote: "The American strain in Winston might be traceable for his lack of simplicity, a taste for self-advertisement, uncommon in any English aristocrat, an unbridled tendency to naked 'bossing' of any 'show,' and for any and other peculiarities which make Mr. Churchill a difficult man for any plain Englishman to 'get on with.' It may also have imparted an extra touch of recklessness and speculation, while giving him also a doggedness which was not visible in his father. It may also have given him a certain impatience for what he once called 'Tory claptrap.' "

[4] Undated letter, Peregrine Churchill Papers.

[5] Sir Frederick Ponsonby, *Recollections of Three Reigns* (London, Eyre & Spottiswoode, 1951).

[6] "I say God bless her for it. Few women would have done it," Daisy, Princess of Pless, wrote in her diary. *From My Private Diary* (London, John Murray, 1931).

[7] Ponsonby, *op. cit.*

[8] The German Emperor had once said of Edward VII, "A Satan—you cannot imagine what a Satan. . . ." André Maurois, *The Edwardian Era* (New York, Appleton-Century-Crofts, 1933).

[9] Margot Oxford saw Queen Alexandra after King Edward's funeral and the two of them "cried together." Trying to divert the Queen's attention, Margot commented how touched everyone was at the sight of the King's dog Caesar at the funeral. "Horrid little dog!" said the Queen. "He never went near my poor husband when he was ill!" Margot said she remembered having seen the dog lying at the King's feet after his death. "For warmth my dear," answered the Queen. But Margot added that the dog had put his paws on the coffin before they screwed the top down. "Curiosity, my dear," said the Queen. Margot Oxford, *More Memories* (London, Cassell, 1933).

[10] That evening Winston dined with the Asquiths, and proposed a toast to the new king. "Rather to the memory of the old," replied Lord Crewe. Philippe Julian, *Edward and the Edwardians* (New York, Viking, 1962).

[11] Unidentified clipping.

[12] Jennie had bought the lease of the house of her friend and former neighbor on Great Cumberland Place, Madame Melba. She then completely redecorated it and soon had a long list of friends wanting to lease it from her. The *Daily Chronicle*, January 11, 1910.

[13] August 4, 1909. Randolph S. Churchill, *Winston S. Churchill*, Companion Volume II, Part 2, 1907–11 (Boston, Houghton Mifflin, 1969).

[14] Unidentified clipping.

[15] Seymour Leslie, *The Jerome Connexion* (London, John Murray, 1964).

[16] H. Hamilton Fyfe, in *Shakespeare Memorial Souvenir of the Shakespeare Ball* (ed. Mrs. George Cornwallis-West) (London, Frederick Warne & Co., 1911). Among

other contributors were George Bernard Shaw and G. K. Chesterton. Jennie edited the contributions and wrote the introduction.

[17] *Frederick Edwin, Earl of Birkenhead, by His Son* (London, Thornton, Butterworth, Ltd., 1933).

[18] George Cornwallis-West, *Edwardian Hey-Days* (New York, Putnam, 1930).

[19] January 18, 1912.

[20] May 27, 1912.

[21] *Literary Digest,* July 6, 1912.

[22] F. E. Smith, later the Earl of Birkenhead, was to be one of the knights in the jousting. "The armour was brought to him for his inspection. It looked very heavy and very hot; at the last moment, he decided to substitute his brother Harold." *Frederick Edwin, Earl of Birkenhead, by His Son.*

[23] Mrs. Patrick Campbell, *My Life & Some Letters* (New York, Dodd, Mead, 1922).

A much quoted line of the time came from an American dancer, Harry Pilcer: "Every woman wants something another woman has got." Ernest Dudley, *The Gilded Lily* (London, Odhams Press, 1958).

[24] *The* [London] *Times*, October 25, 1922.

[25] George Cornwallis-West, *Two Wives* (New York, Putnam, 1930).

[26] *Ibid.*

[27] He travelled as far as Canada for a big game hunt. En route back he was operated on in New York for appendicitis. London *Daily Telegraph*, August 29, 1911.

[28] Anita Leslie, *Lady Randolph Churchill* (New York, Scribner's, 1970).

[29] Charles B. Cochran, *The Secrets of a Showman* (London, Heinemann, 1925).

[30] Cornwallis-West, *Two Wives.*

[31] Unidentified clipping, March 4, 1913.

[32] February 23, 1913.

[33] Unidentified clipping.

[34] Jennie's friend Pearl Craigie had once told Sidney Low that she always tried to "hear" her dialogue when writing it, almost as if she were writing for music. Major Desmond Chapman-Huston, *The Lost Historian* (London, John Murray, 1931).

[35] Unidentified clipping.

[36] Filed as 1483 in Lord Chamberlain's Office. Date of license: March 8, 1913.

[37] Letter from Ayot St. Lawrence, Welwyn, dated June 9th 1913. Alan Dent, *Bernard Shaw and Mrs. Patrick Campbell: Their Correspondence* (London, Victor Gollancz, 1952).

[38] *Ibid.*, letter dated August 11, 1913.

[39] Quoted in Sunday *Express,* July 31, 1955.

[40] April 24, 1913. Randolph S. Churchill, *op. cit.*

[41] Unidentified clipping, July 16, 1913.

[42] *The* [London] *Times*, November 13, 1913.

[43] It was described by *The Times* as a Brazilian diamond necklet.

[44] Lady Randolph Churchill, *Small Talks on Big Subjects* (London, C. Arthur Pearson, 1916).

[45] Anita Leslie, *op. cit.*

[46] Moreton Frewen Papers, Library of Congress, Manuscript Room.

[47] The London *Daily Mirror* (April 17, 1914) printed a photograph of the marriage certificate, on which it described George West is "The divorced husband of Jennie Cornwallis-West, formerly Churchill (widow)."

Chapter 39

[1] London *Daily Express* interview, undated clipping.

[2] Interview with Sir Shane Leslie.

[3] Anita Leslie, *Lady Randolph Churchill* (New York, Scribner's, 1970), letter dated July 24, 1914.

[4] *Ibid.*, July 28, 1914.

[5] *Ibid.*, August 1st, 1914.

[6] Viscount Grey of Fallodon, *Twenty-Five Years* (New York, Frederick A. Stokes, 1925), Volume II.

[7] Interview with Sir Shane Leslie. In a book review of Mrs. Patrick Campbell's Letters, The *Times Literary Supplement* referred to George as "a well-bred scalawag, whose taste was as bad as his debts." Sir Shane defended George in a letter to the editor (May 5, 1961) saying, "I don't think his *taste* was so bad, for he married on his own merits the two most remarkable women of the day, and as for the *debts*—he paid them up for both ladies." After the death of Mrs. Pat Campbell, in 1940, George married Mrs. Georgette Hirsch, a close friend of the former Barbara Hutton. His business firm had gone bankrupt in 1917, with liabilities of £150,000 ($750,000). In 1920, George filed for personal bankruptcy. In 1951, after a lingering illness, he shot himself. He was seventy-six years old. He had called his years from 1895 to 1914 "a supreme vintage."

[8] This was during *Pygmalion*'s American tour. George played the part of Doolittle. He later also wrote an unsuccessful one-act play in which his wife starred.

[9] Jennie mentioned to Leonie that "Charles" had sent her a Cartier clock for Christmas. (December 30, 1913.)

[10] George Lambton, *Men and Horses I Have Known* (London, Thorton Butterworth, 1924).

[11] Letter to the editor, London *Daily Dispatch,* December 16, 1919. Lambton also mentioned in this letter that "it afforded him [Kinsky] great pleasure that 4 of his old favorites were carrying two generals. . . ."

[12] Correspondence between author and Prince Clary.

[13] *Ibid.*

[14] May 17, 1914. Oswald Frewen Papers, courtesy of Mrs. Oswald Frewen. During Jennie's divorce proceedings, Oswald had written in his diary, "I wonder if he [George] will insult *her* if it appears in the press. It is strange, because in many ways he is chivalrous and charming too." When Oswald was at sea on the HMS *Florus,* he recorded hearing somebody yell, "Old Winston's got a nice old mug, like his *Ma!*"

[15] Lady Maud Warrender, *My First Sixty Years* (London, Cassell, 1933).

[16] Lady Randolph Churchill, *Small Talks on Big Subjects* (London, C. Arthur Pearson, 1916).

[17] *Ibid.*

[18] *Ibid.*

[19] Warrender, *op. cit.* Rupert Grayson, in his autobiography, *Voyage Not Completed* (London, Macmillan, 1969), tells an anecdote about the hospital: "This hospital happened to be conveniently next door to our London home at 100 Lancaster Gate. In spite of this, or because of it, Mother wanted to make a hole through the wall so I could be passed through on a stretcher as soon as I was well enough to spend the day with her and the family. She even called on a builder to survey the job. Finally Lady Randolph Churchill, Winston's mother who was in charge, persuaded her that it was a little impractical. . . ."

[20] *Harper's Bazar,* January, 1915.

[21] Interview with Peregrine Churchill.

[22] *Ibid.*

[23] *Ibid.*

[24] When Winston's daughter Diana was christened in 1909, Jennie had sent an old coral rattle and Winston wrote her, "I remember it well."

[25] Warrender, *op. cit.*

[26] Interview with Sir Shane Leslie.

[27] October 20, 1914. Other earlier entries in the Oswald Frewen diary:
"Lunched with Chicken [Clare] and Aunt Jane . . . then Clemmie came and Aunt Jane took her out. . . ."
". . . We went down to Winston's to have lunch with him and Clemmie. . . . Aunt Jane, Winston and Pa had a spirited argument on Free Trade and other topics. . . ."
". . . Went to Ladies Imperial Club, dined with Ma and Aunt Jennie, and went to first night of Strauss' 'Salome' at Covent Garden. . . ."
"Woke up Jack Churchill. We then brutally threw over poor Aunt Jane, and we got two stalls for the 'Wall Stream.' . . ."
". . . Aunt Jane lent us her car. . . ."
". . . Jennie gave me a lift to Buckingham Hotel where Ma smoked a cig. . . ."

[28] This had been a most intimate friendship. Sir John Fisher often began his letters, "Beloved Winston," and signed them, "Yours till a cinder!"

[29] Sir Basil Liddell Hart believes that the whole operation was "a sound and farsighted conception marred by a chain of errors in execution almost unrivalled even in British history." C. L. Mowat, ed., *The New Cambridge Modern History*, Second Edition (Cambridge, at the University Press, 1968), Volume XII.

[30] E. Ashmead Bartlett, *The Uncensored Dardanelles* (London, Hutchinson, 1928).

[31] Seymour Leslie, *The Jerome Connexion* (London, John Murray, 1964); letter dated October 12, 1915.

[32] July 4, 1915, Anita Leslie, *op. cit.*

[33] Winston S. Churchill, *Painting as a Pastime* (New York, Cornerstone Library, 1965).

[34] A. Wallais Myers, *Memory's Parade* (London, Methuen, 1932).

[35] Winston S. Churchill, *op. cit.*

[36] Lady Violet Bonham Carter, *Winston Churchill As I Knew Him* (London, Eyre & Spottiswoode and Collins, 1965).

[37] August 27, 1916; Seymour Leslie, *op. cit.*

[38] *Frederick Edwin, Earl of Birkenhead, by His Son* (London, Thornton Butterworth 1933).

[39] Undated letter. Shane Leslie records in his book *Long Shadows* (London, John Murray, 1966), that in 1915 Jennie made a bet that Winston would become Prime Minister.

[40] *The* [London] *Times,* April 5, 1916.

[41] She was so nicknamed in the press—presumably because of her abundant black hair.

[42] Lady Cynthia Asquith, *Diaries, 1915–1918* (New York, Knopf, 1969).

[43] January 1913.

[44] Article dated January 4, 1917.

[45] Interview with the Baroness.

[46] *Ibid.*

[47] Interview with Lady Betty Cartwright.

[48] Christopher Hassall, *Edward Marsh* (London, Longman, 1959).

[49] Oswald Frewen Papers.

[50] Interviews in Glastonbury with Mrs. Hadley Hucker, Mr. Scott-Stokes and several others who have requested to remain anonymous.

[51] *Glastonbury and its Abbey* (Bristol, T. O. Elworthy n.d.).

[52] Some of these implements are still in the British Museum.

[53] Interview in London *Daily Express,* December 21, 1959.

[54] Lagos *Standard,* March 13, 1912.

[55] An article in the Lagos *Standard* (March 13, 1912) noted that a pet leopard was loose on Bishop Street in Olowogbowo. The article said: "Must have belonged to a white man, for no native would keep such a brute." It had injured several people.

[56] *Daily Express* interview.

[57] Anita Leslie, *op. cit.*

[58] Undated letter, Peregrine Churchill Papers.

[59] Lieut.-Col. C. à Court Repington, *The First World War,* 1914–1918, Volume 2 (Boston and New York, Houghton Mifflin, 1920).

[60] Bernard Falk, *He Laughed in Fleet Street* (London, Hutchinson, 1933), tells of his visit to Downing Street to see the new Prime Minister, Lloyd George. "I shared the coal-fire in the hall with Lady Randolph Churchill, a dainty and attractive figure in becoming furs."

[61] She said the same thing to Oswald Frewen, who recorded in his diary on February 9, 1917: "Aunt Jane to tea, complaining that her children never come near her—'The fierce ingratitude of children's love,' as Goethe used to say."

[62] She was also listed as one of the organizers of a Grand Bazaar at Claridge's Hotel for the "Victims of the War."

[63] Christopher Hassall, *op. cit.*

[64] Interview with Baroness Cedestrom.

[65] "It is quite wrong if anyone has got the idea that I have put my maids into military uniform," she told a reporter for the *Daily Express,* March 15, 1915.

[66] Lady Diana Cooper, *The Rainbow Comes and Goes* (Boston, Houghton Mifflin, 1958).

[67] She was the daughter of George Burke of San Francisco, and the niece of a California millionaire whose money she inherited. Her husband was the grandson of the founder of Cunard Steamship Lines. He was most interested in fox-hunting and horses, and she was not. She once confided to a friend, "No man has ever said to me, 'I love you.'" John Lehmann, *I Am My Brother* (New York, Reynal, 1960).

[68] Seymour Leslie, *op. cit*; undated letter.

[69] Article dated January 19, 1918.

[70] *Ibid.*

[71] Seymour Leslie, *op. cit.*

[72] Repington, *op. cit.*

[73] *Daily Express* interview.

[74] Anita Leslie, *op. cit.*

[75] Repington, *op. cit.*

[76] *Daily Express* interview.

[77] Conversation with author.

Chapter 40

[1] She was the former Adele Grant of New York who married the 7th Earl of Essex. Lady Cynthia Asquith, *Diaries, 1915–18* (New York, Knopf, 1969).

[2] *Ibid.* George Moore had had a frustrated love affair with Pearl Craigie. She had collaborated with him in writing two acts of a comedy, then abandoned it—but they had never been lovers. Susan L. Mitchell later described Moore as a lover who "didn't kiss but told." (Malcolm Brown, *George Moore: A Reconsideration* (Seattle, University of Washington Press, 1955). Moore's caustic comments about Jennie may have been prompted by jealousy of Pearl Craigie's deep feeling for her. Vineta Colby, in her excellent chapter about Pearl Craigie in *The Singular Anomaly* (New York, New York University Press, 1970) refers to George Moore's "vicious scandal-mongering."

[3] *Bystander,* July 6, 1921.

[4] London *Daily Express* Interview, December 21, 1952.

[5] Undated letter, Peregrine Churchill Papers.

[6] The correspondent for *West Africa,* July 2, 1921, also noted, "She took steps to get a passport to Nigeria, but Downing Street refused because of the submarine peril. . . . She pleaded over and over again, but permission was withheld."

[7] Oswald Frewen Papers, Brede Place, Sussex.

[8] Undated letter, Peregrine Churchill Papers.

[9] Interview with Mrs. Hadley Hucker in Glastonbury.

[10] London *Evening News,* May 31, 1918.

[11] Jennie wanted her name regularized by deed poll. She also felt it would help if the King received her at Court as Lady Randolph Churchill, thereby giving the change of name his royal approval. "I have made a name for myself," she wrote. Letter to Leonie, January 20, 1919. Seymour Leslie, *The Jerome Connexion* (London, John Murray, 1964).

[12] Interview with Mrs. Hucker.

[13] Conversation with Mr. Porch.

[14] Interview in *Daily Express*.

[15] Andrew Turnbull, *From Letters of F. Scott Fitzgerald* (New York, Scribner's, 1963).

[16] Interview with Sir Shane Leslie.

[17] George Lambton, *Men & Horses I Have Known* (London, Thornton Butterworth, 1924).

[18] Interview in *Daily Express*.

[19] March 8, 1921.

[20] The pilot was Sir Sefton Brancker and the plane was a DH4.

[21] Interview with Lady Altrincham, the daughter of Jennie's close friend, Lady Islington. She also remembered Jennie asking her, "What beaux do you have?" She recalled that Jennie used a lot of American expressions. "In a sense, she never grew up," Lady Altrincham said. But then she added, "Jennie smoothed the ruffled feathers of the friends whom Winston irritated. . . . If Jennie had been a man, she would have been a real power."

[22] Unidentified clipping. Jennie was an inveterate first-nighter. Her particular penchant was for grand opera and Russian ballet.

[23] London *Daily Chronicle*, February 16, 1921. In a magazine article she wrote called "Art In Dress," she commented that the chief aims of art in dress should be "either the artistic blending of colors, the clever effects that make beautiful the greatest simplicity, or the most gorgeous and sumptuous raiment." And she added, "The abominable practice of wearing long skirts for the street is dying out. . . . The sight of a woman dragging her gown in the street, sweeping up the filth and collecting millions of microbes, is a revolting spectacle; and yet with a long skirt the only alternative is to hold it up, a practice which induces cramp in the arm, as well as cold fingers in winter, and gives a decidedly ungraceful walk and attitude." Jennie also wrote that "Mme de Pompadour once, for a wager, wore radishes in her hair at a court festivity. At the next, most of "the court ladies made their heads into market gardens." *Munsey's Magazine*.

[24] Clare Sheridan, *The Naked Truth*, (New York, Harper, 1928). Clare never saw Jennie again. In America, she did a bust of Charles Chaplin, and there were strong international rumors that the two planned to marry. Chaplin denied this to the press by saying, "Why, she's old enough to be my mother."

[25] From article by Caseur in *The Dispatch*, June 30, 1921.

[26] April 20, 1921; Seymour Leslie, *The Jerome Connexion* (London, John Murray, 1964).

[27] The Duchess of Sermoneta, *Sparkle Distant Worlds* (London, Hutchinson, 1947).

[28] Duchess of Sermoneta, *op. cit.* John Singer Sargent, the noted American artist, had drawn a portrait of Jennie at the turn of the century. Winston much admired that portrait, not only because of the subject but also because of the technique. Sargent was an excellent musician and he and Jennie played duets together. He became so much in demand as a portrait artist that he was quoted as saying, "Ask

me to paint your gates, your fences, your barns, which I would gladly do, but *not the human face!*" Article by Richard Ormond in John Hadfield, ed., *The Saturday Book–25* (London, Hutchinson, 1965).

[29] Duchess of Sermoneta, *op. cit.*

[30] Lady Horner's husband had been killed in World War I. She had a fluent knowledge of Greek, did expert needlework, and had the reputation of having one of the most interesting literary salons in London.

[31] She had always disliked stairs and once actually drew plans for a stairless villa. It had a circular ground floor area, off which all the rooms opened. *Irish Society, July 30, 1921.* She also always had felt that women should be escorted to any dining room. In *Small Talks on Big Subjects* (London, Pearson, 1916), she wrote, "Surely it is a time-honored courtesy which is as graceful as it is convenient; I might slip on the stairs. . . ."

[32] Belfast *Telegraph,* July 1, 1921.

[33] London *Evening News,* June 18, 1921.

[34] *Ibid.*

[35] Oswald Frewen Papers.

[36] Correspondence with Violet Pym, Eleanor Warrender's niece.

[37] Oswald Frewen Papers.

[38] Bourke Cockran died two years later.

[39] Oswald Frewen Papers.

[40] *Ibid.*

[41] The same church where Winston and Clementine were married.

[42] Shane Leslie Papers.

[43] Porch married again in 1926 and lived in Italy until his wife's death in 1938. He then returned to Glastonbury and rented a room from Mr. and Mrs. Hadley Hucker on Main Street. A neighbor quoted Porch as saying, "I've had such a lot of trouble. My first wife died, my second wife died, and now my dog has died." Porch himself died in November 1964.

[44] Lieut.-Col. C. à Court Repington, *The First World War,* 1914–1918, Volume 2 (Boston, Houghton Mifflin, 1920).

[45] H. H. Asquith, *Letters of the Earl of Oxford & Asquith to a Friend,* First Series, 1915–1922 (London, Geoffrey Bles, 1930).

Critical References and Bibliography

Chapter 1

The most definitive source material on the early origins of the Jerome family is the New York Genealogical Library and the Genealogical Room of the New York Public Library. *The New York Genealogical and Biographical Record*, LXXIII, No. 3, (July 1942), 159–66, has an excellent genealogical summary of the family in an article called "Two Famous Descendents of John Cooke and Sarah Warren" by Cornelius Mann. Another valuable reference is *Fragments in the Life of Ambrose Hall* by Gladys E. Caffyn (Palmyra, N. Y., 1956). Vera Curtis has an interesting article about the Jerome family in the Palmyra *Courier-Journal*, December 25, 1947, but unfortunately it has some serious errors. The best book on the subject of Leonard Jerome is Anita Leslie's *The Remarkable Mr. Jerome* (New York, Henry Holt, 1954), but unfortunately, it is also subject to serious error of fact. Randolph S. Churchill's excellent biography of his father, *Winston S. Churchill* (Boston, Houghton Mifflin, 1967), concentrates on his father's British background, and gives only short space to his American heritage.

Mrs. John Sloane of New York City has possession of the Jerome family Bible, as well as an excellent family scrapbook, both of which are invaluable.

The most rewarding intimate material on the family came from interviews with Sir Shane Leslie, Leonard Jerome's grandson, whose book *American Wonderland* (London, Michael Joseph, 1936) has warm and colorful material.

The Jerome family in Rochester is best treated by Dr. Blake McKelvey, city historian of Rochester, in his article "Winston Churchill's Grandparents in Rochester" in the *Genessee Country Scrapbook*, III, No. 1 (Spring 1952), published by the Rochester Historical Society. In that same issue there is a good article on Rochester society of that era by Virginia Jeffrey Smith, "Reminiscences of the Ruffled Shirt Ward." Dr. McKelvey also has dealt with Rochester history and society most ably in his book *Rochester, the Waterpower City* (Cambridge, Mass., Harvard University Press, 1945).

The Brooklyn background of the family is everywhere skimpy and inaccurate. The story of Brooklyn itself at that time is generally disappointing. *Yesterdays on Brooklyn Heights* by James H. Callender (New York, Dorland Press, 1927) has captured little of the flavor of the place; *The Historical Guide to the City of New York* by

Frank Bergen Kelley (New York, Frederick Stokes, 1909), even less. *The Civil, Political, Professional and Ecclesiastical History, and Commercial and Industrial Record of the County of Kings and the City of Brooklyn* by Henry R. Stiles (New York, W. W. Munsell, 1884) is heavy going and not worth much. The same may be said for *History of the City of Brooklyn* by Stephen M. Ostrander (Brooklyn, 1894). Indeed, the best material on Brooklyn has come from interviews with James Kelly, city historian of Brooklyn.

The material on New York City is vastly better. *Incredible New York* by Lloyd Morris (New York, Random House, 1951) is most valuable. *The Diary of George Templeton Strong*, ed. Allen Nevins and Milton Halsey (New York, Macmillan, 1952) has some pertinent color and anecdotes worth searching for. *Courtroom Warrior* by Richard O'Connor (Boston, Little, Brown, 1963) focuses on Leonard Jerome's nephew, William Travers Jerome, but nevertheless provides some fine background on the family and the time. In contrast, *The Yankee Marlborough* by R. W. Thompson (London, George Allen & Unwin, 1953) adds nothing new. Of less value is *Young Lady Randolph* by René Kraus (New York, Putnam's, 1943), which has more fiction than fact.

A good vignette of Leonard Jerome can be found in *Offhand Portraits of Prominent People* by Stephen Fiske (New York, Lockwood & Sons, 1884), even though it is not entirely accurate. Some sidelights into Leonard Jerome's Wall Street manipulations are dealt with briefly in *The Story of Wall Street* by Robert Irving Warshow (New York, Greenburg, 1929). *Good Old Coney Island* by Ed McCullough (New York, Scribner's, 1957) deals slightly with some of Jerome's racing record and *Jersey Lily* by Pierre Sichel (Englewood Cliffs, N.J., Prentice-Hall, 1958) details some of his involvement with Lily Langtry. *Washington Heights, Manhattan: Its Eventful Past* by Reginald Pelham Bolton (New York, Dyckman Institute, 1924) is hardly worth examining. But Ward McAllister's *Society As I Have Found It* (London, Cassell, 1890) has excellent glimpses into the society of the time. So has *The Vanderbilt Feud* by Cornelius Vanderbilt, Jr. (London, Hutchinson, 1957), which has a particularly fine description of life at Newport.

From Gaslight to Dawn by Julie Chanler (New York, Pacific Printing Co., 1956) has only a few scattered references to young Jennie. *Reminiscences of Lady Randolph Churchill* (New York, Century, 1908) is unfortunately skimpy on the early years, devoting only three pages to her early life in the United States; and some of her statements are based on faulty memory. The book, however, is excellent with regard to her later years, except that she herself has said, "There may be some to whom these Reminiscences will be interesting chiefly in virtue of what is left unsaid."

Chapter 2

There is a large library of material on the Franco-Prussian War period in France. Two of the best books I found were both called *The Second Empire*, one by Philip Guedalla (New York, Putnam's, 1922), and the other by G. P. Gooch (London, Longmans, 1960). Even more important as an eyewitness account of the time was *France in the 19th Century* by Mrs. Elizabeth Latimer (Chicago, A. C.

McClurg, 1892). *Democratic Despot* by T. A. B. Corley (New York, Clarkson N. Potter, 1961) is also solid and useful. *The Golden Bees* by Theo Aronson (Greenwich, Conn., New York Graphic Society Publishers, 1964) is interesting because it concentrates on individuals rather than events. *A History of the English Speaking Peoples*, Vol. IV by Winston S. Churchill (New York, Dodd, Mead, 1956) concentrates on events. *The Empress Eugènie* by Harold Kurtz (Boston, Houghton Mifflin, 1968) has much of interest, as has *Miss Howard and the Emperor* by Simone André Maurois (New York, Knopf, 1958). Of little value is *The History of French Civilization* by Georges Duby and Robert Mandrou (New York, Random House, 1964).

The literature on Bismarck is equally large. *Bismarck* by Werner Richter (New York, Putnam's, 1965) is worthwhile, but *Bismarck* by A. J. P. Taylor (New York, Knopf, 1955) is much better.

Chapter 3

There is a whole series of fascinating books on the siege of Paris, but perhaps the best is *Recollections of a Minister to France* by E. B. Washburne, 2 vols. (New York, Scribner's, 1887). The Washburne volumes are excellent source books. Mrs. Elizabeth Latimer's *France in the 19th Century* (Chicago, A. C. McClurg, 1892) also has some vivid first-hand descriptions and anecdotes. Other good books on the subject include *The Siege of Paris* by Robert Baldick (New York, Macmillan, 1964); *The Siege of Paris* by Melvin Kranzberg (Ithaca, N. Y., Cornell University Press, 1950); and *The Turbulent City: Paris* by André Castelot (New York, Harper, 1962). *Europe Since 1815* by Charles Downer Hazen (New York, Henry Holt, 1910) has some amplifying material, but not much. The reminiscences of Otto von Bismarck (New York, Harper, 1899) are very much worth reading. A. J. P. Taylor does not deal with this siege in his biography of Bismarck (New York, Knopf, 1955). Philip Guedalla's book *The Hundred Days* (Garden City, N. Y., Doubleday, 1936) has a short but excellent section on Bismarck and the siege. Guedalla's *The Second Empire* (New York, Putnam's, 1922) has some good material on Napoleon's final days in England. So does Mme. Maurois' book, *Miss Howard and the Emperor* (New York, Knopf, 1955).

The best sources of Jennie's life in Paris and England at this time are *Reminiscenses of Lady Randolph Churchill* (New York, Century, 1908) and Anita Leslie's *The Remarkable Mr. Jerome* (New York, Henry Holt, 1954). There are also some family letters.

There is, of course, a vast library of material on English life at this time. A standard source, and a very good one, is *England: 1870–1914* by R. C. K. Ensor (London, Oxford University Press, 1936). More valuable for social history is *Our Mothers* by Alan Bott and Irene Clephane (London, Gollancz, 1932). *Life in Victorian England* by W. J. Reader (New York, Putnam's, 1964) and *The Victorian Temper* by Jerome Hamilton Buckley (Cambridge, Mass., Harvard University Press, 1951) were both of minimal value for my purpose. *Edward VII and His Circle* by Virginia Cowles (London, Hamish Hamilton, 1956) offers a good, personal biography of the Prince of Wales. Frances, Countess of Warwick, has written several books, all of them revealing of that social strata: *Life's Ebb and Flow* (New York, Morrow,

1929); *Discretions* (New York, Scribner's, 1931); and *Afterthoughts* (London, Cassell, 1931). A more royal view comes from the invaluable *Letters of Queen Victoria*, 3 vols. (London, Longmans, 1930).

G. M. Trevelyan has some interesting material in his *English Social History* (London, Longmans, 1943) and so does Quentin Crewe in *The Frontiers of Privilege* (London, Stevens Press, 1961). The Crewe book is illustrated. But one of the best sources of the mood of the times is a book of *Punch* cartoons, *Society Pictures* (Bradbury, Agnew, n.d.). The files of *Graphic Magazine* also have some excellent material.

The Story of English Life by Amabel Williams-Ellis and F. J. Fisher (New York, Coward-McCann, 1936) was not very useful.

Chapter 4

The bulk of the basic reference material in this chapter came from a big black metal box of family archives in the Muniments Room of Blenheim Palace. It contains everything from letters to the oversize, thick marriage contract. It is invaluable.

Sir Shane Leslie has another large supply of letters, particularly from Leonard Jerome and from the Jerome sisters, which is equally invaluable. So are Sir Shane's books, particularly, *Studies in Sublime Failure* (London, Ernest Benn, 1932) and *Men Were Different* (London, Michael Joseph, 1937), which deal so perceptively with Sir Shane's uncle and godfather, Randolph Churchill; also *The Passing Chapter* (London, Cassell, 1934) and *The End of a Chapter* (New York, Scribner's, 1917), which focus so sharply on the society of the time. His *American Wonderland* (London, Michael Joseph, 1936) is richly rewarding for its material on Leonard Jerome.

The best single book on Randolph Churchill is by Robert Rhodes James, *Lord Randolph Churchill* (New York, A. S. Barnes, 1960). There have, of course, been many other books on Randolph Churchill, including a two volume biography by his son, Winston S. Churchill, *Lord Randolph Churchill* (London, Macmillan, 1906). The Winston Churchill biography is beautifully written and detailed, particularly in the political areas, but it is much less a human document.

Reminiscences of Lady Randolph Churchill (New York, Century, 1908) is surprisingly skimpy concerning this period of courtship, and Anita Leslie's *The Remarkable Mr. Jerome* (New York, Henry Holt, 1954) remains the best source book on the Jerome sisters at this time. Of the courtship, however, Jennie has written a short but revealing memoir, which is among the family papers at Blenheim.

A. L. Rowse, *The Early Churchills* (New York, Harper, 1958), has creditably detailed the early Marlborough history and Winston S. Churchill, *Marlborough: His Life and Times*, 2 vols. (London, Harrap, 1934), has done a superb description of his ancestors. The account in Randolph S. Churchill's biography of his father, *Winston S. Churchill* (Boston, Houghton Mifflin, 1967) is also excellent.

The Dictionary of National Biography and *The Complete Peerage* are indispensable reference books for this period. The files of *The Times* and *The Graphic* were of important use.

Sir Edward Clarke's *The Story of My Life* (London, John Murray, 1918) has a single anecdote on Randolph Churchill at this time that is highly pertinent. The first volume of *Life of Herbert Henry Asquith, Lord Oxford and Asquith* by J. A. Spender and Cyril Asquith (London, Hutchinson, 1932) has an even briefer sidelight. *Leaves from the Notebooks of Lady Dorothy Nevill*, ed. Ralph Nevill (London, Macmillan, 1907) has some fascinating anecdotes of the time. *Offhand Portraits of Prominent New Yorkers* by Stephen Fiske (New York, Lockwood & Sons, 1884) has a fine anecdote concerning Leonard Jerome at this time. But, again, all this is peripheral material—the heart of the chapter comes from the letters in the family archives.

Chapter 5

Blenheim is best described by Winston Churchill in his two volume biography of *Marlborough* (London, Harrap, 1934), but there is also an excellent description by Winston's son, Randolph S. Churchill in *Fifteen Famous English Homes* (London, Verschoyle, 1954) and in a slim undated volume called *Blenheim* (Oxford, Henry Slatter). Consuelo Vanderbilt Balsan, who became Duchess of Marlborough, gives an intimate account of the palace in *The Glitter and the Gold* (New York, Harper, 1952). *Reminiscences of Lady Randolph Churchill* gives an intimate account from another point of view.

The files of *Punch* and *The Graphic* are still superb in picturing the times and the society, but the most revealing insights come from the family archives of Churchill and Jerome letters. The letters of the Jerome sisters to each other are particularly invaluable. Lady St. Hélier's *Memories of Fifty Years* (London, E. Arnold, 1909) and Ralph Nevill's *Leaves from the Notebooks of Lady Dorothy Nevill* (London, Macmillan, 1907) are the important memories of the two outstanding hostesses of the time.

Of Randolph Churchill, the biographies by Robert Rhodes James and Winston S. Churchill are still basic for this period, as they are for the whole of his life. Sir Henry Lucy's profile of Randolph Churchill in *Speeches of Rt. Honorable Lord Randolph Churchill* (New York, Longmans, 1889) is also much worth reading. *Randolph Spencer-Churchill* by T. H. S. Escott (London, Hutchinson, 1895) is better on the later portions of his life. Sir Shane Leslie, *Men Were Different* (London, Michael Joseph, 1937) has a fine chapter concerning him. Also worth looking at for important anecdotes and background are *Life of Benjamin Disraeli* by W. F. Monypenny and G. E. Buckle (London, John Murray, 1929), Vol. II; *Miscellanies* by Lord Rosebery (London, Hodder & Stoughton, 1921), Vol. I; and *The Story of My Life* by Sir Edward Clarke. (London, John Murray, 1918).

Virginia Peacock, *Famous American Belles of the Nineteenth Century* (Philadelphia, Lippincott, 1901) has an excellent chapter on Jennie, backgrounding much of the feeling about Anglo-American marriages. *They All Married Well* by Elizabeth Eliot (London, Cassell, 1960) has more of the same. *The Remarkable Mr. Jerome* (New York, Henry Holt, 1954) by Anita Leslie remains an important source book until Jerome's death.

Winston S. Churchill by Randolph S. Churchill (Boston, Houghton Mifflin, 1967) Vol. I and Companion Vol. I, Part I, are indispensable books. The short biographies in them are equally excellent.

The sources on syphilis come from the files of *Lancet Magazine* in the *Wellcome British Medical Library* in London and the files in the New York Academy of Medicine. An excellent book of detailed background is *Man Against Germs* by A. L. Baron (New York, Dutton, 1957), and another fine one is *Disease and Destiny* by Judson Bennett Gilbert (Los Angeles, Dawson's, 1962). *The Medical Annual of the District of Columbia*, 1955, was also valuable.

It should also be mentioned that Winston S. Churchill's novel *Savrola* (New York, Random House, 1956) should be read for his many revealing descriptions not only of his nanny, but of his relationship with mother and father.

For background on the Prince of Wales and his society, Virginia Cowles' book *Edward VII and His Circle* (London, Hamish Hamilton, 1956) has good anecdotes and details. A book entitled *Kings, Courts and Society* (London, Jarrolds, 1930) has intimate detail which presumes a knowledge, but it unfortunately is anonymous. *The Darling Daisy Affair* by Theo Lang, (New York, Atheneum, 1966) is equally intimate. A. L. Rowse, *The Churchills* (New York, Harper, 1958) is well worth examining.

Chapter 6

The most complete account of the origins of the quarrel between the Prince of Wales and Randolph Churchill is in *Winston S. Churchill* by Randolph S. Churchill, Vol. I. Robert Rhodes James has a shorter but fine account in *Lord Randolph Churchill* (New York, A. S. Barnes, 1960). Leslie's *The Remarkable Mr. Jerome* (New York, Henry Holt, 1954) is intimate on this, but much more sketchy. The letters themselves, particularly those between Jennie and Randolph, are the most revealing source. Winston S. Churchill barely touches the matter in *Lord Randolph Churchill* (London, Macmillan, 1906). George Smalley's *Anglo-American Memories* (London, Duckworth, 1911, and New York, Putnam's, 1912) does not deal with the cause of the quarrel, but with its solution, which differs from that in Randolph Churchill's version. It is possible that both versions are parts of the same piece.

For a general background on the Queen and her relations with the Prince, there are many books: *Queen Victoria* by Elizabeth Longford (New York, Harper, 1965) is good and so is Churchill's *History of the English Speaking Peoples* (New York, Dodd, Mead, 1956). Monypenny and Buckle's *Life of Benjamin Disraeli* (London, John Murray, 1929) and John Morley's *Life of William Ewart Gladstone* (London, Macmillan, 1932) are both valuable sources. Rowse's *The Churchills* (New York, Harper, 1958) has a good summary.

Atmospheric descriptions of the United States at that time can be found in Lloyd Morris' *Incredible New York* (New York, Random House, 1951) and in the files of *The New York Times*, the New York *Tribune*, and the New York *Herald*.

Chapter 7

The only good source of reference for Jennie's life in Ireland is her own *Reminiscences* and the family letters. Rowse's book *The Later Churchills* (New York,

Macmillan, 1958) is skimpy here, and Robert Rhodes James and Winston Churchill, in their biographies of Lord Randolph Churchill, both concentrate on the political focus. *The Life of Charles Stewart Parnell* by R. Barry O'Brien, 2 vols. (London, Smith, Elder, 1898) is essential for another political view of this time and for a discussion of Parnell's relationship with Randolph Churchill.

The family archives at Blenheim Palace, supplemented by Randolph S. Churchill's biography of his father, provides vital personal news of the family. The British newspaper library at Colindale and the newspaper library of the New York Public Library both have files of assorted Irish newspapers which offer some general background.

There have been a number of books about the Empress of Austria, but no one of them is truly good. Some of the better ones: *The Lonely Empress* by Joan Haslit (Cleveland, World, 1965); *Elizabeth, Empress of Austria* by Count Egon Corti (New Haven, Yale University Press, 1936), and *The Empress of Austria* by Carl Tschuppik (New York, Brentano, 1930).

Churchill and Ireland by Mary C. Bromage (South Bend, Ind., University of Notre Dame Press, 1964) surprisingly deals mainly with Winston Churchill and completely neglects any real description of Ireland in Randolph's time.

Chapter 8

All the previously mentioned biographies of Lord Randolph Churchill are important here, particularly Winston Churchill's biography of his father, the Robert Rhodes James biography, and the books by Henry Lucy. Morley's biography of Gladstone (London, Macmillan, 1932), the Monypenny and Buckle *Disraeli* (London, John Murray, 1929), and O'Brien's *Parnell* (London, Smith, Elder, 1898) all have supplementary information.

Reminiscences of Lady Randolph Churchill is particularly good here, as are Lady Warwick's *Discretions* (New York, Scribner's, 1931) and Lady St. Hélier's *Memories of Fifty Years* (London, E. Arnold, 1909). Another interesting book of background is *Fifty Years: 1882-1930* (London, Thornton Butterworth, 1932) written by twenty-seven contributors to *The Times* in London. Shane Leslie in *Long Shadows* (London, John Murray, 1966) has some charming anecdotes about young Winston and his mother, and Winston has even more in *My Early Life* (New York, Scribner's, 1930). G. W. E. Russell, *Portraits of the Seventies* (London, T. Fisher Unwin, 1960) has some material on Randolph, but not much.

Barbara Tuchman, *The Proud Tower* (New York, Macmillan, 1965) is excellent on Balfour and Gladstone, and Cowles' *Edward VII and His Circle* (London, Hamish Hamilton, 1956) has a good description of the Lily Langtry craze.

On Frewen in the United States, Moreton Frewen has written *Melton Mowbray & Other Memories* (London, Herbert Jenkins, 1924) and Allen Andrews, *The Splendid Pauper* (Philadelphia, Lippincott, 1968) reveals him even more intimately in his letters. Again, the best resource are the letters in the family archives at Blenheim Palace.

Chapter 9

The files of *The Times* of London become increasingly important about this time because the Churchills have become increasingly important, and the accounts of the couple are fuller. This is similarly true of the periodicals of the time from *Punch* to *Fortnightly Review*. The previously mentioned memoirs of women such as Lady Nevill are almost invaluable now for the intimate flavor of the time.

The Kinsky material comes from contact with Prince Clary in Venice, who knows the basic background of the man and has the visual memory, and from the Countess Kinsky in London who passed on family stories and memories of her husband. George Lambton's *Men and Horses I Have Known* (London, Thornton Butterworth, 1924) has a few interesting anecdotes, but little more. The family letters, particularly those of Jennie to her sisters, tell more about Kinsky than any other source. There are also a few scattered and most discreet references in Jennie's *Reminiscences*. According to Prince Clary, Jennie's letters to Kinsky no longer exist.

The social life at Sandringham is excellently described in Jennie's *Reminiscences*. The Curzon material comes largely from *Life of Lord Curzon* by the Earl of Ronaldshay (New York, Boni & Liverwright, 1927) and from *Discretions* by Frances, Countess of Warwick (New York, Scribner's, 1931).

Chapter 10

A short but excellent review of the tone of the times in this chapter comes from *The Saturday Book–25*, ed. John Hadfield (London, Hutchinson, 1965). Again, the files of *Fortnightly Review, The Spectator, Punch,* and *The Times* are all indispensable for a proper study of the period.

Lady Warwick's several books of memoirs, previously mentioned, are particularly good for this, but perhaps the best books that connect the Churchills with doings of British society then are the first and second series of *Anglo-American Memories* by George W. Smalley (London, Duckworth, 1911, and New York, Putnam's, 1912). Smalley was not only a trained correspondent and editor in England for the New York *Tribune*, but also a *bon vivant*, an intimate of all levels of British society and his house served as a salon for everybody from royalty to Sarah Bernhardt. Mrs. J. Comyns Carr, herself a celebrated society leader, noted in her *Reminiscences* (London, Hutchinson, 1926): "It was through my friends, the George Smalleys, that I met most of the Americans I knew." Smalley's wife was the daughter of the celebrated American, Wendell Phillips. His memoirs are the works of a trained observer with a sharp facility for the pertinent anecdote.

Sir Shane Leslie's memories and private papers are invaluable for the description of his mother's marriage. The family letters are particularly important here.

Frank Harris' *My Life and Loves* (New York, Grove Press, 1963) has a most revealing anecdote in great detail typifying the relationship of Jennie and her husband at this time.

Jennie's own *Reminiscences* are excellent on the details of the Primrose League, and Robert Rhodes James' biography of her husband is even better. Winston Churchill's biography of his father has supplementary information well worth reading.

Chapter 11

The Kinsky material comes from a variety of sources: Jennie's own letters and the letters of her sisters, particularly Leonie; the letters and papers of Moreton Frewen; Prince Clary and Countess Kinsky; and some small references in a variety of memoirs, including Jennie's own–although the latter is the most spare of them all.

Winston Churchill's novel *Savrola* (New York, Random House, 1956) provides through its heroine an excellent description of his mother. Jennie's friend and rival, Lady Warwick, has some anecdotal material in her several memoirs. Clare Sheridan, Frewen's daughter, describes well in *Naked Truth* (New York, Harper, 1928) their home and atmosphere, and so does Anita Leslie in *The Remarkable Mr. Jerome* (New York, Henry Holt, 1954). But the best material comes from the books and memory and papers of Sir Shane Leslie.

The clothes and style of women of that period are ably described in *Our Mothers* (London, Gallancz, 1932) by Alan Bott and Irene Clephane.

Again, Winston Churchill's biography of his father and Robert Rhodes James' biography ably supplement each other, particularly on the politics. Barbara Tuchman has a short but excellent profile of Lord Salisbury in *The Proud Tower* (New York, Macmillan, 1965). The best account of Jennie's political campaigning is given by Jennie herself, supplemented by family letters and some newspaper reports.

Chapter 12

The three volumes of *The Letters and Journals of Queen Victoria* (London, Longmans, 1930) are most valuable to supplement *Reminiscences of Lady Randolph Churchill* and the several biographies of Randolph Churchill. But best of all are the letters among the Jerome sisters.

Randolph Churchill's *Winston S. Churchill* has the best detailed description of his father's fight with pneumonia at the age of eleven. The strain of Randolph's own life, as well as his illness, are marvelously well described by Dr. Robson Roose in his articles in *The Lancet,* and in his books, particularly *The Waste and Repair in Modern Life* (London, John Murray, 1897), where he clearly uses Randolph's life as a case history but without mentioning his name. The articles and books are available at the Wellcome British Medical Library in London.

Frank Harris' *My Life and Loves* (New York, Grove Press, 1963) has a fine description of Gladstone's famous speech in Parliament on the Home Rule for Ireland. The clearest account of the 1886 election is still in Robert Rhodes James' biography of Randolph Churchill. Lady Randolph's *Reminiscences* is excellent on her own political campaigning experiences.

Barbara Tuchman in *The Proud Tower* (New York, Macmillan, 1965) has a concise but penetrating description of Balfour. Lady Warwick's memoirs add something to this, but not much. The same should be said of Margot Asquith's *Autobiography* (Boston, Doran, 1920–22).

Two books worth looking at for some interesting references to Randolph Churchill at this time are *Randolph Spencer-Churchill* by T. H. S. Escott (London, Hutchinson, 1895) and *The Fourth Earl of Carnarvon, Sir Arthur Hardinge, 1878–90,* (London, Oxford University Press, 1925), Vol. III. Only a few anecdotes or descriptions are offered, but they are choice. The same should be said for *Life of Lord Curzon* by the Earl of Ronaldshay, 3 vols. (New York, Boni & Liverwright, 1927), and the three volumes of Morley's *Life of William Ewart Gladstone* (London, Macmillan, 1932).

The Blenheim Palace Papers are especially important as reference for this chapter. *A Very Great Soul* by A. G. S. Norris (New York, International, 1957) is not very good, but it does have a few interesting observations about Lady Randolph as a public speaker. Lady Randolph's book of essays, *Small Talks on Big Subjects* (London, Pearson, 1916) has some pertinent comment for this time. So do *They All Married Well* (London, Cassell, 1960) by Eliot, and Smalley's *Anglo-American Memories* (London, Duckworth, 1911).

Some warmly intimate material on Jennie comes from her cook, Rosa Lewis, in a biography of her by Daphne Fielding called *The Duchess of Jermyn Street* (London, Eyre & Spottiswoode, 1964).

There are a number of accounts of Randolph Churchill's resignation as Chancellor of the Exchequer, and some of them are conflicting, but Robert Rhodes James makes the most effective case for his version.

Chapter 13

Reminiscences of Lady Randolph Churchill catches much of the love for horses and racing, but it is at its best in the author's penetrating and excellent description of the trip to Russia. *The Times* closely followed the Churchills on that trip, and *The Letters and Journals of Queen Victoria* (London, Longmans, 1930) adds still more to the political aspects of the sojourn, as well as the Queen's personal criticism. Lady Gwendolen Cecil's biography, *Third Marquis of Salisbury,* Vols. III and IV (London, Hodder & Stoughton, 1931–32) has a number of good references.

Sir Algernon West's *Private Diaries* (London, John Murray, 1922) has several excellent comments worth reading, and so does Margot Asquith's *Autobiography* (Boston, Daran, 1920–22) and Lady Warwick's *Discretions* (New York, Scribner's, 1931). Marcel Proust has some revealing description of the Marquis de Breteuil, whom he calls the Marquis de Breuté in *Remembrance of Things Past*. The Kinsky chronology comes from Prince Clary, and the description of Herbert Bismarck comes from a variety of biographies of Otto von Bismarck, none of which are of any particular importance.

Chapter 14

The best descriptions of The Souls can be found in *Portraits and Appreciations* by Viscount (Edgar Vincent) D'Abernon (London, Hodder & Stoughton, 1931).

D'Abernon writes as an insider and, indeed, has written an amusing and revealing long poem about The Souls which can be found in the manuscript room of the British Museum. Lady Warwick deals briefly with The Souls in her memoirs, as does Lady Randolph Churchill in her *Reminiscences,* but Barbara Tuchman is even better in *The Proud Tower* (New York, Macmillan, 1965).

The privately printed poetry of Harry Cust can be found in the main reading room of the British Museum. *The Memoirs of Sir Ronald Storrs* (Putnam, 1937) is excellent on Cust.

Mrs. Tuchman and Lady Warwick ably describe both Balfour and Curzon, although there are a number of biographies of each man worth reading for background. The Earl of Ronaldshay's biography of Curzon is good, and Lady Frances Balfour's *Ne Obliviscaris,* 2 vols. (London, Hodder & Stoughton, 1930) is worth looking into for more personal material. Margot Asquith's *Autobiography* (Boston, Doran, 1920–22) is also good, with reference to both men, as well as to The Souls, of which she was a member.

On the Jerome and Frewen families, Moreton Frewen's *Melton Mowbray & Other Memories* (London, Herbert Jenkins, 1924) is important and so is *Courtroom Warrior* by Richard O'Connor (Boston, Little, Brown, 1963) and Clare Sheridan's *Naked Truth* (New York, Harper, 1928). The family letters of both the Jeromes and the Frewens, *The Splendid Pauper* by Allen Andrews, the Blenheim Palace Papers, and *The Letters and Journals of Queen Victoria* are all vital research for this chapter.

Chapter 15

The British Museum newspaper library at Colindale offers a variety of interesting comment on the Churchill activities at this time, not only in the London papers, but in such papers as the Sheffield *Telegraph* and the Cardiff *Mail,* which had no qualms about sharp editorial comment. In 1890, George Newnes started a small weekly journal called *Tit Bits,* which had more gossip than news, but offers some interesting leads in many areas. *The Review of Reviews* is also highly informative.

Punch Parliamentary critic Henry Lucy in his several books previously mentioned is particularly good on this period. So, as always, is Robert Rhodes James. The Parnell background comes from a variety of sources: James Adams, *Empire on the Seven Seas* (New York, Scribner's, 1940) has a short but good account, and Jules Abels, *The Parnell Tragedy* (New York, Macmillan, 1966) goes into considerable detail. Shane Leslie in *The End of a Chapter* (New York, Scribner's, 1917) has a fascinating footnote on the tragedy.

Arthur Balfour's *Chapters of Autobiography* (London, Cassell, 1930) is well worth reading for his references to Randolph Churchill. So is Margot Asquith's *Autobiography* (Boston, Doran, 1920–22) for her references to Joseph Chamberlain. The Birmingham fiasco is very well described in Lady Randolph Churchill's *Reminiscences* and also in Henry Lucy, *Later Peeps at Parliament* (London, Newnes, 1905).

Chapter 16

The Churchill family letters at Blenheim Palace and the letters held by Peregrine Churchill, many of which have been included in Randolph S. Churchill's biography of his father, plus the letters of Mrs. Oswald Frewen, all form the basic research of this chapter. All are invaluable.

Winston Churchill's *My Early Life* (New York, Scribner's, 1930) has special value here and his *Thoughts and Adventures* (London, Thornton Butterworth, 1932) also has a few pertinent anecdotes. So has the *Recollections* of John, Viscount Morley (New York, Macmillan, 1917), and Rosebery's *Lord Randolph Churchill* (New York, Harper, 1906). W. S. Blunt, *My Diaries: Being a Personal Narrative of Events,* Part One, 1888–90 (New York, Knopf, 1921), has only a few observations on this subject, but they are worth having.

Daphne Fielding's *Duchess of Jermyn Street,* (London, Eyre & Spottiswoode, 1964), the story of the amusing cook of Lady Randolph, is more revealing than one might imagine.

Randolph Churchill's newspaper columns, collected in *Men, Mines and Animals in South Africa* (New York, Appleton, 1892) is well worth examining. The best account of Lady Randolph's concern for music at the Bayreuth Festival is her own *Reminiscences.*

Frank Harris has some fascinating anecdotes in *My Life and Loves* (New York, Grove Press, 1963) and Shane Leslie's books *Film of Memory* (London, Michael Joseph, 1938) and *The End of a Chapter* (New York, Scribner's, 1917) are also excellent.

Chapter 17

Reminiscences of Lady Randolph Churchill, supplemented by her frequent letters to her sisters and her sons, offers the most complete account of the round-the-world trip, which was never fully realized.

The Buzzard Papers of Dr. Thomas Buzzard have a detailed discussion of the final stages of Randolph's disease, and the letters of Dr. Robson Roose have much to add.

Winston Churchill has some moving accounts of this time in *My Early Life* (New York, Scribner's, 1930) and so does Sir Shane Leslie in several of his books, particularly *Salutation to Five* (London, Hollis & Carter, 1951).

There are only a few fragments in *The Life of Sir William Harcourt* by A. G. Gardiner (London, Constable, 1923), Vol. II, and *Uncensored Celebrities* by E. T. Raymond (London, T. Fisher Unwin, 1918), but they are interesting to look at.

Dr. A. L. Baron's *Man Against Germs* (New York, Dutton, 1957) is still the best descriptive book on syphilis that I have found.

Newspaper and magazine accounts of this period are necessary background. There is an excellent collection of representative articles from *The New York Times* describing the United States at this time in *America's Taste,* ed. Marjorie Longley and others (New York, Simon and Schuster, 1960).

Chapter 18

Because this is the second volume of a two-volume biography, there is an obvious overlap in the use of some material. This particularly applies to the big black metal box of family archives in the Muniments Room of Blenheim Palace. The Duke of Marlborough graciously gave me access to the metal box, which is filled with a vast variety of correspondence, memoranda, diaries, etc. It is basic and invaluable to any biography of Lady Randolph.

Similarly invaluable are the private papers of Jennie's grandson Peregrine Churchill. These include a large file of correspondence between Jennie and her son Jack.

Another vital source of information is the Moreton Frewen Papers in the Manuscript Room of the Library of Congress in Washington, D.C. The range of the documents is enormous, but a careful sifting reveals a variety of materials giving fresh insight into Jennie and her relationships with her family and her world. Moreton Frewen admired Jennie and was a good friend to her, and the correspondence between him and his wife Clara offers a source of information about Jennie that cannot be found anywhere else. There are also valuable clippings among the Frewen Papers as well as letters from Jennie and an interesting correspondence between Moreton and Winston.

Indispensable for a biography of any member of the Churchill family are the collected letters in the five Companion Volumes of Randolph S. Churchill's *Winston S. Churchill* (Boston, Houghton Mifflin, 1967). Although many of these letters are elsewhere available, they are here compiled and copied with admirable accuracy.

My interviews with Sir Shane Leslie had an enormous value that is reflected throughout my book. This includes the material and letters he showed me, as well as the books and clippings he made available to me. My correspondence with Prince Clary, Count Kinsky's nephew, which was so important in my first volume, has a continued importance here. Countess Kinsky in London was similarly helpful. Lady Altrincham, the daughter of Jennie's close friend Lady Islington, was kind enough to tell me many things of great value that I had not heard elsewhere. She also made available to me some important material. I am grateful to her son John Grigg for finding a copy of a moving letter about Jennie.

There is, of course, a vast library of excellent books describing England at this time. *The New Cambridge Modern History,* C. L. Mowat ed., Second Edition (Cambridge, at the University Press, 1968) is very good. So is *England, 1870–1914,* by R. C. K. Ensor, (London, Oxford University Press, 1936). There is also some specific information of value in Anthony Sampson's *Anatomy of Britain* (New York, Harper & Row, 1962); H. H. Asquith's *Some Aspects of the Victorian Age* (Oxford, Clarendon Press, 1918); and James Truslow Adams' *Empire on the Seven Seas* (New York, Scribner's, 1940). But of particular importance is the *Annual Register* (Volume 137, London, Longman, 1896), which is excellent not only in recording the important facts of a given year, but in capturing the mood of it.

Holbrook Jackson, *The Eighteen-Nineties* (New York, Knopf, 1922), does a fine job of recreating the literary flavor of the time and Richard Le Gallienne ably abets him in *The Romantic Nineties* (New York, Doubleday, 1925). Virginia Cowles' *Edward VII* (London, Hamish Hamilton, 1956) is very good on the social life of the Prince of Wales. But most valuable are the memoirs of the major people on the scene: Margot Asquith, *Autobiography* (London, Thornton Butterworth, 1920); Frances, Countess of Warwick, *Discretions* (New York, Scribner's, 1931); Duke of Portland, *Men, Women & Things* (London, Faber & Faber, 1930); among many others. I also found many sidelights in *Our Mothers* by Allan Bott and Irene Clephane (London, Gollancz, 1932) that I found nowhere else.

Inevitably a major source is the daily newspapers: *The Times* in London, *The New York Times* and the *Tribune* in New York. The weekly New York magazine *Town Topics* requires careful examining and checking because of its inaccuracies, but it does offer a surprising number of leads and pieces of information which do prove true and which may not be available elsewhere.

Chapter 19

The best book of description of the Paris scene at this time is Richard Harding Davis' *About Paris* (New York, Harper, 1895). It is wonderfully alive.

The major source of facts about the happenings and the people in Paris is the Paris edition of the *New York Herald*. It is not only well edited, but its pages are filled with humor and anecdote, and very little reticence.

Of the American newspapers, the one which seems to have had the largest number of feature articles about Americans in Paris is the *New York Journal*. It is gossipy but informative.

Seymour Leslie, *The Jerome Connexion* (London, John Murray, 1964), has some interesting anecdotes about his great-aunt Jennie in Paris. And Jennie herself records some in her *Reminiscences of Lady Randolph Churchill* (New York, The Century Co., 1908).

For the purpose of this chapter and its subject, there are only a few things of interest in *Empress Eugénie in Exile* by Agnes Carey (New York, The Century Co., 1920) and *The Empress Elizabeth of Austria* by Carl Tschuppik (New York, Brentano, 1930).

Shane Leslie offers rich memories as well as insights in *Long Shadows* (London, John Murray, 1966). There are some good stories in the anonymous *Uncensored Recollections* (New York, Lippincott, 1924).

It is most interesting to read Marcel Proust's fictional description of the Marquis de Breteuil in *Remembrance of Things Past,* Volume I (New York, Random House, 1934).

Chapter 20

The Manuscript Room of the New York Public Library has the most complete collection of the Bourke Cockran Papers. The Irish Historical Society has his personal library, but most of the other many papers, letters, and clippings are in the Manuscript Room. It is a valuable and revealing collection.

There are several biographies of him—*Bourke Cockran: A Freelance in American Politics* (New York, Scribner's, 1948); *Bourke Cockran, American Orator, His Life & Politics* by Ambrose Kennedy (Boston, Bruce Humphreys, 1948)—but neither catches the full quality and drama of the man. He comes much more alive in his letters and interviews, and also in the various newspaper reports from political conventions where he was a star performer. Particularly well written were articles in the Philadelphia *Press* (May 7, 1893 and December 19, 1897), the New York *Sun* (June 26, 1892), the Toledo Sunday *Journal* (June 26, 1892). There are also some unidentified clippings among the Bourke Cockran Papers containing interviews of high caliber.

Shane Leslie in his *American Wonderland* (London, Michael Joseph, 1936) has some of the most intimate material on Cockran. Senator Champ Clark, *My Quarter-Century of American Politics* (New York, Kraus, 1969), has an excellent anecdote about him too.

Chapter 21

The prime source book on Moreton Frewen is *The Splendid Pauper* by Allen Andrews (Philadelphia, Lippincott, 1968). It is excellent. Anita Leslie also has written a biography of him: *Mr. Frewen of England* (London, Hutchinson, 1966), but as a member of the family she is perhaps not as objective.

The Holbrook Jackson book has good background material for this chapter, as does E. T. Raymond, *Portraits of the New Century* (New York, Doubleday, 1928). Lady Randolph's *Reminiscences* are also very useful here, and so is the book of memoirs by her niece, Clare Sheridan, *To The Four Winds* (London, Deutsch, 1955). A few relevant stories can be found in *Time Was: The Reminiscences of W. Graham Robertson* (London, Hamish Hamilton, 1931).

One of the best-written books of this period, and full of fascinating material, is *The Proud Tower* by Barbara Tuchman (New York, Macmillan, 1965). Anybody writing about or interested in this period should read it.

Some Piquant People by Lincoln Springfield (London, Unwin, 1924) is worth referring to for anecdotal material.

The files of *Truth* magazine are also a necessary source of information.

Chapter 22

Here again, the files of the Paris *Herald* offer the most detailed picture of Paris at this time.

Shane Leslie's recollections and writings are of particular importance in this chapter. Peregrine Churchill also had some pertinent comments. His brother, John Spencer Churchill, provides further observations about their father Jack Churchill in his book, *A Churchill Canvas* (Boston, Little Brown, 1961).

The letters between Jennie and her sons take on a growing importance in the book. The letters between Jennie and her son Jack come from the personal papers of Peregrine Churchill, and most of the Winston letters are in Randolph Churchill's Companion Volumes of collected letters.

720 * CRITICAL REFERENCES AND BIBLIOGRAPHY

There is a fairly good summary of French politics in this era in *Modern France* by F. C. Roe (New York, McKay, 1961).

The Duchess of Sermoneta in *Sparkle Distant Worlds* (London, Hutchinson, 1947) has an anecdote about Jennie worth telling. And Clare Sheridan, in another book, *The Naked Truth* (New York, Harper, 1928), has some excellent observations about her aunt Jennie.

A superb book on the social life of American brides in Europe, which was valuable to me in Volume I and again is valuable here, is Elizabeth Eliot's *They All Married Well* (London, Cassell, 1960).

Chapter 23

Two of Winston S. Churchill's books of memoirs—*My Early Life* (London, Odhams, 1930) and *Thoughts & Adventures* (New York, Scribner's, 1932)—provide necessary facts and background for this chapter, as they do elsewhere in this book.

Bourke Cockran's speeches reveal much about the man, but there are few copies of his speeches among his Papers in the New York Public Library Manuscript Room, because he spoke from notes and memory rather than from a written text. One must, therefore, go to the files of the newspapers in the cities where he spoke. Some of them, fortunately, are almost verbatim reports.

The Society conflicts in New York are reported in a number of books, but again, the local newspapers provide a fresh source of information. *The New York Times* then reported such social conflict on its front pages. The New York *World* was similarly thorough and descriptive. Allen Churchill has treated this aspect of New York Society in rich detail in his excellent book *The Upper Crust* (Englewood Cliffs, N.J., Prentice-Hall, 1971). Harvey O'Connor also has done a creditable job in *The Astors* (New York, Knopf, 1941).

On the British side of Society, Frances, Countess of Warwick, *Life's Ebb and Flow* (New York, Morrow, 1929), goes into some fascinating detail. The Countess's frequently caustic approach comes from the fact that she became an avowed Socialist in her middle years. W. Pett Ridge, *I Like To Remember*, remembers his Society more warmly (New York, Doran, 1926). So do *The Private Diaries of Sir Algernon West* (London, John Murray, 1922).

Chapter 24

Winston Churchill describes his youth best in *My Early Life* and in his regular flow of letters to his mother. The large number of biographies of Winston Churchill can be easily avoided here, because they add almost nothing to Winston's superb descriptions of this time of his life.

As for the fringe material, Francis Neilson makes a small contribution in *The Churchill Legend* (London, Nelson, 1954), but can otherwise be dispensed with. Consuelo Vanderbilt Balsan, *The Glitter and the Gold* (New York, Harper, 1952), should be read for the personal sidelights she provides. Margot (Asquith) Oxford,

More Memories (London, Cassell, 1933), is, however, better written and more revealing. Lady Randolph's own *Reminiscences* are more discreet, but informative.

The best supplemental description of Winston at this time comes from a correspondent of The London *Daily Mail*, reprinted in *Churchill by his Contemporaries*, edited by Charles Eade (New York, Simon & Schuster, 1954). This is a very good book of collected memories by those who knew him best.

Chapter 25

Frances, Countess of Warwick, contributes still another book of memoirs, *Afterthoughts* (London, Cassell, 1931), and R. D. Blumenfeld adds his *R. D. B.'s Diary* (London, Heinemann, 1930) to supplement all the other books on London Society already mentioned. Because so many of these people knew each other, each book of memoirs seems to add another piece of mosaic to fill out the pictures. It is particularly interesting to get separate perspectives of some major social event from different memoirs. The best view of these affairs, from the royal side, is Sir Frederick Ponsonby's *Recollections of Three Reigns* (London, Eyre & Spottiswoode, 1951). Ponsonby not only had an excellent vantage point but also an excellent memory. So did Lady Maud Warrender, *My First Sixty Years* (London, Cassell, 1933). As for Jennie, her memory was always very good indeed, but in her *Reminiscences* she follows her son Winston's advice to try not to hurt anybody's feelings. She doesn't.

Aside from the previously mentioned books of Shane Leslie, his *Film of Memory* (London, Michael Joseph, 1938) and his own interviewed memories have special meaning here. And, again, Barbara Tuchman's *The Proud Tower* is of particular value.

Chapter 26

In this chapter, probably more than any other in the book, excerpts from letters between Jennie and her sons provide the best possible description of their relationship. The regularity of their correspondence, their frankness with one another, and their mutual love and trust offer the most open view possible of what they meant to each other. Any interpolative material can only be redundant.

Chapter 27

All the books of the Countess of Warwick are useful in this chapter. Theo Lang, *My Darling Daisy* (London, Michael Joseph, 1966), is of some slight value. Virginia Cowles' *Edward VII and his Circle* is better.

There are a great number of books about the Edwardian era. *The Edwardian Age* by R. J. Minney (London, Cassell, 1964) is interesting, but J. B. Priestley's *The Edwardians* (New York, Harper & Row, 1970) is more crisply written. Michael Harrison has much to offer, for my purpose, in *Lord of London: a Biography of the Second Duke of Westminster* (London, Allen, 1966), more because of the content than the treatment.

George Cornwallis-West, *Edwardian Hey-Days* (New York, Putnam, 1930), is a basic book for this biography, however careful and controlled the author is about his feelings and his relationships. Aside from his letters, this is the only place where George West gives any inkling about himself. His sister Daisy, Princess of Pless, is not so reticent. In her series of memoirs, *Daisy, Princess of Pless, by Herself* (New York, Dutton, 1929) and *From My Private Diary* (London, John Murray, 1931), among others, she is revealing indeed about everybody, and even somewhat about herself. However, she is not always accurate.

Chapter 28

The Berg Collection at the New York Public Library has a large and important collection of letters of Mrs. Pearl Craigie. The British Museum is also a good source of varied material by and about her. Aside from her own books and papers, she wrote considerably for magazines and some newspapers, and these can be consulted. *The North American Review* (October-December 1906) has a good article on her novels. Her father, John Morgan Richards, who idolized his daughter, has collected what is mainly a paean of praise in *The Life of John Oliver Hobbes* (London, John Murray, 1911). Isabel C. Clarke has done a better job in a single chapter in *Six Portraits* (London, Hutchinson, 1935). But by far the best source of information about Pearl Craigie—a portrait that really comes alive—is Vineta Colby's superb chapter in *The Singular Anomaly* (New York, New York University Press, 1971). Earl Curzon of Kedleston, *Subjects of The Day* (London, Allen & Unwin, 1915), has done a sensitive memorial to her.

Mrs. T. P. O'Connor, *I, Myself* (London, Methuen, 1919), also has recorded some vivid memories of Pearl Craigie.

Two other books of general use in this chapter should be mentioned: Vera Brittain, *Lady Into Woman* (London, Dakars, 1953), and Francis Power Cobbe, *The Duties of Women* (New York, Sonnenschein, 1905).

Chapter 29

One must of course read the ten volumes of the *Anglo-Saxon Review*. They tell better than anything else does the high quality of this literary quarterly. They also reveal much about Jennie's own interests. Invaluable here was the large file of correspondence between Jennie and John Lane, which describes not only the relationship between them, but Jennie's concern and effectiveness as a working editor.

Michael Rhodes in London, who has researched deeply into John Lane and this literary period, is an excellent fount of information and references. There is a book, *John Lane & The Nineties* by John Lewis May (London, John Lane, 1936), but the full story still remains to be written.

Jennie's own *Reminiscences* are not very good on the story of the *Anglo-Saxon Review*. The biography of Sidney Low, *Lost Historian* by Major Desmond Chapman-Huston (London, John Murray, 1936), has some references to Low's work on the *Review*, including an excellent short excerpt from his diary. Aside from Jennie's letters to Lane, her correspondence with Winston about her project is perhaps the best source of information. But there is no full account of the development and demise of the *Review*. In fact, a book about literary magazines in England during this period would make intriguing reading.

Chapter 30

The newspapers, again, are important here for facts available nowhere else. The Oldham *Daily Standard* provides small pieces of description about Jennie's political campaigning for her son. There are other comments in other regional newspapers, the Manchester *Evening News,* for example, but they are not as worthwhile.

The letters to her key political friends, including the Prime Minister, indicate better than anything else does the range of Jennie's constant activity on behalf of her son. Other letters indicate clearly Winston's resentment and concern about Jennie's impending marriage to George West. George West's own memoirs are not very good on his romance with Jennie. Since they were written long after the fact, after resentment had set in, his views are more superficial than they should be, and less detailed. His letters at that time are a much better indication of his true feeling. Some of these are used in various places, including Anita Leslie's book, *Lady Randolph Churchill.* (New York, Scribner's, 1970). The original file of George's letters in the Churchill archives is typified largely by the sameness of content: hunting, riding, fishing, and romance, almost in equal proportion.

Jennie had never dealt with her romance with George in any book. Her *Reminiscences* end just before her marriage.

Chapter 31

There is an extensive literature in England on the Boer War, or The South African War. R. C. K. Ensor, *England, 1870–1914,* presents the facts clearly and objectively. Winston's letters and Bourke Cockran's speeches (clippings in his Papers) show greater emotion on the subject. The involvement generated such emotion that there are few memoirs of this period that are not strongly expressive on the subject. Even clearer evidence can be seen in the Letters to the Editor column in *The Times* of London.

Winston's own writing in his books and letters contain some of the best combat description of the war itself. Burdett-Coutts' report on the hospital conditions presents the more grimy side.

The early story of the *Maine* and Jennie's organization of the hospital ship can be found in the newspapers, both in England and the United States. Specific detail on the ship itself and its staff is to be found in the issues of the *Nursing Record & Hospital World,* in the last two months of 1899. Jennie's *Reminiscences* are also quite good on this. The *British Medical Journal* is also of value. The most vivid description of the actual sailing comes from a reporter of *The New York Times,* December 24, 1899. There is also a most interesting letter from Clara to Leonie, reprinted in Randolph Churchill's Companion Volume.

Chapter 32

Jennie has done her finest writing in her description of the *Maine*'s voyage to help the wounded in the Boer War. She wrote it in rich detail as the final section of her *Reminiscences,* and also did it as an article for her own *Anglo-Saxon Review.* She also wrote constantly to her sisters and friends, and did a full report on the trip for the British government.

Mary Hibbard, the Chief Nurse, also wrote a series of articles about the hospital ship for The *Nursing Record,* but they do not have the quality of impact of Jennie's writings. Winston, in his letters and books, wrote about the combat most dramatically indeed. Jack's letters are also very vivid.

E. T. Raymond, *Portraits of the Nineties* (New York, Scribner's, 1921), has some excellent profiles of the important personalities, particularly Kitchener. Sir John Fortescue, *The Post-Victorians* (London, Ivor Nicholson and Watson, 1933), is also good.

A most interesting anecdote comes from Frederic Villiers, *Peaceful Personalities & Warriors Bold* (New York, Harper, 1907). Michael Harrison's *Lord of London,* mentioned earlier, also has some usable material on this subject.

Chapter 33

George Cornwallis-West is very expressive about his Boer War experiences in *Edwardian Hey-Days,* but he is very reluctant to dwell on the family opposition to his marriage to Jennie. For this conflict, we must go to Cornwallis-West's letters to Winston in the Companion Volume of Randolph Churchill's biography. Jennie herself barely mentions the bitterness, but there are no such qualms in the London and American press, or in the memoirs of her friends, already mentioned. *The Diaries* of Daisy, Princess of Pless, are more revealing for what they don't say; much of what she does say simply is not true.

George West does detail the opposition of the Prince of Wales and the military authorities to his planned marriage. Jennie's letters to her sons, reprinted in the Companion Volume, are particularly moving. So is the obvious opposition of her sons. *The New York Times* account of the wedding is better than anything else I found, which is why I reprinted it in full.

For other background, there is some interesting information in Hesketh Pearson, *The Pilgrim Daughters* (London, Heinemann, 1961), as well as other books already mentioned, such as Lady Maud Warrender's *My First Sixty Years,* Lincoln Springfield's *Some Piquant People,* Clare Sheridan's *The Naked Truth,* and Seymour Leslie's *The Jerome Connexion.*

The Berg Collection in the New York Public Library also had a letter from Sidney Low about the *Anglo-Saxon Review,* which explained some of his work.

Chapter 34

In my interview with him, Sir Shane Leslie provided very full descriptions and memories of George Cornwallis-West. He also deals with him at length in several of his books. And there is a letter to the editor of the *Times* written by Sir Shane Leslie in George's defense years after this period.

George West's description of his frustrating business career and his early marriage is surprisingly good in his memoirs. This is amplified by the exchange of letters between Winston and Jack and between Jennie and Winston.

Jennie's letters to John Lane highlight the conflict at this time. None of the books, or magazine articles on John Lane deal with the subject in any way. The best verbal source on the subject, again, is Michael Rhodes, who is currently doing a biography of John Lane.

Shane Leslie's account of the death of Queen Victoria and her funeral–in his *Film of Memory*–is the most moving I had read.

Chapter 35

The books previously mentioned dealing with the Prince of Wales are again most useful in this chapter. This is particularly true of J. B. Priestley's *The Edwardians*. For general background on the new era, there is *The New Cambridge Modern History* (Volume 12), and Arthur Bryant's *English Saga* (London, Collins, 1940).

Two highly interesting books of recollections of this time are E. D. Gramont, *Pomp and Circumstance* (London, Jonathan Cape & Harrison Smith, 1929), and The Duke of Manchester, *My Candid Recollections* (London, Grayson & Grayson, 1932). Not very well written, but very pertinent to the chapter, is *Edwardian Daughter* by Sonia Keppel (New York, British Book Center, 1959). Much more interesting and valuable is *They All Married Well* by Elizabeth Eliot.

George Cornwallis-West is the second best source for a full account of his social life in the early part of his marriage. The primary source is still Jennie, mostly through her letters.

Chapter 36

Reading the files of magazines and newspapers for general background can be unproductive in terms of the results to be achieved for the time spent, but there are some newspapers and magazines of this period that deserve careful attention. The files of *Punch* give a marvelous insight to the mood and foibles of the time. The *Illustrated London News* is excellent because it's so visual, and the highlights are all here. The London *Times* and *The New York Times* are best for the details of major events. *The New York Herald* and *The New York Journal* both give a lot of space to London Society news. There are other specialized magazines in England, such as *Bystander* and *Gentlewoman,* which are worth examining, and the London *Spectator* also deserves attention.

Descriptions of Jennie's tenure at Salisbury Hall come from a variety of her friends' memoirs, most of them already mentioned. George Cornwallis-West's book is good, but the best material comes from family letters.

The Marquis de Soveral Papers in Lisbon are of selective value–the Marquis apparently destroyed a large number of his more private letters. That seems to be the pattern of a great number of surviving private papers, including those of the Marquis Henri de Breteuil. However, enough papers are extant to help complete the mosaic of information.

Edward Marsh by Christopher Hassall (London, Longman, 1959) is very valuable here, but the Marsh Letters at the New York Public Library are a necessary supplement. There are also some important letters in the superb Churchill Collection of the Marquis of Bath. Douglas Plummer's book, *Queer People* (New York, Citadel, 1965) confirms some well-known facts, and a correspondence with the author reveals even more.

Two books by Ethel Smyth, *What Happened Next* (London Longman, 1940) and *Streak of Life* (London, Longman, 1921), both have some interesting anecdotes about Jennie, as well as some fascinating general background.

In relation to his own romance and marriage, it is worthwhile to read Winston Churchill's novel *Savrola* (New York, Random House, 1956).

Chapter 37

The Victoria & Albert Museum has a comprehensive collection of research materials on the history of the British Theater. This ranges from old playbills to clippings and photographs, much of it not readily available anywhere else. In addition to the library at the British Museum, there is also a very good collection of books on the subject at the University of London.

Some of the more useful books for the purpose of this chapter include: William Archer: *The Old Drama and The New* (New York, Dodd, Mead, 1923); A. E. Wilson: *Edwardian Theater* (London, Arthur Baker, 1951); Ernest Short: *Sixty Years of Theater* (London, Eyre & Spottiswoode, 1951); Roger Manvell: *Ellen Terry* (New York, Putnam, 1968).

The most pertinent, and therefore the most necessary, to our subject is Mrs. Patrick Campbell's autobiography, *My Life & Some Letters* (London, Hutchinson, 1922).

Of much less value, but worth checking, is A. E. W. Mason: *Sir George Alexander & The St. James Theater* (London, Macmillan, 1935). Max Beerbohm, *Around Theaters* (New York, Simon & Schuster, 1954) has a review of Jennie's play that should be read. Again, the richest material comes from the newspapers, both in London and Glasgow, where there are not only reviews and articles about the plays, but several excellent interviews with Jennie. This is particularly true of the London *Daily Chronicle*.

Copies of Jennie's plays can be found in the Lord Chamberlain's Office at St. James Palace. They cannot be removed, but they can be consulted.

Chapter 38

All the books about the Edwardian era previously mentioned are necessary reading for the history of King Edward's final years. Of these, though, the best are Sir Frederick Ponsonby's *Recollections of Three Reigns* and J. B. Priestley's *The Edwardians*. Margot Oxford's *More Memories* has an intimate anecdote and André

Maurois' *The Edwardian Era* (New York, Appleton Century, 1933) has a few sidelights of interest, as have the memoirs of Daisy, Princess of Pless. Philippe Julian, *Edward and the Edwardians* (New York, Viking, 1962) also has some pertinent quotes. The Edwardian period is one of the few areas in this book where outside published material is better than personal letters.

The only copy of the *Shakespeare Memorial Souvenir of the Shakespeare Ball* that I could find was at the office of the publisher that printed it privately (London, Frederick Warne, 1911). It is not listed in the British Museum. It is, however, an indispensable source for information about the ball. Jennie edited the *Memorial Souvenir*, and the leading writers of the day, including George Bernard Shaw, contributed to it. Newspapers and magazines gave colorful descriptions of the ball, but they do not compare to the *Souvenir*.

About the Shakespeare's England exhibition at Earl's Court, the biography of *Frederick Edwin, Earl of Birkenhead*, by His Son, (London, Thornton Butterworth, 1933) has an amusing anecdote, and Charles B. Cochran, *The Secrets of a Showman* (London, Heinemann, 1925) has some interesting facts, as does George West's book. The best material, however, comes from the London newspapers and magazines, which are rather full in their descriptions. A good American account can be found in *The Literary Digest* (July 6, 1912).

Neither George Cornwallis-West's book, nor Mrs. Patrick Campbell's book deals very deeply with his divorce from Jennie. Jennie herself was most circumspect about it, even in her letters. The newspapers are the best sources, and their accounts are detailed. George Cornwallis-West's novel, *Two Wives* (New York, Putnam, 1930) is interesting indeed in its obvious parallels.

In this connection, a fascinating book to read is Alen Dent, *Bernard Shaw and Mrs. Patrick Campbell: Their Correspondence* (London, Victor Gollancz, 1952), and The Moreton Frewen Papers at the Library of Congress, Washington, D.C., provide a great deal of tangential information.

Chapter 39

I was fortunate enough to talk to Montagu Porch before he died, and his comments were vital to my description of his marriage to Jennie. There is also an excellent interview with Porch in the London *Daily Express* (December 21, 1959). Other views of the marriage come from interviews with other members of the family: Lady Betty Cartwright, the Baroness Cedestrom, Peregrine Churchill, Sir Shane Leslie, among others, as well as from Mrs. Hadley Hucker, Mr. Porch's closest friend, who had invaluable comments. The Oswald Frewen Papers are very valuable, and there are also some relevant comments in the magazines and newspapers of the time and some books. Of course, Jennie's letters add a necessary dimension.

Absolutely necessary to this chapter are the essays in Jennie's book, *Small Talks on Big Subjects,* (London, Pearson, 1916). The essays are important for what they show of Jennie's ideas and for her illustration of them with specific incidents.

A key anecdote about Jennie's influence on Winston's painting can be found in A. Wallais Myers, *Memory's Parade* (London, Methuen, 1932). Winston's own book,

Painting As A Pastime (New York, Cornerstone Library, 1965) should be read in this context, too.

World War I is treated well in C. L. Mowat, ed., *The New Cambridge Modern History,* Second Edition (Cambridge, at the University Press, 1968), among many other works. The dramatic story of the Dardanelles comes from E. Ashmead Bartlett, *The Uncensored Dardanelles* (London, Hutchinson, 1928).

The information about Count Kinsky during World War I is based primarily on correspondence with his nephew, Prince Clary in Venice, and the books of George Lambton, one of Kinsky's close friends in England. Lambton's book, *Men & Horses I Have Known* (London, Allen & Co., 1924) has an excellent account. There are also several interviews with Lambton about Kinsky in the London newspapers of the time, as well as a very good letter which Lambton wrote to the editor of the London *Daily Dispatch* (December 16, 1919) dispelling some rumors about Kinsky. There are also a few references in Jennie's letters.

The Oswald Frewen Papers are of particular importance, as Oswald most conspicuously enjoyed his aunt's company at this time and faithfully recorded everything in his diary.

Of varying worth are a number of other books: Viscount Grey of Fallodon, *Twenty-Five Years,* Volume II (New York, Stokes, 1925); Lady Cynthia Asquith, *Diaries, 1915–1918* (New York, Knopf, 1969); Lady Violet Bonham Carter, *Winston Churchill As I Knew Him* (London, Eyre & Spottiswoode and Collins, 1965); Bernard Falk, *He Laughed in Fleet Street* (London, Hutchinson, 1933); Lady Diana Cooper, *The Rainbow Comes and Goes* (Boston, Houghton Mifflin, 1958); John Lehmann, *I Am My Brother* (New York, Reynal, 1960).

It was very interesting and often amusing to read the issues of the Lagos, Nigeria *Standard* from the period when Montagu Porch was there.

Chapter 40

All the material relating to Montagu Porch that was mentioned in the preceding chapter is also applicable here. There are some West African magazines that offer a little general background, but not much. The *West Africa* of July 2, 1921 did have some quotable comments.

The most intimate material about Jennie at the close of her life again comes from interviews with and memoirs of her family and her closest friends. There was also a massive amount of worldwide press comment at her death.

The Duchess of Sermoneta in *Sparkle Distant Worlds* provides a good description of Jennie's final visit to Rome. Lady Horner's testimony at the inquest of Jennie's death was most graphic and detailed and was fully reported on in the London newspapers. The best personal accounts come from Sir Shane Leslie, in interview, letters, and books, and from the diary of Oswald Frewen.

But the best summary of her life in a single sentence is the quotation at the end of this book, which is from H. H. Asquith, *Letters of the Earl of Oxford & Asquith to a Friend,* First Series, 1915–1922 (London, Geoffrey Bles, 1930).

Index